Books by Dorothy Clarke Wilson

NOVELS

THE BROTHER

THE HERDSMAN

PRINCE OF EGYPT

HOUSE OF EARTH

JEZEBEL

THE GIFTS
A Story of the Boyhood of Jesus

BIOGRAPHIES

DR. IDA
The Story of Dr. Ida Scudder of Vellore

TAKE MY HANDS
The Remarkable Story of Dr. Mary Verghese

TEN FINGERS FOR GOD

HANDICAP RACE
The Inspiring Story of Roger Arnett

PALACE OF HEALING
*The Story of Dr. Clara Swain, First Woman Missionary
Doctor, and the Hospital She Founded*

LONE WOMAN
*The Story of Elizabeth Blackwell—
The First Woman Doctor*

PLAYS

TWELVE MONTHS OF DRAMA FOR THE AVERAGE CHURCH
A Collection of Religious Plays

FOR YOUNG PEOPLE

THE JOURNEY

THE THREE GIFTS

LONE WOMAN

LONE WOMAN

The Story of Elizabeth Blackwell
The First Woman Doctor

by DOROTHY CLARKE WILSON

with illustrations

Boston   LITTLE, BROWN AND COMPANY   *Toronto*

LIBRARY OF CONGRESS CATALOG CARD NO. 70–97907

SECOND PRINTING

The frontispiece and the illustrations following page 268 are reproduced here through the courtesy of the New York Infirmary.

Published simultaneously in Canada
by Little, Brown & Company (Canada) Limited

PRINTED IN THE UNITED STATES OF AMERICA

LONE WOMAN

October 20, 1847

"THIS MORNING, GENTLEMEN, we will continue with our discussion of bones." The genial, stout little professor of anatomy beamed on his class. "And we'll do our best not to make the subject too dry."

The class snickered. Dull eyes brightened. Lolling figures straightened. The spirited undertone of conversation in the back of the room subsided to a murmur. Good old Webster! He always managed to instill a little spice in the bland monotony of medical instruction. It was rumored that when certain subjects of a delicate nature were approached, with the attendant display of illustrative materials, the professor became more than humorous, even a bit ribald in his treatment. They could hardly wait for this interesting study of anatomy, especially in its female aspects, to arrive. Meanwhile, since even the brilliant Dr. James Webster was scarcely an Ezekiel with the genius for bringing dry bones to life, the class relapsed into its usual boredom, punctuated by fidgetings, scufflings, whisperings, and finally, outright conversation.

Stephen Smith sighed. Sitting in one of the upper tiers of seats in the classroom, he found it impossible to catch the full text of the lecture. As a student who wanted seriously to study medicine, he had certainly chosen the wrong place to do it. But he had liked the sound of this little college located in Geneva, on the northwest corner of Seneca Lake, in upper New York state. It had shown a remarkable courage and pioneer spirit just twenty years ago, in 1827, by establishing a medical department when certain eminent physicians, including Dr. David Hoosac and Dr. Valentine Mott, had been excluded from giving medical instruction in New York City through lack of an affiliating college in the state.

Moreover, it was an institution dominated from its beginning in

3

1822 by the spirit of pioneers whose minds had not run in conventional grooves. At a time when colleges were molded to a narrow denominational pattern, the founders of this institution had been the townspeople themselves, all 1,723 of them, a cross section of many denominations and social strata. Its third president, Dr. Benjamin Hale, was one of the great pioneers of American education. Its trustees included Whiting, a Supreme Court justice of New York state; Rees, who had known General Washington; Burrall and DeZeng, men with practical achievements and inventive vision. Its medical faculty was largely constituted of reputable practitioners from the cities, many of them distinguished teachers and writers as well as doctors.

But its student body! After three weeks of the academic year Stephen Smith had not yet recovered from his first shock and disappointment. The medical class, numbering about a hundred and fifty, was composed largely of young men from neighboring towns, sons of farmers, tradesmen, and mechanics. It was a common saying among the people of the vicinity: "A boy who proves unfit for anything else can always be a doctor." The road to a degree was remarkably easy, involving no more than three short terms of study, with minimum fees. They were here, not because of a compulsive interest in medicine, like himself and a few others, but for lack of any other occupation, especially during the winter months. Their love of fun far exceeded their love of learning. They were rude, boisterous, riotous, both in and out of the classroom. Lectures were accompanied not only by horseplay but by even noisier forms of athletic sport sometimes ending in fisticuffs, which drew ear-splitting shouts from the spectators. Already their crude and noisy behavior outside the school had won them a reputation in the town resulting in several written protests to the faculty. If such offensive disturbances continued, it was threatened, townspeople in the neighborhood would have the college indicted as a nuisance.

Resigned to frustration, unable to follow the lecture sufficiently to take notes, Stephen Smith looked around the room. He wished heartily that he had taken a seat down front, like Francis Stratton, the class chairman, who was leaning forward and writing furiously. Most of the students were not even making a pretense of listening. Several were unabashedly sleeping. One, apparently inspired by the subject under discussion, was loudly cracking his knuckles. Mumbles, snickers in various parts of the room pinpointed the locale of a vulgar joke or spicy story.

4

Over in one corner thumps and squeals gave ominous portent that an even more violent storm was brewing.

Poor devils! Stephen's appraisal changed from disgust to clinical curiosity. What made them act like such boors? Probably most of them came from good, respectable homes. They had been taught decent manners. Their mothers would be shocked to see them, and the boys would be ashamed to have them. If only something would jolt them out of their smart-aleck immaturity, turn them from irresponsible buffoons into men!

A ripple swept over the room, stirring up waves of lively but no less noisy interest. Looking up, Stephen saw that Dr. Lee, the dean of the medical school, had entered and was standing in front of the class. After some desk pounding and stern appeal from Dr. Webster, he managed to make himself heard.

"Gentlemen, I have an important matter to present to you, a *very* important matter."

The dean's ringing voice, geared to the lecture platform, was always impressive. But this time it was more than his voice that compelled attention, more even than his elderly, courtly dignity which was such a contrast to the informality of fat, genial Dr. Webster. There was a gravity about his features, a tension in the fingers which held a piece of paper, above all a nervous urgency in his manner which electrified the class.

"I have a letter here, gentlemen, and I crave your indulgence to read it. It contains the most extraordinary request which has ever been made to the faculty."

Stephen's heart sank. So the neighborhood had carried out their threat. They had asked to have the medical college closed. Well, he couldn't blame them. And he might have expected it. A year gone to waste in his education, one he could ill afford to lose.

"This letter is dated October third," went on Dr. Lee. "It is from a highly reputable physician, a personal friend of mine, Dr. Joseph Warrington of Philadelphia."

Stephen breathed more easily and settled himself to listen, with more curiosity now than foreboding. Therefore the shock of surprise was even more poignant when it came.

Dr. Warrington requested the faculty to admit as a student a lady who was studying medicine in his office. She had been refused admission by several medical colleges, but as the Geneva school was in the country he thought it more likely to be free from the prevailing prejudices against a woman student than others might be. He heartily recommended the applicant as a good student, eminently respectable, and honestly sincere in her desire to become a doc—"

The dean hesitated. "My friend says, 'to become a doctor,'" he observed with his first flash of humor, "but perhaps the word he should have used is — what? A 'doctress'?"

There was dead silence as he finished. It was obvious as he refolded the letter that his hands were twitching nervously.

"The — the faculty has taken action on the communication," he went on, as if searching for the right words, "and they directed me to report their conclusion to the class. The faculty decided — " the whole room seemed to be holding its breath — "decided to leave the matter in the hands of the class, of you gentlemen, with this understanding — that if any single student objected to her admission, a negative reply would be returned. We shall be waiting for your answer. Thank you, gentlemen."

There was silence as he turned and left the room, and until the door clicked shut. Then suddenly the ludicrousness of the situation seemed to seize the class. Pandemonium broke loose. There were whistles, catcalls, stampings of feet, poundings of fists, hoots of incredulity, of derision, of mutual congratulation.

"Men, did you hear that!"

"Shades of Hippocrates — a woman!"

"It's a hoax. Somebody's spoofing us!"

"Woman *doctors!* How about men mothers?"

"I say it's a great idea!"

"Hurrah, we're all for it!"

"No need to hold a meeting. We'll vote right now. All in favor say aye!"

"Aye, aye!"

Little Dr. Webster good-naturedly yielded to the inevitable. He threw up his hands in mock despair. "Gentlemen, gentlemen, that will be all for today. Class is dismissed."

But the session was by no means over. Francis Stratton was on his feet in the front of the room, waving his hands for order. It was a full minute before he could make himself heard.

"Men, men, this is a serious matter. It's not a joke. Strange as it seems, I really believe the dean is serious. We have a decision to make, and we must do it in orderly fashion, in a duly called business meeting. What do you say? Shall we meet here in this room — tonight?"

While the campus stewed over the new development, Stephen and Francis Stratton and some others discussed the possible cataclysm behind closed doors.

"Could it be a hoax? Students of some other college pulling our leg? Or even some of our own! I wouldn't put it past them!"

"No, no. I thought that at first. But Lee's no fool. He *knew* the man who wrote that letter. Didn't you see how upset he was?"

"But it's so impossible — ridiculous!"

"Unheard of. A *woman* doctor!"

"Doctress, my dear man. Or should we say doctoress?"

"You see? It's such an anomaly we don't even have a name for it!"

"Not *it*. Her!"

"What do you wager she's six feet tall, talks in low G, and has an incipient moustache?"

"Seriously — what a spot for the college to be in! If they admit her, they'll be the butt of every medical school in the country, and they haven't too much of a reputation already. The whole staff will be blackballed, maybe even expelled from their medical associations!"

"And if they don't, where are the precious democratic principles set forth by the founding fathers? I happen to know that it was the first principal's boast back in the twenties that the classroom facilities were designed to accommodate *both sexes.*"

"But of course they never expected women to *use* them, even in the classical academic department!"

"Did you notice the date of the letter, October third? This is the twentieth. They must have been brooding about it all this time."

"Dr. Webster must have known about it this morning. Yet the jolly old fraud could sit there calmly talking about dead *bones!*"

"Yeah, they're in a quandary, all right."

"Can't you see? That's why they put it up to us. They're sure we'll vote no. That will relieve them of all responsibility. It's impossible that not one person will vote against it."

"You think so?" It was Francis Stratton speaking. "I'm not so sure."

The meeting that night was one hundred percent attended. The class was in a hilarious mood. From the beginning the sentiment was violently affirmative. The catcalls, whistles, jeers of the morning were not only repeated but compounded. The scene was bedlam.

"Where is she? Bring her in! . . . Let us at her! . . . What a break! One woman to a hundred and fifty men! If she sticks the course out, that will be just about one day for each of us! . . . Wait till we get her in dissection!"

Stratton had to pound the desk for at least five minutes before he could make himself heard. "Gentlemen, gentlemen!"

"Not for long, man. We'll soon be *lady* and gentlemen!"

"You really think she could be called *lady?*"

But a semblance of order finally emerged. Stratton managed to impress on the group the serious nature of the decision they were about to make. It was not a matter to be treated lightly. Not only tradition but the fate of the college might well be in the balance. They must not vote on impulse. And this was a business meeting. If any man wished to speak for or against the admission of Miss — he consulted his notes — Miss Elizabeth Blackwell, let him request the floor in orderly fashion.

The class rose to the occasion. "Mr. Chairman." One man rose, was recognized, cleared his throat, and proceeded with irreproachable, if obviously tongue-in-cheek, dignity. "I wish to speak in favor of the proposition. There has been something lacking here on our beloved campus and in our classroom. Shall we call it beauty, delicacy, refinement, a certain spiritual element which is seldom evident save in the presence of the fairer sex?"

"Hear, hear! Bravo!" The speaker was acclaimed with vigor.

He proceeded at length in the same vein, waxing more and more eloquent as he approached the peroration. The applause was deafening but orderly. Other speeches followed, some short and to the point, but most of them couched, after the pattern of the first, in flowery diction and extravagant superlatives.

They're actually going to put it through! thought Stephen Smith with amazement. What a wry joke on the faculty! Or — was this what they really wanted? Had they actually approved the innovation, yet had known that without the support of the student body it could not possibly succeed? It was hard telling. Perhaps they would never know. But as the meeting progressed he found himself more and more excited. By heavens, suppose they were making history here tonight! Suppose a hundred years from now . . .

"Mr. Chairman."

"I recognize Stephen Smith."

Stephen made a brief but cogent speech about the democratic basis of American society and the ideal of equality in all phases of education. He was applauded but not with such violence of enthusiasm as were the more extravagant speakers.

"Question!" shouted someone, and the demand swept around the room. "Question, question!"

Stratton pounded on the desk. His face was tense and serious. "Gentlemen, I want you to understand several things before you vote. First, this is no small decision. You are voting whether or not to overthrow traditions — customs — which have been in effect since the first medical school was founded in our country, perhaps in the world. Second, this is not an issue to be decided by a whim, or by minds swayed by pretty speeches. Your decision should be based on principle, the spirit of this college as you believe it was envisioned in the ideals of its founders. Third, if you vote to admit this — this *lady*, you are pledging yourselves to conduct yourselves always in her presence like gentlemen. Now — are you ready to vote?"

"Ready. Question!"

"Very well. All those in favor?"

"Yea, *yea*, YEA!" To a man, apparently, the class rose to its feet, shouting in deafening chorus. A barrage of hats hit the ceiling.

When the tumult had subsided, the chairman pounded for attention. "All right. Now those opposed?"

"No." The word came from a single timid voice in one corner.

There was a concerted gasp of disbelief, then a sudden rush as at least a dozen figures converged on the lone dissenter.

"Cuff him!" They were reinforced by a chorus of screams. "Crack his skull!" "Throw him downstairs!" . . . "Traitor! Here, let me at him!" . . . "Say 'Yea,' you Benedict Arnold!"

"Yea, yea — " croaked the victim as he was dragged to the platform.

The vote was declared unanimous.

Stratton pounded again. "I ask your indulgence on one more matter. In case the vote should proceed in this manner, a few of us took the liberty to prepare a statement, to be sent to the faculty and forwarded to the applicant. I ask you to listen while I read it. Then we will vote upon it."

"Hear, hear!"

The chairman read: "At a meeting of the entire medical class of

9

Geneva Medical College, held this day, October 20, 1847, the following resolutions were unanimously adopted:

"1. Resolved, that one of the radical principles of a Republican government is the universal education of both sexes; that to every branch of scientific education the door should be open equally to all; that the application of Elizabeth Blackwell to become a member of our class meets our entire approbation; and in extending our unanimous invitation we pledge ourselves that no conduct of ours shall cause her to regret her attendance at this institution.

"2. Resolved, that a copy of these proceedings be signed by the chairman and transmitted to Elizabeth Blackwell."

The resolutions were passed unanimously and signed by F. J. Stratton, Chairman.

Stephen Smith walked back alone to his room, his emotions a mixture of triumph, unholy glee (What a surprise for the faculty!), and most of all, wonder. Did this — this female (he could not quite bring himself to say "lady") know what she was getting herself into, flouting tradition, custom, accepted principles of society which had been hundreds of years in the making? True, he knew there had been women physicians in history, even famous ones, but not officially recognized, not in modern times, certainly not in America in this nineteenth century! Suppose she actually finished the course and tried to practice. Medicine was a proud and jealous profession. Did she realize that she would be outlawed by almost every doctor and certainly every medical society in the country?

He remembered a crazy story he had once heard about a woman who had hidden herself in order to witness the ritual of a powerful secret order. Discovered, she had been given the choice of death or of submitting herself to the ritual, one part of which was to appear naked before the assembly. This woman must be almost as bold — or as naïve — or as — what?

He stood still and looked up at the stars, swinging placidly above the provincial little town. Heavens above! *What sort of woman was she?* An Amazon? A Joan of Arc? A — a Lady Godiva? He could hardly wait to find out.

Chapter One

WAS IT MERE COINCIDENCE that on February 3, 1821, just forty-two days before plans were completed for a pioneer school in an obscure town of 1,723 people in upper New York state a girl child was born in Bristol, England, the breadth of an ocean away, and that a quarter of a century later the merging of the two would mark a historic event? The child, grown to womanhood, would not have said so. The coming together, she believed, was inevitable. Though refusing to take credit for an achievement as adventurous and demanding as the conquest of Everest and of far greater significance to human progress, she insisted that it had all happened, not because of her efforts, but because of "a large providential guidance in the comparatively trivial incidents of an individual life."

But on the day in the mid-1820's when she stood staring at herself in the mirror of a big mahogany bureau, the making of history was as remote from her mind as the small town across the sea.

"E-liz-a-beth. E-liz-a-beth *Black*-well." She intoned the syllables slowly, lingering on the harsher sounds with sharp emphasis. Then with the same deliberation she mouthed the names of other members of her immediate family: her two older sisters', "An-na," "Ma-ri-anne"; her mother's, "Han-nah"; her father's and baby brother's, "Sam-u-el"; her four Blackwell aunts', "Ann," "Lu-cy," "Ma-ry," "Bar-ba-ra."

"Bar-ba-ra." She repeated the name with some distaste. It confirmed her fears. Only she and her tyrannical Aunt Bar had names that were different, explosive. All the others were soft, mild, gently harmonious, like most of their faces.

Perching on her toes and leaning forward, she studied her own face. It seemed to waver, bodiless, in the vast expanse within the dark ma-

hogany frame intricately carved by Grandpapa Blackwell. The soft fine
light hair was not a bit curly or glossy like Anna's. It hung straight as
straw and almost as pale in color. The cheeks were too thin, the mouth
too wide, the chin too square. But the eyes did not waver. A clear
bluish-gray, they stared back from under the low, too heavy brows
with cool appraisal. No, she was not pretty like Anna and Marianne,
certainly not like beautiful Mamma, who was lovelier than either of
them. She was the odd one, in face as well as in name.

"E-liz-a-beth. Bar-ba-ra." She repeated the two names again, taking
a perverse pleasure in mating the family's unpopular disciplinarian in
the same disdained category with herself. "Aunt Bar — Bar — Bar —
Bar —"

She stopped suddenly, appalled by the sight of a grim face above her
own, framed by the chintz hangings on the high four-poster. It wasn't
Aunt Bar, of course. She was imagining things. Aunt Bar was busy in
the kitchen directing preparations for the big company dinner. On an
impulse, just to prove it wasn't real, she leaned forward still further and
stuck out her tongue at it. Then as a firm hand descended on her
shoulder, her heart sank. It was real, all right. In dumb misery she
watched the Black Book come out of the big white apron pocket.

"So — three marks against you this time, Miss Bessie. One for
disobedience: you are not allowed in the spare room without permission. One for vanity: looking at yourself in the mirror and preening.
And the third, the worst, for impudence. Even your indulgent Mamma
would not stand for the sticking out of tongues at one's elders."

"But — I didn't mean —" As always, words of explanation choked
in the child's throat. Besides, there was little to explain. She *had* been
disobedient. She *had* been impudent, if unintentionally. She *had* been
looking in the mirror, if not preening. Tense with foreboding, she waited
for the pronouncement of penalty. Please — don't let it be something
that would last all day — not through tonight! But it was.

"To the attic with you, young lady, for the rest of the day, and
supper and early to bed in your room. And you'd better spend the time
praying that you may be purged of such naughtiness."

Only a slight quiver and tightening of lips betrayed the bleak
despair that racked her small body. Head high, she marched with dignity from the room and climbed the attic stairs. To have to spend the
first night of May Anniversary Week in lonely solitude was almost more
than she could bear.

She did not pray. If Mamma had asked her to, she would have, but defiance of Aunt Bar's admonition gave her a certain satisfaction. Besides, the enormity of her punishment surely made remorse unnecessary.

She gazed morosely through the windows, which the servants had opened a few inches to dispel the mustiness of winter. The distant view was discouraging, little but red-tiled roofs and chimney pots, and the branches of the tall elm and plantain and sycamore and huge may tree quite hid the courtyard garden below. But sounds and odors drifted up, the murmur of voices, the fragrance of lilacs and passionflowers and jessamine from the plants that hung in masses about the back parlor windows — yes, and the bad smell that came from the little closet where water was pumped up into a washbasin which was connected with a pipe to the little garden pagoda. Somehow it spoiled all the sweetness.

The voices were easily distinguishable. Mamma and Aunt Lucy were sitting under the may tree, Aunt Lucy probably sewing as usual, making some of the bonnets, frocks, or pelisses which drew contemptuous comments from their more fashionable cousins and which her older sisters were so terribly mortified to wear. Mamma hired her to make everything they wore, because she needed the money. "It will keep you from vanity," she consoled gently when Anna and Marianne protested. Elizabeth did not mind wearing the ugly clothes if it helped Aunt Lucy, who was small and gentle and kindly. "And absolutely null," was Anna's caustic summary. In fact, Anna had no use for any of the Blackwell aunts except Aunt Mary. Aunt Ann was well-meaning enough, but "ignorant and ugly." Aunt Barbara, though admittedly neat and orderly and very clever at drawing, was "utterly unbearable." Only Aunt Mary was a "real lady." And Anna's aversion extended to most of the Blackwell family except, of course, Papa.

"I don't see how I came to be mixed up with these people," she had once remarked to Marianne when they were walking in the garden.

Elizabeth did not share Anna's contempt. She liked all the Blackwells, even cantankerous Grandpapa, but she also was partial to Aunt Mary. A pity that her romance with that Mr. Harwood had come to an end, just because they had quarreled over baptism! She would have made such a nice mother! In fact, all the four aunts were to be pitied because they were unmarried. Even at her age Elizabeth knew that from overheard conversations. An unmarried lady, unless she had relatives to support her, like Papa, was an unfortunate creature. She had to sew, like Aunt Lucy, or teach other people's children, like Aunt Ann, or be a governess-housekeeper, like Aunt Bar and Aunt Mary.

"Not much better than housemaids," explained Anna with scathing astuteness, "except Aunt Mary, and she's more like a high-class lady's maid."

Elizabeth shivered, considering the fate that might be hers if she never married. But the gay voices of Anna and Marianne in the play-room below revived agony over her present situation. She could tell by the sounds what they were doing, riding the wonderful new rocking horse which Mamma had bought from the Goddards. It was as big as a pony, with a real mane and tail and a handsome red saddle. Anna would be riding, as usual, on top, with Marianne on the end of the rockers behind. And hers, Bessie's, place on the front rockers would be empty! As usual, they were singing verses from Taylor's *Scenes in Foreign Lands* while they slid over the wooden floor. Now they were singing their favorite, "Mumbo Jumbo," after which would come "Mont Blanc is the Monarch of Mountains, They crowned him long ago." She was even more desolate when the singing stopped, for it meant that Marianne was probably launched on one of her romantic stories, perhaps about the continuous adventures of "The Beautiful Estelle."

Then suddenly she remembered. Anna's telescope! She stole into the garret chamber where Anna was allowed to sleep. Yes, here it was, the beautiful toy spyglass which Anna had purchased for a half-crown at Weston last summer. Wonderful to have it all to herself, not to have to wait her turn, which since she was the youngest was always the shortest! She took it to the window, which looked out on the front garden, gasping because it made everything look so big, the bay tree in the corner, the old apple tree which grew fruit as large as a baby's head, the pear, plum, and red currant trees, and the greengage over the door. You could see every cane of the raspberry bushes at the foot of the wall, though there would be no fruit this summer. Cousin Kenyon had seen to that.

Kenyon and Sam, Uncle James Blackwell's sons, had walked the sixty miles from Worcester to Bristol last summer to make them a visit, arriving with blistered feet but unquelled energy. One morning Kenyon had risen with the dawn, gotten hold of the key, and when he came in to breakfast, proudly announced that he had put the raspberry bed "into perfect order." To Papa's intense vexation he had cut every one of the young shoots, the hope of the coming year! The incident had not added to Papa's already low opinion of his nephew.

Papa had been vexed with his daughters, too, because of this same little spyglass. Anna had discovered that by climbing through the window onto the leads and sitting behind the parapet, she could see much farther across the roofs of Bristol, and sometimes she had invited Marianne and Elizabeth to join her. Elizabeth sighed now, remembering the delights imprisoned in that magic orb. They could even see Bundry Tower on the hills to the right and the Duke of Beaufort's woods far over the fields to the left. It had been almost like flying! But Marianne had had to spoil it. Papa had not dubbed her "Monkey Polly" for nothing! Instead of sitting quietly beneath the parapet, she had insisted on walking the whole length of the leads, and one of the servants had seen her. They had been summarily ordered in and forbidden to set foot on the leads in the future. But so keen had been the delight that they had determined to make one last attempt. Anna, the writer, had penned a little petition to Papa, and they had all signed it. Please would he let them? They would promise to sit perfectly still and not lean over the parapet. Anna had carried the paper to Papa as he sat at his wash-hand-stand, shaving. He had read it through, smiling, laid down his razor, taken a pencil from his waistcoat pocket, and written on the back of the petition.

> *Anna, Bessie, and Polly, Your request is mere folly,*
> *The leads are too high For those who can't fly.*
> *If I let you go there, I suppose your next prayer*
> *Will be for a hop To the chimney top!*
> *So I charge you three misses, Not to show your phizes*
> *On parapet wall, Or chimney so tall,*
> *But to keep on the earth, The place of your birth.*
> *"Even so," says Papa. "Amen," says Mamma.*
> *"Be it so," says Aunt Bar.*

Elizabeth chuckled. Papa had the most painless way of saying no, as when Cousin Maria had come to visit the last time. As usual, Maria had been afraid to sleep alone in the huge four-poster, and Anna and Marianne had taken turns sleeping with her, to the envy of Elizabeth, whose great delight was to mount the little set of steps, mahogany and green baize, and plunge into the mountain of a featherbed, so big that it had cost twenty pounds.

"It's big enough to hold four people," she had suggested with canny innocence.

Marianne, whose turn it was to sleep with Maria, had been dubious, but Anna had seized on the idea. Another note had been delivered hopefully to Papa, who had responded in the same poetic vein.

> *If you four little girls were together to lie,*
> *I fear you'd resemble the pigs in their stye!*
> *Such groaning! Such gruntings!! Such sprawling about!!!*
> *I could not allow such confusion and rout!!!!!*
> *So this is my judgment: 'tis wisdom you'll own,*
> *Two beds for four girls are far better than one!*

And Papa's punishments were as lenient as his prohibitions were painless, as with the little thief one Christmas. Mamma had been returning from market, her black velvet reticule stuffed with oranges for the evening jollification, Anna by her side. Suddenly she had exclaimed, "Oh, you naughty, wicked boy!" and Anna had seen a ragged urchin tearing down Cumberland Street toward Stokes Croft, the big bag dragging at his side. She had charged after him, shouting, "Stop, thief!" at the top of her voice. Everybody within hearing had taken up the cry. The young thief had been caught and convicted. But Papa had found out that the boy's father was a decent laborer and much distressed over his son's conduct and had obtained a lenient sentence for him. But that wasn't all! Papa had later given the boy good clothes and sound advice and sent him to Australia, where he had mended his ways, gotten a good job, and sent back grateful letters.

No, Papa would never have banished her to the attic on the first night of Anniversary Week, which she had been looking forward to for a whole year.

Crouching at the head of the garret stairs, she listened to the preparations going on two floors below. Anna and Marianne were chattering, probably not even missing her. Mamma would be making one of her famous custards, stirring the mixture in a broad shallow brass preserving kettle with a dozen new marbles to keep it from sticking, and since it was a very special dinner party, she would be serving one of her delectable trifles. The table would be set with the best dinnerware, and the handsomest silver would be used, the sauceboat and beautiful epergne, with its trifle dish and accompanying little dishes for jellies and preserves, as well as the silver wire cake basket. Odors of roasting beef and raspberry and currant pies floated up through the hallways. There would be Yorkshire puddings and oysters and mashed potatoes and Bristol's famous Nag's Head Cake, yellow with saffron, bought from the little shop squeezed into the wall of the market. It would be almost like New Year's. Nothing was too good for the visiting missionaries who always came first to the Blackwells' on Anniversary Week.

Her sharp ears heard the turn of the latchkey, and her heart lurched. There was a rush of feet as Anna and Marianne flew to meet Papa coming home early from the sugar house, chortles as baby Sam came toddling after them. Elizabeth squeezed her eyes shut to hold back the tears. She could actually see the tall beloved figure in white work flannels, sidelocks a bit ragged and rumpled, blue-gray twinkling eyes belying the natural austerity of prominent cheekbones and heavy overhanging brows; could smell the steamy fragrance of the sugar house in the moist flannels as the other children twined their arms about his waist and knees. It took no imagination to hear his hearty welcome. His voice, inured to preaching the Gospel to large crowds outdoors "in desolate places," easily penetrated to the third story.

"Ho, my bonny Anna and 'Monkey Polly,' and young Samuel Charles, what mischief has my son been up to today?" Elizabeth waited in tense silence. "And where's my Bessie, my 'Little Shy'?"

A low rumble from Aunt Bar detailed the accounting in the Black Book. Elizabeth tightened her eyelids until they hurt. There would be no leniency from Papa, only tut-tuts and "Dear, dear, what a pity!" He never interfered with his sister's disciplinary decisions.

Jane, one of the housemaids, sympathetic but too busy to spare time for commiseration, came to tell her that supper was served in her room, and after eating it she was to go directly to bed. Elizabeth ate without appetite, even though old Margaret the cook had managed to smuggle a few choice bits of meat, fruit, and sweets into the usual prison fare of tea, thick bread and butter, and the inevitable "toast water," made each morning in the big white and blue "toast and water jug" with a cover and strainer in its spout. Baby Sam, with his bowl of bread and milk and delicious pap made of Norwich biscuits, was faring better in his nursery!

With her usual meticulous care she removed her pinafore, her pretty frock with its embroidered front and little sleeves tied with blue ribbons (put on because guests were coming), her petticoats and white-frilled pantalettes, and folded them all carefully. At least Missionary Week was just beginning! If she was good, she would be wearing them to the chapel tomorrow. But even the prospect of picnicking in the church gallery, where the children would divide their time between listening to thrilling stories of the missionaries and more worldly pleasures, did not atone for present loss. Bleakly she donned her long white nightgown and climbed into bed. But not to sleep! Hours later, it seemed, she tiptoed from her room, stole partway down the stairs, and crouched on one of the steps in the dark, peering through the banister.

She could see clear into the dining room. The big mahogany table had all its leaves in, and the space around it was filled, but dinner was over. She picked out familiar figures. There was Papa at the head of the table, wearing his black, as usual, with his flowing white cravat which he put on clean every day, a yard and a half square of fine muslin ironed to perfection by Mrs. Yandall, their washerwoman. He liked to wear black because it made him look like a minister. In fact he looked more so than Mr. Leifchild, the minister of their own Bridge Street "Independent" chapel, whose "dear ugly face," as Mamma called it, was pitted by smallpox. Grandpapa was there, too, sitting opposite Mr. Leifchild and probably glaring at him the way he did on Sundays. Even without being able to see under the table, she knew that both Grandpapa and Mr. Leifchild were wearing breeches instead of the trousers most men wore nowadays.

The other men were all ministers or missionaries of various dissenting congregations. There were Mr. Unwin from Dublin, who always carried a green silk umbrella with an ivory handle, and Mr. Burnet of Cork, who told the funniest stories and always kept the table in a roar. He was telling one now. It must be very funny, for Papa was writhing in his chair as though it were on fire. Mr. Unwin looked as if he were ready to fall down and roll on the floor. Mamma was laughing until the tears ran down her face. All the aunts, even Aunt Bar, were shaking with laughter and holding handkerchiefs to their faces. And there were Anna and Marianne, sitting at their small table at one side, and the third chair, the pretty mahogany child's chair made by Grandpapa with its horsehair seat and bar underneath with a brass screw for making it go up and down — *her* chair — was *empty!*

She held her breath trying to hear, but it was no use. The words were mere rumbles. She strained her eyes trying to focus the scene between the spokes of the banister, but it floated in a blur of tears. The mirror had been right. She was different, she was the odd one. She was the outcast the missionaries told about. She was the sinner thrust into outer darkness.

She watched and listened until Papa rapped on the table, and the merriment instantly subsided. The servants were called in, and the Bible was brought from the back parlor. The ministers all cleared their throats, straightened their cravats, and put on their pulpit faces. Then she crept back up the stairs, into her dark room, and climbed into bed.

So poignant was her misery that, nearly forty years later, standing in the hall below and looking up, she was to see that little childish face wistfully peeping through the banister.

2

It was while they were living at One Wilson Street, Bristol, England, that Samuel Blackwell's sugar refinery in Counterslip, a short street close to the river, burned to the ground. Elizabeth would never forget the experience. The whole household, Mamma, aunts, children, servants — all except Papa, who was fighting the fire — huddled against the railings at the top of Bridge Street Back, a slip of a street above the river leading down to Bristol Bridge, and watched the feathers of flame mount to the sky, actually feeling the heat against their faces, even coursing into their hands through the railings. For a time it seemed as if the whole of Counterslip must go, but miraculously the fire was confined to the sugar house.

Elizabeth had been born in Counterslip — once called Countess' Slip — and had lived there for her first three years. Now the burning of the refinery brought about the second major change in her life. Not only was it a severe blow to Samuel Blackwell financially, but it necessitated the relocation of his sugar business. Finally he purchased a property on Nelson Street containing two adjoining houses. One became the new sugar house. In order to economize, he moved his family into the other.

Samuel was independent. A Whig in politics, a Dissenter in religion, he chose to be dependent on no other man in his business. He abhorred debts of any kind. But he could not escape them entirely. And one of his most grueling obligations lay in the very nature of his business.

For the sugar trade, which had helped make Bristol the third richest town in the kingdom and the greatest port, outside of London, was rooted in slavery.

True, the traffic in slaves which had thrived for centuries no longer existed. In 1711 the Corporation of the Merchant Venturers had declared that the city's prosperity was founded on her slave trade. A generation later Bristol ships had carried at least one third of the trade. Then had come John Wesley, goading the unawakened public conscience. On March 31, 1739, Wesley entered Bristol at the invitation of George Whitefield, whose father had been a Bristol merchant, and there, "from a little eminence in a ground adjoining the city," so his diary stated, he preached his first open-air sermon. Here in the same year, near St. James' Churchyard, in the Horsefair, was built the "New Room," the first Methodist Chapel in the world. For the first time in the city's thousand years of history its poor had a champion — the blackened Kingswood miner, the laborer with his shilling and sixpence a day, the prisoner rotting in Bridewell or Lawford's Gate or Newgate, the children spinning cotton for a few pence a week, the slaves in the ships' stinking galleys. Wesley preached against slavery, and his name became anathema to the many Bristol merchants who were making their fortunes in the trade. On March 6, 1788, a riot occurred as he preached on the explosive subject. But the conscience of England as well as of Bristol was slowly being quickened, and thanks to the burning oratory of William Wilberforce, by the Act of 1807 the traffic in slaves was abolished. Not the issue, however! Slavery in the Colonies was still the lifeblood of the Empire's prosperity. In that decade of the twenties, all over England impassioned liberal orators were flailing the national conscience with tales of cruel masters lashing their cowering Negro slaves in Jamaica and others of the Colonies.

Samuel Blackwell was an inheritor of this liberal tradition. But by the time his conscience was fully aroused his lifework was chosen, his growing family dependent on an industry which throve on the labor of those same cowering slaves. It was a dilemma which he would never be quite able to solve, though the attempt would take him a third of the way around the world. His sensitive conscience would remain raw and tortured to the end of his life. But he tried to solve it by dedicating all his overpowering energy to the cause of abolition. During Elizabeth's childhood anti-slavery leaders were frequent visitors in the house. Wilberforce was a familiar name almost before she could lisp it, and as heroic as her more romantic favorites — Queen Elizabeth, the huntress Diana, and some of Mrs. Sherwood's heroines. As a feeble gesture against the bonds of injustice which entangled the family, she and the other children actually gave up the use of sugar for a time, an irony which must have twisted a fresh rapier in Papa's conscience.

In her own way Elizabeth was as guilt-ridden as Samuel, and she was conditioned at an early age to be painfully conscious of her personal weaknesses. Her name occurred with distressing frequency in the ubiquitous Black Book. The burden of "original sin" was distributed impartially from the Bridge Street pulpit each Sunday, to be borne by children as well as adults. Repentance was the constant theme of family prayers. What could she do to get rid of her sinful affections? Brooding, she sought an answer in the stories of saints which she had read or heard. How had they got that way? By doing something called "mortifying the body," "despising the flesh." There were the monks in their cells, the prophets in their sackcloth, Saint Simeon on his pillar. Certainly none of them had got holy by sleeping on a soft featherbed!

More than one night she crawled out of bed after Marianne was asleep and slept on the floor. Once she tried to go without food until Aunt Bar decided she must be sick and dosed her with nasty physic. But the entries in the Black Book continued, and the torturing guilt persisted. If she had gone to either of her parents and divulged her worries, they would have ended, for both were wise and understanding. But it would be years before "Little Shy" would be able to communicate her most intimate thoughts.

She was also the inheritor in full of Papa's independence, together with the tenacity with which he clung to his opinions regardless of opposition. Once when she was between four and five Papa had to make a business trip to Dublin, and the whole family went down to the Hot Wells to see him off. Elizabeth had set her heart on going to Ireland with her father and fully believed that he was going to take her. Then to her terrible amazement he said goodbye to her along with the rest. The restraint which had given birth to her nickname kept her silent, but within she was bursting with bitter disappointment. Papa boarded the vessel, and it moved slowly down the river. Anna and Marianne ran on beside it down the bank, waving their handkerchiefs, and Elizabeth followed, but when the vessel quickened its pace and her sisters stopped, she kept on running.

"What are you trying to do?" screamed Anna with vexation, trying

21

vainly to catch up with her. "Do you think you can go with him on foot?"

Impervious to the chorus of remonstrances, Elizabeth raced on. Panting hotly, Anna finally overtook her, seized her shoulders, and spun her around, but though five years older, she was no match in physical strength. Elizabeth wrenched herself away.

"Look, silly!" Anna resorted to reason. "Dublin's in Ireland, an island with water all around it. You could run a hundred miles and still not get to him."

Elizabeth stopped suddenly, turned an outraged face, and submitted, though obviously still at war with necessity, and she spoke not a word all the way home.

"A persistent child," observed Aunt Mary kindly.

"Stubborn," corrected Aunt Bar with compressed lips.

Aunt Bar had her favorites, and Elizabeth was not one of them. At first she had been partial to Marianne, the quietest and most amenable to discipline. But after Henry Browne arrived in 1825, all other loyalties were eclipsed. The small Harry became her pet. She curled his hair every morning with water and a tail comb and reveled in the admiration of doting females when she took him to walk.

Elizabeth could remember scarcely a time in her childhood when Mamma was not nursing a baby. After Harry came two more girls, Emily and Ellen. "All in twos," she thought with philosophic resignation. All except herself. She was isolated in another way because she had come between two boys, both of whom had died. Aunt Browne had been horrified when Papa and Mamma, having lost the first Samuel Charles, had given the same name to their second boy.

"It's fatal. Don't you know the saying, 'The second dies, the third lives'?" She had not been pleased, of course, merely vindicated when the prediction had proved correct, and she had struggled with all the family to keep the third little Sam, almost as delicate as the other two, alive. Since she and Uncle Browne, Mamma's uncle, had had eight sons, all of whom had died of convulsions in teething, she vented her maternal affection on her grandnieces and nephews. The life of her own daughter Elizabeth, she claimed, had been saved by the application of slices of the root of the white peony, bound to the soles of her feet. Elizabeth always regarded her namesake curiously, wondering what possible connection there could be between one's teeth and the soles of one's feet.

Elizabeth loved to visit Uncle and Aunt Browne at their house in Bourton. Uncle Browne was a goldsmith, "a real gentleman," explained Anna with satisfaction. He had high arched brows like Henry the Eighth, and wore breeches, with black silk stockings and silver buckled shoes. He was one of the last men in Bristol to give up the pigtail. Aunt Browne was tall, large, a bit loud, and usually wore black velvet with lace. Elizabeth listened entranced to her stories of her Irish family until the day she started talking about her brother, "Old Dr. Short," who had been an eminent surgeon.

"It's said he once took a man's eye out of its socket," related Aunt Browne with obvious relish, "cut something off the back of it, and put it back in place!"

Elizabeth shuddered and was promptly sick. For weeks afterward she awoke from nightmares, stomach lurching, with visions of a staring eye held in a plump hand.

To the horror of Aunt Browne and others, fate was again tempted when, after Emily and Ellen, came little John Howard, for there had been another baby Howard. He had been Anna's special delight, a beautiful creature, and when Mamma had come to her room one morning saying, "It has pleased God to take our dear little Howard in the night," she had been inconsolable. Elizabeth had received a full report of the tragedy from her emotional sister, how she and Marianne, wearing black dresses and long gauze veils, had held the tiny coffin between them on their knees in the mourning coach to the Brunswick burying ground, where Anna had thrown herself on it in frantic grief, refusing to let it be torn from her grasp.

"I'm sure he comes back to me," she insisted. "I see him, and he gives me messages."

Always when each baby came there would be for weeks the terrible uncertainty. With Aunt Browne's children the death-odds had been eight to one. With many families they were fifty-fifty. Why, wondered Elizabeth, as each tense period succeeded another, did this have to be? God had been especially good to them, Mamma said humbly when the second little Howie had survived the first crucial weeks. A queer sort of God, thought Elizabeth, picturing a frowning giant trying to decide which of his creatures to keep and which to throw away.

Elizabeth had to agree with Anna that Mamma's relatives were more interesting, if not more "genteel," than the Blackwells. Her brother, Uncle Charles Lane, was a prime favorite. Though ugly in appearance and without much education, he made up for all deficiencies by being agreeable, amusing, and generous (the latter usually at Papa's expense). An aura of romance and tragedy hung over Uncle Charlie, who had gone with an army regiment to India and other far places, eloped with the granddaughter of the Duke of Buckingham, and sired two children whom he loved very much but seldom saw.

His infrequent visits were events. Elizabeth remembered one in particular. His first act on arriving was to order a "fly," pack all the children into it, and drive to Lucas's, the pastry cook's, in Wine Street, where he told them to eat whatever they liked. Gaily they gorged on their favorite raspberry tarts and cheesecakes. One day soon after his arrival he arranged a special surprise. When they came into their classroom and were seated for lessons, a big bag which hung from the ceiling opened to release balloons, sweets, kerchiefs, and all sorts of presents descending in a shower. Looking around, they saw Uncle Charlie, grinning, in a corner, a telltale end of string in his hand. Elizabeth noticed, however, that he paid little attention to their shouts of appreciation. His glances were all for their new governess, Miss Eliza Major, a fresh-cheeked, highly educated young woman from Frome. And no wonder, for the governess looked uncommonly pretty, cheeks ruddier and eyes brighter than usual.

The various governesses from Aunt Bar on were far more than tutors. They were mentors, companions, nursemaids, playmates, disciplinarians. Each day, sometimes twice a day, under Papa's orders they took their young charges for long walks about Bristol and the surrounding country. Elizabeth reveled in these daily excursions. Inside her long skirts and frilled pantalettes her thin legs grew tirelessly tough and wiry as they moved to the clatter of pattens (predecessors of rubbers) which lifted her feet above the wet flagstones, or to the quieter rhythms of cork clogs. She trudged the narrow, cobblestoned streets, plodded the roads and paths along the riverbanks to the brook, to Leigh Woods, or raced across Mother Pugsley's Field, with its healing spring, leading out of Kingsdown Parade. She stared fascinated at the ominous Giant's Hole on the face of St. Vincent's Rocks, into whose dangerous depths the valiant Uncle Charlie was credited with clambering when a boy. She stood on tiptoe before the great iron gates of Sir Richard Vaughan's place, pushing back her bonnet so she could better see the preening peacocks.

But she reveled even more in adventures into the world of books.

After the nine o'clock supper of oysters or cold meat, bread, cheese and ginger beer, the two candles would be lighted in the silver candlesticks on the table, the silver snuffers in the tray between them. There would be a great roaring fire in the grate, for Papa never stinted the household on coal, which came by contract from Swansea in a barge every week. The whole room would be warm and glowing. Often Papa would read aloud. One of his favorite authors was Cowper, while Mamma favored Young's *Night Thoughts*. Mrs. Barbauld's poems, in the form of hymns and psalms, were less appreciated by the children, who preferred Mrs. Sherwood's stories, which illustrated the catechism. But whether Papa read aloud or they sat around the table and read to themselves, keeping quiet as mice, always, summer and winter, there would be reading.

It was the quiet Marianne, not the more aggressive Anna, who introduced novels to the three girls, smuggling them in with the help of one of the nursemaids. Hungrily they devoured *The Bandit's Bride*, *The Scottish Chiefs*, and finally, *Ivanhoe*. Then disaster fell. The precious loot was confiscated and taken to Papa. They waited for the dire punishment sure to follow. But to their immense relief Papa began reading them, at first with portentous frowns, then with pleasurable excitement.

"I see nothing wrong with these," he said at last. "In fact, I like them. Go ahead, daughters. Read them all you like."

Papa even encouraged them to write their own poems and stories, suggesting a Christmas Annual, to which everyone old enough should contribute something, to be read on Christmas Eve. Anna and Marianne set to with avidity, spinning out long romantic yarns and verses, copying them in booklet form with many illustrations. Elizabeth, only seven or eight at the time, wrote a stiff little poem and copied it with her usual painstaking correctness. Even Sam contributed a bit of doggerel. The collection was such a success that it set a precedent to last for decades.

As she grew from childhood into girlhood Elizabeth became increasingly conscious that Papa was different from most Englishmen of his time. Sometimes the knowledge came from the chance overhearing of conversations.

"If you ask me, you're a fool, son Samuel, to spend all this money on nonsense teaching for your *girls*. The boys, of course, have to be taught to read and write and add, have to know such things to run a business. But even for them all this folderol — French, mathematics, geography, meta — meta — "

"Metaphysics, Father."

Grandpapa snorted, dust from his carpenter's shop rising in a halo about his riot of white hair. "Huh! In my day physic was something you took when you were sick! You never learned all that nonsense, and I don't see but what you've done well enough!"

"Well enough to support him and Uncle James and all his sisters," hissed Anna in a pungent aside.

The aunts were just as critical. "I always supposed girls, *ladies*, should be taught certain things — music, painting, embroidery, penmanship, and perhaps a bit of French." This in a puzzled tone from Aunt Lucy, who had recently tried to learn French by the "Hamiltonian system," which consisted of reading the Gospel of John in the tongue you were to learn, the English words being inscribed beneath the French, Latin, or whatever. Unable to cope with the pronunciation, she had finally given it up as hopeless.

Aunt Mary, who had tried unsuccessfully to conduct a school for little boys in Brunswick Square (at Papa's risk and expense) was more practical. "Of course a lady needs *some* education, in case she doesn't get a chance" — she sighed — "or some misfortune prevents her marrying."

Elizabeth, who at the age of seven had fallen desperately in love with one of Aunt Mary's pupils, a young Apollo with flaxen curls and rosy cheeks, echoed the sigh. Her idol had not deigned to look at her. Suppose all males proved equally indifferent! Already the frightening ogre of spinsterhood was rearing its head. To be like the aunts, eternally dependent on one's father or brothers!

Aunt Ann shook her head over her interminable sewing. "Embroidery now, and sewing, those are accomplishments which a *lady* can always use, married or not."

Of course Aunt Bar was the most outspoken. "Sheer nonsense, brother Samuel! What possible use can your daughters make of all this education these uppity governesses and masters are forcing down their throats? You know very well they won't need it if they marry; and if they don't, it doesn't take a knowledge of history and mathematics to be a seamstress or a governess — the usual sort of governess, that is, employed by *gentlemen* for the proper rearing of young *ladies*." There was an edge of acidity in the comments of Aunt Bar, whose frustration of spinsterhood had been compounded by the enforced yielding of her duties as governess to the eminently qualified Miss Major.

Papa listened mildly to such criticisms and replied in the same manner to all. "My daughters have as good minds as my sons, and I see no reason why they should not be taught to use them in the same way. As to what use they will put them in later life, that will be for them to decide."

But just how revolutionary were Samuel Blackwell's ideas Elizabeth would not learn until long afterward. Grandpapa and the aunts were right. Education for the masses was still only a vague concept germinating in the society of early nineteenth-century England along with extension of suffrage and reform of the relief laws. Part of the democratic thrust accompanying the Industrial Revolution and the emergence of a substantial middle class, it would come to fruition only after its popular acceptance many decades later through the genius of strong trade unionism.

True, there were a few schools for boys in Bristol, all of them private, most of them affiliated with the established Church of England. No children of Dissenters like Samuel Blackwell could attend them. The few girls who received an education were usually sent to boarding schools, where they learned to read and write a little, possibly to spell, but most of their time was spent in dancing, music, painting, and needlework. The Elizabethan period, when learning had been considered respectable for women, at least those of the upper classes, had long since passed. On the threshold of that strange anomaly to be known as the Victorian Age, woman had entered on an era unique in history, when "modesty," "refinement," "delicacy" became the polite sentimentalities for subordination and male supremacy.

"The whole education of women," declared the French philosopher Jean Jacques Rousseau, "ought to be relative to men. To please them, to be useful to them, to make themselves loved and honored by them, to educate them when young, to care for them when grown, to counsel them, to console them, and to make life sweet and agreeable to them — these are the duties of women at all times, and what should be taught them from their infancy."

Or, as Noah Webster had defined a good education for ladies about 1790, it should render them "correct in their manners, respectable in their families, and agreeable in society. That education is always wrong which raises a woman above the duties of her station."

Samuel Blackwell was indeed a revolutionary, and not merely in concepts pertaining to education.

The knowledge that Papa's religion was different also came slowly. Elizabeth learned at an early age that the family was something called Independents or Dissenters, belonging to those minorities who dared to differ in theology and practice from members of the established Church of England, a body as firmly entrenched in power as was the Roman Catholic Church in countries of southern Europe and in South America. She knew that they were eyed with some contempt by the respectable majority who frequented the Cathedral or the Church of St. Mary Redcliffe on a Sunday morning. But that there were differences more fundamental than those of sect she realized only vaguely during childhood. And only after years of growth in discernment and experience would she fully comprehend the caliber of Samuel's amazing courage and reforming zeal or the effect they would have on the extraordinary lives his children were to lead.

Religion was as orderly a procedure in the family as meals: breakfast at eight, dinner at one, five o'clock tea, supper at nine. On Sundays the whole family went to church at Bridge Street Chapel. Their pew was the one nearest the center entrance, to the left, large and handsomely fitted by Papa, entirely lined, book ledge, door, and all, with green baize put on with brass nails. Papa always sat nearest the door; then came Mamma, then a row of children according to size, the littlest one nearest Mamma. The governess sat at the farther end.

The Sunday services were sources of acute mortification to Elizabeth. First she always stumbled over the straw hassocks set in a row, the tallest for the smallest child. Then, sitting between Marianne and Sam, she was in constant agony for fear his and Harry's sly whisperings would be noticed and bring nudgings from the aunts in the pew behind. She dreaded the family christenings, which came with startling frequency, always fearing the behavior of Sam would be repeated. Unhappily restricted in his long white dress, his cap with its white satin bows, and violently objecting to the cross strokes of the wet finger on his forehead, Sam had disgraced the family by striking with his fists at Mr. Leifchild, kicking, crying, and finally howling at the top of his voice.

She endured with some distaste the boring sermons, the endless learning of hymns and chapters and genealogies, the family prayers morning and evening, when cramped knees sent shooting pains through her body, and toes and nose, far from the fire, became colder and colder. But she rather enjoyed attending the two prayer meetings held at the chapel each week. Papa was always called on to pray, and she swelled with pride listening to him, as on the rare occasions when she heard him preach. Peeping through her laced fingers, she liked to watch his face, handsome, intense, fringe of whiskers framing its rugged features like a halo. He always talked as if God were right there in the room and he was well acquainted with him. Then, too, there were diversions in prayer meeting, as when Mr. Godwin the draper got up to pray. Invariably he would bring in "and-when-we-are-laid-in-the-cold-and-silent-grave" as if it were all one word. The children would listen for it and poke one another with malicious glee.

In spite of its distasteful features, for Elizabeth religion was a beautiful and essential part of life, inseparable from the goodness and gentleness and reverence which characterized the home, from the daily walks, from the stories of Mrs. Sherwood read in leisure hours on Sunday. No need to dwell on their tiresome dogmas and philosophical treatises! Skip over them to the charm of gentle romance, the pictures of breezy commons, lovely woods, clear streams and waterfalls, everything beautiful in nature and daily living!

3

Papa was no bigot. The winds of new ideas blew through the Nelson Street house with refreshing vigor. Unlike most English children of their day, Elizabeth and her brothers and sisters were not banished, when company arrived, to the nursery. Sitting at their small table when distinguished guests were feted, she listened wide-eyed, not only to the hair-curling exploits of missionaries and the lighter anecdotes of certain jolly divines, but to eminent liberal orators, writers, and philosophers. She was especially partial to the famous essayist John Foster, who occasionally dropped in for an evening and sat for a couple of hours at a corner of the fire, wrapped in a huge red, green, and brown Scotch plaid cloak, old and faded.

One evening she sat enthralled as George Müller, who with his associate Henry Craik was planning to start a ministry in Bristol, discoursed on the principles he had been formulating for the Plymouth Brethren. Gazing at the glowing features, listening to the impassioned plea for the right of every man to preach the truth that had been revealed to him, for the relinquishment of all attempt to save money, Elizabeth marveled at the rumor that this holy man could have experienced a youth of precocious wickedness.

An even more voluble guest was the renowned Robert Hall, minister of Broadmeed Chapel, but she was less intrigued by his honeyed discourse than by his ability to imbibe twenty-three cups of tea in succession. The famous Dr. Chalmers impressed her even more with his fiery Scotch eloquence. And once she and her sisters participated in a great party for one of the inventors of phrenology, who took a great fancy to the three and investigated all their cranial bumps for the edification of the company.

"Disgusting," commented Anna, feeling her youthful pride affronted. But Elizabeth thought it highly amusing.

Abolition was not the only social issue on which they cut their intellectual teeth. These were whirlwind days of change when the Industrial Revolution, having spawned untold wealth and opportunity for a new moneyed middle class but untold misery for the masses, was sowing the seeds also of a new and profound concept — political democracy. As a Dissenter, Samuel had had bitter experience with the old Corporation Act of 1661, which excluded all but Church of England men from participation in municipal government, and with the Test Act of 1673, which prevented all who had scruples against receiving communion as administered by the Church from holding government office, either in the civil service, in the army, or in the navy. Not until 1828, when Elizabeth was seven, were these Test and Corporation acts repealed. And the fight was only beginning to insure another basic human right, free elections. For still the majority of the people had no voice in electing members of Parliament.

Bristol, second port of England, center of ship building, sugar refining, glass and porcelain works, brass and iron foundries, soap, rope, tanning, tobacco, and other industries, was a hotbed of social turmoil. Evils abounded. Its prisons — Bridewell, Lawford's Gate, Newgate — were shocking dens of filth and vice. Prisoners of every age and sex were herded together in verminous cells which were little better than the dungeons of old castles. Conditions in the city's grim workhouse were unspeakable. After one outbreak of cholera it was found that six hundred paupers had been accommodated there, with fifty-eight girls sleeping in ten beds, seventy boys in eighteen! Orphanages exemplified all the beggary and sadism to be exposed by Charles Dickens a mere decade later in his scathing *Oliver Twist*.

In Bristol, as all over England, poverty, stark and grinding, was the accepted lot of the majority — accepted, that is, by the well-to-do. The laboring masses were oppressed, child labor exploited. Though in 1802 Parliament had passed a law forbidding cotton manufacturers to work their apprentices (pauper children) more than twelve hours a day, in 1816 Sir Robert Peel had lamented that the children were "torn from their beds, compelled to work at the age of six years from early morn till late at night." A national conscience stirred to wrath by the injustice of plantation owners lashing their slaves to labor in Jamaica had still to be roused to the evil of its own countrymen being whipped to their work. Most Englishmen accepted such evils as a matter of course. Not so Samuel Blackwell. He was concerned with all injustice, and as loyal a dissenter in politics as in religion.

Elections were exciting times in the Blackwell household. The three girls always wore ribbons the color of the Liberal candidates for office, and if they were elected, went to see their "chairing," the triumphal procession of the victors. Most exciting of all for Elizabeth were the victories of Protheroe and of John Bright on the latter's entry into Parliament. Bright, a young Quaker, the son and partner of a Rochdale mill owner, was a passionate orator and argued eloquently against the hated Corn Laws, which levied high import duties on foreign foodstuffs and thereby increased the cost of bread for the common people. Elizabeth wore his colors of red and yellow with enormous pride and shouted herself hoarse at his chairing.

It was the Reform Bill, however, which aroused the family's most ardent enthusiasm. This proposed act, providing for the enlargement of the suffrage and the reform of Parliament to include representation by the new industrial middle classes was hailed with hope by both factory owners and common laborers.

Reform was long overdue. Medieval practices persisted. The power of the old landlord families was almost supreme. "Rotten boroughs," voting precincts whose population had disappeared but which were still represented by nonresidents in Parliament, abounded. The industrial cities were almost without representation. In one instance 84 men nominated 157 members. In another an ancient wall sent two representatives! The plight of the poor was becoming intolerable. After a bad harvest in 1829 had come the severest winter in sixteen years. The death of the tyrannical George IV in June of 1830 and the accession of his more amiable brother, William IV, aroused new hope among the liberals. Elizabeth went with her sisters and Sam to the end of Nelson Street, where on the corner was read the proclamation of the coronation, and they cheered wildly at the big procession. Soon afterward the July Revolution in Paris stirred democratic hope into action. When Parliament was dissolved the same month and a new election called, every liberal in the country was roused to battle.

Though Elizabeth was only nine, she was just as ardent a politician as her older sisters. The house in Nelson Street became a campaign center. John Harwood brought a huge poster, and the girls helped him hang it over the parlor mantel.

"A long pull! *And a strong pull!* AND A PULL ALL TOGETHER!" it demanded in larger and larger capitals.

To their great joy many Whigs were elected, including the fiery Henry Brougham from Yorkshire, supported by Quakers, Methodists, and other nonconformists as a champion of freedom. A scant six years before Brougham had helped found the University of London. Already he had won fame for his fearless and eloquent championship of just causes. Tall, bony, loose-jointed, gaunt of feature, fiery of temper, he was fast vindicating the judgment of his liberal peers: "Of every human right Brougham was a champion; of every human wrong an avenger." Elizabeth was as ardent a devotee of this brilliant champion of justice as was Samuel.

When, after the Tory Wellington's speech opposing all reform, he was forced to resign and the Whigs came at last to power after twenty-three years, there was even greater jubilation in the Blackwell household. Now victory seemed assured. The king approved the Reform Bill. When it was finally passed by the House of Commons, there was a vast celebration. But the battle was far from over. The bill was defeated again and again by the House of Lords!

"Very well," retorted the Whig ministry. "Then we will create enough new peers in favor of the bill to pass it."

With her sisters Elizabeth veered from discouragement to fresh hope. Gleefully the three acted out a skit which Uncle Browne, chuckling, told them was going the rounds of the papers. It depicted William IV as the master of a stable and complaining because his stable boys would not clean them properly.

"If they don't mind what they're about, I'll take the broom [Brougham] to them!" he was made to threaten severely.

But the king suddenly turned about face. He refused to create the new peers. In October sentiment in the country rose to fever pitch. In London a mob vented its rage by breaking windows and making personal assaults on the opponents of reform. Rumors of violence in other industrial centers reached Bristol, and in the city itself there were murmurs of unrest. As the day approached for Sir Charles Wetherell, Recorder of Bristol, to come to the city on October 29 to open the Assizes, the murmurs swelled to an ominous undertone, for Sir Charles was one of the most notorious opponents of the bill. But Papa refused to be alarmed.

"We won't have trouble here," he said confidently. "Our people aren't that sort. We haven't had a mob in town since the Bridge Riot in 1793."

Elizabeth well knew the story of that most famous of all the many riots which had shaken Bristol. The new bridge, completed in 1768, had been built, not by the city, but by a body of commissioners who had been permitted to levy tolls. After twenty-six years of tolls and the accumulation of two thousand pounds, demands were made that the tolls should cease. It was promised that the bridge should be made free after September 29, 1793, but a few days before that time the tolls were again advertised for subletting. A mob gathered, burned the toll gates, and pelted with stones the militia sent to preserve order. The soldiers became furious and fired up High Street. Before the riot was quelled, eleven persons were killed and fifty wounded, most of them innocent bystanders. Ever since, whenever trouble seemed imminent, people had cried ominously, "Give 'em Bristol Bridge!"

The family was still living at Olveston, the village nine miles out of Bristol where Papa had hired a charming house for summer use. They always hated to leave. Nelson Street seemed big and bleak after the lovely stone cottage with its splendid pyrus japonica on its front and its walled garden, a real brook running through it lined with watercress. All winter they would talk nostalgically of the black roses, the figs, the enormous gooseberries almost the size of a hen's egg, the jolly haymakings in John Beard's meadows, even of Ellen's hapless falling into the brook. Papa drove to and from work each day, fearlessly traveling the solitary lane, often after dark, where more than one crime had been committed, Mamma worrying each night until he returned. He had bought the little yellow carriage and gray pony which the carriage builder had used to drive him and other amateur preachers down to Clevedon, and had named the little horse Bessie Gray.

"After you, 'Little Shy,' " Anna had cheerfully told Elizabeth to the latter's acute but pleasurable embarrassment. "You know you've always been his favorite."

Twice a week the three girls rode with him to take lessons of their masters in drawing and other subjects, chief among them Mr. Hartnell, the principal of the Boys' School in the Fort at the top of St. Michael's Hill. They rode with him on the morning of October 29, all four of them crammed into the front seat of the little carriage, the back seat having been removed to make the weight lighter for the small Bessie Gray. When they reached the tollgate at the top of Stokes' Croft on the Gloucester road, the keeper held up his hand in great excitement.

"Better not go any farther, friend Blackwell. The Recorder's here, and all hell's broken loose!"

Papa paled. "You mean —"

"I mean they're all a-rioting. Streets aren't safe. Anybody goes into town this morning takes his life in his hands."

"But — I must go — my house — my business — "

"Then go by a roundabout way. Don't go straight."

Papa hesitated. "I don't want to put you girls in any danger. Perhaps I'd better take you back."

All insisted that they go on. How they reached Nelson Street none of them remembered. Familiar lanes and alleys had become strange, ominously deserted, shops and shutters tightly closed, not a soul visible. But once they came to a lane choked with crowds, and Papa wheeled the pony and whipped her down another. Not before Elizabeth had caught a glimpse of some of the faces, however! They looked wild, savage, like animals on the hunt. But though Marianne cowered beside her and closed her eyes, Elizabeth kept hers opened wide. In spite of her fear she felt almost exultant. This would show Sir Charles! Maybe he would be sorry now for keeping people from getting their just rights!

Papa herded them into the house, ordered them sternly not to leave it on any condition. He would send one of his men to stay with them. In sudden panic Elizabeth threw her arms about him, begging him to stay where it was safe.

"Sorry, I can't, little Bessie. I must go to the sugar house, then to the Guildhall to see what can be done. This madness must be stopped."

When he had gone, it was Elizabeth, not Anna, who took charge. Marianne wept in a corner by the dining room fire. Anna, who always went to pieces in a crisis, rushed about pulling all the curtains. Calmly Elizabeth went after her, pulling them open; then asked one of the servants, who were equally terrified, to bring them tea. Presently William White arrived, one of Papa's oldest and most loyal workers, who every day of his life since Papa's marriage had come to the house each evening after work to clean the knives and forks and shoes of the whole household. He was pale and trembling, scarcely able to speak from excitement.

"Terrible — whole town gone wild — when Sir Charles got to Totterdown — handed into the sheriff's carriage — crowd met him — yells, groans, hisses — got to Hill's Bridge, carriage pelted with stones — "

As the hours passed and William or one of the servants ventured into the street, more news trickled into the house. Unable to hold court because of the uproar, the Recorder had left the Guildhall for the Mansion House, still in his gown and wig, a mob following his carriage. As it turned along the quay at the bottom of Clare Street, they had tried to upset it, but Sir Charles had arrived at the Mansion House safely and shut himself in. . . . The crowd, two or three thousand strong, was attacking the Mansion House. Windows were being smashed. . . . The mayor had come out and tried to read the Riot Act, the law passed in 1714 defining the conditions under which riot, by common law a misdemeanor, might become a felony. Under its provisions, if any unlawful assembly of twelve or more failed to disperse within an hour after a magistrate had read the act verbatim in the prescribed language, they became guilty of felony, punishable by life imprisonment. But the mayor had only been greeted with a volley of stones and brickbats. One had just missed his head. . . .

The hours dragged like lead. Elizabeth left the others and fled upstairs, crouching by an open window. She was sick with worry for Papa. She wished desperately she were a boy; then nothing could have kept her from rushing out and finding him. As dusk fell, noises outside became louder. Bridewell Prison was not far away, and she could tell that the streets between were filling with people. There was the sound of marching feet . . . soldiers . . . yells . . . screams . . . then after what seemed an eternity, silence.

It was two in the morning, Sunday, when Papa returned, clothes disheveled, face gray with anxiety and weariness. Briefly he told what

35

had happened. Soldiers had been sent in, the 14th Light Dragoons under Colonel Brereton. Fortunately they had been ordered not to fire on the mob, merely to disperse it. Now quiet seemed restored. But enough damage had been done! The Mansion House was half destroyed, its windows smashed. Sir Charles had escaped in disguise by climbing out on the roof, passing from one housetop to another. The magistrates were busy now getting the windows and doors boarded up. Most of the troops had been ordered back to their quarters. Thank God, the worst seemed to be over.

But he was wrong. Elizabeth woke to the sound of shouts and running feet. Hastily dressing in the near-November cold, she rushed downstairs to find Anna and Marianne in tears, old William wringing his hands, the servants too distraught to prepare breakfast. Papa had gone. Hell had broken loose again, worse than before. As soon as the soldiers had left the Mansion House, the mob had returned, torn down all the new barricades, plundered everything they could find, sacked the wine cellars and driven themselves to a drunken frenzy. Heaven only knew what would happen now!

It was a day of terror. There was no thought or desire for meals. Elizabeth again crouched for hours at the upstairs windows, Anna often by her side, their cold hands locked, the two joined in a unity of fear and emotion which brought them into a rare closeness.

"Bessie, what shall we do! Suppose Papa doesn't come back — suppose — " Already there was news of several innocent persons having been killed.

Elizabeth tried to be calm, reassuring. It was a strange feeling, knowing herself to be stronger than the clever and competent fifteen-year-old Anna! But she suddenly sensed that in times like this it would always be so. She felt a hardness within her and a satisfaction which for the moment transcended even fear. It was for this feeling of self-conquest that she had lain on hard boards at night and gone without food, believing toughness was a thing of the body, when all the time it was something inside of you!

When flames began licking the sky, the fragmentary reports from outside became more and more terrifying. Poor old William kept running to the gate and back wringing his hands, and the servants were reduced to babbling incoherence.

"They're burning the Mansion House — mayor and magistrates had to escape over the roof . . . whole square is in flames . . . going to

Council House — burning that — looting, destroying everything — drunken mobs filling the streets — looks like half the town is burning . . .

"Heaven help us, they're coming this way — right down Nelson Street! Stopped at the smith's shop, where they got hammers and crowbars. . . . It's Bridewell they're after now. . . . Gate of the prison on Nelson Street side given way, mob lifted it clean off its hinges, threw it into Frome River. . . . demanded Mr. Evans the keeper to release the prisoners taken last night. . . . Prisoners released — tore off their prison clothes — some running about almost naked! . . . All on fire now. . . . God help us, what's going to become of us!"

The three girls stared at each other in horror, each reacting to the terror in her own way.

"Oh — people!" fumed Anna, stamping her foot. "They're all such fools, such — such barbarians!"

"It's terrible," moaned Marianne, retreating to her corner by the fire. "I won't look. I don't want to even hear about it."

While Anna stormed and Marianne wept, Elizabeth crept upstairs again and opened the window wide toward Bridewell. She gripped the ledge with both hands and clenched her teeth hard, as if to keep terror locked inside of her. The street outside the high wall was full of people. She could not see them, only hear their sound, like the sea in a storm, or like the growl of animals. Once a group passed holding sticks with burning oil-soaked rags, trailing fire along the top of the wall. Occasionally words emerged from the medley.

"Damn it, we *will* have reform!"

"The jail next, then the tollhouses!"

"Hill's Bridge — to stop the London mail!"

"Reform — *reform!* The king! No bishops!"

It was raining, had rained all day. Elizabeth felt the cold wetness mingle with the heat on her cheeks, and she shivered. Papa was wearing his white flannels, dressed for the heat of the sugar house. She hoped he had his greatcoat.

The three prisons, came the report, were all in flames. Next came the Bishop's Palace. It wasn't fair that the bishop should get forty thousand pounds a year, while the poor were starving! "They're plundering the furniture, burning the tables and chairs, cutting open the featherbeds and placing live cinders in them!" Then the churches, the Cathedral . . .

Rags of popery! thought Elizabeth. Should she be glad it was burning? But it was so very beautiful! And the Church of St. Mary Redcliffe! She could not bear to think of its being destroyed. Better the old wooden Bridge Street Chapel! . . . But, no, news finally came that both of the beautiful buildings had been saved, although fires had been kindled on the stone floor of the Chapter House and priceless books destroyed. But when the mob had attempted to break through the cloister doors of the Cathedral, two or three men had daringly placed their bodies in the way and somehow held the mob back.

"They're burning people's houses now," reported old William, his face ashen. "Mostly anti-reformers', but many of the big factories and warehouses are being warned ahead. Let's pray they remember that the master is their friend!"

At dusk the rain fell in torrents, but it did not put out the fires, only seemed to make them burn harder. It looked as if the whole city were on fire. Surely they must see the flames as far away as Cardiff!

"Come away from the window, Bessie," begged Anna. "You'll catch your death!" Impatiently she pulled at the slight figure, but it seemed made of iron. Only when she heard Papa's voice would Elizabeth leave her post. Then she rushed down the stairs as if the house were on fire.

He was not wearing his greatcoat, and he was soaked to the skin. His friend and associate Mr. Goodwin was with him. Had he not been there, they might never have heard what happened.

"You should have seen him! Stood there in the doorway of St. Mary Redcliffe and stretched his arms across! Faced that howling mob with their stones and brickbats — might have been killed — and *made* them listen while he talked to them! It was like arguing with a pack of wolves! But by heavens, at last they listened, turned around and went away meek as lambs. I tell you, it was a miracle! Nobody else could have done it. But they knew he was with them at heart, they trusted him."

"It was nothing." Papa held out his hands to the fire; then, as he winced, Elizabeth saw to her horror that they were badly burned. Old William saw too and hurried to find salve and bandages. "I just happened to be there."

"And in the Cathedral — he helped save that, too, put out some of the fires with his own hands!"

"I did no more than others," said Papa. "You did the same yourself."

Elizabeth stared at him with a mingling of shock, admiration, pride, envy. He, a Dissenter, had risked his life for those "rags of popery" which he hated with such consuming passion! Why? Because the churches were so old and beautiful? Because it was his duty as a good citizen? Or because — her child mind fumbled — because he wanted other people to be as free as he was to believe what they wanted to? She was sure of only one thing: she wished she were grown up — and a *man* — so she could have stood beside him!

4

The riots passed, the worst tragedy in Bristol's thousand years, and the mob reverted, somewhat sheepishly, to their accustomed roles as human beings, all but the five hundred or so who were said to have perished either in the fire, from drunkenness, or at the hands of soldiers, plus the four chief prisoners, who were tried and hanged. Eighty-eight others were sentenced to transportation or imprisonment. It was not the beginning of a revolution, as many had hoped, and did nothing to improve the lot of the oppressed masses.

Somewhat to Elizabeth's surprise, Papa did not seem to blame the rioters. In fact, the few snatches of comments she heard sounded more like sympathy than censure. Riots . . . human madness but never without reason . . . people would endure only so much injustice, then explode like a too-tight boiling sugar kettle. . . . Look at the long history of Bristol riots, the one raised by Kingswood colliers in 1709 when the price of wheat rose from four to eight shillings a bushel! They had dispersed soon enough when the price was decently reduced. And the bread riot of 1753, resulting in four deaths and scores of injuries . . . perhaps as well die by the sword as starve! . . . Blind, obtuse governments, would they never learn what happened when legitimate demands of people were ignored or rejected? Would they still be sending soldiers to quell riots a hundred years hence, clamping even tighter lids on the kettles?

Whether in spite of or because of the massive protests, the Reform Bill was passed in June of 1832. Fifty-six rotten boroughs were deprived of their representation, and these seats were divided among the new manufacturing towns and counties. The vote was given to householders paying a ten pound rental in towns, or forty pounds in the country. There was a great celebration in the Nelson Street house. The girls set plants in all the windows and illuminated the whole house with candles. Over the warehouse gates were placed two enormous pans of

39

grease that were kept constantly burning, with a man to look after each one. But though it was a shining landmark in English history, the bill brought little immediate relief to the poor, merely set in motion new democratic processes which would not be fully achieved in most of their lifetimes.

"Poor people," sighed Papa. "They thought it was going to bring the millennium. Instead, no less of taxes or starvation wages, no downfall of a tyrant aristocracy or of a grasping religion; just a few more votes for some middle-class citizens who have plenty to eat and wear, and some improvement in the manner of voting."

Papa had been badly shaken by the riots. Though the part he had played brought him much favorable recognition, even honor, so that he was mentioned as a likely candidate for mayor, he had lost much of his glowing enthusiasm. Indeed, during the winter following the riots, he seemed to become a different person, abstracted, sober, almost morose.

Elizabeth would always remember this winter of her tenth year as the period when she slowly ceased to be a child. For the first time uncertainty, insecurity, and fear had entered her life. The riots seemed to have loosed the lid of a Pandora's box, letting an unwholesome malaise overspread her whole world.

In whichever direction the children fared forth for their daily walks the scars were there — charred beams, blackened stones, vacant windows like the eye sockets of skeletons. She scanned each familiar face warily — Hunt the butcher, old Mr. Lucas who kept the shop on Wine Street where they bought cheesecakes and "whips," the workers coming from the factories — looking for signs of potential savagery. Had they been part of the rushing, howling mob which had broken windows, burned churches, endangered Papa's life? The two little lions on the fountain opposite the Nelson Street house had lost their jolly look. Now that the water no longer poured, their mouths seemed frozen in an ugly leer. Even the billowing sails of incoming ships in the Bristol harbor had a sinister look, for they might well be bearers of the deadly cholera which had been creeping slowly westward from India and across northern Europe. Early that February, the month she was eleven, the curse struck London. Soon it hit Manchester, where a whole family was swept away within twenty-four hours.

But it was the change in Papa which disturbed her most. The uncertainty, worry, indecision she detected in his manner upset her world. She knew vaguely that he had sustained severe losses in bank failures, that for some time the sugar business had been suffering reverses, but to her helpless dismay she could find out no details. Anna and Marianne were equally ignorant. Even eight-year-old Sam seemed to know more than she.

"It's business trouble." He dismissed all her questions loftily. "Women are not supposed to worry their heads about such things."

Then suddenly the blow fell. The reversed fortunes of the family could no longer be hidden. Two of the great sugar importers' houses failed, and all of Bristol knew that Papa had been a very heavy loser. It was rumored that his losses might have approached seventy thousand pounds. Yet strangely enough, Papa seemed more relieved than dismayed by the disaster. He was like a drowning man who, having struck bottom, gains new impetus to forge to the top. He called the family together in the dining room. With a bounding heart Elizabeth saw that his stooped shoulders were straight again, the glint back in his blue-gray eyes.

"How would you all like to go to America?" he demanded abruptly.

The reaction was sudden but as varied as the group assembled.

"You — you mean — not — not leave — England!" gasped Mamma, paling. Aunt Bar grunted. Aunt Ann reached for her smelling salts. Aunt Lucy looked ready to faint. Aunt Mary nervously fingered the bands of sawtooth trimming above the enormous, balloon-like sleeve of her dress. Anna's cheeks reddened with annoyance. Marianne looked sick. The two boys, struggling with the injunction to be seen and not heard, stifled whoops of excitement. Only Elizabeth, eyes fixed intently on Papa's face, revealed nothing of her tumult of emotion.

He strode about the room, fingers alternately tucked in the pockets of his waistcoat or pulling at his sidelocks. In America, Papa expatiated, a man could easily turn failure into quick success. There was room for new ideas, new ways of doing things. He would find more enthusiastic reception for his new vacuum-pan process for refining sugar. Perhaps — he waved his arms as if throwing aside shackles — he could promote the production of sugar beets, so he would no longer be dependent on the hated slave labor of the Indies. There the boys would not be excluded from schools because their father was a Dissenter. It would be a New World . . . sure success . . . unlimited opportunity . . . room for all.

The news aroused as much consternation in the city as in Samuel

Blackwell's own household. Hastily a group of Bristol merchants met in the Merchants' Exchange to discuss the matter. All were agreed that Samuel Blackwell was one of the city's most valuable citizens. He must not be allowed to leave Bristol because of pecuniary problems. They drew up a set of resolutions, which were unanimously voted and delivered at once to Papa. The undersigned, the paper stated, had heard with the deepest regret that it was Mr. Blackwell's intention to move, with his family, to the United States. They regarded the loss of such a citizen as a calamity to the town; they could think of no other reasons than financial why he could possibly wish to leave; and they pledged themselves, individually and collectively, to furnish him with any amount of capital he might name, as a loan, for any number of years at an interest of only one and a half percent.

Though Elizabeth never saw the imposing document, like the other children she knew what it contained; knew also that Papa had expressed his gratitude but had instantly refused the offer. Once she heard Mamma and Aunt Mary discussing the affair in the parlor when they thought no one was listening.

"If only he had been willing!" mourned Mamma. "Why — *why* isn't he ever able to let anybody help him?"

"Pride," replied Aunt Mary. "He's always been like that. It's the one quality he inherited in full measure from our father."

"But — it would have been so easy! He didn't have to ask. They offered."

"I know. They really want him to stay. And if he did, I don't think there's the slightest doubt that he would be elected mayor."

"I don't care about that." Mamma was weeping quietly. "All that matters is our having to leave everything we know and love and go across that terrible ocean to find heaven knows what."

"Does brother Samuel know how you feel?" demanded Aunt Mary.

Mamma looked shocked and hastily wiped her eyes. "Of course not. It's a wife's duty to follow her husband's wishes without complaint. Don't you dare tell him!"

From that moment Mamma's apparent cheerfulness never wavered. She entertained her church Dorcas Society as usual, receiving them early in the afternoon; helped make garments for the poor, listened bright-eyed to the secretary's report (as calmly as if there were many more to come), gossiped with them pleasantly, and served them a beautiful tea about six o'clock, with her special rasp rolls (wonderful small bread with shiny, springy crust), two or three kinds of delicious cake handed around on handsome silver trays, and the most fragrant coffee with a profusion of thick cream. Then after they had gone, without a quaver she packed away the trays and other fine silver in the rapidly growing piles of household goods which must be sold.

Anna and Marianne were not present during the days of most distressing upheaval, when the precious cultivations of a lifetime were being torn out by the roots. Papa thought they should see London before they left for the New World, and he sent them on a fortnight's trip with Uncle and Aunt Blackwell, first to London, then to Worcester. Desolate with envy, Elizabeth saw them off, excessively proud in their new black silk veils, first badges of womanhood.

When they returned, the Olveston house had been given up, the Nelson Street house dismantled, most of it turned into salesrooms. Almost all of the beautiful rosewood and mahogany furniture was for sale — the dining table polished to a mirror shine, the huge bedsteads with their intricate carvings, the inlaid sofa tables, the chairs of rare wood which gave out such a sweetish smell when rubbed. Not the favorite old red sofa, however. Aunt Mary had made a new cover for it of black and red chintz, and with some other articles of furniture it was going with them to America. The best dishes were going, too, the set Mamma had picked out in Uncle Browne's goldsmith shop after her marriage. Elizabeth herself helped to pack it, proud to be trusted with such precious treasures, in thick tresses of Grandpapa's shavings. Lovingly she stroked the delicate porcelain with its intricate pattern of pagodas, of fragile bridges, of pink, red, and blue long-tailed birds, of gold bands and rectangles. There was a family legend that Mamma had refused the fine set Uncle Browne had wanted to give her as too elaborate for the wife of a poor sugar refiner. How, marveled Elizabeth, could it possibly have been any finer than this!

The silver and other small articles were all set out in the back parlor, with prices marked for each lot. Half the women of Bristol, it seemed, came to inspect and bargain.

"Look at them!" fumed Anna. "Pawing everything, trying to beat the prices down! And they call themselves our friends! Vulgar, hateful pigs, all of them! I'm glad we're going away."

Papa had first thought of sailing from Havre, then from London or Liverpool. But finally, to reduce cost, he had engaged passage on the *Cosmo,* sailing from Bristol. For the last fortnight Elizabeth and the other children, with their governess Miss Major, were housed in furnished lodgings in the Hot Wells, not far from the basin where the ship lay. There was little to brighten the ugly little place except the abundance of jessamine which flowered about the windows of their rooms, but they needed no external aids to color their excitement. Change and adventure were in the offing. Like John Cabot who had set out from this same port over three centuries before, they were about to discover a New World. Even rumors that cholera had broken out with fresh severity in London, where five thousand deaths had occurred, and that cases had been found among the Irish emigrants who had crossed the channel to Bristol to await sailing vessels to America, did little to quell their anticipation. If the new disaster inspired hope in some of their elders that the journey would be postponed, they were disappointed. The ship was cleared for sailing, as scheduled, on a day in August.

A great crowd of friends and relatives assembled at the dock to see them off. Many were in tears. Poor old William White, only one of Papa's sugar house men who had served him for years with worshipful devotion, stood sobbing, heartbroken, declaring there was nothing left for him but to die. Uncle Browne, who since the death of his wife had made his home with Papa, was overwhelmed with grief.

"Your going will shorten my life," he said sorrowfully. And indeed soon after their arrival in America they did receive news of his death in the lodgings into which he had moved in Northumberland Street.

Uncle Charlie, who had strongly disapproved of their leaving, was there, looking as much the foppish gentleman as ever. "I'll sell out my business soon and come to see you," he promised the clinging children while casting meaning glances over their heads at the blushing Miss Major.

There was Mr. Finzel, who had begun life in England as Papa's sugar boiler at the Counterslip house and who, taking over the site later and building on it, would in coming years make a fortune out of the sugar business for himself and his sons.

They were all on board at last — Papa and Mamma, the eight children (another soon to come), Aunt Barbara, Aunt Lucy, Aunt Mary, Eliza Major, and the two house servants Harriet and Jane Bryan. Aunt Ann had bravely chosen to stay in Bristol and teach school. Just as the ship was heaving her anchors it was discovered that two very respectable-looking young women who had taken places as steerage passengers were unable to pay for them. Incensed at their apparent dishonesty, Captain Gillespie had them hauled on deck with all their boxes and was about to send them ashore. Papa immediately made it his business to question them. They were dressmakers, he discovered, who had managed to scrape together just enough to buy provisions for the voyage. If they could only get to New York, they believed confidently, they could make a fortune, so they had installed themselves in their quarters, hoping to escape detection and fully intending to pay for their passage as soon as they could. Now they were in despair. Believing in their honest intentions, Papa paid their passage on the spot. His family was not surprised. It was the sort of thing he was always doing.

Elizabeth wept as they passed down the winding river past Leigh Woods and Clifton Downs, but by the next morning, when they passed the huge rock of Lundy Island rising precipitously out of a stormy ocean, she had ills to nurse worse than homesickness. A dose of hot arrowroot jelly with a spoonful of brandy helped but did not cure the terrible nausea, and she was more seasick than most of the others all through the voyage.

There were some two hundred passengers on board, mostly in steerage, half a dozen in the second cabin. The latter comprised a family named Blandy, for whose oldest daughter Isabella Sam, aged nine, formed a romantic attachment. Fortunately for him she was more receptive to boyish favors than their own four-year-old Ellen, on whom their cabin boy Tom, overflowing with reckless jollity, tried to shower demonstrations of regard. She amused them all with her scornful, "Get along, you gustion creetur." Among the steerage passengers was a bricklayer from Bath, a Methodist lay preacher, Dennis Harris and his wife. Papa was much attracted by his resolute, aggressive piety fearlessly displayed among the godless passengers. At first the passenger list also included a cow, but she soon died, and there was no more milk. For the rest of the voyage diet consisted of salt beef, pork, crackers, and brackish water.

The seven weeks and four days on board ship were a nightmare for most of the Blackwells. The stern cabins which they had thought themselves so lucky to secure took the brunt of the ship's tossing, with ten times more motion than those amidships, while the lovely windows they had so rejoiced in rattled and leaked with every wind that blew. The cabin where Anna and Elizabeth were quartered, with four others, had an iron pillar in the middle of it, proving to their horror to be the drain leading from the deck's roundhouse to the water below, and despite the patchings of the ship's carpenter it leaked incessantly. The fastidious and sensitive Anna was outraged.

"Horrid, stinking, filthy hole!" she kept muttering.

Far from escaping the liabilities of the Old World, they discovered that they were carrying one of its worst curses with them, for cholera soon broke out among the steerage passengers, and several died during the voyage. But except for the inevitable seasickness, the family remained in good health.

They made the trip just a little too early, for already an Englishman named Brunel was designing a steamship which he claimed would negotiate a journey between Bristol and New York without refueling.

"Pipedream!" hooted a noted lecturer as late as 1835. "As ridiculous as to talk about making a voyage from the earth to the moon!"

Yet on April 8, 1838, just five years and eight months after the *Cosmo* hoisted its sails for its seven weeks' journey, the *Great Western* was to leave Bristol with seven passengers and steam into New York harbor fifteen days later; leaving on her return trip of only twelve days to the cheers of a hundred thousand spectators!

Poor Elizabeth, stubbornly refusing to yield to the torturing nausea as she staggered wanly about the deck in pursuit of her exuberant brothers! It was well that she could not see this long hard journey as a prototype of adventures yet to come. For it was by no means the last long hard trek into the unknown which would tax all the strength she could muster because she was years ahead of her time.

Chapter Two

THE WONDERFUL NEW GAS JETS were certainly more revealing than the old candles! Or was this guest whom Papa had brought home, this Mr. William Lloyd Garrison, so on fire inside that his features shed light instead of just reflecting it? Studying the brilliant, protruding eyes, the high dome of forehead with its sharply receding hairline, the flaring nostrils and firm yet mobile lips, Elizabeth wondered if his face might not even glow in the dark.

The closed outside blinds and drawn shades, shutting out every encroachment of the New York streets and the April night outside, enhanced the potency of the spell. The secrecy was imperative, for Mr. Garrison had many enemies. Organizer of two anti-slavery societies, founder and editor of the recently introduced Boston publication *The Liberator*, this bold young reformer was arousing almost as much opposition by his fiery and occasionally belligerent vigor as by his extreme views on slavery. The fact that within two years, in 1835, he would be suffering physical violence from a well-dressed mob of sedate and proper Bostonians, would attest even further his robust and provocative personality.

And he had aroused plenty of opposition here in New York! On one of his recent visits his enemies had conspired to prevent his forthcoming trip to England by having him kidnaped and sent to Georgia. However, he had managed to escape them and reach Philadelphia, intending to outwit them by sailing from there instead of New York, but he had arrived too late. The ship had sailed. Since then he had spent the days waiting for his New York sailing by slipping incognito from one town to another, sheltered in the homes of friends.

"On one occasion," he related the details of the incident now with apparent relish, "I was obliged to flee from the blackguards by riding through a rainstorm in an open wagon."

Elizabeth listened to the exciting tale with as much absorption as the adventure-loving Sam and Harry. But she turned curious. This was a strange man. He seemed actually to enjoy having enemies! But he liked having friends, too. She could tell by the way his eyes gleamed when he told about the crowds who had hung on his words in Boston and Providence and Brooklyn, Connecticut; about the colored people who had wept and clustered about him to shake his hand.

"Perhaps," she decided with a shrewdness beyond her twelve years, "he just likes to be in the center of things."

At last Papa had found an anti-slavery passion to match his own. The two men were tinder to each other's emotions. Papa's eager questions and agreements sparked a constant blaze of rhetorical fervor.

"I am awed by the vastness of the cause I have undertaken," said Mr. Garrison in a voice hushed with humility. "Often I dream about it. I stand on a mountain overlooking Africa and hear the agonized screams of the dying. I see slave ships, their wakes littered with the bodies of men, women, and children. I hear the cries of the suffocating victims in their holds. I see the two million slaves in this guilty land, debased, bleeding, calling for a champion. And out of heaven there comes a voice saying over and over in rising crescendos, 'Plead for the oppressed!' And then I know that I *must* obey the voice from heaven, whether men will hear or not."

"Amen," agreed Samuel Blackwell fervently. A dramatic silence followed.

Elizabeth choked with emotion. Looking about the room for responses to match her overflowing fervor, she noted with surprise and indignation that none of the family except Papa seemed as profoundly stirred as herself. Mamma's pretty smiling face was bent over her mending, one ear politely intent on the conversation, the other cocked for the first warning whimper from Washy — George Washington Blackwell — born soon after the family's arrival in New York six months before. Aunt Lucy was busy with her interminable sewing, Aunt Bar frowning over a bonnet she was trimming. Aunt Mary was listening with amiable politeness, but her eyes held a slightly vacant look, as if she were planning her early morning trip to market. Over in the far corner Miss Major, ostensibly boning up on the children's lessons for tomorrow, was surreptitiously penning a letter, the brightness of her eyes and the pinkness of her cheeks suspicious signs that it was to Uncle Charlie. Marianne, always too lively to keep still for long, was fidgeting on the edge of her chair. Even Anna, the ardent and emotional, was stifling a yawn. And Sam and Harry, permitted to sit up beyond their bedtime, were showing signs of overpowering drowsiness. What was the matter with them all? How could they think about groceries and bonnets and — yes, even babies, when a battle for freedom was waiting to be fought!

Now Mr. Garrison was giving an exuberant description of his impending trip to England, asking Papa's advice on which of the great anti-slavery leaders he should approach to solicit help for a manual labor school for indigent colored students. Wilberforce? Brougham? Buxton? Elizabeth swelled with pride as Papa competently gave advice. Buxton was the man to see. He had succeeded Wilberforce as the driving power of the abolitionist movement. But he did not encourage Mr. Garrison in his hope of financial support for his project. England was too concerned at the moment with the problem of slavery in her own colonies. At least, he told the visitor with some satisfaction, he would be received with courtesy and respect. In London he would not be mobbed and threatened with kidnaping!

The bitterness in Samuel Blackwell's voice reflected the partial disillusionment with which six months in the New World had slowly corroded his high hopes. Many of the old problems had not only followed the family but been compounded. The cholera which had fled with them on the *Cosmo*, taking the lives of several steerage passengers, had arrived in New York before them, stripping the streets of life, sending many of the two hundred thousand inhabitants fleeing to the country, barricading most of the rest behind blank shutters.

It had been night when they reached the pier in the East River, too late to disembark. But Papa had taken the two older boys and, walking to a bake shop, had bought some loaves of fresh bread, welcome indeed after the long diet of hardtack and salt beef. The next day he had hired some rooms at two respectable boardinghouses on Pearl Street, side by side, kept by two maiden ladies. No conveyance being available, the family had walked there, their small baggage conveyed in wheelbarrows, a not unimpressive procession of eight somber adults and eight excited children. Soon afterward Papa had met Dennis Harris, the Methodist lay preacher who had attracted his interest on the *Cosmo*, and on learning that Mr. Harris had not yet found work, had forthwith hired him to help transport their furniture to this house in Thompson Street, which he had rented.

The crisis of cholera had passed. Life had flowed back into the cobbled streets — drays, phaetons, a remarkable omnibus such as they had never seen in England, drawn by four horses, carriages as handsome as any in London yet looking oddly unpretentious with no coronets or miters, no obsequious attendants in smart liveries. Shutters, most of them painted a deep and rather ugly green, had opened, and now that spring had come, the starkly plain and colorless house fronts disgorged their occupants *en masse* every evening, to huddle in a smoking, drinking, spitting, and altogether jolly conclave on a small space in front called the "stoop," seemingly a poor substitute for the ubiquitous English garden, tiny though it might be. The hotels swarmed again with life, bustling and rowdy, factory owners and lumbermen from New England, cotton planters from the South, merchants and mechanics from England, Scotland, France, Germany, part of that vast influx of up to fifty thousand foreigners who were disgorged each year from the ships constantly streaming into the harbor.

Samuel's disillusionment sprang neither from unhappy comparisons with England nor from lack of business prosperity. The absence of picturesque cottages, ivied churches and romantic ruins, splendid halls and castles, the substitution of wooden fences and unsightly walls of loosely piled stones for the neat hedges lining country roads, the badly paved highways and inferior hotels — such drawbacks seemed unimportant. He reveled in the clear dry air, the wide streets, the look of vigor and freshness peculiar to Old Country eyes, the look of newness visible on every hand, raw and crude though it often seemed. His pulses quickened to the tempo of the robust and lusty spirit of this conglomerate people. Even their inquisitive brashness, appearing to his British restraint like sheer impertinence, failed to shock him. Already he was penning the report on the new country which he had promised his friends back home.

"It is a land of vast rivers and lakes, rich fertile plains, thriving settlements. Here every man sits under his own vine and fig tree. Poverty is unknown. This is the true crown of American glory."

There were limitless opportunities in the sugar business. He had brought with him letters from leading members of the trade in England and had soon established a successful business in Gold Street, with Dennis Harris rapidly becoming his efficient foreman. Since Samuel was the only man in America who then understood the process of refining sugar by the use of vacuum pans, his prospects looked good for acquiring a large fortune.

Nevertheless Samuel was becoming more and more disillusioned. He had left England largely to loose himself and his business from the bonds of slavery. Now he found that his conscience had escaped the meshes of one trap only to become caught in another one with teeth of steel. In England the evil had been as far removed as Jamaica. Here it was as near as his own doorstep, part of the very fabric of this "free" land. There his bold protests had met with tolerance, if not indifference. Here they encountered bitter and violent opposition. At first his business associates merely looked at him askance, then with growing suspicion. Now he was already sensing in their attitude an active and dangerous belligerence.

"You're joking! Surely you realize that we'd all be out of business if those blacks were free!"

"What are you trying to do, man, drive us all to the poorhouse?"

"Don't let our West Indian planters hear you spout such rot! You'll never get another shipment!"

"What are you, a fool? Look out, or you'll see that sugar house go up in flames some night!"

His attempts to arouse interest in the growing of sugar beets were less explosive but equally discouraging.

"No good. Too difficult and expensive to grow."

"But all those empty spaces," urged Samuel, "and such a wealth of labor! Surely it would be better for the country's economy to employ free men on its own soil than to import the output of slaves!"

They shrugged. And drive the price of sugar sky high? Just try and sell it, with the other kind in competition! And besides, people were accustomed to cane sugar. He was making good profits, wasn't he? Why try to change things?

Samuel was shocked and appalled by his own forced complicity in the hated slave trade. The Cuban planters from whom he bought his supplies said frankly that they made no effort to raise slaves, finding it more profitable to work them out in seven years and fill their places with fresh Negroes from Africa.

"There are twenty-five thousand colored people in New York," noted Samuel for his report. "The smallest hint of colored blood is detected by American prejudice. They are excluded from schools, churches, and charities. People call them 'niggers,' their dwellings 'rookeries.' Their work is mostly drudgery, as porters on wharves and in stores, or as domestic servants. They seem surprisingly docile. The slaveholders strenuously maintain that the Negro will never labor except under the exercise of the lash. I marvel at the audacity which utters and the credulity which receives so false and stupid a dogma. What the future of this people will be and how the controversy between them and the whites will terminate are problems which I pretend not to solve. They are truly portentous questions, involving the very existence of this Union and of deepest importance to the human race."

To add to the irony of Samuel's dilemma, Parliament chose that very year of 1833 to free all slaves in the British colonial possessions!

2

Other members of the family were disillusioned but for different reasons. The high ugly sliver of a house in Thompson Street seemed less than ideal to tastes inured to spacious rooms, generous open coal fires, and English gardens.

"I feel shut in, stifled," complained mild Aunt Mary, usually the uncomplaining one, "as if I couldn't breathe."

"Sixty pounds a year for this!" sniffed Aunt Bar, reluctant to speak in terms of dollars. "It wouldn't bring twenty-five in London. And a kitchen in the basement!"

It was the price of fuel Aunt Lucy deplored. Twice as much as it had been in England, and fires necessary from October to April! No wonder they were cold. And servants! Five to eight dollars a month for a third of the work you could get out of good English help! Poor Harriet and Jane Bryan, struggling up and down steep flights of stairs, training a slovenly cook, dealing with strange shopkeepers and foreign money, lugging drinking water from a wooden pump at the corner of Houston Street, were soon tearfully saving for passage back to England.

"The food is only half as much here," Mamma would remind gently.

She did no complaining. Only two faint lines in her pretty forehead gave indication of the toll of strength the months had exacted — crossing the ocean in company with a deadly plague, arriving in a strange country nearly nine months pregnant, giving birth for the thirteenth time in a strange house in a strange bed with a strange nurse (though Mrs. Christopher amused the whole household with her blunt American ways), hovering anxiously over the cradle to discover if this mite would go the way of the eight living or the four dead, keeping comparative peace in a household of seventeen variant personalities cramped within an unaccustomed small space. But the demands of living, she soon proved to her satisfaction, were much the same in one country as in another. A man needed the same clean dry change of clothes, the same hot food, the same encouragement, whether his sugar house was in Nelson Street or Gold. Shirts must be sewed, pinafores made, socks mended, whether for expeditions to Mother Pugsley's Field or to Washington Parade Ground. Heated arguments over sermons must be cooled or diverted, whether delivered by Mr. Leifchild or by the Rev. Dr. Samuel Hanson Cox at the Presbyterian church the family decided to attend (and Dr. Cox's unfortunate pro-slavery addiction aroused heated arguments indeed!). Moreover, cases of the sniffles engendered by the blasts of Long Island Sound responded to her same time-honored remedy as those roused by the fogs of Bristol Channel.

> *Wrap your head up in flannel down to your eyes,*
> *Put your feet in hot water up to your thighs;*
> *Take a half pint of rum, going to bed, as a dose,*
> *With a candle dip end, well tallow your nose.*

Elizabeth had never felt more solitary, less related to her brothers and sisters. Anna and Marianne, at seventeen and fifteen, were now women, lacing their developing figures into tight, spindle-waisted corsets, stuffing their sleeves with pillowlike padding to simulate enormous balloons, fussing interminably over the decorations of their bonnets, while her wiry, flat-chested body was still bundled into Aunt Lucy's shapeless worsteds and merinos. She took little interest in either their preoccupation with dress or their nostalgic sighings for the superiorities of England.

"These rough filthy streets!" they were always fussing. "A lady can't step out the door without soiling her skirts. Mud, snow, slush — to say nothing of scavenging pigs!" . . . "Not an impressive building in the town except maybe the City Hall and Merchants' Exchange! What a contrast to Westminster Abbey and Parliament!"

Elizabeth missed England, yes, horribly, but here they were and they might as well make the best of it. She thought New York a pleasant Dutch town with its comfortable frame houses and shady parks, its rural suburbs, its simple life and friendly customs. She felt equally removed from the childish exuberance of Sam and Harry, who, since the ship had passed Sandy Hook lighthouse and entered the Narrows where they had caught their first glimpse of the distant shoreline of roofs and steeples rising out of a forest of masts, had lived in an orgy of excitement.

Not that she failed to enjoy all their childish pleasures! She was as excited as they when Papa took the whole family for a sleighride that first winter, away up Bloomingdale Road (later to be known as Broadway), lined with all its country seats and villas, even though none of them had known enough then to bundle up, and they had all returned nearly frozen. She reveled in the sliding expeditions on the ponds up at the Washington Parade Ground (later called Washington Square). She was as thrilled as the boys when their landlord, an old gentleman named Jennings, visited them and told hair-raising stories of the numerous rattlesnakes on his lands in Pennsylvania. And she shared the younger children's intensity of grief when Anna, having heard of the excellence of American pumpkin pie, filled a deep pie-dish with square blocks of pumpkin, added water and brown sugar, and baked it like one made with fruit.

"Horrible!" they all wailed. "Uneatable!"

But it was with her father that Elizabeth was beginning to feel the strongest unity. More perhaps even than Hannah, she sensed his deepest longings and frustrations. Like him, she found the necessary daily activities — school with Miss Major, music lessons, piano practice — of secondary importance. All around her she saw a new world in the making, full of exploding ideas like those pounding at the portals of her own adolescence. As in England with the Whigs in power, reform was in the air. Andrew Jackson, courageous, vigorous, was in the White House, triumphant from a campaign whose rallying cry had been, "Down with the aristocrats!" Out of a frontier West had come the impact of a new democracy, resulting in wider suffrage, and the new masses of voters were demanding shorter hours of labor, reformatories instead of dungeons, more popular education, an end to the senseless custom of throwing men into prison for petty debts. And a few bolder people, like Garrison, Samuel May, and — yes, Samuel Blackwell, were daring to proclaim that no man had the right to own another.

Anti-slavery was a cause readymade for a sober, clear-eyed adolescent, especially when it boasted a heroine like Prudence Crandall, a young teacher in Canterbury, Connecticut, who had outraged her community by daring to take a Negro girl into her school, then flouted every prejudice of conservative New England by starting a school "for the reception of Young Ladies and Little Misses of color." The resultant campaign of intimidation, litigation, and violent persecution exploded into flaming headlines in the anti-abolition press and into the ardently defensive editorials of William Lloyd Garrison's abolitionist newspaper, *The Liberator*.

Elizabeth wished passionately that she were old enough to go to Connecticut and help Miss Crandall teach. She would walk through the streets with head held high and be glad if they pelted her with stones. She followed the news from Canterbury with tense absorption, reading every detail in *The Liberator*: the arrest of Prudence in July on an old vagrancy charge, her trial for breaking a new state law, the conviction and appeal, the final dropping of the case for lack of evidence. She agonized when in September the Crandall well was filled with manure, sweated in sympathy when Prudence's father carried water two miles from his farm to keep the school going, fumed silently when windows were broken and fires started in the Crandall house, felt despair and a bit of shame when Prudence finally gave up the fight and closed her school out of fear for her pupils' lives.

But she could feel only a fierce pride in the part Papa was playing. In October of 1833 Mr. Garrison returned from his triumphant trip to England, where he had aroused American furore by his scathing denunciations of slavery and the colonization movement, and was met by a hostile mob bent on preventing the organization of a New York Anti-Slavery Society. Joining the mob, he was carried to the proposed meeting place, which was found closed and locked. The trustees had denied the organizers the use of the building.

"And all the time," Papa chuckled grimly, "Tappan and the others were at the Old Chapel in Chatham Street getting the society organized. By the time the mob discovered their whereabouts the meeting was almost over. The abolitionists got out the back way. When the mob poured in the front, they found nobody but a solitary Quaker calmly praying in one of the pews!"

It took courage to belong to the Anti-Slavery Society in the following months. Most of the leading citizens — editors, lawyers, clergymen, politicians — were bitterly opposed to the movement. Many were "colonizationists," advocates of the plan to gradually establish freed Negroes in an African colony, but apologists for the institution of slavery. The pro-slavery demonstrations reached their climax in the summer of 1834, when an Englishman, George Thompson, came to New York as a delegate from the British Anti-Slavery Society, denouncing slavery as a crime and slaveholders as robbers and murderers. Elizabeth was present with other members of the family when Thompson spoke in a stone church near their house at the corner of Thompson and Broone streets. Excitement rose to fever heat. A mob gathered outside began to pelt the windows with stones. Amid the crash of falling glass and the howls of the mob, Samuel managed to get his family out and safely home. For three days they stayed locked in the house, all except Samuel who went regularly to his place of business, while the brutal mob attacked the homes, churches, and persons of colored residents and other citizens known to be abolitionists.

"For no other crime," wrote Samuel to his friends back in England, "than presuming to apply to black people the foundations of American freedom, 'that all men are created free and equal.' "

Perhaps it was fear resulting from this ugly temper which caused him to remove his family to a country home on Long Island in the spring of 1834, though for himself he never compromised. One night, to Hannah's dismay, he returned home from an abolitionist meeting with hair disheveled, clothes in disarray, and all the buttons torn off his stylish plum-colored coat. Please, Mamma begged, oh, please do not go to one of those terrible meetings again!

"It's this country," snapped Aunt Bar. "Savages, all of them! Such a thing couldn't have happened in England."

Elizabeth stared at her. Had she forgotten already the riot in Bristol? And did she really think that the man who had kept a mob at bay on the steps of St. Mary Redcliffe would stay away from a meeting because he was afraid?

It was like Olveston again, living in the house on Long Island. There were flower gardens, fruit trees, a barn and carriage house, an orchard, clover fields and pastures, a fowl house, and even a pig sty! Elizabeth reveled in the country air, the wide spaces, the big frame house. It was good to run again, to tumble in hay, to bite into fruit fresh from the trees, to caress animals. She even enjoyed the prevalence of insects, to which the adults found it so difficult to adjust.

"English poets celebrate the night," Papa wrote back to England, "as the chosen season of silence and meditation. Not so here! With the setting sun all America becomes vocal—bullfrogs, locusts, whippoorwills, crickets, mosquitoes!"

He had an even worse complaint, for close to the garden was a marsh, and Papa, who was extremely sensitive to malaria, was soon attacked by bilious fever, the effects of which would remain with him the rest of his life.

For herself Elizabeth had only one regret: it was too far away from the exciting, changing world of ideas and people. She welcomed every opportunity to go back to the city. To reach the ferry and New York from this spot about three miles from Williamsburg, between Newtown and Flushing, it was necessary to have a gig and horses, two of them, and at her suggestion they were named William Lloyd Garrison and Prudence Crandall. Often when they drove into New York, they went by way of Brooklyn, a single street of scattered houses, because at a special bakery there they had found nice plum buns, sweetened cakes containing raisins and currants.

To Elizabeth's relief her participation in anti-slavery activities was not curtailed. In fact, remoteness from the city made possible a most daring enterprise, for Anna and Marianne organized a small school for Negro children living nearby on the banks of Newtown Creek, and she was permitted to help with the teaching. She was also busily involved with Mamma and her sisters in a huge Anti-Slavery Fair which was held at Niblo's Gardens in the city. It ran for several days, and in spite of hostile propaganda many people attended. Even young Harry was enlisted by the energetic Anna to write mottoes for sugar kisses being sold at her booth. One of his efforts was crude but to the point:

> *Hurrah for the banner of Stars!*
> *Hurrah for the banner of stripes!*
> *Get up, you black niggers all covered with scars,*
> *Hurrah for the banner of stripes!*

Elizabeth needn't have worried about their remoteness from the world. The world came to them. Mr. Garrison came, to sit in the flaring lamplight, wiping the sweat from his bald dome and spouting fiery denunciations of slavery like a righteous dragon, then, to Anna's delight, reciting long stanzas of his favorite Russian poetry. Samuel May came, the frail gentle Unitarian minister from Brooklyn, Connecticut, as quiet in his abolitionist zeal as Garrison was fiery, yet equally devoted. Even

Mamma, horrified at first by the invasion of Unitarian heresy, soon decided that his unorthodox lips would not pollute her best teacups.

And then one day in that long hot summer of 1834 there was heard the clatter of horses' hoofs, and a tightly closed carriage rolled up to the door. Elizabeth and the younger children rushed out. To their amazement, for it was early in the day, Papa was first to descend. After him came a man, a woman, and five children. The man looked very pale. The woman and children had been crying. Elizabeth recognized the man as Dr. Samuel Cox, minister of the Presbyterian church the family had often attended.

"Tell your mother we have guests," Papa told Elizabeth. She thought she had never seen him look so stern, and for some reason he rushed the Coxes into the house as if he were afraid someone would see them. "Our friends will be staying with us for a while."

Elizabeth was more pleased with this announcement than she would have been some months before, when Dr. Cox had roused family ire by his pro-slavery sermons. Recently he had been to England to attend a World's Evangelical Conference, and having found abolitionism popular there, he had returned home almost as ardent in his opposition to slavery as he had been heretofore in its defense. Now, while helping Mamma serve tea to the distraught guests, Elizabeth listened with horror and fascination to Papa's account of what had happened. On Sunday Dr. Cox had preached a sermon on tolerance, begging his people to remain sane amid the spate of racial hatred which had overrun the city.

"Jesus himself," he had reminded them, "was a Semite, not a Caucasian. He had a darker skin than ours."

Immediately the *Courier and Inquirer*, New York's leading commercial paper, edited by James Watson Webb, an apologist for slavery, had announced editorially that Dr. Cox in his sermon had denied that the Savior was a white man. Word had then gone abroad that he had said, "Jesus Christ was a nigger." The already inflamed mob, with a sudden unwonted display of piety, had risen in righteous wrath, attacked the church, smashed its windows, and broken into the parsonage. Warned that he was in danger of lynching, Dr. Cox had fled with his family in the closed carriage which Samuel Blackwell, also forewarned, had managed to procure. A little later the minister's brother, Dr. Abraham Cox, who was the Blackwell family physician, joined the exiles.

Elizabeth's first burst of heroic fervor was soon tempered by the complications resulting from the addition of eight persons to an already bulging household. The mere serving of tea each afternoon was a caterer's headache. The girls' French and music lessons from instructors in New York, as well as regular school sessions, had to be suspended. And the excitement of Sam and Harry waned considerably when they found themselves not only sharing food, toys, and books with the five young guests but sleeping rolled up in blankets on the hard hall floor. The girls fared little better on quilts in the stiflingly hot attic.

The two Doctors Cox reacted to the imprisonment according to their variant personalities. The clergyman, already regretting his sally into unpopular reform, walked disconsolately about, sighing deeply and overwhelmed with terror and despair. Elizabeth could scarcely hide her contempt. "Turncoat, coward!" she muttered under her breath. But for Dr. Abraham, irascible and opinionated though he was, she had only admiration.

"Let the mob come! We'll be ready for them!" he announced to the world at large. Whereupon he spent his enforced vacation practicing pistol shooting behind the barn, his zeal greatly exceeding his skill, for several of his bullets landed in the back of the family carriage. Elizabeth endured agonies fearing for the safety of Prudence and William Lloyd. Glad though they were to furnish sanctuary, the whole family breathed sighs of relief when Dr. Cox, venturing into the city after ten days, deemed it safe to move his brood back into the parsonage. Back in his pulpit he hastened to temper his zeal and was never afterward heard of as a reformer. The friendship rooted in the shared experience of the two families, however, was to grow and thrive for many years.

Another guest at the Long Island house was far more welcome. Great was the joy of all when the world arrived at their door in the shape of Uncle Charlie, gay and debonair as ever, complete with exotic gifts from far places, a brand new spate of fantastic tales, and the recently acquired title of "Captain," a promotion which had been his hope and despair for many years . . . also with an unabashed and purposeful gleam in his eye for the blushing Eliza Major.

The children, even sophisticated Anna, listened with rapt admiration to the tale of his latest adventure, when he had been shipwrecked during his return from India in the Persian Gulf, emerging with only one possession: a miniature of his mother which he had badgered his sister Hannah into giving him and which he had managed to hang on to as he swam to shore. The children looked at the poor wreck of a thing, enthralled, trying to trace their grandmother's delicate features through the encrusted mold.

Anna, who had always yearned for acquaintance, if not intimacy, with Uncle Charlie's aristocratic wife and children, inquired eagerly for "Aunt Fanny" and "our darling cousins Edward and little Fanny." Uncle Charlie was vague. He had heard that his estranged wife was dead, and his children were doubtless being cared for by her relatives.

"Oh, dear," his sister Hannah was heard to remark wistfully, "what a nice wife our Eliza Major would make you!"

As the days of his visit passed her hints became more pointed. With an almost incredible naïveté and lack of conventional morality in one so manifestly pious, she actually encouraged a course which her far more weak-minded brother was eager to pursue.

"As you say, the report of her death is no doubt true. And — and even if it were not, dear boy, surely in the sight of God you are free to marry, since she has practically divorced herself from you all these years."

Such encouragement was irresistible, and if Samuel countered his wife's advice with sterner and more legal logic, it had little effect. Charles Lane and Eliza Major were duly married, to the delight of all the children except two: Harry, who endured tortures of jealousy, and Anna, who being old enough to understand the implications of the possible offense, would live for years under the shadow of impending family disgrace. Uncle Charlie renounced his army affiliation with the further advance in rank and pay which must surely have come with time, so surely, in fact, that he felt not the slightest compunction about passing himself off as "Major Lane." He and Eliza opened a school in New York, where the waggish and convivial Charles was soon as thoroughly at home in the Hotel Astor as in his old haunts in London and Bristol. And Anna, now a mature nineteen, was constituted governess of the younger children in place of Eliza, ruling them with a rod of iron.

3

"There are only a few buildings worthy of note," wrote Samuel Blackwell to his English friends after two years in New York. "Just the City Hall and the Merchants' Exchange, of white marble, nothing else striking. There are only two squares which really deserve the name, Hudson and Washington. The Park, in which the City Hall stands, and the Battery, a delightful open space on the extreme southern point of it, with a profusion of beautiful trees and open to the public, are the only promenades. There are excellent marketplaces. The city is indifferently lighted and badly paved, with accumulations of filth which would not be countenanced in a European city, partly due to the absence of public sewers and drains and want of water.

"The shores of the island within the limits of the city with the exception of the promenade and Battery are formed into one continuous quay or wharf. The quays are of wood, destitute of the convenience common in all parts of England, with a mean appearance, and in wet weather they are filthy.

"The island is destitute of bridges. The waters around are too deep and broad to permit of their construction. But steam ferryboats, able to bear carriages fully laden, make transportation easy."

Samuel knew whereof he spoke, for he and his family made almost daily use of the ferries, first across the sound to Long Island, then over the Hudson to New Jersey. It was a Dutch friend, Mr. Alofsen, who persuaded him to make the move to Paulus Hook, soon to be known as Jersey City.

What a relief to exchange the high thin wedge on Thompson Street, even the remote house on Long Island, for a big home set high on a hill above the river, with clean air to breathe, woods and fields close by for walking and romping, and one of the most exciting panoramas in the world spread at your feet! It was like owning a box seat in a huge theater, imagined Elizabeth, though because of the family's religious taboos she had never been inside one. Walking the long porches by the hour, she never tired of the constant flow of action — frigates with lofty riggings, merchantmen proudly displaying strange flags, yachts with bellying colored sails, chugging ferryboats — all moving against the backdrop of New York skyline, its spires and towers and rooftops rising out of a forest of masts.

There were tragedies played on the stage, as on a night in December, 1835, when, safe and warm from the bitter cold outside, they heard the distant clanging of the fire bell across the river. Hurrying to the porch, they gasped, for it looked as if the whole city were in flames.

61

"The sugar houses!" gasped Papa, and hastening to pull on warm clothes, he rushed to the ferry.

There were two sugar refineries now. Just that year Samuel had entered into partnership with a branch of the eminent London firm of Gower, Guppy, and Company, who had put up in their Congress Sugar Refinery on Duane Street the first vacuum pans ever erected in America. Competitors in New York were still boiling sugar over an open fire in a vascule pan and deodorizing with clay and syrup. Business was booming with a margin of seven cents a pound between raw and refined sugar, and Papa and Mr. Stephen Gower, who was representing the English firm in New York, were well on their way to making a fortune. No wonder Samuel had rushed off in panic!

Bundled into a coat and shawl and still shivering from cold as well as fright, Elizabeth walked the porch, stamping her icy feet, clenched fists burrowing into her mittens, and stared with fascinated horror into the inferno. It was the terror of the Bristol riots all over again, the still older nightmare of a small child clinging to the hot railings at the top of Bridge Street when the Counterslip sugar house had burned. It seemed wicked to weigh personal dangers in the face of such monstrous disaster, yet one could not help it. Would Papa return safely? Would the new family security, so dearly won, be wiped out? And what of Aunt Bar and Aunt Lucy, who had remained in lodgings in the city to run a small millinery shop? And Uncle Charlie and Aunt Eliza, with their little boarding school? To say nothing of the Coxes, the Harrises, and all their other friends! If only she could do something, like Papa, not just watch from the sidelines!

It was like looking into the maw of a volcano. While the flames leaped, licking up more and more of the horizon, the hours of night only crawled. After pacing the porch and staring until the cold became unbearable, the girls would huddle by the fire just long enough to thaw stiffened fingers and set toes to throbbing, then return to pace and stare again. The boys spent most of the night down by the wharves. If Papa had not sternly forbidden them to follow him, they would undoubtedly have tried to find some way to get across. Occasionally they returned to warm themselves and report the latest news, picked up goodness knew where.

Starting in Merchant Street among the dry goods stores, the fire had soon spread to Pearl and Water. Engines were slow. Pumps buried in ice had to be thawed with hot water. Flames swept along wooden gutters and shutters, whipped by an icy wind, leaped the narrow streets, roared into the docks and along the piers, set vessels ablaze. The volunteer firemen were almost helpless, the puny streams of water relayed from ice-choked East River by a chain of engines but futile gestures. It was like fighting a giant with toy darts. By one o'clock South Street was gone, by two the proud new Merchants' Exchange with its thick stone walls in ruins. A navy barge braved the raging wind, hoping to fetch dynamite from the magazine at Red Hook in time to blow a space before the holocaust should reach the uptown residential frame houses. Meanwhile the small supply from Governor's Island was used to blow up strategic buildings, but the flames leaped every barrier. That morning six daily newspapers failed to appear because their plants were demolished. Firemen dropped exhausted at their posts, some with clothes frozen so stiff that they had to be cut from their bodies. It was noon before a gap was finally made at Coenties Slip by blowing up a big brick warehouse, and the flames were checked. Though the smoke continued to billow and the flames to devour hungrily, and would for many days, the worst was over.

Not for the Blackwells, however. It was three days — three acts of terrible mounting suspense — before their agony ended. Only then did Papa return, gray and gaunt, clothes stiffened with ice from the pumps he had helped man. The two sugar houses were untouched. Relatives and friends were safe. But relief, sweet though it was, tasted too bitter of tragedy to be savored. The city had been gutted from Wall Street to the Battery. Forty blocks had been consumed, between sixteen and twenty million dollars' worth of property destroyed. Merchants, many with French fabrics on consignment from Lyons, were ruined. Thousands were homeless and destitute. Not for almost thirty years, until the Draft Riots of 1863, would New York again experience such utter tragedy. Elizabeth would be there to witness that, too, only not from the sidelines.

Four days after Christmas she went with Sam and Mamma into the city, and they viewed the shambles. Streets were strewn with charred timbers, broken glass, bits and wrecks of merchandise discarded even by the most beggared looters. Many damaged goods were being sold at auction. Inspecting them hopefully, Mamma shook her head. "They would be dear for nothing," she said sadly.

It was a bitter winter. Elizabeth often slept with a featherbed on top of her as well as underneath. When Sam went to the city to buy her a birthday present the second of February, he was unable to get back, the river was so filled with ice. Papa spent every third night now at his Washington Street sugar house guarding against fire, because all the insurance companies were either ruined or deep in debt, and in case of another disaster there could be no assurance of redress. Sam and Henry, who went to school in New York every day when the river was passable, often spent the night with him.

Elizabeth also was attending a school in New York that year, as well as taking music and French lessons from private tutors. She was an avid student of most subjects, especially history and metaphysics. Only one subject aroused in her acute distaste: physiology. The very thought of dwelling on the physical structure of the body filled her with disgust. One day her professor, attempting to interest his class in the marvelously intricate structure of anatomy, brought the eye of a bullock to the classroom. Elizabeth took one horrified glance at the glazed staring orb resting in its cushion of somewhat bloody fat and fled precipitately to the restroom. For days she could scarcely think of the incident without retching.

Yet, oddly enough, at the same time she despised herself for this physical weakness. She had always felt a peculiar impatience with sickness of any kind. Dutifully she nursed Marianne during her increasingly frequent bilious attacks, held the basin, mopped her sweating forehead, fed her hot gruel when she was beginning to mend, but all the while stifling a surge of contempt and revulsion. When in May she and Emily and Howie all came down with attacks of intermittent fever, she felt more angry and ashamed than miserable. One day she was forced to leave school early, she was so racked with chills. But she did not go home. Instead, after leaving the ferry she walked for miles into the country, head swimming, body alternately shaking and perspiring.

"I won't, I won't give in to it!" she mouthed between clenched teeth. "I'll walk it off, I will, I will!"

When she found she could not, she returned home and shut herself in a dark room, locking the door and refusing to come out or let anybody in until the worst stage of the fever was over. Sickness of any kind, she felt, was no cause for pampering. She would not be like Anna and Marianne, who went to a doctor and got themselves bled every time they felt unwell.

She took a fierce pride in her physical strength, which made her more than a match for all her brothers and sisters. She did not have

Anna's beauty or cleverness. She looked like a wisp of straw, pale hair, pale complexion, even pale eyes, though whenever she became intensely concerned about something, which was often, the blue dominated the gray. She could not be popular like the merry and beguiling Marianne. All verve and sparkle seemed locked inside of her. But the wisp of a body, which stubbornly stopped growing at a bit over five feet, had the strength of a steel rod. The long tramps, the romps with her brothers, perhaps even the nights of lying on a hard floor and the days of going without food, all had contributed to the toughness she coveted. The family, and the boys especially, could testify to that. More than once she would settle an argument by picking up the opposition and carrying him or her about the house until, worn out with laughter and useless entreaties for release, the dissenter would capitulate.

But physical strength could not compensate for her many frustrations. It seemed that she was always the odd one, the one left out. It was Anna and Marianne who stayed frequently with the Coxes in New York, Marianne who was invited to visit the Samuel Mays, their antislavery friends who were now living in Schuylerville. Then when the time came for her to come home, it was Mamma and Sam who Papa suggested should go and fetch her.

"I think it very strange," Elizabeth confided to her new "Private Journal," on the cover of which she had drawn the significant picture of a woman with a scimitar, "that I should be left so entirely out of sight."

She did go to Schuylerville, however, with Mamma and Sam, whizzing up the river at a fine rate. At Troy they stayed overnight in the Mansion House Hotel where in the morning they were served an enormous breakfast. There must have been a hundred people at the table. "Quite inspiring," observed the droll Sam, "to see those long lines of faces, each with its mouth and teeth going like millwheels!" A student of Virgil, he was also intrigued by the "Trojans," but, "mirabile dictu," there was no "pious Aeneas" or "fidus Achates" or "parvus Iulus" in sight.

The journey by packet boat up the canal to Schuylerville took about eight hours, for the horses were slow, but they arrived about seven in the evening and after much wandering found the Mays' house. Too shy to express her joy at seeing her old friends, again Elizabeth felt left out. Watching Sam being hugged by the two boys, George and Charles, smiled on by Irene and Caroline, she wished desperately that she could be more like all of them.

It was her own fault, she knew, that so often she felt excluded, as on the day in July when she went with Uncle Charles and Aunt Eliza, Mr. Gower, Anna, Marianne, Sam, and Harry to see the French frigate *Arctemise* lying in the harbor. It was a splendid vessel, very clean and shining, with two tiers of guns and four hundred and sixty men. "Not to be compared with an English man o' war," observed Uncle in a lofty aside, but to the rest of the party it appeared magnificent. One of the officers put a sort of percussion cap in one of the big cannons and asked Marianne — of course Marianne! — to fire it. She pulled a little cord, and a small hammer fell down, striking a spark. The detonation shook the deck. Anna and Marianne played the piano in the officers' cabin, and Anna talked French to the officers like a veteran, but Elizabeth was too timid even to try, though she understood much that was spoken. Would she feel any less awkward and tongue-tied, she wondered, when she was eighteen or twenty?

Even when she became articulate she was often misunderstood, as on the evening when Papa seemed especially quiet and almost morose. Thinking he was asleep, Elizabeth went up to him and said, "Aren't you going across tonight?" To her amazement Mamma raised a warning finger and shook her head reprovingly. The next day she delivered a severe lecture on the rudeness of calling Papa "cross" to his face. Explanation brought laughs from everybody, but Elizabeth was vexed.

Only to her journal did she confide most of these frustrations.

"January 5. Anna and I had a quarrel. She is so fond of lecturing me I could not bear it any longer."

"January 11. Anna and I not yet reconciled. I am afraid our project of living together in England would be rather uncomfortable put into execution."

"February 27. Mamma told me to get out some butter and sugar. Instead I went upstairs. Papa told Mamma I should not go on with music. I do not think I am treated at all justly, for Papa told me I could learn if I taught Howard and Wash. Mamma will allow Anna and Henry to be as impudent and selfwilled as they please with merely a slight reproof, but directly I do something that does not please, the strongest punishments are resorted to."

"April 4. I began to teach Howard writing. Just as I was getting to bed Anna sent me a most dignified note of forgiveness for my past conduct. Our estrangement of more than three months is at an end."

"May 15. I took a music lesson of our new master Mr. Jones. Don't think I shall like him."

"May 29. I was taken to task for my manners today, Mr. Jones having told Uncle that he 'supposed I did not mean to affront him but really he thought I was a very singular young lady.' Marianne seemed particularly displeased with me and said I behaved in the same manner to every gentleman, that Dr. Cox thought I had taken a great dislike to him. To all this I could only say that I wished they would point out the faults of which I was guilty and that until they did so I should most certainly behave in the same manner, as I considered proper."

"June. Miss Webb says that I am really her favorite and she would like to have me for a friend, she always liked those mysterious sort of persons. I shall care very little about it, even if people think I am a queer."

"July. I wish I could find some good way of maintaining myself, but the restrictions which confine my dear sex render all my aspirations useless."

"October 3. Went to Columbia commencement. How I long to go to college! The Greek oration called up a multitude of thoughts and the melancholy reflection that the enchanting paths of literature were not for me to walk in."

"February 14. Read Foster's essay on decision of character. How I do long for some end to act for, some end to be obtained in this life, for though that most glorious end 'to serve God and enjoy him forever' is before me and I hope and trust I am laboring for that end, yet God has given us talents to be used in earthly pursuits; and to go on every day in much the same jog-trot manner without any object is very wearisome."

Not that she spent her time in self-pity or repining! The years in Jersey City were brimful of activity. After finishing her formal school study in June of 1836 she continued to take private lessons in music and French, pursuing both with a furious intensity. Fortunately Papa did not make good his threat of discontinuing her music study, and lessons continued as compensation for her giving Emily, Ellen, Howard, and Washy the rudiments of education. Her daily stint of piano practice was five hours, but in spite of progress made she often confided discouragement to her journal.

"Alas, I fear it is no good to attempt to make a first-rate player!

"I gave Heig's variations on Weber a regular broadside, and am not yet beaten. Am determined not to give them up. It's intolerable to hear Anna say, 'Of course it is nothing but what I expected.' "

It was Sam, not she, who distinguished himself in French, winning a prize for excellence. Papa gave him three dollars in recognition of his achievement, which of course he spent on books.

In fact, all the older children shared a passion for books. They begged and borrowed them from friends. They gave them as Christmas presents, stinting on actual necessities when times grew harder and money became scarce. For Christmas in 1837 Elizabeth bought Goldsmith's *Poems* for Sam, Watts's *Logic* and Scott's *The Lay of the Last Minstrel* for her older sisters, lamenting because books were so dear. Her own chief presents were Coleridge's *Poems* and a collection of *Spiritual Songs*. But her reading that year contained more substantial fare than poetry. It included Bacon's *Essays*, Jeremy Taylor's *Holy Living*, Harriet Martineau's writings on America, as well as lighter works of current interest. She confessed to neglecting her chemistry, French, and philosophy for *Belinda* and became enthralled with the first installment of the Pickwick Club *Papers*. But *The Bride of Lamermoor* outraged her feminine pride. Lucy's weakness infuriated her.

"If I had been her," she fumed, "I should have knocked down my father, overturned my mother, and fled over my elder brother into my lover's arms."

Such feminine boldness, however, was confined to vicarious imaginings. Since the episode of the small blond boy in her childhood she had seldom been free from romantic flutterings in the presence of personable males, yet she viewed all such instincts with profound distrust. Invariably, if she came to know the subject better, he turned out to be at best an egotist or a prig, at worst an insufferable bore. Better to nip all such emotions in the bud!

"I went to the tabernacle today," she confided once to her journal. "Resolved to act with a little more dignity and not be so taken with the appearance of a young gentleman there. I regarded him with the most stoical indifference, thought of Bacon and Newton, determined that the outside is a worthless casket, that the mind is the standard of the man, lofty imaginations, spiritual, bright beams of genius, and all that."

In fact, the caliber of her own family spoiled her for most other relationships. Papa had always been her idol. Sam and Harry were rapidly approaching her intellectual level. She took long walks with them — twelve miles to a Dutch settlement by the Communipore way, eighteen miles along the hills behind Hoboken. Uncle Charles was an almost daily evening visitor, establishing himself in his customary corner of the red chintz sofa and keeping the family in an uproarious mood with his songs, jokes, and tall tales. Recreation was never a problem. There were contests, reading, music, dancing. Even Mamma liked to dance and was light as a feather on her feet. Always on Christmas Eve and often at other times the whole group played games: consequences, blindman's buff, beast bird or fish, magic music, charades, hunt the rabbit, turn the trencher, how'd you like it. At a party to which Sam and Harry were invited they played a game called "Quakers," but when they tried to introduce it at home it lacked allurement. Small satisfaction in chasing one's sister around a circle in order to catch and kiss her!

Elizabeth did not shine at such social gatherings, whether at home or visiting friends. At least she thought she didn't. ("Afraid I shall never dance gracefully . . ." "Anna and Marianne went to Mrs. Dummer's part of the evening. I thought I would be too many so did not go. I should have liked to do so for the purpose of getting over my feeling of awkwardness." . . . "At Uncle's. Plenty to eat as usual. Had music, but as Anna was the musician, of course it was overdone." . . . "I think sometimes a hermit's life would suit me very well.")

Her religious activities, though faithfully executed, did not fill the void. In Jersey City Papa hired a pew at St. Luke's Dutch Reformed Church, but since family custom dictated attendance both morning and afternoon, Elizabeth often found herself subjected to the ministry of a Mr. Lusk, from whom she derived little benefit. Only to her journal did she confide her spiritual frustrations.

"January 29. Went to Mr. Lusk's twice. How very inanimate he is!"

"March 5. Mr. Lusk so dull I could not keep up my attention. Slept through his second most tremendous prayer and much of the sermon."

"March 27. Mr. Lusk called and talked his peculiar drawl."

"February 9. The more I think on the subject the more I find in Episcopalianism that I don't think right."

But into one activity she could pour all her passionate fervor: antislavery. All the older members of the family were involved, even Sam and Harry. It was one area of community life in which women were permitted full participation, barring the right of public speech, and even this sacrosanct male prerogative was meeting startling challenge. To New York in the mid-thirties came the Grimké sisters Sarah and

Angelina, the ardent abolitionist daughters of a southern slaveholding
family, who had been invited by the American Anti-Slavery Society to
speak at small parlor gatherings of women. More than three hundred
appeared at the first meeting, and still larger groups were soon assembling, some men among them. Immediately there burst a storm of controversy, especially among church leaders. What about St. Paul's injunction to woman to keep silence? What would become of her "mild,
dependent, softening influence on the sternness of man's opinions"?
Fine for her to pray (unostentatiously), to teach in sabbath schools, to
modestly lead inquirers to her pastor for instruction, but to "assume
the place and tone of man as a public reformer"!

"The power of woman," continued a pastoral letter from the Congregational ministers of Massachusetts, "is her dependence, flowing
from the consciousness of that weakness which God has given her for
her protection."

Elizabeth was entranced with the Grimkés, especially beautiful
Angelina, the younger and more eloquent, of whom Wendell Phillips
said, "She swept the chords of the human heart with a power that has
never been surpassed and rarely equaled." Listening to her graphic
description of the evils of slavery, horrified by the story of Angelina's
own little slave who had been afraid to eat for fear she would grow fat
and be eaten by the family, Elizabeth was fired with a burning zeal.
But if it was Angelina who kindled her emotions, it was the older and
plainer Sarah who set fire to her mind. Avidly she devoured every word
of the latter's written responses to their critics.

There was no biblical justification for the inferior position of women,
maintained Sarah. The scriptures were not divine in origin (heretic but
exciting thought!) and they naturally reflected the patriarchal society
which had produced them. She pleaded for equal rights for women,
not because they justly belonged to them, but because women must
have them to join in the urgent tasks needing to be done.

"To me it is perfectly clear," she maintained, "that whatsoever it is
morally right for a man to do, it is morally right for a woman to do."

Elizabeth and her older sisters were active participants at all such
meetings, spending evening after evening in New York at lectures,
study groups, anti-slavery powwows, temperance gatherings. They often
returned unescorted, sometimes by the last ferry, without the slightest
fear, also without a suspicion that they were permitted freedoms un-

heard of for the average woman of their time. Only occasionally did Papa assert his male authority by forbidding their participation even in the most radical of groups. But he did so once, and with vehemence.

The occasion was the arrival in New York of Frances Wright, the English freethinking lecturer who not only dared to publicly espouse the equality of women with men, including their right to equal education, but advocated the even more incendiary idea of the rational basis of all knowledge and the importance of free inquiry, even in matters of religion. If the Grimkés had stirred up a storm, Miss Wright aroused a tempest. Dissenter and liberal though he was, even Papa could not swallow this giant pellet. With one of his friends, Mr. Brown, he went to call on the lady, and she invited him to her political lecture on the following evening. He politely refused.

"A woman with a remarkably intelligent countenance and agreeable manners," he had to admit to the family, "but she is a" — he choked on the word — "an *infidel*. And some of her ideas, like the support of political action by working men, could be most disorganizing." He did not mention the commonest scapegoat of accusations against her, that she was an advocate of free love, probably thinking the subject unmentionable before respectable young ladies.

Elizabeth was unimpressed by the presence of Miss Wright, possibly because she was not allowed to go and hear her. However, the linking of women's rights with the issue of anti-slavery excited her tremendously. She flung herself heart and soul into the women's work of the movement, going with Anna and Marianne to meetings at the Coxes', attending sessions of the Ladies' Anti-Slavery Society, selling articles at a fair in Broadway Hall ("Our table was the handsomest!"), listening to innumerable orators. It was a red-letter day when Mr. Garrison returned home with them to spend the night, quoting long stanzas of Russian poetry all the way on the ferry. But she found another experience even more thrilling.

Returning home from Hoboken one day, Sam found Dr. and Mrs. Cox and their son Johnny in their gig waiting at the ferry. Going home with them, he brought back with him a runaway slave girl who had taken refuge with the Coxes. Believing that her master had tracked her to their house, she was in desperate need of another shelter. She stayed with the Blackwells for several weeks, until it was possible to get her on a ship to England. For Elizabeth they were weeks of almost complete

71

fulfillment. For once she was doing something for the Cause besides attending meetings and selling fancywork. She was helping to free a slave.

And then one day in July, 1837, Anna returned from a meeting of the Anti-Slavery Society with a queer gleam in her eyes. Miss Tappan, she said, had told her that a book of anti-slavery poetry had just been published, and that it was believed to have proceeded from the pen of a lady of their family in Jersey City.

"*You!*" cried Marianne and Elizabeth in concert.

Anna shook her head with regret, mingled with unmistakable envy. She turned to Papa, his head suddenly buried, all except the peak of hair rising from his forehead, in the pages of the last *Liberator*. "There's the poet," she charged, pointing. "Isn't it so, Papa? Tell us."

Papa put down his paper and laughed. He did not deny it. Later he presented each of his children with a volume of his *Slavery Rhymes*. Anna sniffed at them in private, said they were all very well for an amateur but really little better than doggerel. But Elizabeth fingered the slender little collection tenderly, almost with reverence. She had never felt so proud. Surely these wonderful verses would soften many hard hearts and help change the world!

4

Papa's laughter was a memory to cherish, for as months passed it grew less and less frequent. He said nothing to the family when things began going wrong with his business, only seemed at times preoccupied and taciturn. But there were disasters he was unable to hide, as when on a Wednesday night in October of 1836 the greater part of the Congress sugar house burned to the ground, the fire starting in a small wooden annex on the back. The four walls were left standing, but all the inside was burned away, beams, engines, pots, boilers either consumed or left a total wreck.

Mr. Gower, the genial, highly cultured manager of the British firm, as much friend as business associate, closed the business and prepared to return to England. When he left on February 9, they all went to the docks and watched the ship ride through the Narrows under full sails. There was more of sadness than derived from farewell to a friend. Not a one but wished silently that they were all on their way back to the beloved land.

For loyalty to England still ran hot in their blood. When later in July Papa came home with the news that King William had died, Elizabeth felt the new country fall from her like a garment. Instantly with every quickened fiber of her body she was back in England, mourning the old monarch, acclaiming the new. Victoria! A *woman!* Would she prove worthy and capable of governing their great kingdom? Would she be an honor to their sex? Elizabeth closed her eyes and wished ardently, prayed, that it might be so.

They had to do something to show their loyalty. The girls rummaged for black trimmings. Aunt Eliza bought a mourning bonnet, Marianne some black ribbon; even Papa purchased a piece of crepe for his hat. The next Sunday the whole family wore some sign of mourning to church — all but Mamma.

"I'm ashamed of you," she scolded in a lecture of unusual length. "Such want of respect for America!"

Elizabeth was feeling less and less respect for the country these days. Land of opportunity, was it, where everybody had a chance to prosper? Not in this year of 1837! The new president, Van Buren, had scarcely been installed before the country was in the worst panic of its history. The huge boom of prosperity resulting in overspeculation, inflation, reckless "wildcat" banking in the West, burst like a bubble. In May the banks of New York suspended specie payment, and by the end of summer not a single bank in the country could meet its obligations in gold and silver. Unemployment mushroomed. By September nine-tenths of the factories on the eastern seaboard had closed. Businesses were failing right and left.

Papa became more and more taciturn. Worry made him physically sick. Once to Elizabeth's dismay he seemed too unwell even to smell a sweet little bouquet from her garden. He was connected now with only one sugar house, at Washington Street. His nightly vigils increased, once in two nights instead of three, and even on the evenings at home he would go to the porch to look for signs of fire. To the family's dismay he began talking again about beets, bringing home French books on beet production which he asked Anna to translate. Then toward the end of March, even before the worst of the panic hit the country, he exploded a bombshell.

"Papa condescended to inform Mamma," wrote Elizabeth bleakly in her journal, "that he had sold his Washington sugar house concern to

73

Mr. Harris and some other person. What his plans for the future are we do not know. I suppose it will be something about beets!"

"If only we could go back to England!" yearned Anna. "Maybe now he'll realize that we shouldn't have left in the first place."

Elizabeth hoped not. Papa had enough worries for the present and future without being burdened with guilt for the past. He continued to tell the family nothing about his plans, though they could draw some conclusions from his actions. One day he burned his face badly with sugar he was boiling on a small stove in the basement. Then he began covering in one side of the garden, obviously preparing for experiments on a larger scale. Later they learned that he had rented a big sugar house on East Broadway, but since he was almost without capital, he could carry on the business only on a small scale.

The family economy became as cramping and hateful as the fashionable pinched-in waists which Elizabeth despised. They were unable to give Papa presents on his birthday, finances were so low. Finally Mamma felt obliged to get along without a servant, and the girls began to take turns doing the housekeeping.

"This is my day for seeing to the meals," recorded Elizabeth one day in June. "I hate the employment and look with real dread to my week, for we have agreed to take it by weeks. I fear we shall not have much pleasure in life now."

A few days later she wrote, "Papa gave Mamma a little money and told her it must last the week. We all had to go to bed in the dark as we had only a little spirit left and but two lamps trimmed for Papa and Aunt Mary."

Economy in clothes was less painful for her than for the older girls, for she cared little about dress and less about sewing. Still wearing her winter merino in June, she finally yielded to necessity and began altering her old summer frocks, making the pointed waists and tight frilled sleeves which were the current fashion. It was October before she was able to afford a new purple cotton frock. But the necessity of giving up her music lessons was far more distressing.

In spite of hard times the Blackwell hospitality remained bountiful, and the house was often filled with guests. In May came the Samuel Brownes from Cincinnati, relatives of Mamma who had long preceded them to the New World. Mrs. Browne was now on her way to visit England. Papa and Mr. Browne held many conversations about the relative advantages of the eastern seaboard and the West, where, the guest enthused, the present slight depression was only temporary. There was unlimited opportunity for expansion in every sort of business. Sugar? questioned Papa eagerly. Of course, assured Mr. Browne. There was no sugar refinery west of the Alleghenies. Anyone with the courage to pioneer would be assured of a fortune. Papa's admiration did not extend to the fussy and somewhat frumpy wife of his western guest.

"A silly old woman," he evaluated after she had sailed for England and her husband had returned to Cincinnati.

"An old *lady*, Papa," corrected Anna with asperity.

Papa, more testy these days than usual, responded that he did not choose to be reproved by his daughter.

Anna was not to be intimidated. "She is my relative, Papa," she retorted with daring impudence. To Elizabeth's amazement and distress Papa made no reply, only retreated, shoulders sagging, to his interminable experiments.

Tensions in the household were not lessened when Uncle Charles and Aunt Eliza sold their school, auctioned off most of their furniture, and with their two small children Miriam and James moved in with the Blackwells.

"I think they have pretty cheap boarding," recorded Elizabeth, "two rooms, one very large, a closet with a window, another without one, use of the drawing room, whole range of the house and garden for three dollars apiece a month!" Mamma even bought some dishes from Uncle.

"Yes," commented Aunt Mary with unusual tartness, "your Mamma is determined to enrich your uncle at the expense of poor Papa's hard toils."

Uncle Charles was more agreeable as a guest than as a boarder. There was inevitable friction with occasional unpleasant scenes at dinner. Once Mamma and Uncle became engaged in heated argument over abolition, which Uncle did not favor. Papa took Mamma's part. Uncle became offended, left the table, and took tea in his own room.

In September Anna, resigned to becoming a governess, accepted a position teaching music in a Vermont seminary. Seeing her leave by boat with Mr. Crane, the principal, and his wife, Elizabeth felt a conflict of emotions: loss, for it was the first family separation; relief, for Anna had been becoming more and more frustrated and difficult; but mostly envy. What joy to be independent, no longer a burden on poor

Papa, to have some purpose in life! She plunged with renewed vigor into her music practice, wondering if at twenty she could become as proficient as Anna, knowing all the time she could not.

Finances sank to new lows. Mamma advertised three rooms for boarders. "What will we come to next!" despaired Elizabeth. The last of September she recorded with a simplicity which belied her shock and dismay, "Papa is going to give up his sugar house. He is to go to the West and fix upon a location for planting beets, taking Sam and Henry with him to go to some cheap school, Mamma and the four youngest to go to an economical boarding house and Marianne and me to go as governesses." It seemed like the disintegration of all that made life worth living. Mamma, of course, made no protest, but Aunt Mary ventured to inquire timidly why they did not all return to England. Papa's blue-gray eyes softened, but his lips set stubbornly. Sometime they would return, he promised, but not until he had provided security for his children. And again with dogged perseverance he set about making beet sugar in a small silver saucepan on the kitchen stove.

But they celebrated the holidays as usual. Sam and Elizabeth helped Aunt Mary weigh and wash and pick and grate flour, raisins, currants, nutmegs, for Mamma's fabulous puddings. They decorated the house with greens. On Christmas Eve after tea they danced, played hunt the rabbit, turn the trencher, birds and beasts and fishes, how'd you like it, and had toast and ale and cider for supper. The next morning they exchanged presents as usual before breakfast, even though there was little to exchange. The aunts came, and they dined at four, then played charades and ring and traveler. Except that Uncle Charles was not as merry as usual, it might have been any Christmas. Three days later they managed to scrape up enough money to help a runaway slave on his journey.

On New Year's Day Elizabeth helped set the parlor in apple pie order. Uncle's tables were brought down and set with plates of cake, sandwiches, oranges, jugs of wine, cream and sugar for coffee. Twenty-one callers came. They put away the rest of the cake for Twelfth Night, when they burned so many boughs that they set the chimney on fire. Elizabeth even finished making herself a new cotton frock of a beautiful Mazarine blue.

But after that changes came with a rush. Uncle Charles became so deeply offended that he moved his family to other boarding quarters and began making plans to return to England. Mrs. Browne came back, disillusioned with her native country and full of praises for her adopted Cincinnati. Partly through her encouragement, more because of the urgings of an English friend, Mr. Howells, who had also settled in the western outpost, Papa went West on a scouting expedition for more favorable business openings, especially in country adapted to growing beets. Marianne took a position teaching at a Mrs. O'Kill's school. Papa returned with glowing descriptions of the booming young town of Cincinnati and the announcement that they were to move there by May 1.

The news met with a variety of reactions: consternation, excitement, resignation, a vast flurry of activity. But for Elizabeth one emotion was uppermost, well being. It did not matter that they had no meat for dinner, only a stew made of potatoes with a few bones carefully preserved and a one-penny leek. All was well, because Papa was himself again. He made fun of the Jersey City trees which looked like dwarfs beside the luxuriant vegetation of Ohio. He joked about an April snow squall being "the last grin of winter." He painted lavish pictures of the flourishing Rome of the West surrounded by its seven hills and its glistening coil of river.

It was lucky Anna was not there to puncture the bubble of expectancy. Elizabeth knew what she would have said. "He's running away again, just as from England. He should stay and fight it out, just as he should have then. Look at the money the sugar men are making now in Bristol! Mr. Harris will make good here, wait and see."

Elizabeth did not want to hear such innuendos, even though she had a gnawing suspicion they might be true. The glint in Papa's eyes, the spring in his step, silenced any doubts. She plunged with all her abounding energy into the preparations for moving: packing china and glass, storing books in the big lead-colored chest, sweeping out the dining room after the carpet had been taken up, head swathed in a paper bonnet, rubbing, scrubbing, polishing. On the auction day there was a cheery fire in the schoolroom where Papa, Mamma, and Wash slept, and where the family sat and ate their meals. The sale was disappointing. Most of the household goods went for a song. But Papa, lavish in his new gaiety, insisted there was enough to furnish the women of the family with new clothes for the great adventure. Elizabeth bought herself a Tuscan bonnet trimmed with green ribbon and a frock of greenish muslin with reddish spots. On Sunday she went to hear Mr. Lusk for the last two times. She was not sorry. On Monday they sent two loads of household goods to the boat. Tuesday night was spent with the two aunts who lived in Canal Street. They began their journey by boat on Wednesday morning.

It was a long journey, with far more difficulties than crossing the Atlantic. In Philadelphia they stopped overnight at the Red Lion. The following day Papa and the boys sallied forth on business. The others went sightseeing, returning in time to proceed to the railroad station by coach. Papa did not come — and did not come. Elizabeth, driven to assume leadership because of competence rather than age, became frantic. Finally Harry arrived out of breath. Papa wanted them to ride to the station with the luggage but not put it in the railroad car. They did so, then put up a losing battle fending off the bevy of attendants bent on loading their baggage. But at last Papa came, face red as his precious beets, and they boarded the train just in time.

The "Pioneer Fast Line," the advertisement read, "By Rail Road Cars and Canal Packets, FROM PHILADELPHIA TO PITTSBURGH, Through in 3½ days. Starts every morning from the corner of Broad and Race St." It continued in smaller print, "In large and splendid eight wheel cars, via the Lancaster and Harrisburg Rail Road, arriving at the latter place at 4 o'clock in the afternoon, where passengers will take the packets, which have all been fitted up in a very superior manner, after the most approved models of Boats used on the Erie Canal, and are not surpassed by the Boats on any other line."

All day it rained, and though the country was green and fertile, it looked dark and desolate. But when they approached Columbia on the Susquehanna, where the canal commenced, even rain could not quench their delight in the beautiful wide river, lined with its high wooded hills and filled with sweet little islands. Elizabeth was enchanted . . . until they reached the canalboat. "Fitted up in a very superior manner"? She and her mother and sisters were crowded into a room four by six yards crammed with noisy Irish women, almost every one with a half dozen children, who roared in spite of being threatened every other minute with being tossed overboard. Already the sixteen berths and much of the floor were occupied. This from Friday night until Monday morning!

The Pennsylvania Canal had been built only a few years. The whole line was 395 miles long, and it had cost twenty-five million dollars. It was a triumph of engineering. But the thought brought little comfort to the women huddled with the snuffling children in the cabin. Four years later, in 1842, Charles Dickens, making the same trip, reported that the inside of the barge was like a caravan at a fair, "the gentlemen being accommodated, as the spectators usually are, in one of those locomotive museums of penny wonders; and the ladies being partitioned off by a red curtain, after the manner of the dwarfs and giants in the same establishments." But he obviously was not wedged with some forty others into a small space intended for sixteen!

It rained all Saturday morning. They crossed the Susquehanna and continued for some time in the canal by its side. But the skies cleared when they entered the Juniata, crossing it by ropes and pulleys, and Elizabeth escaped from the scolding women and squalling children to walk the decks delighting in a river as lovely as the Hudson. But she was sorry for the poor horses straining to pull the heavy barge, three of them being driven tandem along the side of the canal, and for the sweating Negroes with their long poles, their bodies bent double in an effort to hold the packet in the middle of the stream.

They reached Hollidaysburgh in the late afternoon of Monday. Then began one of the strangest trips any of the Blackwells had ever experienced. The passengers changed to horse-drawn cars on what was called the Portage Railroad, a device contrived to conquer the many slopes and planes of the Alleghenies. The mountains were scaled in a series of five planes. At the foot of the first plane the horses were unhitched and the cars were fastened to a rope passing up the middle of one track and down the middle of the other. Then a stationary steam engine at the head of the plane was started, and the car moved majestically up the long and steep incline. When a level place was reached, the horses were again attached. Sam and Harry were fascinated by this performance and climbed out to watch each time a change was made.

They arrived at the top of the Alleghenies about ten that evening in a blinding snowstorm. They spent the night in a queer hotel, where Papa was able to engage a room with two large beds, enough room for all but Sam and himself. The two of them tried to sleep sitting up in the barroom, redolent with smells of rum and "baccy." However, toward one o'clock the proprietor, seeing them cocked up Yankee fashion against the stove, brought down an old hollow boxlike frame, filled with straw, a blanket, and an old coat. Throwing off coats and boots, they crawled with relief into this chest and slept soundly.

The snowstorm was still raging when they started down the mountains on Tuesday, descending plane after plane by the stationary engines ("What if the ropes should break!" thought Elizabeth with a shudder), running over the levels with the black ponies. Shivering in the poorly heated car, feet bitter cold, she longed to get out and warm herself at one of the boiler fires as the men and boys did, even little Wash, but the *Far West* had no proper door, and anyway, her sex and petticoats forbade. At Johnstown they returned to boat travel full of woeful remembrance of the squalling children afflicted by colds, whooping cough, and measles.

But Elizabeth's spirits, always resilient, were soon soaring again. The snows and cold were left behind. The next day, Thursday, she was able to walk with Papa and the boys and Emily for two or three miles along the canal bank. Spring was again in the air, the sun bright, flowers blooming. Then came another step in the long relay. About twelve miles from Pittsburgh they came to a break in the canal and had to anchor, crowded in among a half dozen other canalboats, only the breadth of a field separating them from the Allegheny River, where they were to proceed by steamboat.

After waiting far into the evening, with no boat arriving, Papa decided the children must go to bed and try to sleep. It was one in the morning, and Elizabeth was lying in her rope berth tense and wakeful when she heard the shout, "Steamboat come!" She sprang up and roused the sleeping children. Hastily the family gathered together all their bags and boxes and struggled across the field in a dense fog, trying to keep together among the milling passengers, all rushing to reach the boat before the best places were taken. No use. The berths in the women's cabin were all full. By exercising firmness Elizabeth managed to find places for Mamma, Aunt Mary, and the two youngest children to lie down, but she and her sisters had to sit the night out huddled against a wall. Discomfort was the least of her worries. She could not forget how utterly fatigued Papa had looked after struggling across the field with their heavy baggage.

But in spite of weariness, when they arrived at Pittsburgh on Thursday, he set off at once to arrange passage for Cincinnati and was able to engage three staterooms on the *Tribune,* sailing at three that afternoon. Elizabeth was thankful this was not their destination, for Pittsburgh seemed a dirty disagreeable city, enveloped in a dense cloud of smoke.

The *Tribune* was a fine river packet, colorful and jaunty in appearance with its red and black sides and white-painted cabin, and even Mamma and Aunt Mary, who had endured all the discomforts of the journey's many stages with resignation if not equanimity, visibly brightened. Fresh frocks emerged from the tin boxes, deep ruffles mussed in spite of careful folding, billowing sleeves stuffed with crumpled newspapers. Mamma's face settled into its normal serene smoothness, and her hair, still thick and black, peeped in its usual well-brushed, glossy wings and coils from beneath her bonnet. Papa donned his new silk waistcoat. The boys looked scrubbed and combed.

The tempo and mood of the journey had changed. No more laboring through snows, toiling through tunnels and over mountains, straining up and down planes. Even the aura of depression beclouding the East was left behind. Most of the passengers on the riverboat were young, gay, boisterous. Some of the men, dressed in the latest fashion, loud checks, flowing ties, colored waistcoats, were obviously adventurers, gamblers perhaps, fortune seekers; some of the women, painted and overdressed and blowzy, had an even more obvious destiny in view.

"I don't like the way some of those young men pay attention to our Emily and Ellen," murmured Mamma, a tiny line scoring her smooth forehead.

Elizabeth was first amused, then sobered. Those little children — young men! She regarded her young sisters with sudden awareness: Emily, sweetly serious, undeniably pretty, and at twelve already showing a poise and confidence which the shy Elizabeth could not help envying; Ellen, ten, gay, sparkling, with all of Marianne's endearing grace and vivacity. How beguiling she looked, chattering away with such ease and abandon, as mature in her sociability as was Emily in her poise! No wonder the young men found their company stimulating, while she, Elizabeth, could walk the deck without eliciting more than the respectful raising of a hat!

But when one of the women on board innocently inquired if Washy was her son, amusement and sober reflection changed to dismay, almost panic. Did she really look old enough, at seventeen, to be the mother of a six-year-old? Was youth going to pass her by? She fled to the cabin and peered surreptitiously in a looking glass. The face under the sober bonnet was surely not unattractive, delicate and oval in shape, eyes blue-gray and very clear, blonde hair neatly parted in the middle and flowing in soft wings into neat coils over her ears, features even and finely cut in spite of the too generous mouth. She was too colorless, that

was the trouble, all pale and strawlike, just as she had been as a child.
But inside she was not colorless. She was like one of the fireworks
Uncle Charles had bought last Fourth of July, the wheel and two
serpents, dull brown on the outside, but within all movement and
brightness and fire. No, not like that, either. The fireworks had exploded
in one little *Splut-t-t!* and then fizzled. What she felt inside her was
more like — like the power in the big engines which had pulled them
up the mountain. Sometimes she felt that if she couldn't let it out, to
use it in doing something worthwhile, she would burst.

But she wasn't one to mope. A whole new world was waiting outside.
With rebounding enthusiasm she drank in every detail of the country
through which they chugged and churned: forested slopes cloaked with
every shade of green from pale lime to deep emerald; gorges with
rushing streams, islands strung like a jade necklace, rustic landings set
in circles of log cabins. Only one thing marred her enjoyment of the
scene.

"Slave country," Papa had waved grimly toward the left when they
had crossed the border between Pennsylvania and Virginia.

Resolutely Elizabeth kept her eyes fixed on the vistas to the right.

They reached Cincinnati about three on Saturday, after a nine
days' journey. As the chugging side-wheeler churned through the last
glistening coil of river, Elizabeth's heart bounded. All her misgivings
vanished. No pall of smoke, such as had hung over Pittsburgh and
Wheeling! No crude log settlement carved from raw wilderness! The
city was beautiful. Its modern, well-built structures clung to the sides of
its encircling hills like the rising tiers of a great amphitheater. The broad
waterfront with its bustling of drays, carriages, phaetons, and wagons;
the river alive with steaming whistling packets, mail boats, ferries; the
shouting lusty swarming life all about; yes, even the mysterious backdrop of slave country . . . all were parts of an exciting, unfolding drama.
On a stage like this, where history was being made, almost anything
could happen. There might even be an important role for a woman to
play!

A blessing that she could not know the lines and business that
would soon be assigned to her.

Chapter Three

PAPA WAS DYING! Elizabeth was sure of it. Heretofore smiling, life had suddenly become a Janus, turning a hideous, frightening face. Attempting to escape it, she fled from the sickroom in a panic of conflicting emotions: grief, fear, furious helplessness, and — yes, revulsion. Not against Papa, of course. Never had he seemed so dear. Against the inevitable Thing which had taken possession of him, filmed the clear eyes, yellowed the ruddy flesh, turned the strong hands, which for seventeen years had shaped her destiny, into groping claws.

In the front parlor outside the room where he lay she stopped short, senses reeling, trying to orient herself in a world gone suddenly berserk. Where — when — ? Time and place wavered. Then familiar objects emerged. Here was the old red carpet, worn in spots. She had sweated one day in terrific heat to help tack it down. There in the corner was her piano. It had been weeks arriving with the other furniture. And against the wall stood the old sofa, still wearing its red cover brought from England. Her gaze clung to them gratefully, and the world slowly righted itself.

Where? The big square stone house on Third Street. No wonder it still seemed strange, for they had lived in it less than a month. When? July — no, August, 1838. Monday the 6th. Was it only three days since Papa had been taken sick, really sick, that is? He had not been well for weeks, months, ever since he had gotten his feet wet back in May soon after their arrival in Cincinnati. There had been fainting fits. After hiring the new sugar house on the edge of the river he had had little energy to get the business started, though his courage had been boundless.

83

"No end to the opportunities once this depression gets over! . . . Great country for beets. Once I can get to Michigan and see some of the farmers, we'll be free of slave labor in no time. You'll see! . . . This water-powered plant will be twice as efficient as the old steam!"

Elizabeth was so utterly fatigued that she had to cling to the banister climbing the steep narrow stairs. She had scarcely slept in three days, since she had been called from her bed late Saturday night. Sam had gone to get Dr. Atlee and she had run to the nearest apothecary shop in Lower Market Street, frantically pulling the night bell beneath the sign of the mortar and pestle until the night clerk sleepily emerged. But all the medicines — calomel, arrowroot, laudanum, brandy — had done little good. They had stood around his bed all night listening to his harsh breathing, trying to ease his terrible fever with constant fanning.

"He'll never leave his bed," Aunt Mary had whispered in a mournful aside to Elizabeth. The girl had stared at her aunt in horror, her sharp exclamation hushed into silence by the, "Sh-h! Your mother must not know."

Sunday had been prolonged agony, with Papa's pulse sinking alarmingly. In the afternoon he had kept asking for Mr. Browne, and Henry had been sent to fetch him. He was in the sickroom now. He would stay, he promised kindly, as long as he was needed. And he had sent Elizabeth to get some rest.

She did not want rest. Climbing to the third story, she mounted the ladderlike stairs to the flat roof. Instantly she caught her breath in wonder. Never had the world looked so beautiful. A great full moon hung just in front of her, seeming only a few yards above the Kentucky hills. Through openings in the treetops and descending roofs the encircling river sparkled like a necklace of gems. To the right a soft mist curled along the valley of the Licking River. And all about and behind rose the roofs and turrets of a fairylike city. It could be Rome, with its seven hills, or Athens — Cincinnati was called the Athens of the West — or fabulous Camelot, or — yes, Bethlehem. On just such a night and on just such hills, the shepherds must have watched their flocks.

Again time and place wavered, and as in the parlor below, she stood still, seeking signs of the familiar. There to the left was the schoolhouse tower; below, the stout roofs and chimneys of the long line of shorefront buildings. There on the hill to the right, boldly probing the moonlight, was the tower of the church to which she had walked on her first Sunday, exulting in the handsome houses, the well-dressed people, the air of respectability and cleanliness, the good organ, and the fine congregation. Dr. Lyman Beecher, however, whom she had hoped to hear, had been away. Later, when she had heard him, he had been disappointing, with a dry-as-dust sermon on "The Presbyterian Schism." Farther up the hill, hidden somewhere in the shadows, was Bellevue, the Brownes' house, where they had stayed for two months. It also had been a house of death, for little Eliza, one of the Brownes' children, had died of measles four days after their arrival.

"I cared more for her than for all the rest put together," Samuel Browne had admitted brokenly, believing his loss a judgment on such partiality.

Elizabeth had spoken comfortingly, with confident assurance. Now, remembering, in spite of the stifling August heat, she shivered. Had she not loved Papa better than anyone else in the world?

She crept down to her room at last and fell into short, uneasy sleep.

In the morning Papa seemed better, his pulse more regular, and like the others, Elizabeth began wildly to hope. The doctor prescribed another dose of arrowroot, laudanum, and brandy. Mr. Browne patiently rubbed the patient's joints with mercurial ointment. Elizabeth sponged him over and over with a solution of muriatic acid and plied him with chicken broth and brandy. He always tried to take everything she brought him, even though she was sure it caused him great discomfort. For the first time he seemed to realize how sick he was.

"I've been an unworthy Christian," she heard him whisper when she sat fanning him. "But I love God. He is my rock, my fortress, my deliverer." Presently his eyes opened and regarded her with their usual affection, though with a certain strangeness. "Don't stay so long with me, I beg you. Try to get a little rest, my dear child." They were the last words she was to hear him speak to her.

A little later she came into the room, a cup of broth in her hand, to find Mamma kneeling beside his couch, his arms around her. He was speaking, clearly, but in a voice painfully low and halting. "I advise you — soon as you can — all go back to England. Only one year — must keep this house. Dear love, sorry — must tell you — no money to leave you — "

"Please, don't let that trouble you, don't be anxious, my husband."

Elizabeth fled back to the kitchen, the broth slopping over and scalding her hands. She was still working over the stove, reheating it, when her mother called.

"Elizabeth! Come quickly!"

Heart beating wildly, she sped up the stairs.

"Papa asked for you," said Mamma in the same calm voice. "He thought it was you beside him. 'Bessie, dear, light of my eyes,' he said. Then, when he saw it was I, 'Oh, I thought it was Elizabeth.' He wants you to read to him the chapter in the Bible with the story of the Annunciation."

Elizabeth hastened to get the book, praying that she could read without her voice breaking. But there was no need to worry. He had sunk into a doze, and she tiptoed away, the book unopened.

The August heat was almost as scalding as the broth. It turned her tight corset waist of cotton twill into a steaming compress. The high neck and long puff sleeves of her voluminous housedress encased throat and wrists like imprisoning chains. No wonder Papa found it almost impossible to breathe! Evening brought no relief, only the additional hot fumes of lighted lamps and a barrage of mosquitoes. Elizabeth sat by the couch fending off insects with one hand while holding Papa's hand with the other, wondering how it could be so cold and fiercely willing it to absorb some of her own body's saturating heat. The whole family were there, with Mr. Browne and their other old friend, Mr. Howells. Once they all knelt around the couch and prayed silently. A little before ten the doctor came. He looked at Papa, and Elizabeth saw him shake his head. Then without speaking he lifted Mamma from her knees beside the couch and led her to a chair.

"No!" Words choked, unuttered, in Elizabeth's throat. "It isn't so. I won't believe it. He's just sleeping, peacefully sleeping."

"It's all over," said Mr. Browne, holding up his hands.

Horrified, Elizabeth put her hand to Papa's mouth. Never to her dying day would she forget the shock of finding that there was no breath. But there was relief, too, in the release from tension. Now they could weep unrestrainedly.

Later Elizabeth and the others went upstairs, leaving the three men to watch in the back parlor. As she entered her dark room, a candle in her hand, wind was swirling the muslin curtains. The fevered heat of the day had broken. She set down the candle, went to the window. The world was restless, full of uneasy shadows, the moon half hidden by racing clouds.

"I wonder," she thought, "if our blessed father has reached home."

86

2

There was no time to grieve. Suddenly Elizabeth found herself the virtual head of the family. Mamma's calmness, part of the studied behavior pattern of a dutiful and loving wife, evaporated into helpless bewilderment. She and Aunt Mary were like small craft bereft of captain, rudder, and compass. The two eldest boys, still in a state of shock, were not yet fully stunned into maturity. Even the funeral on Wednesday was for Elizabeth an occasion for anxiety rather than proper grief. Though Mr. Browne assumed direction of many details, it was she who arranged the back parlor where Papa was laid out, cleaned the house for guests, rummaged for mourning clothes for the family, dispatched letters by mail boat to Aunt Bar, Anna, and Marianne, received the kind callers, tried to explain the mystery of death to tearful six-year-old Washy. She scarcely found time to cut for herself a lock from dear Papa's hair, as did all the others. Only when riding to the burial ground could she yield momentarily to emotion. Then grief became overpowering. She hated the bright beautiful day, the staring people. Afterward the house was filled with kind neighbors. One, Mrs. Thompson, sent in tea. She thought they would never go, but finally, left alone, the family did what they knew Papa would have wanted, had prayers. Sam led them in a timid but courageous quaver, his changing voice a poignant contrast to the confident and resonant tones accustomed to lead them to the throne of grace. On her knees Elizabeth was suddenly racked by awareness and desolation. Never to hear that beloved voice raised again in family worship! At last, in the sanctuary of her own room, she found time to weep.

But she rose at dawn the next day, Thursday, laced herself into her tight stays like a soldier armoring for battle, and prepared to face the responsibility of a family of nine persons, six of them children, a large house with a year's unpaid lease, rent due for the new sugar refinery, doctor's and undertaker's bills, and capital of exactly twenty dollars; also, as she was soon to discover to her dismay, a startling number of debts. For all the available means left her father after the closing of the New York sugar house had been employed for the new refinery. And although various amounts, some large, were still due his estate from several business firms, none could be recovered, many of the parties having gone bankrupt, others managing to elude their obligations due to

the confusion of his sudden death and the inexperience of the claim-
ants. To add to the misfortune, an agent in New York with whom the
greater part of their household goods had been left for sale sold the
furniture and pocketed the proceeds. But as one hurdle after the other
appeared, Elizabeth braced herself with grim fortitude to face it. The
obligations, she determined, should be met to the last farthing.

The second day after the funeral she went as usual to the homes of
several music pupils she had begun to teach, income from whom would
soon augment their funds by twenty-four dollars.

"We'll get jobs," announced Sam and Henry with grim but vague
optimism, and Mr. Emery, the Englishman who ran the emigrants'
office, promised to help them.

Sam, sober and slight of stature at fourteen and almost fanatically
religious, snapped immediately into the premature manhood which
his status as eldest son predicated. Harry at thirteen assumed the
mantle of enforced maturity with more jauntiness than sobriety. Charming, energetic, merry, with curling black hair, blue sparkling eyes, and
teeth so white that they were later to win him the nickname of "Carker"
(when *Dombey and Son* became popular reading in the fifties), Harry,
unlike Sam, would never fit into a conventional mold. Already he was
shocking Mamma with his questioning of religious fundamentals, and
Hannah spent long hours praying for his soul. Sam, Elizabeth knew,
would not suffer too much for lack of further schooling. He read constantly, from Carlyle to Plato, Wordsworth to Italian history. But Harry!
It tore her heart to think of his having to relinquish his dream of
becoming a lawyer.

To her surprise, often by her side these days she found her next
younger sister Emily, making sensible if shy suggestions, relieving her
sometimes of responsibility, quietly sharing tasks that must have been
sheer drudgery for a twelve-year-old. As they stood side by side one
day at the cookstove, she discovered to her amazement that the sturdy
shoulders, the overly broad face with its placid features and frame of
reddish hair, were on a level with her own. Another time she noticed
that they had the same kind of hands, long-fingered, slender, with the
same competent sureness of motion. Musician's hands? Artist's? But
though Emily played well, she was not as interested in music as herself
and Anna, nor in art, like volatile ten-year-old Ellen.

"What would you like to do?" she asked suddenly, "if you could do
anything you wanted to?"

"Do?" The wide eyes were puzzled.

"With your life? What kind of work, I mean."

The eyes flashed scornful fire. "What kind of work *is* there for a woman to do?"

Elizabeth laughed aloud, the first time such a sound had been heard in the house since that fateful Tuesday. She felt a warmth of companionship which she had never felt with Anna, seldom even with Marianne. Suddenly the world seemed less empty.

But it was Mamma who was most surprising. Like a long-sheltered plant whose protecting vegetation has been uprooted, she burst into unexpected vigor. The stunned and helpless apathy vanished. She asked to see accounts and went over them with Elizabeth, making shrewd comments. Soon afterward she called the family together. Carefully groomed as usual, voluminous skirts of her best black silk billowing about her, dark hair parted in the middle, braided, and coiled becomingly over each ear, eyes bright, cheeks pink, she made a striking picture.

"My dears." Though her voice was soft and gentle as ever, it held an unmistakable note of authority. "We are faced with vast problems. We must use all our wits and energies to survive. Not only have we no money, but we have debts. God will help us, but we must work together. Mr. Emery will find work for the boys, positions fitting the status of young gentlemen — I hope" — her smooth brow furrowed momentarily —"but if not, we must make the best of it. Elizabeth has suggested that we start a small school. We must do so immediately, even before your sisters come to join us. I suggest that we have some circulars printed, something nice and genteel. Samuel and Henry can go from house to house, delivering them. No, on second thought" — she looked suddenly startled, frightened, then her small head lifted — "I think it might look more respectable if — if I did it myself. Now, my dears, let us kneel and ask God's help."

Elizabeth felt a boundless relief. She would not have to bear the burden alone. The circulars were printed, and true to her word, Hannah went from house to house ringing doorbells. Results were only mildly encouraging. She returned from her first trip with the certain enrollment of only two little boys. Further expeditions met with little more success. But events moved with startling swiftness. Sam was given a job — yes, it might even be called a *position* — as a sort of bookkeeper in the office of Major Gano, clerk of the Superior Court. Harry brashly assumed the role of cook while the women turned the big adjoining parlors into schoolrooms and prepared the extra bedrooms to accommodate boarding pupils, until Mr. Howells gave him a job as errand boy in his shop. But Elizabeth's relief was tinged with rising panic. Until the arrival of her sisters the major burden of teaching must fall on her, and nothing had been heard from them.

"Marianne must have heard the news," she wrote in her diary on August 21. "Anna, being thirty miles in the country, probably hasn't heard yet. *What* shall we do in the school"? The next day she dispatched a letter to Aunt Bar in New York frantically urging her to speed their departure.

The school was opened at nine o'clock five days later. Aunt Mary taught the little boys in the front room, Elizabeth the girls in the back. In addition to their own younger children there were only four pupils.

Ten days later, fortunately on a Friday when to Elizabeth's vast relief the grind of the school week was over, Anna and Marianne arrived. It was both a joyful and a sorrowful reunion. Elizabeth had to get acquainted with her sisters all over again. Marianne was prettier than ever, but she seemed more delicate in health and had developed a languidness of manner suggestive of either sophistication or a mildly chronic invalidism. For some reason she now insisted on being called "Marian." But these were surface changes, Elizabeth noted with relief. Marianne or Marian, she was still the gay vivid sprite who had spun magic tales of the beautiful Estelle on the old rocking horse.

It was Anna who had really changed. To say that she was more sophisticated would have been putting it mildly. She had become what might vulgarly be called "smart." Her clothes typified the latest in Eastern fashion: incredibly tight waistlines, billowing skirts over heavily padded and quilted petticoats, enormous sleeves extended by a pillow-like padding and pleated into a tapered cuff, collars of fine embroidered muslin, thin woolen shoes laced at the back and trimmed at the top with pleated frills, all in the current fashionable colors, olives and grays and tans. Her dark hair, brushed to shining sleekness and looped over her ears in impeccable coils, framed the thinner and more sharply defined features which Anna herself would have liked to think of as *distingués*.

"Vigor and brilliance," thought Elizabeth, conscious anew of her own pale drabness. "That's what describes her."

The change was not all external. Anna's world had expanded. She had rubbed shoulders with the great, or at least basked in their intellectual shadows: Captain Marryat, Emerson, Horace Mann, the Grimké sisters, Theodore Weld, John Greenleaf Whittier. She had written a long drama, which she let Elizabeth read. They were soon engaging in spirited discussions about ultra-abolitionism, Unitarianism, the right of women to preach.

To Elizabeth's relief Anna liked Cincinnati, was agreeably surprised by the substantial brick houses strung in tiers along the curving hillsides, the clean wide streets with no scavenging pigs running wild as in New York (though with pork one of the chief industries there were plenty of the beasts in captivity), the bustling and colorful Lower Market just below Third Street on Sycamore, the river with its bevy of sidewheelers constantly churning up a dazzle of spray, the roisterous waterfront with its displays of goods covering the whole acreage from Main to Broadway — pork, whiskey, boots and shoes, hides, leather, molasses, cotton, iron, steel, tools, carriages, its hundreds of roustabouts at work with trucks and cotton hooks and drays. She was fascinated by the Arabesque-Grecian-Gothic monstrosity built by the indomitable Englishwoman, Mrs. Anthony Trollope, who had come to Cincinnati in the twenties prepared to take the city by storm with her lavish bazaar, her elegant saloon dispensing delicate refreshment, and her magnificent ballroom — all a woeful flop.

"What a story!" chuckled Anna, her flair for the dramatic instantly aroused as she learned of the lady's outraged and indignant retreat, her scurrilous comments on the city's vulgarity, its pursuit of wealth rather than art, its dripping and stinking slaughterhouses. "And how I would love to write it!"

But she was most impressed by the friends the Blackwells had made in their less than three months of residence. Thanks to the Brownes, the Donaldsons, the Howells, all English in background and abolitionists, they had been introduced to the cream of Cincinnati society. There were the Thomas Emerys, also English and proprietors of what was to become one of the city's greatest estates. There were the Ganos. Major Daniel Gano, a rigid Campbellite and son of one of Cincinnati's first settlers, born in a log cabin in 1794, had become one of its most wealthy and respected citizens. Clad in his long frock coat, the collar of his white ruffled shirt stiffly upstanding above his black silk stock, the last man in the city to wear a queue, he was a commanding figure as he promenaded Fourth Street to or from his office in City Hall. He owned three farms, with a hundred head of horses, imported Arabs and Conquerors, bred sheep, and had experimented with silkworms. Back in 1824 he had entertained Lafayette in his house on East Court Street. All these details were meat for Anna's insatiable appetite for the *distingué.*

The Gano country house was already a favorite visiting place of the Blackwells, and its rosy-cheeked mistress, who leaned toward the Millerites, apostles of the imminent "Second Coming," always made them welcome. Soon after the older girls' arrival not only did Major Gano send his carriage to bring them to tea, but the three were invited to stay overnight, their rooms equipped with a pleasant fire, curl papers for Marian, and a hot brick for Anna.

Then, of course, there were the Beechers, Dr. Lyman, president of Lane Theological Seminary, his son Henry Ward, and his daughter Harriet, who was married to Dr. Calvin Stowe, one of the seminary professors. They all lived in a big house at Walnut Hills near the seminary, about two miles away. Anna could hardly wait to meet Mrs. Stowe, who was reported to have sold stories to a western magazine, but she wasn't likely to very soon, Elizabeth told her, for Harriet was the faithful mother of young twins and very much confined. Anna was still more interested in the rumor that Dr. Stowe was a gifted medium and had held conversations with Goethe, spiritualism being one of the many "isms" which had recently captured her volatile imagination.

Being unimpressed by Dr. Beecher's preaching, Elizabeth took her sister on the first Sunday not to Second Presbyterian but to St. Paul's. But she need not have worried about the excellence of the sermon. Though Anna seemed moderately pleased, she announced that thereafter she would attend Mr. Brooks's church since it was nearer. The quality of the sermon was immaterial, since she never listened, anyway.

"I could make a better one myself," she admitted frankly.

If Elizabeth had hoped to be relieved of responsibility once her older sisters were home, she was doomed to disappointment. Marian was too delicate in health, Anna too mercurial of temperament to make and execute clearheaded decisions. They shared the housekeeping and teaching load, of course. But it was still Elizabeth who kept accounts, budgeted and spent the slender income, planned the meals and often shopped for provisions for the increasing number of boarding pupils. At six in the morning on Wednesday and Saturday she was usually in the market house bargaining with the farmers who had come into town by cart or canalboat with meat, butter, eggs, and other farm produce, knowing just which ones would have the best fowls for five to seven cents apiece, or a roasting pig for twenty-odd cents, or beef at less than three cents a pound. True, she was able at last to hire two servants of a sort, but a few weeks later she confided to her diary, "Servants marched off without saying a word!"

Tragedy was by no means ended. Less than a month after the arrival of Anna and Marian Aunt Mary was taken sick, and four days later she was dead. The funeral was held the same day, a pitiful affair beside Papa's, as anticlimactic in emotion as in ceremony. Only a handful of friends attended. The pastor, Mr. Brooks, insisted on meeting them at the vault instead of at the house, and his reading of the service was both hasty and abbreviated.

"An awful thing is death," Elizabeth recorded with a twinge of guilt. "With dear Papa our feelings were so intense, but now it seemed as if whatever arrived I should never feel again. Not one tear did I shed. Poor Aunt Mary, delirious all the time."

It was only a few weeks later that a letter from Aunt Lucy told of Aunt Bar's death. One by one the physical bonds binding Samuel Blackwell's children to the old life in England were being severed. But not the spiritual bonds! Never since setting sail from Bristol in the old *Cosmo* had Elizabeth been so homesick for her native land as in this blatantly booming outpost of modern progress far from the smell of the sea.

"Lovely, lovely England," she wrote in her diary one night after reading Mrs. Sherwood's nostalgic *Roxobel* to Anna, "when shall I see you again? The more I think of it the more I detest the idea of settling down in America. It would be an insuperable objection to my marrying here."

It was Anna who suggested one day in church that one of the three sisters try to go as governess with the Emerys, who were planning a trip to England, "just to see how it would seem living there again." Elizabeth's blood tingled. She could imagine herself already on the ship with the foam and blue waves dashing around her. So attractive was the illusion that she could scarcely listen to Mr. Johns's sermon. But of course it *was* an illusion. They were tied to the daily grind like the blindfolded oxen she had seen pictured going round and round an oil press.

And for Elizabeth it was a grind. She hated teaching. Each week the five days of classes seemed interminable. During those first months when inexperience battled bitterly with necessity, her journal bristled with secret bursts of revolt.

"Sept. 28. Friday. O be joyful! I'm always delighted when Friday comes."

"Oct. 10. Oh, for a lodge in some vast wilderness, far away from children!"

"Nov. 16. Could not go to Mrs. Pullan's for tea with Anna and Marian, as I had promised the children a period of play. Had to fulfill the promise but shan't do so again, as it compromises my dignity."

"Dec. 20. How we long to send off the boarders! Such stories the girls tell, such sulky looks and impertinent actions! Friday most joyfully dismissed the children until next Wednesday week."

"Feb. 15. Spent most of my spare time in combing the children's heads, a most horrible employment for the state in which they were."

"March 8. Friday. By the time school was over I was almost distracted. I really think if anyone came and offered to me, I should have accepted without any hesitation." Yes, she might have added, even that bothersome Mr. Smith, who liked to accompany the three girls to church but who showed obvious preference for Elizabeth. The following day, however, March 9, the three took a drive with this hopeful young swain down the river, and she gained further insight into his character. He had "associated with low people," she discovered, and had "nothing like refinement or literary taste and betrayed his commonness of mind." His fate as a suitor was irrevocably decided. Not even to escape the apparently sole alternative to marriage — teaching — would she fulfill her rash promise of the day before.

She did not even have her sisters' recourse to sickness as a reprieve. Anna as well as Marian was constantly having to be dosed for some ailment or other. Still contemptuous of weakness in others as well as herself, Elizabeth accepted her role of nurse with less than sympathetic resignation. "Anna unwell. Sent to Mr. Emery for some lobelia. It made her feel so horrible she thought she was poisoned." . . . "Anna took lobelia. I was her ministering angel. She took five teaspoonfuls without effect, then raspberry tea and last of all saleratus. At last in despair she took *le roi* and went to bed."

All the incapacity Elizabeth could manage was a sore mouth, treatment of which with doses of strong limewater burned her throat and brought tears but did not relieve her of one hour of teaching. She was almost disgustingly healthy. And in spite of their fast-developing manhood, her wisp of a body continued to be more than a match for her adolescent brothers'. Her strength was to them more a matter of pride and amusement than of embarrassment, as on the evening when the Emerys came to call.

The conversation turned for some reason to the inferior muscular power of women as compared with men. Mr. Emery, a man small of stature but large in self-confidence, was vehement in his opinions.

"Not only is the male sex stronger than the female," he asserted, "but I'm sure the weakest man, if he put forth his full strength, would prove stronger than the strongest woman."

"Oh, come now." Sam laughed. "That can't be true. Our Elib here, when she chooses, is more than a match for either Henry or me at wrestling or lifting. She can even carry us around!"

The visitor looked contemptuously incredulous. "Well, she couldn't lift *me!* No woman living could lift me against my will." Defiantly he turned to the quiet girl sitting in the background, and settling back resolutely, pressed his feet firmly on the floor. "Try it, Miss Elizabeth! I defy you to move me out of this chair."

Elizabeth slowly crossed the room. With apparent ease she lifted the visitor from his chair, seated him on her left arm, anchored him firmly with the other, and in spite of his frantic efforts to get free, bore him deliberately three times around the room, then set him down amid a burst of merriment.

"You see, sir," she said simply, "that *some* women can be quite as strong as *some* men." Sheepishly the visitor contributed his share of the laughter.

Elizabeth felt no pride in the proceeding. She had not the slightest desire to compete with or be stronger than men. All she wanted — and she was beginning to want it with a fierce concentration — was that women should be accorded the same rights and privileges. That night she recorded the simple, unadorned statement, "I carried Mr. E. around the room."

There were practical advantages as well as entertainment to be derived from physical strength. One day in October she wrote, "I went to Mr. Mills' by myself to hear a lecture on the state of countries. Came home followed by some young man, but as I thought I could knock him down if necessary I did not much mind."

But her strength was as much of the spirit as of the body. Mamma was a good teacher, but sweetness, not firmness, was the essence of her classroom manner. The small children she taught, many of them from uncouth frontier homes, were often her despair. When they became too obstreperous, she would call Elizabeth. The seventeen-year-old girl would come into the room and walk about, not saying a word, merely looking at the children, and somehow under the compelling force of her eye, the mute power of her dignity and authority, the uproar would cease and the most mutinous of the pupils would become as quiet as mice. Little did they know how terrified she was of them and how she was quaking inside!

3

There was one difference between the daily grind of the three Blackwell girls and that of the ox plodding its patient circuit. They were not blindfolded. Eyes were wide open, every sense alert to the frustrating but challenging society in which they functioned.

Their inferior opportunities as women were becoming more and more galling. They encountered the frustration at every turn, in books, in conversations, in sermons, in the bitter realities of daily existence.

"Heard Bishop Meade at St. Paul's," Elizabeth recorded one Sunday. "He gave some rather unjust and quite uncalled for remarks on the inferiority of women."

Again — "Finished *Romance and Reality*. I do not like many of the sentiments at all and think the author is exceedingly unjust to the ladies."

Later — "Anna and I had a talk on matrimony. She fully intends courting somebody if a better fate doesn't turn up. I really could not help crying upstairs when I thought of my situation. When I think of the long dreary years in prospect . . ."

Even the possibility of marriage offered little more hope of freedom — indeed, less. For they had learned long since that few husbands and fathers, even the best of them, were like Samuel Blackwell. If a single woman had few opportunities for improving her economic lot, she might be even worse off if she married. For legally the wife became literally a slave of her husband. Both American and English law were built firmly on Blackstone, whose views of women's rights had been dim indeed!

"By marriage," that eminent jurist had proclaimed, "the husband and wife are one person in law, that is, the very being or legal existence of the woman is suspended during marriage or at least is incorporated and consolidated into that of the husband, under whose wing, protection, and cover she performs everything. . . . Upon this principle, of a union of persons in husband and wife [and that one the husband!] depend almost all the legal rights, duties, and disabilities that either of them acquire by the marriage. . . . A man cannot grant anything to his wife, or enter into covenant with her, for to grant would be to suppose her separate existence."

Worse almost than being a slave, to be considered a nonentity! And if a woman protested such injustice, she was ridiculed as a freak of nature, like Mary Wollstonecraft, writing her *Vindication of the Rights of Women* back in 1792, who had been dubbed by Horace Walpole as a "hyena in petticoats"!

At least, the girls consoled themselves grimly, they could call the pittance they earned their own. Not so if they were wives instead of fatherless spinsters! In most states a married woman's earnings belonged wholly to her husband. She was not permitted to hold property separately from him, to make a will or a contract, to sue or be sued. Yet all such economic slavery was camouflaged under a pretty male vocabulary of "chivalry" and "protection." Harriet Martineau, the English author, visiting America in 1837, had been amazed to find the new democratic nation more backward in its treatment of women than some parts of the Old World.

"While woman's intellect is confined," she had marveled, "her morals crushed, her health ruined, her weakness encouraged, and her strength punished, she is told that her lot is cast in the paradise of women. And there is no country in the world where there is so much boasting of the 'chivalrous' treatment she enjoys. In short, indulgence is given her as a substitute for justice, and marriage is the only object left open to women."

But the right to control their own earnings was bitter satisfaction. For what could they do to earn? The same Harriet Martineau had listed only four occupations that she had found open to a woman. She could teach, make hats or clothing, become a domestic servant, or work in a factory. The fact that the textile mills of New England were employing more than fifty thousand women (all, of course, at a much lower wage than men), that women were engaged in a variety of occupations — makers of gloves, glue, snuff, trusses, cigars, harnesses; laundresses, leechers, soda room keepers — was scant encouragement to the keenly intellectual and ambitious daughters of Samuel Blackwell. Why, they often asked each other, were things so unfair? Here were Sam and

Henry, mere boys with much less education than they, able to step into decent jobs which paid almost as much as the girls were earning altogether, with any number of possible careers open to them. Anna was luckier than the others. Writing also was considered a respectable career for women. There might even be hope for little Ellen, who showed an astonishing ability at painting. But Elizabeth! All the womanly skills she or most of her friends worked so furiously to develop resulted in either mediocre attainment or in frustrated boredom.

"Practiced guitar until my fingers were sore. . . ."

"Mrs. Howells showed us her counterpane. Really astonishing such an industrious waste of time!"

"Learning wax flower making. . . . How sick I am of wax! However, as I wish to arrive at the highest degree of perfection in the art, I must go on."

And much as she hated the daily grind, she flung herself into it with the same furious ardor. Must she teach other people's unruly and often dull children all her life? Then she would become the best teacher possible. She practiced the piano even after giving lessons much of the day, labored to perfect her French with Anna. Always an omnivorous reader, she now read voluminously, not only in English but in French, and less successfully, German: Guizot's *Civilization*, de Tocqueville's *Demos*, Abercrombie's *Moral Philosophy*. She was delighted when Sam brought her half of Gibbon's *History*, borrowed from Major Gano. But most of all she was mentally stirred by Jouffroy's transcription of Cousin's *Metaphysics*. Its introduction to a new world of reason brought her ecstatic delight. Doubt, she suddenly discovered, was a human right, not a sin!

In spite of her doubts, she decided in the winter of 1838 to join Anna and Marian in being confirmed in St. Paul's Episcopal Church. The announcement elicited horrified disapproval from Hannah and Sam, who had joined the Orthodox Congregational Church of which Thornton K. Mills was pastor. "Your poor father, he would turn over in his grave!" . . . "So you're actually going to deck yourself in those rags of popery!" . . . Hannah wept bitterly and indulged in a long dissertation on the state of her daughters' souls.

But, undeterred by all objections, even by the visiting Bishop Meade's derogation of women, the girls persisted in taking the step of confirmation, even picking a $48-a-year pew, which they could ill afford. A disappointment, too, as it turned out, for they discovered on the first Sunday that it was directly beneath a dripping oil lamp! "All gewgaws," Hannah denounced the last communion service they were permitted to witness before their confirmation, lasting from ten until after two. But Elizabeth was deeply stirred, less perhaps by the impressive liturgy than by the fact that Bishop Smith "preached an excellent sermon in favor of women." She and Marian were confirmed by Bishop McIlvaine the following Wednesday, with twenty-one other candidates. "I took the vows," she recorded, "with fear and joy."

Her fears were for her ability not only as a sinful human being to keep the vows, but, unacknowledged perhaps, to give credence to them. She had gone through much troubled soul-searching before answering some of the questions. For Episcopalianism was a creed of conformity, and the children of Samuel Blackwell were born of Dissenters. Pioneer thought as well as action was in their blood. Anna's volatile mind was probing into all kinds of "isms" and philosophies — spiritualism, Swedenborgianism, the rationalism of the New England transcendentalists. Henry was frankly an agnostic. Already the shrewd-eyed Emily was coming to Sam with such questions as, "Sam, how do you know the Bible is inspired?" But in spite of previous doubts, Elizabeth took the vows with all sincerity.

"The constant irritation of an uncongenial and most wearisome life," she confessed in her diary soon after her confirmation, "would make me perfectly pettish, but I hope a higher power has entered into me, and though the freshness of the soul has gone and I know I am most unworthy, I humbly trust that some divine power will enable me to perform faithfully those duties here and then receive me, oh, how joyfully, into that eternal abode where sin and sorrow can never enter."

Hannah should have been well content with her daughters' acceptance of such orthodoxy, even though accompanied with "gewgaws," for there were far greater worries soon to come. Cincinnati was by no means an intellectual backwater, but rather a turbulent stream fed by every popular current of religious and political thought. There were the "Come-Outers," representing dissent from almost every phase of social life. On her first Fourth of July in the city Elizabeth had attended one of their picnics where the Wattles brothers, Augustus and John, distinctive for their long hair and peculiar dress, had been loudly applauded for their condemnation of "Priests, lawyers, and doctors, the trinity of the Devil!" She had been especially intrigued by their "Humanity's Barn," where any human being, even a runaway slave, could find a night's shelter. There were the Millerites who, dressed in white, assembled on hills and housetops to await the imminent Second Coming, always postponed — for some good reason, according to their leader William Miller — to a future date. There were Lutherans, centered in the large colony of German settlers, many of them prosperous brewers and pork packers; Calvinist Presbyterians, spiritually nourished by Lane Seminary on the hill; Strict Baptists, Campbellites, Methodists both white and African, Swedenborgians, Quakers; yes — and Unitarians.

It was the presence of William Henry Channing, nephew of the famous William Ellery Channing of Boston, as minister of this church which exploded a new bombshell in the Blackwell family. To Elizabeth his coming was like a fresh sea wind blowing clean all the foggy crevices where secret doubts had long been shunted. A man of rare moral endowments and eloquence, handsome, elegant in manner and appearance, vibrantly glowing and sincere, he brought with him all the idealism, rationalism, and social dynamism of New England's transcendental thought. For her he opened a new world, introducing her to such kindred spirits as Emerson, Thoreau, Theodore Parker, Bronson Alcott, Margaret Fuller; introducing her also to some of Cincinnati's most intelligent leaders gathered about him, such as James Perkins, C. P. Cranch, William Greene, and Judge Walker. Later she learned about Brook Farm Colony in West Roxbury, Massachusetts, an attempt to establish a cooperative community of like-minded persons dedicated to "plain living and high thinking," and she was so inspired by the idea that belief in such a solution to many of society's problems was to persist throughout her life. She read the *Dial* and the *Harbinger*, new publications stressing need for such social reorganization, and pored over the writings of Emerson, Carlyle, Cousin, and Fourier.

"Sit down," cried Mr. Channing when she came one day to visit him and his wife, "and listen to this!" Then with a glowing face he poured forth extracts from one of Emerson's latest essays.

Affiliation with the more orthodox Episcopalianism was temporarily abandoned, not to be resumed until years later, when she would become a member of the Church of England. The three girls joined Mr. Channing's Unitarian Church. Mamma mourned and prayed. Sam, who had remained rigidly seated during all the risings and kneelings when accompanying them to St. Paul's, refused to darken the portal of this new heresy. Though his diary dutifully recorded that "Anna, Marian, and Elizabeth were at Mr. Channing's" or "went to hear him lecture," the notations were usually followed by such pious entries as, "O Jesus, come and rule my heart!" or "Oh, for a heart broken on account of sin!" His distaste was more explicitly evident when he wrote, "Found to my great sorrow that one of my Sunday School scholars has imbibed the notions of the Universalists from his father."

An even more serious result of this excursion into "heresy" was the consequent dwindling of the school. Unitarianism was regarded as infidelity by the fashionable and conservative society of the city and so was intensely unpopular. Many shocked parents withdrew their children. But the daughters of Samuel Blackwell were not afraid of criticism, even of ostracism. They would rather starve than compromise. Elizabeth was more troubled by her mother's grief than by the curtailment of income.

However, there were issues on which the family was in full agreement. One was the exciting election of 1840, when William Henry Harrison, Whig, native son of Ohio and champion of the rights of the common people, was pitted against the lavish and autocratic administration in Washington. The family made flags, sang lustily for "Tippecanoe and Tyler too," attended rallies. In May one of their boarders, a young man named West, drove Sam, Henry, Anna, and Elizabeth to Dayton, fifty-two miles in a carriage, to attend a great barbecue at a convention. Some of the thousands of visitors were entertained by hospitable people of the city. Others slept on straw beds on the floors of public buildings.

On October 1 all the young Blackwells marched with a rousing procession under the great arch erected on Main Street at the corner of Fourth, with its crowning slogan, "A People to be Free Must Do Their Own Voting, their Own Fighting." The sweeping Whig victory was a triumph almost as thrilling as the "chairings" back in England. And with equal fervor they all mourned together when a few months later the body of Ohio's first president was brought from Pittsburgh on the steamer *Raritan* and after a procession as somber as the former had been riotous, interred in the cemetery at North Bend.

They were united, too, in their ardent support of a lawyer named Johnston, who opposed the reactionary efforts of the Roman Catholic Archbishop Purcell, who appeared before the Educational Congress in Cincinnati denouncing free and equal education for women. Of course the lawyer's efforts were unsuccessful. The Archbishop's position reflected the prevalent views of clergymen, politicians, professional leaders throughout the country. The idea that women's minds might be fit for serious study was to most men as ridiculous as it was revolutionary. It was woman's province to be an adornment to her home and a purifying and helpful subordinate to her husband. A girl should be taught how to run a household and practice the proper graces of a lady — music, dancing, French, embroidery, perhaps even a little history and geography, but not enough to disturb a proper deference to her future husband's opinions. Certainly she had neither the capacity nor the need for formal education.

But, Elizabeth consoled herself, progress was being made. Since Frances Wright had boldly proclaimed a dozen years ago that "until women assume the place in society which good sense and good feeling assign to them, human improvement must advance but feebly," education for women had advanced by a few halting steps. There was Emma Willard's Female Seminary in Troy, New York, the first endowed institution for the education of girls which, to the shock of the pupils' mothers, had even dared to introduce into the course of study the indelicate subject of physiology. At their insistence the modesty of their daughters had been preserved by the pasting of heavy paper over the pages in their textbooks which depicted any part of the body.

There was Oberlin College, founded in 1833 right here in Ohio, the first institution of higher education to open its doors to all regardless of race, color, or sex. There was exultation in the Blackwell house when news came of the first woman graduating in 1841. There was Mount Holyoke Seminary, founded in 1837 by Mary Lyon, who had carried her green velvet bag all over New England trying to raise the needed funds for her bold experiment of making education available to girls of all economic groups, of preparing them for more than homemaking or teaching. In one group that she addressed, a sewing circle in West Brookfield, Massachusetts, had been an impressionable young girl making a shirt to help some young man through theological school. "How absurd," the girl had thought, "for me to be making a shirt to educate a student who can earn more money toward his own education in a week by teaching than I could earn in a month!" She put the shirt away unfinished, and in that small act had charted a course which was to become immutably linked with that of Elizabeth Blackwell and her family. Her name was Lucy Stone.

And there was Catherine Beecher. Daughter of Dr. Lyman, sister of Henry Ward and the literary Harriet, she was Cincinnati's own pioneer in the education of women. Elizabeth knew her slightly. Though her work was in the East, she was in and out of the big house at Walnut Hills and sometimes visited informal meetings which the girls attended. Catherine had conducted a school for girls in Hartford for several years but had had to give it up because of ill health. Now she devoted her time to writing and lecturing. Listening to the vivid and effusive Catherine expound her revolutionary ideas — that housewives, to fulfill their duties properly, needed training as technical as a lawyer's or a doctor's, and that teachers especially should be trained; and her plan to develop what would later be called normal schools in a chain of Midwestern cities — Elizabeth was so enthralled that she forgot her usual reserve.

"Oh, yes!" she burst out eagerly. "If I had only had such training before I started teaching! I was so inexperienced and so afraid of my pupils!"

And she still was. Seeing her standing before them so cool and dignified, her boisterous young pupils had no idea how terrified she was of them, or how gladly she retreated from them to her garret room, from whose southern window she could look out over the curling river and the peaceful Kentucky hills. It was the east window that she liked best, however. Sometimes, reading, she would raise her seat by piling a bag of straw on boxes so she could look out toward the east — England — as the captive Jews had looked west toward Jerusalem.

It was Henry who escaped first from captivity. Dr. Silas Crane, who had been Anna's employer in Vermont, was appointed president of Kemper College in St. Louis, and en route to his new assignment in the fall of 1839 he and his family stayed nearly a month with the Blackwells. Knowing Henry's ambition to become a lawyer, the Cranes offered him a home with them if he wished to attend Kemper. By the summer of 1840 it was decided that the project could be managed financially, and he left by the boat *Gallant* on September 21, with a tin trunk, many moral and religious admonitions from Hannah, and a new suit of clothes which he insisted on wearing against the counsel of the family — also an extra change of clothes in his carpetbag on the advice of Elizabeth. The latter was a happy suggestion, since the five-day trip down the Ohio and Mississippi was to take nearly two weeks because of the low state of the river, and a slight accident was to subject the new suit to an unhappy wetting.

"Oh, dear boy, when shall I see you again?" worried Hannah.

"Maybe on the Judgment Day," grinned the irrepressible and often irreverent Harry, "on the left side of the cross."

Deeply grieved, Hannah mourned constantly over the state of his soul. Anna, however, was more worried lest the dashing and carefree young mischief-maker should fail to take advantage of his opportunities and return the same "impertinent little loafer" who had gone away.

The following year, 1841, the country was again facing financial crisis. French and music became luxuries. The number of pupils decreased even further. Finances became desperate and Harry was forced to return home, surprisingly grown, beard sprouting, voice changed, but no less dashing and fun-loving, certainly no more pious. He went to work again with Mr. Rowland Ellis, owner of a flour mill, as his sole clerk and assistant, a position he was to hold for the next six years.

Anna was next to leave home. Since pupils were so few, she was less needed, and she secured a position as teacher of music, first in Dayton, Ohio, later in Columbus. She was soon gaining some success in writing as well as teaching, though her tempestuous nature often involved her in misunderstandings and even dissension with her employers as well as her friends. Into each situation, each friendship, each new "ism," she tumbled with headlong impetuosity, certain that she had found the ultimate; then too often became swiftly disillusioned. It had been the same with her romantic attachments. They had flared brightly, giving every promise of rocketing sky-high, then spat out like duds. Until Mr. Murdoch.

She wrote about him from Columbus. The die was cast. The "handsome, amiable, learned, wealthy John Murdoch, mayor of Springfield" had "urged anew his claim," and she had "given a pledge she must one day redeem at the altar!" Moreover, he was coming to visit them within a few days on his way to Colorado.

The family was in an uproar. Their Anna was engaged! Excitement was soon charged with doubt, with foreboding, almost with panic. He couldn't possibly be the right man for her, worried Hannah. And his religion hadn't even been mentioned! Probably one of those Swedenborgians, agreed Sam dubiously, or perhaps she was off on some other tangent by now, like mesmerism or spiritualism. Her letters had been hinting of such leanings. A country storekeeper, marveled Marian, even if he was rich and a mayor! Probably a dull sort of bloke, offered Harry cheerfully.

Elizabeth said little, but she witnessed the rising tide of opposition with uneasiness and growing alarm. Shouldn't they wait to see what he was like? she suggested mildly. But long before the encounter he had been judged and found wanting.

The young man came, saw (and was seen), and did not conquer. He was personable enough, well groomed, intelligent, but definitely not good enough for Anna. Stodgy, just as he had expected, was Harry's verdict. Just a little — common, don't you think? offered Marian. Wouldn't commit himself on any religious questions, was enough for Sam. An unsaved soul, feared Hannah.

"He's not a bit like Papa," said Emily with astute finality.

Elizabeth stared at her. That was exactly what she had been thinking. And suddenly she knew that unconsciously she had been applying this same measure to every man who caught her fancy. But it was an impossible test. No other man could possibly be like Papa. If all the five girls applied it, then none of them would ever marry! However, in this case she had to agree with the family. Mr. Murdoch was not the man for Anna, and not because he kept a country store, or was a bore, or was unlike Papa. He was simply too different. It would be like harnessing a racehorse to a family carryall, or confining a young eagle in a gilded cage.

A bombardment of letters went out to Anna by almost every mail boat, strongly dissuading her from the contemplated step. But her decision continued firm. A month later she arrived by canalboat in a state of lively anticipation and immediately began making purchases for the coming event. There were dress fittings, sallies to Mrs. Avis's shop on Walnut Street, which specialized in "fashionable corsets and gentlemen's stocks," and to Mrs. Westerfield's on Main Street, the city's most patronized milliner and mantua maker. But as days passed the lively anticipation visibly waned. Two weeks after her arrival she was writing Mr. Murdoch to defer matters, and a few days later the luckless gentleman called and was given his final dismissal. He accepted the misfortune with gentlemanly grace, asking the return of his letters but begging her acceptance of all other presentations. Since the latter included two hundred dollars which he had apparently loaned her, it was a generous gesture. As head of the family Sam concluded the sad affair by delivering the letters, also the two hundred dollars.

Bidding Anna goodbye each time she left home, leaving the household curiously quiet after a flurry of social activity, Elizabeth felt envy as well as loss. Anna was independent. She knew what she wanted to do. She would probably become a successful writer, a career considered fitting for a lady, while she, Elizabeth . . . What future? Teaching? Marriage? If so, to whom? Some boring, if not vulgar Mr. Smith? The ones who favored her she did not want. With those she might have favored she was always too shy to make them look at her a second time.

Now Elizabeth and Sam were the decision-makers. The house became unsuitable. Already they had moved once, from Third to Fourth Street. Now, in June, 1841, they moved to a smaller one in Eighth Street, and again the old red carpets were nailed down. An ad for boarders was placed in the *Chronicle*, their second piano sold for $150 to defray debts. Early in 1842 the Bank of Cincinnati failed; a mob gathered and tore it down. Family resources sank to a new low. Sam's new job in the flour mill did little good, for his employer was unable to pay his salary. For a time they could not afford even fuel. Without the occasional "paying guests" they would have been desperate indeed. But decrease in pupils meant no lightening of Elizabeth's responsibilities. Marian's ill health made her services undependable. Hannah had been brought up to be a "lady," not a household manager. After a twelve-hour day of teaching, marketing with scant funds, planning meals with insufficient food, directing incompetent servants or doing most of the work herself, keeping the boarders decently warmed and fed, Elizabeth should have been tired enough to fall into bed. Instead she went to a lecture, a church meeting, a study group, an Anti-Slavery Society conclave, or, twice each month on Friday evenings, to the meeting of the Semi-Colon Club, a group of Cincinnati's intellectual and literary elite, where, unlike Anna and Marian, who often contributed amusing little essays or musical numbers, she sat in shy seclusion, basking in the brilliant company and conversation but seldom daring to open her mouth.

4

Perhaps it was because she felt herself a sort of unwilling prisoner that for Elizabeth slavery became more than ever a burning issue. Or perhaps it was merely increased proximity to it. For Cincinnati, sitting like an uneasy lid on the boiling caldron of North-South dissension, seethed with emotions pro and con.

As in New York, the Blackwells were very much involved. In the brief two months of his sojourn Samuel had allied himself fearlessly with old English friends like the Brownes, the Howells, the Donaldsons, and with new ones like the Emerys who were outspoken abolitionists, had sought out churches whose preachers were anti-slavery, had taken his sons to the courthouse to witness trials of abolitionist ringleaders from the East who had stirred up mob frenzy in the city. And his children followed faithfully in his footsteps.

But there was so little a woman could do! Elizabeth envied Sam on the day in 1841 when he went with some eighteen others to Covington across the river as witnesses in a case for establishing the freedom of two kidnaped colored girls. Far better to be in the thick of action, even danger, than to pace the floor, then when Sam returned with lips grim and clothes rumpled, to demand breathlessly, "What happened?"

"Oh — nothing much. We were followed by three villains, and once the people were all ready to mob us. But nothing really happened."

It was even worse on the night in August when after a white man had been killed a mob attacked some of the city's colored residents at the corner of Sixth and Broadway. The firing kept up all night. Some Negroes were killed, many wounded. The mob got hold of a cannon and began firing it. In the morning a citizens' meeting was called. Sam and Henry were there, but of course the women could not properly attend. Again the frustration, the waiting, the longing to do something.

"A man stood on the fence," reported Sam bitterly, "and urged them to pass resolutions and show the world that the people here were no abolitionists. The crowd yelled approbation. Then the mayor took the chair. Resolutions were drafted to condemn abolition and revive an old law of 1807 requiring bond of free colored people. The streets are a shambles. Gangs are hunting down every poor colored man they can find and lugging them into the colored quarter. Want to take away all their weapons and pen them up in a narrow section between Broadway and Sixth and then glut themselves with murder."

"Oh — no!" wailed the girls in horror.

"Yes. Be sure you women stay in the house with all the doors and windows closed."

But Sam and Henry, being males, did no staying in. That night the mob attacked the *Philanthropist* press and threw it in the river. Stores of abolitionists were demolished. Sam and Henry returned, grim but safe, having spent most of the night guarding the flour mill. At least they had been *doing* something!

Elizabeth was even more envious of some of the bolder citizens who operated the underground railroad, helping fugitive slaves from the south to escape across the Ohio River, and by relaying them to various "stations," to reach safety in Canada. Every time she passed it she thrilled to the sight of the building at the northwest corner of Sixth and Elm streets, rumored to be the "dispatcher's office" of the railroad. It impressed her far more than the ornate National Theater with its arched facade or the magnificent Observatory which in 1843 she saw dedicated by John Quincy Adams. In this unimpressive storefront building the Quaker Levi Coffin lived and operated his business, but more important, received runaway slaves, fed them, clothed them, concealed them when necessary, then managed to convey them in carts, carriages, even in funeral coaches, to the next station thirty miles away. Another house of concealment was supposed to be that of Salmon P. Chase, the distinguished lawyer whom she met often in church groups or at lectures, and who would later become twice governor of Ohio, Lincoln's Secretary of the Treasury, and Chief Justice of the Supreme Court. If Papa were still living, their home might be just such a haven.

The Kentucky shoreline held for her a morbid fascination. The sweeping panorama of hills, the charming little towns of Newport and Covington, were beautiful yet mysterious and sinister. They were "slave country." What was her dismay, then, when in early 1844 a position as teacher was offered one of the Blackwell girls in a small school in Henderson, Kentucky! The proposition was hers alone to consider. Marian's health was too poor. Anna, back from Columbus and recovered from the Murdoch incident, was now heading with all her usual optimism for a teaching position in a private school in New York. The thought of venturing into strange territory alone was frightening enough, but to pass beyond those forbidding hills into the uncharted wilderness of slave country — ! She could not accept.

But — could she refuse? She was needed no more at home, was just another mouth to feed. The school had closed a year ago. Sam and Henry both had good jobs, Sam in a new bookkeeping position at Mr. Bradbury's mill that kept him so busy he was unable to pursue his precious reading. Elizabeth's heart ached for Sam, so slight of body, weighing no more than a hundred pounds, yet so strong of will and determination. Now that he had grown a beard, every day he grew to look more and more like Papa, and there was that same dogged bafflement in his eyes. He shared Papa's dream, too, of becoming a successful

sugar manufacturer *without slave labor*. For a long time he had agonized over the offer of a job from Dennis Harris, who had bought Papa's
old factory in New York and turned it into a successful business, before
deciding with grim finality, "I can't do it. I have determined not only to
keep clear of the manufacture of slave products but as far as possible to
forgo their daily use." And again the family ate their porridge without
sugar.

Henry, now eighteen but the same carefree, irreverent young blade,
was still with the flour mills, taking frequent long trips westward over
wilderness trails as the firm's salesman. Emily, grave-eyed and adult at
seventeen, was as capable as Elizabeth of managing the younger
children and helping Hannah and Marian run the household. George
— little Washy — Elizabeth noted with startled awareness, was as tall as
herself and already working at part-time jobs.

No, Elizabeth was no longer needed at home. Nor anywhere else,
she admitted with brutal candor. Suddenly she felt a mounting panic.
She was twenty-three years old, the age when most women were married and had several children. With distaste and horror she contemplated her probable future: earning a little by giving music lessons;
being dependent, as her four aunts had been, on the largesse of her
brothers; pursuing the "ladylike" tasks of helping to run another
woman's household, playing nursemaid to her children.

Thoughtfully, on the night that the offer came from Henderson,
Elizabeth appraised herself in her bedroom mirror. It had to be tipped
forward to give a clear view, for she was still barely over five feet. The face
that looked back was clear-skinned and delicately featured, its broad
forehead unlined. It might have belonged to a girl of seventeen — or to a
woman of thirty. "Nondescript," she thought with dispassion, or as
Hannah had sometimes described her, "wispy." She was quite unaware
of the warm glints which often turned the wide-spaced eyes into jewels
of rare luster, or of the unusual beauty and grace of the slender hands
lifted to the wings of pale blonde hair.

With swift fingers, not a motion wasted, she pulled the big bone
hairpins from the flat coils hiding her ears and with a few brisk shakes
of her head sent the straw-colored mass cascading about her shoulders.
Then, stroke after determined stroke, she brushed it vigorously until it
splayed out like a thing alive, crackled, and almost struck sparks.

No, she would not be like her four aunts. Spinster perhaps, yes.
Dependent, no. She would go to Kentucky.

Chapter Four

As THE LITTLE TOWNS along the Ohio River bank became more and more straggling, dingy, and uninteresting, Elizabeth was increasingly apprehensive. By Saturday morning, with the jaunty little steamer *Chieftain* four days and a hundred miles from Cincinnati, nervousness mounted to actual panic. *Is this it?* she wondered each time the boat rounded a curve and a still more dingy hamlet came into view.

"Madam, we have reached Henderson," said the clerk, approaching her politely.

She gave one glance as the boat swung toward the bank. Three dirty old frame buildings, a steep bank covered with mud, some Negroes and unprepossessing whites gathered at its foot. She looked away hastily. The boat touched, and she was hustled off. Uncertainly she stumbled through the mud toward the group of men.

"Is — Dr. Wilson — "

A rough-looking man came forward and presented his arm. "Howdy, miss." He gestured curtly toward three waiting Negroes. "You there, tote up her baggage."

Elizabeth struggled after him up the bank, clinging to his hand to keep from slipping in the mud. They passed through a straggling little country village, stopped at a small frame house, entered a low, shabby room.

"My wife, Mrs. Wilson." A poorly dressed, tired-looking woman came forward and extended a timid hand.

Head whirling, Elizabeth longed to be shown to her room, but she forced herself to take the proffered seat and utter polite inanities. At last she ventured to ask if she might go upstairs. The daughter of the house came, a girl with untidy hair and clothes but bright, curious eyes.

110

Gratefully she followed the girl up a flight of old crooked, creaking steps and through a bedroom door, then stood stock still, stifling a desire to burst into tears. Incredulously she absorbed the details: rough walls daubed with old whitewash, a rickety bed, a bureau, a commode, a chair, all covered with litter and dust. She felt the eyes of the girl anxiously appraising her and managed a reassuring smile.

"Could I have my trunks brought up?" she asked with surprising casualness.

The girl vanished. Presently her mother appeared, much embarrassed. "I'm sorry. I didn't explain. This isn't to be your home. My niece has gone to make preparations and will take you to her home this evening. I" — she looked around the room — "I know perfectly well you couldn't live in such a — a *hole*."

Elizabeth smiled, relief pouring through her. She washed in the cracked bowl, dried her hands on a clean but frayed towel, smoothed her hair, went downstairs. Her host, Dr. Wilson, was the man who had written to and hired her, one of the group she was soon to dub the "Responsibles." She sought him out immediately.

"I would like to begin teaching," she told him, "on Monday morning."

He looked shocked. Why, this was Saturday! The schoolhouse had barely been selected. Its windows were broken, its floor and walls filthy, its plaster fallen off, the — the trustees not yet appointed, the scholars not notified. It would take at least a week — !

Elizabeth groaned inwardly. But outwardly she showed perfect calm, merely a persistence which was to cause the leisurely Kentuckians both dismay and unwelcome activity. She urged, argued, cajoled, insisted, until finally one man was found to mend the windows, another to clean the floor. The Responsibles were somehow assembled. Yes, they agreed, helpless under the barrage of persuasion, they would see that the scholars were notified, and yes, all should be ready to begin by — hesitation here, but she regarded them steadily, small head lifted with the imperious dignity which had often brought order to the classroom — yes, by Monday.

Presently she followed the daughter of her new hostess, a tall, graceful, sleepy-eyed girl, to her new quarters, a small, high-ceilinged bedroom in a substantial, rough brick house. Relief was tempered with dismay when she found she was to occupy it with three others, but the sight of the two other sisters consoled her. All, as well as the mother, were clean, pleas-

111

ant, attractive. In fact, their chief faults were a kindness and friendliness which made impossible the privacy she so loved. She felt in danger of losing her identity.

On Tuesday, if not Monday, she took her seat in a classroom of fourteen girls and organized her school. The girls were a quiet, pleasant sort, much more gentle than the ones in Cincinnati, and she soon settled into a not too disagreeable routine. After school hours she taught four music scholars, as well as a private pupil in French, which meant that on three days of each week she taught ten hours. And she wished the others had been equally filled. She found not a single soul from whom she could learn or with whom she could enjoy a stimulating conversation.

"Carlyle's name," she wrote home, "has never been distantly echoed here. Emerson is a perfect stranger, and Channing would produce a universal fainting fit!"

Not that people were unfriendly or indifferent. Quite the opposite. They manifested an intense interest and volubility in all that concerned her, even her teeth. "Well, I declare she's got a clean mouth, hasn't she!" A rarity indeed, white teeth, in a community where all used tobacco! She suspected that they were a little afraid of her and detected odd glances from her roommates when they caught her reading German. But she did not discourage this reaction. It was her one insurance of privacy.

And she sometimes wished the townspeople were more aloof. All the important residents called on her, and she had to return their visits. At least one such episode tested all her powers of adjustment. One evening she went to call at the home of one of her pupils. Refreshments were served by a small Negro girl with huge black eyes and teeth even whiter than Harry's. The tray was much too big for her, and she could scarcely help slopping the tea. The hostess, anxious to do everything just right for the teacher, reprimanded the child sharply.

"You'd think," she apologized, "as how that Lily could do things decent by this time. Here we've owned her since she was scarce bigger'n a grasshopper."

Elizabeth choked on her tea. She had suspected that many of the Negroes she had seen about were slaves, but this was the first time she had been sure. Coming in out of the chilly dusk, she had taken a seat close to the open fire, which was blazing merrily. Now she felt the hot blood rushing to her neck, her cheeks, her forehead. She was sure she was going to suffocate.

"Is anything the matter, miss?" inquired the hostess, gently anxious.

"No — no, I — I'm just a bit warm, I guess. That fire is really hot."

"Lily!" The gentle voice turned harsh, peremptory. "Stand between teacher and the fire."

"Oh — no — please! I'm really all right!"

But her protests were of no avail. She had to sit, talking pleasant inanities, while the slip of a Negro girl, barefoot and scantily clad, made of her puny, unprotected body a living firescreen. The heat from such proximity must have been blistering. The coldness Elizabeth felt now was far worse than the heat had been. It did not help to know that her hostess had only meant to be kind and hospitable.

Her hatred of slavery grew every day, even though she knew she was seeing it only in its mildest form. No whipping post in Henderson, no instance of downright cruelty! On every hand she heard mistresses, masters, priding themselves on the advantageous situation of their slaves. "Better off than the poor over in your England and other countries!" "Plenty to eat, roof over their heads, dang blamed critters don't know when they're well off!"

Elizabeth tried to reply mildly, to slide some little truths through the narrow apertures of their minds, but she knew that if she expressed her honest opinion she would shut them up tight, arm all their prejudices. The constant smiling and bowing and wearing a mask provoked her intolerably. Sometimes she felt an almost irresistible urge to go to the other extreme, to rush to the woods, to vilify Henderson, to shout curses at the Whigs, to rail at the orthodox, whose bells had been calling a fruitless invitation to revivals ever since her arrival.

It was only a small typical incident, but it would be etched indelibly on her memory a half-century later. She was sitting with her hostess on their broad shaded veranda one pleasant Sunday morning when one of her roommates, the oldest daughter, came out on her way to church, tall, graceful, beautiful in her floating summer drapery. Just at that moment a shabby, forlorn Negro, one of the family slaves who worked in the tobacco fields, approached the veranda. Of course he did not mount the steps, only stood hesitantly, timidly smiling, eyes pleading, the paleness of his extended palm mutely accenting the shining blackness of his face.

"Please, mum — could I have — clean shirt — Sunday?"

His mistress stopped rocking. Her placid Sunday-go-to-meeting face creased with annoyance. "Stupid dolt! No, of course you can't have a clean shirt. You had one last week. And you know better than to come to the front door. Get along!"

The girl descended the steps, pointedly pulling her draperies aside to keep them from contact with the slouching figure. Meekly the slave turned and went away.

Such evidence of contrast and injustice was more than Elizabeth could stand for long. At the end of her first term she resigned from the position.

2

So great was her joy at being home again that at first it seemed like perfect freedom. She exulted in saying exactly what she thought. She attended lectures on abolition, meetings of the Anti-Slavery Society, night after night. She spent long afternoons with groups of women sewing garments for fugitives escaping by the underground railway. She read back numbers of the *Liberator*, the *Democratic Review*, the *Philanthropist*, until the uncertain light of the oil lamp made her eyes smart. She took long walks with Sam or Harry, the walls of her habitual restraint melting before a torrent of words.

"Never knew our Elib could be such a talker," chuckled Sam after a ten-mile jaunt.

Her newfound freedom was intellectual as well as moral, for in her absence the family had moved to the suburb of Walnut Hills, home of Lane Theological Seminary and center of much of the cultural life of Cincinnati. They shared a roomy house with its owners, Professor and Mrs. Franklin Vail and their beautiful daughter Kate. But of all the stimulating influences which Elizabeth found in this new environment, by far the most exciting and energizing were the Beechers.

They lived in a huge rambling brick house high on the hill, a sturdy structure with high ceilings, many arches, fireplaces with green and yellow tiles, and a wide curving staircase. It needed to be big to house the family of Dr. Lyman, which had included nineteen children. Though all were now grown, seven of them ministers, they continued to stream in and out of the old homestead, charging its atmosphere with all the fresh trends of Eastern thought and culture. Elizabeth was soon introduced to their inner circle. Dr. Lyman was no longer a mere pulpit dignitary, often disappointing in his sermons, so mild in his anti-slavery convictions that some of his more extremist students had left Lane Seminary to found the more radical Oberlin College. He was a brisk, untidy figure, white hair straggling, neckcloth awry and academic robe streaming behind him, sprinting down the woods path to the seminary and thinking nothing of vaulting a fence which got in his way. She marveled at his vitality, laughed at his habit of getting exercise, when no other form was available, by going down cellar and shoveling a load of sand from one corner to another; winced at the monotonous and maddening discords of his violin. She came to know Henry Ward, not only as the noted writer and eloquent preacher but as the towheaded urchin who had often shinnied down the rain pipe of the big house to escape parental discipline.

But it was Harriet who satisfied her deepest need for friendship. Finding that they had a host of interests in common and that she was always welcome, Elizabeth became a frequent visitor at the Beecher home. It was an untidy, noisy household, for Harriet was an indifferent housekeeper, "slack," according to her meticulous husband, a prolific and indulgent mother. Floors were always strewn with toys and children, tables with uncompleted manuscripts. Elizabeth often trotted the latest baby on her knee so that its harassed mother could gain a few extra minutes of writing.

"Lucky I can write anywhere, anytime," Harriet would say cheerfully. "My mind bubbles with stories. Pen and paper are to me what sailing is to a duck. But just let me try to write, and lo, a dozen interruptions! A man brings a barrel of apples, a book agent calls, I have to nurse the baby, then make a chowder for dinner. Writing for me is rowing against wind and tide, but I have to do it."

Seeing the small untidy woman determinedly scratching away, curls bobbing, dark eyes dreamy, children's grimy hands pulling at her skirts, Elizabeth felt admiration, pity, envy. Wonderful to have such an all-consuming urge for self-fulfillment and the talent for achieving it! But to be married to a man like Professor Stowe, nearly ten years her senior, thick-shouldered, baldish, nervous, often irritable, presenting her with another baby almost every year, running off on all sorts of expeditions and leaving her with the whole family responsibility! Oh, of course he was very intelligent and an eminent theologian, but such a staid and prosaic complement to the sprightly and imaginative Harriet! He had married her after the death of his first wife Eliza, who had been Harriet's best friend. It was rumored that every year on Eliza's birthday they sat together before her picture and recalled her virtues. Not Elizabeth's idea of romance!

But she basked in the intellectual aura of the Beechers and Walnut Hills. Again she joined the Semi-Colon Club, which met fortnightly in Samuel Foote's mansion and included such gifted members as Christopher P. Cranch, James H. Perkins, and Salmon P. Chase. Just a year before, Harriet Stowe had published her first book of fiction, *The Mayflower*, a series of New England sketches, which had been written for and first read at the club. The program included contributions by painters, poets, musicians, astronomers from the new observatory, as well as other writers. Slowly Elizabeth began to overcome her shyness, contributed her piano or guitar selections and even an occasional story or essay, then zestfully enjoyed the refreshments and Virginia reel which followed. She would never be such a socialite as her sisters or even as Sam and Harry, who were not only at home in the Semi-Colon Club but were active members in a debating society which included such prominent citizens as Ainsworth Spofford and Rutherford B. Hayes. Still, those months following her return from Henderson were among the happiest she had known.

But the euphoria of self-fulfillment did not last, and one of its prime creators was also its destroyer. For once again she fell deeply, extravagantly in love. This time the recipient was no vulgar Mr. Smith, lacking refinement and literary taste. He was a highly educated and cultured member of her select circle of friends. As usual when prey to such emotions, she was shy to the point of torture in his presence. Feeling herself totally unattractive, without charm, she endured agonies in his company, sure there was no hope of his ever according her more than the most casual politeness. Then, as autumn brought increased social activity to Walnut Hills, they were thrown into a more intimate relationship. He began to manifest an unmistakable interest in her, to escort her home from club meetings and lectures. Hope burgeoned like the prodigal scarlet of the huge maple in front of their house. It was the most radiant autumn she had ever known, the air more exhilarating, stars more blazing bright, colors more sharply blue and gold and crimson. One evening when he came to the house he brought her a bouquet of late blooms, and she nursed it for days in a vase of water, then hid the drying wisps in her bureau drawer.

And then, inevitably, like the bouquet, autumn faded. The leaves fell. The air chilled. The gold radiance fought its losing battle with the brown deadness of winter. The idol, she discovered, was not vibrantly alive, awake to new and stimulating ideas, but cast in the rigid mold of caution and tradition. She shared with him some of her favorite passages from Swedenborg, who at that time intrigued her, loaned him some pamphlets by the French socialist philosopher Charles Fourier, which Anna had sent her to read. Fourier's concept of the ideal harmonious state — often called associationism — to be accomplished by dividing society into *phalanxes*, or communities, with elaborate rules for communal life, made strong appeal to Elizabeth's vigorous idealism. Introduced into the United States by Albert Brisbane in 1842, Fourierism had already given birth to many of these experiments in communal living. Though she scarcely expected her friend to be genuinely in sympathy with such controversial theories — she wasn't sure she was herself! — she was wholly unprepared for his reaction.

"Come now, you shouldn't be bothering that pretty little head about social theories that no woman could possibly understand. Better to leave the reforming of society, if it needs it, to us men who have the responsibility of running it!"

"But —" When she tried to protest, no words came. In fact, there were no words. Criticism she could have countered. Argument she would have eagerly welcomed. But — amusement, *patronage!*

"Suppose I bring you some books — poetry, some nice little essays. They're the sort of things a woman should read, something that — that — " Suddenly he too seemed at a loss for words.

— *that don't require any serious thinking,* she finished for him silently.

"Yes. Please do," she said with polite finality.

The battle between autumn and winter was not only in the world outside. *She* was the gold warmth being dissipated by chill winds, the bright maple being stripped of its leaves. That night, instead of tenderly fondling the wilted blossoms and conjuring up their lost fragrance, she thrust them into a paper sack, labeled them "Young love's last dream," and pushed the packet into a back corner of her lowest bureau drawer.

One evening early in 1845 she sat in a semicircle of Blackwells close to a glowing coal fire, a copy of the *Democratic Review* in her hands. But she was not reading.

Her eyes traveled slowly about the circle: Marian in her old sage green frock, skirts drawn up to show an undignified ankle so her small feet could enjoy the warmth of the fender, eyes dancing to the lilts of Coleridge; Harry in his brown sack, lolling in the big rocker beside the lamp table, legs straddled toward the heat while his ever-roaming mind, aided by the *Family Library*, explored the polar seas. Next came Ellen, face vivid above her dark green robe, apron bunched into a ball under another copy of the *Democratic Review*, eyes merry as she quoted the title of an article, "Satan Montgomery's Absorptions of the Muse." Then came Elizabeth herself, and completing the semicircle, Sam in his black dress coat, black cassinières, and house slippers well ventilated about the toes, grave face bent over his journal while his pen scratched and the dog Sultan sprawled at his feet. What was he writing, wondered Elizabeth. His frustration at being twenty-one and nothing but a clerk? His envy of young Emily, who was now a pupil at St. Ann's School in New York where Anna was teaching, because she was enjoying the coveted luxury of studying ten whole hours a day?

"I observed today," remarked Sam, "that the whole of Front Street from Main to Elm, four long blocks, was well lighted with gas. Thus comes progress."

Elizabeth moved restlessly, her black and yellow striped Henderson dress catching the glint of firelight and rippling like a tiger's coat. Would she still be sitting here ten years from now, reading another *Democratic Review* and rejoicing that gas lights had been extended the whole length of Second as well as Front? A spinster with nothing more productive to do than attend teas and literary meetings, read German and metaphysics, try to din a little music into other people's children? Or — worse yet, perhaps — a wife compressed into a mold of rigid conformity?

Suddenly she pushed back her chair, rose, and rushed from the room. Seizing a black woolen cape from the hall rack, she escaped to the porch and began walking. But the cold air fanned rather than quieted her restlessness. Her feet felt like lead. Life was rushing past her. She was using all her tremendous energy to walk back and forth, round and round, like the plodding ox. If only she had some goal, some all-consuming purpose . . .

Was it sheer coincidence that a few days later she called on Mary Donaldson?

3

She dreaded the visit, had postponed it as long as possible, for Mary, a close family friend, was dying of cancer. The shock was even worse than she had expected. The ravages of disease had been swift. It was like seeing a beloved house, where you had known laughter and love and dancing, despoiled by vandals. The wasted limbs, the sunken cheeks, the pallor stunned her almost into incoherence. It was Papa all over again. She hoped desperately that her face revealed only sympathy, none of that instinctive revulsion which the presence of sickness always aroused.

"My dear, how good of you to come!" Mary's eyes were as dancing with life as ever. "Tell me all that's been happening. See, I've had my bed moved nearer the window, but I can't see half as much as I'd like to. Tell me what you see."

Elizabeth's tension relaxed. They talked naturally and pleasantly of recent events in the city, in the church, the Anti-Slavery Society, the Semi-Colon Club. Finally, fearing she was tiring the patient, Elizabeth rose to leave. But a thin hand reached out to restrain her.

"Wait, my dear. I have something to say to you. It's been on my mind for some time. Perhaps you'll think it's interfering, but I must say it."

Curious, a little wary, Elizabeth sat down again. If Mary was going to advise her about her romance — ! The eyes fixed on hers held a fevered intensity.

"It's a terrible thing, Elizabeth, to die a slow death like this. I hope none of my friends will ever experience it. But for me there is one thing that would have made the suffering so much easier. If — if only I didn't have to be examined and treated by a *man!*"

Elizabeth felt the clawlike fingers tighten. As Mary continued, she had the sensation of being pulled down into chilling waters.

"You're young and strong, my dear. You have a keen mind and like to study. You have health and leisure. Why don't you try to become a doctor?"

"A — doctor!" echoed Elizabeth faintly.

"Yes. If I could only have been treated by a lady doctor, my worst sufferings would have been spared me. So many women must feel this way! Please, my dear, promise me you will at least think about it?"

Elizabeth floundered in silence. It was Mary's eyes, steady and compelling, which brought her slowly to the surface. "I — I promise," she said finally.

The wind had risen. There was snow in the air. Fine flakes stung her face as she climbed the hill toward home, picking her way carefully to avoid the frozen ruts. She was glad of the wind's resistance, the necessity to brace herself against an external force rather than face a swirl of inner confusion. But gradually the driving gusts, the stinging flakes, even the click of her heels on the hard ground, assumed an inescapable rhythm, merged into the clamoring pulsebeat of her thoughts. Doc-tor . . . *Doc-tor* . . . DOC-TOR!

What an absurd, preposterous idea! She had thought at first Mary must be joking and had almost laughed aloud. But there had been no levity in the haunted eyes. Mary had been deadly serious. She did not really know, however, to whom she was talking. Doctor! The very word aroused sensations of distaste, almost disgust; summoned visions of a staring bullock's eye embedded in its cushion of fat; of a beloved face with flesh yellowed, eyes glazed; of repulsive bloodletting; of an endless and impatient spooning of remedies between fevered lips. If there was one thing she had always resisted above all others, it was weakness in the human body. Harden oneself by sleeping night after night on the floor, only to spend one's days soothing the real or imagined ills of people unable or unwilling to leave their soft beds? Kicking at a clod of frozen earth with such force that her toes screamed protest, she relished the sensation of pain.

Anyway, it was impossible. Women did not become doctors. Whoever heard of a female physician? *Female physician.* The words immediately suggested an unpleasant memory. She *had* heard of one only recently. It had been in all the papers. There was a woman in New York, a Madame Restell, who was known by that name. She was a noted abortionist, famous all over the country, skillful, extremely rich, driving a fine carriage and owning a pew in a fashionable church. Though she had often been arrested, she had always been bailed out by some of her patrons. Condemned by an outraged society, she had brashly defended her infamous practices in widely published and inflammatory articles. Elizabeth had read them with horror and revulsion. Such gross perversion and destruction of motherhood, surely the human faculty most closely allied to the divine, filled her with the utmost indignation. Let oneself be classed in the same category with a woman of such vile reputation? Heaven forbid!

And yet — *female physician!* Why should a woman like that be permitted exclusive ownership of such a title? Come to think of it, the fact was an aspersion not only on a noble profession but on womanhood itself. Surely some woman sometime must prove the falsity of such a premise, somebody with the courage of a Prudence Crandall or a Frances Wright or an Angelina Grimké! Somebody, of course, with an interest in scientific study and a keen compassion for the sick. Certainly not — she dismissed the whole matter with profound relief — somebody like herself!

But it would not stay dismissed. During the following days and weeks it kept rearing its head like a persistent jack-in-a-box. It woke her in the middle of the night with Mary's quiet voice: "One thing would have made the suffering so much easier . . . you're young and strong, you like to study, why don't you, why don't you . . ." After an especially useless round of teas or club meetings or sewing circles it would rise up suddenly to confront her: "You wanted a goal in life, a consuming purpose. What could be more challenging, more all-consuming?" It leaped at her from the pages of a month-old New York newspaper which some traveler from the East had left in Sam's office: "The notorious female physician Mme. Restell has again been released from jail to pursue her infamous trade. When will some righteous avenger arise to expurgate this cancerous growth from our society?" But most of all it pursued her as she fled from a torturing encounter with her present beloved, torn afresh between susceptibility to his attractions and repulsion at the thought of life association with such a one: "If you had something to engross your thoughts completely, to fill this vacuum and prevent this constant wearing away of your heart! You can't stifle these feelings, neither can you yield to them. Then why not put an insuperable barrier between you, why not, *why not . . .*"

Why not, indeed? She could give a dozen reasons. She was too old — twenty-four — to start a new life, demanding years of training. She had no money. She was peculiarly unsuited, by taste and temperament, to a medical career. She was a woman, and so far as she knew no woman had ever become a full-fledged doctor. The difficulties might be insurmountable. Moreover, it was the worst possible career for a woman to choose, since it carried with it not one stigma but two, the compounded ignominy of both *female* and female *physician.* Why, then, should the few words of a dying woman set in motion a chain of impulses which ran counter to all reason?

One day she startled Hannah by a blunt, "Mother, tell me what it's like to bear children. You've borne thirteen of them. Is the pain terrible?"

Hannah flushed, floundered. It was a subject no lady would think of discussing with her unmarried daughter. "Why, I — I —"

In spite of her mother's shocked face Elizabeth persisted. "You've had both doctors and midwives at your confinements. Which did you prefer?" Then, as Hannah remained chokingly inarticulate, "Would it have made your suffering any easier to bear if you had had a competent *woman* doctor to attend you?"

The shocked restraint was suddenly unloosed. "Oh — yes! You have no idea. The shame and embarrassment for a lady of delicate upbringing — ! Ask any refined mother!"

Though Hannah was unable to express her emotions in such graphic language, the horror on her face would have done justice to the testimony of a fellow female of the previous century, the Swiss writer Suzanne Necker, who had immortalized her experience in childbirth in a most vivid description.

"I confess," she had written, "that my terrified imagination fell far short of the truth. For three days and nights I suffered the tortures of the damned, and Death was at my bedside, accompanied by his satellites in the shape of a species of men who are still more terrible than the Furies, and who have been invented for the sole purpose of horrifying modesty and scandalizing nature. The word *accoucheur* still makes me shudder. . . . The revolting details of childbirth had been hidden from me with such care that I was as surprised as I was horrified."

Hannah was able to communicate a similar emotion with far less words.

Because of Anna's penchant of the moment Elizabeth was delving deeply into the works of Swedenborg. His theories of the close correspondence between the physical and spiritual world appealed both to her analytic mind and to her vivid imagination. Heaven and hell, according to his philosophy, were not vague spiritual hypotheses of the hereafter but realities here and now. Man's freedom, said Swedenborg, enabled him to choose the good, overcome the powers of hell. Elizabeth became acutely conscious of the heavens and hells all about her. Human suffering was a hell. So was slavery, whether of a black man to his master, or of a woman to her husband. Yes, and so were the gross perversion and destruction of motherhood by a crude opportunist like

Madame Restell, whose usurpation of the name *female physician* so utterly degraded what might and should be a noble position for women. She couldn't "redeem" all these hells, of course, but perhaps she could at least try to redeem this one which had been brought to her notice.

Just when she decided she might try she could not have told. It was not sudden, rather the inevitable sprouting and springing of a seed well planted and nourished. It was one day in the first warmth of spring, after the lilac bushes and shrubs had burst into leaf, when the cherry and myrtle and iris gave every hint of an early blooming, that she quietly but with great inner trepidation broached the subject to her family.

"What would you say if I told you that I am thinking of trying to become a doctor?"

Being Blackwells, her brothers and sisters were neither shocked nor unduly surprised. Harry, always the most optimistic and impetuous, expressed immediate approval. "Great idea! Any other woman, no. But our Elib! To put it bluntly in terms of scripture, 'With most women this is impossible; but with a Blackwell female, all things —' and so forth, and so forth."

"Henry!" Hannah's horror at her son's blasphemy somewhat dissipated her initial shock at the announcement. Perhaps he had intended it to do so.

"Sorry, Mother. All I meant was, if anyone can do it, our Elib can."

Sam took time to ponder, then slowly nodded. "If you really thought it was the thing to do, of course we'd be behind you. I" — his grave eyes smoldered — "I've sometimes thought I'd like to become a doctor."

Marian was shrewdly practical. "You hate taking care of sick people. I know. A doctor should be sympathetic, like our Dr. Cox. He was crude sometimes, too outspoken, not always gentle, but somehow you felt he really *cared*."

Elizabeth did not evade the accusing eyes. "You're right. I've often been impatient with you and unsympathetic. I'm sorry. I've thought about that long and hard. But I believe that both patience and sympathy can be cultivated if you want to badly enough. And — I do care about people, tremendously."

She was glad Anna was not there. She could feel the cool, appraising gaze, the uninhibited frankness, cutting her dream to shreds. "This I would like to see! 'Little Shy' trying to storm a citadel which no other woman in the world has even attempted!" She missed Emily, however.

Somehow she knew that in the wide steady eyes there would have been a warmth of understanding and approval.

"I couldn't stand being a doctor." Ellen shivered. "All that blood — !"

"Will you have to cut people open?" demanded Wash.

Elizabeth's stomach lurched. She dared not look at Marian. "Probably," she tried to sound calm. "That is, if I really decide to do it."

It was her mother's comment which surprised her most. Perhaps seeds sown in their previous conversation had taken unexpected root. "I wish," said Hannah, "that your father could be alive to see his Bessie show such courage."

What next? She had not the slightest idea where to get further information. With even greater trepidation she broached the matter to some of her friends. To her relief and delight Mrs. Vail expressed strong sympathy and enthusiasm.

"If anybody can do it, you can. You'll encounter prejudice, of course. I doubt if any medical school in this country would take you in, but how about the Paris schools? You must talk with Dr. Peck. He can help you."

But Elizabeth was not ready yet to seek professional advice. She wanted more assurance, and she thought she knew where to find it. One day she took the woodland path leading from the seminary up the hill to the Beecher house. Harriet, adventurous, fearless, had always been a kindred spirit. Elizabeth's hopes were high. It was April, and the whole world bloomed lavishly, assailing all her senses with color, warmth, and fragrance. If ever there was a time to start a new and daring life, this was it. She took little skipping steps under the shelter of her wide skirts.

But she saw she had come at the wrong time. Harriet was in the room behind the front parlor on the left of the hall scratching furiously on a sheet of foolscap. The table was piled high with books and papers, the floor littered with toys, dead ashes sifting from the white-pillared fireplace, the tiny-paned windows still streaked with the dinginess of winter rains. Georgiana, aged two and a half, was pulling at her skirts, the two boys Henry and Freddie noisily rushing in and out. Though Harriet was cordial enough and listened attentively, Elizabeth felt her own enthusiasm ebbing like a slow leak in a balloon. There was none of the instant rapport she had expected.

"A — commendable idea." Harriet spoke absently, her pen remaining poised. "A woman doctor. It might be highly useful — if you could do it."

"You — don't think I could?"

Harriet put down her pen. "You're really serious about this, my dear?" Elizabeth's deflation was charged with indignation. It was the tone Harriet used to the Stowe children when one of them was caught in some foolhardy activity, like flying off the roof under an umbrella. "Of course I'm serious!"

"Very well. Then of course I'll do what I can to help. First let me consult my husband. He's much more practical than I."

Elizabeth walked home slowly. The luster had gone out of the day. The path no longer seemed carpeted with flowers. But she had not expected it to be. And in the days that followed interviews with others of her friends proved as exhilarating as that with Mrs. Stowe had been disappointing. One day she shared her hopes with a fellow member of the Semi-Colon Club, a very wealthy woman.

"A most noble purpose!" was the hearty response. "And if you find you are able to carry it out, I shall be glad to help you financially."

Hope again soared. She wrote letters of inquiry to several physicians known to the family, in various parts of the country, as to the possibility of a woman becoming a doctor. And when Mrs. Stowe sent word that she wanted to see her, Elizabeth could not travel the woods path fast enough. This time the stage was set for a more happy domestic scene. The house was tolerably neat. A fire was burning cosily in the green-tiled fireplace in the front room at the right, for though it was now May, the air still held a chill. Harriet was sewing instead of writing. Her face revealed only the deepest interest and concern.

"My dear, I have talked with Mr. Stowe about your plan. I hate to be discouraging, but — he seems to think it entirely impracticable. Commendable, of course," she hastened to add, "and, if you were able to carry it out, of great usefulness to many people, especially women. I, a mother, can well appreciate that. But we both wonder if you realize, my dear, what a strong prejudice exists. You would either have to crush it or be crushed by it."

Yes, Elizabeth assured her, trying not to show her disappointment, she did realize it. Whether she could crush it or not she did not know, but — her small head lifted — she believed she was strong enough not to be crushed by it.

Harriet's black curls bobbed. Her dark eyes held no amusement now, only respect and admiration. Yes, she did not doubt that. But — well, she and Dr. Stowe had taken the liberty of consulting Dr. Reuben Mussey, one of Cincinnati's foremost doctors. He was certain that no medical school in the country would even consider admitting a woman student.

That might well be, agreed Elizabeth quietly, but she understood there were schools in Paris —

Harriet shook her head. "We mentioned that to him, too. He visited the Paris schools some years ago, and at the very idea of a woman's going there he was simply horrified. The method of instruction is such, he declared, that no American or English lady could stay there six weeks."

Elizabeth went home. That night Kate Vail brought some of her young friends to the house, and both families participated in charades. It was a lively group, many of them seminary students, and competition was keen. But Elizabeth had no heart for the gaiety. She scarcely noticed that Harry barely took his eyes off Kate all the evening and looked almost sick when one of the students seemed to monopolize her favor. She left early and went upstairs. By all logic she should have been relieved that an object so contrary to all her natural inclinations should prove impossible of attainment. Instead, the very opposition seemed to make the goal more desirable. What had first been a mildly compulsive urge had now become an obsessive challenge.

Suddenly she remembered Dr. Abraham Cox, their fiery little physician back East. She resolved to write to him. Never one to postpone action, she sat down and penned the letter immediately. The next day she read it to Sam and to Mrs. Vail, her staunch ally, who approved it heartily. Mrs. Vail had consulted another physician, Dr. Peck, about the prospects of a woman in medicine. He also had expressed vehement condemnation of the Paris schools for a woman.

"But he says the most thorough education can be obtained through private instruction," was the more encouraging feature of her report.

It would be more than two weeks before Elizabeth could look for a reply. They were filled with alternating hope and despair. She was not surprised that when answers to her other letters began to come, they were curiously unanimous. Whatever merit there might be in the idea, it was impossible of execution. But Dr. Cox was no timid conformist. She could still see him recklessly pumping shots into the family carriage. He would not be afraid of flaunting convention. She waited with restless impatience for his reaction.

Meanwhile she mentioned her plan to Mr. James Perkins, one of the liberal group who had clustered about Dr. Channing, and to her delight he was enthusiastic. "Splendid! I do wish you would take the matter up, if you have the courage — and you do have courage, I know." He offered to obtain the opinion of Boston physicians whom he knew and to talk with Dr. Avery, another Cincinnati doctor. He also loaned her a book of Jackson's *Memoirs* which contained much information about the French schools. She went home walking on air, feeling as if she could conquer the world.

But again hope plummeted. She wrote in her journal, "I felt cold and gloomy all day; read in Jackson's *Memoirs* and felt almost disheartened at the immensity of the field before me. I hesitate as if I were about to take the veil, but I am gradually coming up to the resolution."

The upsurge of hope which followed was more spiritual than material, for later she wrote, "I thought much on my future course, and turned for aid to that Friend with whom I am beginning to hold true communion. It cannot be my fancy, Jesus Christ must be a living Spirit, and have the power of communicating with us, for one thought towards Him dispels all evil, and earnest, continued thought produces peace unspeakable."

The letter came. Harry brought it home to her one evening past the middle of May, and her hand trembled as she took it. She went upstairs, shut herself into her room, and opened it. It was not easy to read, for the good Dr. Abraham was no better a penman than a marksman. It was a kind letter, but noncommittal. It gave no word of advice. In fact, it was much like her letters from other physicians. The idea was a good one, but it wouldn't work. There was no way for a woman to obtain a medical education. Even if she could find a way to pursue it, such education would be long and expensive. He mentioned a discouraging sum. There were innumerable obstacles in the way. In short, the idea, though a valuable one, was impossible of execution. However, he was glad to give her the information she requested, the names of medical schools, the preliminaries required, the usual manner of procedure.

Elizabeth stared at the bold black scrawl, reading and rereading, searching for some straw of hope to grasp. It was there. Her gaze clung to the words; *The idea is a good one . . . a valuable one.* Impossible to achieve? But surely if an idea was a really valuable one, there must be some way of realizing it! Difficult, of course. But she had never been afraid of difficulties. Indeed, she had welcomed them. The harder the task, the more zest and strength she had brought to it. How much greater the zest and strength if the struggle were not only physical but moral, a veritable crusade! Suddenly words spoken to another woman, a queen in another age, flashed into her mind: *Who knoweth whether thou art come to the kingdom for such a time as this?*

It was in that moment that she made the irrevocable decision. She was no queen, just an ordinary woman. But *she would become a doctor.* And no discouragement, no difficulty, no misfortune short of disability or death, would turn her from her purpose. Already she felt herself set apart, a novitiate, separated from the rest of womankind.

4

The next day she took Dr. Cox's letter and went to see the wealthy friend who had promised to help her financially.

"You told me to come to you if I made up my mind to carry through my plan. I have now decided, definitely. I want to take steps as soon as possible to gain admittance to a medical school."

Dr. Cox had mentioned a probable sum necessary to defray the expenses of a medical education: three thousand dollars. Elizabeth gave her friend the letter to read . . . and waited, hoping and trembling.

"Wonderful, my dear! I admire your courage. I want to help, of course. What other plans do you have for meeting these expenses?"

"Well, I — I thought I might take a teaching position and try to save money."

"Admirable! And I'm sure you can count on your other friends, as well as me. My dear, I shall be glad to loan you a hundred dollars."

Both the hoping and the trembling ceased. Elizabeth's calm face revealed nothing of her terrible disappointment, nor did her steady voice. Could her friend suggest any others who might be interested enough in her plan to make her a — a small loan? No, her friend could not think of any at the moment. In fact, she thought Elizabeth's plan of teaching and laying up money for a few years decidedly the best.

So that was that. But disappointment was not untinctured with relief. Far better not to be dependent on anyone to whom she might later feel an obligation!

Less than a week later a letter came from Anna, offering her a position as a teacher in Asheville, North Carolina. Elizabeth had not the slightest doubt that the opportunity was more than coincidence, for Dr. John Dickson, who was principal of the school, had previously practiced as a physician. As teacher of music she would be living in the

Dicksons' home. Surely this would be an opportunity to at least make a start in her medical studies. She eagerly accepted the position.

But the intensity of her purpose made it no easier to leave home. There was a finality about the act which made it a painful and traumatic experience. Not only was she severing the most intimate ties of life, but she was preparing to act contrary to her strongest natural inclinations. And it was a journey into the unknown in more ways than one. The rivers and mountains she must cross into the new world were literal as well as figurative. There was no railroad, no steamboat to her destination. The roads through Kentucky were little traveled. Several rivers must be forded. There were three lines of mountains to be crossed. Physical barriers as formidable as those other less tangible impediments she would soon be facing! But Family was behind her in the venture all the way. Sam offered to drive her to North Carolina, sacrificing nearly a month's work. Such family loyalty only made the impending separation more agonizing. Leaving for Henderson had been hard, but nothing compared with this. The last night she could not sleep. She rose heavy-eyed at dawn to a prospect of gloomy skies and tearful farewells. They started punctually, three of them, Sam, Elizabeth, and fourteen-year-old Howard. Thanks to Mr. West, Sam's friend and business associate, they were all stowed snugly in a fairly comfortable carriage drawn by an old horse, Fanny. Elizabeth noted the time with a sense of inescapable destiny: six o'clock, Monday morning, June 16, 1845.

"Rosinante," as Sam dubbed the plodding Fanny, was an apt name, for the trip of nearly two weeks was indeed quixotic. But there were raptures as well as discomforts: walks by the roadside in a cool cloudless dawn; the green lawns and opulent homes of Lexington, bringing nostalgic reminders of English country estates; the first glimpse of rhododendrons clustered in their glossy leaves above a clear spring trickling from a moss-covered rock; their surprise and delight after leaving Crab Orchard to see strewn all along the road those round brown rocks, hollow and sparry in the center, which in their English childhood they had called "potato stones"; and best of all, the view from the top of Cumberland Gap, where Virginia, Kentucky, and Tennessee lay spread beneath them in breathtaking panorama.

The next day in the heat of noon Elizabeth toiled up the steepest slope of Clinch Mountain, Howie a little behind her, Sam and Fanny clambering far in the rear. She moved like an automaton, doggedly persistent, heart pumping, ears pounding, sheer willpower keeping one foot ahead of the other. "Good practice," she thought, gritting her teeth, "for the life ahead of me!" Then suddenly she reached the top.

"Oh! O-oh!" Life surged through her trembling limbs. Instead of sinking down in complete exhaustion, as she had expected, she began to caper about in a mood of exhilaration. "What on earth!" Howie stared in astonishment, then he too burst into "Ohs!" and "Ahs!" It was the most glorious vista she had ever seen, a huge amphitheater of hills circling a vast green basin, rising tier on tier to lose themselves in high ranges whose peaks were lost in clouds. Was this a promise, she wondered, of the triumph which might crown her own long struggle? She arrived in Asheville on Friday, the eleventh day, still in a mood of hope and exhilaration.

But no such optimism remained when she retired to her strange new room in a strange new home on the following Sunday evening. Not that either was a disappointment. The Dicksons were cultured and hospitable, the school attractive, their home a fine two-story brick house surrounded by shade trees and gardens, her room pleasant and airy with windows commanding a fine view of village and hills. A far cry from Henderson! But she had just said goodbye to her brothers, and they were returning early in the morning. Severing this last link was devastating.

She stood in the darkness at the open window staring at the dim mountain outlines barely visible in the starlight. Suddenly she was overwhelmed by doubt and dread of the future, terror of the appalling course she had chosen.

"Oh God, help me!" she cried silently out of what seemed a Gethsemane of despair. "Oh Christ, guide, enlighten me!"

And then, suddenly, overwhelmingly, she was conscious of a Presence. Nothing visible, of course, but somehow it flooded her soul with a brilliant light. All doubt as to the future, all hesitation as to the wisdom of the choice, left her. She *knew* that, however insignificant her small individual effort might be, it was in the right direction, in harmony with the purpose of that divine Will attempting to direct human progress.

It was the only personal communication with the Unseen which she would ever consciously experience, her sole revealed awareness of Truth. But it was enough. It would remain with her for the rest of her life.

Chapter Five

IT WAS THE MOST SATISFYING DAY Elizabeth had experienced since coming to Asheville, this Sunday toward the end of July. The evening before, she had performed her first "cure" and was already being dubbed "Dr. Blackwell" by the Dickson household. The patient had been Miss O'Hear, a kindhearted spinster who was a favorite of the family and a special pet of the children. She had just recovered from a severe sickness, which had been aggravated by a sore mouth from calomel.

"No physician should receive his diploma," she declared tartly, "without being salivated, so he may know the torture he is inflicting on his patients."

Elizabeth found Miss O'Hear suffering from a throbbing headache. A wild idea occurred to her. Recently she had been reading some books on mesmerism. "Let me see if I can help you," she suggested.

Sitting beside the bed, she spoke soothingly to the patient, gently smoothed her forehead, concentrated with all her will on relieving the pain. In a half-hour Miss O'Hear declared herself completely cured. "My dear, some good angel must have sent you to me!"

Elizabeth had no illusions of mesmeric talent. Probably the patient would have recovered without her help. Her satisfaction lay in her own self-conquest. For the first time she felt no impatience, no contempt, in the presence of another's weakness, only concern. Somehow she knew that this was more important preparation for becoming a doctor than all the books in the Dickson library.

Now on Sunday afternoon, looking into the faces of the four little girls grouped around her, varying from coal black to warm golden, eyes dull or wary or mildly curious, she was experiencing an even more satisfying moment.

This little Sunday School for slave children was not the fulfillment of her dream. She had resolved on coming here again to "slave country" that she would become another Prudence Crandall, teach all the slaves possible to read and write.

"Sorry." Dr. Dickson had been genuinely regretful, for he was at heart an abolitionist. "It's against the law to teach them."

Elizabeth had looked at him aghast. "You mean — no effort is made to teach —"

The little principal had smiled wryly. "Only an occasional sermon."

But it might be possible, Elizabeth had learned, to start a small Sunday School. She had found four ladies and one man willing to help. Now here they were with twenty-five scholars. The ages of her four ranged from eight to twelve.

"Now," she said smiling, after teaching them a song, "suppose we learn a scripture verse. 'Thou shalt love the Lord thy God with all thy heart . . .'" The four voices parroted her, low and frightened at first but gaining confidence. "'This is the first and great commandment. And the second is like unto it. Thou shalt love thy neighbor . . .'"

She stopped, stricken with a sense of irony. Try to teach these degraded little beings a religion which their *owners* professed to follow while violating its first principles? She looked around the room, staring at the one man and four women preaching to their slaves. Suddenly she wanted to jump up, scream at them, denounce them as blasphemers and atheists.

"Is — is anything the matter, mum?" asked a small pupil timidly.

"No. Nothing." Elizabeth smiled and went on quietly teaching.

The months at Asheville were pleasant, leisurely, mildly stimulating. Dr. Dickson was an alert and energetic principal, aggressive in promoting education not only in his school but in town, county, and state. She found the community as congenial as the Dickson household. There were social gatherings with provocative conversation. Her piano-playing seemed to give satisfaction. At one party she astounded the company by performing magic tricks with draughts, learned in the evenings in Cincinnati, and herself by the ease in which she joined in the activity and conversation. Of course such acceptance in the community was balm for her painful shyness.

But her most satisfying companionship was still found in solitude. As one of her housemates, Miss Amelia, remarked, "Miss Blackwell is never less alone than when alone." During her combings and brushings on Saturday morning she paid imaginary visits to the family, enjoyed a good laugh with them before getting into bed at night. Anna was now her special concern, for in August, after a bewildering turnabout toward her principal at St. Ann's, Anna had left the school in a dudgeon and was now at Brook Farm, the Utopian community founded in 1841 at West Roxbury, Massachusetts, by George Ripley, a disciple of Fourier, and encouraged during its brief five years of life by such intellectual leaders as Hawthorne, Channing, Charles A. Dana, Margaret Fuller, and Emerson.

Elizabeth was fascinated by the experiment. Had her own purpose been less adamant, she would have rushed off to join her sister. Avidly she devoured Anna's letters, enthusiastic over the classes, the plays and lectures, the uniform dress, less fervent in praise of the farm and household tasks required of each member. Elizabeth read every word of *The Harbinger*, the colony's publication, and became an ardent "associationist," even devised a plan of her own for a phalanx modeled on Fourier's ideas, which she detailed at length in a letter to Harry.

"The society to consist of 2000 members, each bringing a thousand dollars contribution . . . organize after three years . . . building should be a real palace, magnificent . . . glorious, totally different from anything hitherto attempted. . . . I abhor this hateful state where the few are happy and the many miserable!"

But Anna's enthusiasm was shortlived. Long afterward she would view the experience through rose-colored glasses, saying, "Those days were the happiest of my life. Everyone was so genial, so happy. It was a sight to see the washing up after dinner, all the prettiest girls doing the work, and the men doing their best to get a share in it." . . . This in retrospect, however. Before the end of the year she was back in New York searching for some other Utopia, and Elizabeth was as concerned over her uncertain future as over the rejection of poor Sam by his latest love, Gabriella, and the failure of Harry to persuade the pious Kate that his honest doubts would make him as satisfactory a husband as the orthodox seminarian who was his rival.

Elizabeth's own future was uncertain. Numbers in the school were dwindling. Surrounded by a predominantly Methodist community wary of entrusting their offspring to the heresies of a Presbyterian, Dr. Dickson was fighting a losing battle. Also, he longed to locate in a free state. Besides this, Elizabeth was making little progress toward her goal. Though the principal was as helpful as possible, loaning her medical books from his library, even borrowing for her use a real human skeleton, for the most part she was just marking time. Yet during these weeks she gained her introduction not only to anatomy but to dissection!

"If it's specimens you want," offered Miss Maria, one of the other teachers, with a hint of mischief, "how about practicing on this? It met its death from long incarceration in my scent box."

Elizabeth looked at the huge limp cockchafer and felt suddenly sick. But she knew she must accept the challenge. Gingerly seizing the insect with a hairpin, she placed it on a white paper and took her small mother-of-pearl penknife in hand. "It's dead," she told herself. "Nothing I do can possibly hurt it." But minutes passed. Her fingers seemed paralyzed. Grimly she sensed that far more was at stake than the dismemberment of a dead beetle. Her whole future, her fitness for the career she had chosen, hung in the balance. At least a half-hour passed. Then with quivering stomach but steady fingers she lowered the knife and with a neat stroke and a sickening crunch severed the head. "No brains," she observed with what she hoped was clinical detachment. Boldly she split it down the middle and laid the parts elegantly in a shell for the doctor's inspection. The revelation was disappointing, nothing but a little yellowish dust. But she knew it was a major victory. Never would she feel such squeamishness again, even when holding a real dissecting knife.

The arrival of the "Christmas Annual" on the morning of December 26 was a golden link between past security and future uncertainty. The cold brilliance of Christmas Day, the evergreens with which she had ornamented the house, the half-dozen raisins which she had insisted the cook boil in the apple pudding — nothing had dispelled the homesickness of this first Christmas away from the family. Then, just when she was about to conjugate the present passive of the verb "forsake," up marched the Annual in its gay holiday dress!

Joyfully Elizabeth plunged into the three volumes of delicate slanting handwriting, trying to figure the author of each anonymous contribution. "A Mother's Wish" was obvious in its pious sweetness. Ellen's poetry was delicate and romantic, easily distinguishable from Sam's. "The Legend of Hickory Hill," by Mr. Nobody, was doubtless Howie's. Wash must have written "The Horrid Calamity." "Sulphurous Blasts, or the Scramulations of a Demon," consuming twenty-three pages, was probably Harry's. Not as extravagantly robust, decided Elizabeth, as last year's Annual, with its "Adventures of a Rat, by Beef Cracklings" and "A Letter from Mr. Destiny traveling in Hindustan to his female friends the Misses Fates." The Blackwells were becoming more serious with increased age and responsibility. Even Harry, the most carefree, was now a partner with Atkins and Blair, owners of three flour and linseed oil mills, a respectable status for a young man not yet twenty-one! But she welcomed the evidence of maturity. Her sole regret was that her own contribution, sent to Anna in November, must have arrived in New York too late to be sent in time to Cincinnati.

Anna's bright promises of finding Elizabeth a position in New York faded. John Dickson closed his school in January. Elizabeth's dismay was lessened by an invitation to go with Mrs. Dickson to Charleston, where she could stay in the home of John's brother, Dr. Samuel Dickson, one of the city's prominent physicians. The opportunity seemed too good to be true. A teaching position could certainly be found in such a large city, and she could continue her medical studies in the doctor's home while she taught.

It was a journey not only from country to city, but from one world to another. She started at two one morning with Mrs. Dickson and her oldest son Flinn. The stage door slammed shut, and away they tumbled in the dark close box, over frozen ruts, silent, sorrowful, sleepy, jolted time after time into the laps of three gentlemen opposite whose pale faces, revealed by the ghostly moonlight through the dirty window, made them look like corpses in La Morgue.

"Bless me, madam!" exclaimed one when tiny Mrs. Dickson was catapulted into his lap with unusual violence. "The roads are very rough!"

But the night was prelude to a glorious morning, when Elizabeth walked with Flinn over the tops of the Blue Ridge mountains dividing the Carolinas. Though impressed by the towering heights disappearing into blue mists, she felt sad to be crossing the border. Exchanging the glorious mountains for swamps and flat cotton fields! Down over the steepest mountain trail she had ever seen, terrace upon terrace, deeper and deeper into slave country! But there were compensations: palmettos and strange gray moss two or three yards long, like gigantic webs or the ghosts of weeping willows; pines, holly, wild orange, live oak, all seeming to give the lie to January; brimming rice fields blue as the sky, hundreds of acres of cotton fields with their belts of evergreens. All were strange and beautiful.

A night in Greenville, another in Columbia, then a rapid railroad journey to Charleston. She was driven by a Negro coachman to a large old-fashioned house, surrounded by a garden full of tall evergreens. In the spacious hall she was welcomed by Dr. Samuel Dickson, his wife, and their eldest daughter. Still swathed in cloak and hood, steeped in smoke and cinders, she was ushered into a handsome drawing room. Anxiously she scanned the features of one of Charleston's most eminent physicians. Would he be like his brother, sympathetic to her daring enterprise, or like all the other doctors she had encountered, amused, contemptuous, discouraging, or frankly hostile?

2

To Elizabeth's great joy Dr. Sam was not only encouraging and sympathetic — he was bold and adventurous, a kindred spirit. Once his shrewd appraisal had satisfied him that in the slight five-foot figure, so modest and delicate in appearance, there were a purpose and will of steel, he put all his knowledge and experience at her disposal. She could have the run of his fine library. He suggested that she learn Greek, indispensable to medical research, and offered to teach her. Realizing that money was a prime essential, he secured for her a position teaching music in the fashionable boarding school of a relative, Madame Du Pré, located in a fine Charleston mansion. So to her satisfaction Elizabeth was adding not only to her growing fund of medical knowledge but to the precious bank account which would finance her more formal education. Every morning before breakfast she devoted two hours to learning the rudiments of Greek; then she taught for several hours, sometimes as many as eight, at the school. Most of her spare time she devoted to the reading and medical study which Dr. Dickson directed. Since he was not only a physician but also a distinguished professor in the Medical College of Charleston, she could not have had better tutelage.

"I wish more of my male students showed a similar intelligence and application," the doctor commended, especially impressed by her progress in Greek.

But, being Elizabeth, she found time for other activities. Except for the constant reminders of slavery, she found Charleston by far the most delightful city she had ever known. In its stately mansions, its courtly manners, its leisurely yet brilliant social life, there was the quintessence of all Southern charm and culture and romance. She took long walks, often between Greek and breakfast, taking nostalgic delight in the winding streets and high narrow buildings which reminded her of Bristol, filling her long-thirsty lungs with the heady tang of the sea. She visited some of the old Huguenot families, relics of an independence which had made Charleston the first Southern city to join the revolutionary movement against the English crown. She attended lectures, one of them an oration on states' rights by John C. Calhoun, marveling at his clever calmness as he completely dominated a rapturously demonstrative audience. "Able, though erroneous," she evaluated the brilliant performance. And whenever possible, she fed her music-hungry soul at the rare concerts which brought the world of genius to the city. Sometimes these feasts were more tantalizing than satisfying.

"I never have been so affected by music before," she wrote Marian after hearing Herz and Sivori. "Yet the first concert made me sad, homesick, discontented. I felt as I do after reading a powerful novel of Bulwer's. It was Sivori's violin that bewildered me. I did not understand it. It seemed to me like a chaos that might become a world of beauty could I only find the word that should reduce it to order. I went home unhappy and indignant at being obliged to pass life in such a stupid place, amongst such stupid people."

But the second concert was more satisfying. "I felt as if I were worshiping in an old cathedral at twilight, and I shut my eyes not to destroy the illusion by the expressionless concert room and faces all around."

Her favorite haunts for worship were not cathedrals, however. When Madame Du Pré moved her school to the cooler environment of Aiken in the summer, Elizabeth reveled in woodland strolls through colonnades of tall pines and oaks, with mosaics of wild peas, sunflowers, and goldenrod blazoned on either side. One Sunday, not caring to make the Episcopal church a second visit and having seen a dark wooden building with a little steeple, she strolled toward it along the sandy wood paths, only to find a deserted schoolhouse of weatherbeaten pine, with a projecting roof and elevated porch. Here, with the rich odor of pines for incense and the hum of insects for a choir, she worshiped so rewardingly that she visited it again and again. The schoolhouse was deserted, she discovered, because the three denominations in Aiken could not agree on the choice of a teacher!

Elizabeth lived three major roles during those months of 1846 and early 1847: teacher, student, and member of a family. The latter consumed hours of letter writing and anxious concern, for the Blackwells were a close-knit tribe. She followed with intense interest Howard's change of teachers, Ellen's progress in piano, gave warnings and advice about Wash's lazy habits and the deplorable state of his infested head. She was as worried over her mother's imagined mortal ills as was Hannah over her children's immortal souls. She lamented Sam's ill luck in toiling hard for a year and coming out a few hundreds poorer. She mourned with Harry over his rejection by his beloved Kate for the more pious seminary student and rejoiced with him on his burgeoning success in business.

Eighteen-forty-six was the year of the Irish famine. The price of flour leaped from $2.25 to $9.00 a barrel. A demand for kiln-dried corn sprang up for the starving Irish, and Harry's company converted one of their mills and ran it for a short time at enormous profit, clearing $45,000 in four months. But the Irish refused to eat corn, preferring to starve on rotten potatoes. The company's large stock tumbled in value, and Harry wound up with only three thousand dollars profit. But with it he bought his mother a little brick house and lot adjoining Lane Seminary. Elizabeth was there in spirit as the old red carpets were again tacked down, the fragile best china tenderly packed and unpacked. She worried about them during the cold winter.

"It seems to me the wind must blow through and through and make a balloon of that little house! And is it possible the kitchen stairs are outside? Alas for poor Marian, sliding up and down. I should think the boiling water would have to be thawed before it reached the end of its long journey!"

But it was Anna who concerned her most. Irritated her also. Anna's translation of George Sand's novel *Jacques*, a frank espousal of free love, shocked her as well as the rest of the family, and she was excessively provoked when Anna sold one of her, Elizabeth's, stories written for the Annual and sent her $4.50 as her half-share of the payment. Elizabeth promptly returned the money, declaring that she considered the Annual sacred to the family. That year she sent her Christmas contribution via Anna, but addressed to H. B. Blackwell, Cincinnati, and *sealed with six seals!*

But always her major concern was toward attainment of her goal. She continued to write letters to doctors, to women she knew to be concerned with the education and advancement of their own sex, like

Mrs. Emma Willard, founder of the Troy Female Seminary. She read dozens of Dr. Sam's medical books, often far into the night, wrapped in her blanket, oil lamp shaded in order not to disturb her roommate Miss Buell. She pored over her anatomy charts, became glibly familiar with every bone in the doctor's dangling skeleton, every specimen in his laboratory, and the whole galaxy of names emblazoned on medical history since the days of the fabulous Egyptian Imhotep.

And to her intense joy she discovered that there were distinguished women among them! The art of healing had often been considered not only a female right but a female prerogative. The Hebrew midwives mentioned in Exodus might well have been trained at the medical school in the Temple of Sais, where gynecology and obstetrics were taught by women. During Greco-Roman history the names of many women appeared, not only as midwives but as medical students and doctors. There was Agnodice, the Athenian midwife, who, brought to trial for breaking the law by attending medical lectures on gynecology disguised as a man, was successfully defended by her grateful patients, the women of Athens. Martial, the Latin poet, referred to the *feminae medicae* in one of his epigrams, a different category from midwives, who on monuments were always described as "obstetrics." There was Aspasia, such a specialist in obstetrics and gynecology that she was quoted in Greek and Latin medical works for over a thousand years. In the early Christian church there were three Roman women, Fabiola, Marcella, and Paula, who devoted their lives to healing the sick, establishing hospitals which became models for institutions spreading all over Europe.

Then in the Middle Ages there was Trotula, who served on the faculty of the first medical school in Europe, at Salerno, at the height of its fame in the eleventh century, and whose books on gynecology were studied for five hundred years. Like many other physicians' wives, she had acquired knowledge as an assistant to her husband in an era when medicine was largely a family occupation. And at Salerno, center of science in all of Europe, there were not only women professors on the faculty but in time the whole department for women's diseases was handed over entirely to women! In the eighteenth century at the University of Bologna there was Anna Morandi Manzolini, who assisted her husband and after his death succeeded to his chair as professor of anatomy.

But to Elizabeth's amazement she encountered an even more fa-

miliar name in the annals of female medicine: *Elizabeth Blackwell!*
She could hardly believe her eyes. Her namesake had lived a century
ago. She had been a Scotswoman who had studied medicine with her
doctor husband. When he had been thrown into jail for debt, she had
continued to practice as a midwife and published a book on herbs
which had become a classic in medical libraries. For Elizabeth the discovery was like the assurance of a signpost on a strange road. It was as
if in choosing this career she were fulfilling a destiny set long before
her birth. Even her name had been given as a sign.

"My mind is fully made up," she wrote Marian in the late fall of
1846. "I am quite resolved to go through with the study of medicine.
I think you attribute to me a foolish sentimental fastidiousness that I
do not possess. You also speak of my want of bodily sympathy being
an objection. I suspect you were thinking of that unlucky dose of
lobelia I once gave you when I grew angry because you groaned and
groaned and obstinately refused to drink the warm stuff that would
relieve you. I think I have sufficient hardness to be entirely unaf-
fected by great agony in such a way as to impair the clearness of
thought necessary for bringing relief, but I am sure the warmest sympathy would prompt me to relieve suffering to the extent of my power;
though I do not think any case would keep me awake at night, or that
the responsibility would seem too great when I had conscientiously
done my best."

Only at one period in her study did she almost lose courage.

"It's time," said Dr. Sam, "that you read some books on surgery.
That is" — his eyes were kind but probing — "I suppose you do in-
tend to become a surgeon?"

"Oh — oh, yes!"

"Then suppose you start with these." He produced two books by
Robert Liston, *Elements of Surgery* and *Practical Surgery*. Liston, Dr.
Sam continued, a professor at University College in London, was one of
the most skillful surgeons living. He chuckled. "And one of the vainest,
roughest, and most cantankerous. It's said that he can amputate a thigh
with the help of only one assistant, compressing the artery with his
left hand and doing all the sawing and cutting with his right. Strong
as a bear and clever as a juggler. I've heard he holds the scalpel between his teeth when he needs both hands to tie a blood vessel. Learned
the trick while watching the butchers in his native Scotland!"

"Thank you." Elizabeth took the books, hoping her hands were not trembling. She fled with them to her room. Months ago she had taken the first step toward conquering the horrors of dissection. But here was no dead cockchafer to be slit with a pearl-handled knife, not even a human corpse to be somehow dismembered. It was living, quivering human flesh. It had taken her nearly an hour to summon courage to attack the beetle. The books on surgery lay untouched for days.

"How's the study of Liston coming?" asked Dr. Sam, then, without waiting for a reply, "I have another for you when you've finished those, *Surgical Observations* by Warren." John Collins Warren, he explained, was one of America's great surgeons, founder of the Massachusetts General Hospital in 1811 and professor at Harvard Medical School. "A remarkable man, master of both surgery and anatomy, trained in London in the days when English surgeons had to become grave robbers to obtain cadavers. They say his favorite portrait shows him holding a skull in his hand. Calm and cool. To see him operate you'd think he possessed no emotion whatever. He doesn't pride himself on speed, which is the only way to eliminate pain, but every movement is planned and cool and skillful."

She opened the books finally, with the same unhesitating precision which had severed the cockchafer's head, and entered the world of surgery. No actual visit to an operating room could have been more realistic, for she had a vivid imagination. Liston was as caustic and blunt a writer as he was a surgeon. Scalpels slashed, blood spurted, flesh quivered, white-hot cautery irons glowed and flashed and sizzled. Elizabeth dreamed of operating chairs which turned into torture racks, scalpels which suddenly became butchers' cleavers, and she woke with the agonized screams of patients still ringing in her ears.

By a strange coincidence it was on October 16, 1846, that an incident took place at Massachusetts General Hospital in Boston. Dr. John Collins Warren was performing an operation on a young man named Gilbert Abbott for a tumor of the maxillary gland and tongue — a rare event, for only the most excruciating agony could tempt a patient to undergo the pain of such an operation. It was a grim experience for observing doctors and students as well as for the patient, and a bed was always kept ready outside for the observer who could not stomach it. This time the circle of spectators' benches was fuller than usual, for it was rumored that a dramatic, possibly amusing experiment was to be tried. They were not disappointed.

"Gentlemen," announced the surgeon in his dry clipped voice, "this morning a Boston dentist by the name of Morton is coming to test on our patient a preparation for which he makes an extraordinary claim. He says that it will render the patient free from pain."

The sarcasm in his voice was not lost on his students. A titter went around the benches. Some remembered an occasion twenty-one months earlier when they had heard a similar claim from another dentist named Wells, only to hear the patient split the air with screams of agony. "Humbug," somebody mouthed audibly.

The patient was strapped into the red plush chair. Dr. Warren removed his faultlessly tailored coat and put on an old black jacket, stiff with the dried blood of many operations. The tools were assembled, scalpel, forceps, various knives, a charcoal burner on which were several glowing cautery irons. Ten o'clock came, the designated hour. No sign of Morton. Amid a ripple of merriment Warren grimly proceeded to begin the operation without him. He had just taken his scalpel in hand when the door burst open and a man rushed in. He carried a globe of glass connected to a tiny tube. Curtly Warren gestured him toward the patient. The man placed a tube in the patient's mouth. "Please breathe deeply and regularly," he said. The air filled with a strong, sweetish odor. The patient's eyes closed. His head fell to one side.

"Your patient is ready, Doctor."

Warren stepped forward, raised his scalpel, and made a swift incision. The room tensed for the scream which was its inevitable accompaniment. It did not come. The operation proceeded without a sound. When he had finished, the surgeon straightened. He stood staring at the patient, who still remained silent, quietly breathing. At last he looked around the room. His cold austere features were suffused with emotion. "Gentlemen," he said in an awed voice, "this is no humbug."

The discovery of what Dr. Oliver Wendell Holmes later called "anesthesia" was reported by one of Warren's assistants in the Boston *Daily Advertiser* on November 18, 1846, almost the exact date that Elizabeth wrote her sister Marian, "My mind is fully made up. I am quite resolved to go through with the study of medicine."

3

Elizabeth had been in Charleston more than a year. She had saved less money than she had hoped, for her small salary had been slow in coming, sometimes nonexistent, Mrs. Du Pré being a poor manager and heavily in debt, but she believed her painfully accumulated bank account was enough to insure her independence during most of her medical course. She had been thrifty to the point of parsimony, and the Dicksons had refused to take more than token payment for her board and room.

As February of 1847 brought her twenty-sixth birthday, she felt like a trapped bird beating its wings against a cage. Tokens of affection from home were pleasant but unsatisfying.

"I always think of old family times on that day," she wrote her mother, "the penny for each year which Father used laughingly to bestow, and the silver that came after, and then the children's party, and all the merry old times. But I am quite satisfied that my childhood has gone. I want to be up and doing, not simply enjoying myself. And if I never succeed in accomplishing all my intentions, I mean to have the comfortable assurance that I have tried hard and done my best."

But how? Acting on Mrs. Willard's advice, she had written in November to a Dr. Warrington, an old Quaker physician in Philadelphia. Though she had not requested a reply, she had given him her address and waited hopefully. Three months passed. When a letter finally came in late February, she tore it open with trembling fingers. It was long and had been carefully copied in his wife's neat handwriting.

"My dear E. Blackwell — Thy letter of November 18 came duly to hand; it has indeed remained unanswered, but not unheeded. I have reflected much on the proposition contained in it; so strong a hold has the communication had on my feelings and sympathies that I feared I might speak imprudently if I should reply promptly to such noble sentiments. I have myself been so circumstanced in life as to be rendered measurably competent to understand the force of promptings to move in somewhat new and little-tried paths. My immediate response would therefore perhaps have been, 'Go onwards' . . ."

Elizabeth's eyes flew over the pages. Bless the old fellow, he was an idealist! "I beg thee to believe with me that if the project be of divine origin and appointment it will sooner or later be accomplished." Ah, but he was practical too! "I have personally appealed to some of the most intelligent and liberal-minded ladies of my acquaintance how far the services of a well-trained educated female would be appreciated. The response uniformly is, 'No female could become acceptable to us' . . ."

Cold doubt suddenly assailed Elizabeth. Was it possible he was right, that women in general felt no desire or need for physicians of their own sex? Or were they too prejudiced by custom and the image of a Madame Restell to acknowledge or even be aware of such need? Uncertainty gripped her. Then she remembered the urgent appeal of Mary Donaldson, the eloquent horror in Hannah's eyes, and warmth returned. Reading further, she smiled wryly. The old doctor did not minimize the difficulties. And he obviously thought that if she felt she must "succor the distressed" it would be better for her to "contribute with all the talents which thy Father in Heaven has so bountifully bestowed the exaltation of a portion of thy sex to the holy duties of *nursing* the sick . . . and let man be the physician." But at least he had answered. And he had invited her to confer with him if she came to Philadelphia. It was more encouragement than most other doctors had given. What more could she ask? She would go to Philadelphia.

She left Charleston early in May, traveling by a merchant vessel for the sake of economy. She took with her her last month's pay (the rest of her precious hoard having been banked by Anna in a bank recommended by Harry in New York), a prized collection of skull and hand bones given her by Dr. Sam, letters from him to several physicians, together with a certificate outlining the study successfully completed under his tutelage, and a determination which stress and opposition had slowly strengthened to the toughness of steel.

Dr. Warrington was like his letter, kindly, devout, honest, generous with positive advice and suggestions. More helpful still was another Quaker couple, Dr. and Mrs. William Elder, with whom she was able to take lodging. Dr. Elder had none of the meekness and mildness Elizabeth associated with Quakers. Big of frame, boisterously genial, and with a mind as broad and agile as his body, he seemed more at home in a sailing brig than a Quaker meeting. In fact, he was an adventure fan with a yen for Arctic explorers. A graphic storyteller, he drew tale after tale from a prodigious memory. His gray-clad and demurely bonneted wife was in her quiet way equally hospitable. Elizabeth was immediately at home and on the first night slept as soundly as the Irish man in one of the doctor's stories, who slept like one "who paid attention to what he was about."

Anna was in Philadelphia being treated by a Dr. Schieferdecker, specializing in the currently popular "water cure." Elizabeth was not impressed by the doctor. Neither did she approve of the extreme views into which her espousal of Fourierism was plunging Anna, though she was strongly committed to associationism, of which the Elders were ardent supporters, and she was favorably impressed by Anna's friend Albert Brisbane, who had translated many of the works of Fourier. Letters from home expressed relief that Elizabeth, with her "cool, unimpassioned judgment," was nearby to exert a stabilizing influence on Anna. Sam, shocked by the theories of free love so brilliantly advocated in his sister's translation of *Jacques*, feared that poor Anna had "thoughtlessly exposed herself to an odium much greater than she desires or anticipates."

He did not know the half of it! Only to Marian did Elizabeth confide the extent of the Brisbane-Fourier influence, and it is certain Marian did not share that June letter with Sam or Hannah, though she failed to follow Elizabeth's final injunction: "Hadn't you better burn this?"

"Anna horrified me greatly with her doctrines and the dreadful pictures of society she unfolded to me. Simple constancy she laughed at, advocated a continual change of lovers as fancy dictated, thought it right that a woman should love one man for his beauty, another for his fortune, or rank, or talent, that it was natural and proper that a woman should unite with a man, because he could make her the mother of beautiful children; when women are better developed, their passion will be as great as man's, and that the highest material enjoyment and most beautiful act of life should be cultivated and refined with the utmost care. She regretted much that she was not of a passionate nature and that all the women of our family were so deficient in that area."

Sam would have been even more shocked when in the same letter Elizabeth, temporarily intrigued by the persuasive logic of Brisbane and other Fourierists, wrote that she began to understand "how rich life might be, where these free beautiful relations prevailed, how ever varying the enjoyment, how grand the knowledge to be gained."

However, she had little time for philosophizing. Philadelphia was the center of medical education in America, with four important medical colleges. Immediately she began exploring every possible avenue leading to admission into one of them. Dr. Warrington lent every assistance possible, outlining the requirements, giving her names of influential professors, making arrangements for her to take lessons in anatomy in a private school conducted by a Dr. Allen. She went to her first lesson aquiver with foreboding, memories of the cockchafer, the nightmares of torture racks and butchers' cleavers returning to haunt her. Suppose this Dr. Allen proved to be a callous egotist, deriving sadistic amusement from shocking a bold female who dared invade his masculine province! She need not have worried. He combined the instincts of the perfect gentleman with the sensitivity of the artist.

"Suppose we start our lesson in practical anatomy," he suggested with great tact and delicacy, "with a demonstration of the human wrist."

What followed was for Elizabeth more than a lesson in anatomy. It was a moving religious experience. She felt as if she were being initiated into the mysteries of creation. The beauty of the tendons, the delicacy of bone structure, the exquisite arrangement of veins and nerves and sinews, turned what might have been distaste, even horror, into wonder and admiration. Later, visiting the finest museums and galleries in Europe, she would stand in awe before the world's masterpieces of painting and sculpture, but never would she be more conscious of consummate artistry. All her life she would be grateful to this sensitive man who made her introduction to practical anatomy an act of reverence rather than a distasteful chore.

Her encounters with other Philadelphia doctors were less inspiring. As she interviewed one professor after the other while making applications to the medical colleges, her emotions ranged through encouragement, disappointment, amusement, hope, despair. On May 27, soon after her arrival, she called on Dr. Jackson, one of the oldest professors in Philadelphia, and found a small, bright-faced, gray-haired man.

"Well?" He lifted friendly, alert eyes. "What can I do for you, madam?"

Elizabeth wasted no preliminaries. "I want to study medicine, Dr. Jackson."

He burst into laughter. "Why?" he demanded.

She told him, wasting no words, ending earnestly, "Surely, Doctor, you must have known women patients who would have welcomed the services of a well-trained female doctor."

He was no longer laughing. "He's interested," thought Elizabeth, her heart leaping. He was. He could not give her an answer then, he told her. There were great difficulties in the way of her proposal, but he did not know that they were insurmountable. He would consult with his colleagues and let her know on Monday. Elizabeth went home with a lighter heart, though she dared not hope. On Monday Dr. Jackson reported that he had done his best, but the other professors in his school were all opposed to her entrance. She consulted others with similar results. Dr. Horner advised her to try the Filbert Street and Franklin schools. A professor at Jefferson College thought it would be impossible for a woman to study there and advised the New England schools.

She felt gloomy as thunder when on June 2 she trudged around to see Dr. Darrach. There was not even a hint of color in her gown and bonnet to lend brightness to her mood. Living with the Elders, she had adopted the Quaker style of dress, with its plain gray gown and poke bonnet. But she took some satisfaction in the knowledge that the wide brim framing her heart-shaped face with its smooth wings of hair was not unbecoming.

Dr. Darrach's face was like a blank sheet of paper. He neither smiled nor frowned. She launched into her little speech, which by now had acquired a parroty glibness. He made no response even in change of expression. Finding the silence uncomfortable, she continued, impatience injecting a note of sharpness in her voice. Suddenly conscious that she had been haranguing him for at least five minutes, she stopped. Still he said nothing.

"Well, sir, can you give me any encouragement?"

He cleared his throat. "The subject is a novel one, madam, and I have nothing to say either for or against it; you have awakened trains of thought on which my mind is taking action, but I cannot express my opinion to you one way or another."

"Your opinion, I fear, is unfavorable," said Elizabeth bluntly.

"I did not say so. I beg you, madam, distinctly to understand that I express no opinion. The way my mind acts in this matter I do not feel at liberty to unfold."

Elizabeth persisted. She *would* get a straight answer! "Shall I call on the other professors of your college?"

"I cannot take the responsibility of advising you to pursue such a course."

"Can you not grant me admittance to your lectures, as you do not feel unfavorable to my scheme?"

"I have said no such thing. Whether favorable or unfavorable, I have not expressed any opinion. And I beg leave to state clearly that the operation of my mind in regard to this matter I do not feel at liberty to unfold."

Elizabeth got up in despair and left, leaving his mind to pursue its ambivalence at leisure.

All her efforts to gain admittance to the four Philadelphia medical schools were unavailing. True, Dr. Pankhurst, professor of surgery in the largest college, offered to admit her to his classes, but only on condition that she would disguise herself as a man. The idea was abhorrent. At first she refused even to consider the possibility.

Equally dismaying but certainly more amusing was the reaction expressed by the dean of one of the smaller schools, who replied to her application by saying, "Surely you cannot expect us to furnish you with a stick to break our heads with!" And she was dumbfounded when her friend Dr. Warrington burst out, "Doctors are knocking their heads against each other for lack of business. One cups, another blisters, and the third gives calomel. Between them there are not enough patients to go around nor enough new fashionable and utterly notorious treatments with which to inveigle them. From their point of view the profession has small need of women physicians added to their woes."

Elizabeth could hardly believe her ears. Did these men actually think the invasion by a few women into medicine would threaten the livelihood of the whole profession? Then they must be either incredibly insecure or incredibly naïve! Later she would be even further amused by this mistaken notion of the rapid practical success which would attend a woman doctor when a professor in a medical college wanted to enter into partnership with her on the condition that he would share profits over five thousand dollars on her first year's practice!

For weeks she marked time, continuing her anatomy lessons with Dr. Allen and attending some of the private classes of Dr. Warrington. The Quaker physician became more and more pessimistic about her chances.

"Elizabeth," he said to her finally, "it is no use trying. Thee cannot gain admission to these schools. If thee must continue in this undertaking, then thee must go to Paris and don masculine attire to gain the necessary knowledge."

"*No!*" Her whole being was revolted. Not that she objected to going to Paris, but to put on male dress, to be forced into achieving a reasonable and just purpose by deception! It was unthinkable. She had entered on a moral crusade, to open the door of a noble profession to other women as well as herself. To accomplish its end, her purpose must be pursued in the light of day and with public sanction. But — *how?* Even if it were possible to obtain private instruction, the enormous expense would make it impracticable, and with the profession so strongly united against her, museums, libraries, hospitals, all such aids, would be closed against her.

She felt alone in a hostile world of men. Anna had left for a log cabin in Pennsylvania to sample a new variety of associationism, and even though they were not often in agreement, Elizabeth missed her desperately. She called on Mrs. Sarah J. Hale, the liberal editor of *Godey's Lady's Book*, but though she succeeded in interesting her in her plans, Mrs. Hale could not see the necessity of thorough training. Surely she could gain enough practical knowledge to start practice soon, within a year! Again Elizabeth turned to her understanding friend Emma Willard, who just a year before had dared to invade the medical sanctum by publishing a scientific treatise on the circulation of the blood.

"Dr. Warrington is discouraged," she wrote. "He joins with his medical brethren in advising me to give up the scheme. But a strong idea, long cherished till it has taken deep root in the soul and become an all-absorbing duty, cannot thus be laid aside. I must accomplish my end. I consider it the noblest and most useful path that I can tread, and if one country rejects me I will go to another."

Paris? She was informed by Dr. Warrington and others that it could be done there, perhaps even without resorting to the abhorrent disguise. Though the free government lectures were confined to men, and a diploma was strictly denied to a woman (even when one of them had successfully gone through the course in male attire), thorough courses of lectures were delivered by able physicians on every branch of medical knowledge, to which she could be admitted without hesitation. But a chorus of shocked physicians vetoed the idea vehemently.

"You, a young unmarried lady, go to Paris, that city of fearful immorality, where every feeling will be outraged and insult attend you at every step! Where vice is the natural atmosphere, and no young man can breathe it without being contaminated! Impossible, you are lost if you go!"

Dr. Warrington was deeply troubled by the idea, even though he had suggested it. "I saw my friend Dr. Ashmead, and he says Paris is such a horrible place that thee must give up thy wish for a medical education. He doesn't even want thee to talk about it."

Elizabeth clenched her small fists. "You can tell your friend," she replied with icy calm, "that if the path of duty leads me to hell I will go there. And I'm sure of one thing. Just because I was in the company of devils wouldn't mean that I had to become a devil myself!"

The good doctor only stared.

But Elizabeth was not as confident as she sounded. Once more she appealed to Mrs. Willard, who had studied in Paris. Was this not a false view, an exaggerated fear? Wasn't it true everywhere that a woman who respected herself would be respected by others? If Mrs. Willard agreed, she thought she would probably sail for France during the summer, in order to improve her familiarity with the language before the winter lectures.

"I have tried to look every difficulty steadily in the face," she ended her letter. "I find none which seems to me unconquerable, and with the blessing of Providence I trust to accomplish my design."

Mrs. Willard did agree, yet in spite of this encouragement Elizabeth postponed her decision. Giving up the struggle here would mean at least partial defeat. The tension of uncertainty was broken one day in July when she looked up to see Hannah, Sam, and Marian standing in the Elders' doorway. Though she had known they were considering an eastern trip, their arrival was unexpected. They had wanted to surprise her. Her joy was overpowering. She rushed at them, jumped about them, kissed them, shouted, wept. Finally, after volleys of questions and answers, a sumptuous tea served by the Elders to the accompaniment of some of the doctor's jolliest stories, and an exhibition of Elizabeth's treasures, the skull and hand bones, the guests were deposited at the Morris House, where Sam treated them all to a grand dinner memorable for delicious Dutch bread. Details of the long trip were recounted: boat from Pittsburgh, stage from Wheeling, train to Philadelphia — which had blinded them with sparks and ashes and bewildered Hannah by its "mad, tearing, headlong whirl at twenty miles an hour."

For a time the grueling struggle was mercifully forgotten while Elizabeth basked in the warmth of family reunion. Anna traveled the 130 miles from the country phalanstery where she was sampling a second variety of associationism. After ten days Elizabeth journeyed to New York with Sam and Marian, and they visited the old Long Island house, saddened to find it dilapidated, fences gone and gardens overgrown. They called at Dennis Harris's sugar factory, now a flourishing concern, and found that his boiler, Mr. Brant, had once worked for Papa in Nelson Street.

"There's a place for you boys," Mr. Harris offered generously, "and a home with my family in case either of you wants to learn the sugar boiling."

After Sam and Hannah left for home via Niagara Falls, Elizabeth spent two refreshing weeks with Marian at the seashore, then returned to Philadelphia to continue her stubborn assault on the schools, both strength and courage revived. She would not go to Paris except as a last resort. To do so would be to admit at least partial defeat. She possessed all the qualifications necessary for admission to an American school, statements verifying the equivalent of three years' study with reputable physicians — everything but the right sex. Attempts to enter the New York schools proved as fruitless as had those at Philadelphia schools.

With Dr. Warrington's help she obtained a complete list of all the smaller medical schools in the northern states, "country schools" most of them were called. She examined their prospectuses and picked out a dozen where full courses were given under able professors, then sent applications to all of them. After toying with the idea of signing her name "E. Blackwell," on the slim chance that once admitted she might browbeat a school into keeping its commitment, she decided firmly in the negative. It would be almost as deceitful as wearing men's clothes. Any devious means of attaining her goal would thwart its fundamental purpose. Twelve times she signed her name in her bold neat slanting script: *Elizabeth Blackwell*. She had now made applications to twenty-nine American medical colleges.

The waiting was torture. Time for the commencement of the winter sessions of sixteen weeks approached, arrived, passed. Still no reply. She went to New York to visit Anna, now installed in a snug little house on 26th Street, with a clean Irish woman to cook and wash for her, and several newspaper assignments which kept her writing furiously. Harry was in New York also, having suddenly decided to take advantage of Dennis Harris's offer to teach him the sugar business, and he was a frequent visitor at Anna's. But Elizabeth found little contentment in their company. She returned to Philadelphia and found a letter waiting from the medical department of a small college in the western part of New York state. It read:

Geneva: October 20, 1847

To Elizabeth Blackwell, Philadelphia.

I am instructed by the faculty of the medical department of Geneva University to acknowledge receipt of yours of 3rd inst. A quorum of the faculty assembled last evening for the first time during the session, and it was thought important to submit your proposal to the class (of students), who have had a meeting this day, and acted entirely on their own behalf, without any interference on the part of the faculty. I send you the result of their deliberations, and need only add that there are no fears but that you can, by judicious management, not only "disarm criticism," but elevate yourself without detracting in the least from the dignity of the profession.

Wishing you success in your undertaking, which some may deem bold in the present state of society, I subscribe myself,

Yours respectfully,

Charles A. Lee, Dean of the Faculty

Elizabeth was not surprised. She had never believed failure possible. But she was immensely relieved. She read the letter of the students with profound gratitude. Immediately she accepted the invitation and on November 4 started on her long trip to western New York state, arriving in the little town of Geneva at eleven in the evening on November 6. It was both the beginning and the ending of a journey.

Chapter Six

STEPHEN SMITH SIGHED. Monday morning, and another week of lectures beginning. Five of the sixteen were gone already. Now, even before the first lecture of the day started, his nerves were jangling, muscles tensed for the effort of strained attention. Hopefully he spread open his notebook titled: *Dr. Lee: Materia Medica,* but the scantiness of previous entries boded ill for the next hour. Even Dr. Lee's resonant voice, geared to the lecture platform, could not penetrate the lusty disorder of his classroom. As well try to listen to a symphony amid a horde of chattering magpies!

The pre-lecture bedlam had already started, with more zest than usual, for Dr. Lee was late. Erasers were flying, dust mounting from scuffles, snickers and hoarse guffaws pinpointing the locations of the latest unsavory jokes and stories. On the window side, overlooking a girls' normal school, some of the wilder students were bunched, avid for glimpses of the less timid females often peeping from behind their blinds at this hour. Waxing even bolder, they were soon raising the windows and accompanying their oglings with catcalls and whistles.

"Hey, you there with the pink ribbons, what's your name?" . . . "Hurrah for the gentle sex!" . . . "Better stay in today, or you'll get those pretty toeses wet!"

"I say, Stratton, I thought *we* were going to have a woman!" Suddenly diverted, one of the students headed for the class chairman's desk. Others followed, and he was soon surrounded. "Yah, how about it, Stratton? Where is she?" . . . "Thought it was all serious, didn't you? Wouldn't believe it was a hoax!" . . . "Didn't we tell you it was some other meds pulling our leg? Gosh, if they ever find out what fools you made of us!"

Like Francis Stratton, Stephen pretended utter absorption in his books. Both hoped the class had forgotten the incident, but no such luck. No doubt about it, somebody must have made fools of them, for two weeks had passed, and the lady had not arrived. They should have known. Who had ever heard of a woman wanting to study medicine! As crazy as a man's thinking he could become a mother! Oh well, they'd just have to grin and stand the gaff. But — it couldn't have been a complete hoax. Dr. Lee had certainly received both the application and a letter from a reputable physician. What had happened? Obviously the applicant must have changed her mind. Stephen felt a vague disappointment. Now his curiosity would never be satisfied. *What sort of woman —?*

The entrance of Dr. Lee caused a hiatus in the disorder. The students all scuttled to their seats. The lull would be temporary, however. Once the dean mounted the platform, settled in his chair and started his lecture, rowdiness would be back full force. But he did not mount the platform. Seemingly in a state of great agitation, he approached the front tier of benches, stopped, opened his mouth, closed it. His face was pale. He fumbled with the buttons of his waistcoat. Thoroughly alarmed, the class subsided into dead silence.

"This is really it," thought Stephen, his heart sinking to an even greater depth than two weeks before. "There's been a court order. They have to close the college. We've been condemned as a public nuisance. And no wonder!"

"Gentlemen." The dean's voice had lost its resonance. It actually trembled. He cleared his throat and started again. "Gentlemen, you will remember a letter about which I consulted you some days ago, about a — a certain application we had received. In accordance with the class vote, the faculty informed the applicant, also the Philadelphia physician, that — that she would be admitted. Gentlemen, I have now to inform you that the — the student has arrived."

Dr. Lee crossed to the reception room and opened the door. Not a sound could be heard in the classroom. The class seemed stricken with paralysis. Yet every eye remained riveted on the woman who entered, followed her across the room to the platform, where the doctor placed a chair for her.

"Gentlemen, may I present your fellow student, Miss Elizabeth Blackwell."

Stephen stared with the others. What sort of woman! His brain reeled, trying to reconcile reality with the picture unconsciously formed. What had he expected? Certainly not this tiny creature dressed modestly in Quaker gray gown, delicate features half obscured and eyes demurely downcast beneath the brim of the plain bonnet! But as she untied the strings, removed the bonnet, and placed it under her chair, he noticed the length and slenderness of the deft, competent fingers. "A pianist's hands," he thought, "or — yes, a surgeon's." And in spite of the delicacy of line, there was a firmness about the features, a poise in the lift of the small blonde head, an erectness in the slender shoulders which belied their apparent fragility.

Amid the complete silence Dr. Lee began his lecture . . . and continued it. For the first time that term he was able to expound his ideas on remedial substances without interruption. Every word carried to the farthest ring of seats.

"First let us review, gentlemen, the circumstances that modify the action of medicine. You will remember that there are ten: age, sex" — his voice stumbled ever so slightly on the word — "temperament, constitutional power, habit, climate, diet, cause, period, and seat of the disease."

The order in the classroom was uncanny. The rowdiness had suddenly turned into the circumspect behavior of a group of clerics, or rather, of faultlessly mannered gentlemen in the presence of a lady.

"The term 'laws of nature' is calculated to mislead us." Stimulated by the silence and apparently rapt attention, the resonant voice assumed a sermonic quality. "A law is nothing but a manifestation of certain phenomena, under given circumstances. Thus the modern discovery by the miscroscope that every organized structure originated in a germ or cell is called the law of cell life, but it is simply the will of the Creator exercised in that way."

For the first time in the course Stephen could have taken complete notes on the lecture, but his notebook remained blank. Like every other student's in the room, his eyes remained fixed on the small figure seated on the platform. Not once did she look toward the class. They might have been nonexistent. The delicate profile revealed no change of expression, only the slightest shifting of attention from the instructor to her notebook. Obviously she was the only student in the room taking notes.

Stephen was more puzzled than ever, curiosity whetted rather than satisfied. An Amazon, a Joan of Arc, even a Lady Godiva — these would have been comprehensible. But this was no mannish freak, no bold crusader. She was a lady if he had ever seen one, cast in the most conventional and acceptable of molds, dainty, refined, modest, even diffident and retiring. There was a firmness, a determination about her, yes. It showed in the set of shoulders, the unwavering profile, above all in the complete detachment from everything except the lecture and her notebook. But it would take more than firmness and determination to storm one of society's most jealously defended citadels. His question was more than ever unanswered. *What sort of woman —?*

2

Her first day in Medical College was over. Her mood was almost as gloomy as the weather outside, where rain continued to beat its incessant tattoo against the windows. She threw another stick of wood in the small airtight stove and huddled over it, chilled to the bone, for the classrooms in which she had attended five lectures had been almost unheated. But it was neither physical coldness nor the gloomy weather which accounted for her mood, nor the complete loneliness which made the small attic room in Miss Waller's boardinghouse seem like a monastic cell. It was frustration. True, she had been permitted to attend all the lectures, and she was not concerned with the difficulty of making up five weeks of lost time. All the professors had courteously offered to lend her their notes or give her private instruction — all, that is, except one. The professor of anatomy had been absent, and the demonstrator had been unwilling to admit her to dissection without his superior's permission.

"A queer duck," she had heard someone characterize the missing Dr. Webster.

Anatomy, dissection! She must have them to fulfill the necessary requirements. Suddenly she realized that admission to a college was no insurance of success. One balky professor could jeopardize her chances of graduation. She was bewildered, too, as well as frustrated. Her head swam from the effort of finding her way about the big college building, with its maze of classrooms, corridors, and doors. She had no books and no idea where she could get any. But as she resolutely began copying notes her spirits revived. At least she was here. She was duly registered in a medical college as Student No. 130. She had attended classes. The students had been faultless in their demeanor, perfect gentlemen. She had acquired a room of sorts in a comfortable boardinghouse, though the latter had been oddly difficult to secure.

She had called on at least a half-dozen landladies suggested by Dr. Lee without success. The responses had all been similar: "Sorry. Rooms are all taken," "No vacancy," "We cater to men only." It had been puzzling, for more than one window had displayed a sign, "Room for rent." At first the landladies had seemed cordial, helpful; then when she had mentioned Dr. Lee and the Medical College, they had turned brusque and dour. Was it possible that the college was in ill repute? Surely not Dr. Lee! It had not once occurred to her that the news of her arrival late the previous night had already been noised through the town. Not until long afterward would she learn that proprietors of many establishments had been threatened with the loss of some of their "best" patrons if she were received. But finally she had found the cheerful and motherly Miss Waller.

"A room? Of course, my dear. Any friend of Dr. Lee is welcome here. I have several empty. What sort would you like?"

"The smallest and cheapest, if you please."

It was small, certainly, and chilly, but, hung with pictures and mementos, it had not seemed too unhomelike. Until tonight. Even a letter from Marian failed to raise her spirits.

The next day, Tuesday, was equally dismal in prospect. The lake below the town was shrouded in fog, and rain and wind whipped her long skirts as she walked to the college. Then the day suddenly turned bright and cheerful, all because of an anatomy professor!

She dreaded meeting him. What was her surprise, then, when Dr. Lee introduced her to a plump little man who shook her hand warmly and seemed to beam all over.

"Capital, I say, this plan of yours. Just what we've needed around here, a lady pupil! The class acted manfully. I wish you could have heard them. Those resolutions were worthy of a congressional committee. Welcome, my dear Miss Blackwell."

Elizabeth could have hugged him. "Thank you, Dr. Webster."

"And what branches have you studied, young woman?"

"All but surgery," replied Elizabeth.

The dean looked alarmed. "But — surely you don't mean to practice surgery!"

"Of course she does," interrupted Dr. Webster. "Think of the cases of femoral hernia, and so many others affecting women. Just think what a well-educated woman doctor could do in a city like New York! Why, she'd have her hands full in no time, her success would be immense! Yes, yes, my dear young lady, you'll go through the course, and get your diploma, too, with great éclat. We'll give you all the opportunities." He rubbed his plump hands. "Yes, and you'll make a stir, I can tell you."

Elizabeth was inarticulate with relief. She felt like a martyr who had entered the arena expecting a ferocious lion, only to find a purring pussycat. She gave him a personal note of introduction from Dr. Warrington.

"Yes, yes, I know him well. Suppose you wait in the anteroom while I read it to my anatomy class. The lesson today is preparatory to one of the most delicate operations in surgery, and — well, I just want to make sure they recall their promise of good behavior."

Elizabeth waited outside. The professor had left the door ajar. There was a surprising amount of noise, puzzling because yesterday the students had been so quiet, but she could hear the doctor's voice reading the letter above the din. There was a shout of laughter when Dr. Warrington referred to the "age and experience" of Dr. Webster, and Elizabeth shared in the merriment, for the little man could not be more than forty-five, and dignity was not one of his assets. When he finished, there was a round of applause. Dr. Webster reappeared, face beaming like a plump sun, and ushered her to a seat on the platform. The lecture proceeded amid the same quiet and orderliness as had all the other classes. Dr. Lee was waiting outside when it was over, face a bit anxious. "Everything went — smoothly, I hope?"

"Oh — yes, sir. And I am very much impressed by the quality of teaching. I think New York and Philadelphia could learn more than one lesson from Geneva."

Dr. Webster came bustling toward them. He seemed bursting with merriment. "You attract too much attention, Miss Blackwell. There was a very large number of strangers present this afternoon. I shall have to guard against this in future."

The dean brightened visibly. Relief made him almost jovial. "Who knows?" he chuckled. "This step might prove a good advertisement for the college. If there were no other advantage to be gained, it could certainly attract notice, and the college needs it right now. I believe I must report the matter to the medical journals."

Who did know, indeed? Certainly the dean could not have guessed that events set in motion by a faculty's vacillation and a student body's bravado would be a century later this small college's chief claim to distinction!

Elizabeth's worries about opportunity to pursue studies in anatomy seemed over. After that first class Dr. LaFord, the demonstrator, now exhibiting the utmost friendliness, explained at Dr. Webster's request the details of one important subject she had missed. It was admirably done, well illustrated by specimens. The next evening she wrote in her diary, "Attended the demonstrator's evening lecture — very clear — how superior to books! Oh, this is the way to learn! The class behaves well, and people all seem to grow kind."

Not quite all, however. It would have been strange if even her studied aloofness had quelled the buffoonery entirely. Once as she sat in the seat reserved for her, quietly looking over her notes, she felt a very light touch on her head. Again, in the amphitheater, while the lecturer was giving a demonstration which a less objective woman might have found embarrassing, she felt something fall on her arm. Looking down, she saw a bit of folded paper, evidently a note, conspicuously white, lying on the sleeve of her black dress. Someone in an upper tier had tossed it with unerring aim. She could guess that it contained some bit of vulgar impertinence, and she felt every eye in the room upon her. A small thing, yet a mistake at this point might make her continuation of the course intolerable, even impossible. She must keep the respect of the students. Without moving or raising her eyes from her notebook, she continued to write. Then, when she had finished her notes, she slowly lifted the arm on which the paper lay until it was well in view of the whole room, then with the merest flick of her wrist let it fall to the floor. The action was both a protest and an appeal, and the students responded. There was even a wave of applause, a few hisses directed at the offender. Such actions were never repeated. However, she continued to keep aloof from all social intercourse, passing in and out without taking any notice of the other students, going straight to her seat, whether on the platform or in one of the front tiers, never looking in any direction other than at the professor or her notebook.

"The notice I attract is a matter of perfect indifference," she wrote Marian. "They might be mummies for all I care. I believe the professors don't exactly know in what species of the human family to place me, and the students are a little bewildered."

But she had not the slightest idea of the commotion she created in the town. The fact that small boys stared at her as she walked the short distance from Miss Waller's to the college she attributed to childish curiosity. But presently she overheard whispers and mumbles accompanying the stares: "Here she comes!" "Come on, kids, let's have a good look at the lady doctor!" Then she noticed that others besides idle boys were staring. As she went through the streets, a knot of well-dressed men or women might gather to look at her, as if she had been some strange animal or a visitor from another planet. A doctor's wife at the boardinghouse table avoided communication with her. Though she soon sensed suspicion and hostility, it was a long time before she discovered the full truth: that she had so shocked the town's propriety that they sincerely believed either that she was a bad woman whose designs would gradually become evident or that, being insane, she would exhibit some manifestation of violence. Feeling their unfriendliness yet unaware of all the gossip, she seldom ventured out except to the college and entered its sure refuge as quickly as possible. It was no sacrifice. Study consumed all her time and attention.

She approached every subject with enthusiasm: chemistry and pharmacy, materia medica and general pathology, medical lectures, lectures on the institutes and practice of medicine. But thanks to the sensitive Dr. Allen and the equally considerate Dr. LaFord (also perhaps to the unlucky cockchafer), anatomy became increasingly fascinating. The wonderful arrangements of the human body excited an interest and admiration which obliterated most of her instinctive feelings of repugnance. Dr. LaFord selected four of the more advanced students to work with her in the private room of the surgical professor, and Elizabeth soon felt almost as much at home with them as with her brothers. In fact, since she was several years their senior, they were soon treating her like an older sister and, conscious of her friendly sympathy, talking freely.

Besides its ample lecture and dissection rooms and convenient laboratory, the school had valuable anatomical, surgical, pathological, and obstetrical collections. Sometimes Elizabeth became so fascinated in tracing the ramifications of different parts of the body that she remained alone after the others had gone, until, struck by the intense stillness, she aroused to the fact that it was near midnight, and the rest of the little town was asleep. Then she took keen pleasure in the short walk home along the street high above the lake, no knots of staring people, no fluttering of curtains at the blank windows, only brisk winter air, scudding clouds, and, often, far below and extending to the horizon, an expanse of frozen magic glittering in the moonlight.

But progress in anatomy was not all a delight. Before many weeks had passed, Dr. Webster was approaching that section of his lectures dealing with the reproductive organs, some of his most important demonstrations. He suggested that she might prefer to absent herself temporarily from his classes. When she protested and he reluctantly gave her permission to attend, it proved as much an ordeal as a triumph.

"That dissection," she recorded one day in late November, "was just as much as I could bear. Some of the students blushed, some were hysterical, not one could suppress a smile, and some who I am sure would not hurt my feelings for the world, held down their faces and shook. My delicacy was certainly shocked, and yet the exhibition was in some sense ludicrous. I had to pinch my hand till the blood came, and call on Christ to keep me from smiling, for that would have ruined everything; but I sat in grave indifference, though my heart palpitated painfully."

She relied on more than prayer to preserve this complete objectivity. Knowing that to finish the course she must somehow make the other students regard her, not as a woman among men, but as one among 158 medical students, confronted only with the dignity and truth of science, she had confined herself to a rigid, almost a starvation diet, believing that such discipline might keep her from betraying embarrassment by change of color. Whether by prayer or asceticism or sheer willpower, her technique succeeded. That day and through the even more difficult ones following, she was able to remain as imperturbable as a statue during all the necessary plain speaking of her medical courses.

The session had been as trying to the genial Dr. Webster as to his class, partly from embarrassment, partly because her presence had proved inhibiting to his customary ribald approach to this normally most popular section of his course. The following day he wrote Elizabeth a note. Since he feared that her presence during the remainder of the present lectures would be embarrassing to himself, restricting his language and illustrations, and to the class, straining the natural modesty of many students, he begged leave to request her absence during the next few sessions.

Elizabeth was not only saddened and discouraged, but annoyed. She wrote the doctor a carefully phrased note. She was there as a student, she told him, with an earnest purpose, and she should be regarded simply as a student. The study of anatomy was to her a most serious one, exciting profound reverence in all its many aspects. Certainly that of procreation and human birth was one of its most sacred and should be approached only with the utmost reverence. Like herself, these students were being prepared to officiate at childbirth, a holy ministry in which they would be sharing with womanhood the most intimate mysteries of creation. But if the presence of a woman's bonnet on the platform during this process of learning was embarrassing to him and the class, she would gladly take her seat on an upper tier of benches and remove her headdress. In fact, she would absent herself from the lectures if it was the desire of the class, though it was not her wish and seemed to her a grave mistake. She was willing to submit the matter to the students' just and thoughtful consideration.

Dr. Webster acknowledged the note in person. He seemed pleased and asked permission to read it to the class. "If all of them were actuated by such sentiments," he said soberly, "the medical class at Geneva would be a very noble one." She waited for the result in the anteroom outside the amphitheater, trembling between hope and fear. Never had the students seemed so unpredictable, such strangers. The orderly decorum which she had always encountered had vanished. Behind the closed doors reigned pandemonium. Hoots, yells, shufflings, scufflings . . . it sounded like Howie and Wash on a rampage, multipled a hundredfold! How could the doctor even make them hear? Then suddenly the confusion ceased. She heard only a faint murmur which must be the doctor's voice. He was reading her letter.

Once more Stephen Smith sighed and put away his notebook. The chair on the platform reserved for Student No. 130 was again empty. That meant there would be no taking notes today and probably for the whole upcoming series of lectures. The transformation of the class from a band of lawless desperadoes to gentlemen because of the presence of a lady had been permanent but conditional upon her presence. Whenever her chair was empty, they reverted to type. Now the mood was sportive to the point of ribaldry. The class had anticipated this stage in the lectures for weeks. Always rollicking and jovial in his treatment of his subject, the plump little professor was noted for his delightfully unchaste and profane approach to those branches of anatomy in which less professional education was normally accompanied by behind-the-barn snickerings and furtive experimentations. Conjecture had been rife.

The advent of Student No. 130 had noticeably tempered the professorial vocabulary and choice of anecdotes. What would it do to his treatment of this most delicate of subjects? The empty chair apparently signified a return to more lusty procedure, and the more reckless students were anticipating the hour with relish.

But the little doctor was far from his jolly self. He looked flushed and excited. In fact, so strange was his manner that it effected what discipline could never have done: complete and immediate attention.

"Gentlemen." For the first time in Stephen's memory Dr. Webster seemed at a loss for words. "I — have a very novel situation to deal with, and since it involves the interests of the class, I — I believe you should be apprised."

After explaining the situation, he read Elizabeth's letter. Stephen Smith looked around the room, hopefully, fearfully. It would take sober men, not slaphappy schoolboys, to meet this challenge. But before the class could register its reaction, Dr. Webster raised his hand for silence. The plump dumpy little figure looked suddenly six feet tall.

"Gentlemen," he said, "I am rebuked. I am humbled. We have in our midst a student of the type of our Greek master Galen, who wrote sixteen hundred years ago, 'The study of anatomy is a perpetual hymn to the gods.' I am profoundly impressed by the good influence Miss Blackwell has exerted on the class, and I believe that the noble stand which she has now taken in the assertion of her rights as a duly registered pupil of the college entitles her to every privilege and honor which the faculty and class can confer. I hope you will agree and act accordingly."

Amid a complete silence the little doctor went to the door of the anteroom, opened it, and with courtly dignity ushered Elizabeth Blackwell into the amphitheater. As she walked to her usual seat, the room shook with such tremendous applause that neighbors in the adjoining houses must have been startled. With a sigh of relief Stephen Smith opened his notebook. The lecture proceeded in an orderly manner, the professor adhering closely to the text. If lewdness and jocularity were noticeably missing, there was ample compensation in lucidity and sober scientific technique. A pattern was set for the entire series. Some of the older students declared that this was the first course on the subject they had been able to follow connectedly, and the professor admitted it was the first in which he had been keenly interested.

Long afterward Stephen Smith, a distinguished physician in New

York City, would recall the sequence of events and write, "This personal experience determined affirmatively in my own mind the question of the propriety of the coeducation of the sexes even in medical colleges."

Levity, however, dominated most current journalistic reports of Geneva's innovation. Even the startled medical profession sensed that ridicule and amusement were more effective weapons than hostility.

"A very notable event of the year 1848," reported the *Boston Medical Journal*, "was the appearance at medical lectures of a young woman student named Blackwell. She is a pretty little specimen of the feminine gender, 26 years of age. She comes into the class with great composure, takes off her bonnet and puts it under the seat, exposing a fine phrenology. The effect on the class has been good, and great decorum is preserved while she is present."

"She should confine her practice, when admitted," commented the sprightly Baltimore *Sun*, "to diseases of the heart."

3

The sixteen-week term ended the last week in January. Eight whole months to the beginning of the next term! Much could happen in that time. Suppose the mounting criticism and publicity caused an about-face in the attitude of the faculty. Suppose the gallant struggle by President Benjamin Hale and his colleagues to keep little Geneva College alive against almost impossible odds should fail, jeopardized perhaps by the scandal of her presence! If only she could continue her study at once without this paralyzing hiatus!

There were small satisfactions which eased the sadness of leaving. One was a letter she received from one of the students. It requested the honor of an occasional correspondence. Amusing as well as cheering! Another student, who had a daguerreotype room, asked her to sit for her likeness.

"Sorry," she replied with genuine regret. "It's annoying enough to have to see my name in the papers without having to publicize my face too!"

Humbly the young man admitted that he had thought of graduating earlier but was glad he had decided against it, since she intended to come back next year. All these little friendly advances from the students, plus an oyster supper given in her honor by Miss Waller, lightened her heaviness of heart. Though still ostracized by most of the towns-people, here in the boardinghouse she was now accepted as a respectable, if not a normal, woman.

She received her certificate for the course from the registrar, Dr. Hadley, attended commencement, then an assembly of the faculty. They talked over her affairs but gave her no important advice. To her disappointment no letters of introduction had been prepared for her, only a promise that some would be sent. She had counted heavily on such letters to provide opportunities for further study during the coming months.

What to do next? She could not return home to Cincinnati. All doors to medical study there were tightly closed. Besides, her finances were pitiably low, and it was no time to burden the family with another mouth to feed. The foundry where Sam had worked had failed, and he was both without income and deeply in debt. Harry had left Mr. Harris and taken some of his old machinery to Cincinnati in the hope of starting a sugar refinery there. His experiments at "blowing up" with the old cisterns and filters were discouraging. Then too, the best sugar he could make with the machinery at his disposal (blow pans) was what was known as "coffee crushed" sugar, which, though greatly in demand in New York, was not yet acceptable in the West. His efforts seemed as doomed to failure as his romance with Kate. The family was talking of selling the house. No, it was no time to burden them with her problems.

She went back to the Elders' in Philadelphia. While exploring medical opportunities, she tried to earn a little money by selling some of the stories she had written for the Christmas Annual and by obtaining music pupils. But medicine, not music or writing, was her consuming interest, and education, not money, was her goal. Already she was becoming surfeited with book knowledge. What she needed desperately was experience. And where, with the door of every hospital and clinic closed to her, could she get it? The answer came suddenly, exciting, terrifying, but revealing as a flash in the dark. *Blockley!* What better place for experience than Philadelphia's huge almshouse, with its enormous hospital wards, its dregs of diseased humanity? In spite of her horrified friends' protests, she obtained a letter of introduction to a Mr. Gilpin, one of the directors.

"Sorry," he said, after listening to her appeal with the utmost kindness, "but I can be of little help. If I, a Whig, should present your application to the board, it would be inevitably opposed by the Democrats and the Native Americans. Your only chance of admission lies in your securing the support of each of those parties, unbeknownst to the others." He shook his head sadly. "Politics, my dear Miss Blackwell."

So Elizabeth began lobbying. After interviewing each political leader with apparently favorable results, she sent her petition to the board meeting. And lo, a miracle! Each party was prepared to fight in her behalf, but there was no one to fight!

"Resolved," read an extract from the minutes of the Guardians of the Poor, Philadelphia Alms Hospital, for February 28, 1848, "that permission be granted Miss Elizabeth Blackwell to enter this institution, enjoy such accommodations as can be conveniently afforded her, and occupy such a position as may be assigned her by the chief resident physician."

A unanimity, she was to learn later, utterly without precedent in the records of the institution!

She was given a room on the third floor of the women's hospital in the syphilitic department, where it was hoped that her residence might have a softening influence on the most unruly patients. It was a big lofty room, with three enormous windows giving a view on the winding Schuylkill River, Fairmount, Girard College, and much of Philadelphia. Its airy cleanliness was a heavenly contrast to the noxious stench of disease, poverty, and bodily neglect which pervaded the huge wards outside. A pleasant serving woman tended the room and brought her meals. Plain though the food was, she felt guilty in taking it, but though she had offered to pay her own expenses, the resolution of the board permitted her both residence in the establishment and use of everything the house afforded. A godsend with her purse in its lean condition!

The unfortunate inmates who roamed the halls outside did not know what to make of her presence. Sometimes she would hear stealthy steps approach and pause at her door. Helpfully she placed her study table in a direct line with the keyhole, to satisfy their curiosity as much as possible.

At first Elizabeth was almost as mystified by her function as they. She wandered bewildered about the huge establishment, the largest in America. She saw so much that she could see *nothing*, and was almost in despair. But slowly details came into focus. The great complex of buildings housed some two thousand people, distributed in the men's and women's hospitals, poorhouse, lunatic asylum, factory, children's asylum, and additional hospitals for the lunatic, the blind, the lying-in, and children. Assigned to the women's hospital, she had free access at all times.

"You would laugh," she wrote Marian, "to see me wandering eagerly about those great wards, timidly inquiring into symptoms, and spearing about for useful knowledge. At first it was very trying — all eyes, and such queer eyes, were fixed on my every movement. But already people are becoming accustomed to the quiet apparition. I find some of the patients like to detail their symptoms!"

Not all, however. Some were as outraged as the interns. "I may be poor and cast out by the Lord," one old crone whimpered, "but I'll have no woman to take care of me in my illness!"

Hannah was as worried now about the state of her body as of her soul. Dutifully Elizabeth tried to allay her fears.

"Do not fear for me. I live simply, do my duty, trust in God, and mock at the devil. At present there is no epidemic in the house. If one should come it would interest me greatly. I am not afraid myself, of sickness, but if I should be ill, I am certain none of their nostrums would go down my uncontaminated throat. I should trust to fresh air, cold water, and nature, and live or die as the Almighty pleased."

Attendance on the sick was divided among six young physicians, who hotly resented her presence. When she walked into a ward, they walked out. They even ceased to write the diagnosis and treatment of the patient on the card at the head of each bed, so she was thrown wholly on her own resources. Only one of these young residents, a Dr. Knight, ever became her friend. But the chief physician, Dr. Benedict, was cooperation itself. When Elizabeth first saw him, she thought him the loveliest man the Almighty had ever created. Tears came into his eyes as he bent down to soothe some dying woman, and his voice was as gentle, his touch as kind as if each patient were his sister. He was as truthful, energetic, and spirited as he was kind.

Elizabeth was appalled by her own ignorance in practical medicine. Soon after arriving she had to confess that this was the first time she had ever seen a person bled. Yet bleeding was considered one of the most effective treatments of most diseases. She hastened to refresh her memory of Dr. Lee's lecture on bloodletting in materia medica.

"If blood could be completely extracted from an inflamed part," she read from her notes, "we could completely arrest the inflammation, for blood is the fuel which feeds the fire of inflammation. The more important the organ, the more necessary to be prompt in bleeding. . . . Children and old people have less tolerance in bleeding. For children leeches should be used. Cups are preferable to leeches where speed is necessary. Leeches can go where cups cannot be applied. . . ."

Elizabeth also made friends with the matron, the only other "lady" in the establishment. (The female nurses she did not include in that category.) The matron was a strange paradox. A pious Quaker, gray hair smooth under her starched white cap, soft dove's eyes as gentle and limpid as Hannah's, she looked like a motherly angel. Then her loud voice would break out in fierce scolding, and Elizabeth would secretly dub her "Mrs. Beelzebub." Seated in her armchair in an immense room at the center of the almshouse, feet propped on a velvet footstool, she would parcel out orders from morning to night, rave at the paupers, dispense clothing, doom the refractory patients to shower baths and straitjackets.

But Elizabeth often took tea with her and learned much, for the woman was shrewd and had seen much of life through dark spectacles. Slowly, through talks with her and Nurse Welch and through her own observation, she wakened to the moral tragedy surrounding her. Shocked and distressed, she absorbed the stories of the unhappy patients, most of them unmarried, many having been in service and seduced in the very households that should have protected them. She was horrified when one young woman, trying to escape by tying sheets together and fastening them outside the window bars, fell from the third story, to be picked up a wreck of broken bones and concussions. Helping to deliver a poor scrap of a Negro baby, she was racked with pain at thought of the unhappy fate awaiting it. The injustice done to helpless women appalled her. Yet she remained incredibly innocent of the extent and meaning of sexual immorality in its effects on the womanhood of her day. Not until twenty years later, when attending a social science congress in her own Bristol, England, would she fully comprehend its social consequences.

She saw enough now, however, to create in her a core of rebellion which would harden slowly into one of the dominating purposes of her life.

"All this is horrible!" she recorded despairingly one day in June.

"Women must really open their eyes to it. I am convinced *they* must regulate this matter. But *how?*"

Could she have looked ahead a half-century and seen the fruits of her own crusade for the betterment of women — how with Josephine Butler she would wage the vigorous and successful campaign to repeal the notorious Contagious Diseases Act legalizing sexual vice in England; how her constant battle against sexual injustice would anticipate and undergird the White Slave Traffic Act of 1902; how with tongue and pen and group participation she would labor with considerable success for forty years to educate the British public conscience to the evils of prostitution, venereal disease, the double standard of morality — the despair would have been partially mitigated by satisfaction. But only partially. For her goals would always be too high for full attainment. Sixty years later she would still be writing to a friend, "Sexual injustice is nowhere fully recognized, I fear, at present."

Now she felt little but despair, for even in the branch of associationism in which she was involved there in Philadelphia she was discouraged by the uselessness and frivolity of its women.

"I hardly know how we must begin to improve women," she wrote Emily, even while eulogizing the joys of "glorious association." "They will not be better until society changes, and society cannot be improved till they are nobler. Then again, the majority of women do not seem to me formed for strong action or high aspiration. There is a great deal of the sweet flower and bright butterfly about them."

But even as she wrote, the first seeds of the revolution she despaired of were being planted. On July 19 and 20 in Seneca Falls, only a few miles from Geneva, the first women's rights convention in the world was being held. In response to an announcement in the July 14 Seneca County *Courier* that women would convene "to discuss the social, civil, and religious rights of women," an incredible three hundred women flocked from a radius of fifty miles to a little Wesleyan chapel. There they listened to Mrs. Elizabeth Cady Stanton, the young wife of an abolitionist leader, Mrs. Lucretia Mott, founder of the first Female Anti-Slavery Society, and other daring pioneers set forth a Declaration of Principles which was to launch a program of reform extending through three generations. Based on the Declaration of Independence, it stated: "The history of mankind is a history of repeated injuries and usurpations on the part of man toward woman, having in direct object the establishment of an absolute tyranny over her. To prove this, let facts be submitted to a candid world."

The facts followed, ranging over every aspect of the status of women: her inability to vote, to control her own earnings, to sign legal papers, to manage her own property, to share in the guardianship of her own children, to even have custody over her own person; the injustice of the double standard of morality, the iniquity which barred her from ninety percent of the lucrative and self-fulfilling occupations of the world. Eighteen grievances were presented. Except for one resolution, "Resolved, that it is the duty of the women of this country to secure to themselves their sacred right to the elective franchise," all were passed unanimously. That one carried by a small margin.

One of the most earnest of the three hundred was a nineteen-year-old girl named Charlotte Woodward, whose grievances as a female glovemaker typified the economic status of many victims of the factory system.

"We women did more than keep house, cook, sew, wash, spin and weave, and garden," she was to write long afterward. "Many of us were under the necessity of earning money besides. We worked secretly, in the seclusion of our bedchambers, because all society was built on the theory that men, not women, earned money, and that men alone supported the family. Most women accepted this condition of society as normal and God-ordained and therefore changeless. But I do not believe that there was any community anywhere in which the souls of some women were not beating their wings in rebellion. For my own obscure self I can say that every fiber of my being rebelled, although silently, all the hours that I sat and sewed gloves for a miserable pittance which, after it was earned, could never be mine."

A hundred women signed the declaration, demanding for women opportunities in education, trade, and the professions, together with rights of free speech, the ownership of property, the guardianship of their children, and — the vote. But only one, Charlotte, would live to see this last goal realized when, seventy-two years later, she would become one of the first women to cast her ballot for the President of the United States.

News of the scandalous convention swept the country, from Cincinnati to Philadelphia. Mankind arose in shocked and righteous defense of the scripturally based right of their lordship over women. Preachers and editors joined in horrified denunciation. Women assuming man's prerogative of public speech — and in a church! Demanding rights which would "destroy their sensibility, weaken their dependence on man, and thereby take away one of the liveliest of their charms!" It was that same year that Senator John Ingalls successfully opposed a bill in Massachusetts giving women the right to hold and administer property while declaring, "The doctrines of female suffrage and the equality of the sexes are undermining the foundation of our social structure."

But it was a man named McIntosh who stated the current male reaction most succinctly. "There is a political inequality, ordained in Paradise, when God said to the Woman, 'He shall rule over thee' and which has ever existed, in every tribe and nation and people of earth's countless multitudes. Let those who would destroy this inequality pause ere they attempt to abrogate a law which emanated from the all-perfect Mind. And let no woman murmur at the lowliness of her lot."

Elizabeth read the stories and comments with mixed emotions. Wonderful for women to be so daring! Nobody knew the courage it took better than she. And yet — why talk about "women's rights" and "men's rights"? What one should be concerned about was *human rights!* Women should certainly be fighting for their God-given rights, but not as women, as human beings. Besides, the adverse publicity and the proximity of Seneca Falls to Geneva made her tremble with apprehension. Suppose all the agitation so alarmed the faculty that they felt forced to deny her admission for her second term! Or — hopefully — might it strengthen them in their bold stand for democracy? Or perhaps, shying from further publicity, would they think it wise to get her through and out of the way as quickly as possible, then make sure they made no such mistake again?

She was worried about others' futures as well as her own. One Sunday in May she met William Donaldson from Cincinnati coming out of church. He told her that he had seen a notice in some paper of the burning of Mr. Blackwell's sugar house. She waited apprehensively for a letter from home. When it came, it brought relief as well as anxiety. The sugar house had indeed burned, but insurance had covered the loss and enabled Harry to pay his creditors. Since the business was doomed to failure, he was well out of it. But she was by no means encouraged when Harry came East, and after visiting her for a day in July, went to New York to consider a position as clerk with Dennis

Harris. Poor Harry! An impossible alliance for a restless, ambitious young freethinker with a narrowly orthodox Wesleyan preacher!

Poor Anna, also, who was responsible for the family's initial exposure to Fourierism! Bereft of the society of her admired Dr. Brisbane, who had sailed for France, she was up in Providence, off on another tangent. This time it was a "magnetic" treatment conducted by a Professor de Bonneville, from which she hoped to "regain the vital power which would enable her system to react upon water or medicine." She was writing articles to pay for her treatment and translations to defray the cost of her board. Elizabeth had no more faith in de Bonneville than she had had in Anna's hydropath Dr. Schieferdecker. The country was full of these exponents of dissident medical systems, as varied as the many philosophical "isms." There were the hydropaths with their "water cures," the homeopaths with their substitution of harmless little pills for drugs, the mesmerists, the physiopaths, the phrenologists. Then there were the eclectics, who claimed to combine the valuable parts of all systems, like their medical predecessors who had coined the name in the first century. As a student in one of the conventionally reputable though smaller schools, Elizabeth shared the well-educated physician's contempt for unorthodox systems. But fortunately Anna's present obsession would be temporary.

The Blackwells' horizon was brightened in July by the arrival of Cousin Kenyon, Uncle James's son. The English Blackwells had not shared their American relatives' adversity. After Samuel had left England, his older brother had engaged in iron manufacturing, and prosperity had burgeoned. His talented and energetic sons Kenyon and Sam had continued to prosper, and now Kenyon, retired with an adequate competence, had come to America to renew family ties, and also to investigate the possibilities of iron manufacturing in the new country.

When he came briefly to Philadelphia to visit her, Elizabeth was pleased with Kenyon, found him intelligent, thoughtful, well read, a happy contrast to the careless young blade who had ruined the raspberries and muddled her father's bookkeeping. Some of his mannerisms brought poignant reminders of Papa. Immediately his presence injected vigor into the sluggish family bloodstream. One of the boys must go back with him and enter the business with his brother Sam. Henry? To Elizabeth's disappointment Henry stubbornly chose to remain with Mr. Harris. Sam? No. Sam was already involved in negotiations for a hardware business. Howie, then? The seventeen-year-old boy jumped at the chance and prepared to leave for the East, tremendously excited. Elizabeth was relieved by this development, for she had been worried about young Howie's manners and morals.

But family worries, even the cometlike flashings of Kenyon between Providence, New York, Philadelphia, and Cincinnati, became secondary to the problems at Blockley. For the disease called "ship fever," usually diagnosed as a form of typhus, came flooding into America — and into Blockley — with a fresh tide of Irish immigrants.

For Elizabeth the emergency spelled both responsibility and opportunity. Sex ceased to be a liability. All hands were pressed into service. Even the hostile young interns grudgingly welcomed her assistance. She had not the slightest fear of contagion. Her trust in fresh air, sanitation, bodily cleanliness, was implicit. She worked tirelessly, often with Dr. Benedict, assisting with examinations, diagnoses, treatment, much of which was experimental. When there were no doctors present she roamed the wards alone, asking questions, observing the disease in all its stages, judging for herself the efficacy of various forms of treatment. And then came the flash of inspiration.

"I'll make this the subject of my medical thesis!"

She compiled voluminous notes derived from books, the doctors' pronouncements, answers to her questions, but mostly from her own observations. In terse plain language, unusual in a period of grandiose expression, she described symptoms of the disease and its progress, the condition of brain, lungs, liver, spleen, as noted in autopsies. She quoted French physicians, Scottish, British, American, as to the nature of fevers, the distinction between typhoid and typhus. But the major part detailed her own observations as to effective treatment both during the various stages and through convalescence.

"Symptoms, then, furnish valuable indication of the method Nature is taking to remedy. But Nature is blind; it must be watched, guided, restrained. . . . Cleanliness, ventilation, and judicious exercise are of the utmost importance. . . . The importance of the hygienic means here referred to cannot be too strongly insisted upon. . . . When the laws of health are generally understood and practiced, when a social providence shall be extended over all ranks of the community, then we may hope to see these physical evils disappear, with all the moral evils which correspond to and are constantly associated with it."

So were born in her thinking and practice those fundamentals of medical approach which were to be her lifelong norms. Little did she realize that generations ahead of her time she was voicing a philosophy which would be hailed by later pioneers in sanitation, public health, preventive medicine, as science's latest discoveries! And she would have been amazed to have her ideas dubbed a *philosophy*. To her they were nothing more nor less than common sense. And they could be expressed in two simple sentences: *It is better to prevent disease than to cure it*. And: *Nature, with its God-given remedies of fresh air, cleanliness, sunshine, exercise, is the world's best doctor*.

She read the thesis to Dr. Elder and was encouraged by his hearty approval. The end of summer and of her painful but rewarding apprenticeship brought a conflict of feelings.

"September 22. My last evening at Blockley. Here I sit writing by my first fire. How glad I am, tomorrow, to go home to my friends! And yet as I watched the beautiful sunset from my great windows, as little Mary Ann pays her willing attendance, and all seems so friendly; as I walked to Dr. Benedict's with my thesis, and felt the entrancing day and the lovely country, I *almost* regretted that I was going to leave. Heaven guide me! May good spirits ever surround me!"

4

Geneva seemed to have stood still in her absence, while she herself had grown older and taller. It seemed gloomy and dull also, perhaps because of the rain which had followed her all the way from New York and now enclosed the little town, turning the green square into a morass, the mellow hues of the fine brick houses into ugly duns and drabs. Or perhaps her sense of expectancy was dulled by the severing of ties in Philadelphia, more likely by distress over a visit with Harry. She liked nothing about his present arrangement, his job with Harris, his tired appearance, his boarding place in a family which seemed to have swallowed him up; worse yet, his too hurried engagement to a girl of the family named Jane. With characteristic urgency for action, she wrote him, dispensing advice in no uncertain terms.

"You must board elsewhere. . . . I am very anxious to hear also that the positive engagement is dissolved for a time."

The mood of gloom persisted. The class was surprisingly small and looked disconsolate in the great rooms of the Medical College. Many professors were late in arriving. Then suddenly all changed. The sun appeared, turning Lake Seneca's long finger into a shaft of dazzling blue.

The professors arrived. The class increased, bringing back familiar faces, all smiling in friendliest welcome. She plunged into study with all her faculties as usual, keeping a rigid schedule, feeling as if she were committing a sin if she took up any book or activity unrelated to medicine. She was equally spartan with her meager resources, denying herself everything possible. Once, refusing to purchase for perhaps six cents a little bottle of eau de cologne which struck her fancy, for she loved perfumes, she felt such physical deprivation that the memory of that little bottle would haunt her for years.

Only in one area did she permit herself a slight relaxation of rigidity, her relations with her fellow students. No longer the need to look neither to right nor left as she entered a classroom, to half starve herself to keep from blushing. The students were as courteous as they were friendly, and her dignity as a woman was unchallenged. Sometimes, as she sat by the doctor during a delicate demonstration and the students were crowding around, standing on chairs, leaning on one another's shoulders, she was conscious of their care to keep a respectful distance from her, drawing back instantly if by accident one of them touched her head or shoulder.

But she was accepted as an equal in hot discussions before and after classes and sometimes contributed to the spirited arguments on free soil, abolitionism, agrarian reform, the spoils system. It was election year, with a sharp contest between the Whigs, who had nominated the slaveholder Taylor, and the Democrats, one faction of whom, the "Barnburners," had formed a new party under the banner, "Free soil, free speech, free labor, and free men." At one meeting in October the class discussed whether Mississippi should be admitted as a slave or free state. The students decided to hold an election to determine their opinion. When the men had all voted, it proved to be a draw.

"Miss Blackwell!" one of them shouted. "She hasn't voted. Let her decide!"

She was given rousing cheers when she went over to the "free soil" side. Then followed a bitter argument concerning the right of a woman to vote, which disturbed her less than the fact that Dr. LaFord, the anatomist whom she so admired, had been on the opposite side.

"Are you really going to vote for that slaveholder Taylor?" she asked reproachfully. Though he was eloquent in giving reasons for loyalty to the Whigs, her admiration suffered severe erosion.

The hostility she had encountered the previous year in the town had subsided to mere curiosity or indifference. Even the pursuing urchins had tired of their old jibes, and when someone managed to think up a fresh one, there was more of amusement and less of taunt in their chantings. "Doctor, doctor in petticoats, do you cure corns or do you cure colds?"

Though she was on moderately friendly terms with the boarders at Miss Waller's, not a single woman in the town had ever called on her. What was her surprise, then, when one day in October two strange women appeared. But they were not from Geneva. They came from Waterloo and were active members of the women's rights convention.

"We were so anxious to meet you, and we think you're so wonderful and brave! You're actually *doing* all these things that we're just talking about."

Elizabeth regarded them with a mingling of interest, admiration, and dismay, her fastidious scrutiny absorbing every physical detail. One was a cadaverous-looking Quaker with all the plainness and none of the neatness of the traditional garb, the other rather pretty but vulgar, with faded artificial flowers and soiled pink bonnet strings. Was this a sample of the bold crusaders for women's freedom? Heaven help the cause if its chief exponents turned out to be extremists, cranks, or — worse yet — dowdy misfits! But these women seemed intelligent enough, and she knew some of their relatives in a respectable Philadelphia family. Almost to her own surprise she promised to visit them.

"I want to find out," she wrote home, "if there are any women possessed of substantial elements of character. There is such a great work for women to do and so few to do it that I am bound to search out any elements that promise to be of value. Anything is to me better than the vegetable life of most women, so I hail with hope any indication of active life, however wild."

Elizabeth sensed only vaguely that, remote though little Geneva might seem from the tumultuous industrial and social change shaking the country in this year of 1848, she was at the very center of one of its most turbulent revolutions. For in this slowly mounting storm soon to be labeled the Women's Rights Movement, she was in the eye of the hurricane.

Seneca Falls, with its double distinction as home of Elizabeth Cady Stanton and site of the world's first women's rights convention, was a scant dozen miles to the east. Even nearer was Waterloo, where Lucretia

Mott and Mrs. Stanton had met with others to draft the notice of this historic meeting, little dreaming that the mahogany table about which they sat would one day be a national exhibit in the Smithsonian Institution. Nearby also lived Amelia Bloomer, that doughty forerunner of women's dress designers who would be forever remembered for the utilitarian garment bearing her name, a loosely belted tunic, skirt no more than knee length, and baggy Turkish pantaloons reaching to the ankles. A little to the northwest was Rochester, site of the second convention and home of Susan B. Anthony, the incomparable organizer who was to pilot the frail craft of women's rights through stormy waters for the next half-century.

Elizabeth was even less aware of tides in the movement already in motion which were to engulf the Blackwell family. Entering Oberlin College, the first and still the only institution of higher learning open to both men and women, in 1843 came that same Lucy Stone who had balked at sewing shirts to support young theologs who by virtue of mere sex could earn more money teaching in a week than she could in a month. At twenty-five she was possessed by the same independence of spirit, only more so. Dissatisfied with the policy of Oberlin, which defined women's high calling as being the mothers of the race and endeavored to confine them to that sphere, she insisted on taking the "regular" instead of the "literary" course in college, a four-year instead of a two-year course. Liberal though the college was for its day, she was in frequent conflict with the authorities. In spite of the college's stand against the abolitionism of Garrison, she became agent on campus for the *Anti-Slavery Bugle*, published by Garrison's followers, and herself subscribed to *The Liberator*. Finding that wearing her bonnet in church gave her a headache, she removed it, and was called before the Ladies' Board. How, she demanded, should she account to God for a wasted Sunday afternoon if she had a raging headache? Routed by this logic, the board agreed that if she would sit in the last row she might remove her bonnet if the pain became unbearable.

Worse even than the heresy of going hatless in church was her stubborn insistence on the right of women to speak in public. With her classmate and best friend, Antoinette Brown, she battled the college rule that required female attendance at a debate held each week by the coeducational rhetoric class but forbade its participation. Losing the battle, they organized a small group of debaters among the more daring females, holding secret meetings in the woods and posting guards to warn of impending danger. Graduating from college in 1847, Lucy dedicated herself to a career as a public speaker.

"I expect to plead not for the slave only, but for suffering humanity everywhere," was her avowed purpose. "Especially do I mean to labor for the elevation of my sex."

Her friend Antoinette Brown further roused consternation by applying for admission to the Oberlin theological school. Shades of St. Paul, whose "Let your women keep silence in the churches" was more recently bolstered by Samuel Johnson's "Sir, a woman preaching is like a dog walking on his hind legs. It is not done well, but you are surprised to find it done at all!" Only her stubborn insistence and the avowed democratic policy of the college finally induced Professor Morgan to yield helplessly: "Antoinette, I think you are all wrong. If I could keep you out, I would, but since I cannot, I will do my best to teach you."

Now, in 1848, Lucy Stone was shuttling back and forth over the country, speaking for the Anti-Slavery Society (and incidentally for women's rights), often to savagely hostile audiences, and spinning a web which would stretch one day to Cincinnati to interweave its meshes with the lives of the Blackwells.

But Elizabeth had little time to concern herself with the infant women's rights movement a dozen miles away, to say nothing of its country-wide exponents. She was too busy trying to vindicate the rights of one woman. Yet the constant application to books was often wearying, for the summer's experience made her impatient for more practical service.

"Study is not to me the end it once was," she confided in a letter to Harry. "I want to live, and sometimes I feel almost angry at the very small portion of my being that is called into exercise."

At least her present preoccupation had effectively stifled that troublesome fascination exerted by the other sex. Though one woman in a class of over a hundred, she felt not a hint of the tender passion for one of them. Not so vice versa! The anomalous presence of the one woman had aroused either embarrassed restraint or the excess of amorous interest which might have been accorded the ugliest of females on a desert island. How much more normal and healthy, she often thought, for women to be accepted as fellow-students with men as a matter of course! All such restraint or excessive romantic interest would soon vanish. And what a pity that women were finding it necessary to found their own female institutions of learning! Surely such segregation should be only a temporary expedient and abolished as soon as possible!

"One poor fellow has certainly fallen into the depths," she wrote Marian. "He waylays me at church for permission to accompany me home. He sits at college with his eyes fixed most inexpressibly upon me and starts and blushes if my eye meets his. He begged me to let him call on me, 'from the purest and most disinterested motives,' and now he is too timid to come. He is to me utterly repulsive, though a handsome fellow. I should be very sorry to let him touch my hand."

Yet — was the old fascination completely stifled? A few weeks later she wrote, "I often feel when I am with the students how beautiful the relations of man and woman might be under a truer development of character, in nobler circumstances. I know that Geneva is a very immoral place, the lower classes of women being often worthless, the higher ones fastidious and exclusive, so there is no healthy blending of the sexes. I don't know if I've told you how deep this matter of licentiousness has gradually sunk into my soul, and that the determination to wage a war of extermination with it strengthens continually. So help me, God, I will not be blind, indifferent, or stupid in relation to this matter, as are most women."

Fortunately all her study was not dull or wearying, far from it. Again and again she experienced the thrill of discovery during Dr. LaFord's clever demonstrations in anatomy. With all the joy of an alchemist she spent hours at the tall mahogany medicine cabinet, delving into the mysteries inside the shining glass door and behind the brass pulls of the narrow drawers, little dreaming that a hundred years later it would be wearing a plaque proudly boasting that it had once been used by Elizabeth Blackwell! The study of pharmacy ceased to be academic when news came of a cholera epidemic in Cincinnati.

"Our physicians confessedly cannot cure it," she hastened to write Marian, giving her a graphic description of the symptoms. "But I will give you a receipt, propounded by the Mesmerist Davis, which he asserts to be a spiritual revelation, but which is so orthodox, being compounded of some of the most powerful of our tonics, stimulants, and astringents, that its origin is a little suspicious. 'Put two gallons of cider brandy in a stone vessel with half an ounce each of carbonate of iron, camphor, kino, African capsicum. Shake it occasionally during ten days. Have it always at hand, with 8 six-pound stones and a tub. On the attack, seat the patient naked in the tub with blankets over. Heat the stones, put in four. Pour the brandy on moderately to fumigate him well, change the stones as they become cool, till perspiration is visible and convulsions cease. Give him one gill of white brandy, put him in bed, and he is well.' "

Elizabeth herself, however, relied on fresh air, exercise, and cold water to keep clear of any disease, including cholera, and she proved their efficacy to her own satisfaction. Geneva was stricken with an epidemic of influenza. She visited a family six miles out of town who were suffering from the disease. She stayed two days and slept with a daughter who had a severe commencing attack. On her return she developed sore throat, headache, dizziness, all the symptoms. But she took long walks in the sharp winter air, slept long, bathed frequently, and escaped the scourge entirely.

Her concentration on medicine had mild interruptions. In November came Howie, on his way to sail with Anna to England and join Cousin Sam in his business. He was boyish and vulnerable at eighteen but handsome as a knight errant going out to conquer the world. How Anna's moody face would brighten at sight of him, for he had always been her favorite! Anna had been offered five hundred dollars a year and her expenses to Europe if she would undertake a complete translation of Fourier. Elizabeth rejoiced for both of them. For some of Samuel's nine children fortunes were looking up.

Not for all, however. Chafing under his job with Dennis Harris, Harry was talking moodily of joining the gold rush to California. Some of his friends had already persuaded him to invest all his small capital in the manufacture of some patent "cradles," or rockers, designed to separate the grains of gold from the gravel by washing. Kenyon, on his way from Cincinnati to persuade Harry to reconsider, stopped to visit Elizabeth during the Christmas holidays. Together they read the Annual, containing Marian's "Mary Erle," Ellen's "Sea King," Henry's "Keys of Heaven," and Anna's "Evening Star." There was nothing, however, from Elizabeth's pen. For the first time in years she had been too busy to write.

But New Year's Eve she spent alone, all the more lonely for Kenyon's visit.

"At night, as I watched the last moments of the year slowly depart, a deep solemnity came over me, a hopeless sorrow for poor humanity. I seemed to hear the heavy resounding bell of time, whilst angels with covered faces waited to receive the finishing scroll of the world's existence, that the fearful record guarded in darkness and silence might at last be unrolled in the terrible light of eternity."

5

It was almost as agonizing a question as whether she would pass her examinations. *Should she have a new dress for graduation?* Deny herself a six-cent bottle of cologne and spend five dollars in silk finery? And yet — the church would be crowded. She would have to mount a platform, where the president would sit in his gown and triangular hat, surrounded by rows of reverend professors. Could she disgrace womankind, the college, the Blackwells, by presenting herself in a shabby gown?

She bought the material and had the dress made, a rich black silk with a cape, trimmed with black silk fringe and with some narrow white lace around the neck and cuffs. A grievous expense, since she already had the audacity to be planning for further medical education in Europe, a project in which Kenyon had heartily encouraged her. She could go back with him when he sailed this spring. If she couldn't afford it, he would be willing to provide her with the money. Her instinctive reluctance to accept charity yielded to his assuring arguments that a family should be mutually helpful, that he was unmarried and had more income than he needed, and that he was heartily in support of the battle she was waging and wanted to have a part in it. With the coming of Kenyon, fortune's tide seemed to have turned for the Blackwells. It was as if Papa, with all his magic charm, had come to life, but with none of the old propensity to failure. Kenyon had succeeded in persuading Harry to at least postpone his flight to California. He was attempting to procure a thousand pounds from England so that Sam could buy a hardware business. He had sent Howie into a promising career, inspired Anna to embark on a new enterprise. And now — herself!

The sixteen-week term ended the middle of January. On the 19th came examinations. It was an experience which brought her even closer to her classmates. She was the first to enter the faculty room to present her certificates and submit to the momentous testing. Familiar though all the faces were, they seemed to have become strangers. She could not have been more nervous if it were the Last Judgment. Though the

examinations were not formidable, the anxiety and effort were as great
as if the fate of her whole career were at stake. When she came from the
room her face burned, her pulses pounded, yet so great was the relief
that her body felt light as air. To her surprise the other candidates waiting their turn broke into applause.

"You needn't tell us. They were easy! It's written all over you!"

"Easy for you, maybe. But how about us?"

"Lend me that pretty little head of yours, will you? I'm going to
need it!"

She was touched by their generosity and chivalry, which had obviously conquered any possible jealousy. They acted as proud of her as if
they were responsible for the whole achievement, as indeed they were.
There would be other examinations before the curators of the whole
institution, who would make the final decision about conferring the
degree, but the worst hurdle had been surmounted. She had reached
her goal, achieved the seemingly impossible. And to crown the triumph,
at least one Blackwell — Harry — was coming for her graduation.

At least, he hoped he was. On the morning of Thursday, January 18,
he began to wonder. Strolling down Duane Street toward the pier to
catch the eight o'clock boat, he stopped at Stewart's to buy a cravat and
a new pocket handkerchief, to add éclat to the great event. He arrived at
the pier at one minute before eight to find that the boat had left! Inquiring at the Housatonic Railroad office, he learned that the cars had
left at the same time. Nothing for it but to wait until Friday. The day
dawned clear but bitter cold. He was delayed again in going up to Pier-
mont by the ice. The subsequent trip by rail was a combination of
more delays, violent snortings and whistlings through the crooked course
of the Delaware valley, and magnificent scenery as they crept along the
spurs of the Alleghenies.

At daybreak Saturday morning he reached Binghamton, then crossed
country by sleigh, reaching Ithaca in the evening. There, no public conveyance being available, he chartered a sleigh in company with a farmer
who lived halfway up the east side of Cayuga Lake. After entertaining
him at his house overnight, the farmer drove Harry across the lake in his
cutter, then around the foot of Seneca Lake and hence to Geneva, arriving on Sunday in time to spend most of the afternoon with Elizabeth reading the Annual. His presence made her enjoyment of the occasion complete — or would as soon as the last dreaded examinations
by the curates were over.

They came on Monday morning. Harry went with her to the college, waiting by the stove in an upstairs room while Elizabeth and other members of the class went through the ordeal in a room below. Students kept drifting in and out. No one knew who he was, and he derived keen enjoyment from watching and listening. Occasionally he heard Elizabeth's name and pricked up his ears. His fears lest they resented her presence were soon dissipated. It was all he could do to keep from chuckling.

"Well, boys," one remarked, "our Elib feels first rate this morning. Notice how pleased she looks?"

"No wonder," responded another. "Wouldn't we all if we'd done as well as she did in the exams on Friday?"

"So Lizzie will get her diploma, after all," volunteered a third. "I wondered if the brass would really let her make it."

"They'd better! If any member of the class gets one, she certainly should!"

"Right!" "Amen to that!" all seemed to be agreed. "She's a great girl."

Here Harry could contain himself no longer. Somewhat smugly he introduced himself, was welcomed with alacrity, and later wrote home that he had found some very gentlemanly and intelligent men among his new acquaintances. That afternoon he was permitted to attend the session where members of the graduating class read from their theses. Not Elizabeth, however, for Dr. Austin Flint, one of the professors at Geneva and editor of the *Buffalo Medical Journal and Monthly Review*, had requested the honor of publishing it, and it had already gone to Buffalo, scheduled to appear in the February issue of the *Journal*.

Tuesday, January 23, 1849. Elizabeth wakened abruptly, eyes flying to the wide-open window, lungs expanding with the heady mixture of sun and ozone which already gave promise of almost spring warmth. The miracle which these northern New Yorkers called "January thaw" had come to pass. Bless her good luck! What a tragedy if she had had to trail that beautiful long silk brocade through the deep snows she had struggled with in December! It must serve as her best dress for years to come.

But perish practical thoughts! This was a day for living, feeling, to be imbibed slowly, every moment sipped and savored like a cup of nectar. For a time she lay very still, eyes closed, letting the symbolic warmth and brilliance seep into her being. Did a bride feel like this, she wondered, on her wedding day? Or a novice on the morning she was to take the veil? It was like standing on that high mountain on the way to Charleston. You had sweated and strained and climbed for what seemed an eternity. Then suddenly you were there. It was for this knife-edge of fulfillment that you had lived until this moment, perhaps that you had been born. But how stupid! As if this day were an end instead of a beginning!

She sprang up, closed the window, stuffed paper, kindling, and a few stout sticks into the little potbellied stove, bathed briskly before the room had even started to heat, went down to breakfast, smilingly but a bit coolly accepting the congratulations of the other boarders (hard to forget the cold shoulders which had preceded this "January thaw"!), shared the distress of the kind Wallers that she would soon be leaving.

Harry arrived, sartorially smart in new flowing cravat and plum-colored waistcoat, curling hair and beard combed and brushed to perfection. "You should see the crowds coming into town, coaches, phaetons, buggies, even oxcarts! Oh, and I met that fat little dumpling of a professor outside."

"Dr. Webster! He's my good angel."

"And does he know it! You'd think this was his triumph instead of yours. Says all this crowd is on account of you and that all the town is turning out to see a lady receive a medical diploma. Sure is in his glory!"

Elizabeth laughed. "He loves a fuss."

"Oh — and he sent you this note, said to be sure to deliver it pronto."

"You *must* march in the procession," the little doctor had written. "Meet us at the college at ten o'clock."

"No," decided Elizabeth, and sent back word that she would be at the church at the proper time, 10:30. Another still more urgent note from the doctor failed to change her mind.

She went back upstairs, brushed and braided her long fair hair, arranging the braids in their usual neat coils over her ears. (Was it her imagination, or had the pale wispy strings acquired a certain burnished smoothness with the years, almost a reddish glow?) She dressed carefully, reluctantly lacing the stays tighter in concession to the wasp-waisted mode, readjusted the heavy corset waist of cotton twill, donned the new fawn-colored, heavily padded and quilted woolen petticoat, and finally topped all with the new brocaded gown, complete with snowy lace collar and cuffs. The final concession to prevailing style was a pair of green silk gloves, so delicate in texture that they were almost invisible. Caped and bonneted, she was now ready for the short walk along Main Street which was to preface the making of history.

Harry was right. The streets swarmed with vehicles, the sidewalks with pedestrians. Elizabeth was puzzled by one thing. There seemed to be no women. Were they boycotting the occasion on her account? Well! She set her shoulders and lifted her small head a little higher. Let them! It was no new experience. In front of the college Dr. Webster swooped toward them, open academic gown flapping like restless wings.

"My dear Miss Blackwell — please — really you must march with us! It's *your* procession of triumph, you know."

"I'm sorry, Dr. Webster." Elizabeth was peremptory in her refusal. "I couldn't. It wouldn't be ladylike."

"It — it wouldn't?" He looked nonplussed. "Why — no, I forgot. I — I suppose it wouldn't." But obviously he was a little dazed. It was arranged that she and Harry would sit at the side of the left aisle and join the procession as it came in.

Graduation was to be held in the Presbyterian Church, a handsome building about to qualify for immortality. It stood about four hundred yards from the location of a future sign erected in 1932 by the state of New York, proclaiming: *Site of Geneva Medical College. Eliz. Blackwell received here in 1849 the first degree of M.D. ever conferred upon a woman.*

Entering the church on Harry's arm, Elizabeth felt instantly engulfed in a flood of female gowns and bonnets. No wonder she had seen no women on the streets! They were all here, crowding the seats even to the galleries, leaving barely enough pews for the graduating class! Evidently ladies had been admitted first, and they must have come from miles around. Inconspicuous though her entrance had been, it was greeted by a flurry of whispers, a rustle of silks and swiveling of bonnets. The old shyness overwhelmed her and she felt defenseless, with no protection for her quaking body and blushing cheeks. Then suddenly she straightened. Her head lifted. This was one of the reasons she was here, to show other women that they could be different. She should be glad they were curious. Harry felt the change in her, the tightening of her slender hand on his arm, and smiled. Even without looking at her, he knew it was one of those times when "our little Elib" seemed ten feet tall.

Once in the seat beside Harry, Elizabeth slipped off her surroundings as easily as her black cape. This was no time to give thought to strangers, only briefly to friends. It was a holy hour. The Presence which had filled her room with light that long-ago night in Asheville became the sole object of reflection and gratitude.

A burst of martial but somewhat rowdy music shattered her solemnity as the procession, led by a band of native Indians, approached the church. It regained proper academic dignity as it entered, President Hale and Bishop DeLancey in the lead, faculty and students following. George Field, a graduate student in her class and an assistant in anatomy, stopped by the pew where she sat and offered his arm. As she joined the class in its march down the aisle and took her seat in the row just behind the other graduates, she was quite oblivious to the swiveling bonnets and staring eyes.

After much confusion, during which the men, admitted at last, crowded every remaining space in aisles and rear, there was more music from a choir with an unpleasantly loud-voiced soprano sharing the spotlight of female notoriety, while Elizabeth suffered tortures. Paul certainly had a point, she thought wryly, ashamed for her sex, with his "Let your women keep silence in the churches." Feeling every eye upon her, she removed her bonnet and prepared for the big moment.

President Hale addressed the class briefly, then donned his velvet cap and seated himself in a large chair. The graduates came to the platform four at a time as their names were called. One of them grasped the bundle of sheepskins. Then all four bowed and retreated. Elizabeth was left until the last.

"Domina Blackwell."

As she ascended the steps the room was so quiet one could have heard a whisper. This time the president did not remain seated. He removed his cap and rose before presenting the diploma. There was a brief moment of utter silence. Perhaps he expected her to bow also and retreat. In fact, she started to do so, then on an impulse turned back.

"Sir," she said in a low but very clear voice, "I thank you. By the help of God it shall be the effort of my life to shed honor upon your diploma."

They both bowed. There was applause from the congregation, initiated and heartily encouraged by the students, but Elizabeth scarcely heard it. She was as remotely exalted as the participant in a holy sacrament. It had been not only a graduation but an ordination for high calling as sacred as the ministry. But as she came down and George Field stood and opened the door of the front row, welcoming her to the ranks of her fellow-graduates, she accepted the invitation gratefully and felt thoroughly at home in their midst. Still she heard little of Dr. Lee's valedictory address which followed. She was too absorbed in heavenly communion.

The presence of so many ladies afforded the dean too good an opportunity to miss. He upbraided them heartily for their encouragement and circulation of quack medicines and strongly denounced many of the current "isms" with their exponents. It would do them no harm, he asserted, to study a little medicine themselves before attempting to practice in a field where they were so profoundly ignorant.

Elizabeth came sharply to attention. Dr. Lee was talking about her. The matriculation of the first woman, he said, had been a most gratifying experiment. She had been the leader of her class. She had passed through a thorough course in every department, slighting none. She had profited to the utmost by all the advantages of the institution, and by her ladylike and dignified deportment had proven that the strongest intellect and nerve and the most untiring perseverance were compatible with the softest attributes of feminine grace. To all these encomiums the students gave hearty concurrence by their applause.

To her astonishment, doubtless even more to that of the conservative spectators, after the ceremonies the faculty of arts, the medical professors, and Bishop DeLancey stopped on their way out to congratulate her. The bishop was not the only church dignitary who would look back with satisfaction on the part he played in the event. Fifty years later William Paret, a bishop of Maryland, was to celebrate the anniversary of her graduation by writing a letter to the president of the college.

"When Miss Blackwell was about to receive her diploma I was a student at the college. The engraved diplomas had not been prepared in the anticipation of women graduates, and the Latin terms were all made in the masculine gender. The authorities of the Medical Department applied to President Hale, and asked whether there were not some student who wrote a very good hand, and was a good Latin scholar, who could draw up on parchment a diploma suited for that particular case. Dr.

Hale recommended me, and the diploma which was given to Miss Blackwell was the one which I so prepared."

Elizabeth put on her bonnet and tied the strings. Harry held her cape, smiling.

"Permit me, *Doctor* Blackwell."

One hand tucked through his arm, the other clutching the precious parchment tied with its blue ribbon and inscribed in beautiful calligraphy with "*domina*" instead of "*domine*," she swept down the aisle and out of the church. Almost all the ladies had stopped outside. Now they opened their ranks and let her pass through. Many of the faces she recognized. She had seen them in church turning away or on the streets coldly staring. She did not return their smiles and nods, merely passed through their midst as if they had not existed. Not that she intended to be catty or spiteful. It was merely that their approval and friendship no longer mattered.

6

"It is to be regretted," noted the *Boston Medical and Surgical Journal,* expressing the prevailing opinion of the profession, "that Miss Blackwell has been induced to depart from the appropriate sphere of her sex and led to aspire to honors and duties which, by the order of nature and the common consent of the world, devolve upon men."

The public press seized on the juicy bit of news, and for a brief time this unprecedented act of female pioneering shared headlines with the male stampede toward California gold fields. Reaction ran the gamut of wonder, incredulity, amusement, ridicule, dismay, outrage, approval. The latter was confined largely to such liberal organs as Garrison's *Liberator* and Horace Greeley's *New York Tribune,* which were already linking the slowly emerging women's rights movement with the hotly explosive abolitionism.

The English press also took note of the event, the *Medical Times* duly observing that a young lady, Miss Elizabeth Blackwell, had been admitted by the General Medical College in the state of New York to a physician's degree, receiving a formal diploma under the title of "Domina," the only feminine appellate which the Senate could find for "Doctor." *Punch* characteristically treated the matter in a lighter vein, gently poking fun in a poem of seven rollicking stanzas which included:

Young ladies all, of every clime,
Especially of Britain,
Who wholly occupy your time
In novels or in knitting,
Whose highest skill is but to play,
Sing, dance, or French to clack well,
Reflect on the example, pray,
Of excellent Miss Blackwell!

How much more blest were married life
To men of small condition,
If every man could have his wife
For family physician;
His nursery kept from ailments free
By proper regulation,
And for advice his only fee
A thankful salutation!

For Doctrix Blackwell — that's the way
To dub in rightful gender —
In her profession, ever may
Prosperity attend her!
Punch a gold-handled parasol
Suggests for presentation
To one so well deserving all
Esteem and admiration.

Even medical reaction in America was not all adverse. A group of doctors of the eclectic school in Rochester and another in Syracuse cooperated to organize the Central Medical College of New York, the first chartered medical school in the world to adopt coeducation as a policy. One of its first graduates was Lydia Folger Fowler, the first American-born woman to receive a medical degree.

Elizabeth's satisfaction over her triumph lasted no more than a day. Her classmates might consider themselves fit to practice medicine after three years of instruction under a legally qualified physician and two sixteen-week terms of academic study, but she did not. She had never performed an operation or personally delivered a baby. Except for the weeks at Blockley her knowledge was all theory, and that all too scant.

She returned to New York with Harry, then went on to Philadelphia. While waiting impatiently for Kenyon's plans to develop, she would stay with the Elders and continue her study wherever opportunities might open in this center of medical education. She was received politely, if without enthusiasm, by the heads of the profession as a professional — what? Not "brother." The word "sister" would probably have choked them. At least they welcomed her grudgingly as an "associate."

She spent some time dissecting with George Field, who was working for a few weeks in the city; listened to lectures at the university by such eminent doctors as Jackson, Hodge, Gibson, Chapman, and Horner. Dr. Lee, who introduced her to the university officials, was both relieved and exhilarated by her apparently cordial reception. She visited the Pennsylvania Hospital, where Dr. Levick gave her a conducted tour, heard Professor Agassiz commence a course of lectures on the animal world. In preparation for the coming trip, she brushed up on her French, since all her medical friends advised Paris as the place offering unlimited opportunities.

There was reluctance as well as impatience in all her preparations, for they wore the solemn aspect of finality. For all these years her native England had been drawing her with magnetic nostalgia. She might never return to America except as a visitor. Nevertheless, she deemed it advisable to acquire American citizenship before leaving, since her degree qualified her for professional practice only in the United States, so she made application for naturalization papers. Now for the first time she discovered an equally strong loyalty to her adopted country. The prospect of impending separation also sensitized the bonds binding her to family. With more sympathy than she had ever shown she tried to allay her mother's constant fears for the state of her soul.

"You urge upon me the importance of religion," she wrote Hannah in February. "Why, bless the dear mother, what am I doing but living religion all the time? Isn't it my meat and drink to do the good will of God? Didn't I used to sit in the lecture room and send up a whole cannonade of little prayers? And didn't a whole flood of answers come straight down from the throne of grace? And what am I doing now? Do you think I care about medicine? Nay, verily, it's just to kill the devil, whom I hate so heartily — that's a fact, mother. And if that isn't forming Christ in one, the hope of Glory, why, I don't know what it is. I live in a good society, the fellowship of hard workers, for however little the result of my actions may be, I have the strengthening conviction that my aim is right, and that I too am working after my little fashion for the redemption of mankind."

She gave further assurance to the worried Hannah by declaring herself whole-souledly for the divine institution of marriage, promising to support it by precept and by example as soon as she got the chance; by qualifying associationists as too often a poor set of people who should commence reforming society by reforming themselves, and by labeling the agnostic features of the French philosophy which Anna was pursuing as "twaddle."

She went home the last week in March after nearly five years' absence, and for nine days tried to forget that she had any other identity than plain Elizabeth Blackwell, third in a family of nine. She admired the tiny house with its pleasant front parlor, its little lawn with two trees, its recent improvements of porch and shutters, paint, paper, and chimneypots. She was lucky to see it, for already it was up for sale, and the family would soon be moving back to rented quarters.

She marveled over George and Ellen, grown beyond recognition, and was amazed by the talent Ellen was revealing as an artist. She rejoiced with Sam over his purchase with two other partners of Christian Donaldson's wholesale hardware business and was as relieved as all the rest that Harry had agreed to return home and become a member of the new firm of Coombs, Ryland, and Blackwell; though she shared Harry's skepticism over the firm's ability to support four partners and lent a sympathetic ear to his worried grumblings.

"A pretty kettle of fish, borrowing a thousand pounds from Kenyon at six percent and sinking it in an old stock of hardware invoiced way above its real value, and paying a ten percent bonus for the goodwill of a concern which hasn't a decent customer!"

Elizabeth delighted anew in Marian's delicate beauty, agonized over her ill health, encouraged her longing for creative achievement. She listened with tender good humor to Hannah's sermons, relieved that the piety which produced such solemn preaching was still paired with a girlish sprightliness which kept her dancing about the tiny living room with as lively gaiety as eighteen-year-old Ellen.

To her surprise she found that it was Emily now, not Marian, with whom she felt the strongest kinship. The five years between them had been dissolved by Emily's consuming desire to become a doctor. Now she fired questions, demanded details, and in their long walks together Elizabeth gave them to her, sparing nothing of the difficulties, the loneliness, the ostracism, and watching her closely for the least sign of weakness. There was none. The wide grave eyes remained unwavering. Emily was earning a mere pittance at teaching. Her pitiful attempts to learn were confined to a few books and fumbling experiments with a handful of charts and chemicals in her garret. Elizabeth encouraged her, gave her more books, suggested that for the present she study German instead of anatomy, promised that someday they might share a practice together.

Of course in spite of all her attempts she could not be just plain Elizabeth Blackwell. Never again. Even her family regarded her with a bit of awe, the boys with increased respect, the girls with ill-concealed envy. And in Cincinnati she was a celebrity. As in Geneva, people turned to look after her in the street, children pointed and whispered. And her friends admired, congratulated, clucked with bewilderment, or — yes — confided to her their various symptoms and ailments and waited hopefully for free advice. She was invited to address the Semi-Colon Club. Of course she visited the Beechers and the Stowes, finding Harriet struggling to create amid a bustling untidiness of manuscripts and children, the current brainchild as usual sharing the growth pains of infancy with the latest baby. Harriet was extravagant in her praise. Having obviously forgotten her discouragement of the venture, she "had always been sure that Elizabeth could realize her ambitions." As for her own achievements, she was far from satisfied. She wished she could write something really worthwhile, perhaps something on slavery. Merely sewing clothes for the underground was a poor substitute for direct action. The dark eyes flashed restlessly between the bobbing curls. Men were able to do such big things. But she shouldn't complain, of course. After all, what more could a woman ask than to be the mother of six fine children and wife of a man like her dear brilliant Calvin?

Elizabeth smiled to herself, remembering the bit of gossip she had just heard. During the recent cholera scare Calvin Stowe, brilliant indeed but inept in household matters, had been away on a trip. Harriet, it was reported, had insisted that he stay away, realizing that the only thing he could possibly do for her was to give her another child to look after!

In spite of their joys, for Elizabeth the ten days were too long. "You can't conceive how intensely I long to be at work," she confided to Sam on one of their long walks together.

She left with Kenyon by boat at noon on Saturday, April 2. The whole family came down to see them off on the steamer for Pittsburgh. As the boat sailed they stood waving, wiping their eyes, Hannah leaning on Sam, the three girls on one side of them, Harry and George on the other. Elizabeth watched them through a blur of tears until the curve of the river hid them. But already her sights were set far beyond Pittsburgh, even beyond Philadelphia, where she spent another few days with the Elders. On April 13 her paper of naturalization was granted at a District Court "holden in Philadelphia, made competent proof by the competent testimony of Sara Elder." She became the second woman to obtain American citizenship through naturalization.

She rejoined Kenyon in Boston, where she had a few richly rewarding hours of talk with her old friend William Channing. She sailed at noon on Wednesday, April 18. Standing with Kenyon on deck, with mingled sorrow and hope she saw beautiful Boston Bay vanish in the distance. Then gradually the water which looked so clear and fresh assumed a gloomy, repulsive look. The people chatting so merrily seemed to grow moody or wildly talkative. The gentle motion of the boat became a powerful upheaving of brain and stomach. The half-remembered nightmare of the long voyage seventeen years ago became horrible reality.

"I — I have no expectation of being seasick," she told Kenyon in an unnecessarily loud voice.

At four the bell rang for dinner, its prolonged loudness jarring every nerve in her body. She walked bravely into the dining room, a long low saloon on deck, with six big tables crowded with people, and was met by an intolerable glare of red, compounded of colored glasses, mirrors, and dazzling plate, people treading on each other, waiters dashing about, loud voices, faces looking either very pale or bright crimson, odors of burned meat, onions, cheese, everything she particularly disliked. A herd of pigs, she thought, come to be fed. Leaning back on her sofa, she waited in philosophical indifference until a plate was set before her. She took one mouthful, made a desperate effort to swallow, rose quickly, and rushed from the room.

For six days and nights she lay in her berth in a small stifling cabin, lighted by a single bull's-eye, with just room for one person to turn in. But she shared both it and her misery with a gentle elderly lady, Mrs. Harper, from Virginia. At first Kenyon paid her frequent visits, advising various remedies, but presently he took cold, and as her health improved, his worsened. His joints swelled and he became crippled with rheumatism. After a week it was Elizabeth, too sick to study but well enough to be up and about, who visited him in his stateroom. Watching him each day grow stiffer and weaker, hunched with cold, finding talk ever more wearying, she wished desperately for the voyage to be over, for his sake now more than for her own.

The end came at last after eleven days, the sight of Cape Clear, then the thirty-mile estuary of the Mersey with its high green banks, then the stone docks and terraces of Liverpool. Kenyon was helped, groaning, on board the tender, and with three cheers they pushed off from the giant steamer. Leaving him in a hotel comfortably ensconced with a cup of chocolate, Elizabeth took full advantage of the half-hour before their train left, exulting in renewing acquaintance with the Old World.

"How finished everything looks!" she marveled. The brick walls so high and thick, the iron railings so solid, all the buildings, even the little shops, sitting with an obvious determination to stand there forever! But she wished she could expose the people to a bright American sun and dry them out!

The railroad journey to Birmingham seemed to her beautiful, though Kenyon declared it the most uninteresting country in England. Again she exclaimed over the finished look of everything. Even the sloping banks by the railroad were covered by soft green turf, smooth as a lawn, filled with rich tufts of primroses. Every little town seemed to be set down in the country, the green fields ending where the streets began. But when they took a chaise at Birmingham for the last eight miles, they entered the mining country, with blast furnaces in all directions, great brick towers, coalpits, smoke-blackened villages of workmen's houses full of shabby women and dirty children. Her spirits sank. No wonder it was called the Black Country! She was as silent with dismay as was Kenyon with weariness.

Then they came in sight of an old ivy-covered stone wall and, beyond, a big stone house half hidden among trees. Kenyon stopped the chaise and insisted on negotiating his slow painful descent before reaching the gate. Together they approached a green gothic door in the high stone wall, and a servant came running to open it. Elizabeth gazed in delight at sloping green fields, trees in spring leaf, a little fishpond, bright neat flowerbeds. This was the England she remembered. She knew then that she had come home.

Chapter Seven

THAT YEAR OF 1849 was one of revolution in Europe. For months the infection of democratic reform had spread from country to country. Proclamation of the Second French Republic had sparked widespread popular uprisings. The emperor of Austria was forced to abdicate. Metternich the supreme autocrat was sent into exile. The German states began clamoring for representative government. The Italian city states instigated their long struggle for freedom. Even Victoria in England had some cause for anxiety, for there were serious riots in Glasgow, and a huge crowd of Chartists demonstrated on Kennington Common. Yet when Elizabeth arrived in the spring of 1849 the high tide of republican reform so hard-won in the first burst of revolutionary zeal was already ebbing. Absolutism was restored in Italy. The new Hungarian Republic was approaching its tragic end. Dreams of a united republican Germany had been shattered. Autocracy was again in the saddle.

Amid all this vast struggle of the common man to obtain his God-given rights one tiny triumph had gone almost unnoticed, and except for a few outraged British males who feared such a precedent might put dangerous ideas in the heads of their own wives and daughters, had been deemed of no importance. Yet it struck as deadly a blow to the domestic tyrant as did the February insurrection to the crowned head of France. A small act it seemed. Even Elizabeth, had she known of it, could not have guessed what importance it would have to herself — the fact that on April 8, 1848, a man named Benjamin Smith bestowed on his daughter Barbara, just turned twenty-one, an income of some three hundred pounds a year. Representing the interest on eight thousand pounds, every three months a certain amount became her sole and personal property, to spend exactly as she chose. That her father retained control of the capital sum by no means detracted from the monstrous uniqueness of his action. Barbara Smith, with an income of her own, subject to no parental or husbandly dictation, became one British woman in a thousand. It would still be over thirty years before the Married Women's Property Act of 1882 would give a married woman the right to own property.

Portway, Uncle Blackwell's country estate, was untouched by either revolution or change. Its brown plaster exterior, battlemented roof, stone-paved hall and staircase winding up to a little stone gallery from which half a dozen pleasant bedrooms opened, were as eloquent with age as the date 1674 on the tablet set in the central tower. Except for its unaccustomed luxury, it was the world Elizabeth remembered from her childhood. Even Uncle Blackwell, short, stout, hale, with his white hair and rosy face, had changed little in the seventeen years.

It was good to see Anna again. Their common horror of the ocean crossing united them in a sympathy they had not felt for years.

"What a grand voyage you must have had!" Elizabeth was greeted on every hand. "Only eleven days and a half, no rough weather, no accident or unpleasant occurrence! Traveling is a mere joke nowadays." Elizabeth could only grit her teeth, share a nauseated glance with her sister, and smile.

Anna was as enthusiastic, scintillating, generous but sharp-edged as ever. Elizabeth thought her health had improved until she saw her standing one morning for ten minutes rubbing a magnetized dollar over the back of her neck to cure nervousness and imbibing a tablespoon of magnetized water to strengthen her heart. But the leisurely life seemed to agree with Anna — breakfast in her room, music, reading, strolling in the garden, in spite of the damp, smoke-riddled air which seemed to clog the nostrils. Even on the few fine days the sun had a pale look, as if shining through an eclipse. But for all drawbacks there were compensations.

"I heard the cuckoo," Elizabeth wrote home one day in May. "What a soft human sound it is! Last night the nightingales were singing sweetly in the twilight. Our garden is full of lovely English flowers, primrose and cowslips, lauristina, and many others, though the weather is a most cold gloomy nurse to the little darlings."

It was good to see Howie, too, dignified in his business black, prosperous and happy in his work at Cousin Sam's ironworks. One day

Elizabeth visited him in his lodgings for tea, admired his pleasant little parlor, encouraged his study of German, marveled at his cleverness in constructing a little furnace for analysis.

But Kenyon's sickness cast a pall over the household even gloomier than the smoke. He required constant nursing. Anna and Elizabeth functioned during the day, Uncle Blackwell, Sam, and a friend, Charles Plevins, at night. The multiple drugs and absurd directions supplied by the doctor who came each day from Dudley only made the patient worse. Boldly Elizabeth threw the medicines away, substituting bread pills and flavored water, and trusting to judicious diet, cleanliness, and patient nursing. Kenyon improved. But Uncle Blackwell discovered the plot. The old weakening treatment had to be resumed.

With Kenyon sick, Elizabeth had to change her plans, for he had promised to take her to London. Now she must go alone. Meanwhile she made every moment of leisure count. She wanted to see everything, make up for the seventeen absent years. One day Cousin Sam took her to his Russel Hall Works close to Dudley, and she saw the casting. Twice a day the melted iron was drawn off from the bottom of the great brick towers they called furnaces. Strong men with faces black as coal, armed with iron poles, guided the sea of fire that rushed out into the molds, drawing out the white-hot masses of cinders and dirt, splashing cold water over the front of the furnace so they could stand there. The heat was so great that she and Sam had to cover their faces. Suddenly the flames burst out from the furnaces and immense volumes of black smoke rolled over their heads. The rushing noise was like thunder. She thought an accident had occurred and looked for a safe retreat, but found it was only the clearing of the furnaces after a casting.

"Within a square of twelve miles," said Sam, "one sixth of all the iron used in the world is made."

Elizabeth was less interested in the casting than in the people involved, including Sam. Though he had the good looks of the Blackwell males, fair complexion, blue eyes, a mass of curling light hair with a slightly darker beard, he was thin, pale, nervous, a victim of indigestion and fits of exhaustion which he tried to negate by working even harder. He could scarcely speak of his dead wife Harriet without tears. Was there a fate inherent in the Blackwells which made them the victims of prosperity as well as failure? Sam was a sensitive idealist like the rest of them. Could he be as guilt-ridden by these sweating blackened bodies necessary to his flourishing business as Papa had been by the black slaves of Jamaica?

But to her relief she did not see as much misery in Dudley as she had expected. She studied the people with far more interest than the ruins of old Dudley Castle, in which she explored every corner, looking up the broad chimneys, peeping through the stone window frames and loopholes and trying to imagine armed men bustling about the court, fair ladies in the upper windows and on the ruined terraces. In Dudley, as in Liverpool, she peered into all the back alleys and odd corners she could find. The towns seemed cleaner than those in America, and certainly there was no more squalor. But, remembering the back country of Kentucky and the Carolinas, she found little satisfaction in the comparison.

Sam was a reformer in spirit, as was his young friend Charles Plevins, but she found their thought fumbling and immature. They had no program of reform. They admired Fichte, Carlyle, Emerson, Channing, all the heroes of her own early days. But how she wished she could inspire them to study Fourier and Swedenborg and others who could help them reach that clear insight which could make their work strong, happy, and practically efficient! For in spite of her assurances to Hannah concerning Fourier's unconventional theories on marriage, she was still an ardent disciple of his associationism.

To her delight Charles, who had admired her medical effort even before she arrived, offered to introduce her to some physicians in Birmingham, where his family was old and highly respected. When Dr. Parker, surgeon to the Queen's Hospital, discovered that she was not the mythical being he had suspected but really a living woman, he invited her to witness an amputation he was performing. She accepted with anticipation. Approaching the building, she saw the windows crowded with peeping students.

"All on the *qui vive* to see the freak of a lady doctor!" she told Charles wryly.

Mr. Parker (surgeons were called "Mr." in England instead of "Dr.") received her politely, his round, rosy John Bull face registering the usual surprise that she was not a gruff-voiced Amazon. After showing her the hospital, which was young and not particularly interesting, he led her to the operating room. It was crammed with students, and as more arrived they would peep about, whisper to their neighbors, and work their way to a place where they could see her better. But, as usual, excitement soon died down. There was nothing unusual in the operation. Mr. Parker performed it skillfully, without chloroform, which he disliked. When the screams started, Elizabeth sensed that the students were covertly, probably hopefully, watching to see her blench, but she kept a stolid face, eyeing the whole proceeding with the keenest interest. Of even more value than the experience was the letter of introduction which Mr. Parker gave her to the famous Roux of Paris.

She visited other hospitals in Birmingham, met other doctors.

"Though I must say frankly," admitted Dr. McKay of the Lying-in Hospital, "that I believe God and Nature have indicated the unfitness of women for such a pursuit as you have chosen, I shall be happy to show you everything within my power."

Dr. Percy, a friend of Sam's, promised to meet her in London and furnish her introductions which would gain her an entrée to the medical world of the metropolis.

London! Though she tried to hide her eagerness to be off and about her work, it must have betrayed itself in the brightening of her eyes, the quickening of her step.

"I believe you're anxious to get away from us," accused Kenyon, still confined to his bed.

"Of course not." She hastened contritely to reassure him. "This has come to seem really like home. I shall be very sorry to leave."

She meant it. It was with genuine sadness that she left Portway on May 16, but, fortunately, not alone. Charles Plevins was spending a few days in London and offered to be her escort. It was a great relief, for the idea of wandering about the vast city an entire stranger had brought desolate thoughts. Now again she was all anticipation.

Charles had an aunt in London, a Mrs. Wilson, and the morning after their arrival, a Sunday, they walked five miles through the city before reaching her home in Devonshire Street. Elizabeth gazed her fill at monuments and public buildings, row after row of pillared edifices, whole streets of palaces, splendid but dingy with age and the all-penetrating smoke. They slipped into Westminster Abbey, where the cathedral service was being chanted, saw the new houses of Parliament from Westminster Bridge. Walking through Regent Street past endless rows of handsome houses in the West End, they came finally to Mrs. Wilson's and were shown in by a footman in crimson plush breeches, white stockings, and claret colored coat with gold buttons.

The walls of the drawing room were lined with figured crimson velvet and the room cluttered with all manner of lounges, tables, and knick-knackery. Their hostess, a handsome brunette with red cheeks and very black hair and eyes, was equally bedizened in blue and black satin with jet ornaments and a lace headdress.

"She doesn't approve of me," thought Elizabeth, sitting very straight and talking quietly. "If I had to live here a week, I would overturn her and her house and smash everything to atoms!"

The morning wore on. Fashionable guests dropped in. A formal lunch was served, all the ladies still wearing their bonnets. Afterward their hostess took them to ride in her barouche through Regent's and Hyde parks and became more agreeable, laughing and chatting merrily about a vast variety of nothings. She set them down at the Zoological Gardens, regretting that she could not invite Elizabeth home because of a dinner engagement and hoping that they might someday have a long, long talk.

"Thank heaven!" exclaimed Charles, venting his frustration by taking a hard run through the Gardens. "That's over at last!"

Other personal contacts she made in London were far more agreeable. She was surprised and delighted by the cordial reception she received from dignitaries in the medical world, though her status was obviously a moot question.

"Should I call you — Doctor?" she was asked over and over.

"Yes," she replied firmly, feeling proper recognition a matter of principle.

There was Dr. Carpenter, who had written admirable works on physiology. She was invited to a pharmaceutical soirée at his house in Regent's Park, an affair as elegant as a ball, with distinguished artists and musicians participating as well as doctors. All were cordial though some seemed undecided what tone to take with such a maverick. Elizabeth was intrigued by the doctor's microscopes, said to be the most beautiful in England, and with his exquisite specimens, including the lung of a frog most minutely injected and a piece of sharkskin seemingly covered with innumerable teeth. But she was amazed that the papier-mâché models in common use in all American colleges were previously unknown here and were being regarded with the utmost rapture.

True to his promise, Dr. Percy arranged many introductions. In company with Mr. Owen, one of its lecturers, she visited the Hunterian

Museum, said to contain the finest collection of comparative and morbid anatomy in the world. An hour passed like a minute while she listened to this man of genius.

Her first visit to a hospital, St. Thomas's, however, was less pleasant. The surgeon to whom she sent her letter of introduction had never heard of her, thought the whole matter indelicate, and merely sent her a brief memorandum to give to one of the nurses, requesting that she not enter any of the men's wards. At first she thought she would not go at all, but, swallowing the indignity, she went, feeling most uncomfortable. However, to her surprise she was met by Mr. South, the senior surgeon, who was most friendly and showed her the whole enormous establishment even to the brewhouse! He invited her to attend his clinical lecture. So at the head of a large body of students, who had been peeping at her from every direction, she passed with him through ward after ward, men's and women's. Though the students preserved perfect order, she could see they were consumed with curiosity. He gave her the fullest description of interesting cases and asked her to examine several. Then, leaving his students to the house surgeon, he conducted her on a tour of the Barclay Brewery, a national curiosity. There, like all visitors, she was asked to sign her name.

"But — you didn't add the M.D.!" protested Mr. South. "Really, you must do so." She had entered the hospital feeling like a meddling intruder. She left it feeling like a royal visitor.

Her five days in London were so full of engagements she had not a moment to think. She must have walked ten miles a day. Sometimes she came home hardly able to move a foot. Then she would wash and dress and in an hour be up again and fresh for new adventure. Once such excitement would have bothered her intensely. Now she discovered reserves of physical strength and social graces she had not dreamed she possessed. She visited Greenwich, sailed up the river to Waterloo Bridge, passing the Tower and St. Paul's. She made a swift tour of the British Museum. Visiting the home of Dr. Wilkinson in Hampstead, she fell in love with the place, its common covered with golden gorse, its little dells, pretty cottages, and old mansions, its hedges of hawthorn and laurel.

"You should spend at least a year in London," the doctor told her regretfully. "Here every idea is represented not by a single individual but by a whole class. The societies you could study would be of inestimable worth in your development."

She was strongly tempted. But she wanted to become a surgeon, and all her American friends had told her that Paris was the place to study. When her passport and other papers arrived by the *Europa* on May 18, all doubts were banished. She sailed for France on the twentieth, parting with her friend Charles on board the boat in a heavy rainstorm. "How can I ever thank you?" But he would take no thanks either for the pleasure his companionship had given her or for his services. He had done nothing.

It rained the whole day's trip across the channel, so, even without the internal qualms which drove her for most of the journey to her berth, she could have seen little, including the White Cliffs of Dover. But she made the acquaintance of an English lady who had lived some time in France and insisted that she join her party. She promised to show Elizabeth the best place to stay in Calais and, if she would travel with her in the cars, give her much information about Paris.

"The French, my dear," she explained, "make a point of cheating the English unmercifully, since they think we are immensely wealthy."

Elizabeth was grateful for companions. Approach to Calais at eight-thirty that evening was heralded by a strong smell of fish. It was dark and raining torrents. They picked their way as well as they could over the stone pier, enclosed by walls on which a lighthouse glared into the dark night. Stepping into the rooms where passports were examined, she knew by the whiskered faces that she was among strangers. The "*Où allez-vous, madame?*" confirmed the fact. With her new friends she spent the night in the miserable little town, returning to the pier the next morning to go through customs. By daylight the people looked even stranger: women in their white caps (for here the common people wore no bonnets); workmen in blue blouses; fishwomen returning from fishing laden with nets, their short muscular bodies clad in a single petticoat scarcely reaching their knees; children with books visiting fishing smacks on their way to school and chattering French with bewildering fluency.

The customs officer was surprisingly lenient. He did not even notice her medical cases, which she had put at the back of a trunk. On the journey by train from Calais to Paris she was all eyes, constantly comparing the country with both England and America. No flatter than between Liverpool and Birmingham, but badly drained and cultivated, with many peat bogs and dwarf willows along the waterways. Scores of villages of light-colored stone, but not one thriving town.

Wooden fences instead of beautiful live hedges. Women digging trenches and working in the peat bogs. The railroad as crude and unfinished as those in America but without the excuse of an immense young country. In fact, she was continually reminded of the slovenly and hasty way in which things were done in America, instead of the substantial neat and finished style of England. But as they approached the city, even the clattering wheels seemed to quicken their pace, assume a heightened rhythm. The horizon lifted to include massed buildings, towers, arches, bridges, and her spirits rose to meet them.

Again customs! This time she felt more uneasiness, for there was political tension in the air. There was a military briskness about these officers, reminding that the Revolution of 1848, resulting in the Second French Republic, was still a live and bloody memory. Though the popular hero and new president, Louis Napoleon Bonaparte, was firmly entrenched in power, the two factions of the working class and the bourgeoisie were still unreconciled, and under the quiet surface hostilities still smoldered. Suppose they discovered the letter she carried in her portmanteau from the associationists in Philadelphia to the poet and republican leader Lamartine! Would they interpret her visit as political and hence suspect? But it was butter and cheese customs were looking for, it developed, not political documents!

She bade goodbye to her friends here at customs, and hiring a carriage, set off for the hotel they recommended. In spite of her years of study and of teaching French, she had difficulty making the driver understand her, and even more in understanding him. She felt like a small riverboat boldly launching into an unknown sea.

2

Paris! The mere name was enough to brighten the eyes and set the pulses racing. World capital of art, of fashion, of music, of romance, of philosophy, as well as of medicine! Yes, and at the moment center not only of political unrest but of disease as rampant as the hosts of rats infesting its miles of reeking sewers. For the mighty fortifications of the Enceinte, less than ten years old, with their twenty-one miles of length and ramparts thirty-two feet high, were powerless against the onslaught of cholera. When Elizabeth arrived in that spring of 1849 the plague was raging, its death toll already at more than fifteen thousand. But had she known the extent of the scourge, she would have come just the same. Cholera was the least of her personal worries. After paying twice as much for a hotel room as she could afford, her prime concern was to find a reasonably priced lodging. On the first morning she boarded an omnibus, map in hand, and set off to find the house of a Mr. Doherty, to whom Dr. Wilkinson had given her a letter of introduction.

She must have been early by Paris standards, for the gentleman was not yet up when her letter was delivered. Presently he emerged blinking sleepily above a horrid coarse beard, wrapped in a blue and red woolen dressing gown, green baize trousers hanging about his ankles. After clarifying the letter he became cordial enough, dressed, breakfasted, and took her out to find a lodging. She was soon installed in a house where he had once boarded on the West Bank, Number 11 St. Germaine, Rue de Seine, with a month's rent paid on a small room with bedroom attached. There were no students — *étudiantes* — boarding in the house, the pleasant friendly hostess assured her.

Elizabeth did not realize the importance of this detail until she was visited by a public official, bringing a registration paper to be filled out. She put her name down, followed by "*étudiante.*" The man stared, then made the most extraordinary grimaces, opening his eyes so wide that the whites showed around them.

"You ugly little brute," thought Elizabeth in amazement, "what on earth are you doing that for?"

Recognizing her astonishment, his manner changed. He tapped her kindly on the shoulder. "*Mon enfant,*" he said, "you must not put yourself down as student. *Rentière* is the word you must use."

Not until long afterward, when she learned something of the corrupt system used in regulating female vice, did she realize that she had been interviewed by the Police des Moeurs!

Her hostess was more than kind landlady. She soon became guide to the city, mentor in language and customs. Elizabeth welcomed her company in walks about the city, chiefly for the sake of chattering with her and accustoming her ears to the strange sounds, practicing her own sadly imperfect French. She had trouble expressing herself with any elegance, yet knew that she could approach no physicians until she had acquired a tolerable command of words.

She was disappointed in Paris. It seemed to consist mostly of narrow business streets with such tall houses that only a modicum of daylight could penetrate. She found nothing handsome, elegant, or gay like London. Yet when she went out to buy a new bonnet, she was astonished at the huge variety of shops, not only streets of them but covered walks, galleries, passages, arcades, all overflowing with beautiful goods. Not a single bonnet to fit her, however! She was unable to squeeze her by no means oversize head into one of them. Fortunately she found a good milliner who agreed to make one of plain gray silk, but unwillingly, for she made effusive reiteration that nobody, just nobody, ever wore that color!

It was a week before Elizabeth felt confident enough of her French to make an appointment with the great Lamartine. Dressing with great care, she arrived at the appointed hour and was ushered through several antechambers into a drawing room, where the poet was entertaining some visitors. Bowing, he requested her to wait a few moments and withdrew with his visitors into another room. While waiting, she looked eagerly about, admiring the rich carpet, the purple velvet couches and chairs, the portraits, the golden chandelier, all suffused by a soft green light from the trees in the large garden beyond an outside balcony. Then Alphonse Lamartine returned. Tall and slender, with gray eyes and hair, he was as graceful as his poetry. Every motion was like music. To her relief he understood English.

"Does the resolution you bring from America refer to the fraternity of the race?" he inquired in his clear, melodious voice.

Replying in the affirmative, Elizabeth presented him with the letters. He seemed grateful, promised to read the material carefully and send her an answer for her friends in America.

But her introduction to the medical profession was less propitious. A Boston doctor had given her a sealed letter of introduction to the great Pierre-Charles-Alexandre Louis, whose insistence on medical, as opposed to vital, statistics had exerted a powerful influence on medicine not only in Europe but in the United States. Oliver Wendell Holmes had been one of his pupils at the University of Paris. Louis's studies in tuberculosis of the lungs based on painstaking research had introduced a new scientific approach, and his work on typhoid fever had given the disease its name. Elizabeth was much impressed with his conclusion that bloodletting was of little value, especially in pneumonia, a revolutionary idea for France, which in the year 1833 alone had imported 41,500,000 leeches! She forwarded the letter to Louis with her card, and waited in an agony of expectation.

The next day a tall, imposing gentleman called on her. It was the great Louis himself! Elizabeth had the uncomfortable feeling that he had come to inspect her. But she rose to the challenge with dignity, telling him of her earnest desire to obtain hospital instruction and experience in both medical treatment and surgery.

"Miss Blackwell," he said finally after they had conversed for some time, "I would advise you to enter La Maternité. There you may in a short time obtain more valuable practical knowledge in one most important branch than could be obtained anywhere else." Then he informed her of the steps necessary to gain admission.

Elizabeth felt as if he had dashed cold water in her face. He thought of her not as a reputable doctor but as a midwife! Her hopes sank like lead. When Louis left, he handed to her the letter of introduction which she had sent him, sealed. There was a hint of ironic amusement in his eyes. "I think you ought to see it." She read with mounting horror. Not only was it written in the most atrocious French, but its idiom was unwittingly couched in phrases which in French conveyed just the opposite meaning from their intention. Its author, a distinguished Boston doctor, would have been infinitely shocked if he had been aware of its insulting character or the effect such a letter delivered to a French gentleman by a young unknown woman was likely to produce. Her cheeks burned with shame. Never again, she resolved, would she present a sealed letter of introduction!

The interview sounded a death knell to her hopes. If M. Louis's reaction was typical, then the doors of every hospital in Paris would be closed to her. She would be permitted no more practical continuation of her education than attendance on lectures, which she could have done in Philadelphia or New York or London. Valuable as they might be under such superior tutelage as M. Louis, she must have experience, assist and perform operations, diagnose cases, deliver babies.

Deliver babies! The death knell suddenly became a clarion note. Where could one possibly acquire more practical knowledge of obstetrics than in La Maternité, the biggest institution of its kind in the world? Suppose it *was* a school for midwives, not doctors. It was not status she was seeking, but experience. It would mean delay in her surgical studies, to be sure, but the time would be far from lost. While in the following days she continued to seek admission to some hospitals, the idea took root.

The first of June Anna arrived, planning to spend six or seven weeks being "magnetized" by the Paris experts. Since Elizabeth had already paid for a month's lodging, they took a new suite of rooms in the same house, arranging to have dinner sent in from a neighboring restaurant and taking their other meals independently. Try as she would, Elizabeth could not reduce her expenses below three dollars a week.

With Anna's presence Paris woke suddenly to gaiety, adventure. Her penchant for novelty, her scintillating wit, her superior mastery of French, her instant enthusiasm for the France of Fourier, worked the magic of rose-colored glasses. Visits to the Louvre or Notre Dame became fresh adventure. Every day something exciting occurred, or they discovered some wonderful old place they must visit. One day they attended the funeral celebrations of Marshal Bugeaud, where there was a whole army of soldiers and an enormous crowd. On another they saw a thousand little girls take their first communion at St. Sulpice, all dressed in white with long veils. For Elizabeth the crowning event was a Sunday trip to Versailles, where for the first time she felt a genuine sense of belonging, a oneness in pride and admiration with the throngs roaming through the spacious galleries and gardens.

She even felt at home at the magnetic seance which she attended with Anna and Mr. Doherty, for the faces were those of reformers, most of them associationists. She liked the appearance of Anna's mesmerist, M. du Potet, who seemed a benevolent and earnest old man, and she welcomed the opportunity to study the medical heresy at close hand.

But they could not quite escape the dark tides of unrest and tragedy which, like the festering sewers, underlay the bright gaiety. One day they had a strange glimpse of a revolution. Anna returned from a walk in the streets, pale, gasping that she had found herself in the midst of an *émeute*, riot. Shouldn't they return to England immediately? Elizabeth ventured out, more curious than frightened. The quai to the National Assembly, more than a mile long, was lined with soldiers with drawn bayonets. The Louvre and the Tuileries were closed and filled with soldiers. She passed through hurrying crowds, hearing fearful reports. Faces revealed all the diversity of seething passions: fear, anger, hope, hatred. Elizabeth well understood the display. The scandal of French politics was on every lip. She had heard it from the boy who arranged their rooms, the market woman at her stall. The fear was for the horrors of another revolution; the anger and hatred for the tyranny of the government, which had violently dispersed a peaceable assembly of two hundred thousand citizens protesting the unconstitutional measures of this new Napoleon; the hope that the democratic goals of the recent revolution might yet be attained. Elizabeth shared all their emotions.

They went to bed that night, July 13, to the rumbling of heavy wagons of ammunition and provisions, shouts, the pounding of running feet. The next morning the city was declared in a state of siege. The democratic press was destroyed. A proclamation was published by the President calling on all good citizens to maintain the authority of the law. And, incredibly, the commotion subsided. The conservative press congratulated the country on its preservation from the dangerous conspiracy of a few seditious demagogues. Fears and angers and hatreds and hopes were again buried beneath the brittle, superficial gaiety of apparent normalcy.

Elizabeth's hopes suffered a similar paralysis. Though she had letters of recommendation to all the principal hospitals, the responses were negative. She applied to Davenne, director general of the hospitals, for permission to follow some of the physicians on their ward rounds. She was refused. She went with both trepidation and anticipation to call on the noted Armand Trousseau, also a faculty professor, who had received the prize of the Academy of Medicine for his treatise on laryngeal phthisis and had been the first in Paris to perform a tracheotomy. He regarded her with brutal clinical keenness but also with the tolerance which made him such a generous interpreter of the ideas of other men.

"There is one way and one only, Mademoiselle, that your request could be granted. If you would don men's clothing —"

"No, sir." Elizabeth's response was swift and indignant. "What I am doing is not only for myself, but for other women as well. Therefore I will undertake the task as a woman, or give it up."

But she would become less uncompromising with the years. Some fifteen years later she was to write to Emily, "I would do differently now. I should tell them just what I wanted, find what hospital suited my purpose, and if by putting on disguise I could get either an assistant's post or good visiting privileges, I would put it on. I don't believe it would be a disguise at all to those you were thrown with, but it would be a protection if advised by intelligent men and would make them free to help you."

Not only hospital attendance, even clinical lectures were out of the question. Rules in Paris, it seemed, were more rigid than elsewhere.

M. Louis was right. La Maternité seemed the only solution. But when she discovered the regulations for entering the institution she was appalled. It would mean three months of complete incarceration! She must enter as an *élève*, pupil. She could not venture out and would be allowed visitors only once a week. She would have poor food and lodging, a minimum of menial services, the loss of three or four nights' sleep every week. But — the benefits! Experience in the world's biggest midwifery school, a thousand cases in three months, many no doubt abnormal, lectures from the most distinguished professors of obstetrics living, an opportunity for constant practice! Worth the sacrifice? A thousand times yes!

There were difficulties. She must present an *acte de naissance*, birth record, and a certificate of vaccination. She wrote to Kenyon, who was at last well enough to assume most normal activities.

"Would it be possible to secure in Bristol a copy of my register of baptism, with a statement of my birthday and my parents, certified by the mayor or some proper authority? I was baptized at Bridge Street by Mr. Leifchild. I was born on February 3, 1821." She waited anxiously for a reply.

There was one bright ray of encouragement. In July she received a cordial letter from Dr. Webster. Her study at Geneva, she learned with relief, had for the most part been passed over leniently, if not approved, by the profession in America. It would have grieved her inexpressibly if Geneva had been condemned for the aid given her. Moreover, he reported, her thesis was commented on in the report on medicine at the National Medical Convention held in Boston and received with applause. At least she had not injured her friends!

3

But in Paris her presence had aroused a furore of which she was only dimly aware.

"The medical community of Paris is all agog at the arrival of the celebrated American doctor, Miss Elizabeth Blackwell," reported the Paris correspondent of the *New York Journal of Commerce*. "She has quite bewildered the learned faculty by her diploma, in all due form authorizing her to dose and bleed and amputate with the best of them. Some think Miss Blackwell must be a socialist of the most rabid class, and that her undertaking is the entering wedge to a systematic attack on society by the whole sex. The ladies attack her in turn. One said to me the other day, 'Oh, it is too horrid! I am sure I could never touch her hand. Only to think that those fingers of hers had been cutting up dead people!' "

A sentiment by no means confined to the ladies! Elizabeth was amazed and shocked, after dining with Mr. Walsh, the American consul, to learn that he had remarked that he could not look at her long slender fingers without thinking of the anatomical work in which they had been engaged.

The reporter continued: "I have seen the doctor in person and must say in fairness that her appearance is quite prepossessing. She is young and rather good looking; her manner indicated great energy of character, and she seems to have entered on her singular career from motives of duty and encouraged by respectable ladies of Cincinnati. After about ten days' hesitation on the part of the directors of the hospital of the Maternité, she has at last received permission to enter the institution as a pupil."

"As a pupil" was only too accurate. Elizabeth was unable to obtain from any persons connected with the Maternité the slightest modification to suit the very different status with which she entered from that of the young French *sages-femmes*. There were some sixty to eighty of these student midwives who lived in the hospital, sleeping in crowded dormitories containing ten to twenty beds. Most of them were poor girls in the late teens or early twenties from the French provinces. Though they were required to have a few years of elementary schooling, their ignorance could be judged by the scores of applicants who had to be sent home each year because they were illiterate. Nothing would have been easier, she found out later, than for the authorities to have given her a little room to herself, permission to go out occasionally, and similar favors which would have occasioned no jealousy or inconvenience, for the very fact of her being a foreigner impressed the French girls, and they would have accepted any differentiation. But all her pleas, also those of the consul general, Mr. Robert Walsh, were refused. Very well. She would enter on any conditions, and by July 1, in order to get used to the place before the annual lectures should commence.

On Friday night, June 29, she attended a theatrical performance in order to take a brilliant farewell of Parisian life. The play was a fairy tale, beautifully rendered, a sip of fantasy before the bitter brew of reality. As she prepared for incarceration the next day, the city, the sky, the people, the gardens, all seemed more beautiful than ever before. But when afternoon arrived, and the papers Mr. Walsh had promised her did not come, she grew uneasy. Delay, she felt, might be a bad omen. Then, unexpectedly, they came, the register of birth and baptism which he had procured for her from the minister of Bridge Street Chapel. Hastily she secured a carriage and rode with Anna to the hospital.

A high stone wall with the tops of old buildings jutting above extended nearly the whole length of the street. They entered through a very small door into a dark little hall, the *portière* on one side and a long room, called by courtesy the *parloir*, on the other. In one corner in a sort of glass box sat the dame who attended to the letters and transacted all the outdoor business for the *élèves*. It was a bleak room, low ceiling, brick floor, rows of wooden benches.

"I suppose this is where I'll entertain my visitors," murmured Elizabeth, "once each week."

"It's horrible," shuddered Anna, who had tried to the last minute to dissuade her.

"Some pretty vine leaves peeping through those diamond-shaped windows," noted Elizabeth cheerfully.

It was too late to see M. Boivin, the director, so an old woman ushered them through this front row of old buildings standing against the wall into the central buildings, through a labyrinth of little passages and long galleries, to the room of Madame Charrier, the *sage-femme* in chief. Her parlor was a tiny curiosity shop, crammed with little chintz sofas, mosaic tables, boxes, china figurines, crucifixes, pictures, embroideries, and everywhere curtains! Madame herself seemed a fitting complement to this museum, tiny, deformed, old, but with cheeks as smooth and bright as painted china. Elizabeth was relieved to see kindness in the bright blue eyes. She would learn soon that Madeleine Charrier was one of the most illustrious midwives in the hospital's long history, practical, bustling, capable, but unscientific of mind and loath to accept new ideas. Having met the superior, Anna tearfully took her departure.

Madame conducted Elizabeth through more circuitous ways to Madame Blockel, superintendent of the *dortoirs*, a little woman with projecting teeth and squinting black eyes, dressed in a black gown and cap and muffled in an old shawl, who conducted her to the student infirmary. "You must sleep here," the new *élève* was informed, "until your affairs are arranged."

Elizabeth was not pleased. She looked suspiciously at the long rows of beds on either side, their white curtains closely drawn. What sort of emanations might proceed from them! The large wood fire on the hearth made the air too warm and oppressive. But she said nothing. Her trunk was brought up, her bed indicated, a little lamp placed on her table, and she was left alone. Hastily she pulled aside each curtain and to her relief found every bed empty but one, which was occupied by an *élève* with a headache. They fell into pleasant conversation.

"Are you from my province?" asked the girl eagerly, a tribute to her French which Elizabeth found most flattering. Finding that she was a stranger who had lived in New York, the only place in America she had heard of, the *élève* was much excited. "Is that an island near Havana?" Elizabeth was to discover later that the pupils were disappointed because she was not black, as they supposed all persons from America were Negroes!

She had no sooner seated herself to write a letter home than Madame Charrier again appeared, this time with a group of *élèves*, to inquire if she would pass the night in the *salle d'accouchements*. Elizabeth of course was willing. Being a *nouvelle élève* (new pupil), she was put in the custody of an *ancienne élève*, who had already studied for a year. Donning the big apron of coarse toweling, she felt more than ever as if she were taking the veil.

"Don't lose it," cautioned her mentor, "or it will cost you three francs."

The delivery room was large, dimly lighted, beds all around, a fire on the hearth, cupboards full of linen, heaps of shining copper and tin utensils, several rush-bottomed chairs and wooden tables, and in the center a large wooden stand on which the little newcomers were ranged, tightly swathed and labeled. During the night eight newborn specimens appeared. It was an amusing sight: eight shapeless little red faces, each peeping from under a coarse peaked cap marked with name and sex; each little figure in a black serge jacket with a white handkerchief pinned across it, and a small blanket tightly folded around the rest of the body. They resembled tiny mummies. A vindication of Fourier, thought Elizabeth, for there was little crying as they lay together. The virtues of associationism! She was amused also, listening to her four young fellow pupils chattering foolish nonsense, then when they were called on duty, to hear the most accurate scientific terms flowing glibly from their lips. She went off duty at ten the next morning, dead tired but triumphant. In a single night she had gained more practical knowledge of childbirth than in all her years of study!

La Maternité was an ancient institution with a long eventful history as a lying-in hospital. Founded in 1625, it had moved in 1814 from the square of Notre Dame into the former Jansenist Abbey of Port Royal. But the convent had lost little of its monastic atmosphere in becoming a hospital. The long cloisters, the venerable church, the pleasant grove were still peopled by beings as completely secluded from the rest of the world as the monks or nuns of previous centuries. No outside influence was permitted to divert the students from the purpose of their residence. Discipline was rigid, food spartan, comforts at a minimum, labor hard both day and night.

The majority of its patients were unwed mothers. Most of them came to Paris from the provinces, often traveling hundreds of kilometers by foot in a state of advanced pregnancy. Some were married women from the most poverty-stricken classes in Paris, and a still smaller proportion were prostitutes. For respectable women or those with means, who gave birth at home, its very name struck a chill note of dread, for behind the high molding walls disease was rampant. At least a quarter of the three thousand patients who entered the drab portals each year were either sick on arrival or contracted some disease during their stay. Epidemics of puerperal fever sometimes killed scores in a month's time. Although syphilitic patients were not supposed to be admitted, records of the institution abounded with cases of mothers and infants horribly deformed by the disease.

For Elizabeth the routine of "prison" life unfolded swiftly. That night she was settled in her "cell" in the *dortoir*, a large room containing sixteen beds, occupied mostly by *anciennes élèves*. By shoving her narrow iron bed forward and fitting her one chair behind, next to a window, hanging up her dressing gown and putting a few books on the floor behind her, she enjoyed a "study," with just enough room to move her right arm for writing and plenty of fresh air. It was impossible to write after dark, however, for the small lamp created more shadows than light. There was little privacy or quiet, for the French girls were great chatterers, addicted to sudden fits of ecstasy or rage. At least once each day there was a big furore, with Madame Blockel coming in to settle some trouble, in process of which she and the accused tried to outscream each other, then, after appearing to be mortal enemies, parting the best of friends.

At five each morning Elizabeth was jolted out of sound sleep by a clamoring bell. The *élèves* were usually up before her, for she lay another ten minutes pretending to sleep, partly out of anger at the raucous bell, partly to display her last shred of independence. Then she sprang out of bed, springing back with equal abruptness. Even in July the little polished hexagonal bricks could feel like ice! After completing the refreshing operations of an American toilette, which astonished her companions considerably, and donning her big white apron with its huge pocket, she hastened to the Salle Sainte-Elizabeth to question her patients, wash them, see that their beds were arranged; then with the other *élèves* accompanied Madame Charrier on her rounds, smiling to herself at the queer picture they must make: fifty women of every age, size, shape, and complexion, hastily dressed in little white caps, colored kerchiefs, long robes or short bed gowns, their uncorseted figures a strange contrast to the trig French figures that would be later in evidence, bright eyes sparkling and tongues wagging.

Hurrying back to her *dortoir*, she had just time to make her bed, snatch a crust of bread, and rush to the amphitheater for Madame's lesson at seven. Elizabeth occupied a chair beside her, Madame being anxious that the foreigner should understand everything thoroughly.

"I wish I could describe that lesson to you," Elizabeth wrote home in August. "It is the most curious spurring-up of pupils I ever saw, and really it makes some of them gallop admirably, though many tumble in the effort. Three pupils are called down every morning, seated on a long bench in front of Madame's table, and undergo an hour's examination. If they answer promptly and well, her satisfaction is extreme, her face grows beautiful, and her *'Bien, très bien!'* does me good, it is so hearty; but if an unlucky pupil hesitates or speaks too low, if intelligence or attention is wanting, then breaks forth the most admirable scolding I ever listened to. Alternately satirical and furious, she becomes on fire, rises on her chair, claps her hands, looks up to heaven, and the next moment, if a good answer has redeemed the fault, all is forgotten, her satisfaction is as great as her anger. There is not the slightest wickedness about her. She puts her whole soul into her lesson, and does not realize how difficult it is for ignorant girls to study a science. At first I was a little shocked by this stormy instruction, but it produces wonderful results."

At eight she hurried to the Salles Sainte-Marie and Sainte-Marthé, where Dr. Gérardin, the head physician, would be going his rounds of the sicker patients. Dr. Nicolas-Vincent-Auguste Gérardin was tall, dry, gray-haired, a bit pompous, but serious and full of common sense. With him was M. Hippolyte Blot, the intern, young, very handsome, dignified, and soberly intent on his business. Listening intently, Elizabeth sometimes gleaned a valuable bit of information, but not often, for the doctor felt no obligation to instruct the *élèves* in medicine. Rounds completed, she would rush to her *dortoir*, seize her little white mug (bought from a woman named Louicadie along with a set of coarse white crockery, a little tin saucepan, a bottle for wine, and a pewter spoon), travel through the courtyard and cloister to the Infirmary of the *Élèves*, where a little tin saucepan of coffee awaited her, costing her two sous each morning. Back to her *dortoir*, where she drank the coffee and set her room in order, then rushed to Dr. Dubois's lecture at nine.

"*Bonjour, Mademoiselle, bonjour, Mademoiselle* . . ." she greeted over and over as she sped through cloisters, courtyard, corridors.

She would not have missed a moment of these lectures. M. Paul Dubois, a little, bald, gray man with a clear gentle voice and benevolent face, understood his subject thoroughly and expressed himself with precision. Though she occasionally received a pleasant word from him, the world of business consumed his attention. That very year he was publishing a book on proper obstetrical procedure.

"You should stay a year and gain the gold medal," he said on one of the rare occasions when he stopped to speak to her after class. "You would be the best midwife, male or female, in America!"

"But I already have a medical degree," she told him, "from a reputable college in my own country." She could tell by his indulgent smile that he considered the "reputable" highly improbable.

Twelve o'clock came at last, with the first meal of the day. Elizabeth sprang to obey the bell with alacrity. Each *élève* was given her full day's supply of bread at noon, to be kept in her bedroom and carried back and forth to meals. She wished the family could see her walking gravely along the gallery with her long loaf wrapped in a napkin under her arm. The round tables in the dining room were speedily encircled, a grace said with such rapidity that she never did make out more words than "*saint usage,*" and the sign of the cross made with wonderful dexterity. The menu was always the same, beginning and ending with soup and salad, the middle consisting of rough-looking meat from the soup, some strangely flavored vegetables, and plenty of bread and wine. On two fast days, Friday and Saturday, the fare would contain hard-boiled eggs swimming in oil and vinegar. After the meal another prayer rocket was sent up, and all crowded out of the hall, loaves under their arms.

Afternoons were filled with more lectures from an *aide-sage-femme*, productive of more versatility in French than of medical knowledge, and if no visitor was expected, a bath, negotiated with the same communalism as other activities. The tubs stood side by side down the middle of the room, six of them, and the withered genius of the bathroom stood by, observing every movement and talking an incomprehensible patois the whole time. Elizabeth would shut her eyes, lie quietly for half an hour, and fancy that she was deliciously reposing on the heaving waters of a soft summer lake.

She blessed fate that she was a Protestant, unobligated to attend morning and evening prayers, vespers, daily baptisms, and regular services, to say nothing of numerous extras on saints' days, though she could not escape their byproducts. During the month of May, Mademoiselle Boisonnet, the sweetly pious *aide-sage-femme*, organized groups to sing canticles to the Lady, to the horror of all Elizabeth's nerves and, she feared, to the serious displeasure of the Virgin. Often, too, walking in the hospital woods and gardens in the evening, she would meet the fat, red-faced priest who always gave her long stares of excessive curiosity.

Nor could she have escaped the incursion of the jolly, youthful, ever chattering *élèves* on her precious privacy, had she wanted to. She welcomed with as good grace as possible the pinches, shakes, and similar tokens of French affection, appreciated the curiosity, the patience with her French, the incomprehension of her desire to be sometimes alone. But sometimes her conviviality was sadly strained.

"Imagine that you have retired early to bed," she wrote home, "after a night spent in hard work and the day in that nervous mystification that follows loss of rest. You have just entered a beautiful dreamland, when you are startled by a scream, a burst of laughter, and the vision of one white-robed form darting past in the twilight, pursued by a similar form. You resolutely shut your eyes and will yourself asleep, when a sudden rolling sound, followed by a violent shock, convinces you of the vanity of your efforts. They are 'promenading the bedsteads.' Our beds are of iron on movable rollers. Often in stepping into bed the slight movement causes the mercurial article to describe a sudden semicircle. This property of these usually sober pieces of furniture is taken advantage of. An impulsion is given to one end of a long row, which is quickly communicated to the whole, or a simultaneous shock given to the two extremities and their force brought to bear on the unfortunate center. But the favorite freak is to place a bedstead at the end of the room and drive it with great violence down the center. The rolling noise is tremendous and accompanied by a Babel of laughter, shouting, and jokes of every description."

Though there were jealousies among themselves, they showed her the utmost respect and friendliness. At first she tried hard to exhibit no superior knowledge, especially in the classes conducted by the *anciennes élèves*. Then one day as she sat in the circle joining in the deadly repetition of anatomical parts and processes, the young instructress became confused. She floundered helplessly in an attempt to explain the circulation of the blood. Elizabeth forgot herself in sympathy.

"Perhaps I can make it clear," she offered, and gave a simple but very clear description of the circulatory system. The young *élève* showed no resentment, only relief and delight. After that many of them came to her for help.

She was even more worried when Madame Charrier summoned her one day to her room. Mademoiselle Mallet, one of the *aides-sages-femmes*, was there with her. "You wrote this report, Mademoiselle?"

Elizabeth inspected the paper. It was the account of a surgical case which she had observed with Mademoiselle Mallet and made notes on at her dictation. Only she had made a private memorandum enlarging on the details for her own satisfaction.

"Yes, Madame." She looked guiltily at Mademoiselle Mallet but saw she was broadly smiling. "I know I added a bit. I'm sorry if —"

"No, no, it is *bon*, good! We are both pleased, my dear. Mademoiselle Mallet will include it in her report. We are proud of your progress. You will make a fine *sage-femme*. A doctor could not have done better."

"But I am —" Elizabeth stopped and smiled ruefully. Madame knew she had a medical degree, yet it was as incomprehensible to her as to M. Dubois that a woman could function as a doctor.

4

As at Geneva, at Blockley, Elizabeth had plunged into the new experience with an intense dedication of all her faculties. She had counted on the involvement of mind, eyes, hands, feet, every facet of her energetic body and person — except her heart.

Her first encounters with the handsome young intern, M. Claude Philibert Hippolyte Blot, were clinically impersonal. Each morning she trailed him and Dr. Gérardin from bed to bed, observing, listening. Assisting with the other *élèves* when on duty in the *salle d'accouchements*, she noticed with grudging approval the competent hands, the dark intent eyes, the sober and almost too perfect features in their becoming frame of neatly clipped sideburns.

"Looks as if he might have a cross temper," she thought idly.

Then there were the Tuesday vaccinations. In the Hall of the Nurses, full already of women and babies, a space would be cleared by one of the windows, chairs placed. In the center would sit M. Blot with his vaccines and knives. On one Tuesday Elizabeth sat beside him while the *élèves* brought baby after baby, ugly little mummies in their coarse swaddling clothes, all performing a terrible concert. It was her task to hold each little patient as M. Blot touched his knife to the screaming victim. Occasionally she asked him a question, but each time he seemed confused, colored, passed his hand through his hair, and avoided her gaze in such an un-Frenchmanlike manner that she stopped disturbing him.

"Embarrassed? Disapproving?" she wondered. "Or — could he possibly be in awe of me?"

But not long after, he deliberately pointed out several interesting points to her in the infirmary and not only answered her questions frankly but loaned her a medical journal. Then to her surprise some days later when she made her usual visit to the infirmary he approached her, flushing, but with obvious determination.

"I wonder — Mademoiselle — er — I mean Doctresse, if you would consider giving me some lessons in English."

Not disapproving, decided Elizabeth, and not really in awe. Perhaps — just boyishly shy. To her own confusion she felt herself blushing.

"Of course. I would be most happy."

So began a pleasant and mutually beneficial relationship. Elizabeth remained after his class occasionally, and they conversed in both languages, each helping the other. The hours in the Infirmary des Élèves became the happiest and most profitable of her whole day. M. Blot was a stimulating teacher both in class and after it. One day he brought his microscope and explained to the class the difference between the *épithélium pavimenteux*, such as covers the tongue, and the *épithélium vibratile*, as in other parts. Most of the *élèves* were either bored or baffled, but Elizabeth remained long after the class was over, poring over the specimens and sharing the young intern's excitement over a paper he had heard read at a medical society the day before, proving that the chemical azote, which in the ox is voided by the excrement, in the cow is absorbed into the milk, and that the difference in the manure of the two is great.

"How wonderful," she thought, "that we, a man and a woman, can talk of such things with scientific frankness and without the slightest embarrassment!"

Yet envy and frustration were mingled with her appreciation of rapport. M. Blot was preparing for an examination of interns. At the moment he was busily engaged with his thesis, "On the presence of albumin in the urine of pregnant women, its connection with convulsions, its influence on uterine hemorrhage after delivery," which his two years at La Maternité had well qualified him to write. Elizabeth read parts and gave helpful suggestions. If he should gain the gold medal, he confided with boyish candor, he could enter any hospital he chose as an intern for a second term, beside receiving his M.D. While sincere in her hope for his success, Elizabeth felt a secret resentment. How terribly unfair! What chance did a woman have, barred from all such practical instruction? Almost defiantly she shared with her new friend her own determination to become a surgeon, and though he was gallant in his encouragement, the skepticism in his eyes betrayed him. But her sole reaction to such discouragement was a grim, "Work on, Elizabeth!"

Sometimes they argued hotly. One day Hippolyte told her of the laboratory experiments of his friend Claude Bernard, later to be known as the greatest physiologist of modern France and the founder of experimental medicine. Bernard had discovered an accessory circulation by which substances were sent directly to the kidneys without traversing the general circulation. In his studies of the sugar-forming functions of the liver he had just made an experiment by which a dog was made to secrete albuminous and diabetic urine, according to the pricking of one or another point of the pneumogastric nerve near its origin.

Here Elizabeth felt the first flaring of a rebellion which was to spark one of the most burning passions of her later life: her fight against vivisection.

"What possible benefit to man," she demanded bluntly, "can result from turning a laboratory into a torture chamber for helpless animals?" And all of Hippolyte's defense of his friend and of animal experimentation as a legitimate means of scientific research failed to change her mind.

However, their areas of disagreement were few. With only two persons had Elizabeth ever felt such perfect rapport, William Channing and her father. Anxiously she anticipated some testing where his behavior would be disappointing, but none came. In an environment where to her anger and distress the humane treatment of patients was at a minimum, M. Blot showed exceptional kindness and concern for each individual. His soothing voice did more to mute the screams in the operating room than the seldom-used chloroform. He was as gentle with a blowsy prostitute as with a timid peasant girl. And he was far more open-minded than his superiors toward the new ideas constantly sprouting in the medical world. When a fresh epidemic of puerperal fever swept the wards, killing scores in a month's time, he was as concerned and frustrated as Elizabeth.

"*Mon dieu*, I do not understand! Why should it be less safe for a woman to give birth in a hospital than in her own home? *Why!*"

"I wonder —" Elizabeth searched her memory. "There is a doctor in America. His name is Holmes. Oliver Wendell Holmes."

"*Mais oui*, I have heard of him."

"About six years ago he published an article, 'On the Contagiousness of Puerperal Fever.' He claimed that physicians who had handled cases should never attend women in childbirth without washing their hands and changing their clothes. All the other doctors pooh-poohed the idea, said it was as silly as to wash and change your coat before doing an operation. But — I've wondered —"

"Hmm!" said Hippolyte thoughtfully.

Some time later he came to her, much excited. "Remember what you said about Holmes? Listen to this." He read to her from a medical journal about a doctor in Vienna, Ignaz Philipp Semmelweiss, who had written, "Puerperal fever is caused through the carrying to the patient of decaying particles derived from living organisms through the agency of examining fingers." By compelling all his students to wash their hands in chlorinated water before entering the maternity ward, he claimed to have lowered the death rate from twelve to three percent. And what's more, he was insisting that the doctors and students in his hospital clean all their instruments after use, instead of wiping them on their coattails!

Elizabeth studied the small, obscure news item. "But — this happened months ago. Why haven't we heard of it before?"

Hippolyte smiled grimly. "Can't you guess? How popular would one of our doctors be if he exploded with an idea like that in this hospital? I'd almost wager this Semmelweiss has to leave his hospital and even Vienna!"

The words were as much history as prophecy, for already Semmelweiss, branded by his chief as a Hungarian traitor, had been relieved of his post at Vienna General Hospital, where his regulations of cleanliness had been immediately abolished as ridiculous. This pioneer in obstetrics was indeed to leave Vienna disgraced and disillusioned, finally to die one of medicine's martyrs. Yet even as Elizabeth pored over the item a young professor of physics in the University of Strasbourg was initiating chemical experiments which in a few years were to vindicate Holmes and Semmelweiss and change medicine for all time. His name was Louis Pasteur.

Just when Elizabeth made her own disquieting discovery she was not sure. Perhaps it was the moment she sensed that she was more conscious of the dark head bent close to hers over the microscope than of the magnified cellule below it. As soon as possible she fled to her room, cheeks burning, emotions in a tumult. The knowledge that her old susceptibility to the attraction of the other sex was dormant, not dead, was both disconcerting and, yes, exciting. Being Elizabeth, even while her pulses pounded and her cheeks burned, she analyzed facts with cool detachment.

So — she was in love again. Again? No. Never before had she experienced this complete involvement of self with another, body, mind, and spirit. It was what she had always imagined the ideal relationship of a man and woman to be, compounded of trust, admiration, mutual interests, shared objectives, and — until now only vaguely conjectured — an ecstasy which set one's brain reeling, one's nerve tips tingling, burned through one's veins like liquid fire. Frightening as well as intoxicating, for she knew that, given the choice at this moment, she would gladly sacrifice everything she had paid such a price to win if she could become the obedient, cherished, utterly feminine and, if need be, subservient wife of Hippolyte Blot!

Fortunately the moment passed, and cool reason prevailed. She was not given the choice. She had no reason to think the young intern shared her emotions, and even if he did, marriage would be out of the question. A Frenchman, a promising young doctor, breaking all the rules of family, creed, tradition, to mate with a heretic foreigner frowned on by his own profession? It might ruin his career! And what about herself? Sever all ties with both native and adopted countries? Spend the rest of her life in this land of wooden fences and dun-colored houses, loose morals and crucifixes, hot tempers and revolutions? *Jeopardize her life purpose!*

Suddenly she felt torn apart, not mind from body, but both split into two conflicting entities, each clamoring to be heard.

"But Hippolyte is not like that. He would never expect me to give up my career. He knows how much it means to me."

"More than his to him? You know how ambitious he is."

"Surely we could work together —"

"As doctors? Doctor and *sage-femme*, perhaps. I thought you wanted to be a surgeon."

"Surely that would still be possible —"

"In France? You know better."

"But he's different, not like most Frenchmen."

"Like an Englishman? And can you imagine an Englishman encouraging his wife, a *woman*, to compete in what he considers the world of men?"

"Papa —"

"Liberal with his daughters, yes. Don't forget your mother was the most subservient of wives."

"But — if being a woman shouldn't prevent your being a doctor, then should being a doctor prevent your being a woman?"

Questions — with no answers. Outside her room a storm was brewing. She lay down and tried to sleep, but the clash of dialogue continued, gaining impetus from the conflict of elements outside. The world also seemed torn apart.

She must have slept, for she roused to feel her shoulder being shaken.

"Mademoiselle! *Le docteur* bids you come. *Une grande chose, une opération!*"

Elizabeth staggered to her feet, pulled on her clothes, followed the smoky flare of Mademoiselle Mallet's oil lamp through the maze of corridors and arches to the amphitheater. As they passed through the cloisters, wind tore at the lamp, and Elizabeth felt the first pin-thrusts of rain. All her weariness vanished. She was a unit again, all conflict resolved, mind and body, like the wind and rain, in harmony.

It must be a big operation indeed, for other *élèves* had been roused. Yawning, grumbling, frumpy and unkempt, they were shuffling toward the amphitheater. The benches were fast filling, not only with *élèves*, but with men students from all over Paris, but Madame had saved a place for Elizabeth to stand on a front bench.

"A lithotomy," explained Madame, almost, thought Elizabeth, with the relish a Roman pleb might have displayed before a bloody exhibition in the Coliseum.

Lithotomy! The word beat against her senses like the rain pounding on the skylight. This operation for the removal of bladder stones was one of the most ancient and painful known to man. Yet people endured it, for unless the stone passed naturally, without it death was inevitable — often with it, for acute fever invariably followed.

The patient was already stretched on the raised cot which served as operating table, its filthy covering streaked and stiffened with remnants of previous surgery. Couldn't they give the poor thing a clean sheet to lie on? thought Elizabeth, her fastidious passion for cleanliness affronted. Judging by the oaths and obscenities punctuating the groans, it was no peasant woman but one of the Paris streetwalkers. Arms tied to the cot with tough bands, she writhed and twisted and swore in protest both at the confinement and at the excruciating pain. Though heavily drugged with wine and perhaps more pungent spirits, she seemed fully conscious, and would remain so. The miracle of anesthesia, barely three years old, had not yet penetrated the charity institutions of Paris.

Dr. Dubois entered with the surgeon, a stranger, for lithotomy was the province of a specialist. Maisonneuve, wondered Elizabeth? She studied the short, thickset figure with the expressionless features, shuddering a little as she remembered that the eminent surgeon was dubbed "the assassin." But probably it was not Maisonneuve. A surgeon of his reputation would hardly devote his talents to a gutter derelict. He approached the cot, inspected the patient with impersonal brevity, and donned the stained and crusted operating coat gingerly held by an assistant. Some strings of catgut dangled from one of its buttonholes. Elizabeth stared, all eyes, as he took his instruments from an old cloth bag and laid them on a table, first wiping each one on his coat, perhaps to remove traces of previous operations. Her stomach lurched. Of course an operation was a dirty business. Both coat and instruments would soon be soiled far worse, but — if she were a surgeon, she would want at least to start clean. Suddenly she remembered Semmelweiss, who had insisted that all his doctors wash both hands and instruments and change their clothes between treatments of fever patients. This patient would develop fever also. Was it possible that there was some connection — ?

But the operation was beginning. Except for a slight improvement in the instruments, the technique of lithotomy had changed little since the Roman Celsus had first detailed the procedure. An assistant shoved a folded rag into the patient's mouth, then held the shoulders in a vise-like grip. Others raised the legs into proper position. The surgeon stepped forward and with deft swiftness thrust a grooved probe into the body, reached for his scalpel, swore when it fell on the floor, berated the nervous assistant who picked it up, seized it, and without bothering to wipe it again on his coat, plunged it with a quick sure motion into the perineum. Neither the gagging rag nor the pounding of rain on the glass skylight smothered the howls and shrieks of pain.

Elizabeth did not faint like many of the other *élèves*. She had seen operations before, though never one like this. It was the longest and one of the most torturing hours she had ever spent. It must have lasted an hour, though in the hurry of midnight dressing she had forgotten her watch. Standing on the crowded bench, muscles stiffening with the cold and dampness, she heard a clock strike one. "The holy noon of night," she thought. But this scene was not holy. It seemed the epitome of all the world's sin and suffering. She might be witnessing some dark pagan rites in an ancient grotto, with the priest lifting his knife to the sacrificial victim. Or — the sticking of a pig in one of the Cincinnati slaughterhouses! The rain beating in torrents, the wind shaking the building, the shrieks of pain, all seemed fitting trappings for this strange spectacle of suffering and of science. Yet while one part of her was revolted, another watched with the keenest interest, knowing that a life was perhaps being saved, that she was witnessing a skilled performance of a rare and dangerous operation.

Triumphantly the surgeon held up his forceps, disclosing a yellowish stone perhaps an inch by an inch and a half. Taking a length of catgut from his buttonhole, he proceeded to sew the incision, wiped his instruments once more on his coat, replaced them in the old bag, surrendered his freshly befouled coat to the gingerly custody of his assistants, and with the bow of an impresario to his cheering audience but without a glance at the moaning patient, stalked impressively from the room. It was a scene which could have been duplicated, Elizabeth knew, in almost any hospital in the world.

"But it need not be like that," she decided, returning slowly to her room. The poor woman could have been permitted privacy in the crucible of her suffering. The surgeon could have treated her as a person, not as a display specimen. He could have given her assurance, shown a bit of human tenderness. Surely an operating room need not embody the brutality of a slaughterhouse! "If tonight the surgeon could have been a woman," her thoughts pursued, then, more succinctly, "*If I could have been the surgeon — !*"

Back in her room she threw up the window. The storm had passed. The wind blew fresh under clear starlight. The elements had resolved their conflicts. And so had her own spirit.

She was even surer of her purpose a few days later when Madame summoned her to the queer little museum of a parlor.

"I have a present for you," she announced, blue eyes gleaming with excitement. "*Your portrait!*"

Elizabeth stared, bewildered, into the pictured face of a woman, strong-featured, distinguished if not handsome, eyes straight and unwavering, lips unsmiling but with a slight upthrust of amusement at the corners. "But — it's not at all like —"

Then she understood. It was a lithograph picture of the first Elizabeth Blackwell, taken from a history of *sages-femmes célèbres*. Fascinated, Elizabeth refreshed her memory with the story of her remarkable namesake who, a little more than a hundred years before, had published a work on medical botany in two large folio volumes, in order to get her husband, a medical man, out of prison, where he was confined for debt.

"*Voilà!* You see?" Madame's small deformed body arched in triumph. *"C'est prédit!* With that name you could not help yourself. You were predestined to be like her, a *sage-femme célèbre!"*

Elizabeth took the picture back to the *dortoir*, pored over it, constructed from it a romance, the story of a beautiful true spirit, struggling with a society too strong to be turned from its ancient habits of evil. Perhaps, as the superstitious little Frenchwoman believed, she *was* predestined to follow in the steps of this bold and illustrious namesake. But not as a *sage-femme*, however *célèbre. As the world's first woman surgeon!*

5

It was hard that October attending Hippolyte Blot's lectures, remaining afterward to study specimens, teach him English, discuss subjects in the medical books he loaned her, work beside him on the days she was assigned to duty in the infirmary, and yet betray not the slightest sign of emotion. It would have been harder if M. Blot's own manner had ever indicated more than gallant friendliness. Only once did he turn the conversation toward personal romance.

"Les familles! Eh bien! Sometimes one's family is such a nuisance! Mine is getting impatient. They want to arrange for me a marriage!"

"Oh?" Elizabeth hoped she sounded politely nonchalant. "Well, you can't wonder at that, can you? After all, you are" — it was almost a question — "older than most French youths when they marry."

"I am twenty-six."

She felt a bounding relief. He was only two years younger than herself! As if that mattered, she chided herself grimly. He was a good friend, nothing more.

"And surely a doctor needs a wife."

He shrugged, one of his few French mannerisms. *"Mais oui.* When — *if* I get my degree and gold medal, I can consider it. Not before."

Again she felt a surge of relief. December! Another two months before he took his examinations, and she would be gone at the end of it. At least, while enjoying his companionship, she need not have to think of him as belonging to another. So valuable was her experience at La Maternité, with its three thousand births each year, that she had decided to remain for another three months. But in spite of Dr. Dubois's repeated urgings, that would be the end. She must find some way to gain training in surgery.

October brought two diversions to her monotonous life. Dr. Lee, her Geneva professor, came to Paris and called to see her. His visit was a delightful breath of freedom, but her joy was tainted by the absurd regulation forbidding her to show him over the hospital. However, the *directeur* escorted him, and M. Blot arranged an introduction for him to the great Philippe Ricord, the foremost authority on venereal diseases since John Hunter.

The second diversion was perfection without taint. She was allowed a whole day of release! So many were the medical people and places she wanted to see that she was almost exhausted by the anticipation, but when the day finally arrived, October 21, and everything worked out right — she was neither *en service*, nor in the infirmary, nor in the reception — she decided to forget medicine entirely and give herself up like a child to the natural pleasures of looking and moving and — yes, eating.

The other *élèves* were as excited as she. One hooked her dress, another fastened her gloves, a third arranged her collar, and others stood about admiring with cries of, "*Oh, que vous êtes belle!*" As nine o'clock approached Elizabeth was on tenterhooks. Suppose Anna was late! For according to the rules Anna must take her out and must bring her back at exactly eight o'clock.

"Sorry." The *directeur* had laughed at the absurdity. "But no exceptions."

"Mademoiselle Blackwell!" came the shout under her window. Anna had not failed. As excited as Elizabeth, she had wakened an hour earlier than usual.

Freedom after four months of incarceration! Elizabeth felt like the poor mayfly which has only one day to live. And, thank heaven, it wasn't rainy! Her chest expanded as she stepped over the threshold and saw no barriers, only the beautiful Luxembourg Gardens on one side, unending streets on the other. The pulsing life, the modish dresses, the cheerful houses, the flowery labyrinths of the gardens through which they walked, the trees in flamboyant dress, the children clattering through dead leaves, all seemed the strange and wonderful components of a new world. Anna had moved into a new *appartement* in the Rue de Fleurus by the western gate of the Gardens, pretty as a jewel case, and Elizabeth admired the elegant furniture, carved ceiling, tapestried wallpaper, all tinted warm gold from the long avenue of trees outside. And the view! Up five flights of stairs it *should* have a good view!

The high point of the day was a magnetic séance at the home of M. du Potet, Anna's current guru, an experience which Elizabeth described the next day in a long letter home, the acidity of her droll satire only slightly tempered by her innate tolerance.

"There is an odd side to all reformers" — the words were a possible thrust at herself — "to all who are pursuing a new idea earnestly, that is very whimsical. I am obliged to laugh at it, and yet I have true respect for M. du Potet. Though he believes in ancient magic, lives in the hope of working miracles, I believe him to be honest, enthusiastic, engaged with his whole soul in pursuing what seems to him the most important of all discoveries. Sometime I hope to really study magnetism."

She fed her hungry spirit on the richness of the Louvre and her hungry body on abundant eatables, Anna's faith in the efficacy of magnetism being healthily balanced by that in "the very best beef." She visited the reading room where Anna pursued her studies of Fourier and of European politics, and for once the two were in complete indignant agreement over the barbarism which seemed for the moment triumphant in European society. Punctually at eight the recluse was again retired from the vanities of the world, but not before Anna had delivered herself of a good dose of her characteristic acerbity.

"*Mon dieu*, aren't you satisfied *yet*? You've done what no other woman has been able to do, get your degree, and now you've qualified yourself to be one of the world's best obstetricians. Yet still you're talking of worming your way into some other place, another prison for all you know, where you'll sure as sin endure more slights and snubs and maybe outright persecution! For heaven's sake, isn't it enough to be the world's first woman doctor? What more do you want?"

"To be a surgeon," replied Elizabeth calmly.

"But *why*? All that bloody cutting up, that butchering —" Anna shuddered.

"That's why. Because I'm convinced that it need not be butchering."

Anna was, as usual persistent. She could cajole, coax, as well as needle. "Come now. Let's go back to England, you and I. We'll take a little place in London. I'll write, and you will practice medicine in a nice ladylike way. We'll go in December, as soon as you're finished with that outrageous prison, and —"

"No." Elizabeth was gentle as well as firm, for she knew Anna was genuinely concerned. "I'm sorry, dear. We each have to live our lives in our own way, and this is mine." Her eyes turned a steel gray, and her lips set. Anna knew the look well. She had seen it on a child of five stubbornly insistent on chasing a ship to Ireland. "I have to become a surgeon. It's my — my divine calling. And nothing, nobody on earth is going to stop me."

But something did.

It was midnight-dark at five on a November morning. Elizabeth struggled out of bed more dazed than usual, and because she was scheduled to spend all day in the infirmary, hurried to make the rounds of her patients. One of them was a baby with a bad case of purulent ophthalmia. She had been treating it for days.

"Poor mite," she murmured, bending over the tiny swaddled shape. Then, noticing that its eyes were tightly gummed, she went for the syringe. It was hard working in the dim light, for the smoky lamp was of little help. She had to bend low over the boxlike container which served as a crib. Whether because of the dark or her drowsy clumsiness she would never know, but some of the fluid spurted into her own eye. She washed it carefully, then in the bustle of her duties and the excitement of witnessing M. Dayau's first application of the serrefine, she forgot the incident, but in the afternoon the eye felt scratchy as if irritated by a grain of sand. She dared not even think what it might be. That night it was badly swollen, but she resolutely refused to panic. Trusting to her all-powerful fresh air and water cure, she managed to sleep. But in the morning the eye was painfully inflamed and the lids closely adherent with suppuration. She went at once to the *directeur* and asked permission to leave until the eye was well, but was refused.

Panic now mounting, she had only one thought: Hippolyte Blot. She went straight to the Infirmary of the Élèves, where fortunately he was on duty. He examined the eye with his usual gentle thoroughness and gravely confirmed her fears. It was indeed the dread disease, extremely infectious and often resulting in blindness.

"They're keeping me prisoner." She would have wept if the effort had not been so painful. "I wanted to go to my sister, but they would not let me."

"*Mon dieu*, it is well they would not!" Never had she heard him sound so severe. "You should know, my dear doctor, how important is early treatment in purulent ophthalmia. The first twenty-four hours may well determine whether you completely recover."

The next hours were a turmoil of pain, of fear, yet of increasing

calmness and relief. She was put to bed in the infirmary at the far end
of one of the long rows of iron bedsteads, to insure greater privacy,
though few of the students were ill at the time. M. Blot, having
obtained permission from his superior, announced that he would devote
his whole time to her until the danger was passed. Mademoiselle
Mallet, her favorite *aide-sage-femme*, was in almost constant attendance. Elizabeth managed to scrawl a note to Anna saying that her eye
was inflamed but bidding her not to worry. The treatments began at
once: leeches applied to her temples (disgusting little things — it had
taken all her courage to handle them here for the first time), cauteriza-
tions, injections of collyrium, syringing of the eye every hour with tepid
water, externally and internally, cold compresses, ointment of bella-
donna, opium to the forehead, purgatives, footbaths, and sinapisms,
with only broth for diet. Though the treatments were excruciatingly
painful, the harsh self-discipline which had driven her to sleep on a
hard floor and to walk off a raging fever, had become wiser but no less
inflexible in maturity. When Anna arrived that first evening, shocked
to find her propped up in bed, both eyes closed, surrounded by anxious
faces, traces of leeches on her forehead, the inflamed eye enormously
swelled, Elizabeth was able to greet her with her usual calmness.

"Oh, Anna, is that you? I didn't expect to see you tonight."

As she was to do many times in the ensuing days, Anna hid behind
the bed curtains to cry. Then, after staying as long as permitted, she
went straight to M. du Potet to learn the best ways of magnetizing
Elizabeth. Permitted to visit her sister three times a day, an hour at a
time, she exercised on her all the magnetic faculties she could muster.
During these miniature séances Elizabeth often could not help laughing. "Wouldn't the folks at home be amused if they could see us!"

"My dear child," chided Anna with indulgent severity, "if they could
see you sometimes when I come, in such terrible pain that speech is
impossible, then in five minutes, when I have set my whole soul into the
effort, see you sleeping quietly, they would thank God for the beautiful
power with which he has endowed us."

Elizabeth did not disillusion her. Not for the world would she have
confessed that the hands of Hippolyte Blot, inflicting pain though they
must, exerted far more of magnetism on her tortured body and spirit
than all the magic of M. du Potet and his ilk. Every two hours the
young intern came, day and night, to give the treatments, and on the
alternate hours kind Mademoiselle Mallet, with her soothing voice, her

fingers of unequaled skill and delicacy. Elizabeth came to know Hippolyte's quiet step, thrilled to its approach in spite of the increase of suffering it portended. Sightless though she was, she believed she would have recognized the touch of his hands, firm, deft, yet indescribably gentle, among a thousand.

One night she was asleep when he came. Drifting slowly up to consciousness, she thought she must be dreaming, for often enough in her dreams she had heard that familiar voice speaking these very words.

"Ma chérie, ma pauvre chérie! Oh, my dear, my dear one!"

She lay very still, hoping the sudden quickening of her heart would not betray her. He must not know she had heard. Presently she stirred deliberately.

"Oh! I'm sorry. I didn't hear you come. I must have been asleep."

When he had gone, she lay and trembled. The throbbing of her eye was so mingled with the pounding of her heart that she could hardly tell where pain left off and ecstasy began. The words had told her less than the timbre of his voice. He had spoken not in pity but in tenderness. Hippolyte Blot loved her, not as a brother but as a man loves a woman. At first she merely savored the knowledge, repeating the words to herself, letting the pain and the ecstasy blend and not caring which was which. She must have spoken, for suddenly the *ancienne élève* assigned to sit by her all night was at her side.

"C'est bien, mademoiselle? Voulez-vous quelque chose?"

"Merci. C'est bien, chérie."

All was well with her indeed. Whatever the future might do to her, it could never deprive her of this hour of pain-mingled bliss. And it was exactly an hour. For after Mademoiselle Mallet came, promptly on schedule, bearing sympathy and syringe, reason asserted itself. No trouble now in distinguishing pain from ecstasy! It was all pain. For nothing had really changed. She had made her decision. The course she had chosen must be pursued with singleness of purpose, not for herself, but for all other women who might come after her. Not that she had a scorn or distaste for marriage! She desired it with all her being. And she believed passionately that wifehood and motherhood were the holiest of all callings. It was simply not for her. Since that night of revelation in the little bedroom in Asheville, she had felt divinely called to this crusade. She had pursued it with the dedication of a novitiate, a priestess, with no other major loyalty. Not that she believed, either, that marriage was not compatible with a career for women; far from it — at least, most careers. But not medicine, not, that is, at this point in human history. So great were the difficulties, the ostracism, facing the pioneer woman doctor that if she wanted to succeed, she must allow nothing, nobody, to come between her and her goal. It was the price she must pay for being a trailblazer, walking the trail alone.

She was awake when the young intern came an hour later. After he had treated the eye with his usual skill and gentleness, she groped for his hand.

"*Mon cher ami*, how can I ever repay you for all you're doing for me? I have a confession to make. I can't help thinking of you as more than a friend." Feeling his hand tense, she hurried on. "You seem to me more like a brother. I have told you that I have four very dear brothers. Now, thanks to you, I shall always feel I have five."

There was a long silence. When he finally spoke, it was in a low, unsteady voice. "I — thank you, Mademoiselle."

"*Mon frère.*" She gave the hand a slight pressure before releasing it. "And I hope you will think of me as your sister. It would give me great pleasure."

"Mademoiselle —" His voice held a sudden note of urgency.

"Please — not that! *Sister!*"

There was another silence.

"*Eh bien*, I am honored. Sister it shall be. *Au revoir — ma soeur.*"

He was gone. Now she could hardly tell where the pain in her eye left off and that in her heart began.

6

Three days . . . three weeks . . . Hard to tell which were the longer. The first were divided by hours, the second by days, but the quotient of pain was the same. No morning, no night, just one continuation of darkness. And the agony of those first three days was enough to last a lifetime.

But they passed, and the weeks of waiting began. The fate of the eye was already determined, probably had been in the first day, but it might be four, five, six weeks or longer before she would know whether she had lost her vision. Not until the diseased part of the cornea had become detached could it be discovered how deep the injury had gone. Now every two hours M. Blot would come and with fine pincers peel off the false membranes constantly forming over the cornea. The wash-

ings, the compresses, the ointments — thank heaven, not the leeches!
— all continued, plus Anna's thrice-daily magnetisms. Everything possible was done for her comfort. Thanks to the huge fireplace at one end
and a big stovepipe running up through the center, the infirmary was
far warmer than the *dortoir*. The concerned *élèves* were almost tor-
menting in their attention. Madame and the other chiefs regaled her
with all the latest news and regrets over the surgical wonders she was
missing.

"Ah, such a *jolie opération!*" "Such a *cas intéressant!*" But perhaps another such emergency would arise later, they would console her
hopefully.

The doctors paid her frequent visits and gave professional advice,
though Elizabeth had complete faith in the skill of M. Blot. Even the
fat, red-faced priest to whom she had taken an intense dislike came to
bless her.

"Surely," she said gratefully to Anna, "there never was a case of
this disease around which such perfectly admirable conditions could
have been united!"

After the first week, graduating from the diet of water and gruel, she
was stuffed with delicacies which Anna, contemptuous of the hospital
food, insisted on bringing her: baskets of fruit, a beautiful fruit pie
glacé, her favorite veal cutlets "in curlpapers," on which, though unable
to use knife or fork, she performed a quick vanishing act through her
fingers. It was poor Anna now, straining all her faculties three times a
day to impart the magnetic "vital fluid," who lost weight, Elizabeth
who worried for fear she would "grow too fat and sensual."

But this was the least of her worries. Her cheerfulness was as much
a mask as the compresses which covered her eyes. Though she constantly
expressed certainty that the eye would be saved, she was by no means
sure. Encouraging as all were, she could sense the doubt, yes, the despair
in their voices. And she was a doctor. She knew all the dangers. She
had wept over more than one baby gone permanently blind from the
disease. And it was horribly contagious. In spite of all their precautions,
suppose the other eye became infected!

She took courage from the fact that the eye was still sensitive to light.
And when Hippolyte bent over her to remove with such an exquisite
delicacy of touch the films that had formed, she could see his face for
a moment clearly. But then to her dismay his features soon blurred,
and she was left in darkness. The waiting, forcing herself to be calm

and cheerful, was more torturing than the earlier pain, yet she knew the very slowness was the sole ground for hope, for if the detachment of the diseased portion came too soon, new membranes would have had no chance to form.

About two weeks after the accident the eye suddenly diminished in volume. Elizabeth sensed the fright and tension in her attendants. Only Anna misinterpreted the symptom. "But it's so much smaller! *Chérie*, it must be getting better!" Knowing that the eye might be literally emptying itself into the resultant cavity, Elizabeth did not disillusion her. Smiling, she tried to relax into complete immobility, and prayed. In an hour or two the diminution ceased and did not again recur.

After three weeks the right eye began gradually to open, though its sight was still negligible. However, she could get up and attend gropingly to some of her needs. Freed from constant attendance, M. Blot was able to return to his regular duties, also to his boning for the coming examinations. Elizabeth deplored the time he had lost on her account. If she could only somehow make amends, do something to show her appreciation of his professional service! She asked the advice . of Madame, and the two had long and spirited discussions.

"*Mon dieu*, I have it!" The *sage-femme* clapped her hands with furious enthusiasm. "Something for his office!"

Elizabeth gratefully agreed. He had to do much night reading. A pair of fine lamps! Madame arranged the purchase for her, and Elizabeth went one evening to see them, bundled into a dressing gown and shawl and feeling very much like a ghost as Mademoiselle Mallet guided her through the corridors. Appraising more by feeling than by sight, she adjudged the lamps fine indeed. They were taken to the intern's room that night. The next morning he came to her, obviously much excited and pleased but too conscientious to infringe on the rules by acknowledging the present. But he talked at length about other things, more intimately than ever before, except in that one moment of self-revelation.

"That long braid of hair — how do you make it so beautifully even and regular, without being able to see?" She sensed rather than felt his fingers on it, and trembled at the contact. . . . "You know I am rather an agnostic. But if I ever did join a church, I believe it would be one of your Protestant religion."

Even when he turned finally to go, it was obviously with reluctance.

He turned back again. "I — I want you to know — " Still his delicacy prevented his expressing the gratitude he felt.

"I'm glad you liked them," she said, taking the initiative. "The thanks should be all mine, *mon ami, mon frère.*"

Later Madamoiselle Mallet told her that the night before he had run in to Madame Charrier to tell her in delight about his present, and on his way out he had paused by the cloisters, evidently longing to enter the infirmary, but knowing he would be breaking rules by acting unprofessionally.

She was gratified by a visit from M. Davenne, the doctor who had peremptorily refused her permission to visit the hospitals. Though she could scarcely see him with her dim eye, she got a vague impression of a short, elderly man standing hat in hand, regarding her with the solemnity accorded the image of a saint.

"*C'est d'une patience!*" he marveled. "*Angélique!*"

Her greatest satisfaction, however, came from a conversation with Dr. Dubois, who confessed at last that he understood the justice of her determination to get a full medical education. He not only gave her *congé*, leave, from the Maternité with his blessing, but extended the hope of her gaining admittance to some of the *cliniques* and study in the Eccentric hospitals! That night she scrawled blindly in her diary, "Heaven has answered my heart-cry."

But all the answers were not to be as kind.

Bandaged and veiled, she left La Maternité the last of November. The *élèves* bade her a sorrowful but voluble goodbye. Mademoiselle Mallet wept. Madame Charrier was brusquely practical, but her kind eyes were bright with unshed tears. M. Blot bent low over her hand and kissed it. A carriage drove to the door and Anna guided her in. Through her dim good eye she caught glimpses of stone walls in a cold dull light. So ended her Maternité life.

In Anna's apartment she looked in the mirror for the first time since the accident. To laugh or to cry? The pale features thin to the point of gauntness, the witchlike wisps of hair, the misshapen eye, its pupil undistinguishable beneath a thick white film, shocked her into numbed horror. She decided to laugh, and all that evening she and Anna, who reluctantly followed her cue, burst sporadically into refreshing, if slightly hysterical, laughter.

But merriment, if such it was, was brittle gloss over mounting fear.

When M. Blot came the next day to treat her eye, the long calmness suddenly shattered.

"Tell me, my friend. I must know the truth. Is — is there any hope?"

His silence was more eloquent than words. "My dear — Mademoiselle," he said finally with pitying gentleness, "whatever life brings to us, is there not always hope?"

"Thank you," she said quietly.

He stood helplessly. "If — if there were only something I could do —"

She tried to smile. "If it's true, this is a loss for which there can be no consolation. I must meet and bear it." But there was no laughing that night. She and Anna wept together.

For two days she lived in black despair, taking little food, seeing no visitors. It was the nearest she had ever come to self-pity. Impossible to believe that this insuperable obstacle had risen between her and her life purpose! As the bitter thought recurred again and again, its very repetition became a negation of doubt. It *was* impossible! Hippolyte was wrong. Doctors, as she well knew, were often mistaken. Something resembling Anna's "vital fluid" began coursing through her veins. What was magnetism, after all, but strength of will, and she had always had that in abundance! Confidence returned. The eye was not dead. She could feel it throbbing with life. Even pain was a welcome earnest of vitality. She could still detect light, sense the shape of a hand passing in front of it. If that was not sight, what was it? She could not, *would* not believe that hope was dead. When Hippolyte came again, as he did each Sunday to inspect the eye and take an English lesson, he found her again cheerful, calm, and confident.

December passed, more torturing weeks of waiting, but brightened by her satisfaction when Hippolyte passed his examinations, winning his degree and gold medal. Her gratitude and friendship for the young doctor — destined to become one of Paris's distinguished gynecologists and obstetricians of the nineteenth century, noted not only for his vast experience but for his scientific work and original research — would be lifelong. She could heartily concur with the eulogy appearing forty years later in the *Bulletin de l'Académie de Médicine* at the time of his death.

"In private life," the article noted, "all knew his kindness, his devotion in time of trouble, his honesty. He hated injustice and lies. Occasionally he expressed himself with rather acid frankness. *C'était, pour tout dire en mot, un charactère."*

Elizabeth was still confident in January when, desperately tired of indoors and idleness, she ventured out for her first walk. The day was bitter cold, the ground covered with a coating of hard snow, but, well wrapped, Hannah's black lace veil doubled over her face, a handkerchief covering her left eye, she could have defied the cold of Siberia. She reveled in the fresh sweet air. Never had a summer nosegay held a more soul-rejoicing fragrance. She wanted to run, to shout. Her poor eye begged to be permitted one bracing breath, but prudence said no. It must content itself with reflex enjoyment from the other eye.

"I feel so well and full of life," she wrote the worried family in Cincinnati, who would rejoice at the sight of her handwriting, "that I long to knock you all down. But I'm afraid I can't repeat the experiment, for the snow, dropping steadily, has already reached three inches." Strange to be thus inhibited, when last year at this time she had been tramping to college through drifts reaching to her knees!

With hope still so warm and glowing, she could even write philosophically, "I am not sad or discouraged at what has taken place, nor is my faith in the least shaken. I suffered according to a grand and beautiful law, that the highest must suffer for the sins of the lowest, and this law of union now so productive of misery will sometime be the source of the most exquisite pleasure. I suffered also from the violation of material laws, having weakened somewhat the vigor of my health. But now see how beautifully the loving Father reconciles his special protection, while maintaining his universal laws. He fills me with a spirit of hope and confidence that reacts continually against the disease and will finally cure me."

But weeks lengthened into months, and there was little improvement. She was able to write for brief periods, but reading was impossible. Though her right eye grew steadily stronger, use of it, even in reading a page, aggravated the left. It became congested, projecting, and often painful. It was an impossible dilemma. If she worked, the sick eye cried out. If she was idle, body and soul both rebelled, and the thought of lost opportunities haunted her day and night. She grew even thinner. Her mirror reflected deep holes where cheeks had been. To Emily, who was now teaching in her old school in Henderson, Kentucky, she wrote wryly, "How true it is that we make our own world!

I who grew fat and rosy in that stupid little village where you are so-
journing for a while, have grown to a mere skeleton in this brilliant,
exciting world-famous city of Paris!"

A city as restless and impatient as herself, however . . . or was it
expectant, hoping that with spring and the March elections there might
be wrought some miracle? Anna, trusting in the prediction of a clairvoyant that foreign troops would enter Paris sometime in March, readied
her passport to flee at a moment's notice. Not so Elizabeth. No possible
revolution was going to drive her out. Their landlady expressed fear
that the democrats would carry the day. Elizabeth hoped they would,
for Napoleon's "republican" government had imprisoned its critics, suppressed free speech, indulged in every sort of petty tyranny. She could
not get much excited, however, knowing that the people would probably make a bad use of any triumph they might gain. Experience had
calmed her enthusiasm for apparently great movements. She must
guard her precious fire for the slow sure work of gradual reform.

The deadly months of waiting would have been unbearable without the constant concern of family. Anna was a bulwark of practical, if
erratic, strength. She was not only translating vigorously but writing as
the European correspondent for several American periodicals, including
Horace Greeley's *Tribune* and the *Pittsburgh Commercial Journal*,
which had agreed to pay her five dollars for an article every other week.
Though Elizabeth fretted under the obligation, the freedom from financial worry was a godsend. Howie visited them for several days, youthful eyes ashine with hero worship for Napoleon, and Kenyon came for a
week. Uncle Charles and Aunt Eliza wrote frequently from their home
in Dinard on the western coast of France, where they were living in
self-imposed exile from England, Uncle Charlie in constant fear lest
his possible bigamy should be discovered by the Horse Guards with the
probable result that he would be expelled from the army and perhaps
imprisoned for years at hard labor. (Later Anna, inspired by pity for
his misery as well as by horror of the possible family disgrace, was able
to ascertain by circuitous inquiry that his wife had indeed died, but
only recently, whereupon Uncle Charlie remarried Eliza legally, and
the unlucky pair were able to return to England.)

"Fate certainly gave me a strange and sudden blow," Elizabeth
wrote her uncle, "but now I am up again strong and hopeful, and
eager for work, and I get Uncle to feel quite sure that a brave soldier's

niece will never disgrace the colors she fights under. As to the more serious consideration — loss of vision — I still hope to recover that in time. I can write without difficulty, read a little, and hope to resume my usual employments. I still mean to be at no very distant day *the first lady surgeon in the world*."

Letters poured in constantly from America, and though she could not read them, Elizabeth lived with their news vicariously. She traveled the well-known route to Henderson with Emily, went with the boys to hear Emerson lecture, mourned with Harriet Stowe over the loss of a beloved child, grieved over the apparent suicide of her old friend James Perkins. She worried over the cholera in Cincinnati, breathed a sigh of relief when it abated, sympathized with Marian's dyspepsia and rejoiced when her sister found one item of food — clabbered milk — that agreed with her. She traveled with Harry over hopeless roads through Indiana and Kentucky behind the new white pony that he had swapped for his old mare and that could "swim like a fish," shivered in sympathy at the below-zero temperatures, but rejoiced at the new hardware orders he was able to bring back for Coombs, Ryland, and Blackwell. But the bit of news most significant for the Blackwells' future she could not relive, for Harry did not mention it.

He was on duty one day in the store when a young woman called with a small draft on Mr. Christian Donaldson, who was treasurer of the Ohio Anti-Slavery Society, for services she had rendered as lecturer to the society. Immediately Harry was attracted by her sweet voice, slender figure, bright smile, and charming personality.

"Sam should see her," he thought. "She looks like a girl he might be interested in."

Concerned because the young woman looked ill, he learned that she was returning east after nursing her brother, who had died of cholera, and that she herself was recovering from typhoid fever. Agreeing to send her the check the next morning, he dispatched Sam to perform the errand. But Sam was not attracted to the young woman, and she returned east without further incident. Her name was Lucy Stone.

But for Elizabeth these months of waiting were not completely wasted. Thanks to M. Boivin of La Maternité, she was given permission from the administration to visit the government hospitals. Her desire at last granted, and she could not take advantage of it! But she did not need eyes to listen to lectures, and fortunately some were free to the public.

She attended an interesting course at the Collège de France, conversations on *accouchement* with a highly educated *sage-femme*. She hired a student as a *répétiteur*, who drilled her in anatomy and at risk to himself smuggled her into the dead house of La Charité, where she did some dissection but, as M. Blot had predicted, found such close application injurious.

The lectures, however, were invaluable. Most interesting were those attended at the Collège de France delivered by Claude Bernard, about whom M. Blot had been so enthusiastic. Bernard was an experimental genius who had discovered the office of the pancreatic juice in dissolving fats. Suppressing her instinctive prejudice against the use of animals in experimentation, she watched, enthralled, while the eminent doctor, who had discovered that he could arrest the increase of sugar production by the liver merely by touching certain points of the medulla oblongata situated close together, produced diabetes in an animal in the presence of the class.

No wonder medical students flocked to Paris! A spirit of adventure, of daring investigation, pervaded young and old. Even Elizabeth, standing on the threshold of attainment, sensed the excitement. Somebody was always on the eve of an important discovery. Some brilliant theory was *almost* proved. New plans of treatment were constantly exciting attention in the hospitals, where discussion was widely spread through great crowds of students (males, of course!) freely admitted. Free lectures were supported by the government. The distinguished men who filled chairs in the medical college had leisure and opportunity for investigation and an audience to cheer them on. Leaving one of these exciting lectures, Elizabeth would sometimes stroll with another student or two into the adjacent garden of the Luxembourg, and sitting at the foot of some noble statue, they would prolong the discussion. There in the sparkling air with the fine old palace in clear view, mind stretched and quickened, spirit akin to trees and wind and water and the crowds moving among the gay flowers, life seemed poised on the edge of fulfillment. Anything was possible. She would still reach her goal, become a surgeon — and soon.

But not without two good eyes. One day in late May she faced the issue squarely, head on. It was the day the letter came from England. For months Kenyon had been using his influence to secure her admission as a student in one of the major hospitals of London. She read with incredulous delight.

At a House Committee held on
Tuesday the 14th day of May 1850

A *letter addressed to the Treasurer from Mr. Paget communicating to him the request of Miss Elizabeth Blackwell, a lady with connections in this country and the United States, to attend as a student in the Wards and other Department of the Hospital was read, when the Treasurer reported that the same had been referred to the Medical Council, and the opinion of all the members of the Council having been read and Mr. Paget having attended and furnished the Committee with such information as was required*

It was Resolved

That in the opinion of this Committee Miss Blackwell should be admitted as a student under such regulations as the Treasurer and Almoners may from time to time deem necessary.

James Paget, Esq.

The miracle had happened! She was admitted to St. Bartholomew's Hospital! Bless Mr. James Paget! The way was cleared now to complete her studies in any department she wished. Surgery, of course.

The upsurge of exultation burst like a bubble. She went slowly to the mirror and with her one good eye looked straight into it, taking note of the new angular line of features, the pale skin, the hollow cheeks. She raised both hands and drew the lids of the bad eye downward and upward, so that the eyeball was exposed. She studied its unnatural whiteness, the thickened state of the cornea affected by the almost constant inflammation, the unpleasant corneal projection which none of the doctors could understand. Ugly-looking, though she cared not a whit about her appearance. Covering her right eye, she turned toward the window. Its light was very faint. Forms she could not in the least distinguish. This was the seventh month since the accident. Why, during all these weeks had she tried to deceive herself? Hippolyte had tried to tell her, but she had not been willing to listen. Stupid optimism, that had been so loath to face facts! Now she did face them. She had lost the sight of the eye. It was gone. Irrevocably.

So — she could never be a surgeon. She felt as if a door had been slammed in her face, and she stood outside, beating her fists against it. She was used to facing the difficult. She knew how to deal with it. Almost never before in her life had she faced the impossible. She was the child of five discovering that no matter how far or how fast she ran she could never reach Ireland. And what had she done then? Stamped her foot, railed at fate, and, retreating, made life miserable for herself and everybody else. Easy now to act like that child. But she was no longer a child.

Leaving the mirror, she went closer to the window and looked out. The gardens glimpsed through the western gate were prodigal with spring. The acacias were coming into bloom. Children raced about the many paths, scampering among the flowers as last fall they had cavorted through the dead leaves. At the end of many converging avenues of trees the ancient palace glimmered. Elizabeth's senses quickened. How wonderful that she could still see such beauty! How stupid to be lamenting the loss of one eye instead of rejoicing in the saving of the other! Suppose she couldn't be a surgeon. There was more than one road to the palace of healing.

Chapter Eight

THE SUCCESSION OF TRAINS crawled and rattled through the fertile fields of Belgium, the romantic hills of Germany, the sandy plains of Prussia. The trip from Paris to Freiwaldau, at the foot of the Gräfenberg on the borders of Austria took five days. M. Blot and others had tried to discourage Elizabeth from making it.

"You're a little crazy, *mon amie.* Taking that long and expensive journey all alone to a half-savage country where a peasant takes the place of a physician! And in your condition!"

"In my condition," replied Elizabeth, "it seems to me very wise."

She had heard of Priessnitz and his water cure from a German woman who, it was reported, had studied medicine in the face of great difficulties and insults, though unable to win a diploma. Elizabeth had written to her, and the two had enjoyed a cordial correspondence. This Maria von Colomb, it developed, had derived great benefit from a three-year stay in Priessnitz's famous establishment. The idea had struck like a spark. Mountains, fresh air, water! Her drained, wasted body had tingled at the prospect. Not that she had faith in the cure itself, though she was curious about its techniques. But it gave promise of the renewing power of nature at its best, and it was for fresh air and living water that she yearned.

Her first glimpse of the mountains was disappointing. She had expected, hoped for, height and wildness. There was height, to be sure, at least seven thousand feet, but the vast smooth sides, gently sloping and joining one another, were cultivated to the very top, little white cottages with brown roofs seeming to make one continuous village. Freiwaldau, occupying a triangular space formed by the slopes of several mountains, was at the bottom of the steep ascent. Arriving on Saturday afternoon,

243

Elizabeth took a room in the Crown Hotel and immediately set out to find Priessnitz's headquarters in the town, where she delivered her letter of introduction. A large, healthy-looking woman with very black eyes and hair, who was taking the cure, advised her to remain there in Freiwaldau, as she was doing.

"Impossible for a lady to stay on the Gräfenberg!" She seemed shocked by the idea. "Why, they are almost all gentlemen there, and they go about in their shirtsleeves!"

Undeterred by this horrifying prospect, Elizabeth determined to see Priessnitz himself before making up her mind, and immediately started to climb the mountain. It was a beautiful walk of half an hour, straight up past innumerable furious little springs, terraces covered with corn and olive trees and a profusion of wild flowers. Near the top was an enormous white house, out of the side of which a huge stream rushed into a stone basin, with other smaller houses around it. As she entered the great stone hall, she was greeted not only by the sound of rushing waters, but, better yet, by odors of baking cakes, and she longed to stay here, regardless of the shirtsleeves. Priessnitz was not at home and she returned to town tired and disappointed. But, learning that he came into town each day to treat patients, she left her name at his headquarters and asked him to call.

Hiring an interpreter the next morning, she set out to find lodgings, a discouraging task, for the town was crowded with patients and their friends. A couple of damp dismal chambers were all she could discover. Moreover, there was no boardinghouse, and she must hire a servant or have meals sent from the hotel, a liability aggravated by the fact that she could not speak a decent German sentence! She returned to the hotel and was sitting in her little upper room feeling very discouraged when the door opened and in walked a middle-sized, elderly man with sunburned, pockmarked face, gray hair, light blue eyes, and a very pleasant expression.

"Certainly, Fräulein," he assured her when she had explained her purpose, "I can make you quite strong in about six weeks, and I guarantee it will do no harm to your eye. And you *can* come, child, to Gräfenberg. Come this afternoon, and bring your things with you."

Infinitely relieved and undaunted by the shirtsleeves, Elizabeth hired a cart to transport her baggage and again climbed the mountain. But she was a bit confounded when shown her quarters, a little room at the very top of the house, with bare rafters for roof and wall, a row of tiny windows a foot high set into the roof over her head, a wooden crib filled with straw, three wooden chairs, a table, a low bureau with a green earthenware bowl. The servant girl must have noticed her dismay.

"Your next-door neighbors are an Italian count and countess," she hastened to inform her. "There are eight ladies and eight gentlemen on this floor, and anyway, you will be out in the woods all day."

When the bell rang for tea, Elizabeth was shown into an immense hall big enough to seat five hundred, gaily painted, ornamented with chandeliers, and was seated, to her amazement, in a row of ladies in grand toilette, their gossamer dresses with shorter sleeves and lower waists than she thought were ever worn, hair dressed with curls and flowers, bracelets and rings to match! A strange contrast to the simple fare of sour and sweet milk, brown bread and butter! The bread was so sour that she could hardly swallow it, but the milk was good, and she did it justice. Since the gentlemen's shocking shirtsleeves were all covered with coats, she was spared that predicted embarrassment.

The water cure began the next morning, with Priessnitz assisting, as usual with a new patient: a packing, a half-bath, a plunge bath, a wet bandage, and some glasses of cold water at six in the morning; an *abreibung*, sitz bath, and another wet bandage at noon; the same at four; and water, water drunk *ad libitum* all through the day. It was the same each day, never varying. The rest of the time was spent walking among the innumerable little paths winding up and down the mountain, through sweet-smelling fields or fragrant fir woods, passing many springs along the way. At each, one would stop and drink, chat with other patients, perhaps sit for a few moments. Routine never varied: bathing, walking, drinking, bathing, walking, eating. She developed a ravenous appetite. Fortunately the diet was not all sour black bread and milk, or even the meat and vegetables served at noon. An old woman opened a white bread shop every morning outside the dining room, patronized by almost all the patients, who came marching to meals with loaves tucked under their arms. Then every morning and evening small strawberry gatherers assembled around the steps, offering bright little wild berries for a very small sum. Eating this plain wholesome food, rambling over the mountains, stimulated by wind and water, she found herself suddenly in vigorous health, her past weakness seeming like a fable.

She was lonely at first, separated from the other five hundred or more *Kurgaste* (cure guests) both by language and by social disparity. Instead of a rustic spot where one walked about barefoot and wore old clothes, as she had expected, she was in a fashionable summer resort, the rage of Germany, where counts and barons and generals played billiards, attended balls and theaters, and dressed in the pink of fashion. There was even a little prince, a poor half-blind child sent to be cured. She had brought altogether too small a wardrobe, and even her best gray silk would have looked like calico among these low-cut velvets and satins. She would have had little in common with them, anyway, for they were scarcely a part of the democratic movement surging through Europe with which she felt such strong sympathy.

However, she made a few friends, an American youth, a Mr. Glynn, nearly blind from amaurosis, who seemed like a brother among all the guttural-voiced strangers; and a French woman, shrewd and lively. And she had some contact with the nobility. One day she was sitting in her loft in slippers and an old dressing gown when a knock came at the door. Outside stood an impressive, black-whiskered foreigner.

"*Madame la Doctresse?*"

"*Oui.*" Gratefully Elizabeth responded to his French.

"*La Doctresse* Blackwell?" Apparently he still doubted her identity. Once assured, he presented the respects of *Madame La Princesse* Obolenska, who hoped that she would call on her when she next came to Freiwaldau. Bewildered but flattered, Elizabeth did so, to find that the visit was not social but professional! Expecting to be accorded honor by the visit, instead she was forced to accept four gulden. But the satisfaction of having given her first professional consultation was greater than any social honor could have brought.

The "patients" represented every sort of ailment, from the jaded ennui of the nobility to complete blindness. But Elizabeth was unable to discover any instances where cures of actual bodily disease were effected. For a while her own resurge of health brought a bounding hope. Surely some of this burst of reawakening life must communicate itself to her poor sightless eye! As the weeks passed, it did indeed, but not in the way she was beginning to hope. Perhaps so much air and water and constantly expended energy proved too stimulating to the sensitive organ. Perhaps such a climax was inevitable, no matter where she was. But one morning she awoke in violent pain, the eye terribly inflamed. It was the agony of La Maternité all over again. Priessnitz was infinitely solicitous, obviously helpless, but encouraging. Doubtless this was one of those "seven crises" which often occurred during the water cure. Dreadful though it seemed at the moment, it could well be a harbinger of favorable change.

But Priessnitz was no doctor, only the high priest of water. Elizabeth knew better. She made arrangements immediately to return to Paris. The five days' trip was sheer torture. No enjoyment this time of the sandy plains, the romantic hills, the fertile fields! Every jolt of the clattering train pounded like a hammer. Even her good eye was affected, since its every motion caused a sympathetic twinge of pain, so even to open it was agony. But the physical torture was nothing beside the mental. From the summit of hope she had plummeted to the depths of despair. For a few brief weeks she had been herself again, felt the old buoyancy of health and readiness for work. What now? As the rumbling wheels bore her closer and closer to Paris, she became more and more afraid of the answer.

Anna was spending the summer out of the city in St. Cloud, and there had been no time for a letter to reach her. After establishing herself in their old lodging, Elizabeth consulted the famous oculist Louis-Auguste Desmarres, noted not only for his treatises on eye diseases but for his advanced techniques in eye surgery. He confirmed her fears. The eye must be removed.

Why should she find this news so dismaying? She did not fear an operation. She had already endured the extremity of physical pain. She was not especially concerned about her appearance. Was it possible, then, that she had still nurtured a stubborn notion that full sight would one day be restored? Whatever the reason, she felt enveloped in darkness, spirit as well as body.

She was operated on the fifteenth of August. Then began the weeks of waiting in preparation for the fitting of her new glass eye. She was by no means deserted in her extremity. Anna came in frequently from St. Cloud. In response to her letters and to Elizabeth's poor penciled scrawls written without benefit of sight, consoling letters poured in from the family: from Portway, with invitations to come immediately to England; from Uncle and Aunt in Dinard; from Cincinnati, where Hannah was struggling with boarders, Sam was recovering from an unrequited love, and Emily, back from Henderson, was filled with terrible self-doubt and frustration; from Brattleboro, Vermont, where Marian, still on the clabber milk diet, was taking another of the famous water cures; from New York, where Ellen, staying with the Alofsens — their old family friends and neighbors from the Jersey City days — was feeling misunderstood and thwarted in her struggle to become an artist.

At least the Blackwells maintained solidarity even in their frustrations and failures! This concerned involvement with family aroused in Elizabeth no bitterness or self-pity. Instead it gave her a sense of increased fellowship with all men.

"I could only understand this accident," she was to write a few weeks later to her old friend Dr. Dickson, "as an illustration of that grand law of the solidarity of the human race, which someday will repay, by its infinite production of happiness, the misery it seems now to inflict on the innocent."

The weeks of waiting passed, six of them, and Dr. Desmarres was skillful. The right eye had been saved and grew steadily stronger. The glass eye, while of no earthly use except as an ornament, restored her appearance almost to normal. Not that it mattered! It was the discovery that she could read again, that she was once more independent and able to work, which filled her with such joy that all sorrow in her loss seemed insignificant. The prospect of the opportunities awaiting her at St. Bartholomew's in London shone like a beacon light. Joyously and hastily she made her preparations, leaving for England early in October. The unfortunate accident was already a thing of the past. Except in that one letter to Dr. Dickson, she was never again to refer to it in writing.

2

"Is it England that has changed," wondered Elizabeth, "or is it I?"

Where were the glamour and glory of London a year ago? Historic monuments looked old and drab instead of dramatically ancient. Houses looked dingy. The people seemed ugly in appearance, their dress vulgar, their manners rude, their work days long and monotonous. She felt sealed in an envelope of smoky fog which sickened her all day and kept her awake at night. Never had she felt more forlorn, more foreign. But it was more than the bright airiness of Paris which she had left behind. It was a world which, in spite of discomforts and tragedy, had held friends, adventure, romance — in fact, the world of Hippolyte Blot.

"How strongly my life turns to him!" she confessed once to her diary. "And yet that terrible suffering has put a distance between us that nothing can remove."

The occasional letters they exchanged, one containing news of his betrothal, another of his marriage, both assuaged and aggravated the sense of loss. *"Chère demoiselle et bonne amie, ou, plutôt, chère soeur, puisque vous voulez bien m'appeler votre frère . . ."* Eh bien, she had done her work well that night, sealing their relationship with finality as that of "brother" and "sister."

A week in Portway, where she made friends with Kenyon's new wife Marie, whom he had married in August, only postponed her painful adjustment to the new environment. The notoriously unpleasant ilk of lodginghouse keepers seemed even more exasperating than usual, making the most absurd claims for the dingiest and least desirable of rooms. "Occupied by a colonel in the army and a clergyman of the Establishment," was the glowing description of two miserable little rooms off a courtyard, "and at this very moment I have on the third floor Mrs. Captain Popper, with an income of five hundred pounds a year!" But she was finally settled in two rooms on the drawing room floor of a house in Thavies Inn, which in spite of its name was not an "inn" at all but a very respectable little street entered by an arched passage and containing a number of houses grouped about an inner court, an especially desirable location for a single lady, since the iron gates at the archway were locked at night, with a porter always on guard in a little house at the entrance. And though her bedroom windows overlooked an old churchyard as gray and lifeless as if it stood in a primeval forest instead of on Holborn Hill, they also gave a glimpse of the giant dome of St. Paul's gleaming through the mists. Not that she had time to be either depressed or exhilarated by the view!

To her relief her appearance at classes at St. Bartholomew's excited no more vexatious reaction among the students than curious stares and ripples of polite astonishment. James Paget, her sponsor, was doubtless even more relieved, for he must have had serious misgivings.

"It was thought rather bold," one of his published letters confessed later, "that a lady was admitted to attend my lectures; the courtesy of the students at that time showed that at least one could be safe."

Mrs. Paget shared both his concern and relief. "Well, we have our 'lady doctor' here at last," she wrote one of her friends in October, "and she has actually attended two of James' lectures, taking her seat with perfect composure. The young men have behaved extremely well, and she really appears likely to go on her way, and unmolested. She breakfasted here one morning with several of our students and last evening we had a few medical friends to dinner, and she joined us in the evening. Her manners are quiet, and it is evident her motives for the pursuit of so strange a vocation are pure and good. So let us hope she will become useful in her generation."

Elizabeth reacted to these social overtures with mixed emotions. The breakfast at the Pagets' home, inside the hospital boundaries, was pleasant. The other students invited, about a dozen, were curious but gentlemanly. But the dinner party at the same house in honor of the distinguished Professor Kölliker, where there were three other women guests beside herself, was more ordeal than pleasure. The shock of all three at her unconventional status was apparent. But she was equally shocked and repelled, for the ladies were in full dress — short sleeves, gowns so low that more than a third of the bosom was visible, stiffness which made balloons of their petticoats, all manner of scarves and "flyaways"! Women so dressed did not resemble rational beings and should not be treated as such. Englishwomen, she decided, were disappointing, with few exceptions. Mrs. Paget was both sensible and agreeable. Mrs. Twomley, wife of one of Cousin Sam's friends, was warm and sympathetic. But the Twomleys lived five miles away on the other side of Regent's Park. Elizabeth prepared herself for a winter devoid of female companionship. Though her days were soon filled with hospital duties and medical studies, her evenings promised little but solitude and loneliness.

How wrong she was! One dull afternoon she was sitting in her big lodginghouse front room, bare in spite of its six chairs and a table, recalling pleasanter environs of study under the bright skies and spreading trees of the Luxembourg Garden, when a knock came at her door, not the timid tapping of the service girl or the nervous *rat-tat* of the landlady. There was a verve about this knock, a rhythmic vigor like the insistent summons of a drum. Instinctively Elizabeth's pulse quickened as she hurried to obey it.

Three young women stood on the threshold, *very* young, she qualified, feeling the weight of her own twenty-nine years. They were radiant with youth, exploding with energy, especially the one in front, a girl with glowing color and a mass of golden hair.

"Dr. Blackwell? I'm Barbara Leigh Smith. This is my sister Nannie and our friend Bessie Raynor Parkes. We've heard so much about you, and we think you're so wonderful, and we just had to come and see you. We do so want to become your friends!"

The three girls entered, injecting into the dull room all the magic of Paris sunshine and the color of the Luxembourg Garden. Later they were to hang its walls with charming paintings, fill it with the fragrance of hothouse flowers, but the transformation had already been effected by their mere presence.

"We've heard all about you," repeated Barbara with tempestuous eagerness, "and we admire you tremendously. We want to be just like you if we can, become pioneers in some activity that will help change things for women. We feel our society is so terribly unjust, and we want to do something to encourage the responsible and practical work of women in the various duties of life."

It was almost too good to be true. An intelligent and joyous rebellion in this stultified female society! Even the dress of these young rebels was delightfully unconventional. Amid styles which aped the flamboyant magentas and billows of Napoleon's Countess Eugénie, their gowns, though tasteful and obviously expensive, were both discreet and practical, and, if Elizabeth was not mistaken, their healthy young bodies were unimprisoned by corsets! She was even more intrigued by their description of a trip Barbara and Bessie had just taken through Belgium, Germany, Austria, and Switzerland, unchaperoned, Barbara further flouting convention by blue-tinted spectacles which had aroused great mirth among German *hausfraus*, Bessie eliciting almost as great merriment with a pair of hobnailed but extremely utilitarian boots.

During the eager sharing of experiences and yearnings Elizabeth studied the young women with mounting interest and appreciation — Nannie, a slightly muted replica of her sister; Bessie, thoughtful, reserved, poetic — but her gaze always returned to the vivid Barbara. She was like a flame. She literally glowed. Perhaps it was partly her hair. Later George Eliot, using Barbara as a model for *Romola*, was to describe it as a "reddish gold color, enriched by an unbroken ripple such as may be seen in the sunset clouds on grandest autumnal evenings." But it was much more than hair. Her fire came from within, a burning passion for living life to the full and for expending self in worthwhile endeavors.

"What must their fathers be like!" marveled Elizabeth, mindful of her own vast debt to the radical Samuel.

She was soon to discover, for that afternoon's visit sparked friendships which were to endure for a lifetime. She not only became a frequent visitor at the Leigh Smith house at No. 5 Blandford Square but was drawn into an intimate group of liberal intellectuals which included Lady Noel Byron, William Morris, Sir John Herschel, Christina Rossetti, Professor Faraday, the celebrated author Mrs. Jameson, and the Honorable Russell Gurney.

No wonder Barbara was a firebrand of reform! Her great-grandfather had shocked England in the previous century by sympathizing with the American colonists. Her grandfather, William Smith, had not only aided Wilberforce in his campaign for the abolition of the slave trade but had almost lost his life through avowed sympathy with the ideals of the French Revolution. Her father Benjamin, a Unitarian and the Radical Member for Norwich in the House of Commons, had assisted in the repeal of the Corn Laws. Like Samuel Blackwell, he had acted on the belief that his daughters should receive the same education as his sons and had further shocked Victorian society by sending them to a Swedenborgian school where they rubbed shoulders with the ragged children of London slums. Exiled Poles, Hungarians, Italians, Frenchmen, as well as the intellectual elite, swarmed through the house in Blandford Square, exposing the children to every cult and creed as well as erudite philosophy. Adding to the popular horror was his habit of bundling his family into a big carriage built like an omnibus and drawn by four horses, and taking them each year on a long journey, to Ireland, to Italy, to France, where, equipped with books, sketchbooks, and adult mentors, they inspected all aspects of society, evil as well as benign.

Most shocking of all, however, to his contemporaries was the aforementioned act of bestowing financial independence on his daughter Barbara the day she became of age. Friends and relatives could hardly believe their ears. For it struck at the grass roots of the Victorian family. Sons might be given such independence, yes, but never daughters. Economically the woman was utterly dependent on a man: husband, father, brother. Politically she did not exist. If unmarried, she was the virtual property of her father, plaything or servant to suit his whim. If married, she was in still worse bondage, without legal entity. Not until 1857 would she be able to obtain a divorce. Her husband might beat her, commit adultery, deny her access to her children, yet remain within his legal rights. There was more truth than jest in the old witticism: "My wife and I are one, and I am he."

In fact, the position of the typical British male had been vividly enunciated about the time of Elizabeth's birth by Thomas Carlyle in an ultimatum to his future wife, Jane Welsh.

"The man should bear rule in the house and not the woman," he had announced, proceeding to amplify: "I must not and I cannot live in a house of which I am not head. I should be miserable myself, and make all about me miserable. Think not, Darling, that this comes from an imperious temper; that I shall be a harsh and tyrannical Husband to thee. God forbid! But it is the nature of a man that if he be controlled by anything but his own reason, he feels himself degraded, and incited, be it justly or not, to rebellion and discord. It is the nature of a woman again to cling to the man for support and direction; to comply with his humors, and feel pleasure in doing so, simply because they are his; to reverence while she loves him, to conquer him not by her force but by her weakness, and perhaps (the cunning gypsy!) after all to command him by obeying him."

That the marriage following this announcement to a spirited young woman was turbulent was not surprising, but that it occurred at all was testimony to the current futility of female rebellion.

No wonder, then, that even the isolated instance of a young woman becoming financially independent, hence self-supporting, provoked Benjamin Smith's fellow-gentry to shock and horror! Suppose it put ideas in other women's heads!

Obviously it had, especially that of Bessie Parkes, whose parents were of such "respectable" breed that their daughters, according to custom, dared not ride in an omnibus or go out alone in the street — indeed, were not permitted to drive down Regent Street in a hansom cab. By all rights Bessie should have sat in the drawing room all the morning embroidering, playing the piano, reading wholesome literature, or pursuing some other elegant hobby, and making genteel visits the rest of the day. But to the amazement of her indulgent father she did nothing of the kind. She refused to embroider, read every heretic book she could get hold of, talked (though hazily) of following a profession, and was even known to go to an evening party without gloves!

Elizabeth reveled in this rare air of independence. It was the climate in which she herself, to a lesser degree, had been reared. She welcomed her new acquaintances, recognized that in spite of their intellect and character, they were confused and without an aim in life, and hoped she could help them. The aid was mutual. When Barbara insisted on sharing her generous income to help her meet expenses, Elizabeth was both embarrassed and relieved. Barbara's arguments were persuasive. "But you're doing all this for us! How can we promote the cause of women any better than by helping educate someone who can really show the world what women can do? And besides, my father wants to help too. He admires you tremendously." Elizabeth accepted the help gratefully, though insisting that it be considered a loan. Now that Kenyon was married, she hated to depend on his largesse, and she knew Anna could ill afford the small amounts she had been sending. As usual, Elizabeth was thrifty to the point of niggardliness.

Her evenings became filled with social gatherings. Not even in Cincinnati in the old Semi-Colon days had she feasted on such rich viands of music, art, literature, or in such distinguished and scintillating company. In spite of its fogs and smoke London became as bright and colorful as Paris, the life she was constructing as original and exciting as the huge structure of iron and glass being reared for the Great Industrial Exhibition in Hyde Park. Her energy was boundless. Often she would walk home from Blandford Square between twelve and one at night, being too poor to engage a cab, then rise the next morning at seven-thirty, not exhausted but invigorated for the day's work.

For the evenings were but sweetmeats supplementing the solid viands of her days. Each morning she walked down Holborn Hill, took a shortcut through the once famous Cock Lane, and in about five minutes reached the first gate of St. Bartholomew's, avoiding more than a side glance at the nearby Smithfield Cattle Market with its present screaming of bulls and pigs, and worse yet, its past memories of the fearful fires of persecutions. Then, a small dark figure clad in doctor's sack with writing case under her arm, she made her way through a mass of assembling students who politely, but gaping and curious, stood aside to let her pass, and went to the museum, where she intently studied the specimens lining the walls until the time of Professor Paget's physiology and pathology lecture at nine-thirty. James Paget, soon to publish his distinguished *Lectures on Tumors* and later to become sergeant surgeon to the Queen, was already one of England's eminent surgical pathologists. He had graciously explained her presence to the class, about sixty men, before her arrival, whereupon she had entered the small amphitheater, bowed, and received an encouraging round of applause. Her seat was always reserved for her. It was the most gentlemanly class she had ever attended.

"You will find, my dear Doctor," the professor had warned her, "that you will encounter much more prejudice from ladies than from gentlemen." Elizabeth knew that already. She had discovered it in his own house! Prejudice thrived on intellectual blindness, and most of these Englishwomen remained tightly wrapped in their traditional cocoons. She was by no means daunted. The work of ages must not be hindered by individual emotions. In a hundred years, please God, women would be different.

She took only the one course of lectures. There were more important things to do. St. Bartholomew's was one of the oldest and richest institutions in London. It contained nearly six hundred beds and the previous year had treated over seventy-seven thousand patients. She had been given the full rights of a student, with permission to visit all the wards, follow the physicians, or pursue private study. The superiors were for the most part friendly and cooperative: the chief physicians, Doctors Hue, Roupell, and Burrows; the chief surgeons, Messrs. Lawrence, Stanley, and Lloyd. On one occasion Dr. Hue took her by an underground passage to Christ's Hospital to taste the excellent pea soup for which that institution was famous! An introduction to Dr. Oldham brought a most interesting visit to Guy's Hospital. Dr. Oldham expressed great friendliness toward women's study of medicine, and when Elizabeth told him that her sister was just beginning her medical studies, he beamed approvingly.

"Should she come to England," he promised, "and wish to obtain entrance to Guy's Hospital, I should be glad to assist her."

From only one department at St. Bart's was Elizabeth excluded from professional instruction, that of *women's diseases!* The professor of midwifery and diseases of women and children could not exclude her from his wards since visiting permission had been granted by the governors, but he wrote her a polite note saying that he entirely disapproved of a lady's studying medicine and begged her to consider that his neglecting to give her aid was owing to no disrespect to her as a lady but to his condemnation of her object.

Not that anyone, students or professors, except perhaps James Paget, really understood her! Some apparently thought she must be an extraordinary intellect overflowing with knowledge, others, a queer eccentric. Nobody seemed to realize that she was merely a quiet sensible person who had acquired a small amount of medical knowledge and who wished by patient observation and study to acquire considerably more. But as time passed she slowly observed signs that they began to consider her as an ordinary mortal, worthy of their respect. One old doctor was especially helpful, giving her many useful hints from his experience. She spent three or four hours each day in the wards, chiefly medical, diagnosing diseases, watching the progress of cases, accustoming her ear to the stethoscope.

"Already," she wrote Emily late in November, "I feel that I have made progress and detect sounds that I could not distinguish on my entrance. I advise you, Emily, to familiarize yourself with the healthy sounds of the chest. When you go home, auscultate all the family. You will find quite a variety in the sounds, although all may be healthy persons. Lay a cloth over the chest and listen with the ear simply. It is as good as a stethoscope with clean people."

By this time also she was writing case histories, detailing her day-to-day observations.

Nov. 22. Wilson, a laundress of London, unmarried, 21 years of age, entered Nov. 22nd. A blonde, with high colour, large and plump. . . . Constant pain in lower part of chest . . . cough and expectoration of blood.

Nov. 23. The following is the condition of the patient the day after her entrance into the Hospital: The pulse cannot be counted at the wrist. . . . Auscultation shows a striking derangement of the heart action.

Nov. 24. Cough with brownish water mucous expectoration, speckled with crimson. . . . Great exhaustion. . . . Milk diet prescribed and tinc. digitalis . . .

The history carried through in detail until December 13, when great improvement was noted.

But Elizabeth was by no means in agreement with all she saw and learned.

"I am obliged to feel very skeptical as to the wisdom of the practice which I see pursued every day," she wrote Dr. Dickson only two days after completing this case history. "I try very hard to believe, I continually call up my own inexperience and the superior ability of the physicians whose actions I am watching; but my doubts will not be subdued, and render me the more desirous of obtaining the bedside knowledge of sickness which will enable me to *commit heresy* with intelligence in the future, if my convictions impel me to it."

Yet she was as dissatisfied with the "heresies" as with the present conservative approach to medicine, so dependent on drugs. Neither hydropathy nor mesmerism substantiated the claims of their enthusiastic votaries. She had not heard of one case of perfect cure at Gräfenberg. She wished she could study magnetism further, also homeopathy. It was the spirit of adventure, of experimentation, which she missed most in England. No wonder students thronged to Paris instead of to this immense smoke-ridden London! Here there was no excitement. All moved steadily forward, constantly but without enthusiasm. No theory set the world on fire until it was well established. Everything was stamped by good sense, clear substantial thought, but, oh, how she longed sometimes for a visit to the Collège de France, where somebody was always on the threshold of exciting discovery!

Hygiene, the prevention of disease rather than its cure, she became more and more convinced, should be the true basis of medicine. Her acquaintance with Professor Georgii, Swedish exponent of kinesipathy and a disciple of Brandt, whose consultation rooms she often visited in Piccadilly, strengthened her faith in the employment of hygienic measures rather than a complete reliance on drugs.

"I have come to this conclusion," she wrote Emily, hopefully her future partner. "I must begin with a practice which is an old established custom, which has really more expressed science than any other system. Nevertheless, as it dissatisfies me heartily, I shall commence as soon as possible building up a hospital in which I can experiment. And the very instant I feel *sure* of any improvement I shall adopt it in my practice, in spite of a whole legion of opponents!"

Scarcely an unexpected reaction from this sort of woman!

3

In England Elizabeth was always recognized as an American, which was strange, for in America she had been recognized as English! And yet perhaps not so strange, for she was both . . . and neither. Every nationality she met seemed a bit alien, for though she admired all of them, she was forced also to criticize each.

She had no difficulty detecting an American even without his peculiar intonation and use of words. He revealed himself as a wide yet shallow thinker with a great readiness to express himself on every subject. In America, she felt, reform ideas were more loudly advocated but by persons with stronger heads than hands. Those with the power to accomplish reform expended their energies in making money or toeing a party line. Englishmen might be slow to act and unimaginative, yet they showed greater depth of thought. Many men whom she met — Mr. De Morgan, a professor in London University, Mr. Morell, a government inspector of schools, the attorney Mr. Twomley — seemed open to progressive ideas yet ununited for action. Sometime, perhaps in their children, such ideas might reach a perfect development.

But English*women!* With few exceptions they showed little thought at all. They were immersed in trivialities, embroidery, art dabbling, warming their husbands' slippers, *dress.* At Christmas Elizabeth was amazed by the loaded shop windows, piled to the ceiling with flyaway petticoats, their delicate black gauze embroidered with blue, gold, silver, and endless flowers; with mantles or paletots of poor quality velvet, some trimmed with plush a foot wide; habit shirts with embroidered collars and ribbon bows for less than four shillings. Starving pay it must be for the poor needlewomen!

The exceptions were heartening. Barbara and Bessie with their group of ardent young intellectuals were floundering rebelliously, struggling toward goals which they had not even yet envisoned. Elizabeth longed to imbue them with purpose, something of the spirit which seemed to be activating a few hardy women in America. For across the ocean ideas were crystallizing into action. The Elders wrote that a medical school *for women* had actually been started that year in Philadelphia. A letter from Marian told of a big women's rights convention which she and Ellen had attended in Worcester, Massachusetts.

Elizabeth was only mildly impressed by these developments. She was glad the school had not been in existence three years before, though she would have welcomed it at the time. Far better to have demonstrated the right of a woman to share equally with men in a regular course of instruction! And if she had been in America, she would not have attended the convention. After carefully reading through its proceedings and admiring its high emotion and energy, though deprecating its lack of strong clear thought, she tried to summarize her own views in a letter to Marian.

"My head is full of organization, and the organization of women, but not as women in opposition to men. I cannot sympathize fully with an anti-man movement. I have had too much kindness, aid, and full recognition from men to make this attitude of woman otherwise than painful to me, and I think the true end of freedom may be gained better another way."

Far more than their attendance at this great pioneer assembly Elizabeth envied Marian and Ellen their present winter in Boston, where they were constantly exposed to the invigorating ideas of William Channing. Already she was dreaming of a grandiose organization which would far exceed the bounds even of his associationism. She wanted women to have their rights, yes, but not as women, as human beings. And she was less concerned with their legal and intellectual rights than with their moral freedom.

For she was appalled by the public evidence of immorality which pervaded London. It weighed fearfully upon her conscience. In Paris prostitution had been legalized and hidden, a recognized and profitable branch of the government, and though she had lived with its deplorable consequences at La Maternité, she had been less aware of its presence. Here in London it had been left alone to take its natural course. At all hours of the night she saw groups of derelict women standing at every corner, decked in their best, usually a faded shawl over a tattered dress, attempting to earn their living by the only occupation permitted an ignorant or impoverished woman. Looking into the thin hungry features, she detected aching hearts. Such exploitation of womanhood by a dominantly male society seemed an evil equivalent to slavery.

Women must be organized to fight this evil, yes, but not women alone! Like slavery, it was a cause demanding the noblest souls, both men and women. Her dream was of a grand moral reform society, the remedy to be sought in every sphere of life, radical action, not foolish panaceas. There would be many sub-branches, working through education, industrial occupation, clubs, homes, social unions, an effective press, all so combined that their influence could be brought to bear on any prominent evil, and its head should be no less a personage than Queen Victoria herself! She had other still more radical ideas.

"We must leave the present castaway," she wrote Marian, "but redeem the rising generation." How? Mainly by education. And that must include — heresy of heresies — sex education.

She could not share such ideas with her young friends. Even girls

259

like Barbara and Bessie, daughters of men like Benjamin Smith, would have blushed at the mere mention of the word "sex." That was one trouble, decided Elizabeth shrewdly. The young, especially girls, should be educated in the plain facts of life, and their parents were the ones to do it. Already she was thinking hazily of compiling some of those facts in writing, a project which a quarter of a century later was to shock her generation even more profoundly than her study of medicine.

But she found one kindred spirit with whom she could discuss even these forbidden subjects. When an invitation came through her friend Miss Montgomery to visit Lady Noel Byron at Brighton, she could not resist. The widow of the brilliant but dissipated poet was a romantic figure, revered by English society as the innocent victim of a tragic marriage. Moreover, the invitation hinted of keen interest in medicine and gave promise of a visit to Brighton's excellent hospital.

Elizabeth arrived on a bright windy afternoon in March. In the parlor of a large stone house facing the full fury of Atlantic winds and spray she was greeted by a slender, rather small, venerable-looking lady of sixty, with fair complexion, delicate features, gray hair. The longer they conversed the more Elizabeth's interest and admiration mounted. Never had she met a woman with greater scientific interest and knowledge. Lady Byron possessed the deep wisdom of long and tragic experience. She had never recovered from the blow caused by the conduct of her husband, whom she had worshiped with real idolatry. Not only was she well versed in medicine, but she had a deep social concern, having promoted the organization of some excellent labor schools on her own estate.

For Elizabeth the three days' visit was a physical and intellectual feast. She exulted in the salt tang of sea, the glorious sunsets, the wild fury of wind howling around the house at night. She met Mrs. Jameson, the noted Irish author, heard Fanny Kemble read *Macbeth,* magnificent in black velvet trimmed with ermine, her great black eyes as impressive as her deep voice. On a rainy day with the wind battering their carriage she went with a Dr. King to visit the hospital. It was with genuine regret that she had to leave on Sunday afternoon. Lady Byron, lovely in a purple velvet mantle lined with white silk, a rich dress, and a purple satin bonnet trimmed with black lace, escorted her to the train and put her in the second-class carriage dictated by the rigid necessity for economy.

The friendship did not end there. In the weeks following they exchanged many letters, continuing their spirited discussions. Not always were they in agreement. When Lady Byron implied that women physicians must occupy a secondary position, Elizabeth was firm in her opposition.

"There is nothing in the preparatory studies that requires so unusual an energy as to render women incapable of obtaining the necessary qualifications," she insisted. "All the difficulties which I have encountered have been *moral* ones, which would exist no longer when a college, hospital, and all the necessary arrangements should exist to welcome the woman student as they do the man, instead of obliging her to force her way through opposition, suspicion, and vulgar curiosity." Neither, she maintained, was the health of a *healthy* woman so variable as to prevent study or proper attention to the medical practice. In fact, had not midwifery, the most fatiguing department of medicine, been pursued successfully throughout the ages by women?

Neither were they fully agreed on the "duty" of woman. Lady Byron, in spite of her tragic experience, still maintained that "a life of devotedness to one man, to the highest objects for that one, is Woman's Duty." Elizabeth stoutly affirmed that it was idolatry. And to say that woman's highest fulfillment was to develop the divine in man's nature was almost as much a denial of her "woman's rights" as the legal status which made the wife her husband's chattel.

But on most subjects they were agreed, and to Lady Byron Elizabeth poured out some of her most intimate thoughts and dreams, concepts as foreign to her day as the expectation of travel to the moon but which a hundred years later would be accepted almost as truisms.

"Charity is a false principle. It brings human beings into untrue relations to one another. Those institutions seem to me peculiarly worthy of interest which, while founded by charity, contain in themselves elements of growth which will speedily absorb the charity and develop into free independent associations. I look for the time when religion and government and every institution which is based on the wants of our human nature shall spring from the people themselves continually and not be an external thing, a tradition of the past forced upon them."

Well that she could not know how many generations would elapse before society would awake to the corrupting influence of the "Lady

Bountiful" concept, both on giver and recipient, whether practiced by individual, church, charity organization, welfare agency, or nation!

"I hope some day to arrange a hospital on truer principles than any that we have yet seen, a center of science and of moral growth. I should want my hospital to cure my patients spiritually as well as physically, and what innumerable aids that would necessitate! I must have the church, the school, the workshop (kitchen, studio, etc.) to cure my patients, a whole society!"

A pity she could not see that in another century not only her own hospital but all the most progressive major medical complexes would be employing all these resources to attain these very goals!

"I went today to the Foundling Hospital. . . . What could be a more complete interference with Nature, which defines so well the true method of education? Children growing up without love, without freedom, all those traits of genius effectually crushed out!"

Strange that she who would never use the professional jargon of psychiatry — anomie, the ego, the id, complexes, the unconscious — should have so clearly and simply articulated some of its basic concepts!

"I believe fully that this age is marked by an increasing aspiration which will prove the animating principle of those wild struggles for freedom that we see in every country and which seem to many such a fearful sign. . . . I believe fully that we shall discover the science of society, which is now our essential want. I shall strive to aid its advent by preaching after my fashion unlimited freedom of action for every human being, joined to an ardent aspiration for the highest good."

Surely words that could have been written verbatim with even more startling pertinence a hundred years and more later!

An idealist she was, a Utopian, yet she suffered no illusions.

"I suppose it is in this way that we shall gradually reach that brighter state that some call the Millennium, some the Future, and which Fourier calls Harmony, and though these transitional efforts must contain much that is false, that is unavoidable in the passage from a false state of society to a true one. We could not convey the pure idea of Beauty to a savage. Swedenborg says he 'saw a truth let down to Hell, and it became a lie.' That seems to me to express in his strange imagery a most important fact. It enables me to work on, when without this clear perception I should feel paralyzed by the impossibility of leading a true life, of realizing our Ideal."

4

Elizabeth studied the young woman who shared the warmth of her fire. Though she had met this cousin of Barbara Leigh Smith before, this was her first opportunity for real acquaintance.

Her name alone was enough to warrant interest, to say nothing of all the curious rumors about her. *Florence*. A queer name, given because of the city where she was born, but it suited her. The oval face in its circlet of rich brown hair and silken bonnet conjured up visions of finely chiseled marble and gold-framed masterpieces, just as the soft silvery voice was suggestive of the unusual surname. *Florence*. Elizabeth savored it silently, little realizing that because of this woman hundreds of children would soon be bearing the name. *Florence Nightingale*.

"She's like a pale candle flame," she thought, noting the slender willowy figure, the delicate complexion, the pensive gray eyes, "but a restless one caught in the currents of many variable winds."

"I had to come," said Miss Nightingale after the pleasant amenities had been exchanged. "There are so many things I have to ask you, about yourself, your study, your home, your family. Especially your family. I hope you won't think me meddlesome, but I have to know. Your father and mother, what are they like? What did they think of your studying medicine?"

The words poured out in a hot flood, as surprising as tears gushing from a statue. Not like a candle flame, decided Elizabeth swiftly, more like a raging fire. Instead of curiosity, she felt compassion now and understanding. She also had been possessed by a consuming purpose, like this girl, but it had been governed by a will of steel, not by burning passion. She did not consider the questions meddlesome, for she knew what prompted them. She told about Samuel, who was like Barbara's father, only poor instead of rich, and who would certainly have encouraged her if he had lived; about Hannah, gentle and timid yet amazingly tough, fearful for the welfare of her bold brood yet never opposing their ventures; about her brothers and sisters, who had loyally supported her in her struggle, contributing from their slender funds to help eke out her expenses.

"Suppose," said Florence Nightingale when she had finished, "they had not approved. Suppose they had fought you at every point. What then?"

Elizabeth considered. It was the first time she had faced the question, and she knew why it was asked. Barbara, much troubled, had told her about Florence.

"She's always been queer, or at least most people have thought so. Instead of doing all the proper things a young lady should, she does things that drive her family, especially her fashionable mother, crazy. Says she'd rather scrub floors than dance. Up at their big summer estate at Lea Hurst she would spend all her time visiting the poor and sick in their cottages, taking them food, medicines, clothing. And sometimes she really does act queer. You can be talking to her, and all at once she isn't listening. Her eyes look all strange and far away. And sometimes," Barbara had laughed apologetically, "she acts as if she really heard voices, like Joan of Arc."

"Perhaps she does," Elizabeth had said soberly.

"And for years now she's been daft about hospitals. She used to study all the Blue Books on health and the hospital reports, got up before dawn and wrote by candlelight, until they say she knows more about hospitals than any other person in England. She'd go to work in one in a minute if her family would let her. But you can imagine how they feel about that!"

Elizabeth could. No one knew better than she what hospitals were like. No wonder people who lived in decency would often prefer to die at home rather than enter one. They were places of filth and evil smells and squalor. Many of the patients came from slum hovels rife with cholera. They were crowded into bare, unaired wards in beds less than two feet apart, fifty or sixty to a room. Sheets remained unwashed from patient to patient, mattresses seldom cleaned. The wooden floors, saturated with organic matter, could never be scrubbed clean. Plastered walls and ceilings dripped impurities. Liquor was often smuggled in, and drunken brawls frequently had to be settled by the police. Even at St. Bartholomew's, one of the best, Elizabeth was often so sickened by the sight and smells that she had to flee for a breath of air.

"They simply can't understand her," Barbara had continued, her own brows furrowing. "She's beautiful, and she's had more than one chance to marry. One of her suitors, Richard Monckton Milnes, is a philanthropist and reformer as well as a rich and talented poet. But after seven years she finally refused him. And now she's absolutely possessed by the idea that she wants to be a *nurse!*"

Even Elizabeth had been startled. Nurses were a degraded and notorious lot. Most were hopelessly immoral. As Florence Nightingale herself was to write years later, "It was preferred that the nurses should be women who had lost their characters, that is, should have had one child." They had no other home than the filthy noisy wards, where they slept, lived, even cooked their meals. Usually they were as addicted to drink as the patients. No wonder her rich and aristocratic family had shuddered with the shock!

Now, remembering all this, Elizabeth hesitated. Her response, she realized, was of vital importance. It might even change the course of a life. The gray eyes were compelling magnets. They demanded an honest answer. Elizabeth gave it.

"It would have made no difference," she said firmly. "I would have done it just the same."

Suddenly her visitor's face was transformed. The sober lips broke into the sweetest smile imaginable, revealing a row of dazzling perfect teeth. The blazing eyes dissolved into soft, merry glints. "Thank you," said Florence joyously.

In April Elizabeth went down with her new friend to Embley Park, the Nightingale winter estate near London. The house was a mansion, able, as Florence described it wryly, "to receive five able-bodied females with their husbands and families and all their belongings." The gold moldings, imported carpets, sky-blue ceilings, silks and damasks of red and blue and purple impressed her far less than the delicious country air, the view of the sea with the Isle of Wight in the distance, the peasants going to church in their picturesque scarlet cloaks, the laurels in full bloom. She spent long hours walking with Florence in the gardens, talking of their futures — Elizabeth's imminent departure for America, Florence's dream of going to Kaiserswerth, a deaconess training school for nurses in Germany.

The family was polite but warily suspicious. Elizabeth sensed the tensions, the jealous possessiveness of Florence's sister Parthe, the resentment of her beautiful socialite mother Fanny. Of course they considered her a threat, embodying all the horrifying possibilities of Florence's mania. Elizabeth's involvement with the "infernal" life of La Maternité, where it was rumored the female pupils were generally the doctors' mistresses, her loss of an eye there, her present connection with a hospital, which so aroused Florence's envy, shocked them unspeakably. She could sense their involuntary shrinking as they courteously extended their hands.

As they walked Florence unburdened herself of years of frustration.

"You have no idea, the horror of life for an English gentlewoman. Spending the morning sitting at a table, looking at prints, embroidering, reading senseless little books, taking a little drive in the afternoon, maybe a party after tea! I used to lie down every night exhausted, just from doing nothing, and wishing I were dead!

"We Englishwomen can study anything under the sun that we desire to acquire, not the slightest objection is placed in the way of our becoming learned to any extent; but any attempt to turn this knowledge to account, to work with it, is met with the bitterest opposition, is ridiculed, sneered at, frowned on. Yet the greatest impetus to study, the natural issues of study, lie in some noble career.

"Do you know what I always think when I look up at our house and see that long row of windows? How I should like to turn it into a hospital ward, and just how I should place the beds!

"Oh, my hospital would be clean, *clean!* I'd scrub it on my hands and knees if necessary. Sanitation — that's the important thing in medicine — don't you agree?

"Don't go back to America! Stay here and let me work with you. Then I'd be perfectly happy."

Elizabeth was tempted. She was deeply attached to her native land. But there were strong reasons against it. She had no money and a horror of running into debt. Here there was no immediate family to aid her. Moreover, she firmly believed that it was in America, not Europe, that woman would first be recognized as man's equal. To the French and Germans the idea of the coming change was like so much gibberish. Their minds were so completely warped that they seemed to have lost the power of forming a large conception with regard to women. In England, where the idea could be intellectually comprehended, there was a deep-rooted antagonism to its practical admission which it might take years to modify. She had not yet found there a single advocate of women's essential equality with men. But in America many of the best thinkers were giving the subject their earnest attention and sympathy.

Moreover, her own success had already produced results in America. In both Philadelphia and Boston attempts were being made to establish medical schools for women, and many of her sex had already entered medical study. She must give all the aid possible to those preparing to follow in her steps. Even more important, there was Emily, ready to start her medical studies and depending on her help and future partnership. She had to go.

Yet never had England seemed more alluring. Perhaps never again to see an English spring? The fogs had dissipated. Even the smoke failed to dim the brilliant opening of the Great Exposition on May 1. Thanks to Cousin Sam who was an exhibitor, Elizabeth marveled at the sights of the great building resplendent with products from all over the world, so vast that the sounds of its huge organ were lost in the immensity. As she saw the Queen, holding Prince Albert's arm, with the young Prince of Wales on one side and the Princess Regal on the other, followed by a great train of nobility, tour the building and declare it open, she felt a surge of pride and loyalty which her adopted country would never quite arouse.

The final weeks in London were both sad and triumphant. She parted from Florence, who, in spite of violent scenes with her family, left for Kaiserswerth. "I must expect no sympathy or help from them," she had decided at thirty-one years of age, after a decade of struggle. "I must *take* some thing, to enable me to live." In July, living a spartan life, eating peasant food with only ten minutes for each meal, working rigorously at her nursing training from five in the morning to late at night, she was writing, "Now I know what it is to live and to love life. I wish for no other earth, no other world than this."

Elizabeth said goodbye to her doctors with regret, receiving testimonials from Burrows, Hue, Rigby, and Paget. Now that she was leaving, they were all compliments and kindness. Mrs. Paget called her a "benefactor of the race," and her husband was eloquent in his regret at losing her. The letter from James Paget (later Sir James) was one of her most valued souvenirs.

I certify that Miss Elizabeth Blackwell, M.D., attended very regularly my course of lectures in General and Morbid Anatomy and Physiology in the Winter Session 1850–51, having been admitted, by the Committee of Governors of St. Bartholomew's Hospital, to the privilege of attending as a student the Practice and Lectures in the Hospital.

James Paget.

Now, Elizabeth learned with ironic satisfaction, she might do anything she pleased at St. Bart's, even in women's diseases! She would learn later, with less satisfaction, that, having once said farewell to Elizabeth Blackwell, St. Bartholomew's would stand firm against all subsequent invasion by women. Not until almost a hundred years later, in 1947, would it be compelled by the Universities Grants Committee to admit women students!

Anna came over from France to bid Elizabeth goodbye, and wept. "When will I see her again?" Elizabeth wondered, stricken by the thin unhappy face. It caused her almost as much grief to part with Barbara and Bessie.

She spent several days at Dudley with Cousin Sam and Howie, enjoying lovely weather. Never had the English countryside looked more beautiful. She and Howie rode up the Worcestershire Beacon on donkeys, visited Worcester Cathedral, where they looked in vain for the Blackwell crest of arms, said to be on one of the windows. With Cousin Sam she toured a big cotton mill in Manchester, where eight hundred looms in one room were tended by women and very young girls. The noise was deafening, the dust and heat oppressive. The women were sallow and perspiring, their faces dull and lifeless, mouths projecting like those of lower animals. What had the new industrial society done to women! Instead of spinning and weaving and churning and cooking for their families in the kitchen, wives of profiting manufacturers were now embroidering curtain-pulls with lily-white hands in the parlor while their poorer sisters, who had once earned a pittance doing piecework by hand in their homes, were for a lesser pittance crowded like animals in factories. It had made parasites of one class and slaves of another.

She left pale good Cousin Sam standing in the street of Dudley, watched dear Howie running up the railway bank and waving as she rushed off in the train. Her ties with England had been severed. The very sight of the ship at Liverpool made her sick, and her only concern was to get through the journey. That Saturday night, July 26, 1851, she was on board the ship out in the Mersey. She wrote in her diary, "Another most important page in life fairly closed! Adieu, dear friends! Heaven help us all!"

Dr. Elizabeth Blackwell.
Photograph of sketch made by the Countess de Charnacée, 1859.

The New York Infirmary for Women and Children,
126 Second Avenue, New York City, 1861-1874.

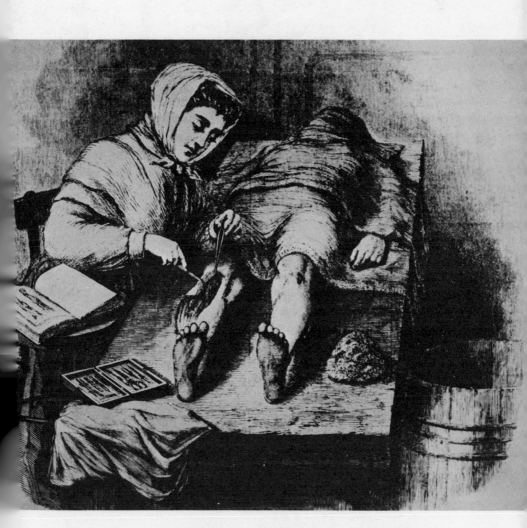

Medical student of New York Infirmary Women's Medical College dissecting
leg in one of the first anatomy classes (illustration from Frank Leslie's
Illustrated Newspaper).

*General Lecture Room, New York Infirmary Women's Medical College, show-
ing Dr. Rebecca Cole, America's first woman Negro doctor, reciting
(illustration from Frank Leslie's Illustrated Newspaper).*

Dr. Elizabeth Blackwell in her seventies.

New York Infirmary on Stuyvesant Square.

Chapter Nine

"BUT — YOU ADVERTISED ROOMS for the use of a doctor. See, the sign is right there in your window!" Drawing herself up to her full five feet of womanly dignity, Elizabeth fixed her cool gaze on the outraged landlady.

The hatchet features sharpened to a cutting edge. "A *doctor*. Not a *woman*."

"But I *am* a doctor. Here, let me show you my diploma."

The door slammed shut even as she started to open her reticule. Elizabeth sighed, turned away, and continued her trek through the New York streets looking for other rental signs. The reaction was typical of dozens encountered in the past month. "Female doctor! You think I run *that* kind of a house?" . . . "If I let a woman doctor's shingle be shown on my premises, a mob would come and wreck the place!" At the end of the day she returned wearily to her temporary lodging at No. 3 Leroy Place, Bleecker Street.

At least she need not face Hannah tonight. Her mother, who had come to New York with Marian and Ellen to meet her boat and was still holding a room in a boardinghouse close by, was visiting friends. And her sisters had left the city. They had seen her triumphant and confident, fresh from her brilliant coterie of friends in London. Even the tragedy of her lost eye, they had noted with obvious relief, had not changed her looks too much. She was glad now that they need not share her mounting frustration.

Was it only a month ago that she had written with such confidence to one of those friends back in England? "This morning is one of those cool, delicious crystal days when merely to live is blissful. And I am quite disposed to set to work, seek out the good side of everything, and do my duty heartily in America. I have no doubt of the propriety of my decision to commence my career in this country."

Had she been wrong? In London at least she could have found a place to work, would have encountered indifference rather than hostility. Soon after arriving in New York she made an application to be received as one of the physicians in the women's department of a large city dispensary. She submitted her credentials from Geneva, Paris, London, as well as letters of recommendation from the distinguished doctors at St. Bartholomew's. The application was refused.

"We would advise you to form your own dispensary," came the curt suggestion.

Her tireless search for lodging was finally rewarded. She secured rooms at No. 44 University Place, but was obliged to rent a whole floor at an exorbitant price. To furnish it her last funds, remnants of Barbara's insistent generosity, were exhausted. But a bit of good news which the family had brought her proved a godsend. Without her knowledge they had submitted one of her Christmas Annual stories, "Aunt Esther," in a magazine contest, and it had won a prize of a hundred dollars. Marian and Ellen had also submitted stories, all of them anonymously. Oddly enough, the three top prizes had been won by the three sisters, and the editors, in a quandary lest the public should suspect partiality, had insisted on pseudonyms and begged the three to keep the coincidence a secret. Elizabeth's pen name had been Florence Brandon. Neither name nor honor mattered a whit. The money, however, was a gift from heaven.

So far, so good. At least she had a place to receive patients. The high-ceilinged rooms were in a red brick house overlooking Washington Square, a respectable, once genteel neighborhood. Overriding her landlady's horrified objections, she hung out her modest shingle: "Elizabeth Blackwell, M.D." She went to the office of the *New York Tribune*, introduced herself to its editor, Horace Greeley, as the sister of Anna Blackwell, his European correspondent, and was received with instant cordiality.

"I know you are a liberal." She came bluntly to the point. "But how liberal are you? Enough to publish an advertisement for a woman doctor?"

Mr. Greeley was indeed that liberal. The following day the paragraph which Elizabeth had prepared appeared: "Miss Elizabeth Blackwell, M.D., has returned to this city from a two years' residence abroad, which she spent at the hospital of La Maternité in Paris and at St. Bartholomew's in London. She has just opened an office at Number 44, University Place, and is prepared to practice in every department of her profession."

A few weeks later, on October 15, the same paper published the encouraging item: "We lately announced the establishment of Miss Blackwell in our city as a practitioner of medicine at Number 44, University Place. We are happy to learn that she meets with much encouragement from our citizens and is extremely successful in her practice."

Whether inspired by misinformation or by wishful thinking, this editorial comment was grossly inaccurate. That fall and winter were for Elizabeth a nightmare of loneliness, discouragement, and waiting. Without the small sums which her brothers were able to contribute, she could not have managed financially. She counted lumps of coal, nearly starved herself. After her mother returned to Cincinnati in November, she was completely alone. Worst of all was the waiting. Day after day she sat behind the lace curtains of her front parlor and hoped for patients, while courage, calm, and money dwindled. And in the evenings, released from the waiting but not from the discouragement and loneliness, she walked downtown to the Battery, uptown to Madison Square and even beyond to Reservoir Park.

New York was no longer the "pleasant little Dutch town" which had welcomed her nearly twenty years ago. The rows of red brick houses with their homey stoops and pocket handkerchiefs of grass had lengthened into monotonous marching ranks, regimented into endless avenues and streets and alleys. The pleasant commons where the Blackwell children had romped were fast becoming parks, tree-planted, fenced, and formalized. Even the old Jersey City shoreline visible from her westward walks along the Hudson was beginning to take on the aspect of a growing city.

But there were other changes more profound. Walking eastward toward the East River, she heard a conglomerate of languages and dialects, half strange, half familiar — German, Irish, French, Italian; saw ragged children romping in the alleys, a half-dozen families huddled on a single shabby stoop; smelled the unmistakable odors of overcrowding and poverty. Walking southward toward the Bowery, near the foot of Houston and Rivington streets, she saw what seemed like thousands of filthy, half-naked children picking rags and bones from the street, obviously to sell. She was almost mobbed by a crowd of screaming candy and match peddlers and newsboys. There seemed to be hundreds of the latter, ranging from tiny tots to twelve-year-olds. Once when she walked to the river for a whiff of sea breeze early on a morning when a brisk east wind was blowing, she saw at least a dozen of them huddled asleep in a printing house alley, curled together against the brick wall for warmth; another was crawling from a wooden box where he had apparently spent the night.

"Where are their parents, their homes?" she wondered at first. That was before she discovered that most of them had no homes, no parents. They were relics of the waves of deadly cholera or of tuberculosis, that most killing of all diseases, or of some other bodily scourge, or perhaps of sheer starvation.

Walking down Ninth Street one day, she saw a little girl with a very sweet face but looking so sad that she halted involuntarily.

"My dear — is anything the matter?"

"Oh, no, ma'am, nothin'." The child looked terrified. "You — you ain't come to take us to the poorhouse?"

"No, of course not."

Fears allayed, the child willingly answered questions. Her name was Elly. She was thirteen. There was no father or mother. She had three younger brothers and sisters whom she supported.

Elizabeth was dumbfounded. "But — how?"

"I sews on check-shirts, ma'am, and on flannel shirts. I gets five cents for the checks and nine cents for the others. But now they won't let me have no more flannel because I can't deposit the two dollars."

She invited Elizabeth into a cold damp basement. Three young children were crouched about an almost cold stove. All had sore eyes and running noses. A drab, soggy wash drooped from a line between two walls. In the little back room was one bed, where the whole family slept. There were only two blankets for warmth. Fuel had to be picked up in the street. Before leaving, Elizabeth gave the child two dollars to buy flannel, an amount she could ill spare. But there was little solace in seeing the sad little face alight with gratitude. She knew that in the network of streets outside there were hundreds of Ellies.

Slowly, through questions, observation, reading, Elizabeth absorbed the details and causes of the appalling poverty. During the last twenty years immigration from Europe had represented a population shift unparalleled in history. Almost 600,000 had poured into New York during the thirties, 1,700,000 in the forties, and the rate was steadily increasing. In one year alone over 300,000 aliens had landed in New York, at the rate of a thousand a day for every weekday. Some of them had spread out over the country, contributing much to its quality. But the poorest, staying here where they landed, had piled up in worse slums than they had left behind. Poverty and overcrowding, as throughout history, had stimulated laziness, vice, dissipation, crime.

Society was attempting to solve the problem through voluntary effort. By 1850 there were organizations for the relief of indigent females, of poor widows, of small children; orphan asylums, homes for the friendless, a few industrial schools. Elly had learned her craft in one of these. A list of New York benevolent associations included ninety charities, twenty-two asylums, eight hospitals, seven dispensaries. But as Elizabeth walked and walked, she saw little of their benefits, especially of the two latter. They might be applying a few poultices, but they were doing little to remove the causes of the sores. She yearned over the suffering she saw, especially of the mothers and children. She longed to scrub the dirty little hands and faces, strip the swaddlings from the puny babies, throw open the windows of the dingy tenements and let in the small amount of fresh air available, cover the open drains and the fly-infested jars of food set to cool on the dirty windowsills.

"If only someone could teach them better ways of doing things!" she brooded.

Walking in the other direction, uptown, she was equally disturbed. What had become of the American women she had known, the sturdy, red-cheeked, pioneer stock who had trekked westward with their husbands, churned, baked, washed, spun, wove, or, becoming more prosperous, skillfully managed their households? Independence they had lacked, to be sure, but at least they had had health and initiative! Not like these mannequins floating languidly along Fifth Avenue in their billowing hoops and innumerable layers of petticoats, waists strangled to the contours of an hourglass, pale faces smothered under protecting veils! The young girls looked as tight-laced as their elders. Remembering her own untrammeled childhood and youth, the ten-mile tramps, the rowdy games, Elizabeth was appalled. What could their mothers be thinking of? Were they ignorant of the most elemental laws of life? If only someone could tell them! If only —

An idea began to germinate. Why not? Nowhere, she believed, was there such a deplorable system of female education as in the United States, and the increasing feebleness and disease among young women were terrible proof of its folly. The common plan, it seemed, was to cram the intellect and entirely neglect the body. The knowledge given to girls in youth was superficial, objectless, and forgotten as soon as school days were over. The physical strength lost by overtaxing the mind could never be regained. Surely it was her unique responsibility, as a woman physician, to rouse attention to this subject, not that the evil might be *cured*, but that it might be *prevented*.

But how? By publishing her thoughts in writing? No, there were some things which she would prefer to share with a few women than publish to the world at large. Lecturing, then? Heaven forbid! All her old shyness and reserve rose in horror at the idea. Yet she knew it was a wrong feeling, a form of pride or self-consciousness, unworthy of one with an important work to accomplish. Resolutely she set herself to a task almost as repellent as had once seemed the study of medicine.

Now the routine of her days changed. She still waited for patients, yes, but no longer in discouragement or frustration. Hour after hour, page after page, she wrote, tore up, rewrote, revised, weighing each word carefully, for she knew she was expressing radical views on controversial subjects. But she was accustomed to treading on the toes of tradition. In her firm legible hand the ideas marched across the pages, and she grew more and more excited.

Meanwhile a few daring patients began to come. Dr. Greeley's *Tribune* was a mighty leavener for all liberal ideas as well as anti-slavery, and as a result of the advertisement she received several invitations from ladies to make professional visits. Soon there were perhaps a half-dozen families in which she had one or more women patients. But this meager success gave prejudice and hostility fresh impetus. Her landlady became even more disagreeable, refusing to either give or receive messages. The modest shingle, she announced darkly, was a blot on her house and must be removed. No "respectable" woman would want to live in a building occupied by a woman doctor. Elizabeth began receiving insulting anonymous letters. Obscenities were flung after her as she walked along the street. It was the persecution of Geneva all over again, but now, since she was a practicing physician instead of just a student, a hundred times worse. Why! What strange perversity of values equated "woman doctor" with such prevalent deviants as "abortionist," "mesmerist," "clairvoyant," or, worse yet, with "streetwalker," "woman of loose morals," even "harlot"? Surely the shadow of Madame Restell, though she was still plying her nefarious practice in New

York, could not be so far-reaching! Yet Elizabeth was constantly glad that it was she, and not another, who had to bear the brunt of this pioneer work. She was strong and could take it. Surely her going first would make it easier for others, especially *for Emily.*

The thought of her plucky young sister in far-off Cincinnati, gallantly struggling to follow in her footsteps, helped to assuage her terrible loneliness. For years Emily had taught, scrimped, studied, taken private instruction from a preceptor, and managed to save one thousand dollars for her medical education. Now she was bursting with eagerness and frustration. After being encouraged by the Cleveland Medical School, which had graduated one woman doctor, Nancy Talbot Clark, soon after Elizabeth received her degree, Emily had been refused admittance. Further refusals came that winter from Columbus, from Castleton. Patience, counseled Elizabeth in the letters they constantly exchanged. Surely conditions had changed in the four years since her own multiple refusals! Some twenty women had received medical degrees of a sort, though only two, her own and Dr. Clark's, had been awarded by regular schools, untainted by such medical deviations as homeopathy or eclecticism. Emily stubbornly refused to seek admittance at one of the "irregular" schools, including the newly formed Female Medical College of Pennsylvania. Even little Geneva she left as a last resort. As unyielding a perfectionist as her sister, she was determined to graduate from an established institution. A woman doctor had too many strikes against her without the added liability of an irregular alma mater.

Though Elizabeth hoped Emily's struggle might be less painful than her own, she made no attempt to minimize the difficulties. Once she wrote with almost brutal candor, "A blank wall of social and professional antagonism faces the woman physician and forms a situation of singular and painful loneliness, leaving her without support, respect, or professional counsel."

It was this lack of stimulating fellowship which made her feel most lonely. The letters from her friends in England were some compensation: from Florence Nightingale, who had at last managed to spend a few "completely satisfied, completely happy" weeks at Kaiserswerth but was now back home in her soft, suffocating cage, beating her wings by writing about the boredom and vacuity of life for a typical young English lady called "Cassandra"; from Barbara and Bessie, who were flouting convention by starting a shockingly advanced school in a poor district near Barbara's London home, where boys were taught with girls, Jews with Catholics and Unitarians, children of a wealthy doctor with those of cockney workmen; from Lady Byron, whose interest in magnetism led to a detailed description of a new discovery called a "magnetiscope."

But letters were poor substitutes for companionship. Most of all Elizabeth missed the professional rapport she had known in London. Here she was completely ostracized by the medical profession. Her requests to visit hospitals were refused. For months she had not a single doctor friend in the whole city. Then one happy but amusing experience made a small breakthrough.

One of her patients, an elderly Quaker woman, fell severely ill with pneumonia. Though almost certain she would recover, Elizabeth wished uneasily that she could secure the advice of another physician. She asked the family if they would permit a consultation, and they agreed. Now what to do? Whom to call? She had little doubt that any doctor she might approach would take keen pleasure in rebuffing her. Suddenly she remembered the kind physician who had been present in Cincinnati at her father's last illness. She recalled hearing that he had moved to New York. To her relief she was able to locate him, and after some hesitation he agreed to visit her patient. After making his examination he accompanied her into the parlor. There he began to walk about the room in a state of great agitation.

"A — a most extraordinary case!" he exclaimed in great perturbation. "Such a one has never happened to me before. I — I really don't know what to do."

Elizabeth was amazed. Was it possible that her diagnosis had been at fault? "But — it's a clear case of pneumonia, isn't it?" she inquired in bewilderment.

"Oh — oh, yes, pneumonia, of course. That's not —" Finally he blurted out, "I — I'm just not sure of the propriety — consulting with a lady physician!"

Elizabeth struggled with a conflict of emotions — relief, vexation, amusement. The first and last triumphed. Controlling her impulse to laugh, she smiled reassuringly.

"Then let's not call it a consultation," she said brightly. "Let's just say you called on me as an old friend of the family, for a little talk."

"Yes, yes, of course." His relief made him almost jovial. "That's the way it is, isn't it? An old family friend. Now, as to this pneumonia patient, Miss — *Miss* Blackwell —" Forthwith he gave her his best advice, and the episode ended happily. The patient swiftly recovered. Henceforth Elizabeth had no difficulty in procuring the assistance of this able physician for a "consultation." Could she have a chat with her old friend about a little problem that was bothering her? Of course, my dear, of course, glad to be of help. It was one of the greatest satisfactions of her career when, after coming to recognize her professional competence both in diagnosis and in treatment, he forgot himself one day and called her "Doctor."

Something else happened that winter to help dispel her professional loneliness. One wild snowy morning a woman came to her door. Her features were as purely delicate as the snow crystals clinging to her bonnet, and at first glance she looked fragile enough to have blown there on the wind.

"You are Dr. Elizabeth Blackwell." It was a statement rather than a question. "And I am Ann Preston."

Once the visitor was inside and out of her long damp cape, Elizabeth hastily revised her estimate. Refined and delicate, yes, but not fragile. In the ramrod-straight figure she recognized a wiry toughness akin to her own. But they found themselves akin in more ways than one. Ann Preston had just completed her first year at the Female Medical College of Philadelphia. With the other thirty-nine students enrolled in its first class she had endured a barrage of jeers and mud from other medical students in the city, who had sworn no woman in Philadelphia would ever get a medical degree. Their opposition was shared both by the medical establishment and by the city's clergymen, who would refuse to a man to offer prayer at Ann Preston's graduation.

"Will woman gain," demanded the Philadelphia County Medical Society, "by ceasing to blush while discussing every topic as it comes up with philosophic coolness, and man be improved in the delicate reserve with which he is accustomed to address women in the sickroom? The bounds of modesty once passed in the professional intercourse, will the additional freedom of speech and manner thus acquired impart grace and dignity to woman in her new character?" In other words, came the ultimate argument, "God never intended women to be doctors."

The dreams Ann Preston shared with Elizabeth that day would be fulfilled during her distinguished career, first as professor of physiology, later as dean of her college, soon to become the Woman's Medical College of Pennsylvania. It must be made truly "regular," she vowed passionately, on a par with the finest medical schools of the country.

"You'll succeed," predicted Elizabeth, little knowing that nearly fifty years later, for the jubilee of this major institution, she would be writing, "The courage and hope of that fragile lady, who came to me out of the wild snowstorm, were an omen of success."

But their communion of thought was even more fundamental, for Ann Preston, like Elizabeth, was an early apostle of hygiene. Her graduation thesis, stating that "food, air, sleep, exert a chemical action upon the system," was a foretaste of preventive medicine. Long before germs were even thought of, these two women were expounding the efficacy of cleanliness, fresh air, exercise, and other elementals of hygiene, generations ahead of their time.

Satisfied at last, Elizabeth finished her many pages of writing. On March 1, 1852, an item in the *New York Times* announced that Dr. Elizabeth Blackwell would deliver a course of six lectures in the basement of a certain church. Tickets could be procured for two dollars each at a Broadway bookshop. The subject of the lectures would be "The Laws of Life with Special Reference to the Physical Education of Girls."

She went to her first session terrified. All her innate shyness arose to taunt her. *Lecturer!* She had never made a public speech in her life. Would anyone come? If they came, would they be able to hear her? If they heard, would they be willing to listen? Her ideas would be new, startlingly so, to most women. Though she looked unperturbed and confident as she made her way to the church in a brisk March wind, her limbs under the voluminous black silk skirts were shaking.

People came, many of them highly intelligent women from the Society of Friends. They were able to hear her. Surprisingly, once she was before her audience she felt no nervousness. Her voice, though low in timbre, was resonant and clear, its appeal augmented by the occasional emphasis of beautiful, expressive hands. She spoke with simplicity, firmness, and confidence, evidencing even in this first public appearance the qualities which years afterward would lead a certain French correspondent to write, "The incomparable clarity of her pronunciation places her, in my opinion, above all orators sacred or profane whom I have heard in England or in America, and I will add that I have heard in France only Rachel to whom I would want to compare her for exquisite simplicity of diction."

Elizabeth would have scorned such appraisal as meaningless. All she wanted was to get her ideas across. Though elementary a hundred years later, for her day the lectures were sensational. Though only a few months in the writing, they had been thirty years in preparation, for they embodied her basic philosophy of life. Flowing through them were the wisdom of Samuel, the homely common sense of Hannah, the free-thinking of Fourier, Emerson, Swedenborg, and Channing, the smoldering genius of Florence Nightingale, the stark realities of Blockley and La Maternité. They were scholarly but not pedantic, idealistic yet intensely practical. The present industrial age, she told them, had lost sight of the profound truth which ancient societies like the Greeks' had considered elemental: that life to be complete must be a unity of body and spirit. Their concept of beauty had equated purity of form with vigorous physical well-being. Weakness, infirmity, sickness, were all discordant with the natural laws of life. Surely also the Christian concept of man created in God's image visioned a potential of bodily as well as spiritual perfection.

She described the sheltered and pampered city girl, imprisoned in a soft and meaningless existence, a "strange anomaly in creation, a being having nothing to do, envying inferior and almost inanimate forms of life, the flower, the torrent, the bird, which in dispensing perfume, song, the melody of motion, realize the joy of fulfillment." She urged reform in the whole gamut of a girl's education from infancy — the tearing-off of swaddling clothes; the encouragement of climbing, running, riding, dancing, and free play in childhood; freedom from strangling corsets and swathing veils; training in skills which would give her a worthwhile goal in life, prevent a too early marriage often resulting in invalidism; courses in all schools and colleges in science and sanitation.

"The education of children," she emphasized, "should not merely not injure, it should do physical good. If lessons produce headache, lassitude, inactivity of functions, if they make the child pale, quiet, spiritless, then the lessons are bad. If the course of study is not positively beneficial to the bodily organism, it is positively injurious."

Then — shocking finale to many of the suppressed females in her audience — she launched into *instruction in the processes of sex, of birth, of the structure and functions of their bodies!*

"Preparation must be laid in childhood. Yet women shrink with repugnance from physiological instruction. Everything should be done to cultivate the taste for natural history and science latent in every child. Their fondness for animals indicates this taste, and the care of animals should be encouraged and directed. . . .

"Physical passion is not in itself evil; on the contrary, it is an essential part of our nature. It is an endowment which, like every other human faculty, has the power of high growth. For good or for evil, sex takes a first place as a motive power in human education." She explained in detail the physical basis of reproduction, noted that it was important to recognize that the nerve connection between brain and sexual organs existed even in children, that — boldest declaration of all — man was no more sexed than woman.

Huge and bitter doses for these Victorian ladies to swallow in a day when sex was a synonym for vice and even the word "body" was taboo! Some choked and did not come back. Yet many returned for more.

They got it. She took them into the back streets and alleys of New York, Paris, London, Liverpool, painted graphic pictures of overcrowded tenements, airless rooms, unsanitary and unwholesome food, rampant disease, underpaid seamstresses, women forced into the streets because of economic exploitation, the double standard of morality. Throughout she emphasized respect for the body, which was only another form of respect for the human spirit and for the divine laws inherent in the unity of both.

The lectures, plus the social and professional connections resulting from them, gave a genuine impetus to her professional life. Several of the Quaker women became her patients. One of the group was Mrs. Stacy B. Collins, wife of a prominent printer and publisher. In time Elizabeth became the physician of the whole Collins family, including the daughter, Mrs. Cornelia Hussey, whose daughter Mary was the first baby she delivered in New York. Significantly, years later Mary was to become a doctor, and Elizabeth's friendship with the family would encompass three generations.

"Those lectures must be published in a book," insisted Mrs. Collins.

With the encouragement of another friend, Dr. Bellows, Elizabeth did publish later in 1852 *The Laws of Life in Reference to the*

Physical Education of Girls. In the book she stressed again the unhealthful restrictions on girls' activities. "The school hour closes, the child returns home, but not racing merrily along, with shout and frolic; for the little girls must not run, or slide on the ice like a boy. . . . Can there be a more melancholy spectacle than that of the girls in a boarding school taking their afternoon walk? There is no vigor in their step, no pleasure in their eye; the fresh air is certainly good for their lungs, but the unattractive exercise is of most questionable benefit. . . .

"Until a girl is sixteen, it is much more important that she should possess a healthy body, an honest, loving heart, good sense, and a clear intellect, than that she should be able to answer questions on every science, play tolerably on the piano, speak French and embroider, if these acquisitions are to necessitate physical and mental weakness in after life."

Though the little book was greeted with shocked horror in some quarters, from many it received warm approbation. It even came to the attention of the eminent Charles Ruskin, who placed on it the golden stamp of his commendation.

Even more gratifying to Elizabeth was the testimony of her old friend Dr. Lee.

"I would not flatter you," he wrote, "but I hope I may say that in my judgment you have done yourself and Alma Mater a very great honor, and rendered a most important service to your sex and to society at large."

The only fly in this soothing ointment was the salutation of his letter, for it was addressed to Miss, not Dr., Blackwell.

But the shock and horror far outweighed the approval. In the society of the fifties sanitation was an affectation of the well-to-do. The body was a necessary evil to be tolerated, subjugated if possible, certainly not pampered or glorified. And sex was an unmentionable vice quite divorced from the respectable but mysterious process of propagation. The very fact that a female had the experience, knowledge, and boldness to write, plus the audacity to speak publicly, on such subjects, was full vindication of the depravity ascribed to the words "woman doctor."

"It has taken fifty years," one of America's first pediatricians was to say a half-century later, "for even the foremost of the medical profession to catch up with her ideas."

After exchanging affectionate greetings, the two women appraised each other, the one anxiously, the other warily.

"Has she grown enough?" wondered Elizabeth. "Has she the strength and perseverance to batter this terrible iron wall? Or is she too tranquil, too sensitive of disposition?"

"Can we really work together?" worried Emily. "She's always been a little strange, withdrawn. I don't expect much sympathy or companionship from her. But — *can we work together?*"

The two sisters had not met for four years. Emily was now twenty-five, Elizabeth thirty-one. They were as different in appearance as in temperament: Elizabeth short, slight, swift of motion, pale sandy hair drawn back in unruly waves from the high, full forehead and prominent cheekbones, the one good gray-blue eye seeming to have absorbed all the burning intensity of the other; Emily taller, broader of shoulder, rounder and calmer of face, sandy hair glinting with a hint of red, cool tranquil eyes revealing almost nothing of the ebb and flow of passion beneath.

Some time before, in Cincinnati, a popular clairvoyant, applying letters of the two women to his forehead, had given an uncannily astute delineation of each. Of Elizabeth he had said, "A very superior person, with an intense thirst for knowledge, not a passive character, but restless, great enthusiasm, a powerful aspiration, great perseverance, much determination, a very glowing character, much order, much idealism, great sweep and breadth of thought. If it be a lady, then there is much more vigor and power than they generally possess."

"You think it is a lady, then?" Harry had asked.

"I don't know. I thought so at first, but it seems to me now too powerful for a woman."

Of Emily he had commented, "Great intellectual capacity, keenness, and clearness of intellect. This is a more passive character than the last, there is tranquility, a fine balance. I do not see the same sweep of thought, the mind is more practical, rapid in decision, first judgment generally the best. This one is more fit for business, much industry." He had summarized, "Keenness and penetration of intellect, balance and tranquility of character."

A description of her outside, Emily had felt, not her inner self. She had written in her diary, "He did not remark the intense longing for perfection, the passion for intellectual pursuits, and the stormy restlessness of my disposition. I always seem to myself to act for the surface. There is an intense reserve below that hinders me from showing my real nature. I do not think my brothers and sisters know me at all."

But that evening she and Elizabeth came closer than ever before to mutual understanding. Emily's long years of teaching, her study under various doctors, her passionate desire to obtain a medical degree, her present frustration, all were for Elizabeth a reliving of her own experience. Already Emily had applied to a dozen colleges and been refused, including — to Elizabeth's dismay — Geneva! Dr. Lee was no longer there. The bold innovation, frowned on by the little college's older and bigger sisters, had never been repeated. Now, following the advice of her mentor Dr. Mussey, Emily was on her way to Hanover, New Hampshire, seeking admission to Dartmouth.

"Five years!" In a rare burst of self-revelation she let some of her long bitterness and frustration spill forth. "So much work and so little to show for it! Imagine, Bessie! At fourteen Harry was able to step right into a job at six hundred dollars a year, while I at twenty, who had prepared him for high school, thought myself lucky to get half as much! Oh, I've felt as if a mountain were on top of me, trying to crush all my hopes and dreams!"

"I know." In turn Elizabeth shared many of her most intimate experiences, including her despair when the loss of her eye had precluded specialization in surgery.

They spent a week in close fellowship, one of the happiest Elizabeth had ever known. It was a family reunion, for Marian was also in New York in quest of some kind of work. Then Emily left for Hanover, and Elizabeth suffered again all the old agonizing suspense. A week later, on the eleventh of August, Emily was back again. Elizabeth read the news in her tired, angry face.

"Milly! You poor unfortunate child! So they've refused you."

It was the old story. Emily had taken her letters of recommendation to several doctors. The decision had been against her. Wearily she had packed, spent a sleepless night, risen at dawn, and left Hanover at six in the morning. For once her tranquility was dissolved. She had reached a nadir of fatigue and despair.

Elizabeth was not surprised. True, New England had spawned Garrison, Emerson, the Channings. It had produced pioneers in female education: Prudence Crandall, Emma Willard, Mary Lyon. But it was the home also of Puritanism. Its clergy were among the most adamant defenders of the preservation of woman's ordained role of subservience and obedience to man. She had not forgotten her own rejection by seventeen colleges, including Harvard, Bowdoin, Yale. She knew also the struggle of Harriot K. Hunt, Boston-born, who, after practicing medicine with competence but without a diploma for a dozen years, had applied repeatedly but without success for admission to Harvard.

"Shall mind or sex be recognized," Miss Hunt had demanded in a letter to the faculty in 1850, "in admission to medical lectures?"

And though the faculty, under the deanship of Dr. Oliver Wendell Holmes, had decided to recognize "mind" and allow Harriot Hunt to attend medical lectures with no promise of a degree, the student body had effectively vetoed the decision in two uncompromising resolutions:

"Resolved, that no woman of true delicacy would be willing in the presence of men to listen to the discussions of the subjects that necessarily come under consideration of the student of medicine.

"Resolved, that we object to having the company of any female forced upon us, who is disposed to unsex herself, and to sacrifice her modesty by appearing with men in the medical lecture room."

Elizabeth sighed. It was well she could not know that twenty-six years later, in 1878, Harriot Hunt (long blessed with a bona fide doctorate from the Woman's Medical College of Pennsylvania) would make one last attempt to induce Harvard to admit women to its school of medicine, this time bolstered with the offer of a bonus of ten thousand dollars. Since it would take about four hundred thousand dollars to get them into Johns Hopkins School of Medicine in the 1890's — a condition of the endowment of nearly half a million dollars by Miss Mary Garrett — Harvard's immunity to such inducement was understandable!

"Don't be discouraged." Elizabeth's counsel was cheerfully based on experience. "We'll get you in somewhere. Meanwhile you mustn't waste time. Why not try to get you in as a visitor in Bellevue Hospital?"

She took Emily to call on her friend Horace Greeley, the most influential man she knew. He promised to see Mr. Draper, a member of the board of directors. Some days later Emily went back to see Greeley, found him in his bare parlor writing at a small table buried under a mountain of papers. He looked up, greeted her pleasantly, eyes startlingly blue under colorless lashes and brows, but never once did he stop writing. Yes, he had seen Mr. Draper and thought it could be arranged. He was glad he had been able to help, sorry he was so busy, but wouldn't she sit down? Emily looked around, saw that every chair in sight was covered with papers, and murmured a polite refusal.

She went at once to see Mr. Draper. He thought she could visit Bellevue without objection, but the doctors must decide about permitting her to accompany them on their visits. Emily returned home encouraged. To crown the week's success, Elizabeth had had three patients yielding the fabulous income of twenty-five dollars! The sisters celebrated with veal cutlets "in curlpapers" and one of Marian's fruit custards. After dinner, instead of taking their usual walk, they boarded a horsecar and rode north to the broad green expanse of Madison Square.

During the next two months Elizabeth forgot her own successes and failures in a vicarious sharing of Emily's adventures. At least five years had brought about some change. The doors of no New York hospital had opened to her own knocking, even to visiting the wards, much less accompanying the doctors. Emily's reports of the days' activities ran the gamut of frustration, triumph, amusement, vexation.

"What a confusion! So many rows of little blue beds! Such a confused mass of diseases! . . . Saw my first post mortem, and three doctors in the dead house were very friendly. . . . When Dr. Parker gave a lecture today, I waited discreetly outside until he had finished exhibiting the syphilitic cases, then I seated myself in a corner and listened with much satisfaction. . . . The most awful thing happened! I put up a prescription wrong! The mixture might have killed the patient if the assistant hadn't been watching!"

Only to her diary, however, did she confide one private observation.

"Last Sunday Elizabeth and I took a pleasant little excursion to Staten Island. We sat among the pines on a hill overlooking the bay and read Hawthorne's *Blithedale Romance*. I find E. a very noble disposition and a good head. She has nervous streaks, however, that seem to me to point out delicate health."

Elizabeth would not have appreciated this comment. Delicate she might look, and nerves she undoubtedly possessed, but that either should be considered indicative of weakness would have vexed her beyond measure.

A book was published that year of peculiar interest to the Blackwells. Harriet Beecher Stowe, who had moved to Brunswick, Maine, where Dr. Calvin was a professor at Bowdoin College, had at last written a book on the slavery issue. *Uncle Tom's Cabin* was kindling fresh fires among the pros and cons from Maine to Texas, the slave states of the southeast to the free state of California. Elizabeth read it with a burning fascination. Though the scene was not laid in Cincinnati and Simon Legree was a Vermonter, she could hear the muffled oars and muted hoofbeats of Levi Coffin and his underground beating like a pulse through every page. The Fugitive Slave Act of 1850, tightening the legal control of southern owners over their runaway slaves, had effected temporary compromise but left a seething volcano beneath the surface. The undercurrents of conflict between abolitionists and pro-slavery factions in the North ran even hotter than those between North and South, and the new book fed their explosive fires. Elizabeth was stirred by all her old anti-slavery fervor. Even the problems of young women doctors seemed small by contrast.

"The deep anxiety of every true-hearted American," she wrote Lady Byron that summer of 1852, "is in relation to slavery, and I am watching the discussion of this subject with more grief than hope. The great rallying cry is the preservation of the Union, right or wrong, at any sacrifice of principle. This acknowledgment has a demoralizing effect on the people. It substitutes expediency for right under the name of Law and consequently undermines all law. Hence we have Cuban invasions, Mexican conquests, anti-Kossuth demonstrations, and a low tone of morality in business."

She was appalled by the ascendancy which the slave interests had gained during the years of her absence. Pulpit, press, mass meetings, all seemed to teach concession. The two rival candidates for President stood on pro-slavery platforms. But the crowning betrayal of principle was reached when a gentleman of Philadelphia asserted publicly that "slavery is part of American liberty"!

Yet for the moment her efforts at reform must be confined to the smaller area of medicine, and it was Emily's problems which were her deepest concern. As September drifted into October, bringing Emily's twenty-sixth birthday, Elizabeth sensed the turbulence under her sister's placid exterior. Medical terms were beginning all over the country. Another year's postponement would be intolerable. But miraculously a door opened. A doctor at Rush Medical College encouraged her to seek admittance there, and Emily immediately made plans to leave for

Chicago. When word came that she had been admitted, Elizabeth's relief was intense.

"Dr. Brainerd thought I should have no difficulty," came the report, "and by his advice I started to see the other professors. After two weary days of trotting through wind and rain I saw all, everyone agreed, and on Saturday, October 30, I attended my first lecture. I went in with Dr. Davis, who at the end of the lecture informed the class, 'I have introduced into the lecture room, with the cheerful consent of the faculty, a lady who proposes to spend the winter with us. To save all inquiry I will inform you that it is Miss Blackwell, sister of Miss Elizabeth Blackwell who studied some years ago at Geneva and subsequently in Europe. The Americans have a reputation of being a very gallant nation. I need not tell you you will be expected by your conduct this winter to maintain the national character.' The doctor's speech was much applauded."

But Emily's problems were only beginning. Like Elizabeth before her, she soon came head on into those lectures considered too indelicate for a lady to comprehend, much less hear discussed in the presence of men.

"This present lecture will probably be the most unpleasant in the course," a student informed her with unmistakable relish. Emily was dismayed. Had he been deputed to warn her not to be present — or else? She went to Dr. Evans, the instructor, and suggested that she absent herself. No, no, he would not hear of it. She must attend all if she wished to attend any. She went, managed to keep her color from changing — she hoped! — during the explicit demonstration of the male external generative organs. There followed days of anxiety and a vast relief when the gentlemanly attitude of the other students seemed unchanged.

To her delight she was given a chance to work in Dr. Brainerd's office, keeping his records, preparing medicines, meeting his patients. It seemed a heaven-sent opportunity — until, due to the objection of some of his patients, it ended two weeks later. In her disappointment she wrote, "I grow disgusted with people, weary of medicine. A kind of breath from a high ideal life passes over me, and I find myself alone in a desert." But the frustration was temporary. She wrote a few days later, "I should like to be a surgeon, and I would choose certain branches, make myself the most skillful surgeon in America in some one department."

Meanwhile Elizabeth's sense of accomplishment was meager. She began to have serious doubts. Could it be that the world was not yet ready for a private woman doctor? Could she use her talents more effectively in some other way? Also her conscience stabbed with ever-increasing sharpness. She was making no impact on the appalling suffering of women in the teeming·society about her. Yet she knew they were in desperate need of the healing skills, even more of the education in health and disease prevention, that she had to give. Doubts gave way to pondering, pondering to resolution.

Early in 1853 she again approached the directors of the City Dispensary, requesting a post.

"It would not promote the harmonious working of the institution," she was again told, but this time with even more curt finality. "If you want to work in a dispensary, start one of your own."

"Thank you," replied Elizabeth with equal curtness. "I will do just that."

With the financial help of some of her Quaker friends, she hired a small cheap room on Seventh Street, near Tompkins Square. Mrs. Cornelia Hussey, the daughter of the Stacy Collinses, actively assisted in arranging drugs, covering a screen, providing the simple furnishings. Elizabeth announced that she would receive patients there on three afternoons each week and treat them — *free.* A modest sign bore the words, *Dr. Blackwell.*

It was one of the worst slum districts of the city. The Eleventh Ward, running from Fourteenth Street south to Rivington, east to East River and west to Avenue B and Clinton Street, lacked medical service of any kind. It contained 213 acres, and its population in 1854 was over fifty-three thousand, nearly twenty thousand children under fourteen. Three-quarters of its residents were foreign-born. Many knew no English. Many of the vast influx of immigrants during the past decades had settled here, in souring, decaying buildings, and becoming more and more disease-infected. Families of ten or twelve existed in one or two rooms. Four families or more were crowded into each floor of the noisome tenements, with no sanitary conveniences except a common sink in the hallway. Many lived in dank cellars. Refuse was flung into the narrow alleys, where it stank, decayed, and spawned millions of flies. Epidemics of cholera, brought in by almost every boat of immigrants, abounded. But worst of all its liabilities were its slaughter pens located in rear buildings among the densely packed tenements.

Not only were the droves of swine permitted free run of the slaughter-house yards as scavengers, but they freely roamed the streets, creating further disorder, filth, and congestion. The stench was almost more than Elizabeth, with her sensitive nose, could stomach.

"For me, only two hours three times a week," she told herself sturdily, acclimating herself each time to the mounting redolence by holding a square of delicate cambric to her nose. "These sisters of mine have it all the time."

Here also she sat and waited. A woman doctor was as suspect here as on Madison Avenue. But finally a woman came, so sick that the word "doctor" inspired a courage transcending fear. When Elizabeth was able to help her, the surprised and grateful patient told others. Word was passed around that there was a queer "doctress" on Seventh Street who could help people. Though Elizabeth despised the word "doctress," she welcomed the fact that her reputation was slowly spreading.

If she had wanted patients, experience, she had them now. Women were soon swarming to the little dispensary. She was over-whelmed with work, not only during the three afternoons but on other days and sometimes into the night. Often she was called to attend patients in their homes and went at all hours and into all sorts of places to deliver babies. More than once she found the expectant mother lying in a cellar on a heap of burlap bags, with a dirty, ragged, whimpering brood of other children clustered helplessly about. The death rate in childbirth, as well as the infant mortality, was appalling.

Elizabeth was as unorthodox in her ideas of proper procedure in childbirth as in many other medical concepts of her day. The prevailing notions about pregnancy shocked her profoundly: that the expectant mother should eat for two, should not exercise, should be bled and purged frequently, should wear tight corsets to protect her child. She scorned the use of most of the common remedies, opium, calomel, aloes, leeches externally applied, blistering, purging — believing them to increase rather than alleviate pain and do little to cure most ailments. In cases of pregnancy and childbirth she followed the dictations of Frederick Hollick, whose *Manual of Midwifery* was already revolutionizing Victorian attitudes, and of her own common sense. Fresh air, wholesome food, exercise, cleanliness, generous quantities of soap and water — all were basic in her methods of practicing medicine.

"Avoid drugs — and *doctors!*" was to become her lifelong admonition to relatives and intimate friends, often to their vast amusement.

Desperately she tried to get these hygienic ideas across to her patients, for reform was in her blood. To these mothers of the slums, as to her more prosperous patients, she exhorted, demonstrated, lectured; urged them to remove the stifling wrappings from their babies, expose them to fresh air and sunlight; explained to them their bodily functions; taught them to keep foods covered and away from flies; tried incessantly to rouse in them a passion for cleanliness. Only in small measure, of course, was she successful.

And her personal problems multiplied. The ill-natured gossip increased. She continued to receive anonymous letters. The visits to homes of her patients, often necessitating night walks through unfrequented streets, created unpleasant encounters. Though she never met with serious difficulties, there were many annoyances. A well-dressed man might walk by her side along Broadway, finally saying to her in a low voice, "Turn down Duane Street to the right." When she walked straight ahead with no sign of hearing or turning, he would vanish in the dark. Once while she waited for a horsecar at midnight by the City Hall a policeman tried to take her hand.

"Thank you," she said with cool politeness, brushing him away. "I can manage quite well without your help."

"See that lone woman walking like mad!" a group of revelers once shouted.

But always her experience gave proof that with common sense, self-reliance, and attention to the duty at hand, any woman could pursue the medical calling without undue risk.

Not without loneliness, discomfort, and pain, however!

"Oh, dear!" she wrote one of her sisters that summer. "It is so hot I can hardly write. I was called this morning to Flushing to see a sick child, and then attended my dispensary, the thermometer varying from 86 to 90 in the house, and it stood 102 in some rooms down town. Walk as deliberately as I would, it made my brain seem too large for my head. Flushing reminded me of the Sahara. It lay breathless under a cloudless sky, leaden with haze."

Far worse than the heat were the anonymous letters, the mischievous gossip.

"These malicious stories are painful to me, for I am woman as well as physician, and both natures are wounded by these falsehoods. Ah,

I am glad I, and not another, have to bear this pioneer work. I understand now why this life has never been lived before. It *is* hard, with no support but a high purpose, to live against every species of social opposition. I *should* like a little fun now and then. Life is altogether too sober."

3

The woman question! All through the fifties, along with the anti-slavery and temperance campaigns, it kept rearing itself, a three-headed monster causing shock and dismay to that timid majority which always cries havoc at every threat to the status quo. In spite of her distaste for the much talking and little acting which she associated with the women's rights movement — especially at its innumerable conventions — Elizabeth was forced to view it with increasing respect. Yet when Harry came to New York in the spring of 1853 to attend an anti-slavery convention and to try to find a publisher for his by no means mediocre poetry, she little dreamed how profoundly the "woman question" would be linked with the destiny of the Blackwells.

"Here are women," she wrote Lady Byron soon after her return to America, "who meet together and say, 'We are human beings possessing every faculty and capable of every development of humanity. We demand full freedom to develop and apply these faculties as seems to us best, responsible only to God. We refuse to acknowledge the right of any human being to arrange our destiny for us. We plant ourselves on Divine Right, we will not be ruled by so-called Expediency!' "

She even found kind words to say about the innumerable conventions.

"This is essentially the statement, not of hundreds but of thousands of women, scattered over our wide eastern and western states, women who do not care one straw for the ridicule of the whole army of newspapers but who are constantly increasing in numbers and bent upon continued agitation. It is a singular spectacle, such as no nation has ever witnessed before."

For the first time Elizabeth saw the leaders of the movement in action, for so closely were the three spearheads of reform allied — anti-slavery, temperance, and women's rights — that the occasion of a World Temperance Convention held in New York in May, 1853, saw the assembling of prominent workers in all three areas. She saw the strength of women's participation also, when some of the few women delegates to the temperance convention attempted to speak and there was such a furore of objection from the conservative majority that it was voted to exclude the women, even though their credentials had already been accepted. There followed such a storm of argument that the convention finally disbanded, its core of conservatives planning to hold another world convention in September, when no women would be admitted.

"World convention!" exclaimed one liberal minister who had been expelled from his pulpit for anti-slavery preaching. "With no women allowed? Better call it a half-world convention!"

Undaunted, the women and their supporters held a great mass meeting in Broadway Tabernacle, at which they planned a similar meeting in September, to be called, fittingly, a Whole World's Temperance Convention. And in spite of, perhaps because of, this furore of opposition, women's voices arose loud and strong that month in New York. Elizabeth went with Harry and Ellen to an anti-slavery meeting held at the Chinese Museum on Broadway, where the chief speaker was Miss Lucy Stone, who had attained a high reputation as an orator.

In spite of her own modest sally into public speaking, Elizabeth was prejudiced. Lecturing to a select group of women was quite different from standing on a high platform and boldly addressing hundreds, thousands, of both men and women. Surely any woman of such daring must be a bit lacking in feminine dignity! Her first sight of Miss Stone did nothing to allay this suspicion. Attractive, yes, small, dainty, on fire with enthusiasm, and with a silvery voice which, in spite of its soft timbre, penetrated to the farthest corner. But — to Elizabeth's horror, *she wore bloomers!*

Reform in women's dress was sadly needed. No one knew it better than she. The pinched waists, giving no chance to breathe or bend over, the huge burden of petticoats weighing in combination up to twelve pounds, the trailing skirts sweeping dirt from floors and streets, the suffocating veils — all seemed designed to make women the helpless playthings men desired. But — *this?* No wonder *Punch* had pictured it in such chortling caricature! That short skirt reaching barely to the knees, those baggy trousers gathered at the ankles! It was actually obvious that — that a woman possessed two legs! But — how very comfortable it must be! To be able to walk without feeling like a pony in the frame of an elephant!

Lucy Stone was eloquent. She held her audience enthralled by the recent incident of a slave mother who had been fleeing from her pursuers with her baby on her shoulder when a shot struck the baby's head, scattering its brains on the poor mother's face and neck as she ran. Elizabeth was impressed like the others, but she was unprepared for Harry's excess of enthusiasm.

"What a woman!" he marveled as they walked home along Broadway. "She was beautiful and charming when she came to my office in Cincinnati, but now — !"

"You've met her before?" asked Elizabeth in surprise.

He related the circumstances. "I told Sam about her, thought they might take to each other if they could only get acquainted. Seemed she might make him a good wife. But he didn't seem impressed."

"I doubt if she would make any man a good wife," said Elizabeth emphatically.

"So? And why not?" He sounded almost resentful.

"Any more than I would." Sensing his antagonism, she spoke more gently. "We're both of us wedded to a cause, something that commands our first loyalty. No man, or woman, can serve two masters."

"Marriage shouldn't be master and servant," he insisted scornfully.

"Of course not." Eagerly Elizabeth launched on a discussion of her favorite subject, the family. "Man wasn't intended to be a master, and certainly not a god to be worshiped, the way he usually is in our society, but an equal companion with whom a true relationship can be preserved only by giving as much as the woman receives."

"And you think a woman like Miss Lucy Stone wouldn't be able to give?"

"Not the way a wife should."

"And why not, I'd like to know."

Elizabeth fumbled for words. "I believe profoundly in the family life, in — in the sacredness of home ties, the central nature of woman's influence, which is — which must be moral and spiritual, working from within outward, to transform the family. The true wife should be a spiritual factor, not — not a driving force. Anyway," she threw logic to the winds, "how could any woman be a good wife and mother running all over the country, wearing pants, and making speeches?"

Harry threw back his head and roared. "Bessie, Bessie, you're a fraud! *You* — turning Puritan with the old cliché that 'the little woman's place is in the home'! But it isn't the first time."

"What do you mean?" retorted Elizabeth hotly. "And please — not so loud! You're drawing attention to yourself."

"That day in Geneva!" He chortled. "After defying tradition, breaking every hidebound code, what do you do? Refuse to walk in the procession with the other students because 'it wouldn't be ladylike'!" He slapped his knee. "I can still see old Webster's face."

Elizabeth flushed. She stifled an almost uncontrollable desire to lift him off his feet and shake him, as she had more than once. Then suddenly she laughed with him.

To her further surprise Harry continued his eulogy after they reached the apartment.

"Not a dry eye in the house! She held every person in that audience right in the hollow of her pretty little hand."

"I believe Harry is in love," said Ellen slyly, adding pertinently, *"again!"*

Elizabeth glanced sharply at her brother. In the years since their last meeting he had matured into a fairly successful and much traveled businessman, self-assured and urbane in manner. He could match tales with the most hardy adventurers: floods and wrecks on riverboats, horseback rides over rough forest trails as he peddled hardware on the frontier, encounters with fortunehunters, con men, even desperadoes. His latest adventure had involved land speculation, traveling to Wisconsin to survey and purchase for a friend fifty thousand acres of wild land offered by the government at ten cents an acre on long-term credit, receiving ten percent of the certificates himself. Since payment had to be made in gold, he had made the journey by stage with the gold coins stored between layers of cotton batting in an old horsehair trunk tied with a complication of strong knots. When he arrived in the frontier country of Wisconsin, he had left the trunk in the hotel entry and gone for three weeks prospecting in Bad Axe County, riding through deep snow on horseback, navigating pathless forests with only a compass; chosen his land; persuaded a mass meeting of indignant frontiersmen that, since the land sale would benefit them through taxation, he was a public benefactor, not a grasping speculator; made the purchase; returned home. Yes, Harry had most certainly grown. At first Elizabeth had hardly recognized him.

But now, flushing self-consciously, he was the charming roguish boy she had always known, the blue eyes as innocent and sparkling, the teeth as white, the black hair topping the full beard as luxuriantly curling as when Aunt Bar had twisted it into ringlets. Poor Harry, she thought. In and out of love a half-dozen times, from Kate Vail to the silly little daughter of his landlady in New York, and always so unfortunate in his choices! And this infatuation, if it really was such, was surely the most unfortunate of all.

But she soon discovered it was far more than infatuation. Disappointed in finding a publisher for his poems, Harry went on to Boston, where in June he attended a petition hearing in Representatives' Hall, and again Lucy Stone was one of the speakers, capturing her audience of Garrison abolitionists in general and Harry in particular by her "beauty, charm, and eloquence."

"I shall endeavor to see more of her before I come West, if practicable," he wrote Sam in a letter containing an urgent request for fifty dollars, "as I decidedly prefer her to any lady I ever met, always excepting the Bloomer dress, which I *don't* like, practically, though theoretically I believe in it with my whole soul." Pursuing her acquaintance was not easy since she was traveling about attending conventions, "having been born locomotive, I believe." But Harry had not sold hinges, flatirons, screws, bolts, shovels, to hardheaded pioneers for nothing. He went to see Mr. Garrison and boldly announced his intentions to pay his addresses to Miss Stone.

The shrewd old "Liberator" shook his head. "You're not likely to succeed, son. Lucy Stone is determined not to marry. She's so devoted to her work that she's declined several other worthy suitors." Worthier than Henry Blackwell, his tone implied. But he gave Harry a letter to Miss Stone, also one to Deacon Josiah Henshaw, the leading abolitionist of West Brookfield, where Lucy lived.

No sooner obtained than put to use. Harry found the deacon plowing in his field. He read the letter, then eyed the young man with a wise twinkle. Miss Stone was away lecturing, Harry learned, but was expected home that afternoon. He dined with the Henshaws, took a long walk, then climbed Coy's Hill to the Stones' farmhouse. He found Lucy mounted on a table in a short dress, whitewashing the ceiling of her parents' living room. She greeted him cordially, having heard of his anti-slavery interest and knowing Elizabeth as a pioneer much admired in the women's rights movement. She introduced him to her parents. They walked together to the top of the hill above the house, talked of anti-slavery and women's rights. Harry urged her to come west and lecture, offering to make all the arrangements. And, being

Harry, he did not confine his remarks to anti-slavery and women's rights. He told her exactly why he had come, that he had fallen in love with her and wanted to make her his wife.

She was both kind and frank. "Thank you for the honor, Mr. Blackwell. But what you ask is impossible. I have consecrated myself to work for the equality of women, and I have resolved never to marry."

Harry was not discouraged. "But I also believe firmly in women's equality with men, Miss Stone. Don't you see that together we might do more and better work than you could do alone?"

She did not see. However, she graciously agreed to permit him to arrange a series of lectures for her in the West, also to exchange letters with him occasionally on the subjects of reform to which they were both committed. So began Henry Blackwell's long and difficult courtship of Lucy Stone.

Elizabeth heard of these developments with dismay. Letters from Cincinnati during the following months did not ease her worries. Harry was arranging the lectures, in Cincinnati, Pittsburgh, Wheeling, Columbus, Sandusky, Toledo, Louisville, St. Louis, Madison, Indianapolis, Terre Haute, Lafayette. Lucy's addresses were taking the public by storm. No hall would hold her audiences. In each place she was giving three lectures: The Social and Industrial Disabilities of Woman, The Legal and Political Disabilities of Woman, The Moral and Religious Disabilities of Woman. While in Cincinnati she was staying at Walnut Hills with Hannah, who took to her immediately and with her usual graciousness and amiability greeted her like a daughter. Marian and Ellen, Samuel and George, all seemed to have fallen under her spell.

"A most admirable woman." Though the exact words recorded in Sam's diary did not reach Elizabeth verbatim, she sensed their fervor in his letters. "By her quiet decision, steady purpose, and lofty principles she reminds me strongly of Elizabeth, and by a certain precision and distinctness of utterance and personal neatness and judgment. We have quite adopted her."

Cincinnati was a-buzz with gossip. Harry's sudden interest in women's rights, his attending all the conventions, even making his maiden speech at a big one in Cleveland, were all noted with both amusement and approval. The city's little group of abolitionists — the Ernsts, the Harwoods, the Burnets, Levi Coffin, the Donaldsons, the Heatons, the Pullanes — all became ardent supporters of the freedom of women as well as of slaves.

Poor Harry indeed! Was he to be disappointed in love again? Surely a woman like Lucy Stone, who so eloquently protested the legal and moral subjugation of women in marriage, would not bend her neck to the scorned yoke! And if she should, what kind of life would such a union bring to Harry? Running around the country at a woman's beck and call, making speeches at her dictation, submitting to the whims of a bloomered freak who should be at home bearing and raising his children?

Elizabeth stopped short, aghast. "Are you really a fraud?" she asked herself. "Demanding freedom for yourself but condemning it for another? Believing it right to deny yourself marriage to study and practice medicine, but wrong to do it for the purpose of defending other women's rights?"

That September of 1853 she had a chance to see another leader of the women's rights movement in action. It was the month of New York's Great Exhibition, its center the Crystal Palace in Reservoir Park, a huge Greek cross of glass housing wonders of art and science from all over the world. Hannah came to visit. Emily, Ellen, and Marian were also there that month, and the family invested in several weeks' tickets, taking turns in using them.

The exhibition aroused memories of that other Crystal Palace across the ocean, of London and Paris. Going home to her stifling rooms, Elizabeth imagined the fragrance of an English spring and walked in fancy the shaded paths of the Luxembourg Gardens. Perhaps it was this nostalgia that aroused other memories, for while Emily sewed that night, Elizabeth talked and talked of her Parisian experiences and for the first time emptied her heart to another human being of all the bittersweet memories that remained of Hippolyte Blot.

The whole world poured into New York that month, and with it the two disparate temperance conventions postponed from May, plus an anti-slavery and a women's rights convention. They aroused in Elizabeth all her old aversion to conventions in general and women's rights conventions in particular.

"I think it will always be found a universal law of this life," she once wrote, "that thought which does not constantly shape itself into action has a tendency to degenerate, and thus that conventions which constantly meet for the mere discussion of abstract principles, or rights, will soon lose the high spirit in which they may have originated and become mere displays of vain oratory or the theatre of vanity and petty ambitions. Every soul must have its body in this world. Had these conventions given rise to working associations, their existence might have continued, perhaps under other names, but they have not contrived to establish even a newspaper. They have constantly degenerated in moral force, from the first assemblage in Worcester, and must finally be dropped from the sheer absence of all true vitality."

In all fairness she did not apply this criticism to the lecturing of such women as Lucy Stone, who had the God-given power to influence public sentiment. "Your earnest personal appeal in a lecturing tour," she was later to write Lucy, "where individual force comes out in its full power, is worth more for influencing public sentiment in the right way than all the conventions which have been held."

Lucy Stone, of course, was in New York that September. Not only had she organized the women's rights convention, but she had been one of the prime promoters of the rival Whole World's Temperance Convention. Present also was her closest friend, Antoinette Brown, who had graduated with her from Oberlin, persisted in her theological studies, and was soon to become the first woman in the world to be ordained, having recently accepted a call to become the pastor of the Congregational Church of South Butler, New York. But her ordination, held on a wild stormy day that same month and denounced by almost every newspaper (The *New York Independent* declared that any woman who would allow herself to be ordained was an infidel!), startling innovation though it was, could not compete in excitement with the furore she aroused in New York.

The orthodox body, dubbed the "Half-World Convention" by its opponents, had insisted it would accept accredited women delegates. Antoinette Brown had brought respectable credentials from her church. Her credentials were accepted, but when she rose to assume a delegate's right to speak, the meeting broke into an uproar. For two hours she stood on the platform waiting for the disorder to subside . . . in vain. The next day she asked again to be heard and was recognized by the chairman. Again she was shouted down by a group near the platform who incessantly kept raising points of order. On the third day, when she tried again, the meeting passed a vote that no woman should be allowed to speak from the platform.

Reported Horace Greeley in his unorthodox *Tribune:* "First Day, Crowding a woman from the platform; Second Day, Gagging her; Third Day, Voting she should stay gagged. Having thus disposed of the main question, we presume the incidentals will be finished this morning."

Harriet Beecher Stowe, whose fame as the author of *Uncle Tom's Cabin* had swept the country, was even more pungent in her defense of Antoinette Brown's right to speak in public and, if she wished, to preach. "If it is right for Jenny Lind to *sing* to two thousand people, 'I know that my Redeemer lives,'" she remarked with asperity, "is it wrong for Antoinette Brown to *say* the same thing?"

Elizabeth admired Antoinette Brown, felt toward her none of the peculiar antagonism she felt toward Lucy Stone. Why? Because she did not wear bloomers? Because she was strikingly beautiful with her dark hair and vivid coloring, poised and calm in her demeanor in contrast with Lucy's intense and dominating vivacity? Because, like herself, she was courageously trying to free women by action instead of words? Or — more likely — because she did not threaten the happiness of a member of the Blackwell family?

Elizabeth did not know, of course, that three years later Antoinette Brown would be Mrs. Samuel Blackwell!

4

That autumn of 1853 saw the abrupt dashing of Emily's hopes. She had visited during the summer at Bellevue in spite of the timid conservatism of some of the doctors, taken private lessons in chemistry, worked furiously on her thesis, and — hopefully — arranged fittings for her graduation dress. Then came one setback after another. She applied for an assistantship at the hospital, to begin after her graduation. She was refused. Then she learned that her friend Dr. Brainerd, who had been largely responsible for her acceptance at Rush Medical College, was not returning to Chicago. Would his absence affect — prevent — her last year of college?

"The future looks black," she wrote in her diary on her twenty-seventh birthday, "but with a golden glow beyond it."

She left for Chicago in November, loath to think of Elizabeth facing the lonely, poverty-stricken winter. Arriving at the college, she found her worst fears confirmed. The first evening she called on two influential members of the college board. "I find I shall have more to contend with than I supposed," she recorded with laconic restraint. The next day she found that a meeting had been held without notifying her and that the

Medical Society of Illinois had censured the Chicago faculty for admitting a woman. She was *out*. It was small satisfaction to know that Horace Greeley published in his *Tribune* a scathing article on her refusal.

But Emily, like Elizabeth, was not one to sit down and mope. On the first day of December she left for Cleveland, where, to her great surprise and delight, she was admitted to the Western Reserve Medical College. At last all obstacles to securing her degree were removed.

For Elizabeth the winter was indeed lonely and poverty-stricken. And the loneliness was far worse than the poverty. Marian was keeping house for the Alofsens in Jersey City. All the rest of the family were scattered and far away. She dreamed constantly of having most of them with her, making a center for them here in the East. There was poor Sam with his intense craving for the ocean, and Harry, sick to death of his lonely and often dangerous treks over Indiana and Illinois, always in pursuit of some will-o'the-wisp which might better his fortunes! Luckily the hardware partnership would soon be ending, and she hoped they would think twice before renewing it. Ellen could pursue her art studies, George and Sam and Harry could all find some profitable business, Marian could keep house for them all, and Hannah, still pink and pretty in her frilled cap and snowy kerchief, could preside over the household with all her fuss and worry and delightful graciousness. Huddled in shawls and blankets to economize on precious fuel, Elizabeth dreamed and hoped and planned.

Perhaps it was partly such musing that led her to a major decision. Her position as a tenant was becoming more and more intolerable. The rented rooms were all expense with little income. Her landlady was increasingly hostile and uncooperative. There seemed to be only one solution. She must buy a house. After some searching she found a satisfactory one at 79 East Fifteenth Street, though larger than necessary. Her friend Mr. Alofsen loaned her the necessary funds. She moved in, renting most of the house to a family which kept boarders and reserving for herself only a front room downstairs for office purposes and living quarters in the garret. At least now she had a place of her own. Proudly she hung her sign on the house front, knowing that, no matter how great the new neighborhood's hostility, no landlady's disapproval could force its removal.

Lonely though her life continued to be, she was by no means idle. She studied, worked on a new series of lectures, wrote, rewrote, revised. And the dispensary in Tompkins Square was taking more and more of her time. Its acceptance by the poor women of the Eleventh Ward was now fully assured. It must now be established on a more permanent basis. Hesitantly, almost apologetically, she approached some of her new friends, for she knew the public support of her unpopular project would take moral courage. Already most of them were supporting the dispensary financially and tacitly giving it their backing. Would they be willing to act as trustees if it was incorporated? She was both flattered and humbled by their agreement.

A meeting for organization was held. Theodore Sedgwick, a distinguished author-lawyer, whose grandfather had been Speaker of the House under Washington, prepared the certificate of incorporation. Charles Butler, another lawyer and philanthropist who was to serve New York University in a legal capacity for sixty years, also helped procure the act of incorporation and served as the first president. The document, dated December 13, 1853, was filed in the office of the Department of State January 20, 1854.

The list of trustees was impressive. Butler and Sedgwick, Richard H. Bowne, and Edward C. West were lawyers. Robert Haydock, who became secretary-treasurer, also Simeon Draper and Charles W. Foster were auctioneers, the latter an importer of French goods and director of the Crystal Palace Exposition. Richard Henry Manning, Robert White, and Marcus Spring were prominent merchants. Dennis Harris was, of course, a sugar refiner. Stacy B. Collins was a publisher. Horace Greeley, Henry J. Raymond, and Charles A. Dana were editors. Cyrus W. Field, later of Atlantic Cable fame, was a business tycoon and eminent philanthropist. Most of them were young men, broadminded, adventurous, as yet unknown. Officially the little room at 207 East Seventh Street was opened as a dispensary in March.

The certificate of incorporation read: "That the particular business and object of such Society shall be the providing and furnishing medicines and medical and surgical aid to such persons as may be in need thereof and unable by reason of poverty to procure the same; also the training of an efficient body of nurses for the service of the community; and also the employment of medical practitioners of either sex, it being the design of this Institution to secure the services of well-qualified female practitioners of medicine for its patients."

A bold program indeed! "Training of efficient nurses!" "Well-qualified female practitioners!" All were dreams for the future, of course. Meanwhile, Elizabeth was thankful to secure the services of a few male physicians who agreed to serve as consultants on her staff. Most had been acting as friends and advisers for months.

It was no mean list: Dr. George Philip Camman, noted diagnostician, who had perfected the vinaural stethoscope in 1840; Dr. Richard S. Kissam, noted for his cataract operations and special skills in ophthalmology; Dr. Isaac E. Taylor, one of the most noted obstetricians and gynecologists of his day, founder and lifetime president of Bellevue Hospital Medical College; Dr. Valentine Mott, Quaker surgeon, teacher, author, who became an authority on surgical anesthesia while it was in its infancy and of whom Sir Astley Cooper said, "He has performed more of the great operations than any man living or dead"; Dr. Willard Parker, professor of the College of Physicians and Surgeons in New York; Dr. John Watson, chief of staff of the New York City Dispensary and one of the organizers of the New York Academy of Medicine.

But the favor of these distinguished men by no means removed the professional stigma surrounding, isolating, the woman doctor. All acted as individuals, secure enough in reputation to defy the grim disapproval of organized medicine. And while vastly reassuring and helpful in cases of emergency, their sanction did little to ease the daily rigors of poverty and loneliness. It was Elizabeth, not her sponsors, who trudged three afternoons a week through snow, mud, indescribable litter, to the small room in the Eleventh Ward, distributed medicines with chilled fingers, endlessly repeated instructions that she knew would not or could not be heeded, climbed rickety stairs or descended into moldy basements to deliver babies, returned home to huddle in shawls and blankets, waiting vainly for the doorbell to announce a rare paying patient.

But spring brought a burst of new life even to the side streets and alleys of New York. As she walked to the dispensary she detected, or imagined, a faint breath of cherry blossoms mingled with the pervading stench of the slaughterhouses. And as if the revival of warmth and new life had spurred similar activity in her own small world, exciting things began to happen.

In late February Emily graduated from Western Reserve, not only the one woman in her class but with almost incredible success. The highest number usually attached to a student's performance was ten. By way of special honor Emily was rated eleven. In addition to the diploma a paper of special commendation signed by every member of the faculty was voluntarily presented to her, an honor accorded only to the best students. When she passed her preliminary examinations, the censor, an old doctor who had been strongly opposed to her admission, said as she went out, "That is the only student you have passed whom I could introduce to practice in my family." At her graduation all her professors and fellow-graduates shook hands with her, as well as Dr. Nancy Clark of Boston, who was also present. Old Dr. Kirkland, another diehard opponent, invited her to his office and presented her with a bouquet from his hothouse, saying, "It isn't often that roses bloom in winter, and it isn't often we have the pleasure of graduating a lady." Honors from home were humbler but no less appreciated. Ellen made her a brilliant hood, and Hannah sent one of her inimitable puddings.

"She has graduated not successfully," said Dr. Clark, "but triumphantly."

Back in New York in March, Emily helped in the newly organized dispensary while concluding her plans for study in England. Money had to be borrowed, notes arranged, and Elizabeth even wrote a letter to a Boston friend, Miss Parsons, asking her to find some friendly person to "escort her and her trunk on board, giving her the strong arm and kindly countenance which is so pleasant in the bustle and confusion of departure." Of her sister she added, "She is most thoroughly in earnest, and her cooperation with me is the brightest thing in my medical life."

Emily was even more loath to leave Elizabeth alone than before. The work at the dispensary was becoming more and more time-consuming, and the big house with its tenants was no mean responsibility.

"I have an idea," she broached one day before leaving. "Why don't you take one of those little orphan girls and train her for house service? It would serve two purposes, keep one of the little beggars off the streets or out of a wretched asylum and get some of the household help you need but can't afford to hire; three purposes, in fact, for you might not be quite so lonely. A lot of people, you know, are taking them."

Elizabeth did know. The new Children's Aid Society, formed the previous year, had been placing many homeless children, often taking them off the streets or even out of prison, where they had been placed for vagrancy. Just in the last year the society had placed 164 boys and 43 girls, 20 of whom had been in prison, in friendly homes where they would be removed from the overwhelming temptations resulting from poverty and neglect. Other institutions, like the Juvenile Asylum and the orphanage for abandoned immigrant children on Randall's Island, specialized in the same service. But she did not wholly approve of the idea. Too many women she knew had taken advantage of the scheme merely to provide themselves with free help, making little slaves of their charges. Yet such a relationship, if assumed for the right motives, could be mutually beneficial.

"I'll — consider it," she promised, though with reluctance.

Emily reached Liverpool on April 8 and started work as an assistant under Dr. (later Sir) James Simpson, professor of medicine at Edinburgh University. Her good fortune was almost incredible, for Simpson was already a front-rank surgeon and specialist in female diseases. He was noted for the discovery of chloroform. One of the first physicians in Europe to employ anesthesia in surgery, he had been the first to use it in childbirth, having administered it in 1853 to Queen Victoria on the birth of Prince Leopold. However, it would be seventy-six years before normal maternity cases in English wards were accorded similar surcease from pain and then only through the intervention of a prime minister's wife, a postponement possibly due to the violent opposition to the innovation by the Scottish clergy, who maintained that pain in childbirth was ordained by scripture: "In sorrow thou shalt bring forth children." Sir James had countered with some scripture of his own. When Eve was born, he maintained, God cast Adam into a deep sleep before performing on him the first costectomy. Thus anesthesia had received scriptural sanction long before the first child had ever been conceived! Such experimental boldness no doubt accounted for the eminent surgeon's willingness to take a woman for his assistant.

Any young male doctor just out of medical school might well have envied her — and did. But Emily was not *any* young doctor. Possessed of robust health, abundant energy, superior intelligence, a remarkable memory, and in addition to her medical knowledge, trained in mathematics, Greek, Latin, German, and French, she was soon justifying the doctor's confidence in unexpected measure. If she was occasionally disappointed in him, it was for nonprofessional reasons.

"I was annoyed by Dr. S.," she wrote once, "when he introduced me to a Lady Agnes Duff, a cousin of the Queen who asked to see me and then, as I thought, was very rude. It's astonishing how rank impresses these people! Dr. S. seemed to deem her condescending to stare at me with impertinent curiosity quite an honor!"

But any such minor annoyance was more than canceled by the

doctor's tolerance and sense of humor. Not only was he cheerfully willing to shock his colleagues and patients by his defiance of tradition, but he derived a wry amusement from doing so. On one occasion when his office was filled with waiting patients of aristocratic lineage, Emily was doing some translating for him in the innermost room of the suite.

"Dr. Blackwell," he called to her in a low voice, then a little louder, "*Dr. Blackwell!*" Assured that the attention of all his patients had been aroused, he thundered, "Dr. Blackwell!" Then from the corner of his eye he watched with intense amusement the expressions of surprise and dismay on the faces of his distinguished patients when they saw a *lady* quietly issue forth in obedience to the summons.

But the slight dent made by a young woman physician in the cast-iron mold of British tradition was nothing compared with the shattering blows which in that same year of 1854 were to split it in two. For in March, the month that Emily sailed, England and France declared war on Russia. And in October a young Englishwoman, appalled by tales of sick and wounded soldiers dying like flies in the barracks at Scutari on the shores of the Black Sea without doctors, nurses, or even old rags to dress their wounds, left with thirty-eight volunteer women for the Crimea.

At last, thought Elizabeth, reading with deep satisfaction as the months passed of the miracles being wrought — the vindication of the competence of women in nursing, the triumph of revolutionary concepts of cleanliness and sanitation — the torture and restlessness were ended. Florence Nightingale was realizing the fulfillment of her heart's desire.

5

When Elizabeth awoke on the morning of the fifteenth of May, she smelled the sea. Her spirits rose like a gull soaring. Portent of storm it might be, with the wind in the east, but for her it always presaged an invigorating surge of energy. With the tang of the sea in her nostrils, she was equal to any discouragement, any herculean task. This morning she felt the added presentiment that something of unusual interest was about to happen. A letter from home, from England? A new patient?

To utilize the energy, she established herself at her desk, every window opened wide, and tackled the most disagreeable task possible, the balancing of accounts. It was an all-morning job, endless in fact, for the debits and credits could never be made to balance. Practicing medicine for a woman in New York in 1854 was a losing proposition. By eleven o'clock the high energy was flagging, the smell of the sea was absorbed into the humid and dusty miasma of another impending hot summer, and nothing exciting had happened. Then the doorbell rang.

A woman stood on the stoop, looking up at her with warily hopeful, extremely intelligent dark eyes. She was not attractive, unprepossessing, in fact. Except for the eyes, deep-set beneath heavy black brows, the face was almost ugly, its broadness accentuated rather than tempered by the wide full mouth and over-large nose. In turn the visitor saw a rather short but stately lady, blonde with wavy hair, eyes for some reason a bit strange, but lips smiling and face radiating kindness.

"Dok-tor Black-well?" The accent was unmistakable. Like the voices of many of her immigrant patients at the dispensary, it transported Elizabeth immediately to Gräfenberg. "Yes," she replied in her very inferior German. "I am Dr. Blackwell. Can I help you?"

The heavy face brightened, like a dark crag lit with sunlight, looked almost beautiful. The woman burst into a volley of German, out of which Elizabeth caught one name, Miss Goodrich, matron of the Home for the Friendless.

"Ah, yes. Miss Goodrich told me about you. You are Fräulein Zak —" She hesitated, trying to recapture the unpronounceable word.

"I — Marie Zakrzewska."

Not so unpronounceable, after all, the way she said it. *Zak-shéf-ska.* She invited the woman into the office–reception room, bare except for the mere essentials of furniture, and tried to put her at ease. Thanks to her German immigrants, Elizabeth could understand most of her speech.

"You are interested in medicine, I know, and you came here from Germany about a year ago." The visitor nodded. She had come from Germany where she had received her training, though by nationality she was Polish. She had arrived with her sister Anna the previous May, hoping to study medicine in the United States. She had been interested in it since childhood, for her mother had been a midwife, and she had accompanied her on many of her cases since the age of ten. Later Marie had studied midwifery herself as the protégée of the eminent Dr. Schmidt, chief director of the Hospital Charité in Berlin. He had been very kind to her and had secured for her a responsible position in the School of Midwives. But there had been criticism of a woman holding such a position, and her good fortune had ended when he had suddenly died.

"May fifteenth," she said simply. "Today is the anniversary of his death. My day of greatest misery. But, now that I have seen you, my day of greatest hope."

She had come to America, believing that in the New World women would have greater opportunities. And she had heard of a new college in Philadelphia where women could study medicine. She had delivered her letters of introduction to a German, Dr. Reisig, who had known her mother. He had told her that female physicians in this country were of the lowest rank, of less repute than a good nurse. Depressed but not diverted from her purpose, she had sought various means of support until somehow she could attain her goal.

Expending all but their last twenty-five cents for good German wool, she had found a market for little worsted tassels and had employed thirty girls to make them. But this spring the demand for worsted goods had ceased. Then she had undertaken the making of imitation coiffures out of silk. But suddenly, two days ago, she had awakened to the fact that she had been here a year and was no nearer to achieving her goal! She could find nothing about the college in Philadelphia, and none of her German friends could tell her. She simply could not, it seemed, learn English. Then she had heard of Dr. Elizabeth Blackwell. So here she was.

As she listened, Elizabeth became more and more excited. Was it because they had so much in common — a sister named Anna, interest in medicine, a fierce enough purpose to surmount all difficulties — that she felt such an immediate kinship with this strange woman of another language and culture? Whatever the reason, she was suddenly sharing her own experience, her secret dream of founding a hospital for women in connection with the dispensary just opened, her hoped-for partnership with Emily.

"My sister has just gone to Europe to finish what she began here," she said, "and you have come here to finish what you began in Europe."

She asked to see Marie's credentials. Reading them, she was amazed. This woman had held one of the most distinguished positions in a great Berlin hospital! She had been chief accoucheuse, head professor in the School for Midwives of the Charité, largest hospital in Prussia! No wonder after the death of her patron her male associates had managed to oust her from the post!

That summer Elizabeth was no longer lonely. She became Marie's medical preceptor, as well as her instructor in English, and in turn the girl became her invaluable assistant in the dispensary. The English proved almost hopeless. The scientific brilliance and competence in midwifery which far exceeded Elizabeth's did not extend to language. Sometimes she felt that she learned much more from her pupil than she imparted.

As summer heat soared, the volume of work in the dispensary rose with the mercury. One woman told another of the cleverness of the woman doctor, whose services could be secured — *free*. The presence of the new woman who knew their ways and could speak their language fluently brought more German immigrants. But the beneficiaries were not always grateful. On the contrary!

One day the settees in the hall of the dispensary were filled with patients waiting their arrival. Outside the building on the curbstone two decrepit old women were also waiting. Elizabeth and Marie were unavoidably detained and were fifteen minutes late in arriving.

"There come the dispensary women now!" shouted one of the old crones as she spied them turning the corner of Second Avenue. As the two came closer, she greeted them with aggrieved reproach, "Those ladies in the hall have been waiting a whole hour already!"

Elizabeth learned other things from her pupil than new techniques in midwifery. The silk wig fad soon lost favor, and Marie had to find other support for her family, which now included another sister from Germany. She procured a commission for embroidering caps, an industry centered in Water Street which gave employment to thousands of unfortunate women. The wholesale dealer paid seven cents each, plus three cents for making up the cap. To make a dozen a day, a woman had to work for sixteen hours. Receiving the cut cloth from the wholesale dealer, she gave it with three cents' worth of silk to the embroiderer, who received three cents for her work. Then she pressed and returned them, making one cent on each for herself. Giving out about six dozen daily, she earned perhaps fifty cents a day, as did her employees.

"How can such women live!" exclaimed Elizabeth.

"They don't," replied Marie caustically, "not for long. Perhaps for a little while until health fails or the merchant says the work has come to an end. But for many of them there is another way."

"You — you don't mean —"

"*Ja!* The merchants tell every woman who is a bit attractive that it is wrong for her to work so hard, that many a man would be glad to care for her, and that many women live quite comfortably with the help of a 'friend.' Oh, they make it sound very nice, these pious and respectable gentlemen! It is the same in Berlin. *Ja,* I learned plenty from the prostitutes in the hospital how good and educated women become what they are!"

"And I in Paris," Elizabeth could have added, "and in London. And now in New York."

She received a further education in the subject when she called on one of her lawyer friends to inquire if something could not be done to prohibit Madame Restelle, the notorious abortionist whose name was on every tongue as the typical "female physician," from pursuing her profitable but unsavory trade. He shook his head somberly. "She is a social necessity, and she will be protected by rich and influential personages. I'm afraid there is no way to stop her."

The conviction which had long been needling Elizabeth's conscience was becoming a sharp sword-thrust of determination. This was *her* anti-slavery crusade. She must fight against this slavery of woman. For woman was almost as much a slave in this enlightened Western civilization as the Negro — legally, economically, physically, morally. Leave it to the Garrisons, the Greeleys, the Elizabeth Stantons, the Lucy Stones, to work for her legal and economic freedom. Those were imperative. But who could best battle for her physical and moral freedom? Clergymen? Men doctors? Moralists? No. Clergymen preached. Men doctors were bent on curing. Moralists philosophized and wrote books. It must be a war of prevention, of education. And who could wage it more effectively and intelligently than the woman physician? She had joined battle with her lectures on the education of girls, but it had been only a skirmish. She vowed it would become a lifetime crusade.

"Collect all the information you can about maternity, the relation of the sexes, and kindred subjects," she wrote Emily. "We have a vast field to work in this direction, for reliable information is desperately needed."

All that long hot summer, with the thermometer sometimes soaring to 102, Elizabeth trailed her long skirts through the dusty streets, sweated inside her voluminous petticoats and tight corsets and chemise and shirtwaist and black doctorial sack; gave free service, often unthanked, in the dispensary; delivered babies in Flushing or Jersey City or respectable uptown bedrooms or downtown reeking tenements; treated her few private patients; instructed Marie and, after much correspondence and many failures, secured her admission to the Cleveland Medical College.

Meanwhile the cap embroidery went the way of the worsted tassels and silk wigs, because, employers explained blandly, "the Southern trade has failed"; in reality because Marie had remained deaf to more subtle blandishments. But thanks to her new friends, one of her sisters had found employment. The other was to be married to another German immigrant. Freed from family responsibility, Marie Zakrzewska left for Cleveland on October 16 with medical textbooks supplied by Elizabeth, twenty dollars to cover travel and matriculation fees, and in addition, exactly thirty dollars.

In spite of her delight over this development Elizabeth had never been more lonely or discouraged. The dispensary was not functioning as she had hoped. The early enthusiasm of its patrons, including their contributions, had swiftly waned. Pledges had not been paid. With the room open for only a short time three days a week, patients forgot the days and hours and failed to come. Closed so much of the time, the room was chill and damp. It looked as if she must close it for the winter. Yet how desperately it was needed, not one small room six hours a week, but an efficient, full-time institution!

Even family seemed to be deserting. Anna was trying to persuade Emily to settle in England, offering to subsidize her until she should get her practice established. Barbara Leigh Smith was urging her to go to the Crimea with Florence Nightingale. Marian was returning to Cincinnati for the winter. Harry was going on a journey which would probably "decide his fate for life." The long cold winter ahead looked desolate. Was it a prototype of all her coming years? Friends, relatives, all flying off on their own tangents, no one who really belonged in her little circle?

It was that autumn that she came slowly to a decision which would change her life.

Chapter Ten

ELIZABETH'S GAZE KEPT RETURNING to the child standing in the window, hands clasped behind her, eyes fixed with an almost painful intensity on the fast-fading brightness of the setting sun. She was not a pretty child, thin face sharply aquiline, shoulders a bit stooped from leaning forward, arms and legs like pipestems, hair so jet black and riotous that it gave her a witchlike appearance. Out of the four hundred children in the orphanage at Randall's Island, the respository for pauper waifs from the immigrant depot, she was certainly one of the least attractive and desirable. During her several visits to the orphanage Elizabeth had reviewed parades of far handsomer and healthier-looking urchins, listened to commentaries on their backgrounds, apparent possibilities, and habits, even been treated to exhibits of their gums and teeth.

"Like a horsetrader," she had thought with deep embarrassment, "or, worse, a purchaser at the slave block."

But always, as today, her gaze had turned like a magnet to the thin sober little figure who was never permitted to join the parade. Now she deliberately interrupted the current sales talk of the matron.

"Tell me about that child there, please, the one looking out of the window."

"Oh, but you wouldn't want her!" The matron looked shocked. "She's a good little thing, but plain, as you can see, and quite stupid. Now this one here —"

"I'd like to know more about her," insisted Elizabeth.

There was little to know, it seemed. She was between seven and eight, of Irish parentage, an orphan, with no living soul to claim her, and even her name, Katharine Barry, was slightly doubtful.

Marian, who had accompanied Elizabeth, was registering anxiety and dismay. "Not *her*, Bessie! Surely you don't want a child like that!"

"Why not?" demanded Elizabeth. "Look at her. Have you noticed how she's been fairly drinking in that sunset?"

"Why *not*! When you can have any one of these others?" Marian spluttered her amazement and indignation. "She — she's almost ugly! And — and she looks weak and pindling. I — I thought you were looking for a nice strong intelligent child that you could train up to be a — a valuable little domestic."

"I thought so too," was the sober reply.

"Then what — why —"

"Because — this child needs me more than any of the others," said Elizabeth simply.

Suddenly she went toward the window, stood for a moment looking down at the intent little face, then gently disengaged one of the small hands.

"How would you like to go home with me, dear, and be my little girl?"

The eyes lifted to hers were startlingly bright, as well as clear and swift in their appraisal. "Yes," came the almost instant reply, "but could we please wait until the colors fade?"

Elizabeth felt her hand squeezed tightly. She dropped to her knees before the window, and together the woman and child watched until the crescendo of brightness had diminished and stilled to a pale yellow glow. It was a communion of sharing which was to mount to its own harmonious crescendo through more than half a century.

"No difficulty was made," Elizabeth wrote Emily on the first of October. "I gave a receipt for her, and the poor little thing trotted after me like a dog. Instead of being stupid, I find now that she is withdrawn from blows and tyranny, that she is very bright, has able little fingers that are learning to dust and wash up and sew, and much perseverance and energy for so small a child. She is a sturdy little thing, affectionate and with a touch of obstinacy which will turn to good account later in life. Of course she is more trouble than use at present and quite bewildered me at first, but still I like on the whole to have her, and it is quite pretty to hear her in the morning, sitting up in bed, waiting for permission to get up and singing, 'Oh, Susanna, don't you cry for me, I'm going to Alabama with me washboard on me knee.' She is not pretty but has an honest little face, something like Howard's when a young child, and it is growing brighter every day under happier influences than she has yet known. So you can imagine me now attended by small Kitty, attired in my colored Paris straw bonnet, and a black silk cape of mine that hangs over her like a mantle."

A "valuable little domestic"? Hardly! Elizabeth knew that on the very first night, when she carried the small angular body up to bed in her arms. In spite of what she wrote Emily, even then her feeling toward the child was not that of mistress to servant but of mother to daughter. She told her about her family, about the long struggle to become a doctor, and, because she was sure the child eyes missed nothing, about the misfortune to one of her own eyes. Though she did not say, "Don't speak of it," Kitty never did except once, perhaps thirty years later. They were having a guest for luncheon, and Elizabeth, who found the artificial eye very tiring at times, had not "put in her toilet," as she called it. Sensitive Kitty, knowing how shy she was of others' staring, took the guest aside and told her about the loss of the eye. It was the only time in their long life together that she mentioned it.

That night was the beginning of a new contentment for Elizabeth. For the first time she felt a unity within herself, a resolution of the two conflicting elements of her woman's nature. Taking the child was only a substitute for marriage and motherhood, yes, but it helped sate her hunger for complete fulfillment as a woman.

"I have recognized the truth of this part of my nature," she was to write Barbara a little later, "and the necessity of satisfying its wants that I may be calm and free for the wider work."

For Kitty that winter also was a time for blooming. Under Elizabeth's careful regimen the thin body rounded, the stooped shoulders straightened. The angles disappeared. Far from stupid, she responded amazingly to the mental stimuli of Blackwell erudition, and as Elizabeth had foreseen, the awareness of a sunset's beauty had given earnest of deep sensitivity and artistic perception.

"You'd better pay attention to what that child says about clothes," advised Marian, who, with Hannah, had always taken a dim view of Elizabeth's contempt for style. "Her eyes are sharp and keen."

And they were keen to notice things other than clothes.

"Your hands," Kitty said once to Elizabeth, impulsively lifting one of them to her own cheek. "They're beautiful. Such long fingers. And they're cool to feel, but not — not moist. And I like the way you always warm them before you touch a sick person. It must keep them from being frightened, especially the babies."

"You noticed that!" exclaimed Elizabeth, surprised.

At first the child did not call her "Aunt Elizabeth" or "Aunt Bessie," as she was to do later, but always "Doctor" or "My Doctor." Once she happened to be present during the call of one of Elizabeth's friends, a physician. After he had gone she exclaimed with a very puzzled face, "Doctor, how very odd it is to hear a *man* called Doctor!"

Elizabeth was determined to give Kitty every advantage. She enrolled her in the primary department of the 12th Street Public School for Girls, then considered the best school in the city and patronized by old New York families such as the Stoats, Phelpses, and Putnams. When the streets were banked by deep snows she would tuck the child under her arm and carry her over the long crossing from the corner of 15th Street across the end of Union Square to the corner of 14th Street and Broadway. From there she could walk down two streets to the school. Then, even though it meant closing the office in the afternoon, she would go to fetch her.

Not that her practice suffered, for patients continued to be few. She was obliged to close the dispensary as she had feared, but in emergencies some of the poor women sought her out at home, expecting the same free treatment. She did not discourage them. And she refused to let interest in the project die. Under her constant proddings the trustees were stirred to fresh activity. A little more money was raised, and on January 1, 1855, the dispensary was again opened, this time in quarters a little better, at No. 150 Third Street, between Avenues A and B, opposite a large Catholic church. Poor women and children, she announced, might be sent from any part of the city to receive medical aid, it being free to all.

At the end of February she made her first annual report. Over two hundred poor women had received treatment. All had gratefully acknowledged the help offered them, and several of the most destitute had tendered a few pennies as an offering.

"With all these patients," she emphasized, "the necessity of cleanliness, ventilation, and judicious diet has been strongly urged, and in many cases the advice has been followed, at any rate for a time. A word of counsel or information too has often been given to the destitute widow or friendless girl who was seeking work as well as health;

the best methods of seeking employment have been pointed out, suitable charities recommended and pecuniary aid sometimes rendered."

But the report did not end with past achievements. It made the daring announcement of a campaign to raise five thousand dollars, a prodigious sum, to be invested as a permanent fund, with "the hope of the founders of this charity to make it eventually a hospital for women and a school for the education of nurses." Already Elizabeth had her eye out for possible desirable locations for the enlarged enterprise. Nor did she wait for the trustees to initiate the campaign. Men of their importance were too involved in their own businesses to give prime attention to a hobby of charity. This was a project *for* women, and it must be promoted *by* women. As a beginning she inspired some of the good Quaker ladies to organize sewing circles, where pincushions, mats, baby bootees, and hair tidies were turned out in vast quantities and then sold at small bazaars held on Thursdays.

There was no time to lose. Marie Zakrzewska would have finished her work at Cleveland in another year, and Emily would be returning from Europe. She had not been swayed by Anna's temptings, nor, thank heaven, had she gone to the Crimea with Florence, an "inane suggestion," Elizabeth felt, for the sensible Barbara to make.

"For Florence Nightingale," she had written Emily in November, "the episode might be an instructive and every way useful one. She will probably thus sow her wild oats in the shape of unsatisfied aspirations and activities and come back and marry suitably to the immense comfort of her relatives." Words which she would soon be obliged gracefully to swallow! Wild oats indeed! For already in Scutari Florence Nightingale was expending her burning latent energy in accomplishing miracles, organizing the machinery which was to revolutionize medicine in armies throughout the world, introducing order in a chaos of blood and filth and death, forever establishing female nursing as an honored profession, and assuring her own immortality as the inimitable Lady of the Lamp.

But Emily had wisely chosen to follow her own star, finishing her year of study under Dr. Simpson with remarkable distinction.

"I have rarely met with a young physician," he wrote her in a testimonial letter, "better acquainted with the ancient or modern languages, or more learned in the literature, science, and practical details of his profession."

Now she was continuing her training at Children's Hospital and

St. Bartholomew's in London, studying under the great Sir William Jenner, and from there she would go on to Paris, working for some time at the Hospital Beaujeu under Pierre Charles Huguier, and at other Paris hospitals. Elizabeth followed her progress with an almost fierce interest, giving her frequent advice on doctors who could help her, strongly urging against La Maternité in Paris unless it proved absolutely necessary (it did, and Emily took the full course!), making sure the loans promised by Dennis Harris were remitted as needed.

This vicarious involvement was a godsend, for her own practice crawled at a snail's pace. But there were a few encouraging signs that her struggle in behalf of other women doctors was bearing fruit. That winter the New York Hospital opened its doors to a class of eight women, all from Dr. Troll's hydropathic institute, permitting them to attend regularly the clinical visits and lectures with all the other students. Messrs. Trimble and Collins had argued earnestly for the innovation, assuring the reluctant doctors that they would soon conquer their bashfulness. It was a step unique in the history of the world.

"A pity, though," Elizabeth wrote Emily, "that the girls have to come from quack auspices!"

But of her own discouraging practice she wrote, "I'm getting desperately weary of medical starvation and will unhesitatingly change my course if I find it has been a wrong one. This is the last year I will try the waiting plan."

Fortunately others of the Blackwells were more successful in their pursuits. Harry especially. It was one specific act which effected his success.

He was attending an anti-slavery convention in Salem, Ohio, a center of the Garrisonian abolitionists, who differed from the more moderate political, or "Liberty," abolitionists by repudiating political action as a compromise with sin, and openly urged separation from the slaveholding states. Harry was in sympathy with both groups. He had written a poem for the occasion at Salem and was in the act of reciting it when a telegram arrived announcing that a young slaveholder and his wife had just left Pittsburgh by rail en route from Baltimore to Memphis, Tennessee, with a little colored girl, a gift from the wife's mother, acting as nurse to their baby. Abolitionists believed strongly that slaveholders should not be permitted to carry their slaves across free soil and contended that a slave so brought was entitled to emancipation. What an opportunity to make a test case of this hypothesis! At once the convention adjourned to the depot to seize the Negro girl, Harry one of its ringleaders.

As the train would stop for only a few minutes, every car was boarded simultaneously on the moment of arrival. Harry happened to enter the right car and was one of the first to lay hold of the Negro child. Asked if she wished to be free, she said she did. Amid a great hullabaloo and cries of "Thief! Murder!" from the startled and indignant passengers she was hustled out and spirited away. It happened that one of the car's passengers was Dick Keyes, an excitable young Kentuckian, with some of his conservative acquaintances. They rushed out on the platform and, recognizing Harry as the one participant they knew was involved, denounced him with virulent threats. As a result, when he reached Cincinnati the next day, he found the city buzzing like a hornet's nest. He was at once indicted for kidnapping. In Memphis a reward of ten thousand dollars was offered for his capture, dead or alive.

But the case was placed by the owners in the hands of the eminent law firm of Taft and Mallon. Judge Mallon was a personal friend of Harry's. The firm informed him that they were satisfied slaves could not be held on free soil, when brought with consent of owners, and that they had so advised their clients. No suit was ever brought against him. But for months he was the object of curiosity, and men kept coming from Kentucky and other border states to get a good look at him, so that if he was ever found south of the Ohio River, he would be recognized and lynched. Surprisingly the incident lost the hardware firm little patronage, though many of their customers in Indiana and Illinois were Southern men.

For Harry the gain would have far outweighed any loss, for no happy accident was ever more richly rewarded. It was the deciding factor, Lucy Stone later acknowledged, in his long and persistent courtship.

Elizabeth received the letter announcing his engagement in December. Though she must unconsciously have long been expecting it, it surprised her as much as if she had never heard of the matter. Why? Had she really believed Lucy so committed to her cause that it would make her incapable of marriage, or had her own disapproval blinded her to the possibility? Had her prime objection been a fear for Harry's disappointment, and, if so, why should she not rejoice with him now in his exuberant happiness? And surely she did, if he had actually found a nature which could unite with his in the whole breadth of his aspirations, leaving him solitary nowhere, no more alone in the universe. *If . . .* Mercilessly she probed her conflicting emotions. She did not know Lucy. So far she had seen her only in the eccentricities and accidents of the American phase of this convulsion of women — declaiming from a platform, organizing and running noisy conventions, hooted at in the street for wearing bloomers. She smiled wryly, remembering how often she herself had been hooted at. Could it be that she had doubts just because *they were so much alike?*

She wrote Harry a letter of congratulation, wrote Lucy a kind note extending the hand of sisterly affection, and acknowledged to herself frankly that she might well have been wrong. She had been. For the marriage was to encompass thirty-eight years of one of the most happy and harmonious partnerships known to history. Together they were to work tirelessly for the cause of women's rights, from Massachusetts to California, as lecturers, as co-editors of the powerful suffrage paper, *The Woman's Journal*, as political agitators for reform in many different areas. Not as Mr. and Mrs. Henry Blackwell, however. For Lucy publicly refused to take the name of her husband at the time of their marriage. She remained, and would remain all her life, Lucy Stone, forerunner of a vast number of professional women who would insist on keeping their maiden names in all situations related to their individual careers and who would still, a hundred years later, be dubbed "Lucy Stoners."

"A bit ridiculous," thought Elizabeth with her usual scorn for nonessentials, "refusing to use the name of a man you had chosen in preference to that of a father you had *not* chosen!" But she kept all such thoughts to herself.

There were other distinctive features about the wedding, most of them related to laws governing the economic status of the wife. In recent years some state laws had become more lenient. In 1846 Connecticut had enacted a provision that "whenever any married woman shall hereafter earn wages by her own labor, payment may be made to her for the same, and when made shall be good and valid in law as though made to the husband." A Vermont statute of 1847 secured to the wife the real estate owned by her at the time of marriage or acquired by gift or bequest afterward; but the husband's consent remained necessary for sale or conveyance. In 1848 New York had granted equal property rights without reservation. Massachusetts, Lucy's state, had been slower to act. In 1842 it had authorized women to make wills, in 1845 to hold property separately and to sue or be sued on contracts made with reference to such property as if unmarried, in 1846 to give a valid receipt for their own wages. But most state laws still gave the husband complete control over his wife's person and property and the guardianship of their children.

As they stood together before the ceremony Harry read a protest which they had written and which they now signed. It declared their dissent from the unjust laws which oppressed the wife and confirmed their own conception of marriage as a "partnership of equals, with reciprocal rights and duties." They pledged themselves not to appeal to those unjust laws in case of a disagreement but to refer such disagreements to arbitration. The protest was especially against those laws which gave the husband: (1) the custody of his wife's person; (2) the exclusive control and guardianship of their children; (3) sole ownership of her personal and real estate; (4) absolute right to the product of her industry; (5) laws which gave the widower so much larger and more permanent an interest in the property of the deceased wife than they gave to the widow in that of her deceased husband; and finally (6) against the whole system by which "the legal existence of the wife is suspended during marriage."

Elizabeth was not in favor of this protest and told Harry so in no uncertain terms when he sent her the text before their marriage.

"First of all, if you please," she retorted, "I protest against a protest, and my short answer to 'Why?' would be, it's foolish and in bad taste. The bad taste seems to me to result from the dragging of one's private, personal affairs into public notice. I think that Lucy and you, too, have protested enough both by public and private parlance to define your position."

Elizabeth had never liked verbal protests. For some reason they always made her laugh. Even Harriot Hunt's frequent pronouncements against the medical bigotry of Harvard aroused in her mirth rather than respect. It was the application of individualism to a task for which it was totally inadequate and inappropriate. Action, not words, she believed, was the right method of reforming the world.

"Much is said of the oppression woman suffers," she said on one occasion. "Man is reproached with being unjust, tyrannical, jealous. I do not so read human life. The exclusion woman suffers has risen naturally, simply because woman has desired nothing more, has not felt the soul too large for the body. But when woman, with matured strength, with steady purpose, presents her lofty claim, all barriers will give way, and man will welcome, with a thrill of joy, the new birth of his sister spirit, the advent of his partner, his co-worker, in the great universe of being."

In spite of her arguments Henry proceeded with his "protest," though he did revise the text according to her suggestions. And though Lucy was unwilling to take Henry's name, she was surprisingly malleable in acceding to his wishes in the matter of dress. With relief as well as meekness she discarded the Bloomer costume which she had worn for three years and returned to the confining stays and long billowing skirts of the prevailing style.

"Never," she confessed later, "did I have three years of such physical comfort and such mental misery!"

Elizabeth was unable to attend the wedding, which took place May 1, 1855, at Lucy's parents' old farmhouse on the rocky hillside above West Brooksville, Massachusetts. In fact, none of the Blackwells attended. A pity for Hannah not to be there to relinquish her first wedded child, presiding in all her smiling glory, with white cap and satin ribbon! But the couple came straight to New York, arriving at Elizabeth's in time for a party of welcoming friends — the Alofsens, the Harrises, and others — which she had planned for the occasion. But poor Lucy, almost prostrated by a severe headache, was unable to enjoy it. It was a disappointment not without its compensations. Putting her immediately to bed, treating the illness with all her patient skill, Elizabeth developed an affection for her which it might have taken years to nurture. This was no platform Amazon, no virulent crusader. It was a very tired and no doubt frightened young woman, overwrought with excitement and worried sick over her new role and the anxiety she was causing her husband. "Poor Henry, what will he think of me — and all his friends — spoiling his party!"

Competent, understanding, Elizabeth tucked her in, put cooling packs on her head, dosed her, soothed her fears, as she had often done for Kitty. When the wedding party left for Cincinnati the next day, Lucy smiling wanly but gratefully, she knew she had gained a sister.

It was less than a year before she gained another, for the next January Sam was married to Antoinette Brown, who after a year of preaching had given up her pulpit in sorrow and disillusionment, having been unable to imbue her rigidly orthodox congregation with the slightest awareness of a God of love. Presently she had rejoined Lucy on the lecture platform, arriving finally in Cincinnati where, like Lucy, she was entertained in the Blackwell home. Soon the sober and business-like Sam, badly smitten, was following the convention circuit with an avidity as intense as Harry's, since it offered the only opportunity for courtship. It was Lucy who had capitulated first, much to the disgust of such single-minded crusaders as Susan Anthony, who called them both "little dunces."

"I do feel it is so foolish," Miss Anthony wrote Antoinette, "to put oneself in the position of maid of all work and baby tender. What man would dream of going before the public night after night tired and worn by such a multitude of engrossing cares?"

Antoinette was as hard to win as Lucy. About the time of the latter's wedding she was writing Sam, "Our relations, though they might strengthen and deepen by association, could not, I am sure, ever so far change as to realize a hope which you have sometimes expressed. I should learn to love you dearly, by sharing thoughts, interests, and confidences, as I have loved but few friends ever, but this is all!"

But her capitulation, when it came, was even more complete than Lucy's. Swiftly the salutations changed from "My Friend" to "Dear Sam" to "Dearest Sam." The following December she was writing him a genuine love letter and talking of getting married at once. "In that case, Sam, do you care about a wedding dress? It might be a pleasant souvenir. If you think so, we'll have one. If not, I'll get a good sensible merino, put on my bonnet and shawl, have father say the ceremony, kiss and goodbye all round and leave at once."

Like Lucy, she would willingly have given up wearing the Bloomer dress to please her husband, but she had never worn it. It seemed more in place on the lecture platform than in the pulpit. And she was arousing enough horror simply by preaching without compounding it by unimportant gestures. She had no desire to keep her maiden name. When Sam humbly suggested it, she set his fears at rest.

"You asked one day if it seemed like giving up much for your sake," she wrote before their marriage. "It will not be so very hard to have a dear quiet home with one husband to love and be loved by, with his big heart full of sympathy and an active spirit ready to co-operate for everything good. And remember to tell Lucy that I like your name much better than my own and have no possible objection to having it added."

For Elizabeth the new year came with a burst of fresh hope and energy.

"My thirty-fifth birthday," she wrote in her journal on February 3, 1856. "Two years since I last wrote. I have not had the courage to write before. Now on this bright Sunday morning I feel full of hope and strength for the future. Kitty plays beside me with her doll. She has just given me a candy basket purchased with a penny she earned, full of delight in Doctor's birthday! Who will ever guess the restoration and support which that poor forlorn little orphan has been to me! I desperately needed the diversion of thought she compelled me to give. It was a dark time, and she did me good. Now I look forward with much hope to the events of this year. Heaven guide us all and make the gray hairs that are coming plentifully to me the sign of wisdom!"

2

"Von year from dis day yoost," said Marie Zakrzewska, "ve open our new hospital, *ja?*"

Elizabeth drew a deep breath. The buoyant energy of the young Polish woman was even more heady than the spring winds sweeping across Weehawken Heights. Not since she had tramped these same New Jersey hills and later those in Ohio with Sam and Henry had she felt the contagion of such abounding vigor. These long walks with Marie in Staten Island, in Jersey Heights, sometimes as far north as Hackensack, were as stimulating as adrenalin. Youth flowed again in her veins like sap in the budding trees. Courage flared high to match the flaming sunsets.

A hospital by May, 1857? It seemed impossible. The charter had been obtained, yes. The house had been chosen, the old Roosevelt home on Bleecker Street on which she had long cast a coveting eye. Her lawyer friends of the dispensary trustees had arranged an option on it. It would be available for purchase as soon as the necessary funds — about ten thousand dollars — could be raised. Ten thousand! As well dream of a million! But on a day like this, walking briskly beside Marie Zakrzewska, all things seemed possible.

"*Ja!*" she agreed with reckless abandon.

"Dr. Zak," as most people called her for convenience, had been back in New York less than two months, having earned her medical degree in a two-year herculean struggle against language, opposition, and poverty. Though her knowledge and experience were prodigious, enough to warrant graduation in only one year, the battle with English, especially the writing of a thesis, had proved almost insurmountable. Had the latter not been exceptionally well done, she might have failed, for her marks were only mediocre. Three other female students graduated with her, but opposition had been virulent as in Elizabeth's college days. The four women were shunned at all church or social gatherings, stared at from behind half-shut blinds, ostracized by the male students, who, after violent protest, were assured that the college would admit no more females. Only through the efforts of a Mrs. Severance, a friend of Elizabeth's who was president of a physiological society interested in medical education for women, was Marie able to find lodgings. Mrs. Severance and her "crowing hens," as the group was derisively called, helped in other ways, provided funds, drilled her tirelessly until her English was at least intelligible. To pay her way Marie taught German, kept house for the family of a liberal minister, signed a note for lecture fees of one hundred and twenty-five dollars. But after commencement Dr. Delamater, the friendly dean, handed back the note as a gift, wishing her a thousand blessings.

The contradictions Dr. Zak had found in the intellectual circles of Cleveland were ludicrous: women who heartily endorsed the women's rights movement even to the political franchise, yet were prejudiced against their sisters who attempted to step out of the domestic sphere; women who spoke freely and intelligently as Free-Soilers or abolitionists, yet abhorred the female medical student and would not be seen with her on the street; men who could listen with respect to their wives' differing political views and encourage them in independent thinking, yet in the next moment seriously ask Marie, "Do you want to turn women into men?"

Back in New York her appreciation of the ludicrous was all that saved her from despair. The shadow of Madame Restell was long and menacing. It was Elizabeth's experience all over again. "Parlor to let for a physician," a sign would announce, but as soon as it was discovered she was a woman she was not even allowed to look at the advertised rooms.

"Come with me," Elizabeth finally suggested. It was not an ideal arrangement, for heaven knew there were not patients enough for one doctor, but she welcomed the association. Dr. Zak moved into the Fifteenth Street house on April 17, using the back parlor as her office, with the understanding that their practices should be separated. Not their interests and plans, however! Dr. Zak had come to America with the dream of founding a women's hospital. Her fresh young ardor was like tinder to Elizabeth's smoldering purpose.

Marie had little patience with the Fair meetings held every Thursday, when the few interested women met to knit and sew articles for the contemplated Fair in December. Watching them come week after week to resume the knitting of a baby's stocking, then lay it aside after an hour or two with little progress made, she would fidget helplessly. Ten thousand dollars! Not even ten thousand cents!

"Tomorrow," she would fume to Elizabeth on a Wednesday, "ve have Fair meeting. I vonder — vill dere be two and a half vomen here, or maybe tree and tree-quarters."

After they came to their mutual decision Marie became even more impatient. "In von year from today, ve say, must our infirmary open, and ve have toward it only two pair half-knit baby stockings!"

But the cause received a bit of fresh impetus when Miss Mary L. Booth, who was serving her apprenticeship as a journalist on the *New York Times*, asked the two doctors for an interview. She also was encountering obstacles in pursuing a career suspect for women, being forced to hide her sex by signing only her initials to what she wrote. The publicity her article gave their plans won a few new friends and revived the interest of some of Elizabeth's Quaker patients. But the new subscriptions were a mere dribble when a flood was needed.

Again Marie fumed in silence, a dynamo storing up fresh energy. Though she had come to revere Elizabeth above all others, she recognized her limitations. They were complements of each other, not counterparts: Elizabeth the philanthropic philosopher, Marie the practical physician; Elizabeth the reforming spirit, Marie the organizer. As Elizabeth was to express it years later in a letter recalling those turbulent days, "I work chiefly in Principles, and you in putting them into practical use; and one is essential to the other in this complex life of ours."

If the hospital was ever to become reality, Marie recognized, she must make it. She mulled possibilities as she waited for patients, treated one at rare intervals, meticulously signed M.E.Z. at the bottom of a few prescriptions, was amused when each time she did so the apothecary sent a messenger to inquire the meaning of the mystical signs. Her initials, she explained, because her name was too long to write in full. But nobody signed prescriptions, she was told, or wrote for whom they were intended. Like Elizabeth, she continued to do both, in order to establish her full responsibility.

Then came a break. Dr. Harriot Hunt sent a patient to Elizabeth. With her came Dr. W. H. Channing, who, though not in practice, tended the patient with her. Hearing him talk ardently of Boston as "the hothouse of all reforms," Marie got an idea. She proposed that Elizabeth immediately search for a house which might suit their purposes, get an estimate of the rent and expense of furnishing it. Spurred to action, Elizabeth did so, and found that the Roosevelt house on which they had an option could be rented for three years at an annual sum of thirteen hundred dollars and furnished for five hundred dollars, plus another one hundred dollars for fuel. But even these sums seemed out of the question.

Not to Marie. "Good!" she approved. "I go to Boston. I try to get half of rent pledged for tree-year lease. You raise half from friends here. We hold Fair to raise six hundred more."

The next day was Thursday, when the women, six or seven of them, came to sew. Marie zestfully outlined her program. Her eagerness acted like a warm soft rain on a field after long drought. The babies' stockings, to her immense relief, were laid aside. Bigger projects were discussed for the Fair. So great was the enthusiasm inspired that Elizabeth and Marie already imagined themselves walking among neat white hospital beds.

"Who does thee think we should ask to make the speech at the opening?" inquired one overeager optimist. "Henry Ward Beecher or a physician of high standing?"

Marie went to Boston in July. Only three months since she had left Cleveland? It seemed three years. She visited her friend Mrs. Severance, who had moved there from Cleveland. She approached the list of liberal women given her by Dr. Channing: Miss Lucy Goddard, Miss Mary Jane Parkman, Miss Abby May, Mrs. E. D. Cheney. A three-years' promise of six hundred and fifty dollars a year?

"But why," they all asked, "can you not raise this small sum in rich New York?"

Over and over she made her explanation. Only a very few women of New York's society dared to connect themselves openly with "such radical reformers." The idea of women not only becoming doctors but daring to take on the responsibility of a public institution seemed utterly monstrous to New York men and women. They were far behind the intelligent and liberal leaders of Boston who had started a school for the education of midwives in 1850, which had since become the small but promising New England Female Medical College.

"But why," came the second question, "do you want and need a dispensary and hospital for women physicians?"

Marie explained this also, how impossible it was for female medical students to get practical experience even in treating the poorer patients of their preceptors; how Ann Preston, graduate of the Philadelphia college, had refused to practice because she was able to get no clinical training and had taught physiology instead; how many, including the Blackwells, had felt obliged to go to Europe for clinical study.

In spite of their regard for Dr. Harriot Hunt, the Boston matrons were not without prejudice. Marie discovered later that, when she visited in the home of Mr. Joseph Sewall, Miss Lucy Sewall had gone upstairs and examined the visitor's cloak, bonnet, and gloves, to see if a woman physician was capable of proper dress!

Nevertheless, Marie returned to New York with pledges of six hundred and fifty dollars, half the rent annually for three years. Vastly encouraged, the two doctors set out to raise the other half. Except among their few friends, they encountered a storm of protest.

"Who would think of letting a house for such a purpose!"

"Female doctors would be looked on with such suspicion that surely the police would interfere!"

"What if deaths occur? Your death certificates would not be recognized."

"Without men physicians, how could you possibly control the patients?"

"Think of the disreputable persons you would have to deal with!"

One lady invited Marie to dine, explaining that she would be all alone and they could talk over plans without fear of ridicule by her husband and sons. Their financial position, she added, made her and her daughters the equal of a duchess in Marie's country, and they must be careful about associating with reformers without a thorough knowledge of their plans. Calmly Marie assured her that her ancestry would perhaps balance her hostess's fortune, since she could trace her forebears to the year 911. Fine. The lady was much relieved, and could she tell her friends, as an explanation of her interest in Miss — Miss Zak — ?

But most wondrous of all was the interview with Fanny Kemble, who at the time was giving a series of Shakespearean readings in New York. Having met the famous actress at Lady Byron's home, Elizabeth resolved to ask her to help, perhaps hold a benefit performance for the infirmary, since she often rendered generous service for charities. She and Marie visited her at her hotel. The actress was all graciousness. Yes, she remembered Elizabeth, listened with kindness to an explanation of their visit and the needs of the projected infirmary. But when she learned that the physicians of the institution were to be all women, she sprang up to her full height, turned on them her flashing eyes, and favored them with the full impact of her histrionic genius.

"Trust a *woman* — as a DOCTOR!" she declaimed in tragic tones. "NEVER!"

There were vanguard groups in New York as well as Boston that were in sympathy with progressive movements. With many of them Elizabeth did not feel in harmony and had no part with them. But the curious and gregarious Marie visited them all: the open house of Mrs. Elizabeth Oakes Smith attended by musicians, artists, and the rare press women; the Sunday evening conversation circles of Alice and Phoebe Cary, patronized by such leaders as Greeley, Colfax, Ripley, Garrison; the so-called Free-Lovers, frequented by all persons who represented any "ism"; the Spiritualists, featuring the wonderful feats of the Fox sisters; the admirers of the socialist Fourier, among whom were the Theodore Welds, Sarah Grimké, Elizabeth Peabody, and Mrs. Horace Mann; a women's club called the Alpha whose members were striving for the advancement of women; the Philanthropic Circle, smallest of all, which Elizabeth strongly supported along with Mr. Charles Brace, Mr. Peter Cooper, Elizabeth Peabody, and the Sedgwicks.

While many members of these groups gave the infirmary project all the support possible, unfortunately they were not well-to-do, and their assistance was in the form of goodwill and best wishes. But during this year of long struggle both were needed and welcomed.

The fund crept toward its goal. Meanwhile another dream of Elizabeth's was realized. Sam and Henry had sold their hardware business in the spring, leaving them no richer in money but slightly so in land, a prairie farm near Chicago having been given in exchange. That summer and fall Lucy faithfully followed her prospector husband from Chicago through the wilds of Wisconsin, from Bad Axe and Coon Prairie to La Crosse, where Harry owned several more tracts of land and opposite which brother George, also bitten by the land bug, had bought a mill site and laid out the town of La Crescent. Cheerfully, with the hardihood of a pioneer, she endured the rigors of stage and horseback and jolting carriage, the discomforts of farm boardinghouse, frontier hotel, and rented room, where she kept house without help, a new experience indeed for a woman thirty-eight years old, accustomed for years to literary and intellectual pursuits. But in the late fall they came east and, to the joy of Elizabeth, moved into the big house in Fifteenth Street.

Here also came Hannah, Sam, and Antoinette, who was expecting her first child. One evening in November fifteen carts drew up in the street outside the house. One held the poor old piano. The rest bore all the worldly possessions of the Cincinnati Blackwells. The unpacking was like opening treasure trove, especially for Kitty. Already a book lover, she gazed entranced at the huge array of volumes strewn helter-skelter, for Sam was an atrocious packer. Most of all was she intrigued by the square tin box in which was packed Grandma Blackwell's wedding china, for already she knew its story, how Grandma had chosen the pattern and Uncle Browne had had it made. Elizabeth watched as she reverently held one of the fragile cups in her hands, stroking the intricate pattern of pagodas, fragile bridges, pink, red, and blue long-tailed birds, with the same wide rapt gaze of herself at the age of nine.

"It's going to be ours," she told the child gravely. "Grandma says so, for I am the only daughter who has a real home." She continued with sudden impulse, "From now on you shall have the care of it. It's very precious, you know."

If she had had doubts of her wisdom, they were swiftly set at rest. The child's face became suffused with a solemn radiance. With the reverence of a priestess handling sacred relics she transferred each delicate piece from its wrappings to the cabinet shelf. It was a trust she was to discharge faithfully for more than half a century, finally turning the set over *almost* intact (one piece was stolen, a cup and saucer given away by Dr. Emily) to the first son born to one of Hannah's children, a boy named Howard, the son of George.

Even greater than the delight in possessions was the joy of Family, a sweet-faced grandmother with bright eyes and pink cheeks, white curls peeping from the edges of her cap; Miss Marian, gracious and beautiful in spite of her frailty, to run the household; and, one other day in November, the most fascinating addition of all. Kitty was on her way to bed when she met Dr. Zak coming downstairs.

"Vould you like to see a baby?" asked the doctor, smiling.

"Oh — yes!" Kitty knew that both her doctors had the remarkable faculty of helping to produce babies, but never before had the miracle happened here. "Where is it? Where did it come from?"

"In big room upstairs. And it came out of a — a cabbage."

Kitty gave her a scornful glance. "Nothing so nice as a baby ever came out of a cabbage!" She rushed upstairs. There on a large pillow before an open fire lay the new arrival, very tiny indeed. "Don't step on my baby!" cried Uncle Sam jovially.

The baby was born on a Friday. The following Sunday all the family sat around the fire, Aunt Nette lying in bed, and Uncle Sam read out a list of five hundred girls' names which he had put down. Kitty wanted her to be called Mary. But My Doctor suggested Florence, after her friend Miss Nightingale. Of course, it must be Florence! So the firstborn of the Blackwell clan joined the hundreds of other new arrivals bearing the name of the famous Lady of the Lamp.

Grandma Blackwell instructed Kitty in the proper holding of the baby, very carefully, to support its back, and thereafter on every fair day the two of them carried it to Union Square for a walk in the sunlight. Kitty mourned like a bereft mother when Uncle Sam, secure in his new job as a corporation treasurer, took Aunt Nette and Florence and moved out to Newark, where they lived for a time in a house on Orange Street. It was tall and slim, perched on the top of a very high bank, dubbed by Uncle Harry "The Pepper Box."

For Elizabeth the coming of Family was a good omen. She reveled in having the big house bulging with the old familiar life and laughter. And with all contributing generously to the expenses, for the first time she was able to save money, make more than token payments on the house mortgage. Her private practice was increasing also. If such good fortune continued, the whole sum could be paid off in a few years.

And surely now her other fondest dream, for a hospital, must come true. All now depended on the December Fair. The women had been sewing furiously. Emily had enlisted the help of friends in England, and a quantity of articles had arrived for an "English table." The Philadelphia friends assisted by bringing articles to the house of the William Elders. Marie's Boston friends sent contributions. Every little mat and pincushion was an occasion for joy, bringing the goal fifty cents nearer.

"Oh, the golden time of Youth and Hope!" Marie was to write of the memory years later when calmly announcing that ten thousand dollars must be raised at another fair.

But there were setbacks. No church or public building would give space for the occasion. Finally Robert Haydock, one of the early Quaker supporters and a trustee, loaned an unfinished loft at Stuyvesant Institute and offered his services as auctioneer. His wife Hannah loaned one of her crystal chandeliers. Connected to the gas piping, it softly illumined the evergreens and flowers that hid the unplaned boards with their knots and nails. Other women loaned rugs and draperies. Horace Greeley furnished publicity with a long article outlining the work of the dispensary and the function of the new project.

The Fair was a success. Ten cents admission was charged, and there was a good attendance for four days. The magnificent sum of six hundred dollars was raised! It was enough. The dream so long in embryo could at least be born and assured a year of life. Elizabeth had not spent so happy a Christmas since her Cincinnati days. Hannah concocted one of her inimitable puddings while the small Kitty helped with the stoning and chopping and peeling and beating, peered into the steaming boiler, and absorbed the rudiments of a skill which in years to come were to make her the family high priestess of its mysteries.

3

The New York Infirmary for Indigent Women and Children was formally opened on May 12, 1857, almost meeting Marie's deadline of May 1. Since Elizabeth had been living in the house since March completing its arrangements, the difference in date was negligible. She chose May 12, the birthday of Florence Nightingale, as a tribute to the friend who had been its inspiration. To her delight Emily returned from Europe in time for the great event, and the three doctors prepared for the day with tireless labor, much anticipation, and some trepidation. Would any people come? Would there be room for all who did come? Would the opponents of the project make trouble? Would the speakers put in an appearance?

"There!" On the morning of the 12th Elizabeth looked about with anxious appraisal. "Thank heaven, I believe everything is ready!"

"Thank yourself even more," threw back Emily caustically. "Until I saw what you two have done, I couldn't believe it. Such a thing couldn't happen yet in London."

The practical Marie went about giving the white beds a final pat and smoothing. *"Ja!"* she expressed her satisfaction in one short syllable.

The old Dutch mansion built around 1820 on Bleecker Street at the corner of Crosby by old James Roosevelt, great-grandfather of a future President, Franklin Delano Roosevelt, had been transformed, its four floors which had seen two generations of gracious and aristocratic living metamorphosed into plain but sparkling clean utility. The lower front room was the dispensary, with consulting desk, an examination table behind a large screen, shelves for medicines, and a table for compounding them. Thanks to the publicity of reporters like Mary Booth, donations had come from several wholesale druggists, and secondhand furniture had been cheaply acquired.

The front entrance hall, arranged for waiting patients, was relieved of its bareness by a few antiques and brocaded settees donated by friends. Beyond the partition separating the front hall from the back was a large stove which heated the stairways, there being no furnace in the house, and dining and kitchen areas.

The second floor was arranged for two wards, each containing six beds; while the third floor had been made into a maternity department, with a little hall room serving as a sitting room for the physicians. One small bedroom had been converted into an operating room by replacing a tiny window with a larger multi-paned one. The fourth, or attic, floor contained two large and two small rooms, living quarters for the resident physicians, servants, and — hopefully — four or five medical students. Open grate fires provided the only heat for all the rooms. A skylight above the center would provide proper ventilation. The furniture, donated or purchased secondhand, was a hodgepodge of elegant antiques, cheap stands and tables, hospital beds, all such material as benevolence provided. But to the three doctors it was magnificence unqualified.

The guests came, filling the space around 64 Bleecker Street with every sort of conveyance: landaus, phaetons, sulkies, four-horse carriages; women sweeping street and sidewalk clean with billowing skirts and hiding from the May sun under ruffled parasols; men dignifying the occasion with morning coats, top hats, and canes. Seated on Dr. Zak's snowy white beds, they filled the tiny wards to overflowing. Represented among them were members of the board of consulting physicians, men of high standing in the profession, who had given the institution the sanction of their names: Drs. Valentine Mott, John Watson, Willard

Parker, R. S. Kissam, Isaac E. Taylor, and George P. Camman. Reporters were present to record the historic ceremonies: Horace Greeley, Charles A. Dana, Henry Raymond, James Gordon Bennett. Henry Ward Beecher rose from his seat on one of the second-floor beds to give the main address, recalling how one of his ancestors, the "Goodwife Beecher," had ridden through the wilds of Connecticut performing her services of midwife and dispensing her simple homely remedies of violets, roses, mint, and anise.

Elizabeth squirmed as the eloquent cleric deduced from this bit of personal folklore the peculiar fitness of women to practice medicine. Couldn't the man see that identification of women with midwifery was just what this day's event hoped to end for all time? But she relaxed as he waxed into flowery oratory praising the foresight of the courageous young friend of his family whose career they had followed with the utmost sympathy and encouragement.

"Does he remember," wondered Elizabeth with amusement, "the opinion his family gave me twelve years ago when I asked them for advice? 'The idea is a good one, but quite impossible of achievement.'"

She relaxed still further as her good friend Dr. Elder from Philadelphia, always the champion of freedom for men and women in all areas, condemned the "fogeyism and humbug" which he believed were characteristic of most of the medical profession. At least men were being accorded their professional liabilities as well as women!

Her own part in the proceeding was brief and modest. Stepping forward in her doctorial sack, she gave a short dignified report of the work accomplished by the dispensary in its three years of service, then pointed out that in three of its functions — providing women physicians, giving clinical training to women medical students, and training nurses — the new infirmary would be unique in the country.

"The full thorough education of women in medicine is a new idea," she concluded, "and like all other truths requires time to prove its value. Women must show to medical men, even more than to the public, their capacity to act as physicians, their earnestness as students of medicine before the existing institutions with their great advantages of practice and complete organization will be opened to them. They must prove their medical ability before expecting professional recognition."

Would she have spoken with greater confidence could she have envisioned the complex structure which would rise from this small begin-

338

ning through a hundred years and after, still bearing the name the New York Infirmary and embodying in its multiple services not only the finest contemporary techniques of medicine but specialized departments for social outreach, education in sanitation, hygiene, disease prevention — all those preposterous concepts in which she was in her generation such a lonely pioneer? Probably not. The vision would have brought satisfaction, a sense of vindication and fulfillment. But since she knew this was the right, the sensible step of progress they were now taking, she already had an abundance of confidence.

At the last minute the Rev. Dudley Atkins Tyng, who had recently been ousted from his Philadelphia pulpit for preaching anti-slavery, rushed in, carpetbag in hand, just in time to give the project his blessing and pronounce the benediction. Elizabeth was grateful, knowing that he had left pressing duties to give the unpopular cause a hearty Godspeed.

It was finished . . . and begun. With the sign boldly affixed to the front door the three doctors sat down to wait, but not for long. Soon came some of their old patrons of the Tompkins Square dispensary, timidly at first, awed by the more stylish neighborhood, but reassured by the familiar faces. They brought others. Before a month passed the beds were filled and there was a daily dispensary attendance of thirty or more. Each of the three doctors attended the dispensary two mornings a week. Elizabeth was the director, Emily the infirmary surgeon, Marie the resident physician, superintendent, housekeeper, and — hopefully — instructor of medicine.

The hope was soon partially realized, for presently four students from the Female Medical College of Philadelphia came to live in the hospital, spending the summer between terms as interns, apothecaries, and pupils of nursing. There were also two nurses in training, one for the general wards and one for the maternity department, both unskilled, who fortunately considered the education more than sufficient pay for their services. Thus the New York Infirmary became the first training school for nurses in America.

Of course the brunt of the daily burden of operation fell on Dr. Zak, who shouldered it with her usual energy and ebullience. A record of one day's work was typical. At 5:30 A.M. she started out in an omnibus for the wholesale market to buy the week's provisions, and at eight she was back for breakfast, which consisted, for all inmates except patients, of tea, bread and butter, Indian mush meal and syrup. On

Sundays coffee and bacon were added. After breakfast she made her visits to the patients in the house with two of the students, while the other two attended Elizabeth or Emily in the dispensary. Then a confinement case arrived, which involved examination and orders to students and nurses. Then she descended to the kitchen, where the provisions had arrived, and helped the cook dispose of them to insure their preservation, also settled the diet for both staff and patients. Then she took another omnibus trip to the wholesale druggist's, begging and buying the needed supplies for dispensary and hospital, arriving home in time for the one o'clock dinner, which consisted of soup, soup meat, potatoes, one kind of vegetable, and fruit. On Sundays there would be a roast or steak.

After dinner, like Emily and Elizabeth, she would attend private patients, if any, for these were their sole means of personal support, since the four dollars a week charged to paying hospital patients were barely enough to cover the actual cost of medical service. Tea was served at seven, consisting of bread and butter, tea, and sauce or cheese or fresh gingerbread. Another round of patients, and it was nine o'clock. But the day was not ended. Assembling the students in the little hall room, she cut and sewed towels or pillowcases or other articles needed for the house while hearing them recite their lessons and giving them instructions in midwifery. The day was finished, except for emergencies, by eleven-thirty.

For all three doctors the strain of intense activity, plus the meager diet, was immense, and Elizabeth insisted on some relaxation. During the summer they all went on a picnic once a month in the hills across the Hudson. In the winter they went to a good theater once a month, seeing performances by such actors as Joseph Jefferson, Laura Keene, Karl Formes, or Brignoli. Not only were such diversions refreshing, but they were cheap!

And heaven knew money was scarce! Mr. Haydock, the infirmary treasurer, allowed only twenty-two dollars for weekly expenses, including groceries, gas, wages, and food. Donations were often in the form of crockery, toweling, stationery, instead of cash. The "indigent" patients for whom the hospital was intended were far more numerous than the paying ones. And though the private practice of each doctor was developing even faster than the morning clinics, most of their house visits were among the poor. Typical was a delivery case in a Negro quarter, where one evening they entered a room filled with people, faces shading from pitch black through all colors to one which seemed pure Caucasian. The latter was the patient in one corner, near the table on which stood a small smoky lamp. At least eight of the swarming children belonged to her, and there must have been a dozen others. After delivering the little new mulatto, the doctors went home, completely fearless, through the squalid streets at one in the morning.

Of course there were problems. On the occasion of her first operation at the hospital Emily had asked a well-known surgeon of the city to be present as a consultant. All was ready, and he did not come. She and the nervous patient were kept waiting a whole hour. Finally he appeared. He had spent the hour consulting with one of his colleagues about the propriety of attending an operation performed by a woman! Such suspicion extended to the patients. Suppose the woman operated on *did* recover. Wouldn't it have been better if the surgeon had been a man? And if on a rare occasion she *died* — !

And there were crises. Fortunately both Elizabeth and Emily were in the infirmary when a fire broke out in livery stables just behind the house. Smoke billowed about the ward windows, and the patients were thrown into almost as great panic as the forty stampeding horses whose terrified neighings rose above the clamor of fire bells and shouting crowds. While Marie organized volunteers to keep sparks from igniting the roof, Elizabeth and Emily quieted the patients. Fortunately the wind was in the right direction, and the infirmary was saved.

Still more threatening were the fires of opposition. Even the loyalty of indigent beneficiaries was not proof against it. In spite of Elizabeth's insistence on cleanliness and sanitation in accordance with the radical views of Dr. Semmelweiss, puerperal fever sometimes developed after childbirth. One woman died of it. Though her relatives had been informed of the seriousness of the case and one of her kin had been at her bedside for sixty hours before her death, they seemed unprepared for the shock. An hour after it occurred, one morning, Elizabeth was startled by a loud commotion outside. Leaving her dispensary patients, she hurried into the hall to the outside door. There in the street was a crowd of people, hooting, yelling, pushing toward the house. Hastily she closed the door and locked it, but not before she had caught a confused glimpse of brandished hoes and shovels, raised fists, and threatening faces, some of them familiar — the sisters and aunts and cousins who had watched by the bedside of the dead patient. They must have rounded up all their male relatives and neighbors! "You killed her, you killed her!" she heard a woman's voice scream. As she leaned, breathing hard, against the door, she could feel it shaken, beaten, pounded. Out of the clamor other shouts were distinguishable.

"You in there! Female doctors! . . . No doctors, killers! . . . Kill women, that's what you do! . . . We'll show you what we do to murderers!"

Marie appeared, dark eyes burning in her white face. "Dey're filling de yard. I've locked all doors, but ve can't hold out long. Dey'll beat dem down. Vat" — for once the inimitable confidence was shattered — "vat ve do?"

Elizabeth pressed back so hard against the door that her knuckles showed white, but her face remained calm. "Perhaps I could go out and talk to them —"

"No! Dey kill you! Did you see faces — like beasts!"

Elizabeth went back into the dispensary and tried to calm the waiting patients. "It's all right. Nobody wants to harm any of you. Get over there, please, all of you, away from the windows." They obeyed her like children.

Carefully she pushed aside a curtain, peered through one of the small wavy windowpanes. Drawn by the commotion, an immense crowd had gathered, filling the whole block, it seemed, from Bleecker Street to Broadway. Chill memory smote her. She was a child again, looking out the window of the house in Bristol — ugly faces, smoking torches, hoarse cries, good, kind, common working people welded suddenly into an unruly composite far stronger and more dangerous than the sum total of its units! Marie was right. They were beasts, not men and women. It would be madness to face them, as mad as — as Samuel had been standing in the doors of the church with his arms outstretched. Her lips tightened. He had risked his life to save a monument in which he had no faith. Could his daughter hide behind a window curtain when the very substance of her life purpose was at stake? She heard a shatter of glass, saw a big workman come toward the front steps brandishing a crowbar. She must stop him, open the door before he broke it down!

She was turning decisively from the window when she stopped, recognizing the burly figure with the crowbar. It was an Irish workman whose wife had been treated at the old Tompkins Square dispensary. Pushing his way through the crowd, he mounted the steps.

"You there! By the saints in heaven, what the divil's goin' on? What do youse think youse doin'?"

It was his booming voice rather than the menacing crowbar which compelled attention. Shovels, hoes fell to lower levels. The clamor subsided, then rose in excited hubbub as all the relatives tried to explain at once.

"*Quiet!* Saints help us, one at a time!" Finally, piecemeal, he got the story. "I see. Your woman had a baby, and she died. So what? Lots of women die in childbirth. What's all this hullabaloo?"

The clamor swelled again. "Women doctors . . . killed her . . ."

"*Quiet!*" Again the booming voice prevailed. "Now youse listen to me. I know these doctors, and lots of you know them too. My wife had pneumonia, and they made her well again, same as they've made lots of your women well. Ain't it so?" Heads nodded. Anger on some of the faces changed to sheepishness. "I ask youse, too, what other doctors ever done nothin' for youse, give yer medicines, go into yer lousy houses to deliver yer bairns, care whether youse live or dies? Saints help us, ain't you got no brains? Doctors ain't God. Don't you know there ain't no doctor what could keep everybody from dyin' when they gets sick?"

Like the tension of the crowd, Elizabeth's clenched hands relaxed. Presently two policemen came running, one from Broadway, the other from their own Bleecker Street beat. But the trouble was already over. The brandished weapons had become tools again. The welded entity had melted once more into its component parts, become curious, worried, happy or unhappy human beings. Relieved, thankful, pitying, she watched them slowly disperse, the more stubborn relatives lingering to the end but looking more sheepish than sullen as they finally slunk away.

It was not the last incident of its kind. During those early months another patient died of a ruptured appendix. The helpful Dr. Kissam had been in every other day for consultation on the case and had recommended a treatment much in vogue at the time, cold water compresses. On the morning following the day on which the patient died a group of men appeared before the house demanding entrance, and again a crowd gathered, curious and inquiring. What was it? Why all the excitement? These murderous female doctors, was the angry reply. An institution of some cranky women who killed people with cold water! This time Marie was able to send a messenger out the back door to Dr. Kissam, who hurried to the infirmary in time to prevent the mob's doing physical damage to the place. Addressing them calmly, he advised them to have a coroner sent for to make an examination of the

343

dead patient in the presence of twelve of their own number to serve as a jury. The leaders of the mob agreed. An autopsy was performed.

"It was a sight to behold," marveled Dr. Zak, recalling the scene years later, "those poor distraught men in overalls, with dirty hands, disheveled hair and grim faces, standing by during the autopsy, and at its close, declaring their satisfaction that death had been an unavoidable consequence of the disease."

"It's all right," Elizabeth told the apologetic relatives after each such episode. "You could not help yourselves. We women doctors have to prove ourselves."

Surely the infirmary could not have survived this first difficult year without the cooperation of these courageous consulting physicians, all of whom defied the sneers and frowns of their colleagues by acting as consultants. Dr. Kissam, a prominent obstetrician, was only a partial convert, believing that the Drs. Blackwell and Zakrzewska were exceptions to all womankind. The influence of these liberal physicians in time procured for the infirmary students attendance at some of the larger dispensaries.

And to their surprise these eminent doctors learned much from their women colleagues. When the visiting students expressed amazement because no records of cases or prescriptions were kept in the large institutions they visited, the doctors inquired into the infirmary system and discovered that every patient treated there could be traced — name, residence, diagnosis, treatment, result; moreover, that no doctor or student was permitted to give a prescription without signing her name to it. It was a revelation to them.

That first year was one of intense struggle and economy. In spite of the simple diet and plain living, debt hung constantly over their heads. Another sale was held before Christmas, this time in the infirmary wards, the patients having been removed for a whole week, and the twenty-six hundred dollars necessary for the year's running expenses, not including the rent, was somehow raised. But it was Dr. Emily who made the greatest contribution to the cause. The New York Legislature had voted to appropriate one thousand dollars a year to each dispensary in the city — the "regular" ones, that is, run by reputable male physicians.

"There's no reason why we shouldn't have it, too," insisted Emily.

"Yes," agreed Elizabeth. "But how?"

Taking with her one of the infirmary trustees, a woman, Emily proceeded to Albany. There they first won over their representative, Mr.

Varnum, and other members of the Finance Committee. Then Dr. Emily went to interview Judge Hogenbaum, who was the special advocate of economy, and was expected to oppose their request. Calmly, but inwardly quaking, she told him about the need for the infirmary, how glad the poor women were to be able to consult a woman, how much more could be done with greater resources.

"I'll consider it," was his terse reply. The two women had little hope of success, but to their surprise when the matter came up the judge supported the motion, and it was carried. Each year thereafter the infirmary received its one thousand dollars. Also on Elizabeth's appeal to the city council, an allotment was voted for the support of charity patients treated at the hospital.

Success was gratifying, though modest. The morning dispensary attendance totaled over eight hundred for the year. Indoor patients numbered about a hundred. But there was a large home practice, one of the four students, Dr. Mary Breed, attending fourteen childbed cases in a single month. Already two nurses, one a German, the other an American, were being trained. Applications were being received constantly from students who wished to share the experience of practice, some of them extremists: women in Bloomer costume or with hair cut very short; some anxious to use the institution to promulgate a particular fad or "ism" — the cold water cure, mesmerism, homeopathy. All had to be meticulously screened, since popular prejudice could be overcome only by following the most conservative procedures.

Thanks to Elizabeth's philosophy of hygiene, the students became missionaries as well as healers. Sponges and soap, along with medicines, were carried in their satchels and dispersed with useful information. Far more revolutionary to medical procedure than the keeping of accurate records was the novel idea that sick people should be bathed and kept clean, that fresh air was not killing, that both cleanliness and ventilation might even prevent sickness from occurring!

4

These were confusing and exciting times for small Kitty. Blackwells passed through the Fifteenth Street house with bewildering frequency. After Uncle Sam, Aunt Nette, and Florence were gone, there were still Uncle Harry and Aunt Lucy, only for some reason her name wasn't Blackwell but Stone. She was away a lot lecturing, and Uncle Harry was trying to find work, a "business position" he called it. Finally he got one with a Mr. Moore, who published agricultural books. Then they tried to find a house. They looked everywhere, all over northern New Jersey, the Bronx, Long Island.

"If we only had money to offer in exchange instead of western land!" Uncle Harry would lament. But finally they found one, a cottage on Cone Street in Orange, whose owner wanted to move west. Uncle Harry managed the sale with five hundred dollars cash loaned by a friend of Aunt Lucy, two hundred and forty acres of Wisconsin land, and a mortgage of twenty-one hundred dollars, and they moved into it in the spring of 1857.

Kitty was even more disappointed when Dr. Emily returned one day in the fall with her little black doctor's bag announcing that Uncle Harry and Aunt Lucy had a baby. Surely they could have arranged to have it, like Uncle Sam and Aunt Nette, here at Fifteenth Street! Kitty was sure now that cabbages had little to do with the origin of babies. Though her knowledge was still woefully incomplete, she suspected that they issued somehow from the little black bags. Once when My Doctor was bound for a "baby case" she surreptitiously examined the bag and its contents but to her disappointment found nothing.

There was again great discussion over the new baby's name. Should it be Stone or Blackwell? At last they decided on both names. But what else? They thought about Sarah, but Aunt Ellen, whom Kitty had never seen because she was studying art over in Europe, wrote that she had been christened Sarah Ellen and had dropped the first name as quickly as possible. Finally they settled on Alice, Alice Stone Blackwell. Little did Kitty know, gazing at the red-faced mite with all her baby-loving fervor, how next to her beloved My Doctor, this young foster cousin was to become the great love of her life.

After the aunts and uncles left, Aunt Marian again took boarders. The New York Medical College was just behind the house, in Fourteenth Street, and for a while she housed and boarded a half-dozen Southern medical students. Kitty found their presence fully as obnoxious as that of the Vails, who had stayed there for a time in 1856, bringing with them their grandson Willie, who was not only an imp, but, brought up in the South, a loud advocate of slavery. It had been election time, the candidates Frémont and Buchanan. Kitty, already a thorough Blackwell, had been all for Frémont, the champion of freedom, Willie for Buchanan. Their arguments had been hot and heavy. On election evening the two children had rushed to Mr. Vail, demanding the result. "Alas!" He had shaken his head sadly. "It was Buchanan." While Kitty raged helplessly, the imp had capered in delight.

Still Blackwells continued to come and go. One snowy night came an Uncle George carrying a pair of saddlebags and wrapped in a big blanket shawl. His coming seemed to give My Doctor great satisfaction. Now all her family, except those in Europe, were in or around New York. Uncle George settled into the hall bedroom and began reading law with a firm in William Street, one member of which had the same name as Dr. Kissam. Finally Aunt Marian, tired of keeping boarders, moved to New Jersey with Grandma, first keeping house with Uncle Harry and Aunt Lucy, later buying a little house of her own in Roseville. The house in Fifteenth Street then seemed strange indeed, with Aunt Elizabeth and Aunt Emily and Kitty crowded into the three garret rooms, the back parlor and its extension used for their offices, and all the rest of the house rented to a Quaker woman, Mrs. Dame, and her daughter, who immediately set her cap for Uncle George and tried ineffectually to capture him through their mutual interest in chess. Kitty was sure Miss Dame did not approve of her, partly because she moved with such lightning swiftness, always turning up when least expected.

Though the two doctors were constantly busy with patients, Kitty was never lonely. Some of the patients were her good friends, especially the two youngest children of the Bleecker Street Stacy Collinses, Stacy and Gertrude, who shared her love of poetry. Once she met Gertrude coming out of the Friends' Library on Irving Place, in dire disgrace, explained Gertrude, for she had asked for a volume of Swinburne's verses, and the librarian had been shocked to death. And her father a trustee of the library, from which Swinburne was banned!

Kitty's own appetite for literature was equally omnivorous. Though she had not known a letter when arriving, soon afterward one of My Doctor's friends, Miss Catharine Sedgwick, a noted novelist, was amazed to see her sitting on the floor in one of the long windows of the front parlor, reading aloud. She had scarcely needed to be taught. Her affinity for books was as natural as that for the citron pies sold in the bakeshop on the northeast corner of Fifteenth Street and Third Avenue. She tried all the books except the medical ones, reveling in the long row called *The Modern Traveler* and the sixteen volumes of Mrs. Sherwood.

It was at the bakeshop that the tragic accident happened. One of the men, swinging his bread basket to his shoulder, knocked her big Swiss doll to the floor, and her china head was smashed. Given her by one of My Doctor's patients, it was the only doll Kitty had ever cared for, with two perfect Swiss costumes, one for working days and one for gala days. There were other gorgeous dolls given her by the patients, all of whom bore grand names bestowed by My Doctor — Lady Carolina Amelia Skiggs, Lady Mary Wortley Montagu — but she cared nothing for them. When a leg or arm broke, she buried them with great pleasure in the back garden.

If Elizabeth's original intention had been to secure a little housemaid rather than a daughter, she had chosen well, for Kitty was as swiftly adept at domestic skills as at reading. She was soon paying some of the household bills, notably the bread bill at Simpson's, on the corner of Fourth Street and the Bowery. Since she liked bread even better than her favorite citron pies, My Doctor once told Simpson that her small ward was made up of his bread, so the next time Kitty entered his shop the grocer accorded her unusual interest. Leaning on the counter until he could just see the top of her head, he twinkled down at her.

"So you're the little girl made of Simpson's bread!"

But Kitty had long since outlived all status as a domestic. When she visited the New Jersey Blackwells she was almost as accepted a member of the family as the idolized Florence. Elizabeth's patients and close friends, like Miss Theodosia Prevost who had a farm in Hackensack where they spent delightful weekends, were as likely to call her "Blackwell" as "Barry." And when Barbara Leigh Smith came to America in the summer of 1857, Kitty was proudly introduced as "my dear little daughter-niece."

Kitty had heard all about this vivid young Englishwoman and regarded her with intent interest. Only she wasn't Leigh Smith any longer. She had a queer new French name, Madame Bodichon. Kitty was even more intrigued with her husband, who was a very brilliant but eccentric scientist and reformer. Once she discovered him sitting cross-legged on the floor wrapped from head to foot in something called a burnoose and apparently deep in thought. Even My Doctor seemed a bit nonplussed when the radiant Barbara described him as "the handsomest man ever created." But he was certainly different, with a magnificent head, thick black hair, and skin as brown as desert sand, which was fitting, since Barbara had met him in Algeria. They had come to America on their honeymoon. Barbara especially wanted to learn the truth about American slavery. To the granddaughter of William Smith, apostle of freedom, and to Eugène Bodichon, who as a member of the House of Deputies in Algeria had worked tirelessly until slavery in that country was abolished, the fact of its existence in free America was an incredible paradox.

Kitty listened avidly to the conversation between My Doctor and Barbara, the stories Elizabeth told of her past — the little Negro girl who had served as firescreen, the underground in Cincinnati, the price on Uncle Harry's head. When the Bodichons returned to New York after their tour, Barbara also had stories to tell. She had interviewed a slave named Polly in a plantation cabin, discovered that she had been sold twice, had had three children, one of whom her master had promised to keep, then sold without telling her. She had attended a slave auction in New Orleans.

"It was awful!" Barbara read notations from her diary. " 'Fine gal, Sara. Twenty-two years old. Has had three children. Healthy girl. Good washer. House servant. $600.' . . . 'Likely girl, Amy, and her two children. What! Only 700 for the three? That's giving them away!' "

Kitty stopped her ears. When she gingerly removed her fingers, the subject had changed.

"Please, Elizabeth, you must come back to England, if only for a visit. We need you. Women there have made no progress in medicine compared with here. But they're interested. You have hosts of friends. We can arrange lectures for you, help with finances. Please — won't you come?"

"But — how could I leave here?"

"With two other doctors? Of course you could. Promise you'll think it over."

Kitty waited tensely for the answer. "I promise," said Elizabeth slowly.

Kitty felt cold all over. If My Doctor went to England, what would become of her? Would she be farmed out to members of the family? All, she knew, had not approved of My Doctor's taking her. Stashed at the infirmary? Horrible thought! She liked Dr. Zak, but Rosalia, her sister, was there, and once Rosalia had locked Kitty in the bedroom, telling her she must stay there until she said she hated Dr. Blackwell. "My Doctor!" Kitty had spouted indignantly and had remained incarcerated until Dr. Zak, after calling for her vainly in her loud penetrating voice, had finally discovered the locked door and let her out. And suppose My Doctor liked England so well that she never came back! *Would she be sent back to the orphanage?*

But months passed, and she almost forgot the dire possibility. Then came spring, with snatches of conversation overheard.

". . . only be gone a few months. . . . Sure you and Dr. Zak can manage? . . . Barbara very insistent . . . many there who might help our cause . . ."

Sudden excitement postponed her fear when My Doctor left with her little black bag for New Jersey. There was consternation when she returned, for Aunt Nette, it seemed, had had another baby, and it had died. For some time the word "England" was not even mentioned.

Then the dreaded moment came. The coldness in her small body was like ice.

"Kitty, dear, I have decided to go to England, not for long, just a visit. I hope you will be happy about it. You know I want you to be happy."

"Yes." The ice in her throat made it sound like a croak.

"We haven't long to get ready. We must begin preparations at once."

"*We?*" The word exploded in an upsurge of wild hope.

My Doctor looked surprised. "Why — yes, dear. You're going with me."

They sailed in August on the Cunarder *Persia*, the same ship Dr. Emily had come back on from Europe, a combination of sails and steam, considered by some dangerous because it was so long and narrow. "Ah, but she was a good ship!" Kitty was to exult over seventy years later. Even seasickness did not ruin her enjoyment. She promenaded the long decks with My Doctor and Captain Judkins. She lay in the deck chair and watched the billowing sails. At night she loved to hear the watch call out, "All's well ahead!" and hear the cry pass from prow to middle watch to stern.

At Liverpool she met another Blackwell, Uncle Howie, burned brown from having just been in India, a small man who looked like Uncle George. In London she met still another relative, Aunt Ellen, who had been studying art in France and England. And here the idyll ended. For she was sent off to a boarding school in Ockham, Surrey, a very modern school for both girls and boys.

Kitty did not like the school. She liked nothing about it.

"How well you speak English!" one of the pupils said in surprise.

"What should I speak?" retorted Kitty.

She disliked the discipline, the food, the senseless English manners. If you came late for breakfast or prayers, you might be sent to bed for a whole day. All the other pupils were fond of a pudding called treacle, with a thick bottom, side and top crusts as thick as boards, and the inside filled with syrup. She loathed it. She despised having to make curtsies to the ladies and gentlemen they met on walks. Once in Ockham Park, when she was playing games with a boy about her age and she said indignantly that he was cheating, his nurse told her that was no way to speak to his lordship. Why not? She knew nothing about lordship, but she knew well enough when someone was not playing straight.

My Doctor was in France. She had given Kitty stamped envelopes to write her in case of emergency. When Kitty discovered that a letter she had written had not been sent, she made use of one of the envelopes, and when the pupils walked one day as far as Ripley, dropped it in a mailbox. Action was prompt. Word soon came from My Doctor that she was to go and stay with Aunt Ellen. Her prison term was over. Then, when word was sent that she was to come to Paris, Kitty's joy was complete.

But there were difficulties. She must have a passport. Charles Francis Adams, the American minister, and Mr. Moran, his chief of legation, both said it was impossible to give a child a passport. Uncle Howie took her to the office many times.

"Now, Kitty," he said once, "if they say this time they will give it to you, you must take off your righthand glove when they give you the book, to swear."

Success! They had decided to give it. "Little girl," said Mr. Adams's deep voice, "do you understand the nature of an oath?"

"Yes, sir," she replied. "It's to tell the truth and nothing but the truth."

They gave her the passport. Fourteen years later, when she went to the same office for another passport, Mr. Moran was still there. Being told who she was, he said, "We never did such a thing before or since, and if anything had happened to the child, the United States Embassy would never have heard the last of it."

One dark morning Uncle Howie roused her at an unearthly hour and took her to Waterloo Station. In one pocket of the cape to her pelisse was the passport. In the other were the addresses in Paris and Dieppe where she would have to stop. She traveled second class. Arriving at

Newhaven, she followed the stream aboard the boat. She sat down on a bench and watched all the preparations for starting. When they were out of Newhaven Harbor, a sailor came and asked if she would not go below to the cabin. She went to the head of the stairway, but did not like the exuding smell.

"No thank you," she told him with dignity. "I will stay here."

He carefully wrapped her in tarpaulins, yet when she arrived at Dieppe she looked like a drowned rat, wet from her swansdown hood to the bottom of her pelisse. She marched off the boat between a file of soldiers and a curious crowd. As they neared the Custom House, a lady approached her. It was one of Aunt Anna's friends. At her flat the *bonne* carried off her clothes to dry and press. Kitty knew enough French to thank her. Again she was put on a train, reaching Paris at two A.M. No one was there to meet her. After her trunk was examined, there was a great gathering of porters and officials to contemplate her, but she showed the address given her to the station master, asked for a *fiacre* to go there, and presently was deposited in a cab, all the officials regarding with obvious alarm the spectacle of a small black-eyed, black-haired youngster driving off alone.

Kitty was equally alarmed. She had read too many tales of the French Revolution. She fully expected to be carried to the Conciergerie, and when the cab suddenly stopped, she thought the hour had come. Looking out, she saw another cab coming in the opposite direction. "Is that you, child?" asked a familiar voice.

Elizabeth was far more relieved than Kitty. She had gone to the wrong station. When she reached the right one, Kitty had gone, but all the officials at the Chemin de Fer de l'Ouest had been able to offer her plenty of information. Now, riding along in her cab, she had recognized Kitty's small trunk on the top of another and stopped her own. Never would she forget the sight of the little dead-white face with its frightened black eyes and frame of jet-black hair.

Another relative, a woman with a beautiful face but restless eyes and thin, melancholy lips, Aunt Anna. A small flat with a lovely white sheep's-fur rug on the floor and a bright fire in a grate. Eating a good lunch and, after it, tumbling into a nice soft French bed. But it was none of these things which made it all seem like heaven to Kitty. It was just being with My Doctor again. The country, the house, the surroundings, the time did not matter. She had come home.

Chapter Eleven

ELIZABETH COULD HARDLY BELIEVE her good fortune. The Countess de Noailles, noted for her generous support of benevolent enterprises and now wintering in Italy, had written to her sister-in-law Madame Standish, asking her to arrange an interview with Miss Blackwell to explore certain possibilities.

"I wish to direct all my efforts to this object. Let me know as soon as possible what it would cost to establish a small hospital for· women and children in either France or England, under Miss Blackwell's direction."

Elizabeth prepared for her interview with Madame Standish with the utmost care. "She's the daughter of the Prince de Poix," warned Anna in the tone which signified, "Be careful what you wear."

For Anna was as acutely discriminating in dress as in the wording of the articles she dispatched to periodicals in America, England, Australia. No sooner had they arrived than she had pounced with devastating censure on the wardrobe Ellen had picked for Kitty in London and, to Kitty's secret delight, when they were away one day had burned two of the most offensive items, a brick-dust dress and a green bonnet, without, however, offering to replace them.

Elizabeth did not like Anna's taste in dress but disliked a quarrel. She was glad, therefore, when her sister left for the country, leaving her to a very ladylike dressmaker to have her wardrobe replenished. Now, fortunately, with the coming trip to England demanding respectability, she had clothes both suiting her own taste and fitting this occasion: a beautiful gray cloth coat, half circular, half mantle, a new hoop skirt, a skirt with very narrow lines topped by a velvet bodice, and a bonnet of dark brown *velours royale* trimmed with black lace,

353

made by a milliner for fifty francs. Later for the London lectures there would be a rich dark brown silk with high and low body, to be worn with black tulle pelerine in the evening, a black *velours de laine* skirt to wear with her old cloth jacket, which was still thick and outstanding, and a black velvet headdress, which would give a little height and importance to her head. Horrible expense but probably worth it, for, as the dressmaker told her, "in your position, you must make a ladylike appearance." Now, preparing for the momentous interview, she was glad for the part of the wardrobe already completed.

Madame might be a princess, but she seemed merely a stout, black-eyed Frenchwoman of forty-five, cordial in manner, speaking English almost as well as French. For two hours they had a serious and spirited conversation. She was much interested in the entrance of women into medicine, having observed much moral degradation among her women acquaintances resultant from their being treated by men in female complaints. Oddly enough, the fact which impressed her most in all Elizabeth told her was Emily's amputating of a breast. "*Merveilleux! Quel miracle!*" This one fact proved to her intense satisfaction what she wanted to believe, that one could actually have faith in a woman physician. She had some extreme ideas. She thought women doctors should never marry. She would be shocked to see Elizabeth dancing in a ballroom with a garland on her head. They should be dedicated to their calling like sisters of charity. After attempting vainly to broaden her conception, Elizabeth gave up, realizing that the idea of abnegation was inherent in this Frenchwoman's nature.

"I shall write to *la comtesse* this very day," declared Madame. "And may I tell her that you are not committed to go back to America, even though you have accomplished there such a *chose merveilleuse?*"

Elizabeth hesitated only a moment. "I am not committed," she replied soberly.

She wrote Emily at once. "I feel convinced that I shall have some proposition in relation to my (or rather our) establishment in London. What, then, ought we to say should such an offer arise? I will accept nothing that is not offered to us both, on that I am quite determined. We cannot separate in practice."

Uncertainty again! The future loomed almost as vague as had Paris during the severe autumn fogs when she and Kitty had walked, sometimes unable to see across the street, groping their way along and feeling delighted when they ran into a gendarme, who could set them straight in their direction. She had come to Europe to help women here make a start in the medical profession, not to remain herself. But fortunately nothing need be decided yet. She tried to apply herself single-mindedly to the writing of her English lectures.

It was a troublesome business. Her first ones were adapted to an American, not an English, audience. She wrote with pleasure but discouraging slowness, only able to write in the morning when she felt fresh. Sometimes a day produced a page, sometimes none. With Anna still in the country and Kitty at a boarding school for American children conducted by Miss Faunce MacDaniel, she had long hours to herself. Now the fogs had lifted, Paris was again a dream city. Though Anna's lodging was in a wretched street, the walk she had to take often to Boissonneau's was beautiful, across the Invalides, along the Quai, pont, and Place de la Concorde to the Madeleine. She never tired of gazing down to the Tuileries and up the Champs Élysées over the water to the setting sun.

Not that she remained a recluse. She paid visits to La Maternité, became acquainted with Dr. Ulysse Trélat, one of the city's distinguished physicians, authors, and politicians. He had been mayor of the twelfth arrondissement in Paris, and during the political upheaval of 1848 had been vice-president of the Assemblée. Now director of La Salpêtrière, a women's mental hospital and prison which was the largest institution of its kind in Europe, he was an authority on mental disease and hygiene. This was the period before La Salpêtrière became a great school of experimentation and was still only a benevolent refuge, where the well-being and kindly protection of its inmates formed the prime object of its director. Elizabeth visited the doctor and his wife at the hospital, learned much from his methods, and made them her staunch friends for life. She visited other hospitals, interviewed former doctor friends, haunted libraries to find facts for her lectures. But, though her pulses often quickened at sight of a possibly familiar figure, she made no attempt to arrange a meeting with Dr. Hippolyte Blot.

As always, she was surprised to find herself a celebrity. When one of Anna's friends, the Countess de Charnacée, insisted on drawing her likeness, she was almost embarrassed. Reluctantly she donned her doctorial sack and sat for the talented artist. The Countess was particularly charmed by her subject's delicate hand, hence the informal pose which showed it raised, fingers curled, against the cheek. Elizabeth would have been even more surprised to know that the resulting black and white sketch would hang for many years at Versailles and that copies of it would adorn books and articles celebrating her achievements for the next hundred and more years!

Kitty came home for Christmas, full of excited tales about her fellow pupils, a teacher Miss MacDaniel, and her irate old mother, who believed the millennium close at hand and Paris the best point from which to ascend in her white robes. Kitty, who had a hot temper herself, was often in disgrace for returning to the old lady a dose of her sharp-tongued criticism. She was amazed that most of her fellow pupils were unable to read properly. In fact, she confessed with frank objectivity, she was the only one who could read with any understanding.

They spent Christmas at Mrs. Woolley's, an English woman with whom Anna since her return to Paris was boarding. The French maid was much interested in the compounding of the plum pudding, to which all the English boarders lent a hand. At last the pudding was pronounced done. The beef and turkey were served, then all the guests proceeded to the kitchen to see the pudding lifted. But the French cook, on hearing that it was done, had cut the string, releasing the contents of the cloth into the water. She was unspeakably astonished to learn that they had expected to eat that solid mass in the cloth. Meekly they ate plum soup instead of plum pudding. But Kitty's joy was immune to disappointment. Not only was she with My Doctor again, but she had a becoming new dress whose color she had been allowed to choose herself, a dark but warmly bright shade called "Waterloo blue."

After Christmas Elizabeth made a hurried trip to England. Florence Nightingale had sent an urgent request to see her. Arriving in London, where she stayed at the home of Kenyon and his wife Marie at No. 73 Gloucester Terrace, Hyde Park, she went almost immediately to Malvern to visit her friend.

The shock of her appearance was staggering. Florence lay on a couch, bolstered among pillows, beautiful in a blue gown, hair tastefully arranged, but a mere shell of her former self. Except for her eyes, Elizabeth thought, trying to hide her shock in inanities of greeting, she might be laid out for burial! But the eyes, which had once reminded her of glowing candles, were blazing fires. The frail body had burned itself out in the Crimea, but the spirit had become pure energy. There was no restlessness in them now, no frustration. They were the eyes of a woman accustomed to giving dictation to members of Parliament and prime ministers, capable at times of wielding as much power as the Queen.

Marveling at her incredible achievements, Elizabeth was stricken into silence. The iron will had revolutionized the whole health program of the British army, engineered the Royal Sanitary Commission on the Health of the Army and another on the same in India, drawn up regulations for a school to provide training in military hygiene and surgery, instigated reforms which had shattered the iron wall of British bureaucracy. Now, with her prodigious knowledge of hospital conditions in London, Paris, Berlin, Rome, Alexandria, Constantinople, Brussels, she was turning her genius to civilian needs. Her *Notes on Hospitals,* just published, drew a shocking picture of damp walls, dirty floors and beds, unsanitary disposal of waste, inadequate food, wretched nursing. Hospitals were doing people harm instead of good, she maintained. And their high rate of mortality was preventable and unnecessary.

Elizabeth's silence went unnoticed. Florence Nightingale had not summoned her for idle conversation. She had a proposition. She wanted to found a school for the training of women nurses. It would be the first one, except possibly Kaiserswerth, in the world. She would be the patroness and organizer. She had the Nightingale fund of forty-five thousand pounds at her disposal. And she wanted Elizabeth to be its director.

"Don't give me an answer now." As Elizabeth hesitated, she lifted a small peremptory hand. "For six months I shall be too involved with other matters to proceed. Meanwhile observe English life carefully. Make up your mind as to whether you can give up America. I know it is a serious matter."

Elizabeth sensed that the raised hand was a gesture of dismissal, but she had to know more. Could her sister be associated with her in such an enterprise? Could they pursue private practice in connection with it?

Miss Nightingale was explicit. Her sister, of course. She knew Dr. Emily's reputation. She frowned. But private practice, no. And, anyway, why should they want it? "To do things just because men do them!" she exclaimed scornfully. "Why should we want to imitate and emulate men? Don't we have enough important work to do as women?"

Elizabeth showed no irritation. In essentials, she knew, they were still of the same mind, and she well understood what it meant to be driven by a single purpose. She took Florence's nursing plan home to read and promised to consider the proposition, but she suspected already what the answer must be. She also had heard voices, and they were not the same ones which had called Florence Nightingale.

Elizabeth had other business in England. She was determined that the name of a woman doctor should be included in the new Medical Register of Great Britain. The Medical Act of 1858 permitted physicians with foreign degrees to register without examinations *if they had been in practice in Great Britain prior to October, 1858.* Arriving in August, she had carefully acceded to the requests of some of her friends to treat them professionally. On the Medical Council, of which Sir Benjamin Brodie was president, were old friends of her St. Bartholomew's days. Now, through an interested lawyer, Mr. William Shaen, she presented the various testimonials of her American and Continental study and made application for her name to be included. Success in this attempt would be a major triumph for women in the profession.

Returning to France, she went to the Riviera for a face-to-face encounter with the Countess de Noailles. The two women were instantly *en rapport.* To Elizabeth's delight the Countess was easily convinced of the value of hygienic knowledge in the treatment and prevention of female diseases. She willingly promised a thousand pounds toward a hospital for the treatment of women. Moreover, at Elizabeth's suggestion, she offered five thousand pounds more for the endowment of a sanitary professorship in connection with it, provided a sufficient sum could be raised to place the institution on a permanent basis.

Elizabeth uttered a prayer of thanksgiving. It was more than she had dared hope. Back to Paris now for a final revision of her lectures, then on to London, where she was greeted by the formal invitation she had been led to expect, together with a surprising letter of welcome. She read it with a warmer upsurge of emotion than she had felt in years.

Dear Madam,

We wish to offer you a heartfelt welcome on your return to England. We have heard of your unremitting exertions during your eight years' absence, to open the study and practice of medicine to women. We have appreciated the zeal, judgment, and perseverance you have shewn in following your noble object, and we are encouraged by the success attending your efforts to hope that in this your native land

358

obstacles similar to those you have experienced in the United States may be overcome, if we can be assisted by a fuller knowledge of the course you have pursued. It seems also most desirable that the public should be better instructed as to the benefits which would result from the diffusion of sounder physiological views among parents, teachers, and women in general, than are commonly held.

Knowing your qualifications for explaining the laws of health and the means of preventing or mitigating disease, we venture to suggest that you should give, during your stay in London, a short course of lectures on these subjects, as also upon the advantages of opening the medical profession to women, and the best means of accomplishing that object.

Should you kindly comply with our request, we engage to provide the necessary accommodation.

> *We are, Madam,*
> *Your friends . . .*

It was signed by fifty names, a roll call of some of the most distinguished and enlightened women in England, including Lady Noel Byron, Barbara L. Smith Bodichon, Mary Howitt, Theodosia Lady Monson, Bessie Parkes, Emily Gurney, and the Countess de Noailles.

2

Her name also was Elizabeth. Perhaps that was why young Elizabeth Garrett read with such absorbed interest the article about the first woman doctor in *The Englishwoman's Journal*, finding it even more fascinating than stories of other eminent career women in the series: Florence Nightingale, Rosa Bonheur, the great Rachel.

The Englishwoman's Journal, first appearing in 1858 under the editorship of Bessie Parkes, was a revelation to bored and dissatisfied young women like Elizabeth Garrett and her best friend, Emily Davies. Elizabeth was the daughter of a wealthy businessman, Emily of an English rector. Like Barbara and Bessie before them, they rebelled with all the vigor of their intelligent minds and energetic bodies at the empty and purposeless lives they were expected to lead. In the *Journal* they read of other women working under wretched conditions as governesses, dressmakers, factory hands, of the need of educated women like themselves to work in prisons, hospitals, and asylums, and the challenge stirred them to the depths.

When Elizabeth Garrett read in January, 1859, that Dr. Elizabeth Blackwell was visiting England, her pulses leaped with excitement. Newspaper comments were by no means all favorable.

"It is impossible," ranted one columnist, "that a woman whose hands reek with gore can be possessed of the same nature or feelings as the generality of women." When her father, Newson Garrett, reported one such comment with amusement, Elizabeth hotly protested.

"How can you judge a woman of whom you know nothing?" she demanded with some of his own asperity. "You could at least find out about Dr. Blackwell before you make up your mind!" She further suggested that he write to a London business friend, Mr. Valentine Leigh Smith, whose cousin Barbara Bodichon knew both Emily Davies and Elizabeth Blackwell intimately, and find out something about her before he criticized.

Newson Garrett, like Samuel Blackwell and Benjamin Smith, was an unusual man. He encouraged independence in his daughters, and he good-humoredly did as she suggested. In reply came a letter of introduction from Mr. Smith to Dr. Blackwell. Elizabeth learned also from Emily that Barbara would like to meet her. The letter safely in her pocket, she departed for London and went with Emily to call on Madame Bodichon, who was also visiting her family in the city. Immediately she was attracted to the tall vivacious woman with the masses of reddish-golden hair.

"Of course," said Barbara, "you must meet Dr. Blackwell. I'll arrange a meeting for you here in my house. And you must come to hear her speak. She's giving three lectures on 'Medicine as a Profession for Ladies,' for the purpose," she laughed, "of opening the medical profession to women before we are all dead."

At her suggestion also the two girls called at the office of *The Englishwoman's Journal* at 14–A Princes Street, Cavendish Square, where a group of young women, surprisingly stylish and attractive, had organized a Society for Promoting the Employment of Women. Conscious of the desperate need of unmarried working-class women, they had started a training school for shop assistants, founded a small printing press, were placing a few women as clerks, printers' assistants, children's nurses. But in one area, the most important, they were failing.

The entire field of professional careers — law, medicine, higher education, executive positions — were as far from attainment as ever.

Elizabeth Garrett was enthralled. Here was a Cause worthy of all her superior intelligence and perseverance. Immediately she joined the society and declared, "The passion of my life shall be to help women." And on the second of March she sat in a front row in Marylebone Hall among the large group of alert and intelligent women gathered to hear Elizabeth Blackwell's first lecture. The hall, hired by Barbara and Bessie, was tastefully decorated, the reading desk festooned with primroses and wreaths of green brought up from Barbara's Sussex cottage. It was in almost an agony of excitement and expectation that Elizabeth Garrett approached this actual encounter with her namesake and heroine.

Her first glimpse was disappointing. This slight modest figure the indomitable force which had battered the iron wall of male prejudice? She looked like a demure little Quaker in her plain bonnet and simple gray silk with its snowy linen collar and cuffs. The features framed by the blonde graying hair looked drawn and colorless, and there was some queer disfigurement about one eye. It remained steadily fixed while the other roamed animatedly about. But when she rose to speak, Elizabeth Garrett swiftly made reappraisal. Unattractive? Demure? Colorless? From the first word in the low resonant voice, the first gesture of the slender, expressive hands, the girl was held captive. Her eyes, raptly fixed on the quiet, intent features, never wavered. Once during the lecture the good eye met hers, kindled into brightness, and the gaze of the two locked together.

Elizabeth Blackwell told of her experience in London, Paris, New York, and of the contribution the infirmary was making not only in treating the sick but in educating wives and mothers in the prevention of disease through more healthful living. She discussed the useless life pursued by most ladies and painted a glowing picture of the satisfactions they might experience by becoming active, cooperating units in an intelligent effort to create a new society instead of living a "crippled and isolated life."

"She's talking straight to me," thought Elizabeth Garrett.

She listened with deep interest to Elizabeth Blackwell's plea for women volunteers in the field of medicine, not to exercise their God-given right as men's equals but to fulfill a function which was their peculiar God-given service to society. "The fact that more than half of the ordinary medical practice lies among women and children would seem to be at first sight proof that there is a great deal women could do for themselves. . . . Though they may be few in number, they will be enough to form a new element, another channel by which women in general may draw in and apply to their own needs the active life of the age."

Still under the exalting spell, Elizabeth Garrett followed members of the audience to a party at Barbara Bodichon's house in Blandford Square, where the lecturer was the guest of honor. Hesitantly she presented her letter of introduction.

"I noticed you in my audience." The doctor smiled. Again the good eye quickened and glowed, and the girl felt a responsive kindling in her own gaze. "I could tell how interested you were."

"Yes. I — I want to know more about it. I felt as if you were talking directly to me. I — I want so much to be like you." Then, eagerly, she was asking questions about the study of medicine, and the doctor was answering, taking all the time necessary, as if they two were the only persons in the room.

Suddenly the girl felt a cold premonition. "She thinks I've made up my mind to be a doctor!" she sensed with dismay.

"You have the intelligence and courage," said the other Elizabeth confidently. "I know. I can tell. Who knows? Perhaps sometime we'll be working together!"

Murmuring a hasty good-night to the guest and her hostess, Elizabeth Garrett took her departure. She crossed the square swiftly to her friend Emily's house, as if fleeing from a pursuing fate. What had she done? What had she said? She felt confounded, as if suddenly thrust into a world that was too big for her. At least she had not committed herself — or had she? She was young, only twenty-three. She had almost no experience of the world. Though well educated, she certainly had no particular genius for medicine, or for anything else, for that matter! And yet — *You have the intelligence and the courage. . . . Perhaps sometime we'll be working together!*

Had Elizabeth Blackwell somehow sensed that this eager young girl with the intent bright eyes, this other Elizabeth, would become the first woman in Britain to qualify in medicine? That Elizabeth Garrett Anderson would found the country's first women's hospital? That fifteen years from that day the two would together be involved in the founding of England's first medical school for women?

3

It was while living with Aunt Ellen in London that Kitty discovered her passion for dogs. Foxey was a black and tan Eskimo dog who belonged to James, the footman at Cousin Kenyon Blackwell's. Aunt Ellen, who was attending an art class taught and criticized by John Ruskin, borrowed him to sit for his portrait on the stones outside the house door.

"It's not a right place to keep a dog," remonstrated Kitty, "on cold stones!"

Almost all the tenants of the house at 5 Osnaburgh Street had a dog. Besides the landlady's two, there were Nippy, the khaki-colored terrier, a brown and white spaniel named Rob, and a dirty white little terrier called Rattle. On Saturday, Adelaide, the good-natured servant girl, collected them all, took them into a back kitchen where an extra fire was laid to heat water, and gave each one a bath. Nippy was Kitty's favorite. He hadn't liked her on arrival, a very seasick little traveler, but in two days he was her intimate friend and protector. Every day he walked with her to the day school kept by a Miss Bridges near Fitzroy Square and was always waiting to escort her home. She liked day school better than boarding school, though there were embarrassing moments, as when Miss Bridges asked, "Who was the bard of Avon?" There was complete silence until Kitty piped up, "Why, it was William Shakespeare." Miss Bridges was very indignant that the question could be answered only by a small American.

Uncle Howie had rooms in the same house as Aunt Ellen, on a lower floor, and often came up in the evening, lying on a sofa and reading aloud the installments of Mr. Dickens's latest, *A Tale of Two Cities*, as they came out in a magazine. He had come home from India on account of the Mutiny, and finally, unable to find any business opening in England, he reluctantly went back to India to continue his engineering and coal mining work. They all went to Southampton to see him off.

Always on Sunday afternoons and sometimes for days at a time Kitty stayed at Cousin Kenyon's with My Doctor. She liked it there.

The part of the household she liked best was the kitchen, where the French cook, Madame Vernon, let her watch all the dainty and exacting ways of preparing meals. "*Mais non, la petite*, she is no trouble. Mademoiselle, she touch nothing, she ask no question, but she watch all." Kitty liked the food there, especially the salmon and Welsh mutton, for Cousin Kenyon, being chief inspector of mines for Great Britain, got all sorts of special provender for his town house. At first James the footman always filled a glass of wine for her, which of course she never touched, but still he kept filling it until she learned to lay her hand lightly over the top of the glass and so defeated him.

She liked Cousin Kenyon, who let her roam at will through his big library and run the stepladder along the shelves and read any book she chose. One day when she was in the library there was great excitement. James the footman put his head in at the door and said, "My Lady Byron, sir, to see the Doctor." Up jumped Cousin Kenyon and ran out bareheaded to open the door of the brougham. Then Kitty, running after, saw him give his arm to an old lady in black with very white smooth hair, whom he escorted upstairs to the drawing room, where My Doctor met her.

"A very distinguished lady," he told Kitty solemnly.

"I know," said Kitty, "the wife of Lord Byron, one of your greatest poets." She almost burst with pride because My Doctor was a friend of such people.

Kitty did not care at all for Cousin Kenyon's wife Marie, who wore very fussy clothes and always wanted to muddle with her long black pigtails. Kitty loathed having her hair touched. Sometimes she could have screamed, it was so trying. Even Cousin Marie's admiring comments that she would like to have hair just like it did not help. Her hair was dark but not really black — midnight black, Madame Bodichon called it — like Kitty's. Cousin Marie was always having parties, and for one of them Kitty paid dearly all the rest of her life.

One evening Cousin Marie had invited a small girl to come and give an entertainment to her guests, and Kitty was asked to come and give her encouragement. She sat in My Doctor's bedroom waiting to be summoned to the drawing room. The bedroom was sumptuously furnished, but it had no light except a candle. Gas was still a novelty in England, and even the wealthiest houses had no good light. She read and read, waiting to be called. It was midnight when My Doctor came up, aghast to find her still reading. The fine print and poor light had caused eye strain for which Elizabeth would never forgive herself. Immediately she began to consult the best doctors in London, but the damage had been done. A weakness had developed which all her scrupulous care and treatment would never quite eradicate.

Salt water was the most comforting medicine for the pain in her eyes. Kitty discovered that when they spent Easter on the Isle of Wight, where Aunt Anna had taken lodgings at the Niton Bath and Lodging House. There was no railroad on the island, so they went everywhere by coach. It was wonderful having My Doctor free from lecturing for a whole week, even though she was busy revising her *Laws of Life* to be printed by Sampson, Low and Company, who had offered her half the profits after 250 should be sold. They roamed the country together, treading the velvet turf that covered the hills clear to the water's edge, exulting in the variety of the flowers — primroses, forget-me-nots, hyacinth, ground ivy. One day they gathered enough cowslips to make a grand cowslip ball, which excited My Doctor as much as Kitty.

Every morning Aunt Anna would work at her newspaper correspondence. Then she would cry out, "The voice of duty, Elizabeth!" That meant that My Doctor would start reading her *Laws of Life* aloud, and Aunt Anna would correct and improve them. While they worked, Kitty would wander on the beach. One day she met a beautiful black retriever. They immediately made friends, and he walked with her up and down or sat by her on the sand. After that they met each day. When the "voice of duty" had been attended to, Aunt Anna and My Doctor would come to the beach. The first time they saw her sitting with her arm around the neck of a big black monster, Aunt Anna screamed. She always expected every dog to bite her, or at least somebody. But My Doctor only laughed.

The black retriever, like Nippy before him, made Kitty's happiness complete. Predecessors they were of the thirty dogs she was to own and love in her lifetime — from Lion through Clyde, Queenie, Toy, Capitan, Laddie, and on to Don, Burr, Khaki, and Jock. My Doctor and a dog — for the next half-century they would be Kitty Barry Blackwell's two prime ingredients for happiness.

4

The success of Elizabeth's lectures exceeded her wildest dreams. For all three of them the hall of the Marylebone Literary Institute was filled. Many of the most important women in London were present. Mrs. Jameson, the well-known author, introduced her. Simply, earnestly, Elizabeth presented the basic tenets of her medical philosophy, dwelling at length on the laws of health, stressing the importance of physiological knowledge to women, and the need to *preserve* health and *prevent* sickness. She pointed out the necessity of acquiring good and avoiding wrong habits of thought, all radical ideas for the Victorian society of the mid–eighteen hundreds.

"Mental and moral progress," she said, "are so intimately connected with the physical condition that no person is worthy of the name of education who does not carefully observe the action and reaction of the mind on the body and vice versa."

There were two classes of people, she told them, most widely separated in society but most prone to disease and death: soldiers and fine ladies. Ah, that surprised them? Surely not the soldiers, for all had read the scathing descriptions of army life in the reports of Miss Nightingale. But the fine ladies? The smiles and faint ripples of merriment vanished as she presented stern facts about the monotony of life, vitiated air, deficiency of exercise, want of duties and employment, injurious lack of care and self-dependence which were devitalizing the health of women like themselves.

Later in the series she spoke on the profession of medicine for women, expounding ideas which she was to express many times during the next forty years.

"What special contribution can women make to medicine? Not blind imitation of men, nor thoughtless acceptance of whatever may be taught by them, for this would endorse the widespread error that the human race consists chiefly of men. Our duty is loyalty to right and opposition to wrong, in accordance with the essential principles of our own nature.

"Now the great essential fact of woman's nature is the spiritual power of maternity. What are the principles involved in this special creation of half the race? They are the subordination of self to the welfare of others; the recognition of the claim which helplessness and ignorance make on the stronger and more intelligent; the joy of creation and bestowal of life; the pity and sympathy which tend to make every woman the born foe of cruelty and injustice; and hope — the realization of the unseen — which foresees the adult in the infant, the future in the present.

"There is no line of practical work outside domestic life so eminently suited to these noble aspirations as the legitimate study and practice of medicine."

As she spoke, two faces in her audience became etched on her memory; one directly in front of her, that of Miss Anna Goldsmid, elderly, benevolent, tears running down her face; the other young and intense, broad high forehead springing upward toward smooth wings of chestnut hair, hazel-brown eyes fixed on her with an almost frightening comprehension and hope.

Chambers' Journal reported: "Dr. Blackwell proposes to establish a hospital in London for herself and her sister to work, for diseases of women and children. We understand, through newspapers, that a lady has offered 8,000 pounds toward this object."

It was true. Soon after the lectures a meeting was held at the St. John's Wood residence of Mrs. Peter Taylor, over which Mr. Shaen presided. A committee was formed to consider the possibility of starting a work in England similar to that being done by the Blackwells in America. Encouraged by the offer of the Countess de Noailles, it prepared a circular stating the object and inviting support. Lady Byron, the Honorable Russell Gurney, the Recorder of London, and the Honorable W. Cowper were among the signers, and sixty-six names of well-known women were gradually added. The plan provided for a hospital "for a class of diseases, the ordinary treatment of which too frequently involves much avoidable moral suffering, to be placed under the direction of competent women physicians, in connection with a Board of consulting physicians and surgeons." It also called for the endowment of a sanitary professorship and the raising and investment of an additional ten thousand pounds, plus an annual subscription list of not less than five hundred pounds to assure the hospital's permanent basis.

Elizabeth rode high on the wave of enthusiasm. It was expected, of course, that she would remain in England, that Emily would join her, and that together they would establish the hospital. It was an intriguing picture. For a time she let herself bask in its roseate glow.

"The more I see of work in England," she wrote Emily in April, "the more I like it. From the Queen downwards I see signs of favor. On all hands we make converts. I believe we could get into general practice. We could shape the whole matter in the right way, for people welcome true ideas. There is no limit to what we might accomplish here."

Her circle of distinguished friends increased. Marian Evans —

George Eliot — invited her to her country home for a visit. "You are one of the women I would choose from all the rest of the world to know personally," read the enthusiastic invitation. The reaction inscribed in the famous author's journal, however, after their meeting was not so complimentary. "Esteemable for the courage and perseverance she has shown in studying medicine and taking a doctor's degree," wrote the novelist on June 26, 1859, "but very repulsive and schoolmistress-like in manner." Fortunately most of her new friends did not share this appraisal.

The Russell Gurneys, bold reformers in the fight to raise women's status by making better education available, were staunch supporters of the crusade for training women doctors. Mrs. Bracebridge — who had accompanied Florence Nightingale to the Crimea — and her husband arranged for a repetition of Elizabeth's lectures in Birmingham. She was entertained and feted by many of London's great. Not that her head was at all turned by such personal honors. She accepted them gratefully not as tributes to herself but as hopeful portents of the expanding circle of reform.

Of necessity the high wave of elation ebbed. Success was dependent on strong and often divergent personalities. Patiently Elizabeth catered to the insistent and often eccentric demands of each one.

She responded to urgent messages from Lady Byron only to find that the urgency involved was not the progress of the hospital project or even her good friend's health, but a bit of gossip about Florence Nightingale. ("Her ladyship has paid me two pounds for my consultation but not followed one of my directions, though she thinks of perhaps doing so!")

She tried to mitigate her refusal to head Florence's projected nursing school by consulting her in plans for the new hospital, hoping that a union of the two projects could be effected. "Your idea of a Nurses' College seems to me *the thing* wanted now, but it must be in connection with a great hospital, and all our medical women must pass through the nurses' college into the medical. But in my coming speech I cannot say anything about our big hospital or your college. I will propose first the founding of a female hospital, second the founding of a sanitary professorship, third the organization of nurses in connection with it, fourth the introduction of *élèves*, rich and poor, to pass through the whole nurses' hygienic training, fifth the elevation of the educated who have passed through this probation into a complete medical course."

But Florence Nightingale was not interested in women becoming doctors. In her view, women made third-rate doctors and first-rate nurses.

In spite of their great friendship she nourished a secret contempt even for Elizabeth, whom some three years later she was to characterize as "inferior as a third-rate apothecary of thirty years ago." And the following year, 1860, she would write to John Stuart Mill, "Female M.D.'s have taken up the worst part of a male M.D.ship of fifty years ago. The women have made no improvement, they have only tried to be men, and they have succeeded only in being third-rate men."

It was well for Elizabeth's peace of mind and for the sake of their friendship that she never learned of these comments. She would have resented them not as a personal affront — the reference to herself would have amused rather than vexed — but as a bigoted and wholly unjustified generalization.

However, it was Madame de Noailles, "angel" of the enterprise, who proved most unpredictable. When the Countess suddenly insisted that the hospital be located *in the country*, Elizabeth was aghast. Leave London with its tremendous needs and medical advantages for the dubious benefits of pure air, quiet, and isolation? When she communicated the news to the committee, they too were disappointed, but it would not have proved an insurmountable discouragement provided Elizabeth decided to remain as its head. The Countess also displayed one of her "crazy fits, of which she has too many," when Elizabeth wrote her that she had been urged to begin practice in London on a "personal basis."

"Dear friend," she wrote in a huff, "lest the personal *basis* of which you speak become a personal *baseness*, let us put the whole matter on its true *basis* again." It was undignified, she protested, for Elizabeth to take fees for medical service. She cared nothing for female physicians, she continued, only for health cures, and signed herself, "*une folle*, who became such on the 1st of April in consequence of much worry."

Though the letter was followed the next day with one of contrite apology, Elizabeth could not ignore its import. This was the woman on whom the whole success of the project depended. Without her support the committee would never have the courage to attempt the raising of ten thousand pounds. Her first enthusiasm cooled to more calm appraisal. Give up the sure if small foundations in New York for an alluring but vague dream structure erected on uncertain promises? Slowly, regretfully, she came to a decision.

"After carefully weighing everything," she wrote Emily in May, "I have made up my mind to return, at any rate for some time."

Even the highly successful provincial trip — lectures in Manchester, Birmingham, Liverpool — did not alter her decision. She encountered a great surge of interest. Mothers begged her for instruction in health, three young women professed an eagerness to become medical students, some wise old physicians begged her to "break up" certain fashionable London practices by starting one of her own. But the enthusiasm unloosed only the tight knots of mental prejudice, not those of purse strings.

"The sympathy is intellectual only," she wrote Lady Byron, back in London in June. "Practical reception and familiarity with the new position of women must be of slow growth. It must be, in fact, a life work. The children of the present generation will grow up accustomed to women doctors, respecting and trusting them, but the large majority of the adults will only hold a half-faith, and this will be a gradual growth."

She did not add what she had already written to Emily, that Lady Byron herself "has not lifted a little finger nail to support me"!

Determined that the success gained should not be lost, she led the committee in revising its program for slower but constructive growth. The Countess gladly agreed to leave her thousand-pound contribution in Elizabeth's trusteeship, the income to be used for the New York Infirmary and the principal to be kept for such time as work might become practicable in England. With a resurgence of exuberance she rode her pet hobby in another direction.

"As the central hospital already exists in New York," she wrote happily, "if you will allow me to help in beginning a sanatorium in country air I should be able to realize my idea at once. I think you might obtain some house or farmhouse for the purpose in the course of the autumn or spring. The importance of convalescent hospitals in the country is beginning to be recognized in England. Let women be the first to set the example of one in America!" To this Elizabeth gladly agreed.

A committee was appointed to test and select students to be sent to the New York Infirmary for training, a long-term campaign set in motion for distributing literature and raising funds for the projected hospital. Regretfully she resigned leadership to as willing and efficient persons as were available: Barbara and Bessie, Mrs. Bracebridge, Emily Gurney. But her emotions were not all regret. Much as she loved England, there was little that she minded leaving. Ellen, in poor health and tired of her art course, had already left for America. Howie was in India. With Anna she had always felt more unease than rapport. With Kenyon and Marie she now had little in common. Uncle Charles had been dead now for some years. (At least Anna need worry no longer about his shameful bigamy being blazoned to the world and disgracing the Blackwell name!) She had not even visited Cousin Sam on this trip. And a pathetic little letter from Aunt Lucy, who had returned long ago to Bristol and married an irately possessive schoolteacher who would not let her out of his sight for even a brief trip to London, must be answered only with regrets. Aunt Lucy, as well as Bristol, belonged to another era. There was no time to return to it now.

Already she was focusing her sights across the ocean. Did Emily think a hundred dollars could be spared from infirmary funds for the beginnings of a library and museum? She ordered from Paris a selection of papier-mâché models designed in wax by Vassourie ("His models are the most exquisite things I have ever seen but horribly dear!") to be sent direct to New York by sailing vessel. She purchased a microscope in London.

But her greatest triumph in England was yet to come.

"I have only one piece of information to send," she wrote Emily jubilantly on June 17, "but that is of the highest importance. The Medical Council has registered me as physician! This will be of immeasurable value to the future of medical women in England."

How great a triumph it was even she did not realize at the time. Only after it had happened did the Medical Council itself fully comprehend what it had done. As one observer commented at the time, it was a case of Dr. Blackwell's "walking through a door that officials hadn't realized was open." Hastily they slammed it against any further possibility of a woman getting her dainty shoe inside, not realizing, however, that another door was left slightly ajar: possible entrance through examinations given by the Society of Apothecaries. Six years later, in 1865, Elizabeth Garrett would edge through with an equally determined foot. Then all doors would be firmly closed, and for twelve more years the names of only two women would be entered on Britain's Medical Register.

A hundred years later Elizabeth's achievement would still be noted as a significant landmark. For in *Scope Weekly*, the issue of February

11, 1959, an eminent doctor, Annis Gillie, would be quoted as saying, "Her achievement was significant not only for women, but as part of the far larger struggle of all those debarred by virtue of creed, as well as class and sex, from the franchise, from the services, and from universal education in England."

Chapter Twelve

THE PALL OF SLAVERY hung over New York like the fog over London. It was as tangible as the August heat waves quivering above the familiar skyline and radiating from cobblestone streets and red brick walls as Elizabeth rode with Kitty in a hansom cab to the house in East Fifteenth Street. In the weeks that followed her return she was more deeply conscious of it than ever before. She saw its evidence in worried, tortured black faces, in screaming newspaper headlines, in the mutterings of church congregations, in hot arguments between "pros" and "cons" in shop, in omnibus, on street corners. In that summer of 1859 it was spreading over the country like a miasma, creating uneasiness, tension, fear of some vague disaster just around the corner.

Of course people did not call it that. They blamed "the times," "business unrest," that "wishy-washy Southerner Buchanan in the White House," "those damned troublemaking abolitionists." But to a daughter of Samuel Blackwell it had only one name, *slavery*. Fresh from the slow-moving, polite, unemotional, intellectual society of England, Elizabeth was all the more conscious of the boiling undercurrents of emotion beneath the surface. Yet, though she knew they spelled danger, perhaps of volcanic intensity, after the first surge of dismayed apprehension she became immersed in lesser problems. Emily was her greatest concern.

"What have you been doing, Milly?" she reproached, noting the gauntness of the once-round cheeks, the weary droop of the broad shoulders. She was almost as conscience-stricken as when Hannah had exclaimed accusingly at first sight of Kitty, "Oh, what has that child done to her bright eyes?"

But she knew very well what Emily had been doing. Dr. Zak had left

373

the infirmary at the end of May, persuaded by her Boston friends to undertake the organization and direction of a clinical department in connection with the New England Female Medical College. It had seemed a wise and progressive step. She had fulfilled her promise of contribution to the infirmary of two years' gratuitous service, and the preceding year had proved that the work of the infirmary could be sustained by two doctors, not only without loss but with a continuance of steady progress. Also Dr. Zak's health, which had become uncertain under the strain of work, had demanded a change from the grueling regimen both habit and necessity would exact in New York. So in addition to maintaining both her own practice and Elizabeth's, Emily had been burdened with the full responsibility of the infirmary.

But the wanness was due not only to hard work. Elizabeth was shocked as she came to realize the privations economy had dictated. While she had been feted by friends in England, Emily had been living in her garret, keeping in a bureau drawer bread, oranges, dates, and a few other simple staples, making most of her meals on them, sometimes cooking a little meat over an alcohol lamp or taking a small leg of lamb to the infirmary for roasting, making both last a long time. Only occasionally had she permitted herself the luxury of dining at a cheap basement restaurant. Elizabeth well knew the routine. She herself had practiced just such privations for years on end. Still she reproached herself.

But the infirmary had prospered. Finances had made such satisfactory progress under the guidance of supporters like Stacy B. Collins, Robert Haydock, Merritt Trimble, and Samuel Willetts that expansion was indicated. The three-year lease on the old Roosevelt mansion was running out. Plunging into the work with all her renewed vigor, she began searching with Emily for more adequate quarters.

The year abroad had stimulated her awareness of all sorts of possibilities. They must greatly enlarge their program for training nurses. Already they had made a good start. Three nurses had been trained in 1858, ten would have completed their training in 1859. But three, even four months were not enough. She had come back imbued with all the intense fervor of Florence Nightingale. Even though unable to yield herself to Florence's demands, which would have meant complete subordination and loss of identity, she was a thorough convert to her friend's objective. When Miss Nightingale's little book *Notes on Nursing* was published, she read it with absorbed interest.

"It makes me regret more than ever," she wrote Barbara, "that her poor health prevents her carrying out her nursing schemes, and I see how impossible it would have been for me to do her work. The character of our minds is so different that minute attention to and interest in detail would be impossible to me for the end proposed — nursing. I cultivate observation with much interest for medicine, but I have no vocation for nursing, and she evidently has. It is a capital little book in its way, and I shall find it very useful. But did you notice her little sneer at the hospital? How difficult it is for people to understand others' work!"

Secretly, however, she regarded the book as ill-tempered, dogmatic, and exaggerated, readable and valuable though it was. "Florence can't write a book," she confided to Emily. "All she can do is throw together masses of hints and experiences." A pity she couldn't have had Anna to help her revise it!

But Elizabeth's plans included more than training nurses. Already sixteen women had resided as medical students in the infirmary for periods varying from six months to two years. This program must be enlarged. There were the students who, she hoped, would be coming from England. If no "regular" school could be found to give them instruction, what then? The infirmary could provide clinical training, was already providing it for a few students from the Female Medical College in Philadelphia and, with more adequate facilities, it could take more interns. But Elizabeth was still far from satisfied with the education obtainable in any school admitting women. Was it possible that they would be forced to start one of their own?

And there was Madame de Noailles's sanatorium. This was the most alluring plan of all. For it could be not only a small hospital for convalescents, but that "place in the country" she had always dreamed of, perhaps center of a homestead for the whole Blackwell clan. Most of the family were now living in the area. Henry and Lucy had returned from Chicago, where Henry had completed his work of selling agricultural libraries and Lucy had lost a premature baby boy, and they were living in northern New Jersey. Hannah was with Marian, who was desperately trying to keep the small house she had bought in Roseville and, with her brothers' help, to make ends meet. Ellen was installed in a small studio in New York where she was teaching art pupils. Sam and Nette were near Harry in New Jersey. Elizabeth dreamed of a Utopia of fresh air, rolling hills, and green fields where each segment of the family could have its own little place, a minute prototype of that associationism for which she had always yearned. With the dividends from an American investment which the Countess had put at her disposal for this purpose, about eight hundred pounds, she started looking for it.

No wonder that, immersed in all these plans and problems, she took little notice of certain momentous signs and portents: In October the attempt of a man named John Brown to start an insurrection of slaves at Harper's Ferry. In November his death sentence. In December his execution at Charles Town, Virginia. The passing of a bill by the New York legislature, thanks to Elizabeth Cady Stanton and other women's rights leaders, giving wives the right to collect their own wages, sue in court, inherit property at their husbands' death. And as the months passed, a look of quiet desperation in Emily's eyes.

Winter brought physical discomforts as well as other problems. Neither the rising fortunes of the infirmary nor the largesse of patrons like Madame de Noailles added appreciably to the Blackwells' daily well-being. Their work at the infirmary was solely a labor of love. An income derived from a small private practice, a few lectures, and the rental of extra rooms permitted the barest of necessities, for every extra penny was applied to payment on the mortgage. They continued to sleep in the garret and cook their meager fare in the basement. The big drafty house on Fifteenth Street absorbed cold like a sieve. Elizabeth felt the cold keenly. Neither London fogs nor the chill of unheated Parisian *pensions* could penetrate one's bones like these icy winds from the north Atlantic. Shivering through the streets or crouched in a blanket in her garret room, she thought longingly of her snug quarters last winter in Thavies Inn and of the fur traveling coat Barbara had insisted on lending her the winter before in Paris.

The miles between them only increased Barbara's solicitude. Her letters, exuding the warmth of Algiers' constant sun and hot sirocco winds, were full of appeals and plans for her friend's return to England. And without Elizabeth's knowledge or consent, she was working to implement those plans.

"You know how much I love and esteem Dr. Elizabeth Blackwell," she wrote her friend Marian — George Eliot — on Christmas Day 1859, "and how much I wish her to come to England for the purpose of opening the medical profession to women before we all die (of course it will be open someday), and because she is not strong enough to bear the inclement winter of New York." Whereupon Barbara proceeded to ask Marian for the loan next spring of a hundred pounds toward a fund to help finance Elizabeth's first two years in England until her practice could be established. She would pay five percent, and Dr. Bodichon or her sister Nanny would sign the IOU with her so that if Barbara died she would not lose it. Barbara was trying to get her sisters and Bessie to *give* money toward the fund, so she could not borrow from them.

"The weather must be very cold in New York," she continued, "and I know how much she suffers from the cold. I remember last year in Paris she was obliged to sit in a room without a fire because she was not rich enough to have one. I cannot bear to think that if we are dilatory in cherishing her, it may come too late. She is not so strong as she was. Her lonely, hardworking life tells on her."

Elizabeth would have been annoyed, as well as amused and touched, by this solicitude. That anyone should think her too lacking in strength to face the exigencies of a normal American winter — or should feel it necessary to beg in her behalf! And return to England now would have been as unthinkable as giving up medicine merely because it caused one to lose an eye. There was work to do here.

They found a house at 126 Second Avenue, at the corner of Eighth Street. It had been occupied by a Frenchman who had laid it out in suites, an arrangement happily suited for a hospital. They persuaded the trustees to buy it. Having experienced all the inconvenience and expense of living in one place and working in another, Emily ventured to make a suggestion.

"Why not sell this house and both of us move into the infirmary? There would be room for offices, and it would reduce both labor and expense."

Elizabeth considered. She had clung stubbornly to the big house as a symbol of family unity. True, only George was living there now, unmarried and completely immersed in his law and business. He would scarcely notice the change. But — all the others! Sam, Harry, Marian, Ellen, Hannah — always moving about, chasing will-o'-the-wisps, wrestling with finances! She had taken a peculiar joy in feeling herself their protector, her house their haven in a storm. But there was also Emily. She took time, briefly, to observe her sister, surprised that the wanness and weariness were still apparent, and — was there something else? Surely not discontent, dissatisfaction! Why, Emily and Dr. Zak had accomplished wonders in her absence, increased the clientèle amazingly, put the whole project on a sound financial footing!

But undoubtedly she was tired. And her suggestion made practical sense. Somewhat reluctantly Elizabeth let herself be persuaded. The mortgage on the Fifteenth Street house was now practically paid off. She sold it, investing the profit in real estate ventures in northern New Jersey recommended by either George or Harry. George especially was exhibiting an astuteness in business management which was unusual for this branch of the Blackwells. In years to come he was to manage her investments with such skill and good fortune that she would have a small but steady income, enough to make her frugally independent.

She and Emily moved into the new house the first of May, and in the excitement of remodeling — preparing reception rooms, lecture rooms, wards, dispensaries, rooms for nurses and interns — Elizabeth forgot her brief anxiety over Emily. Two women students were expected — a Dr. Hughes, a graduate from Philadelphia Female Medical College, and Mary Putnam, daughter of the publisher. Again the two sisters slept in the garret, cooked and ate in the basement. There were difficulties in organizing the household, insufficiency of funds, the clashing of rival interests among the supporters, but all seemed nothing beside the advantages of increased space, big clean roomy wards and dispensary, the hope of raising an educational fund of about two thousand dollars a year which might secure the right of women to study in a male medical college in New York.

During that year of 1860, when Florence Nightingale was just initiating her plan to start a school of nursing in connection with St. Thomas's Hospital, Elizabeth had the satisfaction of seeing their own course of nurses' training, now well established, extended to thirteen months under the supervision of the head nurse and the resident physician. Dr. Emily became responsible for the running of the hospital, supervising wards and dispensary and performing all surgery, while Elizabeth, though assisting in the infirmary, devoted her time to private practice and education of the public through her increasingly valuable lectures.

She exulted in the sheer joy of hard labor.

"How good work is — work that has a soul in it!" she wrote Barbara. "I cannot conceive that anything can supply its want to a woman. In all human relations the woman has to yield, to modify her individuality. The strong personality of even the best husband and children compels some daily sacrifice of self, some loving condescension to the less spiritual and more imperious natures. But true work is perfect freedom, and full satisfaction."

She was as heartened by news from England as by their own success. In January of 1860 an open letter from her pen appeared in Bessie Parkes's *The Englishwoman's Journal* addressed to "Young Ladies Desirous of Studying Medicine." It described the four years of a medical course, one year of medical reading directed by a respectable medical practitioner, a second year of six months' work in a laboratory and six months in hospital as a nurse, a third spent in a college, and a fourth of practical experience, including six months in midwifery. Elizabeth Garrett read this letter with intense eagerness, for, spurred on by her friend Emily Davies, she was determined to study medicine. But it was June before she broke the news to her wealthy and indulgent father. Newson Garrett exploded.

"The whole idea is so disgusting that I could not entertain it for a moment!"

"But why?" she countered quietly. "Why should being a doctor be any worse for a woman than being a nurse? People think Florence Nightingale a heroine for going to the Crimea, and they admire the ladies that went with her."

Mr. Garrett finally capitulated, less because of approval than because all his inquiries revealed the apparent impossibility of her ever being admitted to a college or of being permitted to sit for examinations in order to practice legally. He was as stubborn as his daughter and as used to getting his own way. Immediately Elizabeth Garrett consulted Dr. Blackwell's committee, headed by Mrs. Russell Gurney, who arranged a meeting for her with William Hawes, who was not only a business friend of her father's but a governor of Middlesex Hospital. He suggested that, to prove her powers of endurance, she spend six months in nursing training at Middlesex, assuming all the arduous duties of a surgical ward.

In New York Elizabeth followed the adventures of her namesake with an absorbed interest, sympathizing in all her problems, even that of clothes. Wishing to emphasize her status of medical student, not nurse, Elizabeth Garrett shied from the nurse's uniform. But what should she wear? Ordinary clothes? The season's typical garb for women was a flounced crinoline with tight heavily embroidered bodice and long pointed sleeves with undersleeves of white lawn. Hardly appropriate dress for the operating room where, five years before Lister's experiments in asepsis, the surgeon still wore his oldest frock coat, so stiff with blood and pus that it could stand alone! She finally compromised with plain dark frocks and a good supply of white aprons. The thought of young and lovely Elizabeth Garrett, chestnut hair smooth and shining, hazel eyes clear and steady and unafraid, feet firm on the arduous road which she had made a little less difficult, she hoped, was for Elizabeth Blackwell compensation for all the long struggle, ostracism, loneliness.

To crown her satisfaction in the year's achievement, Elizabeth was able to find and purchase exactly the site she wanted for Madame de Noailles's sanatorium, a tract of land in West Bloomfield, New Jersey (later a part of Montclair), not far from where Harry and Lucy were living in a remodeled farmhouse. Often on a Sunday afternoon she would take Kitty out, and together they would roam the wide green acres while she painted glowing pictures of the cottage she planned to build, first of the many units which should someday make the place both a sanctuary of healing and a permanent domain for the Blackwells.

So confident was her sense of well-being that she was struck numb when the blow fell.

"I think I will abandon medicine," said Emily one day abruptly.

Elizabeth stared at her, sure she had not heard aright. "You — *what?*"

"I have been considering the matter for some time. I feel that it may well have been a mistake my studying medicine in the first place."

Elizabeth felt as if she were living a bad dream. She heard her voice speaking, but the words came without thought, almost without volition. "Milly, dear child, you don't mean that. You *can't* mean it! You're a wonderful doctor, much better than I am. Think of all the things Sir James said about you, and your other professors. And your patients — they worship you! I know some of mine were sorry when I came back. And what you've done with the infirmary — !"

The words trailed off as she realized suddenly that they were nothing but words.

"Yes," said Emily calmly. "I know I am a good doctor. But I might have been fairly good at something else, too — art, perhaps. Who knows?"

Elizabeth was stunned. Now that the implication of her sister's quiet statement had fully penetrated her mind, she had no words. She felt nothing but incredulity, bafflement, cold emptiness. Wonderingly she studied the quiet familiar features bent over the book holding the day's case records. Was it possible that she had never really known her sister, that the tranquil exterior hid turbulent depths of emotion of which she had been completely unaware?

It was indeed. It always had been. No one, least of all Elizabeth, had even suspected the doubt which at times had tortured Emily Blackwell all through her training and since.

"A terrible trial has fallen upon me," she had written in her diary on the very threshold of completing her studies. "An agony of doubt has burnt in my heart for months. Is the end of all my aspiration, of my prayers and dreams, to be that this long earnest struggle has been a mistake, that this life of a physician is so utterly not my life that I cannot express myself through it? And worse — worse — that I might have done more in other ways! Oh, my Father, Thou who seest how pure and true were my motives, leave me not! 'My God, my God, why hast Thou forsaken me?' I could bear anything but the feeling of failure. Show me the way, be with me!"

She raised her head now, and Elizabeth looked full in her eyes, saw there the look of quiet desperation. It could not be a new look. How long had it been there? She must have been blind not to see it, not only blind, selfish. Too immersed in her own problems and hopes and self-pity — the success of the infirmary, the building of a sanatorium for a foreigner, the sudden torture of inflammation in her one good eye which for weeks had made reading and writing impossible! It was because of her, the dominant successful older sister, that Emily had decided to be a doctor. Had she been blind and selfish then, too, trying to create a replica of herself rather than encourage the self-fulfillment of another human being? If so, God forgive her!

"Milly," she said humbly, "tell me — what would you like to do?"

"I'm not sure yet, but I think I shall study art and travel." The generous mouth, so like Elizabeth's, twisted humorously. "But don't worry. It won't be for some time yet. I can't do either without money. That seems to be the bane of us Blackwells. First I'll have to lay by a small competence. I won't desert your work yet." The eyes dropped again to the records.

The word, innocently used, cut Elizabeth to the quick. *Your* work. She had always supposed, taken it for granted, that it was *ours.*

"I'll help, Milly dear," she said gently. "We're making a little money now, living here. We'll make more." She longed to lay her hand on the proud head, slip her arm across the broad shoulders. With Marian she could have done so naturally. But there had never been a display of affection between her and Emily. "It's you who mustn't worry," she added with a lightness she did not feel. "We'll make your dream come true — and soon. I promise."

Not soon, however, for the plans and promises of individuals, even of institutions, were about to be swept away in the flood of conflict which would engulf the country.

2

Shocked suddenly into full awareness of the approaching storm, Elizabeth hardly knew whether to feel alarmed or exultant. Since the execution of John Brown, Northerners had become amazingly united, not against slavery, she was unhappy to admit, but against the spirit of Southern rebellion. Of course the liberal intellectuals of New England — Emerson, Louisa May Alcott, Garrison, Henry Wadsworth Longfellow — reacted to the incident as might be expected.

"This will be a great day in our history," Longfellow had written on the day of the execution, "the date of a new revolution, quite as much needed as the old one. Even now, as I write, they are leading old John Brown to execution in Virginia, for attempting to rescue slaves. This is sowing the wind to reap the whirlwind."

It was the about-face of many pro-slavery or neutral elements which was both astonishing and heartening, even though in most cases the conversion was political, not moral. John Brown was a Northerner and a martyr. His conviction on grounds of treason and murder acted as a catalyst to hostile and divergent groups. The dissension now was not between pro-slavery and anti-slavery elements, abolitionists and colonizationists, Garrisonians and "politicals," but between an aroused North, shocked by the martyrdom of a heroic reformer, and an outraged South, certain that it had merely executed justice on a lawbreaker and black murderer.

The election of 1860 was a trumpet call to all the Blackwells. Elizabeth thrilled to the campaign of t' aunt maverick from Illinois with all her youthful exuberance at the "chairing" of Bright and Protheroe, and the unexpected triumph of Abraham Lincoln, with its swift aftermath of crises, was as pregnant with drama as the Bristol riots. Yet there were both disappointment and confusion mingled with joy over the apparent victory. The pronouncements of sympathizers in her long hatred of slavery were disappointing.

"In so far as the free states are concerned," spoke Henry Ward Beecher in a speech on November 27, "I hold that it will be an advantage for the South to go off."

Said Horace Greeley in a November editorial, "If the cotton states shall decide they can do better out of the Union than in it, we shall insist on letting them go in peace." Elizabeth could not understand their reasoning. If slavery was an evil, then was it not as wrong in the South as in the North? How could they let it continue to exist without a protest?

The whirlwind had arrived and raged with mounting fury. On December 20 South Carolina seceded. Christmas Day brought the horrifying warning that Washington was in danger. In January six more states seceded, and on February 4 the Confederacy was organized. In Springfield the President-elect denounced the proposed plan for the revival and extension of the Missouri Compromise line. Slavery must not be tolerated, he unequivocally declared, in any of the territory of the United States. Elizabeth applauded. But his first public utterance in Washington sounded a knell to the hopes of abolitionists, for he pledged his administration to the faithful execution of the Fugitive Slave Law and noninterference with slavery in the South.

"In your hands, my dissatisfied countrymen, and not in mine, is the momentous issue of civil war."

The South accepted the challenge. On April 12, 1861, the first shot was fired at Fort Sumter, and war had begun. On April 15 the President issued a proclamation calling for a militia force of seventy-five thousand men. Response was overwhelming. Mass meetings were called in cities, towns, hamlets. Within twenty-four hours thousands of volunteers were on the march toward beleaguered Washington — farmers, scholars, businessmen, laborers. They were untrained, ununiformed, unexamined, unequipped. The officers were as ignorant as the men. It was more of a mob than an army, but all were eager, dedicated, fused together in a white-hot crucible of zeal. From all over the free states, responding with one accord, came men — *and women.*

For the mothers, sisters, wives, daughters of this motley cast refused to sit passively in the audience. Most, like their men, played bit parts, crowd scenes — sewing makeshift uniforms, scraping lint for bandages, waving flags and handkerchiefs. But some saw major roles in the script for which they had long been rehearsing on smaller stages — anti-slavery, temperance, women's rights — and, relieved that their long waiting in the wings was over, sprang loyally to play them. Among them were names destined to be starred in history.

Clara Barton. A restless, vigorous clerk in Washington, unattractive, frustrated, she responded to the first shot like a racehorse. The first act of this future founder of the Red Cross was to take a pistol, go to the Monument grounds, put up a target, and, one after the other, place nine balls within a space of six inches from fifty feet away. But she was soon involved in more constructive labors, distributing supplies for wounded soldiers.

Louisa May Alcott. Daughter of the fiery liberal Bronson and his wife, who had once hid a runaway slave in her oven, she first had a good cry because she was not a man, then vented her furious enthusiasm in the Concord women's society whose members numbered Mrs. Emerson, Mrs. Alcott, and Mrs. Horace Mann, assembling supplies and rushing them to the front. Later she was able to serve more actively as nurse in an army hospital in Washington.

Anna Ella Carroll. Daughter of a governor of Maryland and ardent student of law and politics, she first celebrated the election of Lincoln by freeing all her slaves, which she could ill afford, then prepared for her major role in the conflict by battling with her pen to keep Maryland in the Union.

Dorothea Dix. On April 19 this grim reformer, nearing sixty and already well known for her work in combating the horrors of insane asylums, arrived in Washington, went at once to the War Department and proposed to R. C. Wood, the acting Surgeon-General, that she organize an Army Nursing Corps made up of women volunteers, with herself at their head. Perhaps because of her reputation, more probably because Florence Nightingale had become a living legend, the harassed officer accepted her proposal.

Mary Ann Bickerdyke. A poor widow over forty years of age, vigorous, gifted with nursing ability, she was sent to the army camps by the church of Dr. Edward Beecher (brother of Henry Ward) in Galesburg, Illinois. A "cyclone in calico," as one of the doctors called her, she scrubbed, cooked, bandaged, bucked surgeons and bullied generals, created comfort and cleanliness out of misery and filth, and from her "boys" won the high accolade of "Mother Bickerdyke."

And *Elizabeth Blackwell.*

The smoke of cannons at Fort Sumter had scarcely cleared when she said to Emily, "Do you realize, Milly, that the infirmary is the only place in the country where nurses are seriously being trained? They are going to need nurses, well-trained ones. The scandal of the Crimea must not be repeated."

"Yes," said Emily. "And I know exactly what you're thinking — Esther."

"Esther?" Elizabeth looked puzzled.

Emily's eyes, freed suddenly of the look of quiet desperation, were dancing. " 'Who knoweth whether thou art come to the kingdom for such a time as this?' "

After discussing the problem with some of her friends at the home of Mrs. Henry Raymond, Elizabeth called a meeting of the managers of the New York Infirmary for Thursday, April 25, to discuss the need for women nurses in the war. She had no intention of making the meeting public, but Henry Raymond put a notice of it in the *Times*. The response was startling. Not only were the parlors of the infirmary crowded to the doors, but a queue of women formed outside in the street. Several men attended, among them Dr. Elisha Harris, a prominent physician deeply interested in sanitation, and Henry Bellows, a Unitarian minister of great energy and devotion to humanitarian causes.

Armed with all the weapons supplied by her association with Florence Nightingale, Elizabeth found them unnecessary. The group was already convinced and demanding action. Knowing the opposition leadership of a woman doctor would arouse in the medical profession, she determined to keep in the background, letting the eager and willing males brandish the torch she had lighted. A formal meeting was organized, but it was felt that the movement was too vast to be conducted entirely by so small an institution. A letter was therefore drafted and sent to the newspapers calling for a public meeting at the Cooper Institute on April 29. Though Dr. Bellows received credit for this remarkable document and it bore unmistakable signs of his verbosity, Elizabeth's clear thinking and experience dominated it throughout. It was one of the most important contributions to philanthropic progress of the decade.

It stressed the need of thorough investigation and dissemination of the needs of the army, that all forms of benevolence might be coordinated and channeled wisely and economically through proper channels. It warned of the total uselessness of permitting zeal and sympathy, rather than skill and training, to become standards for choosing women volunteers. It strongly urged the creation of a central organization to which all nursing applicants could be referred and their fitness judged by a committee of examiners, and the immediate establishment of a school where competent instruction in nursing could be given all successful applicants.

"Many may be rich and many poor," it stated. "Some may wish to go at their own charge, and others will require to be aided. But the best nurses should be sent irrespective of these distinctions, as only the best are economical on any terms."

There must be a central organization, it insisted. And all the women of New York and of the country should have a direct opportunity of giving support.

"Shall we sign it?" asked Emily after giving it her approval.

"No," was Elizabeth's prompt decision. "It's radical enough already without bearing the extra stigma of support by women doctors."

The meeting at Cooper Institute on April 29 met with a colossal response. Between three and four thousand women attended. An organization called the Women's Central Association for Relief was formed, and Dr. Bellows was again vigorously in the forefront drafting a constitution. He was not so successful, however, when he approached the army medical purveyor in New York in an attempt to discover the needs of the new troops and establish liaison with the military. War, said the irate purveyor, was soldiers' business in which civilians had no right to meddle.

It was the same military obduracy which Florence Nightingale had combated furiously for years in Britain. The women were no less obstinate than Florence. They sent a committee of reputable physicians to Washington, resolved not only to clarify the relationship which Northern women might assume to war activities, but to extend the plan devised for New York to national proportions. They were determined to lay the foundations of a national sanitary commission. It was a long and torturous battle. The army had no concept of disease prevention or health maintenance. Its medical responsibility began only when a soldier became sick or wounded. And it needed no outside help.

Nevertheless, prodded by the insistent women back home, the doctors persisted. The influence of the Administration was brought to bear. After much hemming and hawing, buckpassing, and grudging concessions, there was brought into being the American Sanitary Commission, forerunner of a long succession of government and civilian innovations, including the American Red Cross and the United States Department of Public Health. Though the new organization's activities were restricted to inspection and advice, it became a brilliant vindication of the revolutionary ideas of the brave doctors and their women backers. That it had all started with her little meeting in the infirmary parlors was to Elizabeth a source of satisfaction but not of personal pride. The real credit, she knew, belonged to Florence Nightingale.

In New York the Ladies' Sanitary Aid Association became furiously busy. Women worked every day at Cooper Institute, receiving and forwarding contributions of comfort to the soldiers; cutting, rolling, fastening old cloth into bandages; keeping the one precious sewing machine whirring; scraping wool rags with sharp knives or glass fragments to create the mountains of lint so popular for packing wounds. But thanks to Elizabeth, its primary duty was to pick, train, and forward nurses to the seat of war.

As chairman of the registration committee she sat day after day rigidly screening numerous candidates, choosing the most promising, sending them to the infirmary for a month's training, brief theoretical instruction, then for a month's practical training to Bellevue or New York Hospital, both of which had consented to receive relays of volunteers. In her absence Kitty or Dora Howells, a niece of William Dean Howells, sometimes kept the office, though of course they could not pass on candidates. After the two months' brief instruction the nurses were sent on for distribution to Miss Dix, the superintendent of nurses in Washington. Two months! The course of thirteen months which the infirmary had been conducting seemed short enough! In a series of nine lectures Elizabeth tried to condense it into a capsule: ventilation, cleanliness, food, care of helpless patients, observation of symptoms for report to physician, surgical dressings, bandaging, personal habits and precautions for nurses, and moral and religious influence of nurses.

If the training seemed brief, it was far more than was given other members of Miss Dix's Army Nursing Corps. Though she also had rigid requirements for admission, neither training nor experience in nursing was one of them. Applicants must be at least thirty, plain, severely dressed in brown or black, with no curls, bows, jewelry, or hoop skirt, and preferably Protestant. The morals of the troops were of higher priority than their bodies. She insisted also that all nursing activities be subject to her supreme authority. It was fortunate for Elizabeth that she consistently insisted on working in obscurity, for she was one of the few to whom Miss Dix was willing to delegate some responsibility. It would have been to Miss Dix's advantage and that of the country had she delegated more, for Elizabeth possessed the experience and ability for organization which the zealous and courageous reformer sadly lacked.

But Elizabeth never sought nor expected positions which thrust her into the limelight unless such publicity might further her cause.

"It makes me indignant," one of her Quaker friends once said to her, "that thee has not received more credit for what thee has accomplished in the training of nurses!"

Elizabeth only smiled. "Does thee suppose I care for the credit, so the work is done?"

By July five nurses had been sent, two of them professionals, well trained in the infirmary, capable of instructing others and directing large wards. Seven more soon followed. Elizabeth was not satisfied merely with sending them. She insisted on reports as to their progress, and in August she sent two members of her committee to Washington to consult with Miss Dix as to the fitness of her volunteers. She never obtained much satisfaction. The office of the Nursing Corps seemed as muddled and disorganized as other branches of the military. Letters came pouring in from men in the field, shocking the women with incredible conditions in the camps: semi-cooked food, strewn garbage, rats, dysentery, typhoid, shoes that wore out in a day, clothes made of "shoddy," tents pitched in malarial marshes.

Elizabeth nodded approvingly as the women's outraged sputterings changed to planning; to the efficient stepping up of more substantial supplies — food, clothing, medicine, some even packing their carpet-bags and traveling to the camps to make sure the supplies got there; better yet, to the exertion of pressure on government through the sanitary commissioners to reform its long outmoded practices. And reports from the Sanitary Commission itself were heartening. The greeting "Hello, Sanitary!" announcing in camps and hospitals the arrival of women with supplies of jelly, fruit, clothing, soap, and other welcome articles from home, became famous. Before the war was over it represented seven thousand local societies which raised and spent the amazing sum of fifty million dollars! There was little talk now of "women's rights." They were too busy asserting them, and in areas where their knowledge and experience gave them a preeminent right of authority: the feeding and clothing and nursing of their men. Perhaps the conventions had prepared them for this contingency, Elizabeth had to admit, taught them organization and leadership. But their actions now, commanding both amazement and respect from raw privates and toughened generals, would do more for the cause of women's rights than a decade of resolutions and speeches.

By the end of January, 1862, Elizabeth had been able to send fifty nurses, all carefully picked and with a modicum of training and experience. Her judgment in choosing was not always right. For instance, there was a German woman who seemed so excitable and feeble that Elizabeth gave her kind but firm rejection. The woman went to Washington on her own and finally made her way to the front. So intense was her zeal and devotion that Elizabeth, apprised of her story, would cite it years later as the one incident of these days worthy of comment.

"After the battle of Gettysburg she spent two days and nights on the field of slaughter, wading with men's boots in the blood and mud, pulling out the still living bodies from the heaps of slain, binding up hideous wounds, giving a draft of water to one, placing a rough pillow under the head of another, in an enthusiasm of beneficence which triumphed equally over thought of self and horror of the hideous slaughter."

Other women were distinguishing themselves in that first year of the war, one of whom was to be closely associated with the future of the Blackwells. Anna Ella Carroll, who had helped win the adherence of Maryland to the North and had been chosen by Lincoln to journey west ostensibly as a woman writer but in reality on a trip of military inspection, returned to present a brilliant military strategy which salvaged the dark prospects of the North after Bull Run and succeeded in winning the West for the Union. Hearing of the exploit from Mary Livermore and others of the women who were constantly visiting the camps and making reports, Elizabeth would have been startled to know that a quarter of a century later her sister Ellen would be publishing a book about this same Anna Ella Carroll, brilliantly but unsuccessfully defending her claim on the United States Government for expenses incurred through her service to the Union.

Though Elizabeth saw nothing firsthand of the horrors of blood and mud and slaughter into which she sent her nurses, she endured a grind of activity which consumed every waking hour and sent her to bed aching with weariness. Fortunately her eye improved, for it was subjected to constant strain. She was far more worried over Kitty's eye trouble than her own. But other personal concerns became negligible. No time to think now of Emily's impending desertion, or even of the distressing postponement of her promise to provide medical training for aspiring English women. All her energies were expended in the effort to atone for the disorganized confusion in Washington by providing as many well-trained nurses as possible.

"There is a mania of women to 'act Florence Nightingale,'" she wrote Barbara, "without system or discrimination or practical knowledge."

To Barbara also she confessed her distress that the struggle of the North seemed solely to preserve the Union and not for freedom of the slaves. But the attitude of the British distressed her even more, for fears arose that England would join in the struggle against the North in order to establish Southern independence and free trade. The very thought that her native country might support slavery for the sake of trade was intolerable.

The summer of 1862 seethed with heat, anger, unrest, rumbles of defeat, rumors of stinking battlefields strewn with rotting carcasses. Women like Clara Barton were bitterly berating a military establishment which made little provision for its wounded and let them die like flies. Instead of colorful parades and rousing regimental marches, the streets of New York echoed grumbles of mismanagement and demands for victory. Equally loud were the voices of abolitionists like Horace Greeley attacking the President for not disavowing slavery. Elizabeth shared their impatience. Even the signing of the Emancipation Proclamation in September was not wholly satisfying, for it exempted those slaveholding states which had remained loyal to the Union.

The tension of life was briefly broken during these months by the arrival from England of Herman Bicknell, a fellow student of her St. Bartholomew days, who had sat beside her in the lecture room. Brilliant, eccentric, he was not only a skilled physician, a Fellow of the Royal College of Surgeons, but also a world traveler, clever poet, and Persian scholar. She and Emily, and Ellen as well, listened with fascinated interest to his stories of adventures in the East: life as an army surgeon in the Indian Mutiny, a pilgrimage to Mecca in disguise, experiences in the native quarters of Cairo. His wife had recently died, and Elizabeth noted with some uneasiness his apparent attraction to the poetic and artistic Ellen. A Quixotic globe-trotter as a husband for the beloved little sister? Almost as disturbing as Marian's onetime involvement with a young missionary to India! But she need not have worried. Mr. Bicknell returned uncommitted to England, and the flame of romance, if it had been such, flickered out.

The months rushed past at a fevered pace. During 1862 the infirmary treated nearly seven thousand patients, twice as many as in 1860. Many were Negro refugees from the South. But if opposition had been violent against Elizabeth and Emily as women doctors, in this new capacity it was redoubled. For to an increasing number of citizens the war became insufferable, Negroes scapegoats, and abolitionists anathema. It was in July, 1863, that the unrest rose to a climax.

Elizabeth was on her farm in West Bloomfield, New Jersey, where she had finally been able to erect a small cottage, first — hopefully — of the sanatorium units, when the news came. Riots were blazing in the streets of New York. Immediately she made plans to return. Both Kitty and Alice were with her. Fortunately Henry's house was close by, and she could send Alice home, but Kitty refused to go with her. If there was danger, she stoutly insisted, she would share it with My Doctor. They crossed the ferry in a dusk compounded by drifting smoke, toward a skyline lurid with creeping fires. At the dock they had to wait an hour to find an empty hansom cab. Riding through the streets, Elizabeth felt herself transported to another land and era. This was not New York, 1863. It was Bristol, 1831. The figures glimpsed under the dim lights were the same — sinister, unhuman; upraised hands brandishing hammers, brickbats, crowbars, shovels, flaring torches; faces inflamed more by a wild gleeful excitement than by passion, which would come later. Occasionally there was a crash of glass, a burst of flame, a rush of shouting, struggling silhouettes as one shop after another was fired, pillaged. They passed reeling carts, drays, wheelbarrows piled high, lone figures staggering under burdens of loot, each trying to protect his store from other looters. It was every man for himself, a grim yet riotous defiance of society's restraint. Elizabeth pressed Kitty's cold fingers and tried to reassure her.

"Don't worry, dear. We're quite safe, I think. We'll soon be through the worst of it."

She was wrong. As they neared the infirmary, closer to the Negro and immigrant sections, tension mounted. It was no longer every man for himself. There was a fusion of purpose. Homes were being fired, doors battered down, but not for looting. Suddenly Elizabeth put an arm about Kitty, pressed the girl's face hard against her shoulder. But she could tell by the convulsive shudder that she was too late. Kitty had already seen the limp figure dangling from the lamppost, black face horribly distorted under the flaring gaslight, lifeless eyes still bulging with terror.

Emily met them at the door, white-faced but calm, unnaturally voluble with relief. "Thank heaven, you've come! I was afraid I couldn't manage alone. The furore is infecting the hospital. The white patients are uneasy — demanding that we oust the Negro women. Of course I refused. We need your help."

So began three days and nights of horror. Did they always come in threes, wondered Elizabeth, remembering the Bristol holocaust. The Draft Riots, they were called later, because the armed mobs were ostensibly protesting against conscription, but they swiftly turned into concerted violence against the popular scapegoats, the Negroes and the abolitionists. The limp figure hanging from the lamppost was only one of many. Negroes were beaten to death as well as hanged. The homes of known abolitionists were burned, ransacked, looted. Vandalism swept the city. The doors of a Negro orphanage were battered down and the building set on fire, its two hundred occupants miraculously spirited away to doubtful safety through a back door and rendered destitute and homeless. The city streets, especially those in the Eleventh Ward, were turned into a shambles.

It was an outburst of savagery unique in New York's long history. Not even a hundred years later, with the violent eruptions of a new and restless generation, many of whom would artlessly assume that they had coined the word *riot*, would the city be racked by such wholesale and devastating rebellion.

Elizabeth and Emily dared not confess their fear, even to each other. If the frenzy continued, mounted, it must be only a matter of time before some vandal recalled that the infirmary housed not only the despised women doctors but Negro patients and abolitionists. Hiding their apprehension behind a calmness as impenetrable, they hoped, as the ground floor shutters, they tried to pretend that all was as usual. Elizabeth delivered her lectures to the nervous probationers, quietly adding explicit directions for the evacuation of the patients in case of fire or other emergency. Again and again she made the rounds of the wards, reassuring the terrified patients.

"It's all right. We'll take good care of you. The house is locked and shuttered. Its doors are strong and solid."

Words. What security strong doors against a howling mob, locks and shutters against mad incendiaries?

The second night was the worst. The rioters moved closer, burning eleven houses only a block north of the infirmary. And as if human savagery were not enough, a severe storm raged. Thunder mingled with the frightening clamor, and lightning lent a diabolic leer to the flames' inferno. All night Elizabeth went from bed to bed comforting the patients, adjusting the sheets again and again to shut out the terrifying glare from their hypnotized gaze. Like the storm, it would soon be over, she kept repeating, and indeed the drenching fury of the one did quell the blaze of the other. Certain that approaching disaster was inevitable, Elizabeth felt her whole body tensing to meet it, as Samuel's must have done on the steps of St. Mary Redcliffe. If it were only her life that was imperiled, instead of all that her life had accomplished! For if the infirmary were destroyed now, she knew, it would never be rebuilt. Without the assurance of Emily's support, how could she possibly find courage to begin all over again? Would Emily be relieved, she wondered, to be set free from this millstone which she, Elizabeth, had hung about her neck? And what about herself? What might her own future hold? Emily was not the only one torn between two driving urges.

To be Woman or simply a woman? It was a dilemma which had plagued all the daughters of Samuel, the reason why none of them had ever married. Never had Elizabeth been more conscious of it than during this night when her life's achievement seemed to hang in the balance. Under her calm exterior as she went from bed to bed, comforting, assuring, there raged all the combat of the two storms outside. Did people think she had *wanted* to be different, shunned, a "lone woman walking like mad" through dark hostile streets? No! Tonight, one by one, came all the loves she had yearned over, tested, rejected, from a blond cherub in the streets of Bristol to a man murmuring endearing words in a Paris hospital. A woman . . . and Woman. Love, marriage, family . . . and the fulfillment of one's God-given capacities as a human being. Was it an irreconcilable conflict? Lucy and Nette seemed to have solved it. Just two months ago Lucy had presided at a convention here in New York, and Nette had delivered a stirring address showing the impossibility of reconciling two such contradictory ideas as democracy and slavery. But they were two unusual women married to two unusual men. The sisters of those men had not been so fortunate.

The night was half over when one of the nursing trainees came running toward her, face pale with more than fear of riots.

"That woman — she's in delivery — Dr. Emily says come!"

Elizabeth hurried to the tiny delivery room, where Emily was already grimly bent over the patient, a Negro refugee slave brought to the infirmary by some of their abolitionist friends just before the riots started. Labor promised to be difficult, complicated by near-starvation and the rigors of her escape and long weeks of hiding. Quickly Elizabeth changed into a clean white doctorial sack and washed her hands in the carbolic solution prescribed by the heretic Dr. Semmelweiss and her own common sense. Both practices were decried by most of their male compeers in this medical world still four years remote from Lister's "On the Antiseptic Principles in the Practice of Surgery."

All the rest of the night they labored, the three women, combining the elemental instincts of motherhood with the knowledge and skills of centuries as summated in the teachings of Sir James Simpson and La Maternité. Only when the child was safely delivered, washed, oiled, laid in its basket by one of the nurse trainees, the young mother safely back in her bed, wan, pain-ravaged, but eyes radiant with the image of a healthy son born into freedom, did the two doctors relax their grim struggle. Then, dirty, disheveled, deathly tired, they exchanged smiles of complete concord and satisfaction. It was more than a moment of concord between two people. Elizabeth felt a rare harmony within herself, all conflicts resolved. She had experi ʌ ed the whole passion of creation, suffered travail, given birth, just as surely as this poor despised creature — this precious human being — whose life she had helped save. For a brief moment, at least, she was both Woman and a woman.

She was almost surprised to find that day had come, the doors and windows were still intact, the fires, though blazing no farther than a block away, apparently under control. Safety, continuity, seemed almost an anticlimax. A welcome one, however. And though the riots raged for another day and night, by some vagary of chance — or was it a miracle? — the infirmary remained unscathed.

3

The news from England was both good and bad. Though Elizabeth Garrett was pursuing her object of obtaining qualification as a doctor with all the persistence of Elizabeth herself, plus the machinations of a stubborn and wealthy father, she was encountering the usual stone wall. Her studies at Middlesex Hospital, where she had finally succeeded in gaining admission to some special courses of lectures and demonstrations, had abruptly ended when a memorial requesting her exclusion was presented by the students to the faculty. She was out. As in America, the strongly entrenched medical profession fought her every effort to gain admission to a medical school. Its journal, the *Lancet*, along with diatribes of nonessentials, produced one incontestable argument: There was no examining body which would admit women to degrees. Therefore a woman would be unable to practice legally. But the University of London was applying for a new charter. The inclusion of women to its degrees was vital not only to medical students but to all women now unable to receive any official recognition of their intellectual attainments. Emily Davies, the ardent pioneer for women's higher education, joined Miss Garrett in an attempt to have women included in the new charter. Fifteen hundred letters were sent out. Prominent men, including Gladstone and Richard Cobden and Russell Gurney, supported the women's position. The vote of the senate was ten to ten, and Lord Granville cast the deciding vote — *against!*

"Perhaps," Elizabeth Garrett wrote Elizabeth Blackwell, "when they get another charter eight or ten years from now, we may try again."

With doors all slammed in England, the indomitable Miss Garrett attempted to storm the citadel in Scotland — Edinburgh, St. Andrews — to no avail. "What shall I do?" she appealed to Elizabeth. "Come to America?"

"No," Elizabeth strongly advised. "Only as a last resource."

There was one other loophole. The Hall of Apothecaries included in its charter the statement that it would examine "all persons" who conformed to the regulations. To be sure, its examinations offered only a certificate, not a degree, but it assured a license to practice. Elizabeth Garrett grasped at this frail fingerhold. Now, in 1863, she was preparing through private coaching for the examinations of the Hall of Apothecaries.

Suffering vicariously with her English namesake, Elizabeth fumed with impatience and frustration. Her goal of bringing students to America, gaining admission for them in a good medical college and giving them clinical instruction at the infirmary was as remote as ever. No "regular" medical school would admit women. True, women were being graduated from eclectic schools. And there were two small medical schools for women — in Boston and Philadelphia — gallantly attempting to give standard education, but they did not satisfy Elizabeth. Their standards, though high, did not yet conform to the best "regular" schools. If women were to compete with men in medicine, they must be equally or better trained. Moreover, in order for the infirmary to provide clinical education, the medical training should be given in New York. Yet repeatedly they had tried to induce some good New York medical school to admit students guaranteed by the infirmary, to no avail. There seemed to be but one solution: *They must start their own medical school for women.*

"I don't like the idea," she said to Emily. "It would be far better to work in cooperation with schools already established than to add another female school to those already existing. But — what other choice have we?"

"None," said Emily promptly. To Elizabeth's surprise and relief, her sister was in complete agreement.

No step could be taken, it seemed, until the war was over. The program of nurses' training, in addition to the increasing burden of hospital and dispensary, consumed every ounce of energy. Another project demanding more imagination and courage than any before tackled? Impatiently Elizabeth resigned herself to wait.

But others, unfortunately, were not waiting. Dismayed, she heard the news that another medical college for women was to be opened — and only a few blocks from the infirmary! Founded by Dr. Clemence Lozier, a graduate of the eclectic school of Syracuse, it had obtained a charter for the New York Medical College and Hospital for Women, a feminine counterpart of the Homeopathic Medical College of the State of New York. The project had the support of Elizabeth Cady Stanton and some of her associates in the women's rights movement. A pity, deplored Elizabeth, Mrs. Stanton could not have confined her efforts at reform to women's rights in the abstract rather than dabbling in a concrete mixture of which she knew nothing! — then chided herself wryly. Wasn't she the one who had always decried speech without action? Respectable and sincere though she knew Dr. Lozier to be, the idea of an "irregular" school on their doorstep, producing graduates who would type the term "woman doctor" for the New York medical profession as "sectarians" and "outsiders" was unbearable. The leading physicians interested in the infirmary urged her to take action. War or not, it was time to set the project in motion. The new homeopathic school opened on November 1, 1863, in rented rooms at 724 Broadway with a class of seven students. On December 19 Elizabeth called a meeting to consider the organization of a medical college for women.

In her address she told of the fruitless attempts made by herself and Dr. Emily to find a reputable school to train women guaranteed by the infirmary. She described in detail her own idea of what constituted a good medical education, compared it with the brief and slovenly training at some of the schools then in existence, the haphazard system of examinations, the granting of degrees after only ten months of study without a day's practical experience.

"The practice of medicine by women," she declared, "is no longer a doubtful but a settled thing. But there is not in the whole extent of our country a single medical school where women can obtain a good medical education!"

Let this not be construed, she hastened to qualify, as an attack on the women's schools already established. But a school was needed, formed on a different plan, organized on a much broader scale.

"Consider how women stand in this matter; how alone, how unsupported; no libraries, museums, hospitals, dispensaries, clinics; no endowments, scholarships, professorships, prizes, to stimulate and reward study; no time-honored institutions and customs, no recognized position; no societies, meetings, and professional companionship. One can hardly conceive of a more complete isolation."

There were four points in which a medical school for women should differ from any already established: thorough examinations, complete education, friendly relations with the profession, and a substantial endowment. These were the improvements women needed and which the public had a right to demand.

Action was taken. On April 13, 1864, the infirmary's charter was amended, enabling it "to grant and confer the title of Doctor of Medicine." The first step had been taken, but on a ladder reaching high into the clouds, for a goal of one hundred thousand dollars was set, at least thirty thousand dollars of it to be pledged before any of the pledges should be called in.

Meanwhile the war crawled on. Nursing applicants were interviewed and trained. In spite of Miss Dix's horror of subjecting wounded men to the sight of a pretty girl, women young and attractive as well as courageous were wading through blood and mud, dressing wounds, manning hospitals, obstinately filtering into forbidden front lines, often to the acute displeasure of army surgeons and generals — at Chattanooga, at Cold Harbor, at Spotsylvania. Names like Clara Barton, "Mother" Mary Ann Bickerdyke, Dr. Mary Walker, Mary Livermore, were already blazoned in heroic letters on the war's history.

In June, in recognition of her outstanding service, Elizabeth was invited to go to Washington on an inspection tour of the Nursing Corps and the Sanitary Commission. Her satisfaction in riding through Maryland, now a free state, was unbounded. In Baltimore there were all the old colored men busy as ever on the sloops and about the wharves, grown gray in toil, but now, thank heaven, free! And there were the colored teamsters she remembered, driving their long lines of horses, their curious expletives immortalized by Dickens — "Hi, ho, jo, jiblen, hi, jiggy, jibblin, jo-o-o!" — sounding far more joyous coming from the lips of freed men!

It was a holiday as well as a professional trip. Her old friend Dr. Elder, who had an office in the Treasury Building, helped plan a round of sightseeing. She inspected the new Capitol which at Lincoln's inauguration had been but "blocks of marble and piles of iron castings," now with its House and Senate wings completed and its majestic dome a symbol of national unity and achievement. She walked miles along Pennsylvania Avenue, to the Observatory grounds, to Washington Monument. In the Library of Congress she received a hearty welcome from the Blackwells' old Cincinnati friend Ainsworth Spofford, now chief librarian, and wished she had longer to browse among his eighty-four thousand volumes. She visited both houses of Congress, but was by no means edified at the conduct of affairs. With Dr. Elder she walked through the War Department, but they did not interrupt Stanton, who should have been, and probably was, excessively busy. But the villages of tents and baggage trains, the constant stream of wagons bringing wounded soldiers from the wharves, one steamboat alone bringing fourteen hundred, the disabled men thronging the lobby of her hotel, Ebbett House, sobered all joy of holiday.

Of course she visited Miss Dix in her room full of flowers, observing — without enthusiasm — her manner of working. One of her own trained nurses came in, just back from Fortress Monroe, and Elizabeth was gratified by the high praise Miss Dix accorded her.

But the high point of the trip came when, with Dr. Elder, she visited the President's house. As they were leaving, Judge Kelly of Philadelphia met them.

"Why don't you go up and see the President?" he asked. "He's all alone, and it's a good chance for you."

So up they went. Judge Kelly swept aside the usher and opened the door of a large comfortable square room on the second floor, announced "Dr. Elder and Miss Blackwell of New York," and then, to Elizabeth's discomfiture, left them.

"A tall, ungainly loose-jointed man was standing in the middle of the room," she wrote Kitty. "He came forward with a pleasant smile and shook hands with us. I should not at all have recognized him from the photographs. He is much uglier than any I have seen, except a little one which was given me yesterday in the Treasury and which I supposed then to be libel. I never should have given him credit from a passing view of the ability to regulate affairs and to write excellent documents. His brain must be much better in quality than quantity, for his head is small for the great lank body, and the forehead very retreating."

"Miss Blackwell," explained Dr. Elder in the course of their brief conversation, "was the second woman to become a citizen of the United States by naturalization."

Elizabeth smiled. "But I believe Queen Victoria reserved the privilege of shooting me."

"Yes." The responding smile lit the craggy face like a burst of sunlight. "That was the chief cause, I believe, of our War of 1812."

"Then," Elizabeth's letter to Kitty continued, "he plumped his long body down on a corner of the large table that stood in the middle of the room, caught up one knee, looking for all the world like a Kentucky loafer on some old tavern steps, and began to discuss some point about the war, while we stood criticising him. A fat clerk came into the room with papers and stood fidgeting about, evidently wishing us in Jericho, so of course we said good morning, and he and his clerk were seated at his work table (which stands in a lovely south window with the broad Potomac in full view) bending hard over the papers, before we were fairly out of the room. Altogether it was a most characteristic little peep, immeasurably better than any parade glimpse, so I considered myself quite in luck."

She little realized that within months, amid her rejoicing over the end of the war, she would be lamenting with a shocked nation the death of the strange and lonely leader who, as she wrote Barbara, "expressed the American heartbeat and was transparent to their will."

4

The war was ended . . . and just beginning. The slaves were not the only ones who had won a certain amount of freedom. Women also had obtained a new and hard-won status. They had proven not only that they could leave the shelter of the home and take part in the world's activities with feminine dignity and virtue unscathed, but that they had impressive leadership abilities extending even to executive administration and the efficient handling of funds. They had also proven to themselves the power of effective organization. Again the women's rights movement, dormant through the war, reared its head — or, rather, its two heads, for already there was appearing that conflict of direction among its leaders which was to determine the purpose of Lucy's and Harry's lives for the next two decades.

The convention of 1863 in New York at which Lucy had presided, organizing the National Woman's Loyal League, after hot debate had linked the two causes of women's rights and freedom for the Negro. As long as the war lasted unity had prevailed, and by February, 1864, four hundred thousand signatures had been collected in petitions asking Congress to pass the Thirteenth Amendment. But after the war two conflicting viewpoints emerged. The wording of the Fourteenth Amendment, specifically giving "male inhabitants" the right to vote, and that of the Fifteenth, asking that the vote should not be denied "on account of race, color, or previous condition of servitude" defined even further the split between the cause of women and that of slaves. As time passed, the wedge between two opposing viewpoints of the means to obtain women's rights, especially that of the franchise, was driven deeper and deeper.

"Let others fight the Negroes' war," was the decision of Elizabeth Stanton, Susan Anthony, and other militant suffragists after a valiant but unsuccessful battle to see women included in these definitions of equality. "Women must fight for themselves."

"No," maintained Lucy firmly, "we must stand for justice for all, or we are lost." With her in this opinion stood such staunch reformers as Abby Kelley Foster, Mary Livermore, Wendell Phillips, and Garrison.

With the end of the war Elizabeth's battle for the rights of women was also just beginning. In 1865 the founding of a medical college seemed as formidable a task as the reconstruction of a bitter and war-torn South. But the infirmary showed gratifying progress. That year 31,657 patients were treated, 640 of them hospital in-patients. Only five of the number had died, the remarkably small percentage being due, Elizabeth was sure, to the strict hygienic supervision always maintained. Thorough ventilation, care of water closets, the personal cleanliness of beds and patients, all rendered the place far different, even in smell, from the ordinary hospital, redolent of reeking bandages, unwashed linen, moldy floors and walls, lack of sewage disposal, and — yes, caked and stained doctorial sacks. There was an assistant physician, Dr. Lucy Abbott, and a junior assistant, Miss Blackmer. Two capable women had been thoroughly trained as nurses during the year. And — a sop to Elizabeth's vast impatience — twenty-one thousand dollars had been subscribed toward the fund deemed desirable for the college endowment. Only nine thousand dollars more to go before the subscriptions could be called in!

Many of her friends, like Barbara, questioned the wisdom of such preoccupation with a charity hospital which could promise little of distinction or pecuniary success. Why not establish her reputation as a respectable physician in private practice? Because, Elizabeth tried to make plain, this was the best way, not only to serve where the need was greatest, but to further the cause of women in medicine.

"We are now fair average practitioners," she wrote Barbara in a long exhaustive letter explaining why she could not at present come to London, "with rather less than the average medical initiation, but rather more than the average judgment and common sense. It is an important question with us, how to cope with the distinct medical difficulties of our profession and become authorities, instead of having in every emergency to yield to others. We must be able to command all the exceptional and difficult cases. We must be able to say of every dangerous case, 'I understand this fully. I recognize all the symptoms, I foresee the issue. I know all the dangers to be guarded against. I have watched many such cases. The usual remedies are unavailing. I shall now do so and so.' The same with surgical practice. We must have actually done it all again and again in order to be able to speak out with authority. Private practice will never give us this experience. Directly a case becomes dangerous, when an operation becomes necessary, in 99 cases out of 100 the family will call in a man, and they are right to do so, for not only has the man more experience, but more boldness and scrupulousness, and consequently efficiency. The fact is that until women have a very large experience, their conscientiousness will stand in their way, and they will be either less reliable or more reliable physicians than men, for when the conscientiousness is properly supported by thorough culture and practical experience, then they will become the better physicians. . . .

"It is this perception which interests us so in our hospital. We see in it our only chance, the sole way by which we may gain that amount of positive medical knowledge which is indispensable for our purpose. Almost all our own family, almost all our friends, think we are wasting our time and taking wrong methods in laboring so heavily at this poor little lazar house. 'Why waste your efforts so? Push a private practice,' is their constant cry. But they cannot see, how with our woman's nature, our outside professional position, we cannot push private practice as a man can and can never attain more than unsatisfactory results. Last week at the infirmary we had a case of convulsions, of high application of the forceps, and of perforation of the cranium in one of the most formidable complications of obstetrical surgery. Now in private practice the case would have been instantly taken out of our hands. But here our kind consulting surgeon stood by, and I supported Emily with all my power, and she had a grand experience, accomplished it all by herself, and the woman is getting well."

Elizabeth's impatience was mitigated by the satisfaction of seeing progress made in other places. Slowly but surely throughout the world women were following in her footsteps. Dr. Mary Harris Thompson, a graduate of the New England Female Medical College, who had trained for a year at the infirmary and worked with the Sanitary Commission, was able to open the Chicago Hospital for Women and Children in 1865, with fourteen beds and a free dispensary. In 1862 a hospital for women had been opened in Philadelphia, a major step in Dr. Ann Preston's avowed intent of bringing the women's college there to increasingly higher standards. And not only in America! In Russia in 1861 several women students had been admitted to the St. Petersburg Academy of Medicine, though in a separate class. And in 1864 the University of Zurich had opened its doors to women. Dr. Lucy Sewall of Boston went there to study.

But in England the battle had still barely been joined. After five years of preparation for the examinations of the Society of Apothecaries, promised her in 1862, Elizabeth Garrett's efforts to qualify were threatened with disaster. Waking with dismay to the discovery that a woman actually intended to qualify, the society reversed its decision. They could not examine. However, the belligerent Newson Garrett instantly took action, threatening a lawsuit if his daughter was not admitted to the finals. Hastily the society consulted lawyers and were informed that their charter did not exclude women. Faced with the dilemma of boycott by the medical profession or a disastrous lawsuit, the society withdrew its objections while hastening to alter its regulations as quickly as possible so such a calamity could not occur again. Miss Garrett passed the examinations with ease, two of the examiners agreeing that it was fortunate they did not have to list the names in order of merit since they must have put her first. She became the first woman in British history to pass through a recognized course of medical training in England. Her name joined that of Elizabeth Blackwell on the Medical Register, where the two were to remain, the only women permitted (by accident) to storm the citadel, for the next twelve years.

That fall another young Englishwoman arrived at the infirmary, vanguard, Elizabeth hoped, of the band of students for which she was still preparing. Sophia Jex-Blake was darkly beautiful, brilliant of intellect, full of spirited energy, impassioned with the desire to gain occupational freedom. Daughter of rigid and stiffly orthodox parents, she had shocked her mother by her willful and abounding energy and her father by desiring to earn her own living by teaching mathematics in a London girls' school. Honorable and right to work, but not to accept money for it! But somehow she had escaped both, had taught as a volunteer in London and Germany, and now, desiring to start a girls' school of her own, had come to America to study educational methods. In Boston, however, she had met Dr. Lucy Sewall and Marie Zakrzewska and with a tremendous surge of enthusiasm had decided to become a doctor. Here was a cause worth fighting for, a challenge to her restless spirit and overflowing energy.

She spent some time living and working at the infirmary, but Elizabeth could see that she chafed under their spartan way of life. She was not used to sleeping in a garret and eating frugal fare in a basement. But in spite of her temperamental moods, Elizabeth was drawn to her. Here was a bold spirit with a will akin to her own and a toughness far less sensitive to the censure of society.

"Why don't you get together a class of young Englishwomen," she suggested before the guest's departure, "and bring them back when our infirmary opens as a college?"

"Perhaps." Elizabeth sensed a slight scorn in the noncommittal reply. She smiled to herself as the girl added with an airy nonchalance, "I had thought some of Harvard."

She would have been even more amused if she could have read one of Sophia Jex-Blake's comments in a letter home: "English ladies are not given to dine in kitchens and on poor kitchen fare!"

The next year, 1866, brought another "first" to the infirmary. The country sanatorium had not proved practicable, but the Countess de Noailles graciously permitted the income from her fund to be used for another project. One of Elizabeth's long-time dreams was realized in the appointment of a "sanitary visitor." Though antedating the New York Visiting Nurse Service and the Bureau of Child Hygiene by at least four decades, the work of this "sanitary visitor" was but an extension of the education in hygiene and preventive medicine in which Elizabeth herself had been involved for years.

Her function was to visit among the poor, her exclusive object the *prevention*, not the *treatment*, of disease, by the instruction of poor women in practical hygiene. She would follow to the homes of those who obtained medical prescriptions from the dispensary, the prescriptions serving as an excuse for calling without seeming to intrude. Entering into conversation with the mother or father, she would ascertain facts relating to the physical condition of the family. Where there were children, it was entered on the record. In successive calls she would bring up the subjects of ventilation, cleanliness, warmth, food, clothing, making practical suggestions. Sometimes she taught them how to cook or choose food with economy. Sometimes she showed them how to air their bedding or open windows without drafts. Nuisances found on the premises would be reported to the proper authorities. Employment was sought for those who needed it. During her second year 158 families including 332 children were recorded and visited, all residents of tenement houses paying rent of from six to twenty dollars a month.

"Mary G.," the entries would read, "5 children, 4 dead, 1 sick; Mary K., 2 children, 1 dead, 1 sick; Ann H., 7 children, 5 dead, 2 sick; Catherine W., 10 children, 5 dead . . ."

"Children are born to live, not die," was the text on which Elizabeth constantly preached.

It was a startlingly novel program and derided, of course, in most medical circles. But the "sanitary visitor," forerunner of the vast network of district nurses, social workers, public health workers, and a host of other such functionaries, would remain a unique contribution of Elizabeth Blackwell and her infirmary to a century yet to come.

One of these early "sanitary visitors" was Dr. Rebecca Cole, a graduate of the Woman's Medical College of Pennsylvania, young, tactful, intelligent, the first Negro woman in history to become a full-fledged doctor. During her nine years of service, the "Out-Practice Department" was responsible for 10,442 visits, either by the resident physician or by infirmary interns. Later the work would be taken over by Dr. Annie S. Daniel, who for the next sixty years would run the department with what one of her colleagues described as "an efficiency and medical acumen that were an inspiration to those who served in this active field."

This fulfillment of one of her dreams was a highlight of triumph for Elizabeth. But the year brought sorrow as well as satisfaction. When in March, 1866, the news came reporting Howard's sudden death, the two sisters exclaimed almost with one accord, "Oh! Poor Anna!" Concern over her reaction transcended their own grief. For the second time Anna was suffering the loss of her best-beloved, a young brother named Howard. Always lonely, never quite attaining happiness, what would this do to her? Her dream, they knew, had been to make a home someday for Howard, if he ever decided to stay in one place long enough. Her letters, when they came, were as desperate as they had feared — "My darling Howie, my idol, for whom I would have joyfully given my very life!" — more so, for guilt was mingled with her grief. He had come back from India sick, and she, busy with her writing in Paris, had not gone to him. She had not known of his illness, a severe infection which had ended in an intestinal rupture. He had notified her, too late, that he was not getting proper care at the water-cure sanatorium where he was being treated. If she had known, she might have saved him.

Family letters, Elizabeth knew, would be poor consolation, especially those of Hannah, whose rigid creed permitted little hope of future blessedness for a blithe and unorthodox spirit like Howard's. It was doubtful if she would give Anna even the doubtful assurance which had accompanied her announcement of that other tragedy long ago, "*It has pleased God to take our little Howard in the night.*"

"One of us should go to her," said Elizabeth to Emily. "You or I or Marian."

"Not I," replied Emily. "You forget. There are ten years between us, and Anna and I were never close. Besides, my place is here."

Elizabeth suddenly tensed. For five years, it seemed, she had been waiting in trepidation for this moment. The words so casually uttered shattered a silence which had long suppressed all questions like a coating of thin ice. *My place is here.*

"Milly," she said quietly, "this could be your chance."

Emily looked puzzled. "Chance for what?"

"To get away. Give up medicine. Study art, travel. The things you said you wanted to do. Anna could help you at first. She's earning good money with her newspaper work. Think of it — Paris, the art center of the world! You could —"

She stopped, silenced by Emily's look of utter astonishment.

"What an idea! Why on earth should I want to go to Paris and study art?"

"B-But — you said — surely you remember —"

"One says many things. Besides, that was five years ago."

"Then you mean — you're no longer planning to — to give up medicine?"

Emily's features had resumed their usual tranquility, but she kept her eyes averted. "I'm forty years old," she said calmly. "I spent many long hard years learning to be a doctor. No one knows that better than you. Surely it would be stupidity, if not madness, to think of another career now. Besides, I'm needed here."

Elizabeth's bounding relief was mingled with an unwonted humility, like that of a child who has been rebuked. For the first time in their relationship she felt herself pupil rather than mentor. With a gaze suddenly aware of detail, she studied the familiar face and figure with a new respect, seeing her not as an older sister, but as strangers, her pupils, might see her.

"Tall, broad-shouldered, and commanding in her presence," Dr. S. Josephine Baker was to write of Dr. Emily years later, "she was a striking figure, but I think few of us thought much about her general appearance. It was her face and head that arrested your attention. I dislike to use the word 'noble' in a physical description, but it is the only adequate way to portray her face. Her hair was white when I knew her, and her whole personality was so striking and dominant that when she entered a roomful of students, there suddenly seemed to be only one person in that room, and that person was Dr. Blackwell."

Elizabeth should have been satisfied. Emily was not going to give up medicine, leave the infirmary. Her uncertainty and worry for five long years were over. But there was still one burning question. She asked it hesitantly.

"Milly, tell me — are you sorry you chose to become a doctor — like me?"

The reply was enigmatic. "Choice," said Emily, "what is it really? An accident of birth, one's peculiar inheritance, one's set of relatives or friends or circumstances. . . . Who actually chooses the life he's going to live?"

Elizabeth sighed. It was no answer. And the tranquil face remained averted. She could not see if the eyes still held that look of quiet desperation. She was the "relative," the "circumstance" which had influenced her susceptible young sister. Did Emily regret it, blame her for it? She would never know.

It was Elizabeth who went abroad that summer, accompanied by George. She could easily be spared. Emily was the indispensable one at the infirmary, the physician in charge, the surgeon. Kitty was accompanying Harry, Lucy, and Alice to Martha's Vineyard, where Harry had gone first with his Walnut Hills friend Ainsworth Spofford, now chief librarian of the Library of Congress; he had fallen in love with the place, and determined to make it the Blackwell summer retreat. George, now by far the most prosperous member of the family, having shrewdly invested in New Jersey real estate during the war years, always to good advantage, was a welcome companion.

But it was not a pleasant trip. The weeks Elizabeth spent in Paris with the grief-stricken Anna were scarcely less harassing than the dreaded ocean trip. She found her sister as beautiful, as clever, as generous, as obstinate, as impractical as ever, but with each quality more sharply defined by an almost ascetic melancholy. Grief over Howard's death was becoming slowly mitigated by a fresh interest in spiritism — through which she hoped to make contact with the beloved, and in reincarnation, of which she had become an ardent disciple. Delving furiously into the Vedas, Buddhism, Zoroastrianism, the Koran, testimony of Egyptian, Mexican, Grecian, Norse, Druid, and Christian philosophers, she was hard at work on a *Philosophy of Existence*, subtitled "The Testimony of the Ages," in which she was attempting to prove the antiquity and universality of the doctrine of reincarnation. She was also blessed with a new financial security, since she was her brother's sole heir.

Elizabeth passed the time visiting favorite places and friends, and since her eye was too bothersome to permit reading, in renewing her study of music. In England she spent three delightful days in Sussex, where Barbara Bodichon had a charming brick cottage on top of a hill in a thick hazel copse, made trips to Battle Abbey and Hastings and, with George, visited Greenwich Park, where they set their watches by the observatory time and meditated on being at the center of all things. But the four months of her absence yielded little of permanent value. Even Paris, capital of art and fashion, added little to her personal assets: a piqué sack, a colored petticoat, some jet ornaments, a little book of Paris buildings, a fan, a small satchel — oh, yes, and two lessons in hairdressing, a skill which she promised to practice on Emily and Kitty immediately on her return.

But the visit produced one unexpected encounter.

"You remember your old friend Hippolyte Blot?" asked Anna casually. "I have met him and his wife occasionally through the years. I thought you might like to renew the acquaintance, so we are driving to his house this afternoon."

No, Elizabeth wanted to cry out, not that! She felt as if an old wound, long healed and forgotten, had started to twinge. Wordlessly she made ready for the visit, dressing carefully in her best black silk, ribboned bonnet, and shawl, noting almost with surprise in her mirror the changes of sixteen years — the graying waves of hair, the careworn face, the unsightly staring eye.

But she need not have worried. The premonition of pain was an illusion. M. Blot also had changed, become a successful, slightly bald, eminently respectable physician. She had met many of them in her career. His *"Mon amie, je suis heureux!"* was the effusion of a cultured French gentleman, nothing more. They chatted pleasantly of old times, their differing careers, recent developments in medicine. Had Mademoiselle Blackwell been following the experiments of the French scientist Pasteur? His detection of strange living organisms in fermenting wines had led only in the past year or two to the discovery that these minute organisms could be kept from multiplying through a process of heat sterilization. Now he was asking, what about the decay of living tissue, so like fermentation? Was this also the work of invisible evil organisms, these tiny particles called "germs"? Why, there were no limits to the possibilities! Such discoveries might in time revolutionize the practice of medicine!

"Yes," agreed Elizabeth, her keen mind already toying with the implications of such a theory. Those fly-infested jars of milk and spoiling food on tenement sills! Was there an even more cogent reason than she had supposed for their appearing suspect? Cleanliness, the number one tenet of her medical creed! Might it prove more fundamental to health than even she had imagined?

They discussed the experiments of Louis Pasteur as, sixteen years before, they had discussed the work of Claude Bernard, Elizabeth the pupil, Hippolyte the teacher, and in almost identical language. The master, asserted Hippolyte eagerly, was on the verge of a great discovery. It would immortalize him!

Elizabeth was stimulated, amused, warmed by her friendly reception, but untouched by even a hint of wistful sentiment. She liked his polite, intelligent wife, his two charming children, but never once thought, "I might be in her place. They might be my children." She and Hippolyte Blot were two friends renewing acquaintance after many years, two doctors sharing mutual concerns, but not a man and a woman.

5

Kitty was nineteen that first summer she went with the Blackwells to Martha's Vineyard, a sedate young lady in appearance — long skirts, neatly parted black hair drawn tightly back into a braided pug, a few premature gray strands already visible — but at heart still the lively, merry, adventurous child. Under Elizabeth's careful tutelage she had grown straight as a slender reed and as keen of mind as she was quick of motion. A constant, slightly roguish smile saved the thin aquiline features from any hint of sharpness. In spite of their chronic weakness, the unusually deepset eyes still managed to look brightly curious and alert. Also thanks to Elizabeth, her skills were many. She was a good pianist, spoke French almost as well as English, was an omnivorous reader, and loved to cook, especially French dishes. No wonder she was always a welcome guest in the homes of all the Blackwells!

She arrived by the New Bedford boat on a pitch-dark night, and Aunt Marian had a carriage waiting. It was before the days when vehicles had to carry lights, and she felt as if the carriage were driving right into the ocean, there was such a roaring of waves. There was no gate, and they had to climb a five-barred fence. The driver managed to get her trunk over it and several packages she had brought from New York by request for Grandma — a real Cheshire cheese, a box of McKenzie's biscuits, and a dozen bottles of Bass's Pale Ale. Uncle Sam, a strictly temperate man, had demurred at the ale, but Uncle Harry had insisted. Grandma was ill, with a carbuncle on her back, and Uncle Harry would have got her Burgundy or sherry if she had wanted it.

They stayed at Cliff House that summer: Grandma, Uncle Harry and Aunt Lucy, Aunt Marian, Alice and Florence, and two domestics, Mary O'Toole and Margaret Diamond from Gay Head — oh, yes, and a cat given them by Captain Ephraim Mayhew, a tortoiseshell that liked to kill snakes but never ate them. Sometimes he would drop them under the table in the little writing room at the left of the front door. Once, to Kitty's violent disfavor, he left a large brown one in the middle of her bed, but he was an intelligent cat. When she brought him to the place and indicated her wishes, he understood and carried it away.

Uncle Harry had adopted the island with all its appurtenances. In fact, he had furnished the rented house by a form of petty burglary, entering unoccupied houses and helping himself to silver, china, bedding, and other incidentals, leaving a note saying, "Captain Blackwell has taken such and such things." Most of them were houses of unmarried men who had gone whaling. Of course all such objects were duly returned at the end of summer. Some of the things were acquired honestly, like those given or loaned by Aunt Jedidah Stewart, among them Kitty's featherbed and red and green coverlet.

It was heaven for Kitty, if any place could be that with Doctor away in England and France. She had a passion for children, was the idol of all the young Blackwells, especially Alice. In fact when Alice was about four, the two had made a pact to become "engaged," and the loyal friendship thus begun was to last for the rest of their lives. Alice and Florence were constantly at her heels. The three were free to go anywhere and everywhere on the island so long as they respected neighbors' property (more circumspectly than Uncle Harry!). On most such expeditions Kitty wore her gymnastic dress from the New England boarding school she attended, a short full skirt of blue and white check, blue knickerbockers, and a blue blouse called a "Garibaldi." Once when she was climbing a five-barred fence, a voice hailed her.

"Be you one of Captain Blackwell's gals?"

"Yes," she sang back. "I'm the oldest of them."

And indeed Uncle Harry seemed like the father she had never known. He always made her feel a Blackwell, a part of the clan. There was no bell at Cliff House, so he would stand at the foot of the stairs and call:

> *Alicia B.,*
> *Come down to tea!*
> *Florentia B.,*
> *Kitteea B.,*
> *Come down to tea!"*

And, though the B. could have stood for Barry, she felt somehow that he intended it for Blackwell. Uncle Harry made life fun, different from the intense sobriety of the infirmary, even from the beloved house in West Bloomfield, for Doctor was not one for joking.

"How do you cook potatoes?" Uncle Harry asked one day when Aunt Lucy had gone for a drive and he had volunteered to oversee the kneading of the bread and to cook the dinner. "Do you put them in hot water or cold?"

"I don't know," replied Kitty, who sat on the front doorstep shelling peas.

So what did Uncle Harry do? Used half boiling water and half cold!

Then there was the wonderful grape jelly he made to take back to New Jersey. There being insufficient jars to hold it, he bought a number of chamber pots at West Tilsbury and filled them with jelly. "Don't tell anybody," he warned. "When we get back to Roseville, we'll melt it again and store it properly."

Fortunately the two children were not at her heels when she had the accident. She was carrying a pail of salt water up the high cliff path for the use of Grandma when a big stone came rolling down and broke one of the small bones in her foot. But she carried the pail safely to the top of the cliff, hopping about courageously, and no one knew that the bone had been broken until after it had healed. By then the damage had been done.

When Doctor came back from Europe late that year and saw the slight limp and the queer twist to her foot, Kitty thought she was going to cry. It made her conscience-stricken. It seemed that she was always causing pain to Doctor, first the trouble with her eyes, then a bad time with her ears, which had left her quite deaf. And now this!

"And I thought I was going to make you well and strong," Doctor spoke in a tone that begged forgiveness, "and look what I've done to you! Those bright eyes, those swift dancing feet — !"

Kitty tried to make her understand, how she would rather be lame, deaf, and completely blind if necessary, rather than be anything but what Doctor had made her. But it was no use, of course. Some things couldn't be said. Perhaps if she was given time enough, she might be able to *live* them.

Alice lived with them at the infirmary that year of 1867, while her parents were traveling out in Kansas campaigning for equal suffrage, holding meetings, handing out tracts, trying to persuade the new state in its fall referendum to give both Negroes and women the right to vote. Kitty was amused that Alice actually trembled with awe in the presence of the kind and diminutive Aunt Elizabeth, while the far more imposing Aunt Emily aroused no such emotion, possibly because she gave the child chocolate drops.

"I know Aunt Elizabeth is kind and wouldn't hurt anybody," confessed nine-year-old Alice, "and she's almost as short as I am, and yet —"

"And yet," admitted Kitty, "sometimes she can look at least six feet tall."

Kitty was at Martha's Vineyard in 1867 and 1868, but the latter was most perfect, for Doctor was there also. In fact, by now the whole family had made it their summer home, including Uncle Sam and Aunt Nette with their tribe of five little girls, Florence, Edith, Grace, Agnes, and Ethel. That summer, however, Aunt Ellen was in charge, for Aunt Marian had gone to Europe with Mr. Alofsen and Frances, who since Mrs. Alofsen's death had for many years been her special charge. They stayed at Aunt Jedidah Stewart's house that summer, which Kitty enjoyed better than Cliff House, it contained so many lovely things. Especially she loved the delicate cups, of real eggshell Chinese china, without handles, set in deep saucers. Her sensitive instincts were outraged when Aunt Nette made jelly in them.

It was that summer that Kitty felt she had really become a Blackwell, for she became indispensable to its most important member. She was the only one who could make Grandma's bed to suit her. The maid would not put the blankets the way she wanted them. She wanted the blanket next to her to come clear to her shoulders, the next one a little lower, and so on, so she could draw them up one by one if she felt cold. "I want Kitty to make it," she insisted. "She understands."

Grandma was often cold these days and complained of a "niggling" pain. Though her cheeks were still china-pink and her white curls as saucily bobbing as ever, she was getting infirm and old. Not too old, however, or too infirm to keep sharp and wary vigil over her children's souls, especially those of the errant Henry and the suspectedly unorthodox Elizabeth, or to preside over the mysteries of the Christmas pudding. Or that coming fall to anticipate by a little more than fifty years a woman's right for which certain of her children would spend the rest of their lives fighting. Two years later her obituary would include mention of that unusual but typically adventurous act performed that fall of 1868.

"Mrs. Blackwell will long be remembered in New Jersey for her testimony at the polls on the occasion of General Grant's election. In company with her daughter-in-law Lucy Stone, and leaning upon the arm of her son, the venerable lady, aged 74, walked quietly to the place of voting in Roseville, and offered a straight Republican ticket. The Inspector of Election received it respectfully, but declined to let it be deposited in the box."

Though Kitty would spend many months at Martha's Vineyard in coming years, that summer of 1868 was the most halcyon one of all. For, though she did not know it at the time, nearly forty years would pass before Doctor would be there again.

She was beginning, however, to suspect the coming of change. Just when she sensed the slight increase in tension she could not be sure. Everything in the infirmary was running smoothly. Plans for the medical school were progressing. Doctor seemed very sure how everything should be done, and being older than Dr. Emily and the acknowledged head of the institution, she usually had her way. Yet Kitty, whose instincts were as sensitive as nerve ends, sensed that they were not always in agreement. It wasn't that they argued about things, though they did occasionally. Silence could be more pregnant than words. It was something to be felt rather than seen or heard — a vibration in the air as of strings drawn too taut. And then came the conversation she overheard between Doctor and Aunt Marian. It happened in the fall of 1867, before Aunt Marian went to Europe.

Kitty did not mean to be an eavesdropper. She had a horror of such people. She had come in from her singing lessons at the Conservatory of Music and was sitting in her attic bedroom next to Doctor's with the door open.

"If Kitty were here," she heard Aunt Marian say, "I'd ask her advice about this green merino. She has such good taste."

Kitty was about to announce her presence when, to her dismay, the "conversation" started. By the time she realized what Aunt Marian was saying, it was too late. Her hearing, in spite of its weakness, was suddenly all too acute.

"Bessie, there's something I must say to you before I go. I hope you won't mind if I'm perfectly frank about something."

Doctor's voice was an agreeable murmur.

"I wonder if you know, Bessie, how much you have alienated and are constantly alienating Emily. There seems to be something about the way you do things that rubs her the wrong way. You always were very positive, you know. Perhaps you don't realize it, but she always had reservations about your working together before she came to New York. You're such a — such an intense, determined person. She was afraid you might not be able to get along together. I think you ought to know —"

Kitty refused to hear any more. Cheeks burning, she clapped her hands over both her ears.

6

The Woman's Medical College of the New York Infirmary was formally opened on November 2, 1868, the result of fifteen years of careful planning, patient work, much faith, and the long tedious raising of nearly thirty thousand dollars.

"It is an easy thing," said Elizabeth in her address to the assembled group, "to found a poor college. Our liberal legislature grants a charter to anyone who asks for it, and an audience can always be gathered together by speeches and music to witness the presentation of learned-looking parchment scrolls to a class of well-dressed students; but character and diploma do not necessarily guarantee the fitting education of a physician. To found a really good college is a work of great difficulty and up to the present time has been impossible, for want of professional assistance, of skillful teachers, and ample clinical provision. To this difficulty has been added another — the want of funds. People will give to a charity of popular enthusiasm, but very seldom to a principle, more seldom still to such an unpopular idea as the education of women in medicine. . . .

"We are so accustomed to be 'despised and rejected' that encouragement, welcome, success, seem unaccountable. It is like breathing a new and delightful atmosphere, which is, nevertheless, strange and dreamlike; and one almost fears to wake up with a shock, and find again the gloom and struggle all around.

"A weighty responsibility rests on all those who introduce women into medicine to see that they are fitted to fulfill the trust worthily. . . . We propose therefore to adopt the most advanced plan of instruction and have arranged a progressive course of study which will require for its completion attendance at college during three winter sessions of five months each which we hope eventually to extend to eight months."

Then came the most important part of her speech, the oft-repeated statement of her credo: the need to stress prevention instead of cure, the concern women should feel for the frightful mortality among children.

"Did the women of our city resolve to save these children, they might be saved. Year by year the mortality might be lessened by the sanitary knowledge diffused by women — thousands of useful lives saved to their homes and country through this aid!" To implement this concern she announced that the new medical college would become the first such institution in the world to establish a chair of hygiene.

Dr. Willard Parker, the distinguished surgeon who had been a long-time friend of the infirmary, also gave an address. A doctor was born, not made, he reminded, and the natural doctor was common to both sexes. And, now that "woman was taking her true and proper place as co-worker with man, he, in the name of his profession, stretched out to her the right hand of fellowship."

He could not speak, however, for the profession or the general public. The new institution received publicity, plenty of it, from the press, whose cartoonists delighted in portraying women students at work in the dissecting rooms, aprons over their hoop skirts, gingerly carving up cadavers; from the public, still both shocked and fascinated by these new editions of Madame Restell; expecially from the medical establishment, which deemed the innovations of the upstart institution a criticism of the "system." What! Three sessions of five months each, with a plan of increasing to four, when only two, a total of ten or twelve months, were considered quite sufficient for male medics? A chair of hygiene! What on earth was that? Poppycock! The whole idea seemed tomfoolery in this era four years before the formation of the American Public Health Association and thirty years before the American Medical Association concerned itself actively with the improvement of medical education.

But many of the younger and best-trained doctors of New York were willing to serve on the faculty, among them Dr. Albert Strang, the first instructor in anatomy, whose two daughters, Elise and May, were to serve the infirmary for many years. Of the eleven professors and instructors only three were women, the two Blackwell sisters and Lucy Abbott, who taught clinical midwifery. Dr. Emily was professor of obstetrics and diseases of women. Elizabeth, of course, held the chair of hygiene.

Another important innovation of the new college was the establishment of an examining board, exclusive of the teaching staff, one of whose duties was to pass on requirements, long before such a board became a compulsory state measure. The members of the board included some distinguished names: Dr. Willard Parker, first to perform cystotomy for rupture of the bladder and first in America to operate for appendicitis; Austin Flint, an authority on medical practice and auscultation; Alfred Loomis, soon to become the author of the best American textbook on *Physical Diagnosis*.

But of all the eight examiners the choice which pleased Elizabeth most was that of Dr. Stephen Smith, her much-admired classmate at Geneva, now not only a prominent New York physician but one of its foremost advocates and promoters of hygiene. For Stephen Smith also the new relationship must have been oddly significant. At least by now his question of twenty years ago was answered to his full satisfaction: *What sort of woman?* Was it perhaps his respect and admiration for this most famous member of his class which spurred his interest in a phase of medical science the importance of which at that time was either scorned or derided by most of his fellows? For in years to come the excellent status of the Department of Health of New York City would be due largely to his altruistic service. Stephen Smith had been one of the most serious and gifted members of Elizabeth's class. His presence now on the board as examiner in anatomy seemed peculiarly fitting, binding together her first and last achievements in American medicine. For already she knew that the American phase of her life was ending.

"I will remember," Emily was to record long afterward, "the first time the board assembled at the infirmary, the touch of amusement and surprise with which the different members met each other in the novel position of examiners for women students! Also the encouragement our young faculty derived from the hearty and cordial endorsement they gave to the result of our labor when the exams were over."

They had been able to rent the house adjoining the infirmary, 128 Second Avenue, for the use of the new school. There were seventeen students in the first class. Though the three-year course had to be optional at first, a number of the students chose to pursue it. A full year's course of lectures cost $105, plus $5 for the demonstrator's fee. Graduation fee was set at $30 and a matriculation ticket at $5. First-year students received instruction in such elementary subjects as anatomy, physiology, materia medica, and chemistry, with practical work in anatomy and pharmacy. The second year would include full instruction in medicine, surgery, and obstetrics. The third year would continue with practical medical work, including clinical reports on cases attended.

Each student would be expected to perform all the principal surgical operations on the cadaver, under the supervision of the professor and two trained assistants. The laboratory had tables for thirty-six, supplied with gas and hot and cold water. There were two fume closets, slate-lined, connected with the laboratory and lecture room. The students took turns at being apothecaries, making their own tinctures, ointments, and suppositories, filling some one to two hundred prescriptions daily. In place of the compressed tablets bought by the thousands from wholesale druggists, they weighed out and put up bulky packages of simple bitters composed of boneset leaves, camomile flowers, and quassia chips.

"These packages were much prized by our old ladies," reported one early student, "who, after adding water as directed, stored the brew in the icebox and cheerfully drank their cupful three times a day, confident that it removed all ills."

The startlingly novel course in hygiene, begun by Elizabeth and continued later by Emily, consisted of forty lectures, with many practical demonstrations. They dealt with sanitary investigation of air, water, and soil; ventilation and heating; the study of food and clothing; sterilization and disinfection; disposal of sewage; climatology; sanitary relation of habitations to soil, drainage, and general household hygiene; and, even in these early years of the revolutionary discoveries of Lister and Pasteur, with the relation of disease-producing microorganisms to practical hygiene.

To Elizabeth's delight Sophia Jex-Blake returned from England to become a member of that first class, a chastened Sophia who had explored many avenues to her goal of opening the medical profession to English women, with no success. Only that summer she had written a brochure entitled *Medical Education of Women*, in which, after reviewing the history of women in medicine and the achievement of Elizabeth Blackwell, she had bitterly denounced her native country for its backwardness in women's education.

"It is hardly gratifying to one's national pride to find that England has never accorded such encouragement to female learning as was found in Italy, Germany, and France; and it is still more painful to realize that this country, almost alone, stands still aloof from the movement of liberal wisdom that has now in all these lands as well as in Switzerland and even in Russia, granted to women the advantage of university education and degrees."

In spite of her earlier disdain of the infirmary's plebeian accommodations, Sophia managed to adjust to the rather grueling schedule.

"My routine is pretty regular throughout the week," she recorded in her diary. "I go to the dissecting room at 9 A.M. and work to about 11:15. At 11:30 comes a lecture on Anatomy and Physiology on alternate days, and I get home for lunch a little before one. The afternoon lectures begin at 2 P.M. and continue (except Saturdays) until 5, three lectures of an hour each. I have just put in a petition to Dr. Emily Blackwell (who manages everything and is very nice) for a five-minute space between each two lectures, for opening windows and a walk up and down the corridors, to which she instantly assented as desirable."

But Sophia soon had to leave, called home by the illness and death of her father. Elizabeth was intensely disappointed. Regretfully she bade her farewell, fearing this would be the end of her impulsive and tempestuous medical career. "We are so sorry, my dear, not only for your great loss, but for ours. Please — don't let this end your hope of studying medicine!"

The dark eyes flashed. "Don't worry, I won't. I *will* become a doctor yet."

And indeed she would. For, though Sophia Jex-Blake had all the fiery restiveness of a spirited racehorse, she had also its iron persistence once the gun had sounded. Never would she lose sight of her goal. Before the fall of 1869 she had gained admission for herself and four other women to the medical department of the University of Edinburgh, thanks to the support of Sir James Simpson and other liberal members of the faculty, with the proviso, however, that they be taught in separate classes. Later the number of the group increased to seven. But the triumph was too good to last. When it was discovered by their opponents that the female brain was not, after all, inferior to the male and that the women were actually going to stick out the course — one of them, Edith Pechey, even having the effrontery to qualify for a chemistry prize awarded the best student — a storm of opposition arose which shook all Scotland and raged over into England. Unfortunately Sir James died before the real trouble began. Students joined in harassment and heckling. The women were dubbed "The Shameless Seven," and a "Song of the Seven" to the tune of "The Whale" became popular, running for innumerable stanzas and ending:

*Now should the sweet Seven take advice, they'll go for change of
air,
To Middlesex or Zurich, or to any otherwhere.
Or, as Miss Garrett has saved herself from leading a garret life,
So let each Medical Miss become a Mrs. and a wife.
So here's an extra chorus, Boys, for all those students' friends
Who guard our interests as their own and frustrate hostile ends.
Brave boys! With a fal, lal, etc.*

Finally the men students resorted to outright violence, slinging foul
language, mud, and decayed vegetables as the women unfalteringly
moved toward Surgeons' Hall for their examinations. Many of the professors were on the side of the women.

"Let it alone," said Professor Handyside when the students thrust a
stray sheep into the hall during the examinations. "It has more sense
than those who sent it here."

Sophia remained calm and adamant. When the same professor
suggested that he could let the women out the back door, she announced firmly, "I am sure there are enough *gentlemen* here to see that
we get home unmolested." And there were.

It was an ironic commentary that in the same year that Sophia
found closed doors in Victorian England, a Russian lady, Mademoiselle
Kaschewarow, had the degree of M.D. conferred on her by the Medico-
Chirurgical Academy of St. Petersburg, arousing so much enthusiasm
among the male students that they greeted her with cheering which
lasted seven minutes and, placing her in a chair, carried her in triumph
through the hall!

The battle raged. Sophia initiated expensive litigation on behalf
of the women's rights; lost her temper and her discretion in accusing
Dr. Christison, the professor who was the archenemy of the women's
cause, was sued for libel and fined a farthing and costs; did not have to
pay them, however, for friends sent money from all over the country.
Hopes of success flared . . . receded. For years the contest went on.
Public opinion, much of the press, branches of government were all
on the side of the women, yet on the very eve of their graduation their
cause was defeated. Sophia Jex-Blake in her effort to open the medical
profession to English women had lost . . . and won. For the public
had been thoroughly aroused. The fiasco of Edinburgh had made
medical education for women a burning issue. Though it would take

Sophia, the "lion-hearted pioneer," twelve years to finally earn her medical degree, and she would do it not in her own country but in Switzerland, she would achieve her purpose. If the citadel of British medicine could not be stormed from within, she would do it from without. The London School of Medicine for Women, which she was to found in 1874, would be the instrument. Its board of governors would include such names as the Earl of Shaftesbury, Charles Darwin, Thomas Huxley, Dowager Lady Stanley of Alderly, Sir James Stansfeld, M.P. And one of her staunchest supporters and coworkers would be Dr. Elizabeth Blackwell.

It was the presence in England of such pioneers as Sophia Jex-Blake and Elizabeth Garrett that made Elizabeth's own irrevocable decision easier. After Marian's unexpected revelation she had been for a long time uncertain, hurt, and not a little bitter. Antagonizing Emily! But as the months passed and she learned to regard the situation more objectively, she saw that it was so. Emily was the efficient administrator, the clever surgeon, by far the more naturally gifted doctor. Yet she, Elizabeth, the pioneer, the older, the founder — yes, and perhaps the more intractable — was bound, often unwittingly, to assume undue authority. Emily would not protest. She would merely withdraw beyond a slowly deepening rift. The truth penetrated like the first hint of winter cold: *She had done her work here. She was no longer needed. The college and infirmary could progress even better without her.*

She wrote to Barbara about her problem.

"Come to England," was the immediate reply. "You know you always planned to settle here sometime. And we need you desperately. Come and help us do for the women of England what you have done for the women of America."

It was the answer. It dispelled the coldness like the first warm breath of spring. She was not yet fifty years old. She would give the rest of her life to her native country, practicing medicine, yes, but even more important, helping other women to practice it, lecturing, turning her attention to the social and moral problems which had long been pulling at her nerve-strings. Already a half-dozen ideas for lectures and articles, perhaps even books, suggested themselves. She would fight to the death the terrible evils of vice and prostitution, even more firmly entrenched in Europe than in America. She would start a new crusade for hygiene, sanitation, the moral education of the young, perhaps even organize concerned persons into a group to promote better health and disease prevention throughout the country — yes, already she had a name for it, the *National Health Society!*

Emily seemed only dismayed, aghast, at her announcement. No sign of relief, though Elizabeth's good eye probed the tranquil features with merciless dispassion. Could Marian have been wrong? No matter. She had made the right decision.

"But — you can't leave now — with the school just started!"

"*Well* started," amended Elizabeth. "You're perfectly capable of directing it now with all the help you have."

"But — I'll be lost! We've always worked together."

Elizabeth smiled. "And perhaps we will again sometime — in England." But she knew it was a vain thought. "And we'll be working together now, for the same end, the opening of the medical profession to women."

"And you really want to go?"

Elizabeth hesitated only an instant. "Yes." Her voice was firm. "And I couldn't do it if you weren't here to take over. My work here is done. There's something in me, Milly, that likes to start things anew. I guess I was born to be a pioneer."

If she had had doubts, regrets, they were all gone now. She not only wanted to go. She *had* to go. True, she had no idea what the new adventures would hold in store, whether of success or failure. She could not know that she would not only be instrumental in opening the medical profession to English women, aid in founding another hospital and medical college, actually organize a National Health Society, but that for forty years she would wage fearless and often successful battle for innumerable just causes and against some of the most virulent social evils of her time. She knew only that she was as divinely called to this new mission as to the battering down of other walls nearly a quarter century ago. An era had ended, yes, but another was beginning.

7

It was an evening in July, 1869. The heat of the day still clung to the ceiling and walls like a steam compress. The little attic room was stifling. Kneeling on the floor, Elizabeth sweated and strained over the straps of a large box, repository for the leftovers from her trunks. There! Mopping her face, she leaned back and surveyed the piles of baggage. In the morning the dray would come to take it all to the docks. It was done. Nothing to do now but cut the strings of one life and go groping after the strings of another. She felt suspended between two worlds.

Most of the strings had already been broken. There had been innumerable teas and parties given and attended by friends uptown, former patients (already she must use the word *former!*), trustees, physicians connected with the infirmary and college. A constant stream of poor women had come to the dispensary, tearful, chattering a medley of tongues, kissing her hand, bringing all sorts of poor little gifts. Those goodbyes had been hardest, harder even than family, for the strings binding to family could never be broken, only stretched once more to reach across an ocean. Except one string. Looking at Hannah, growing older and frailer-looking by the day, smiling in spite of her spells of dizziness and "niggling" pains, Elizabeth had given cheerful promises of an early return, meekly accepted the last adjurations for the good of her soul, and then gone away and wept. Her one consolation was that a part of herself — Kitty — would be left for a while to help care for her mother. Later, as soon as she became fully established in the new life, Kitty would join her in England.

Harry did not really approve of her going. "Is it possible," he was to write later, "that your transplantation to Europe is on the whole a gain? I shall be at once glad and sorry if so. Glad on your account, sorry on ours. But surprised, for I have not imagined such medical changes so late in life likely to conduce to happiness."

Yet Harry was contemplating plenty of changes in his own life! The split in the women's rights movement was now wide and deep. In 1868 Elizabeth Stanton and Susan Anthony had organized a new body, the National Woman Suffrage Association, meeting secretly and without authority with the express intention of excluding Lucy and all her supporters. Stricken and heartsick, but always loyal to the cause, Lucy had been driven to action. That fall she and her sympathizers had gathered women of more moderate views into another organization, the American Woman Suffrage Association, designed to "unite those who can work steadily to one end, who will not injure our claim by opposition to the Fifteenth Amendment, or chase after side issues." And Henry was as active a participant as Lucy, foregoing his own business plans to travel with her, speaking, lobbying, setting up state and local associations. Already they were planning the founding and editing of a new paper, *The Woman's Journal,* to counteract the more flamboyant and sensational *Revolution,* started by the Stanton group in January, 1868, and subsidized by an erratic and violently anti-Negro millionaire, George Francis Train.

Yes, Henry's future was already set in patterns of increasing change. Within a year he would be disposing of his interests in New Jersey and moving to the Boston area. His name would become as firmly linked with the women's rights movement as his wife Lucy's. *The Woman's Journal,* which they would edit and publish together, would for nearly half a century speak with an eloquent but dignified voice for the rights of women. Not in Lucy's lifetime, however, or in Henry's, would its most difficult and persistent battle be won. It would be Alice, Lucy's equally spirited and dedicated daughter, who would cast her first woman's vote in a national election just fifty years after the first issue of the magazine appeared.

Elizabeth had no dread of change. She reveled in it. It was only in these restless interims that she felt thwarted, at loose ends, like a wild animal shut up in a stall.

Her plans for the future were vague. Kenyon had died in May. She must spend some time with the bereaved relatives, and of course with Marian and Anna. Herman Bicknell, her fellow-student at St. Bartholomew's, had arranged for her to attend the Social Science Congress in Bristol in September. A fitting beginning for a new life which she hoped to devote to social questions of vital importance, and what a place to begin — Bristol! It was like starting life all over again. Beyond that, who could tell? There were Barbara and Elizabeth Garrett and Sophia Jex-Blake, all expecting her help in opening the medical profession to English women. But she was nearly fifty years old. Did she have the daring, the energy, to take up the struggle all over again? Suddenly, almost for the first time in her life, she felt timid, afraid. Life loomed ahead of her with all the menacing imminence of the dreaded ocean trip.

The attic room was stifling. She knew she could not sleep. Tomorrow night, perhaps, and many succeeding nights — if those sickening waves would let her — but not tonight. She tiptoed through the hall, hoping that Emily, who was working on her new course of lectures for the medical students, would not hear her. The farewells tomorrow would be hard enough on both of them without further emotional rapport tonight. Elizabeth still felt guilty leaving her with all the multifold responsibilities: dean of the medical school, professor of obstetrics and gynecology, president of the medical board, infirmary trustee!

Quietly Elizabeth descended two flights of stairs, past the delivery room and nursery, the tiny operating room, down to the wards on the second floor. Nodding to the nurse in charge, she went about among the beds, patting a hand here and there, giving a low word of encouragement, making sure each patient had all the air possible, and feeling all the time a strange sense of finality. Who could tell when she would make the rounds of a hospital ward again — if ever?

"The patient at the end seems fevered and uncomfortable," she said to the nurse. "You might sponge her hands and face with cool water, and perhaps move her bed a little nearer the window."

"Yes, Doctor." The girl's eyes filled. "I'll be glad to. I don't know what we'll do when — when you —"

Feeling the need of coolness herself, Elizabeth went on down the stairs, thinking to get a breath of fresh air on the stoop. But she found activity in the lower hall. A small boy had arrived from one of the tenements saying his mother had "started and doctor come quick!" The assistant physician, with one of the nursing trainees, was getting ready to go out on the case. She looked terribly fagged, and no wonder, after a morning in the dispensary, ward rounds, and an afternoon of calls. Suddenly Elizabeth felt a surge of excitement.

"Let me go," she offered. "Please — it may be my last chance for a long time."

The young doctor was willing enough. Elizabeth hurried upstairs, fetched a doctorial sack and her medicine case, tied on her bonnet, told a surprised but understanding Emily where she was going, and hurried down again.

The small boy was so charged with urgency that he almost ran ahead of them. The young nurse found difficulty in keeping up. Not Elizabeth! Her feet were almost as accustomed to the uneven pavements as to the hollows in the infirmary stairs. These side streets and alleys of the Eleventh Ward traced the pattern of her life for the past sixteen years. She was glad the route took them around Seventh Street, through Tompkins Square. There was the building with the little room where it had all started, the tiny struggling first dispensary. She could still see those timid first patients, frightened of the "woman doctor," yet desperate; the reproachful women crouching on the curb as she and Dr. Zak came late around the corner; the expressions of hopeless despair when the dispensary had had to close; the tearful joy when they had succeeded in raising the necessary fifty dollars to open it again.

The ward seemed to have changed little except for the worse. There were the same molding tenements, refuse-strewn alleys, swarming ragged children, family groups huddled on their stoops in the half-light of the dim streetlamps, the same stench of slaughterhouses. The sixteen years might never have been. No, not quite. For as she passed, even in the dim light she was recognized.

"Look, it's Doctor!" "Heaven bless you, *Fräulein!*" A woman with a beaming face and a healthy child at her breast came down her steps to greet her. "See, Doctor! My others all die, but this one live well, thanks to you and your hospital!" A child with a cleaner face than the others ran up and shyly touched her hand.

They climbed the stairs to the top floor of a dingy tenement. Not in a cellar this time, but in an attic! The last flight, unlike the others, was clean and unlittered. She entered a room lighted by a single gas jet. Unlike most tenement rooms, it smelled clean and well-scrubbed. The windows were open wide, letting in all the fresh air possible. The food containers on the sills were covered. There were several children, all younger than the boy who had brought them, and all, Elizabeth noted in her first swift glance, looked clean and fairly healthy. A man came forward, face distorted as much by relief as by anxiety.

"Ah, Doctor — you come! Thank heaven! My wife — bed — I make all ready, like Negro lady said — much hot water, clean cloths —"

Elizabeth donned her doctorial sack, washed in the basin brought by the clumsy laborer's hands, entered the one adjoining room, issued a few concise directions to the nurse and the distraught husband, and set herself, like myriads of far less expert and qualified women before her to that peculiarly feminine function of helping to bring a new human being into the world. It was not a difficult birth. The sanitary visitor had done her work well. But it was near midnight when Elizabeth was ready to leave, the mother resting comfortably, the new son squalling lustily, washed but unconfined by traditional tight swaddlings, in his basket. The young nurse would stay with the patient at least until morning.

Elizabeth walked home alone through the deserted streets, as she had done innumerable times before. She felt almost as drained of creative energy as if she herself had given birth, yet deeply content. Could she have chosen any act of fulfillment for this last night of a completed portion of her life, she would have chosen this. As usual, she walked without the slightest fear. Once a man moved out of the shadows, seemed about to accost her; then as she walked steadily into the circle of a street lamp, he saw her face and with a mumbled apology stepped aside. A burly policeman spied her, moved forward belligerently, swinging his club.

"You there — woman — don't you know I won't have no damned streetwalkers . . . saints forgive, ma'am, it's you, the little doctress! Pardon *me!* But it's late, ma'am. Hadn't I best walk you home?"

"Thank you, officer, no. I'll be quite all right."

She walked swiftly until she came in sight of the infirmary. There, about a block away, she stopped and drew back into the shadow of a building. Good to take her farewell of it like this! There would be little time tomorrow. There it was, the only tangible fruit of her long and difficult travail. The rest was in human lives — newborn mites such as she had just left, a few children with cleaner, healthier bodies and women with brighter faces, some students for whom she had perhaps made the way a bit easier.

She stood looking at it, the set of high narrow buildings with their four tiers of windows, the wards' faint glimmers, one brighter slit beneath the roof where Emily still worked, another in the adjoining house where a medical intern was burning the midnight oil. When after tomorrow would she see it again? And how long would it remain? Ten years? Twenty? Perhaps even forty? She laughed at such brash optimism, then dizzily ventured further into space. Might as well wish for the stars while about it! *A hundred?*

Ten, yes. Twenty. And forty. Through four decades she was to follow all the details of its remarkable growth with an intense wonder and interest, like a mother learning of the incredible exploits of a gifted absent child. But always in her mind's eye only, for after tomorrow she would never see the infirmary again.

However, her mind's eye had always been by far the keener. With it she would see both infirmary and college steadily expand to meet the increasing needs of both patients and students, outgrow the present buildings; see the hospital move in just six years to a new site at Livingston Place, far more pleasant, with Stuyvesant Park in front, a large yard and open square to the rear, into a big spacious house which could accommodate twice as many patients; see the college move to adjoining land eleven years later, in 1886, where a new fine building would be reared; see a tragic fire wreck this same college building in 1897 and within a year a new and better one rise phoenixlike from its ashes. In 1876 she would see the college become second after Harvard in making its three-year course obligatory instead of optional.

With Emily she would rejoice when news came that Cornell might open its medical college in New York to women and when their old friend Dr. Stephen Smith, who was a personal friend of the president of Cornell, arranged for a planning meeting held at Emily's house; when the college, after thirty-one years of service and the graduation of 364 women doctors, turned its students over to Cornell in 1899, having fulfilled its purpose. Yet still, after half a century, the infirmary would be the only place in New York City, except one small homeopathic hospital, where poor women could be treated by physicians of their own sex.

She who had helped the infirmary and college instigate so many "firsts" — first to train nurses, to supply a "sanitary visitor," to create a chair of hygiene in a medical college, to set up an examining board independent of the teaching staff, to train the first woman Negro doctor, Rebecca Cole — would exult as through the years they reported other "firsts." Some would come in her lifetime, others later: first to require a four-year course of study; first to create an "out-practice department" to give medical treatment in homes; first to use X-ray to discover a foreign substance in the human body; and — still farther in the future — first cancer prevention clinic and first department for the treatment of cancer by women.

But it would always be the out-practice department, extension of her own "sanitary visitor," which would intrigue her most. When Dr. Annie S. Daniel would take over the work in 1881, to pursue it for the next sixty years, making over ten thousand visits in seven years, Elizabeth would follow her with pained nostalgia: climbing the four to six stories of the rotting tenements, some housing as many as one thousand immigrants in indescribable congestion, often walking six miles a day; carrying chicken legs and other tidbits to replenish bare cupboards; bravely coping with the economic tragedies of the nineties, with their evils of home manufacturing — a child of three suffering from pneumonia forced to string beads, a twelve-year-old girl and her ten-year-old brother finishing pants at six cents a pair, the average wage per week of the workingman only six dollars; teaching the pupils who accompanied her to make meticulous reports, face death, meet emergencies, arrange for funerals, hunt jobs, as well as heal the sick.

With another member of the out-practice staff, Dr. Sarah McNutt, Elizabeth would rush in imagination through the streets, clutching her instruments, in wake of a boy whose brother was choking to death; would kneel beside his straw pallet, depress his tongue, see the "great black mass filling the passage"; seize her knife and cut quickly; then as the youth fell forward, endure an agony of fear lest the carotid artery had been cut.

"For an instant I saw the rope dangling before me." Reading the report, Elizabeth would agonize with her. "But it was only an instant, for my finger was on his pulse, and I recognized that the beat was regular and forceful, that his black face was becoming red as air rushed into his lungs."

With other graduates of the institution Elizabeth would also identify: Dr. Mary Putnam (later married to Dr. Abraham Jacobi, father of American pediatrics), who, returning from the École de Médecin in Paris, would give the infirmary and college twenty-six years of distinguished service; Dr. Elizabeth Cushier, who, after study in Zurich and Vienna, would serve as attending and consulting surgeon, achieving an outstanding reputation in surgery and gynecology; Dr. Gertrude Kelly, who would direct surgery for many years; Dr. Martha Wollstein, head of the department of pathology, who was to publish a monograph on *Congenital Tumors in Infants* which would form the basis of reclassification of this type of neoplasm; Dr. S. Josephine Baker, graduate of 1898, who would pursue a distinguished career in public health, serving as director of the Bureau of Child Hygiene, a model for the future Children's Bureau in the Federal Department of Health, Education, and Welfare; Elizabeth's own nieces Edith and Ethel, Sam's children, who would graduate in 1891 and 1895.

And of course Emily, always Emily, guiding the institution through all its many crises with consummate skill, dignity, and superb poise. It would be her quiet efficient leadership that placed the New York Infirmary and College in the front rank of medical institutions in the country in the thoroughness of its instruction, that would inspire one of her associates, Dr. Gertrude B. Kelly, to say, "I have never known a man or woman with a clearer brain, a sounder judgment, a wider outlook, a more wholehearted dedication than had Dr. Emily Blackwell."

Nor could any tribute to her service be more significant than that which Dr. Stephen Smith would give at her memorial service forty years later.

"For upwards of a score of years I was one of the Committee of Examiners of the graduating classes and was at the same time a professor in another college where only men were admitted. As to the qualifications of the two classes, both technical and practical, the graduating classes of the women's school averaged the highest. I may say that the best-qualified medical graduate whom I ever examined was a young Chinese woman educated at this school."

Elizabeth stood very straight in the shadows. Already, it seemed, she could compass the forty years with her mind's eye.

And the hundred? A pity that she would never see them also — the ten-story building of shining whiteness erected in 1954 on the site at Stuyvesant Square, filling a whole block, its twelve-story counterpart, opened in 1965, just across the way in Fifteenth Street! How she would have exulted in all the reception rooms, wards (none containing more than four beds), delivery rooms and nurseries, gleaming antiseptic operating theaters, efficient laboratories, scientific kitchens and cafeterias, pathological museum, well-stocked library, apartments for staff and students, many of them from far countries serving under scholarships from the United Nations, departments with strange names yet with functions not at all strange to her vigorous imagination — pediatrics, physical medicine and rehabilitation, anesthesiology, psychiatry, neurology, cardiology, radiology — social work agencies, clinics!

Especially the clinics, for in many of them she would recognize the outgrowths of her own intense concerns, education in hygiene, prevention rather than cure, lowered mortality in childbirth, the conviction that "children are born to live, not die." They would have marched before her vision like the fulfillment of all her dreams: the clinic of "preventive therapy," the child guidance clinic, a psychiatric clinic for babies; the Strang Tumor Clinic opened in 1933 as the result of the outstanding work in pathology of Dr. Elise Strang L'Esperance, to be followed in 1937 by the first clinic in the world devoted to the prevention of cancer; the adolescent clinic established in 1941, supplemented later by a language diagnostic clinic, a remedial reading clinic, all ministering to the child's physical, mental, and emotional needs.

And then, to crown it all, the choice of her New York Infirmary in 1968 as the "back-up hospital" for the Northeast Neighborhood Association, an exciting pioneer project of more than seven thousand families living in the Lower East Side of New York uniting in a group plan to provide medical care and education to their whole overcrowded, underprivileged community complex!

Yet perhaps she did see them, vaguely, like the substance of a dream, for it was on the foundation of her own dreams that the structure had been built. Perhaps she even looked beyond to greater dreams, seeing that with the critical dearth of doctors a hundred years later, at least forty thousand, and the shortage of perhaps four hundred thousand hospital beds, the New York Infirmary would be in a unique position to help meet these needs, assuring qualified women in medicine an equal opportunity to train and serve with men.

To only one detail in that long sequence of the future would she have given scant significance: that all the vast complex of achievement resulted from the work of one small persistent dedicated woman!

"Ah, and what about women in medicine?" Elizabeth would be sure to wonder on that night in 1869. "What will be their status ten, twenty — yes, a hundred years from now?"

In her own lifetime she would see many developments. By 1889 there would be three thousand women doctors in the United States, by 1896 over forty-five hundred. By the turn of the century the medical departments of fourteen state universities and many other schools, including Johns Hopkins University School of Medicine in Baltimore and the Cornell University Medical College in New York City, would be admitting women students on the same terms as men. By 1900 there would be about seven thousand women physicians and surgeons in the country.

And in fifty years, seventy, a hundred? Not until 1945 would Harvard break its traditions of 163 years and admit women to its medical school. A year earlier, 1944, *Time* magazine would report: "U.S. prejudice against women in medicine is still evident. The percentage of women doctors in the U.S. is 5 percent, as against 17 percent in Britain." Only 6 percent of the students of the United States medical schools would be women, compared with 21 percent in Britain and 85 percent in Russia. And there would still be four all-male medical strongholds: Georgetown, St. Louis, Dartmouth, Jefferson. Jefferson would be the last to change its policy and admit women, in 1960.

It would be ninety-five years until the Civil Rights Act of 1964 would officially ban job discrimination on the basis of sex. "Yet job labeling — for men and women only — is still pervasive," a noted woman columnist was to write almost a full century after Elizabeth Blackwell stood that night in the shadows. And the Washington, D.C., *Evening Star* in an article entitled "Women Doctors Lag Behind Here" would report the same old prejudiced replies from a sample of men asked about their attitude toward women doctors: "Women M.D.'s irk me." . . . "Women were created to be wives." . . . "I'm glad my daughter isn't neurotic enough to want to become a doctor." . . . Only 7 percent of United States doctors and 8 percent of her medical students would be women. By contrast, in Germany three out of ten would be women; in the Netherlands, 20 percent; in England 15 percent; in India 25 percent; in Russia 75 percent.

Elizabeth would have been neither surprised nor dismayed. Emancipation, whether for slaves or for women, had always been a slow and painful process. She would have been far more amazed to know that her own small achievement would be remembered, that half a century after her storming of the gates at Geneva her alma mater would be naming a new dormitory for women in her honor; that a hundred years afterward it would mark the centennial of her graduation by honoring twelve of the distinguished women who had followed in her footsteps.

The citation would read: "In recognition of the contributions made by the women doctors of our own country and the rest of the world to the science, practice, and teaching of medicine, Hobart and William Smith College are proud to honor for their own great achievements these twelve distinguished women physicians as we celebrate the 100th anniversary of the graduation of Dr. Elizabeth Blackwell from the Medical Department of what is now Hobart College. Today we honor twelve of her most notable successors, women who have contributed in a multitude of ways to the extension of our medical knowledge, to the arts of medical practice, to the development and expansion of our public health services, and to the constant improvement of medical education. In spite of past prejudice and their many continuing difficulties in attaining professional independence, these women have brought victory to their sex, and we are indeed proud to celebrate this triumph. In the home, in the hospital, in the laboratory, in the classroom, and in government service, these women have brought glory to their profession and inestimable benefits to mankind.

"Nominated by the deans of all American and Canadian medical schools, by several professional bodies, and by other leaders in the fields of medicine, these women have been selected by their peers for this distinction. In the name of Dr. Elizabeth Blackwell we cite them for their achievements."

The twelve were: Dr. Alice H. Hamilton, first woman member of the Harvard faculty; Dr. Martha May Eliot, associate chief of the United States Children's Bureau; Dr. Helen Marion Macpherson Mackay, first woman to be elected fellow of the Royal College of Physicians (British); Dr. Helen Vincent McLean, one of the founders of the Institute for Psychoanalysis in Chicago; Dr. Florence Rena Sabin, first woman to graduate from the Johns Hopkins Medical School and to become a full member of the Rockefeller Institute for Medical Research; Dr. Helen MacMurchy, for many years chief of the Division of Child Welfare in the Department of Health in Canada; Dr. Thérèse Bertrand Fontaine, a notable French practitioner; Dr. Helen B. Taussig, associate professor of pediatrics at the Johns Hopkins Medical School; Dr. Elise S. L'Esperance, first woman to become a professor in Cornell University Medical College; Dr. Priscilla White, clinical teacher at Tufts College Medical School and widely known for her research in the field of diabetes; Dr. Gerty T. Cori, third woman to receive the Nobel Prize in medicine for her share in the synthesis of glycogen; Dr. Margaret D. Craighill, head of the Women's Division of the Army Medical Corps during the Second World War.

Nine years later, in 1958, when William Smith College celebrated its fiftieth anniversary, Hobart and William Smith Colleges would institute an annual Elizabeth Blackwell Award for "outstanding service to mankind, to commemorate the life and works of Elizabeth Blackwell, Hobart alumna M.D. 1849, first woman of modern times to graduate in medicine." The award, a simple gold medal bearing her portrait, would be given each year to a woman whose life exemplified Elizabeth Blackwell's with its spirit of "unselfish devotion, sense of dedication, and reverence for life."

"My picture on a gold medal!" Elizabeth would have exclaimed in deprecating wonder. "A house bearing my name! Citations in my honor!"

And if someone had told her that night in 1869 that after a hundred years she would still be remembered and honored, have books written about her, she would have laughed in disbelief.

She became suddenly aware that she had been standing gazing for — how long? The light in the student's window had gone out, but Emily's was still burning. She chided herself ruefully. Perhaps Emily was not working, but waiting up for her. How thoughtless she had been!

Emerging from the shadows, she moved swiftly along the pavement. As she hurried into the orbit of a streetlamp, a group of rowdy boys passed by on the other side of the street. One of them pointed at her, shouted something, and the others burst into loud guffaws. She did not hear the words, but they aroused a memory. Just so, on another night there had been just such a group, and one had shouted:

"See that lone woman walking like mad!"

Elizabeth chuckled. How well it had described her — still did — always would! *Lone woman.* What else had she ever been, in family, in classroom, in hospital, in profession — yes, even in the world of ideas? And she had certainly gone through life *walking like mad!* Chuckling again, she quickened her steps. She was no longer afraid of cutting strings, stretching after new ones. She was ready for tomorrow.

1910

KITTY TURNED THE KEY and opened the door on more than half a century of memories.

Rock House was just as she had left it. In fact, it had changed little since they had first taken possession of it one day in March, 1879, with snow falling and a bitter northeast wind threatening to shake it from its rock foundations. Most people would have been timid about living in this eagle's eyrie clinging to the top of Hastings' West Hill, with a sheer drop on one side of hundreds of feet. But not Doctor. And not Kitty. Dozens of times in the past thirty years she had been wakened by the shaking of her bed, been lulled to sleep by the roaring and pounding of the wind. Was it living with Doctor for a half-century that made her exult in storms and high places, in walking sure-footed along dizzying mountain paths, battling a gale on the Esplanade with the rollers rushing almost to her feet? But there were no winds or storms today. The world outside seemed as devoid of life and motion as the house itself.

The rooms were hot and stuffy. With an automation born of fifty years' conditioning Kitty hastened to open windows, walking on tiptoe from force of habit, until she suddenly remembered. No need any longer to move softly for fear of disturbing someone's rest. No need of putting on gloves and feeding coal into the grates by hand instead of pouring noisily from the hod! Still full comprehension had not come. She wandered through the house as if searching in all the most likely places . . . the high four-poster immaculate and impersonal under its snowy coverlet; the deep comfortable chair between the fireplace and book-lined wall, an empty dog dish set close beside it, the chair back and seat hollowed by decades of frequent use; the upstairs terrace. It was here in the best-loved retreat, looking down, down over the tumbling roofs and chimney pots to the shimmering harbor with its hundred or more bright-sailed little fishing boats, beyond it the giant bulk of East Hill thrusting itself toward the sea, that she awoke to full comprehension. Doctor was gone.

Until now there had been little time to comprehend. Since that agonizing moment on the last day of May when life for herself as well as for Elizabeth had suddenly stood still, Kitty had been too busy to think. Time had consisted of automatic motion: letters and cables sent; the service here in Old Hastings in St. Clement's; the long trip with the precious burden by rail and steamer to Kilmun in Argyllshire, Scotland; the second funeral in ancient St. Munn's Church; the burial in the "Auld Kirkyaird" where for four centuries the dukes of Argyll had been interred and where Doctor had so loved to walk.

"Either in the Campo Santo of Genoa or in Kilmun," she had once said, "I would like to be laid to rest."

Kitty had chosen Kilmun, where they had spent so many happy summers since the turn of the century; Kilmun, with its sweet pure air, its gales and mists and gulls, its green terraced slopes which Doctor had dubbed the "Delectable Mountains," its Holy Loch glistening in the sunlight. Surely she would rest peacefully there, under the close-cropped carpet of heather and the white stone monument with its Celtic cross and its simple summation of her achievement, philosophy, and faith.

In Loving Memory
of
Elizabeth Blackwell, M.D.
Born at Bristol 3rd February, 1821
died at Hastings 31st May, 1910

The first woman of modern times
to graduate in medicine   (1849)
and the first to be placed on the
British Medical Register   (1859)

It is only when we have learned
to recognize that God's law for the
human body is as sacred

as — nay, is one with — God's law
for the human soul that we shall begin
to understand the religion of the heart.

Love seeketh not her own. (I Cor. xiii:5)
The pure in heart shall see God. (Matt. v:8)

For fifty-six years Kitty's life had been merged in another's. Their relationship had been far closer than that of most mothers and daughters. As one of the Blackwells had once said, she had "fitted into Elizabeth's angles like an eiderdown quilt." Now she felt like that same quilt, suddenly emptied, limp, useless, meaningless.

Yet there was relief mingled with the sense of loss. At least Doctor had lived to see another English spring, the horse chestnut trees come to full bloom, the broom and lilacs in glorious blossom. And she had wanted to go. She had not been herself since her headlong fall down the stairs at Kilmun Inn three years ago. The strong body which in the last forty years had trekked over mountainsides of southern Europe, journeyed tirelessly back and forth between Hastings and London, joined furious and fearless battle over numerous causes and moral issues, dauntlessly crossed the ocean in 1906 for one last Blackwell reunion at Martha's Vineyard, had spent all its vigor. The keen mind had become clouded. She had sat lost in silence in the big chair by the fire or on her beloved terrace, and though her eyes had lighted at sight of a friend's face or the wagging devotion of the dog Khaki, the response had sprung from instinct rather than full awareness. It was doubtful if she had really understood when Kitty had read her Alice's letter of a year ago telling of Henry's death. Outliving Lucy by sixteen years, he had continued to battle for women's independence and human rights until the last.

"He lived with protest on his lips," Alice had written, "and resistance in his will, against everything that harmed or hindered humanity."

There were few Blackwells left now of Elizabeth's generation. Sam and Ellen had been gone nine years. Poor Anna, embittered and deluded by a fraudulent quest for buried treasure in an old castle in southern France, in which she had gullibly invested much labor and borrowed money, had spent her last years here in Hastings, where she and Marian had maintained separate establishments in a double house in Dudley Road, perhaps a half-mile from Rock House. Anna had been

437

dead ten years, Marian three. There were left only Emily and Antoinette, George and his wife Emma.

Also mingled with Kitty's overpowering grief was a sense of satisfaction and achievement. Doctor's nearly ninety years had spanned an unprecedented development in the causes to which she had given her vast pioneering energy. As one of her admirers had written, "She lived to see the river of her individual life expand into the ocean of a world movement." A place for women in medicine was now assured, not only in the United States but in England.

And here, as in America, Elizabeth had tasted victory as well as the brunt of the battle. She had seen Elizabeth Garrett Anderson found her New Hospital for Women and, accepting Lister's recent discoveries as "one of the greatest glories of science," become a pioneer in proving the efficacy of antisepsis. She had joined with Sophia Jex-Blake and Dr. Anderson to found the London School of Medicine for Women, accepted the chair of gynecology, served for many years on its council, and seen its success finally assured by its affiliation for teaching purposes with Royal Free Hospital. She had shared the triumph of other women doctors when in 1892 the British Medical Association had finally expunged its twenty-year-old resolution barring women members, with only three or four out of three hundred voting against the motion. She had lived to see 550 names of women added to her own and Elizabeth Garrett's on the British Medical Register.

"Scientific work and the study of medicine are now so easy to the rising generation," a young woman doctor had written her in 1895, "that some people are in danger of forgetting at the price of what courage, fortitude, and perseverance they are gained."

Doctor's little autobiography, Pioneer Work for Women, told some of the details of that grim battle. It was Kitty who had finally persuaded her to write it, and after fifteen years it was still in print. But in spite of Kitty's frequent proddings, the last chapter, the story of almost forty years, had never been written. Not in a book, that is. But words for the story were not lacking. They were all about her, here in Rock House, thousands, millions of them, in letters and diaries, in Doctor's writings and lectures, in reports of boards, committees, conferences, congresses. As Kitty in her loneliness gladly plunged into the task of cleaning, sorting, packing, preparatory to recasting her life, she began a long reminiscent pilgrimage back through the forty years.

She was not quite alone. There was Khaki, the wagging, loving, living link between Doctor and herself. In Kitty's life there had always been a dog. Doctor had loved them too, especially Don. "A very gentlemanly dog," she had described him, "with a fine moral nature." She had loved him so much that over and over she had remembered him in her diary.

"July 6, 1897. A year ago I tried to chloroform my poor suffering Don."

"July 17, 1897. A year ago my dear old Don died. How keenly I miss him!"

"July 18, 1899. Three years ago my dear old Don died. Buried dear little Burr beside his father. How we miss them!"

Doctor's love for animals had not been confined to dogs. The diaries bore witness to her long lifetime of sensitivity.

"Aug. 22, 1904. Watched hundreds of sheep driven onto the cattle boat. Dreadfully frightened, poor things!" Year after year she reported shock at this disturbing spectacle at Kilmun.

Was it this love and concern for all living things which had made Doctor such a fervent anti-vivisectionist during the last years of her life, a position which to many of her scientific friends seemed incredibly regressive for such a pioneering spirit? And yet sixty years after the publication of her book, *Scientific Method in Biology* in 1898, deploring the employment of animals in biological research, the Congress of the United States would just get around to passing a Laboratory Animal Welfare Act, an attempt to establish minimum standards for the care of dogs and other animals used in medical research.

But if in this one area her scientific friends thought she had seemed stubbornly blind to progress, in others they knew she had been far ahead of her times. Her battles for sanitation, maternal and child health, elimination of venereal disease and the white slave traffic, sex education for the young, social justice in the relations of capital and labor, reform in municipal government, would be waged far into the twentieth century. As Kitty packed away the numerous books, pamphlets, and lectures which Doctor had written, the titles read like the beat of her small sturdy marching feet. *How to Keep a Household in Health, The Religion of Health, Medicine and Morality, Christian Socialism, Wrong and Right Methods of Dealing with Vice, The Purchase of Women, Christianity in Medicine, Essays in Medical Sociology, The Moral Education of the Young, The Human Element in Sex. . . .*

Kitty's eyes twinkled. What a furore those last two little books had aroused! It had been hard enough to get a publisher to print *The Moral Education of the Young!* Twelve had refused it with horror. They had simply dared not touch it. After reading it, the local curate had refused her request to use the vestry for a lecture. One of Doctor's friends, Miss Shaen, had told her that if she published it she would be the most abused woman in England. But Doctor had cared little about abuse if only mothers would read it! She had finally had it printed at her own expense.

Kitty chuckled as she recalled the reception of this innocent-looking little volume with its frank descriptions of generative organs and functions, both male and female, of current abuses, of physical laws governing passion in women as well as in men, of the dangers of venereal disease, a subject even male doctors hesitated to discuss in medical journals; its denunciation of trade in the human body as a social crime; its eloquent appeal for premarital chastity as the basis of a healthy society. How Victorian bosoms had shuddered, the eyebrows of shocked papas upreared, clergymen and other bewigged custodians of female virtue emitted "Tsk! Tsk!"s of horror! Even the liberal Henry had expressed dismay.

"I read it first," Alice had written Kitty in January, 1883, "then Papa. Then Mamma came to me privately, with wide eyes, and asked me if I thought it was a book which would do harm. That was Papa's dictum, and it astounded her. I told her no, that it had seemed to me very good and sensible. Papa's idea is that Aunt B. has made reference to all the abominations of the continent and that he would not for the world have it circulated on this side of the water among young people, as it might put into their heads varieties of wickedness which they would never think of!"

But there had been enthusiastic approbation as well. The *New York Star* of November 16, 1879, had said of her book *Counsel to Parents on the Moral Education of their Children*: "Coming from a woman, this book is unique, but its testimony is so bravely given, its arguments are so dispassionately and calmly piled up, without even the bias of sex, and its physiological authority is so complete, that it must be welcomed by all sincere moral workers as one of the ablest appeals in behalf of chastity and sexual nobility of life."

Many English papers had approved it. A committee of clergymen had voted the book their commendation, and it had been given wide circulation.

But Doctor had been used to opposition, even vituperation. Delivering a series of lectures on health to a group of London working people, she had been misquoted and slandered by factory owners who feared their employees would become dissatisfied with working conditions. She had been maligned for writing a pamphlet addressed to the poor, exhorting them to stop having such large families. She had fearlessly defied powerful pressure groups by writing of the scandalous labor conditions endured by match makers exposed to phosphorus poisoning, ragpickers, seamstresses shut up long hours in airless lofts. She had championed unpopular reforms like sickness insurance and old age insurance, better housing, cooperatives to help the poor buy food at more reasonable prices.

And she had done more than write books and give lectures. In July, 1871, she had organized a National Health Society, "whose object shall be the promotion of health amongst all classes of the population." For more than thirty years it had been publicizing information on health, holding classes for working women, training voluntary health workers. Here was its thirty-seventh annual report, received the month of Doctor's death, listing as its president Her Royal Highness Princess Christian and among its patronesses and vice-presidents the names of other princesses, ladies, bishops, dukes, and countesses.

There were boxes and boxes of such reports, marching orders of all the social causes Doctor had championed through the years — the Moral Reform Union, the Federation for the Abolition of State Regulation of Vice, the Home Colonization Society (Doctor had remained an ardent associationist to the end), the Christo-theosophical Society, the Local Electors' Association, the Congrès International de Bruxelles, minutes of the local Poor Laws' Guardians (Doctor had been the first woman to stand for election in the Hastings' Guardians, though twice unsuccessful, and she had engaged in active campaigns for reform in the local municipal government), documents on land reform.

Many had been lost causes, or such long-term hopes that they would take generations for fulfillment. But Doctor had been used to frustration.

"The years seem to move more swiftly on as the sands run out," she had written in 1887 to her fellow-crusader Antoinette, "and to me more and more joyfully. The new hope for the world that I see dawning with the advent of womanhood into the realm of independent thought and equal justice makes me very happy.

"And in the midst of the immeasurable woes of society I can work on with unfailing courage and clear conviction that good is stronger than evil, and there is a grand moral purpose in creation, infinitely larger than our tiny intellects can grasp."

Kitty sorted, dusted, packed, nailed the lids on innumerable boxes containing the library of more than eleven hundred books. The letters took longer, for there were hundreds of them. Blackwells were voluminous letter-writers, and no one of them had ever thrown a missive away. Her own correspondence with Alice — her beloved "Pic" — would have filled volumes, for they had written at least once a week, sometimes ten or twelve pages of close, fine handwriting. It was slow work, for her sight was growing steadily poorer, but she scanned them all.

As she pored over the pages of letters, riffled the leaves of diaries, names leaped out at her, many of them already famous: Charles Kingsley, who had called Doctor "one of my heroes"; Florence Nightingale, who at this very moment, deprived of memory, sensation, sight, lay slowly dying; Barbara Bodichon, dead now for almost twenty years; Herbert Spencer, Dante Gabriel Rossetti, Lady Noel Byron, George Eliot, William Morris, the Herschels, Faraday. For Doctor had been thoroughly at home in England's Hall of Fame.

But it was other names — places, people less well known — which brought the forty years alive. Bordighera, Nice, Turin, Lucerne, Zurich, Como, Milan. Kitty could close her eyes and see them all — the cheap little lodgings and *pensions* where they had spent winter after winter following Doctor's severe illness in 1873 which had made a full load of private practice in London impossible; mountain slopes carpeted with yellow polyanthus, blue gentians, orchids; lakes shining beneath snowy mountain peaks; art galleries and cathedrals; the intense ineffable blue of the Mediterranean. She did not need Doctor's numerous sketchbooks of pen drawings to make them live again.

"I can sit here," she was to say long afterward to Alice when completely blind, "and go through all of Switzerland and Italy and parts of France, and through England and Scotland, and look at the scenery all about me."

Other names evoked faces. Some were relatives. Henry, Emily, Sam's children Florence, Grace, and Ethel, George and his son Howard with the latter's wife Helen, had all visited Rock House. Others — the Trélats, Mrs. Butler, the T. L. Brownes who were active anti-vivisectionists, the teacher and reformer Miss Jebb - - had been Doctor's special friends. One, frequently recurring, brought a heightened color to Kitty's thin aging cheeks — Alfred Sachs. He had been one of "our boys," the young men with problems who had seemed to gravitate to Doctor's mother-figure.

"I would like to adopt six young sons," Doctor had often said gaily.

Alfred had been one of these "sons." A wealthy handsome young Viennese of twenty-five, victim of the prevailing Continental moral code which assumed the necessity of brothel patronage for young unmarried men, he had roamed with them the mountain slopes of the Tyrol gleaning from Doctor the advice, both physical and spiritual, which she was so willing and able to dispense, while Kitty, mousy and already graying at twenty-nine, had discreetly walked ahead or behind them, knowing that her presence would inhibit the flow of professional exchange. Only to Alice had she confessed her secret, that she was hopelessly in love with the profligate young Viennese. Doctor had never guessed. It had been the one and only romantic passion of Kitty's life. Now, both sighing and smiling a little, she packed it away with her other memories.

It was a long task. Long before it was completed news came that Aunt Emily had followed Doctor, in death as in life, just three months after that fateful last day of May. In another few months George, last of the generation, would be gone also. But at last the task was finished, the forty years neatly stacked, labeled, and packed away.

What now? Not Rock House. It belonged to Kitty. Doctor had deeded it to her long ago, in 1894, for her security. But — no. It held too many memories. America? Alice wanted her to come and spend the remaining years with her. Later, perhaps, but not now. *Kilmun.* Yes, that was what she wanted. She would take Khaki, the books, the diaries, the letters, all the little personal possessions of her own and Doctor's, like the picture painted by Madame Bodichon of Lake Windermere, and the two other pictures by Faulkner of which Doctor had been especially fond, the *Haunt of the Kingfisher* with its pond and trees and waterlilies, and *Solitude,* with its lone heron rising upward out of a moonlit mountain lake; like the ebony box with its inlaid ivory Apollo driving his chariots on a cloud, given to Doctor in Rome by the United States ambassador George P. Marsh; like the ruler inlaid with Bristol stones which they had bought on one of their rare visits to Elizabeth's birthplace. She would go to Kilmun and live in the two upstairs front rooms which she and Doctor had so long occupied, looking down on the Holy Loch, surrounded by the "Delectable Mountains," close to the ancient churchyard with its simple Celtic cross.

And Rock House? She would sell it, but to someone who would love it and not change it too much, someone who would be willing to have Doctor still remembered by those who might want to visit it. Already her friends were talking of a tablet to be placed on the outside wall commemorating its most famous occupant. Kitty knew the lines she would have inscribed on it, from Browning's *Asolando*, revised just a little. Doctor had loved them, and — none but Kitty could know better — she had lived them.

One who never turned her back but marched straight forward,
  Never doubted clouds would break,
Never dreamed, though right were worsted, wrong would triumph,
  Held we fall to rise, are baffled to fight better,
    Sleep to wake!

Acknowledgments

The author wishes to make the following grateful acknowledgments:

To Mr. Howard Blackwell, son of Dr. Elizabeth's brother George, and his wife Helen, of Cambridge, Massachusetts, for their cordial sharing of family reminiscences, also of pictures, books, and other personal possessions of Dr. Elizabeth.

To Miss Mary C. Honaker of the New York Infirmary office for invaluable help in furnishing historical materials and for a critical reading of the manuscript.

To research experts whom it is impossible to name, in England, in France, and in the United States.

To the curators, librarians, and other custodians of Blackwell papers and pertinent resource materials in many repositories, including:

> The Library of Congress
> The Arthur and Elizabeth Schlesinger Library on the History of Women in America, Radcliffe College, Cambridge, Massachusetts
> The Sophia Smith Research Room, Smith College, Northampton, Massachusetts
> Columbia University Library
> The New York Infirmary
> Library, Hobart and William Smith Colleges, Geneva, New York
> Cincinnati Historical Society
> Central Reference Library, Bristol, England
> Royal Free Medical School Library, London
> Fawcett Society Library, London
> Medical Library, St. Bartholomew's Hospital, London
> Medical Women's Federation, London
> Central Reference Library, Hastings, England
> National Library, Paris
> Library of the Faculty of Medicine, Paris
> Paris Public Assistance Archives
> Woman's Medical College of Pennsylvania, Philadelphia

Bibliography

Adams, Mildred. *The Right to Be People.* J. B. Lippincott, New York, 1967.

Anderson, Louisa Garrett. *Elizabeth Garrett Anderson, 1836–1919.* Faber and Faber, London, 1939.

Aspinall, A. *Lord Brougham and the Whig Party.* Longmans, Green, London, 1927.

Baines, J. Mainwaring. *Historic Hastings.* Parsons, Hastings, England, 1955, 1963.

Baker, Rachel. *The First Woman Doctor.* Messner, New York, 1944.

Bankoff, George, M.D. *Milestones in Medicine.* Pitman, New York, 1961.

Bell, D. Moberly. *Storming the Citadel: The Rise of the Woman Doctor.* Constable, London, 1953.

Blackwell, Alice Stone. "Because These Women Dared." *The Civic Pilot,* March 1924.

———. "An Early Woman Physician" (article on Dr. Emily Blackwell). *The Woman's Journal,* September 10, 1910.

———. "The First Woman Physician." *The Woman's Journal,* June 12, 1909.

———. "Loved the Vineyard" (article on Kitty Barry). *The Vineyard Gazette,* 1934.

Blackwell, Anna. "Elizabeth Blackwell" (letter to the editors). *The English Woman's Journal,* February 14, 1858.

Blackwell, Elizabeth, M.D. *An Era Begins.* Address on November 2, 1868, at the opening of the Women's Medical College of the New York Infirmary.

———. *Essays in Medical Sociology.* Ernest Bell, London, 1892, 1899, 1902, 2 vols. Reprints of previously published writings:

Volume 1

Counsel to Parents on the Moral Education of Their Children in Relation to Sex, under Medical and Social Aspects. Hatchards, London, 1879; Brentano, New York, 1879; George Bell, London, 1913.

The Human Element in Sex. J. and A. C. Churchill, London, 1894.

Rescue Work in Relation to Prostitution and Disease. Fowler and Wells, New York, 1882.

The Purchase of Women: The Great Economic Blunder. London, 1887 (publisher untraced).

Medical Responsibility in Relation to the Contagious Diseases Act. Address to the Medical Women, April 27, 1887.

447

Volume 2

On the Decay of Municipal Representative Government. Moral Reform Union, London, 1885.

The Influence of Women in the Profession of Medicine. George Bell, London, 1889.

The Religion of Health. London, 1871 and 1879 (publisher untraced).

Christian Socialism. London, 1882 (publisher untraced).

Scientific Method in Biology. Elliot Stock, London, 1898.

Why Hygienic Congresses Fail. Address to members of the International Congress at Brussels, September 1891.

———. Christianity in Medicine (pamphlet). Moral Reform League, London, 1891.

———. The Corruption of Neo-Malthusianism. 1888 (publisher untraced).

———. The Criticism of Gronlund's Commonwealth. 1887 (publisher untraced).

———. The Laws of Life, in Reference to the Physical Education of Girls. Putnam, New York, 1852.

———. Medicine and Morality. Reprinted from The Modern Review, October 1881.

———. Pioneer Work in Opening the Medical Profession to Women (autobiography of Dr. Elizabeth Blackwell). Longmans, London, 1895; Dutton, New York, 1895; Everyman's Library, London, 1914.

———. Wrong and Right Methods of Dealing with Social Evil. D. Williams, London, 1883.

Blackwell, Dr. Elizabeth and Dr. Emily. Address on the Medical Education of Women. Address to a meeting at the New York Infirmary, December 19, 1863. Baptist and Taylor, New York, 1864.

Blackwell, Dr. Emily. Public Demands and the Medical Education of Women. Address on the need for opening Johns Hopkins to women.

Blackwell, Sarah Ellen. A Military Genius: Life of Anna Ella Carroll. Judd and Detweiler, Washington, D.C., 1891.

Bode, Carl. American Life in the 1840's. Doubleday, New York, 1967.

Borgese, Elizabeth Mann. The Ascent of Woman. Braziller, New York, 1962.

Branch, E. Douglas. The Sentimental Years. Peter Smith, New York, 1934.

British Medical Journal, Feb. 1, 1902. "Is the Lady Doctor a Failure?"

Brodrick, Hon. George C., D.C.L. Political History of England, vol. 11 (1801–1837). Longmans, Green, London, New York, 1906.

Brown, H. G., and P. J. Harris. Bristol, England. Burleigh Press, Bristol, 1964.

Burton, Hester. Barbara Bodichon, 1827–1891. John Murray, London, 1949.

Chambers, Peggy. A Doctor Alone. Bodley Head, London, 1956.

Children's Aid Society, New York. Annual Reports, 1854–1859.

Cincinnati Historical Society. Historic Cincinnati (pamphlet).

———. Henderson's Historical Sketches, January 1922–June 1922.

———. Topographical Map of the City of Cincinnati. Doolittle and Munson, Cincinnati, 1831.

"Conteur" in Cincinnati Enquirer. "Interesting Facts from a Newspaper of the Forties," August 19, 1923.

———. "Recollections of the Wagon and Carriage Industry in the Early Days of Cincinnati," March 16, 1924.

———. "Sign of the Mortar and Pestle," September 4, 1921.

Daniel, Annie Sturgis, M.D. "A Cautious Experiment: The History of the

New York Infirmary for Women and Children and the Women's Medical
College of the New York Infirmary, also its Pioneer Founders, 1853–1899."
Medical Woman's Journal, May 1939, December 1939.

De Lancey, Margaret Munro. "Dr. Elizabeth Blackwell's Graduation: An Eye-
Witness Account." Letter owned by the Museum of the City of New York,
quoted in *New York History*, April 1962.

Delaunay, P. *La Maternité de Paris*. Librairie Médicale et Scientifique Jules
Rousset, Paris, 1909.

De Sault, C. "Les Femmes dans la société Anglaise: Elizabeth Blackwell,
Docteur en Médecine." *Revue Européenne*, Paris.

De Tassy, Garcin. Letter containing poem by Mir Awlad Ali about Elizabeth
Blackwell. *Continental Gazette*, Paris, 1867.

Dykman, Roscoe A., and John M. Stalnaker. "Survey of Women Physicians
Graduating from Medical Schools, 1925–1940." *Journal of Medical Education*, vol. 32, no. 3, part III, 1957.

The Elizabeth Blackwell Award, Hobart and William Smith Colleges, Geneva,
N.Y., August 1963.

Fancourt, Mary St. J. *They Dared to Be Doctors: Elizabeth Blackwell, Elizabeth Garrett Anderson*. Longmans Green, London, 1965.

Flexner, Eleanor. *Century of Struggle: The Woman's Rights Movement in the
United States*. Belknap Press of Harvard University Press, Cambridge, Mass.,
1966.

Garrison, Fielding H., A.B., M.D. *An Introduction to the History of Medicine*. W. B. Saunders Co., Philadelphia and London, 1929, 1966.

Gillis, Annis. "Elizabeth Blackwell and the Medical Register of 1858." *British
Medical Journal*, November 22, 1958.

Grayson, Frank. "Historic Spots in Greater Cincinnati." *Cincinnati Times-
Star*, December 12, 1932; March 7, 1933.

Guedalla, Philip. *Bonnet and Shawl*. Putnam, New York, 1928.

Haight, Gordon Sherman. *The George Eliot Letters*, vols. 3 and 4. Yale
University Press, New Haven, Conn., 1954–55.

Handlin, Oscar. *This Was America*. Harper and Row, New York, 1964.

Hayes, Carlton J. H. *A Political and Social History of Modern Europe*, vol. 2.
Macmillan, New York, 1920.

Hays, Elinor Rice. *Morning Star: A Biography of Lucy Stone*. Harcourt, Brace
and World, New York, 1961.

———. *Those Extraordinary Blackwells*. Harcourt, Brace and World, New
York, 1967.

Health Bulletin for Teachers, November 1945. "Elizabeth Blackwell, the First
Woman Doctor of Modern Times."

Hughes, Muriel Joy. *Women Healers in Medieval Life and Literature*. King's
Crown Press, New York, 1943.

In Memory of Dr. Elizabeth and Dr. Emily Blackwell. Speeches at memorial
service at the Academy of Medicine, New York, January 25, 1911.

Jex-Blake, Sophia. *Medical Women*. Olyphant, Anderson and Ferrier, Edinburgh, 1886.

Johnson, Oliver. *William Lloyd Garrison and his Times*. Houghton Mifflin,
Boston, 1885.

Johnston, Malcolm Sanders. *Elizabeth Blackwell and Her Alma Mater: The
Story in the Documents*. W. F. Humphrey Press, Geneva, N.Y., 1947.

Journal of the American Medical Association, December 16, 1961. "The Lady Doctor from Geneva."

Journal of the American Medical Women's Association, March 1949. "Centennial of a Trail Blazer: Elizabeth Blackwell, First Woman Doctor."

Kerr, Laura. *Dr. Elizabeth.* Thomas Nelson, New York, 1946.

Klein, Benjamin F. *Cincinnati Souvenir.* Cincinnati Historical Society, 1960.

Langdon, W. C. *Everyday Things in American Life.* Scribner's, New York, 1937.

Leymaster, Glen R., M.D. "An Answer: A National Center for Medical Education for Women — Forecast or Fantasy?" *American Medical Women's Association Magazine,* April 1965.

The Liberator, March 14, 1851. Article about Miss Harriot K. Hunt.

Lovejoy, Esther Pohl. *Women Doctors of the World.* Macmillan, New York, 1957.

Lowther, Florence DeL., Ph.D., and Helen R. Downes, Ph.D. "Women in Medicine." *Journal of the American Medical Association,* October 13, 1945.

MacDougall, Elizabeth. *St. Munn's Church, Kilmun, and the Holy Loch District* (unannotated pamphlet).

Macfarlane, Catharine, M.D. "A Challenge: Cherchez les Femmes." *American Medical Women's Association Journal,* April 1965.

Manchee, Thomas John. *The Origin of the Riots of Bristol.* Simpkin and Marshall, London (undated).

Manton, Jo. *Elizabeth Garrett Anderson.* Methuen, London, 1965.

Martindale, Dr. Louise. Pamphlet telling of the finding of a memorial tablet formerly on Rock House, Hastings.

McCormack, Patricia. "Women Doctors Lag Behind Here." *Washington Evening Star,* September 18, 1969.

McCormick, Elsie. "Trail Blazer in Medicine." *Reader's Digest,* November 1948.

Mead, Kate C., M.D. "The Seven Important Periods in the Evolution of Women in Medicine." *Bulletin, Woman's Medical College of Pennsylvania,* vol. 81, no. 3, January 1931.

Medical Woman's Journal, January 1926. "Elizabeth Blackwell, M.D."

Merrill, Walter M. *Against Wind and Tide: A Biography of William Lloyd Garrison.* Harvard University Press, Cambridge, Mass., 1963.

Mesnard, Dr. Elise-Marie. *Miss Elizabeth Blackwell et Les Femmes Médécins.* Imprimerie G. Gounouilhou, Bordeaux, 1889.

Moral Reform Union. *Fifth Report,* April 3, 1886, to April 27, 1887.

Mosher, Eliza M., M.D. "Elizabeth Blackwell." *Woman's Medical Journal,* October 1910.

Muzzey, David Saville. *United States of America,* vol. 1. Ginn, New York, 1922.

National Health Society. *First Annual Report,* June 12, 1873.

Neatby, William Blair, M.A. *A History of the Plymouth Brethren.* Hodder and Stoughton, London, 1902.

New York Herald Tribune. April 8, 1956: "A Century and a Half of Medicine in the City of New York." April 18, 1943: "Courage and Service."

New York Infirmary Publications, including: *Annual Reports,* 1858–1868; Biographies of Early Trustees (mimeographed sheets); *New York Infirmary, 1949: New York Dispensary, 1790–1949* (booklet published with annual report, 1949); *New York Infirmary: A Century of Devoted Service, 1854–1954.*

New York Journal of Commerce, 1849. Letter from Paris correspondent telling of Elizabeth Blackwell's arrival in Paris.

New York Times, June 2, 1910. "Dr. Elizabeth Blackwell."

Ostler, Fred J. "America's First Woman Doctor." *Coronet,* February 1949.

Paget, Sir James. *Memoirs and Letters.* Longmans, London, 1901.

Ross, Ishbel. *Child of Destiny: The Life Story of the First Woman Doctor.* Harper, New York, 1949.

Sanitary Commission, *Report No. 32.* Concerning the Woman's Central Association of Relief at New York to the U.S. Sanitary Commission at Washington. October 12, 1861.

Scarlett, Earle P., M.D., F.R.C.P. "One Hundred Years of Medical Progress." In collection of essays for the Centennial Volume of the Royal Canadian Institute, Toronto, Canada, 1949.

Scope Weekly, London, February 11, 1959. "Medical Distaff: First Registered Woman M.D. Honored in Britain."

Sinclair, Andrew. *The Emancipation of the American Woman.* Harper and Row, New York, 1965.

Small, Edwin W. and Miriam R. "Prudence Crandall, Champion of Negro Education." *New England Quarterly,* December 1944.

Smith, Stephen, M.D. "Medical Coeducation of the Sexes." *The Philanthropist,* August 1892.

Tabor, Margaret E. *Elizabeth Blackwell: The First Medical Woman.* Sheldon Press, London; Macmillan, New York, 1925.

Thomas, Benjamin P. *Theodore Weld.* Rutgers University Press, New Brunswick, N.J., 1950.

Thorwald, Jürgen. *The Century of the Surgeon.* Pantheon Books, New York, 1956, 1957.

Time, October 9, 1944. "Medicine: Daughters for Harvard."

The Times, London, June 2, 1910. "Dr. Elizabeth Blackwell."

Titres, Services, et Notices Analytiques de M. H. Blot. Martinet, Paris, 1862.

Todd, Margaret. *Sophia Jex-Blake.* Macmillan, London, 1918.

Vaughan, E. "The Early Days of Elizabeth Blackwell." *Fortnightly Review,* November 1, 1913.

Vietor, Agnes S., M.D., F.A.C.S. *A Woman's Quest: The Life of Marie Zakrzewska.* Appleton, New York and London, 1924.

Wagenknecht, Edward. *Harriet Beecher Stowe: The Known and the Unknown.* Oxford University Press, New York, 1965.

Whittier, Isabel. *Dr. Elizabeth Blackwell: The First Woman Doctor.* Brunswick Publishing Company, Brunswick, Maine, 1961.

Wilson, Robert. *Aesculapia Victrix.* Reprinted from *Edinburgh Review,* January 1888, Chapman and Hall, London.

Woodham-Smith, Cecil. *Florence Nightingale.* Fontana Books, London, 1964.

Woody, Thomas. *A History of Women's Education in the United States.* Science Press, New York, 1929.

Woolf, Virginia. *Three Guineas.* Hogarth Press, London, 1938.

———. *A Room of One's Own.* Harcourt, Brace, New York, 1929.

Young, Agatha. *The Women and the Crisis: Women of the North in the Civil War.* McDowell, Obolensky, New York, 1959.

LONE WOMAN

Most of the Blackwell family papers are located in two repositories: the Library of Congress, Washington, D.C., and the Arthur and Elizabeth Schlesinger Library on the History of Women in America, Radcliffe College, Cambridge, Massachusetts. Other letters and documents may be found in Fawcett Library, London; Sophia Smith Research Room, Smith College, Northampton, Massachusetts; Library of Hobart and William Smith Colleges, Geneva, New York; Boston Public Library; New York Infirmary; Medical Library, St. Bartholomew's Hospital, London; Royal Free Medical School Library, London. The Bodichon letters are in the Columbia University Library, New York.

Family letters are too numerous to catalogue here individually; the following are mere suggestions of the voluminous source materials:

Blackwell, Anna

Letter to Henry on reminiscences.
Letters to family, especially from France.
"A Strange Story," written from Nice, 1889, telling details of her search for buried treasure at Triel.

Blackwell, Alice Stone

Innumerable letters, especially to Kitty Barry.
Interview with Antoinette Brown Blackwell, containing memoirs of latter.

Blackwell, Elizabeth

Diaries for 1836–1839, 1875–1908.
Sketchbook, 1875.
Diploma from Geneva Medical College, original in Queen Margaret College, Glasgow; facsimile in Geneva, New York.
Passports and naturalization papers.
Ship Fever, paper written on experiences at Blockley Almshouse for graduation thesis.
Notes on patients at St. Bartholomew's Hospital, London, 1850.
Correspondence with Lady Noel Byron, 1851–1859.
Correspondence with Barbara Bodichon, 1855–1869.
Correspondence with friends, including the Countess de Noailles, Florence Nightingale, George Eliot, Mrs. Russell Gurney, Emma Willard, Elizabeth Garrett Anderson, Marie Zakrzewska, Mary Putnam Jacobi.
Hundreds of letters to and from members of the family: Hannah, Anna, Marian, Sam, Henry, Emily, Ellèn, George, Kitty, Lucy, Nette, etc.
Christmas Annuals, 1844–1845, 1847–1849.

Blackwell, Ellen

Diary, 1852.
Family letters.

Blackwell, Emily

Diaries, 1851–1853, 1855.
Family letters.

Blackwell, Hannah

Letters to Henry, Elizabeth, brother Charles.

Blackwell, Henry

Diaries, 1845–1846.
Autobiography, transcribed by Alice Stone Blackwell.
Letters to Hannah, Sam, Elizabeth.

Blackwell, Kitty Barry

Reminiscences taken down by Alice Stone Blackwell, from her dictation.
Voluminous correspondence with Alice Stone Blackwell.
Correspondence concerning last days and burial of Elizabeth.
Business notations, household details, and other family correspondence.

Blackwell, Samuel

Two Years in New York, letter to friends in Bristol.

Blackwell, Samuel Charles

Diaries, 1836–1837, 1840–1851, 1853.
Family letters.

Geneva Medical College

Elizabeth Thalman, letter to Mrs. Limbosch describing curriculum of Geneva Medical College in 1848. Library, Hobart and William Smith Colleges, Geneva, N.Y. March 5, 1948.

Index

Abbott, Dr. Lucy, 401, 416
Adams, Charles Francis, 351
Agassiz, Jean Louis Rodolphe, 190
Agnodice (Athenian midwife), 139
Alcott, Louisa May, 384
Alofsen family, 61, 306, 326; Frances, 413
Anderson, Elizabeth Garrett. See Garrett, Dr. Elizabeth
Anthony, Susan B., 177, 327, 423
Asheville, N.C., 130
Aspasia (early physician), 139

Bacon, Roger, Essays, 68
Bacon, Dr. S. Josephine, 407, 429
Baltimore Sun, 164
Barry, Katharine (Kitty), 317–320; description, 317, 334–336, 391, 392, 409; childhood, 345–352; in Paris, 356; in London, 363–365; and dogs, 363, 365, 439; eye weakness, 365; at Martha's Vineyard, 409–414; at Rock House, Hastings, 435–444; and Alice Stone Blackwell, 442
Barton, Clara, 384
Beecher, Catherine, 102, 103
Beecher, Henry Ward, 92, 115, 338, 382
Beecher, Harriet. See Stowe, Harriet Beecher

Beecher, Lyman, 85, 92, 114, 115
Bellows, Dr. Henry, 286, 385, 386
Benedict, Dr. (Philadelphia), 167, 173
Bennett, James Gordon, 338
Bernard, Claude, 219, 220, 240
Bickerdyke, Mary Ann, 384
Bicknell, Herman, 390, 391, 424
Birmingham, England, 198, 199
Blackstone, Judge William, 96
Blackwell, Agnes (daughter of Sam), 413
Blackwell, Alice Stone (daughter of Henry), 346, 410–412, 424
Blackwell, Ann (aunt), 11, 13, 14, 26, 41, 43, 44
Blackwell, Anna (sister): childhood in England, 11, 14–17, 21–23, 25, 30, 34–38, 41, 42, 46; appearance, 12, 90, 268, 352, 407; personality, 13, 23, 35, 46, 49, 60, 75, 90, 99, 104, 196, 207, 233, 353, 407, 408; desire for gentility, 13, 60, 75, 90; emotionalism, 23, 35, 49; belief in spiritualism, 23, 92, 408; love of books, 25; trip to London, 43; youth in America, 49, 53, 54, 57, 59, 60, 64–66, 69, 72, 74, 75, 77; school for Negro children, 57; fluency in French, 66; governess in Vermont, 75; in Cincinnati,

457

Blackwell, Anna (*continued*)
90–94, 98, 100, 101; writer, 91,
138, 151, 180, 238, 365, 408; confirmation, 98; interest in "isms,"
99, 104; romance, 104, 105; teaching in Columbus, 104; teaching in
New York, 108; at Brook Farm,
133; translation of *Jacques*, 138;
involvement with Fourierism, 145,
180; interest in magnetism, 172,
196, 228, 233; in England, 180,
196; in Paris, 227, 228, 247; with
Elizabeth during sickness, 230,
233–237; newspaper correspondent in Paris, 238; at St. Cloud,
247; in England, 316; and Howard's death, 405, 406; interest in
reincarnation, 408; pursuit of buried treasure, 437; life in Hastings
and death, 437, 438

Blackwell, Antoinette (Mrs. Samuel
Charles; Nette. *See also* Brown,
Antoinette), 326, 327, 350, 394,
413

Blackwell, Barbara (aunt), 11–14,
17, 21, 26, 41, 44, 48, 52, 56,
62, 93; move to America, 44; millinery shop in New York, 62

Blackwell, Edith (daughter of Sam),
413, 429

Blackwell, Elizabeth (woman of
eighteenth century), 140, 225

Blackwell, Dr. Elizabeth: admission
to Geneva Medical College, 3–10;
birth, 11, 19; childhood in Bristol,
England, 11–44; early education,
24–26; riots of 1831, 33–39 (*see
also* Bristol, England); cholera epi-
demic of 1832, 40; journey to
America, 44–46; childhood in New
York, 47–61; house in Thompson
Street, 52; summer home on Long
Island, 56; later education, 59, 64,
67; in New Jersey, 61–78; New
York fire of 1835, 61–63; trip to
Schuylerville, 65; panic of 1837,

Blackwell, Dr. Elizabeth (*continued*)
73, 74; journey to Cincinnati,
78–82; father's death, 83–86;
teaching in Cincinnati, 88, 90,
93–96; teaching in Henderson,
Kentucky, 110–114; decision to
become a doctor, 119–128; teaching music in Asheville, N.C., 131–
135; first medical study with Dr.
Dickson, 136, 139–141; teaching
in Charleston, S.C., 136–144; in
Philadelphia, 144–152; attempts
to get into medical college, 145–
152; medical college years, 156–
188; effect on students, 155, 163;
hostility of town, 160, 176; subjects studied, 160; press reaction,
164, 209; in Blockley Almshouse,
165–174; thesis on ship fever,
173; graduation from Geneva,
183–188; naturalization, 190, 193;
in England, 194–203; in La Maternité, Paris, 211–235; loss of
sight of one eye, 229–242, 247,
319; water cure in Gräfenberg,
243–247; in London, 248–268;
study at St. Bartholomew's, 249,
254–257, 267, 268; friendship
with Lady Byron, 260; and Florence Nightingale, 263–267, 356–
358; return to America, 266–268;
difficulties of early practice in New
York, 275–277, 280–283, 296,
308; lectures on physical education
of girls, 284–286; first dispensary
in Tompkins Square, 294–296;
purchase of house, 306; becomes
foster mother of Kitty, 317–320,
328, 348, 412; dispensary at 150
Third Street, 320, 321; opening of
New York Infirmary, 330–338 (*see
also* New York Infirmary); in
England and France (1858–1859),
353–372; picture at Versailles,
356; lectures in England, 361, 362,
365, 368, 370; name on British

Blackwell, Dr. Elizabeth (*continued*)
Register, 371, 372; with New York
Infirmary, 374; house in the country, 380; work in the Civil War,
382–395, 398–400; in the draft
riots, 391–394; visit to Washington, 398–400; founding of Woman's Medical College of the New
York Infirmary, 396, 397, 401,
415–418; work in Infirmary, 401,
402; in Paris and England, 407–
409; professor of hygiene in college, 416; decision to return to
England, 421, 422; vision of the
future, 427–434; last forty years
as reviewed by Kitty, 435–444; in
Rock House, Hastings, 435, 436;
death and burial, 436, 437; professor of gynecology in London
School of Medicine for Women,
438; travels in later years, 442;
memorial at Rock House, 444
PERSONAL: appearance, 11, 12,
65, 81, 82, 109, 136, 147, 155,
175, 184, 210, 248, 288, 312, 319,
320, 361, 368, 408, 412; sense of
isolation, 11, 22, 53, 54, 65–69;
family loyalty, 17, 248, 306, 334,
335, 347, 376; shyness, 17, 21, 34,
66, 106, 116, 132, 185, 280;
strength of will, 21, 22, 98, 128,
144, 149, 150, 156, 219, 228, 229,
231, 236, 263, 288; independence,
21, 67, 128, 256, 257, 265; self-
discipline, 21, 35, 36, 64, 96, 131,
134, 161, 175, 230, 277; aversion
to sickness and bodily weakness,
23, 64, 94, 120, 141, 287; physical
strength and courage, 24, 34, 65,
95, 159, 342; love of books, 25,
98; romantic interests, 26, 68, 94,
116, 117, 121, 178, 179, 221, 222,
226, 230, 234, 248, 249, 303, 393,
394, 408, 409; dignity, 159; voice
and hands, 284, 285; taste in dress,
353, 354; modesty, 388

Blackwell, Dr. Elizabeth (*continued*)
PHILOSOPHY, 286, 366, 367,
436, 437; religion in childhood,
28, 29; religious faith, 69, 99, 127,
130, 186, 187, 190, 191, 237, 442;
religious affiliations, 98, 99; and
transcendental thought, 100; and
Swedenborgism, 122; and Fourierism, 145
SOCIAL CONCERNS: political democracy, 31–33, 207, 208, 238,
246; anti-slavery, 48, 49, 54, 55,
57, 69–72, 82, 106–108, 112–114,
132, 292; economic and intellectual freedom for women, 96, 97,
102, 252, 253, 258, 268; associationism, 100, 117, 133, 169, 198,
212, 441; preventive medicine,
167, 173, 174, 180, 284, 415,
416; crusade against sexual injustice, 169, 259, 315, 441; women's rights movement, 171, 258,
259, 297–299, 303, 304, 325, 326,
389; sanitation and hygiene, 173,
174, 223, 224, 257, 295, 296, 341,
345, 404; antivisection, 220, 439;
physical and sex education for
girls, 260, 279, 280, 285, 366;
vision of an ideal society, 262;
improving slum conditions in New
York, 277–279, 294–296; medical
education for women, 355, 362,
396; organizing National Health
Society in England, 441; other organizations, 441
WRITINGS: *Laws of Life*, 286,
287, 365; *Pioneer Work for Women*, 438; critical reception of
Moral Education of the Young,
439, 440; *Scientific Method in
Biology*, 439; other titles, 439
Blackwell, Ellen (sister), 22, 33, 45,
303, 391; personality, 81, 118;
painting, 98; pupil in New York,
118; as artist, 191; in New York
with Alofsens, 248; in women's

Blackwell, Ellen (*continued*)
rights movement, 258; in Boston, 259; studying art in Europe, 346, 350, 351; teaching art in New York, 375; author of *Life of Anna Ella Carroll*, 389, 390; death, 437
Blackwell, Dr. Emily (sister), 22, 64, 80, 81, 109, 247, 303, 336, 414, 442; appearance, 88, 191, 288, 407; teaching in Henderson, 237; struggle to get into medical college, 281, 289–292; character, 288, 289, 310, 429, 430; in Bellevue Hospital, 291; at Rush Medical College, 292; at Western Reserve Medical College, 306; graduation, 308; in Edinburgh with Dr. James Simpson, 310, 311; in London and Paris, 321, 322; opening of Infirmary in New York, 339; first operation, 341; work in Infirmary, 344, 345, 373, 374, 376–378, 380, 381, 392, 393, 402, 406, 429, 430; teaching in Medical College, 381, 424; relations with Elizabeth, 407, 414, 422; death, 443
Blackwell, Ethel (daughter of Sam), 413, 442; a doctor, 429
Blackwell, Florence (daughter of Sam), 335, 410, 411, 413, 442
Blackwell, George Washington (Washy; brother), 48, 109, 138, 191, 407, 408; business in the West, 334; in New York, 347; in law and business, 377, 378; death, 443
Blackwell, Grace (daughter of Sam), 413, 442
Blackwell, Hannah Lane (mother), 11, 12, 13, 16, 22, 23, 41, 48, 63, 65, 66, 263, 275, 375, 410, 413; dutiful wife, 42, 87; cheerfulness, 52, 53; remedy for colds, 53; anti-slavery activities, 57; extreme piety and orthodoxy, 58, 88, 98, 99, 191, 406; naïveté, 60; gaiety and love

Blackwell, Hannah (*continued*)
of dancing, 69; appearance, 79, 80, 89; husband's death, 85, 86; strength of character, 89; on child-bearing, 122; visit to Philadelphia, 150; and Lucy Stone, 302; in New York, 334, 335
Blackwell, Henry Browne (Harry; brother), 22, 28, 48, 49, 54, 58, 60, 68, 79, 116, 123, 180, 410, 411, 442; poet, 57, 297; school in New York, 64; in Cincinnati, 84; appearance, 88, 118; religious questioning, 99; at Kemper College, 103, 104; in flour business, 104, 109, 135, 138; romance with Kate Vail, 126, 133, 138; in New York, 151; sugar business, 165, 171, 172, 174; at Elizabeth's graduation, 182–186, 188; hardware business, 191, 239, 300; romance with Lucy Stone, 239, 298–301, 323; personality, 300; anti-slavery activities, 322, 323; marriage to Lucy Stone, 324–326; economic agreement at marriage, 324, 325; with Elizabeth in New York, 345; in Orange, N.J., 346, 375; work in women's rights movement, 423, 424; in Boston, 424; editor *Woman's Journal*, 424; death, 437
Blackwell, Mrs. Henry. *See* Stone, Lucy
Blackwell, Howard Lane (son of George), 334; at Rock House, 44
Blackwell, Mrs. Howard Lane (Helen), 442
Blackwell, James (uncle), 14, 43, 196, 197
Blackwell, John Howard (infant), 23, 406
Blackwell, John Howard (Howard, Howie; brother), 23, 64, 129, 138, 173; in England, 180, 196, 197, 268; in India, 350; with Ellen in London, 363; death, 405, 406

ıckwell, Kenyon (Uncle James's son), 14, 172, 180, 181, 191, 193, 194, 209, 363, 364; illness, 194, 197; marriage to Marie, 249; in London, 356; death, 424

ıckwell, Mrs. Kenyon (Marie), 249, 364

ıckwell, Lucy (aunt), 11, 13, 14, 26, 41, 44, 48, 52, 62, 371

ıckwell, Maria (cousin), 15

ıckwell, Marian (Marianne; sister), 11, 18, 21–23, 25, 28, 34, 36, 37, 40, 43, 49, 303, 318, 410, 414; personality, 49, 65, 66, 90, 123; appearance, 53, 118, 191; school for Negro children, 57; ill health, 64, 92, 106, 191, 239, 247; teaching in New York, 77; visit to Philadelphia, 150, 151; in women's rights movement, 258; in Boston, 259; in New York, 289, 346; with Alofsens, 306, 413; house in Roseville, N.J., 347, 375; in Hastings, England, 437, 438; death, 438

ıckwell, Mary (aunt), 11, 13, 14, 22, 26, 41–44, 48, 52, 75, 76, 79, 80, 84, 87, 90; death, 93

ıckwell, Samuel (father), 11, 14, 21, 66, 71, 77; poetry, 15, 16, 72; character, 16, 19, 20, 34–39, 40, 42, 45; appearance, 17, 18; sugar refining business, 17, 19, 41, 50, 51, 62–64, 72–74, 83, 84; religion, 17, 19, 28–30, 85, 86; liberal philosophy, 19, 25, 27, 29–31; anti-slavery, 20, 48, 49, 51, 52, 57–59, 69–72, 82; in Bristol riots (1832), 34–39; decision to go to America, 41, 42; report on America, 50–52, 60, 61; in New York fire, 62, 63; sickness and death, 83–86

ıckwell, Mrs. Samuel (mother). See Blackwell, Hannah Lane

Blackwell, Samuel (grandfather), 12, 13, 18, 26

Blackwell, Samuel (Cousin Sam), 14, 172, 267, 268; personality, 197, 198

Blackwell, Samuel Charles (infant), 22

Blackwell, Samuel Charles (Sam; brother), 11, 17, 25, 28, 40, 45, 84, 87, 123, 412; in New York and New Jersey, 48, 49, 54, 59, 63, 65, 68; school in New York, 64; trip to Cincinnati, 79; appearance, 88, 108, 118; studious nature, 88; religious orthodoxy, 88, 98, 100, 101; business in Cincinnati, 89, 106, 165, 191; anti-slavery activity in Cincinnati, 107; in Cincinnati society, 116; romances, 133; visit to Philadelphia, 150; on Lucy Stone, 302; courtship and marriage, 326, 327; business in West, 333; in New York, 334; in New Jersey, 335, 375; death, 437

Blackwell, Mrs. Samuel Charles (Nette; see also Brown, Antoinette) 326, 327, 334, 335, 345, 346, 350, 394, 413

Blockel, Madame (at La Maternité), 211, 213

Blockley Almshouse, Philadelphia, 165–168, 173, 174

Bloomer, Amelia, 177; bloomer dress, 298, 326

Blot, M. Claude Philibert Hippolyte, 215, 218–222, 226, 227, 243, 408, 409; appearance, 215; treating Elizabeth's eye, 229–237; gynecologist in Paris, 236, 237

Bodichon, Barbara Leigh Smith (see also Smith, Barbara Leigh), 348, 349; leader of women's rights in England, 359, 360; concern for Elizabeth, 376, 377; house in Sussex, 408; death, 442

Bodichon, Dr. Eugène, 347, 348

Booth, Mary L., 330, 337
Boston, Mass., 141, 183, 193, 259, 266, 331–333, 375
Boston Medical Journal, 164, 188
Bowne, Richard H. (trustee of Infirmary), 307
Brainerd, Dr. Daniel, 293, 305
Breed, Dr. Mary, 345
Bright, John, 31
Brisbane, Albert, 145, 172
Bristol, England, 11, 17, 19, 424; birthplace of Elizabeth, 11; Counterslip, 19; and slave trade, 20; prisons, 20, 30, 35, 37; landmarks, 21, 24, 35; schools, 27; churches, 28, 37, 38; social evils of, 30, 31; Bridge Riot (1793), 33; riots of 1831, 33–39; science conference in, 168
Brook Farm, 100, 133
Brougham, Henry Peter, 32, 49
Brown, Antoinette (*see also* Blackwell, Mrs. Samuel Charles), 177, 178; in theological school, 178; lecturing in New York, 304, 305; ordained minister, 304; appearance, 305; courtship and marriage, 326, 327
Brown, John, 376, 382
Browne, Elizabeth (cousin), 22
Browne, Henry (mother's uncle), 22, 23, 32, 43, 87
Browne, Mrs. Henry (Aunt Browne), 22, 23
Browne, Samuel (mother's relative), 74, 75, 84–87
Browne, Mrs. Samuel, 74–76
Browne, Mr. and Mrs. T. L., 442
Bryan, Harriet (servant), 44, 52
Bryan, Jane (servant), 17, 44, 52
Buffalo Medical Journal and Monthly Review, 183
Burnet, Mr. (minister from Cork), 18
Burrall, Thomas Davies (trustee of Geneva), 4

Burrows, Sir George (physician at St. Bartholomew's), 255
Butler, Charles (trustee of Infirmary), 307
Butler, Josephine, 169, 442
Buxton, Sir Thomas Fowell, 49
Byron, Lady Noel, 252, 359, 442; visit of Elizabeth to home in Brighton, 260; their correspondence, 261, 262, 282; visit to Kenyon's house, 364; Elizabeth's impatience with, 368, 370

Cabot, John, 44
Calais, France, 202
Calhoun, John C., 137
Camman, Dr. George Philip, 308, 338
Carlyle, Thomas, 253
Carpenter, Dr. William Benjamin, 200
Carroll, Anna Ella, 384, 389
Cary, Alice and Phoebe, 333
Chalmers, Thomas, 30
Chambers' Journal, 367
Channing, William Henry, 100, 133, 193, 259, 331
Charleston, S.C., 136, 137; Elizabeth's teaching in, 136–144
Charrier, Madeleine (chief *sage femme* at La Maternité), 211, 212, 214, 217, 225, 234, 235
Chase, Salmon P., 108, 116
Cheney, Mrs. E. D., 331
Children's Hospital, London, 321
Christmas Annuals, Blackwell, 2?, 134, 135, 180, 276
Cincinnati, Ohio, 82, 84, 91; water front, 82; Walnut Hills, 92; religious groups in, 99; shops, 10?; observatory, 108
Clark, Dr. Nancy Talbot, 281, 309
Coffin, Levi, 108, 292
Cole, Dr. Rebecca (first Negro woman doctor), 405, 428

Collins, Stacy B., 294, 307, 322, 374
Collins, Mrs. Stacy B., 286, 294
"Come-Outers," 99
Cori, Dr. Gerty T., 433
Corporation Act of 1661, 30
Cosmo (ship), 43
Cox, Dr. Abraham, 58, 59, 126, 127
Cox, Dr. Samuel Hanson, 53, 65; with Blackwells on Long Island, 58, 59
Craighill, Dr. Margaret D., 433
Craik, Henry (*see also* Plymouth Brethren), 29
Cranch, Christopher P., 100, 116
Crandall, Prudence, 54, 55
Crane, Silas (president of Kemper College), 103
Cushier, Dr. Elizabeth, 429

Dana, Charles A., 133, 307, 338
Daniel, Dr. Annie S., 405, 428
Darrach, Dr. (of Philadelphia), 147
Davenne, Dr. Henri Jean Baptiste, 208, 235
Davies, Emily, 359, 395
de Charnacée, Countess, 355, 356
De Lancey, Bishop, 186, 187
Democratic Review, 114, 118
de Noailles, Countess Antonin, 353, 358, 359, 369, 375, 404
Desmarres, Dr. Louis-Auguste, 247, 248
De Zeng, William Steuben (trustee of Geneva), 4
Dickens, Charles, 79, 398; *Oliver Twist*, 31, *Pickwick Club Papers*, 68; *Dombey and Son*, 88; *A Tale of Two Cities*, 363
Dickson, Dr. John, 128, 132, 133; Elizabeth in his home in Asheville, 128–135
Dickson, Mrs. John, 135
Dickson, Flinn (their son), 135
Dickson, Dr. Samuel, 135, 136, 140,

Dickson, Dr. Samuel (*continued*) 141; Elizabeth in his home in Charleston, 136–141
Dix, Dorothea, 384, 387, 388, 399
Donaldson, Christian, 191, 239
Donaldson, Frank, 91
Donaldson, Mary, 118, 119
Donaldson, William, 171
Draper, Simeon, 307
Dubois, Dr. Paul, 215, 226, 235
Dudley, England, 198
du Potet, M. (proponent of magnetism) 207, 227
Du Pré, Madame (proprietor of school in Charleston), 136, 137

Elder, Dr. William (of Philadelphia), 144, 165, 174, 335, 338, 398, 399
Elder, Mrs. William, 144
Eliot, George (*see* Evans, Marian)
Eliot, Dr. Martha May, 433
Emerson, Ralph Waldo, 90, 133
Emery, Thomas (of Cincinnati), 88, 89, 91, 93, 95
Englishwoman's Journal, The, 359, 360, 379
Evans, Marian (George Eliot), 251, 367, 376, 377, 442

Faraday, Michael, 252, 442
Female Medical College of Philadelphia (*see also* Woman's Medical College of Pennsylvania), 258, 283, 290, 339
Field, Cyrus W., 307
Field, George (classmate at Geneva), 186, 190
Flint, Dr. Austin, 183, 417
Fontaine, Dr. Thérèse Bertrand, 433
Foster, Abby Kelley, 401
Foster, Charles W., 307
Fourier, Charles, 117, 133, 145, 333
Fowler, Dr. Lydia Folger, 189
Fuller, Margaret, 133

Gano, Major Daniel, 89, 91, 92
Gano, Mrs. Daniel, 92
Garrett, Dr. Elizabeth (Dr. Elizabeth Garrett Anderson), 359–362, 371, 403, 438; medical study, 379, 380, 395, 396
Garrett, Mary (benefactor of Johns Hopkins), 290
Garrett, Newson (father of Elizabeth), 360, 379, 403
Garrison, William Lloyd, 47–49, 177, 301, 302, 401; editor *The Liberator* 54, 55; and Russian poetry, 57
Geneva, New York, 3, 151, 174, 176
Geneva College (*see also* Hobart and William Smith Colleges), 3, 4, 164; early trustees of, 4
Geneva Medical College, 3, 209; student body, 4; courses and facilities, 160; Emily's rejection by, 289
George IV of England, 32
Gérardin, Dr. Nicolas-Vincent Auguste, 215
Gibson, Dr. William, 190
Gillie, Dr. Annis, 372
Goddard, Lucy (of Boston), 331
Goldsmid, Anna, 367
Gower, Guppy, and Company (Samuel's sugar firm), 62
Gower, Stephen, 62, 66, 72
Gräfenberg, Germany, 244
Greeley, Horace, 188, 276, 277, 290, 305–307, 336, 338, 382
Greene, William (of Cincinnati), 100
Grimké, Angelina, 69, 70, 90
Grimké, Sarah, 69, 70, 90, 333
Gurney, Russell, 252, 368
Gurney, Mrs. Russell (Emily), 359, 370, 379

Hale, Dr. Benjamin, 4, 164, 186
Hale, Sarah Josepha, 149
Hall, Robert, 31

Hamilton, Dr. Alice H., 433
Harris, Dennis, 49, 50; sugar business in New York, 73, 74, 109, 150, 171, 172; trustee of dispensary, 307; loan to Emily, 322; at Elizabeth's, 326
Harris, Dr. Elisha, 385
Harrison, William Henry, President 101
Hastings, England, 435, 436
Hawthorne, Nathaniel, 132; *Blithedale Romance*, 291
Haydock, Robert, 307, 336, 340, 37
Haydock, Mrs. Robert, 336
Hayes, Rutherford B., President, 11
Henderson, Kentucky, 108, 109, 23
Herschel, Sir John, 252, 442
Hobart and William Smith College (*see also* Geneva College), 432 433; memorials to Elizabeth, 43
Hollick, Frederick, *Manual of Mic wifery*, 295
Holmes, Dr. Oliver Wendell, 14 205, 220, 290
Home Colonization Society, 441
Hoosac, Dr. David, 3
Horner, Dr. William Edmonds, 19
Howells, Edward (Cincinnati friend), 77, 86, 90, 91
Hue, Dr. Clement, 255
Huguier, Dr. Pierre-Charles, 322
Hunt, Dr. Harriot K., 290, 325, 33
Hussey, Cornelia, 286, 294
Hussey, Mary (Cornelia's daughter 286

Ingalls, Senator John, 171

Jackson, Andrew, President, 54
Jackson, Dr. Samuel (Philadelphia 146
Jacobi, Dr. Mary Putnam (*see* Put nam, Mary)
Jameson, Anna Brownell, 252, 26 366
Jenner, Sir William, 322

Jersey City, N.J., 61, 67, 69, 277, 306

Jex-Blake, Dr. Sophia, 403, 404; struggle for medical education, 418–421; founder London School of Medicine for Women, 438

Johns Hopkins University School of Medicine, 290, 431

Johnson, Samuel, 178

Kaiserswerth (deaconess training school), 265, 267, 357

Kelly, Dr. Gertrude, 429

Kemble, Fanny, 260, 333

Kemper College, St. Louis, 103

Keyes, Dick (Kentucky slavery agitator), 323

Kilmun, Scotland, 436, 443

Kingsley, Charles, 442

Kissam, Dr. Richard S., 308, 338, 343, 344

La Crescent, Minn., 334

La Crosse, Wis., 333

La Ford, Dr. (anatomy demonstrator), 159, 160, 175, 179

Lamartine, Alphonse, 205

La Maternité, Paris, 206, 209–211, 213; Elizabeth's study there, 210–235

Lane, Charles (Uncle Charlie, mother's brother), 23, 24, 44, 66, 69, 76, 238; marriage to Eliza Major, 59, 60; school in New York, 62; living with Blackwells, 75; death, 371

Lane, Mrs. Charles (see also Major, Eliza), 62, 75, 238

Lane Theological Seminary, 92, 114

La Salpêtrière (hospital in Paris), 355

Lawrence, Sir William (surgeon), 255

Lee, Dr. Charles Alfred, 5, 6, 153–155, 157, 158, 167, 168, 187, 190, 227, 287

Leifchild, John (in Bristol), 18, 28

L'Esperance, Dr. Elise Strang, 416, 430, 433

Levick, Dr. James Jones, 190

Lexington, Kentucky, 129

Liberator, The (see also Garrison, William Lloyd), 114, 188

Lincoln, Abraham, President, 383, 399, 400

Liston, Dr. Robert, Elements of Surgery, Practical Surgery, 140

Livermore, Mary, 389, 401

Liverpool, England, 194

Lloyd, Eusebius Arthur (surgeon), 255

London, England, 43, 199, 201, 248, 254, 360, 363, 370, 371

London School of Medicine for Women, 421

Longfellow, Henry Wadsworth, 382

Loomis, Dr. Alfred, 417

Louis, Dr. Pierre-Charles-Alexandre, 205, 206

Lozier, Dr. Clemence, 396

Lusk, Rev. Mr. (Jersey City, N.J.), 69, 77

Lyon, Mary, 102

McKay, Dr. Eric, 199

MacKay, Dr. Helen Marion Macpherson, 433

McLean, Dr. Helen Vincent, 433

MacMurchy, Dr. Helen, 433

McNutt, Dr. Sarah, 429

Maisonneuve, Dr. Jacques Gilles, 223

Major, Eliza (see also Lane, Mrs. Charles), 24, 44, 48, 49, 59, 60

Mallet, Mlle. C. (at La Maternité), 217, 230, 231, 235

Mann, Horace, 90

Mann, Mrs. Horace, 333

Manning, Richard Henry, 307

Manzolini, Anna Morandi, 139

Marryat, Captain Frederick, 90

Martha's Vineyard, 407, 409, 413, 437

Martineau, Harriet, 68, 97
Massachusetts General Hospital, 141
May, Abby, 331
May, Samuel, 57, 64, 65; children of, 65
Mayhew, Captain Ephraim, 410
Medical Act of 1858 (British), 358
Medical Register of Great Britain, 358, 371
Mill, John Stuart, 369
Millerites, 92, 100
Mills, Thornton K. (minister in Cincinnati), 98
Moral Reform Union (British), 441
Morris, William, 251, 442
Morton, Dr. William, 142
Mott, Lucretia, 169, 177
Mott, Dr. Valentine, 3, 308, 337
Müller, George (*see also* Plymouth Brethren), 29
Murdoch, John, 104, 105
Mussey, Dr. Reuben, 125, 126, 289

National Health Society (British), 441
Necker, Suzanne, 122
New England Female Medical College, 332, 374
New York Anti-Slavery Society, 55
New York City, 47, 50, 52–55, 60, 61, 151, 275, 276, 279, 297, 298, 303, 304, 329, 373; landmarks (1830), 53, 54, 57; description by Samuel, 60, 61; fire (1835), 61–63; social conditions in the mid-nineteenth century, 277–279, 294, 295, 314, 373; Crystal Palace, 303; Children's Aid Society, 309; draft riots, 391–394
New York *Courier and Inquirer*, 58
New York *Independent*, 304
New York Infirmary, 336; opening at 64 Bleecker Street, 336–339; nurses' training, 339, 374, 378; opposition to in early years, 341–344; success of first year, 345; early

New York Infirmary (*continued*)
social work, 345; medical students, 375; move to 126 Second Avenue, 377, 378; in Civil War, 385, 387, 388, 391–394; description (1865), 401; "sanitary visitor," 404, 405; opening of Woman's Medical College at 128 Second Avenue (1868), 415–418; growth of, 427–430; "firsts" accomplished by, 428
New York *Journal of Commerce*, 209
New York *Star*, 440
New York *Times*, 284, 330, 385
New York *Tribune*, 188, 238, 276, 277, 280, 304
Nightingale, Florence, 263–267, 281, 321, 335, 356, 357, 378, 442; in the Crimea, 311; *Notes on Hospitals*, 357; opinion of Elizabeth, 368, 369; *Notes on Nursing*, 374, 375

Oberlin College, 102, 115, 177, 178
Oldham, Dr. Henry (London), 255
Orange, N.J., 346
Owen, Sir Richard, 200

Paget, Sir James, 241, 249, 250, 254, 255, 267
Paget, Mrs. James, 249, 250, 267
Paret, Bishop William, 187, 188
Paris, France, 149, 150, 203–205, 207, 240, 247, 352, 354–356; landmarks, 207; political unrest, 207, 208; Luxembourg Gardens, 227, 250, 303
Parker, Dr. Samuel William Langston, 198
Parker, Dr. Willard, 308, 338, 416
Parkes, Bessie Raynor, 251, 253, 281, 359
Parkman, Mary Jane, 331
Pasteur, Louis, 221, 409
Paulus Hook, 61
Peabody, Elizabeth, 333
Pechey, Dr. Edith, 419

Peel, Sir Robert, 31
Pennsylvania Canal, 78
Percy, Dr. John, 199, 200
Perkins, James H., 100, 116, 126, 127, 239
Philadelphia, 78, 144, 145, 165, 166, 172, 174, 266, 283
Philanthropist, The, 107, 114
Phillips, Wendell, 70, 401
Pioneer Fast Line, Philadelphia to Pittsburgh, 78
Pittsburgh, Penna., 80, 322
Pittsburgh *Commercial Journal,* 238
Plevins, Charles, 197–199, 202
Plymouth Brethren, 29, 30
Portage Railroad, 79
Preston, Dr. Ann, 283, 284, 332, 403
Prevost, Theodosia, 348
Priessnitz, Herr (*see also* Gräfenberg), 243–245
Protheroe, Edward Davis, 31
Providence, R.I., 173
Punch, poem on Elizabeth's graduation, 189
Putnam, Dr. Mary (Jacobi), 378, 429

Raymond, Henry J., 307, 338, 385
Reform Bill (1832), 31, 32, 39
Restell, Madame (abortionist), 120, 121, 123, 144, 280, 315, 329, 416
Ricord, Philippe, 227
Ripley, George, 133
Rock House, Hastings, 435, 443, 444
Roosevelt, Franklin Delano, President, 337
Roosevelt, James, 337
Roseville, N.J., 375, 413
Rossetti, Christina, 252
Rossetti, Dante Gabriel, 442
Roupell, Dr. George Leith, 255
Rousseau, Jean Jacques, 27
Rush Medical College, 292, 305
Ruskin, Charles, 287

Sabin, Dr. Florence Rena, 433
Sachs, Alfred, 443

St. Bartholomew's, London, 241, 248–250, 255, 256, 264, 267
St. Louis, Mo., 103
Salem, Ohio, 32
Schieferdecker, Dr. (of Philadelphia), 144
Schuylerville, N.Y., 65
Scope Weekly, 371
Scott, Sir Walter, *Bride of Lamermoor,* 68
Sedgwick, Catharine, 347
Sedgwick, Theodore, 307
Semi-Colon Club (Cincinnati), 106, 116, 192
Semmelweiss, Ignaz Philipp, 220, 221, 341, 394
Seneca Falls, N.Y., 169–171, 176
Seneca, Lake, 174, 182
Severance, Mrs. Caroline M., 329, 331
Sewall, Dr. Lucy, 332, 403
Shaen, William (lawyer), 358, 367
Shaftesbury, Earl of, 421
Sherwood, Mary Martha, 29, 93
Simpson, Sir James, 310, 311, 321, 419
Smith, Barabara Leigh (*see also* Bodichon, Barbara), 195, 196, 251–254, 264, 281, 316, 348, 349
Smith, Benjamin Leigh, 195, 252, 253
Smith, Elizabeth Oakes, 333
Smith, Nannie Leigh (sister of Barbara), 251
Smith, Dr. Stephen, 3–10, 153–156, 162–164, 417, 428, 430
Smith, Valentine Leigh, 361
South, John Flint (surgeon), 201
Spencer, Herbert, 442
Spofford, Ainsworth, 116, 398, 407
Spring, Marcus, 307
Standish, Madame, 353
Stanley, Dowager Lady, 421
Stanley, Edward (surgeon), 255
Stansfeld, Sir James, 421

Stanton, Elizabeth Cady, 169, 176, 376, 396, 401, 423

Stewart, Aunt Jedidah, 411, 413

Stone, Lucy (Mrs. Henry Blackwell), 102, 304, 345, 394, 410, 411; at Oberlin, 177, 178; appearance, 298; lecturing in New York, 298, 299; romance with Henry, 298-301, 323; lectures in West, 302; marriage to Henry, 324–326; birth of Alice, 346; schism in women's rights movement, 400, 401, 423; editor of *Woman's Journal* in Boston, 424

Stowe, Dr. Calvin, 92, 115, 192

Stowe, Harriet Beecher, 92, 115, 116, 124, 125, 192; *Uncle Tom's Cabin*, 292, 305; on Antoinette Brown, 305

Strang, Dr. Albert, 416

Strang, Elise (*see also* L'Esperance, Dr. Elise Strang), 416

Strang, May, 416

Stratton, Francis, 4, 6, 7, 8, 10, 153

Swedenborg, Emanuel, 99, 122, 252, 285

Tappan, Arthur, 55

Taussig, Dr. Helen B., 433

Taylor, Dr. Isaac E., 308, 338

Taylor, Jeremy, *Holy Living*, 68

Taylor, Zachary, President, 175

Thompson, George (English abolitionist), 56

Thompson, Dr. Mary Harris, 402

Time magazine, 431

Trélat, Dr. Ulysse, 355, 442

Trimble, Merritt, 374

Trollope, Mrs. Anthony, 91

Trotula (early physician), 139

Trousseau, Dr. Armand, 208

Tyng, Rev. Dudley Atkins, 339

Uncle Tom's Cabin (*see also* Stowe, Harriet Beecher), 292, 305

Vail, Franklin, 114, 346

Vail, Mrs. Franklin, 114, 124, 346

Vail, Kate, 114, 126

Van Buren, Martin, President, 73

Versailles, 207

Victoria, Queen, 73, 259, 267, 310

von Colomb, Maria, 243

Walker, Dr. Mary, 398

Waller, Miss, 156, 157, 164, 176

Walnut Hills, Cincinnati, 114

Walsh, Robert (American consul in Paris), 210

Warren, Dr. John Collins, 141, 142

Warrington, Dr. Joseph (Philadelphia), 5, 143, 145, 148, 149, 158

Washington *Evening Star*, 432

Waterloo, N.Y., 176

Watson, Dr. John, 308, 337

Wattles, Augustus and John, 99

Webb, James Watson, 58

Webster, Dr. James, 3–10, 156–158, 161–163, 184, 185, 209

Webster, Noah, 27

Weld, Theodore, 91, 333

Welsh, Jane (Mrs. Thomas Carlyle), 253

Wesley, John (in Bristol), 20

West Bloomfield, N.J. (later Montclair), 380, 391, 411

West Brooksville, Mass., 326

West, Edward C., 307

Western Reserve Medical School, 306

Wetherell, Sir Charles (Recorder of Bristol), 33–36

White, Dr. Priscilla, 433

White, Robert, 307

White, William (sugar house worker), 35–38, 44

Whiting, Bowen (trustee of Geneva), 4

Whittier, John Greenleaf, 91

Wilberforce, William, 20, 49, 252

Wilkinson, Dr. James John Garth, 201, 204

Willard, Emma, 102, 139, 149, 150
Willetts, Samuel, 374
William IV of England, 32, 33, 73
Wollstein, Dr. Martha, 429
Wollstonecraft, Mary, 97
Woman's Journal, The, 324, 424
Woman's Medical College of the New York Infirmary (*see also* New York Infirmary), 397, 398, 415–418
Woman's Medical College of Pennsylvania (*see also* Female Medical College of Philadelphia), 281, 283, 403

Woodward, Charlotte, 170
Worcester, England, 14, 43, 268
Worcester, Mass., 258
Wright, Frances, 71, 102

Zakrzewska, Dr. Marie, 312–314, 349, 403; work in dispensary, 314; in Cleveland Medical College, 316, 328, 329; work in opening New York Infirmary, 329–332, 336, 337; work in Infirmary, 339–344; in Boston Female Medical College, 374, 375